C000184027

MOTORCYCLE GRAPHICS

OUTSIDER ART, GRAPHICS AND ILLUSTRATION

Published in 2013 by Graffito Books Ltd,
32 Great Sutton Street, London EC1V 0NB, UK
www.graffitobooks.com

ISBN 978-1909051003

Art Direction: Sam Ratcliffe
Designer: Tristan Baliuag

British Library cataloguing-in-publication data:
A catalogue record of this book is available at The British Library.

Printed in China.

MOTORCYCLE GRAPHICS

OUTSIDER ART, GRAPHICS AND ILLUSTRATION

GARY INMAN

GRAFFITO

CONTENTS

INTRODUCTION

BARRAS · 8

BRØNDUM · 18

BRUSCO · 24

CHAPPELL · 34

DIRTY DONNY · 42

GEE · 48

GILBERT · 56

GLERUM · 62

GÜREL · 70

LAPIN · 76

LEACH · 84

LEVIATHAN · 92

LORENZO · 100

MCKINNEY · 108

MCLEAN · 114

MERINERO · 122
NICKEL · 130
PATERNOSTER · 140
PATROCINIO · 148
PETIT · 156
PIERCE · 164
QUICKFALL · 170
RAGGIAS · 178
RAID71 · 184
RAULOWSKY · 190
RICKARD · 198
SCHUURMANS · 204
TOKYO GUNS · 212
TUCKWELL · 220
WATSON · 228
WRIGHT · 238
APPENDIX

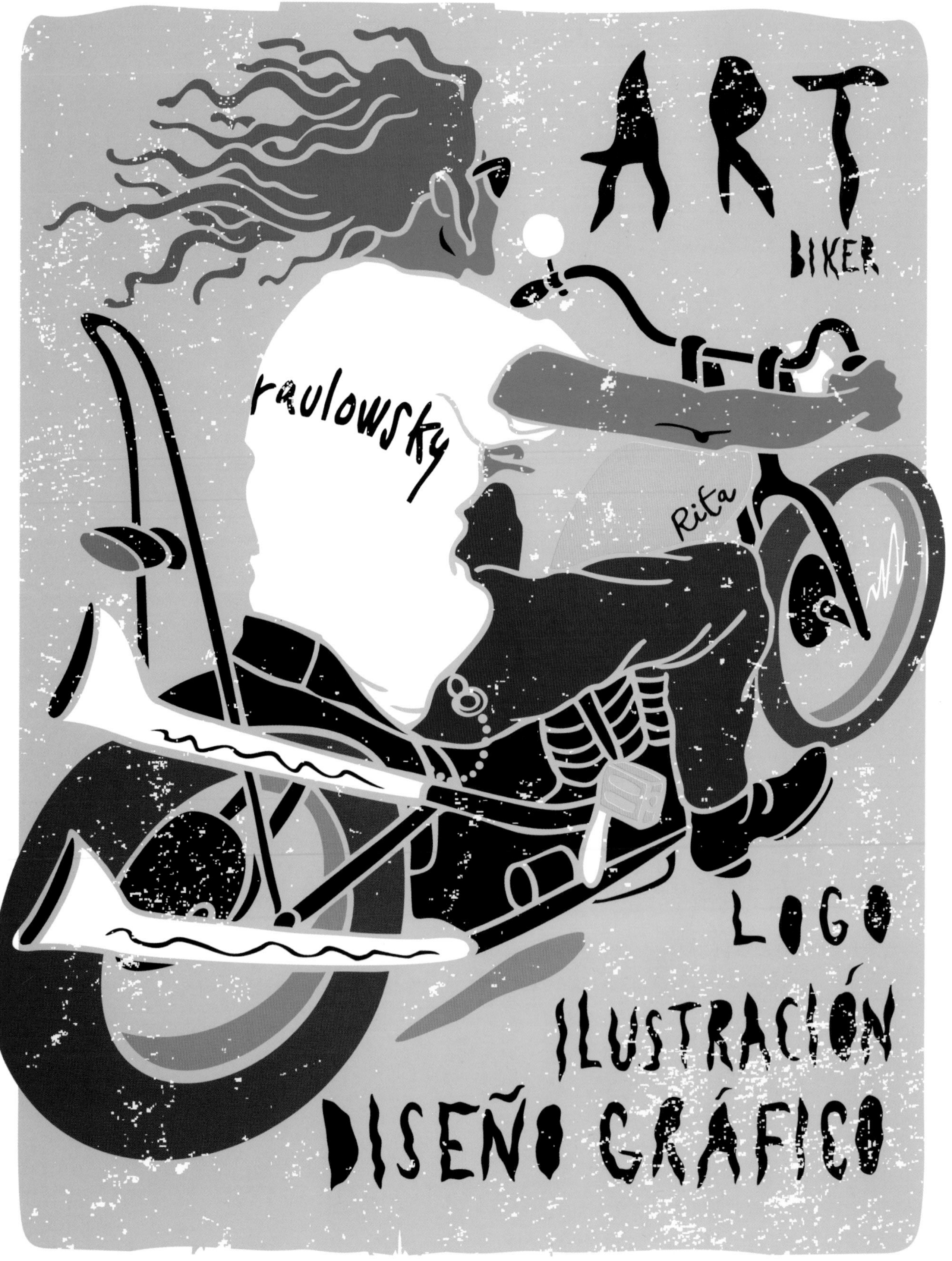

ABOVE: ***Shiralee, alli estare*** **by Raulowsky.**
Ink on paper, digital.

INTRODUCTION

This book of motorcycle art is not about characters, scenes or graphics airbrushed onto motorcycles. Neither does it feature machines that builders or onlookers, rightly or wrongly, label as art. It is purely depictions of motorbikes, their riders and the gamut of related props, tools, equipment and uniforms, on 2D surfaces. It is a whole generation of contemporary artists' efforts to turn the all-encompasing experience of stretching a throttle cable and holding on tight, till the wind turns your eyes into puddles and sets your forearms on fire, onto paper, screen, canvas or cotton.

The artists featured come from four continents and could only be included if they had a body of motorcycle-related work to pack a chapter. That means there is a mixture of specialists: those whose work is almost exclusively moto-related; others, hooked enough by the subject that they have produced a whole compatible series then moved on; and lastly those who are fascinated and sufficiently fizzed-up by the subject that they keep returning to it as artists, rather than as helmet-wearing enthusiasts.

The artwork deals with tribalism and sub-cultures. And the motorcycle world has more than its fair share of easily-identifiable clans. There are the chopper builders, the grand prix legends, the outlaw bikers, the commuters, dirt demons, illegal street racers and off-road voyageurs... And that's before we enter into the world of the paranormal, for zombie, devil dog or alien bikers.

The art that follows explores the bio-mechanical marriage of man and machine. How they work together, how one moves the other. How clenched fist and right wrist, twisting just an eighth-of-an-inch, turns 30mph into 130mph. It deals with unity and separation: being part of a gang but shunned by the mainstream, but also the unhappy occurrence of being sat on a bike one minute, and sliding down the road on your arse and elbows the next.

Because the artwork, on the whole, is produced by people who have spent the majority of their lives owning, riding, crashing and building motorcycles, the images on the next 250-odd pages convey both the dreams and realities of every motorcyclist in the world. The moments of glory outweigh those of confusion and desperation, but they are all there.

Yet, while the majority of the 30 artists featured own and ride bikes, some admit they have barely even sat on one, further proving the magnetic draw of two wheels and an engine.

However much they enjoy the creative process, these are all depictions and reminders of what the artists would rather be doing: riding or wrenching. Because every, single one of them knows they spend too many hours working. I'm glad they do. Work buys bikes, parts, petrol. Sometimes art can even be traded for motorcycles. The joyous rides that follow, when everything is so perfect the bike feels like it's hovering six inches above the tarmac, or when bike and rider split lanes of gridlocked, over-heating misery, as quickly and beautifully as a raindrop running down a pane of glass, restock the inspiration banks for future work. So do the hours covered in oil and grease, or the desperate hard shoulder grapple on hands and knees, giving the mechanical equivalent of the Heimlich Manoeuvre to a recalcitrant V-twin. Art buys motorbike, motorbike informs and inspires art. It's a virtuous circle of vicious cycles.

Start riding early enough and do it for long enough – both in terms of your time on the planet and each day in the saddle – and you'll be given graphic reminders that all life comes down to sex and death, and if you don't agree that those are the ingredients at the core of a motorcycle, then you're riding the wrong one.

Gary Inman

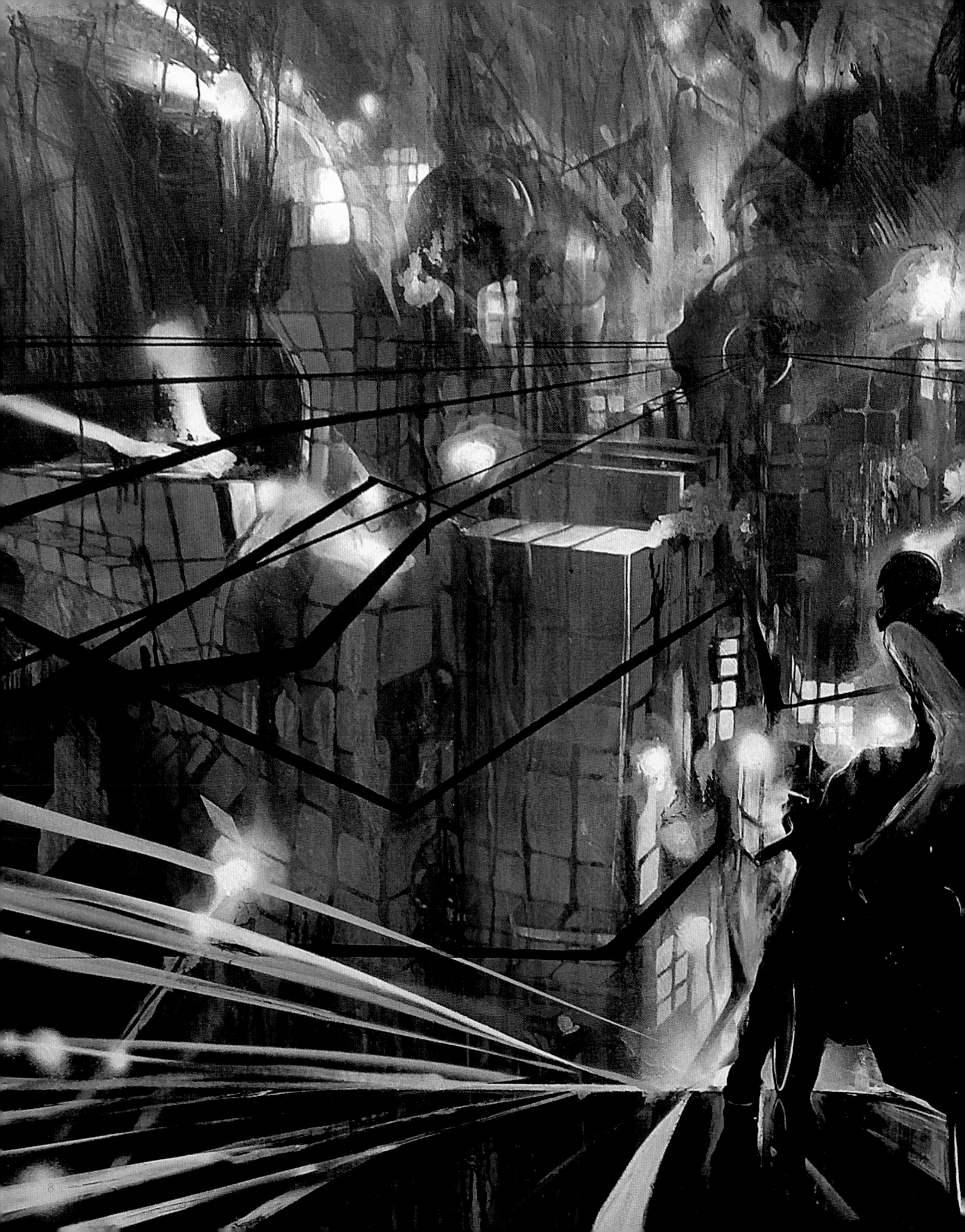

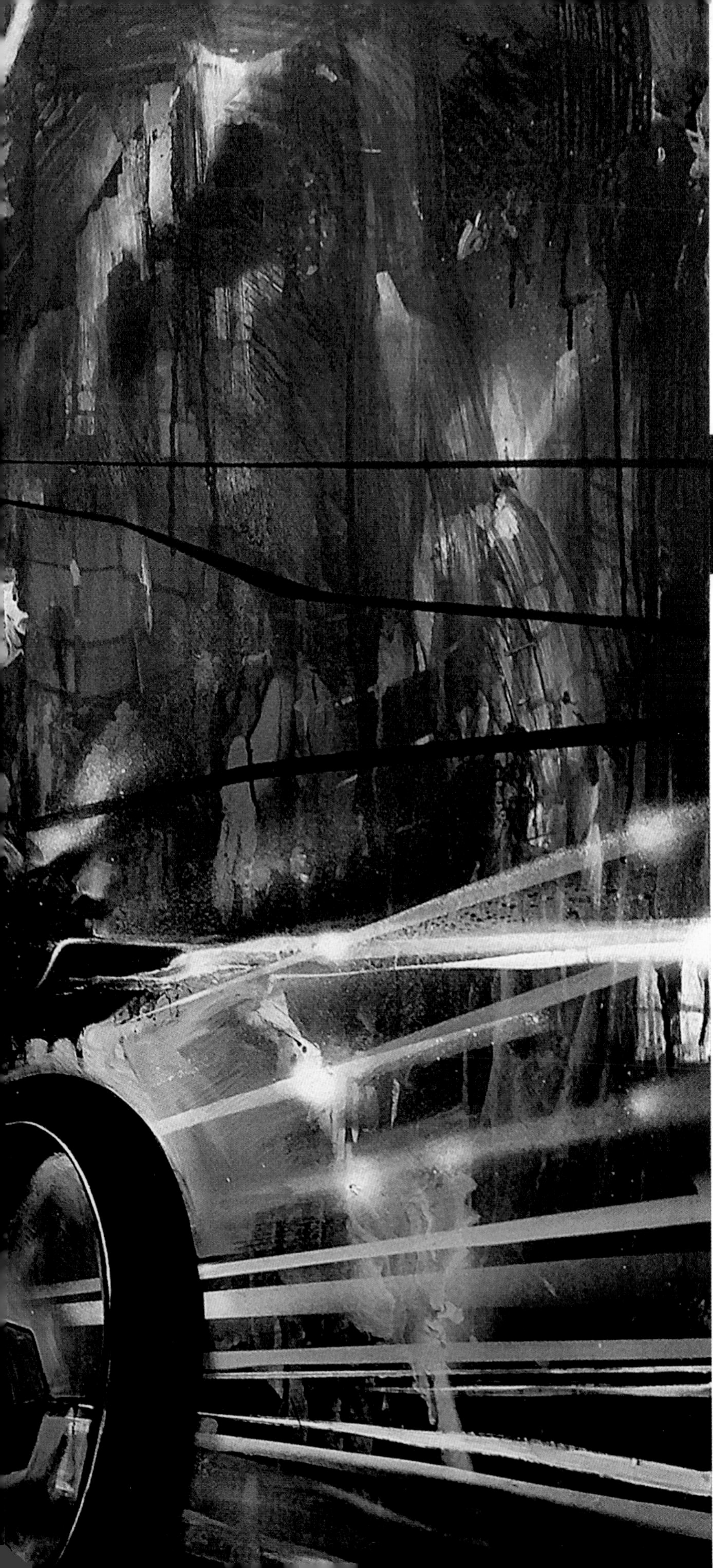

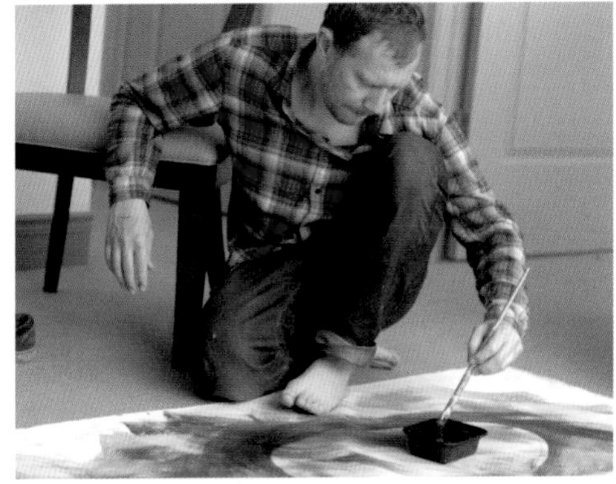

WILL BARRAS

"I've always been interested in capturing figures with speed and movement" says Will. "When I was growing up my dad raced a modified MG Midget. He was always in the garage and I used to go to help and watch the races. We went to watch the Le Mans 24-Hours, and speedway, a load of times. I was really into it."

Will went on to art college, but with unintended results: "I lost my passion for drawing." It was while working at a call centre that he started doodling again. "By sharing ideas and inspiration with two friends from those days, Steff Plaetz and Duncan Jago, I rediscovered a love of drawing. From there I decided to become an illustrator." Will uses a variety of different media and styles, but often returns to motorcycles, particularly moving ones, in his art. "There is something about the way a figure looks on a bike, especially with a passenger. I love this dynamic, I would say it's almost more about the figures than the machine, like a figure on horseback. I like that sense of freedom, of escape and the journey, and the way it looks when someone is hanging on for dear life, or when the riders are talking, yelling at each other at speed. You know that feeling."

LEFT: ***Opponent.***
Acrylic and spray paint on linen.

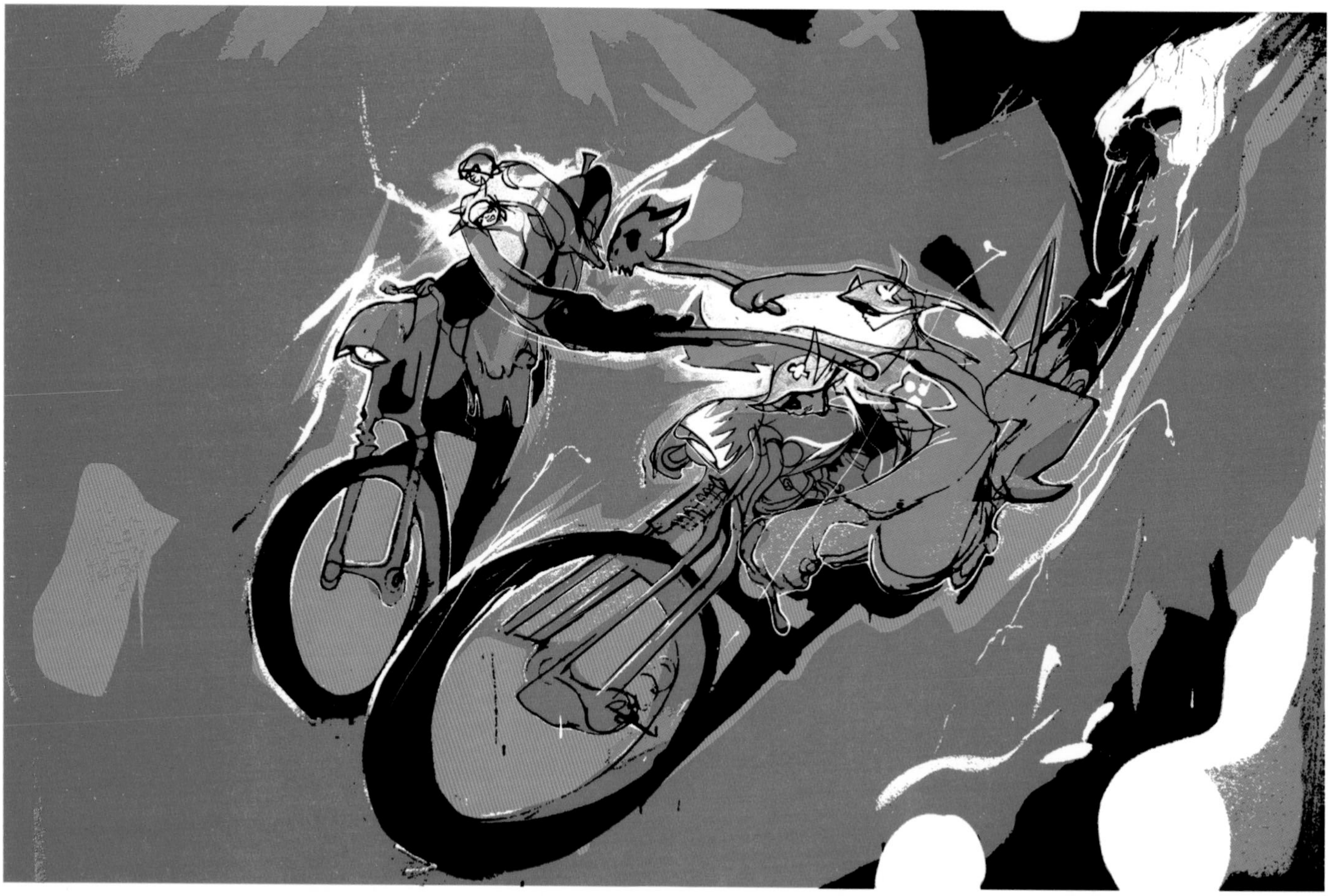

ABOVE: ***Into the Valley.*** Acrylic on wood.

RIGHT: ***Recorded Delivery.*** Acrylic and spray paint on canvas.

MIDDLE: ***Cambiario.*** Acrylic and spray paint on linen.

FAR RIGHT: ***Lost Key.*** Acrylic and spray paint on canvas.

OVERLEAF: ***Headless Pillion Passenger.*** Acrylic and spray paint on canvas.

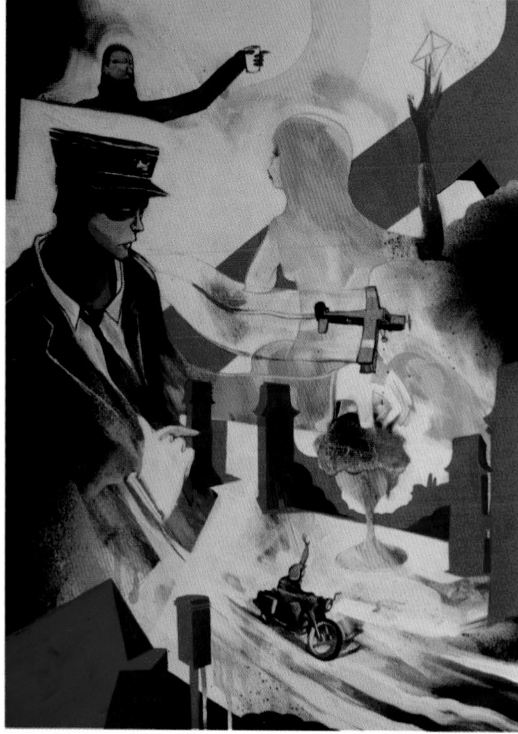

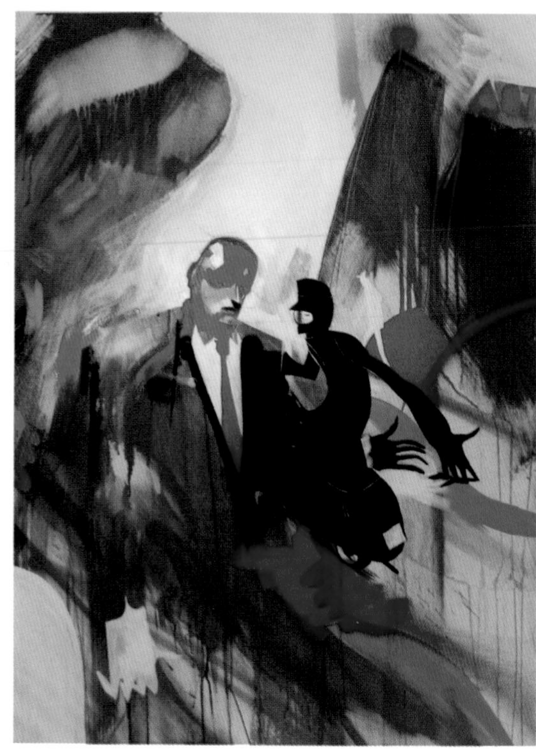

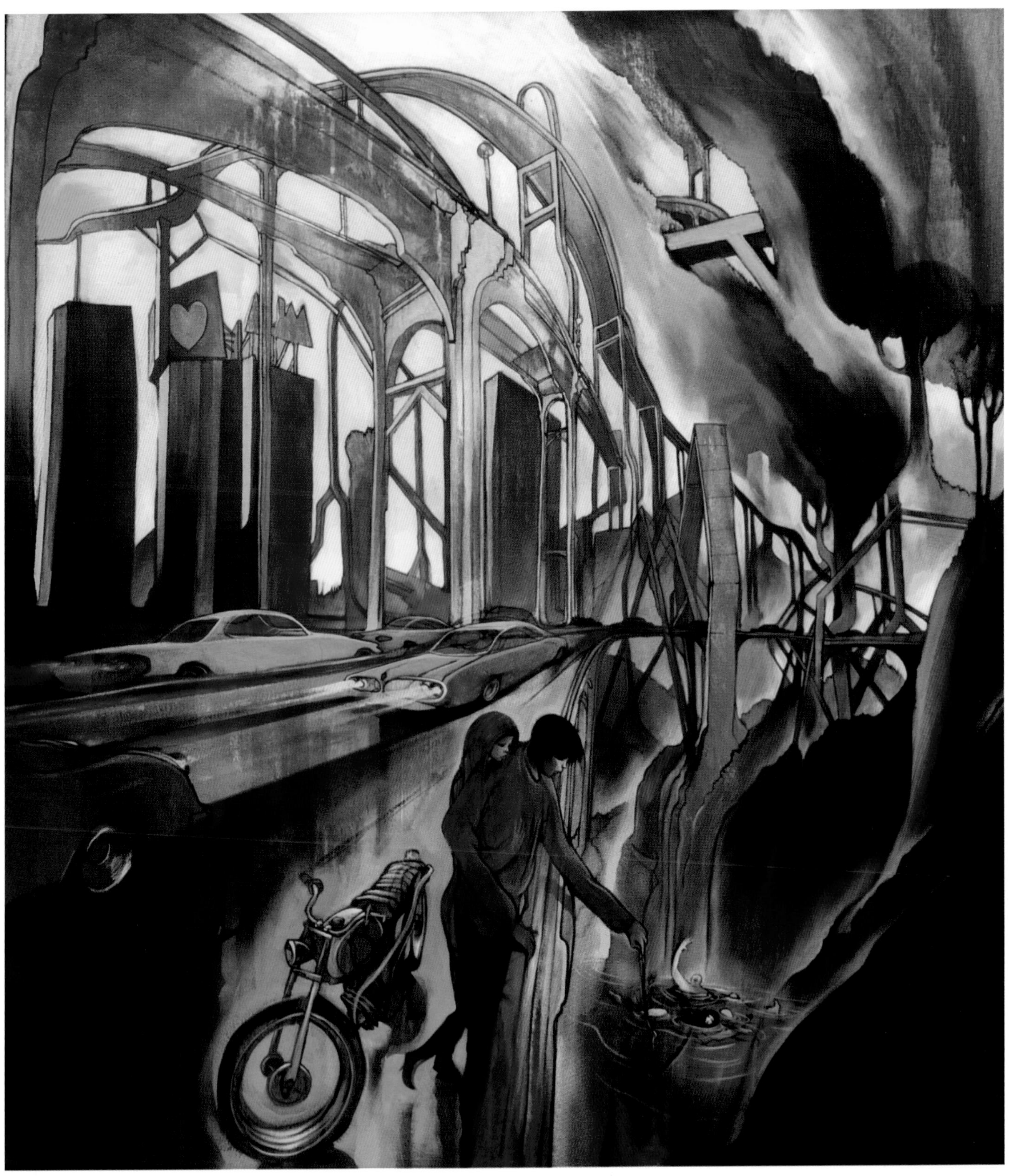

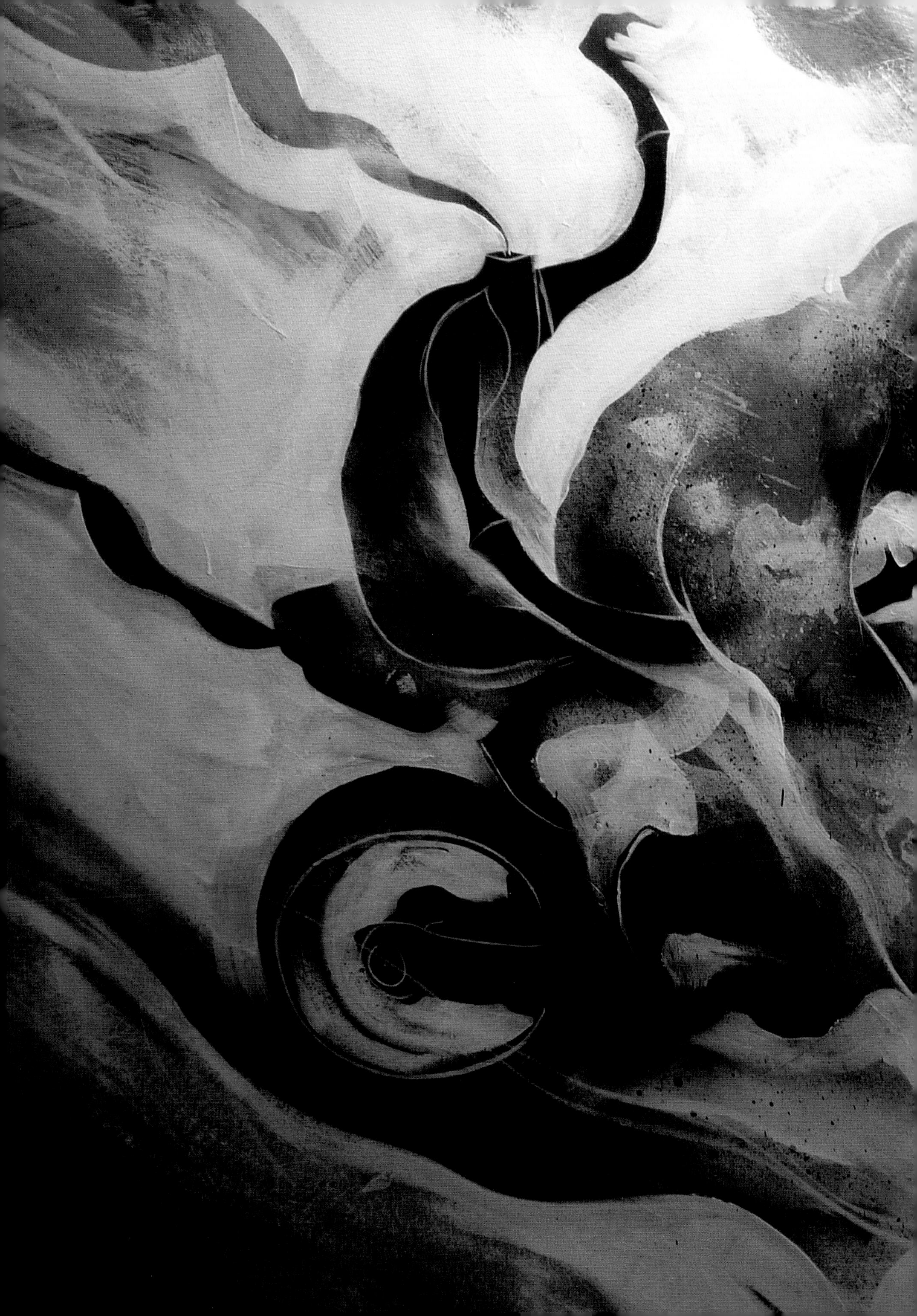

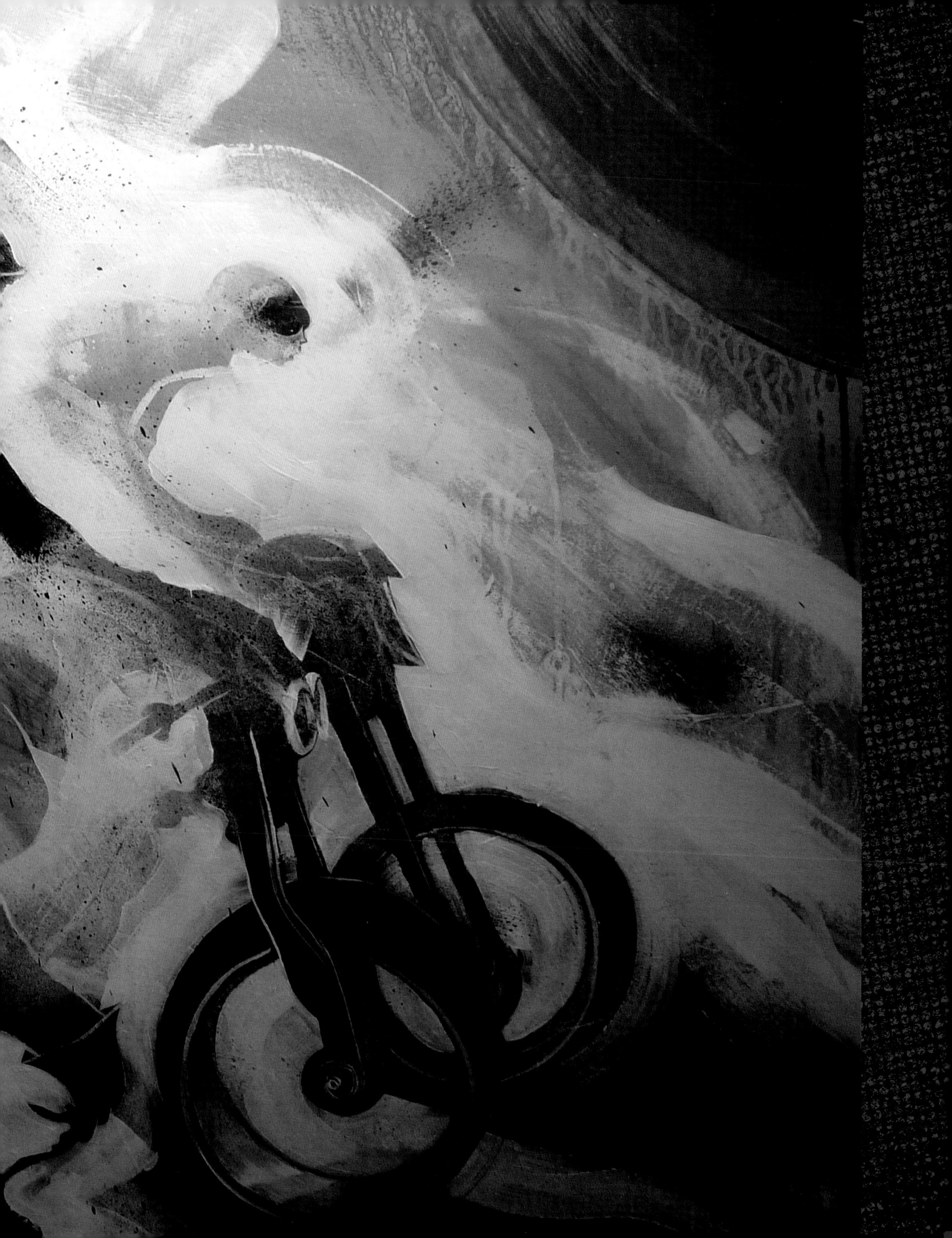

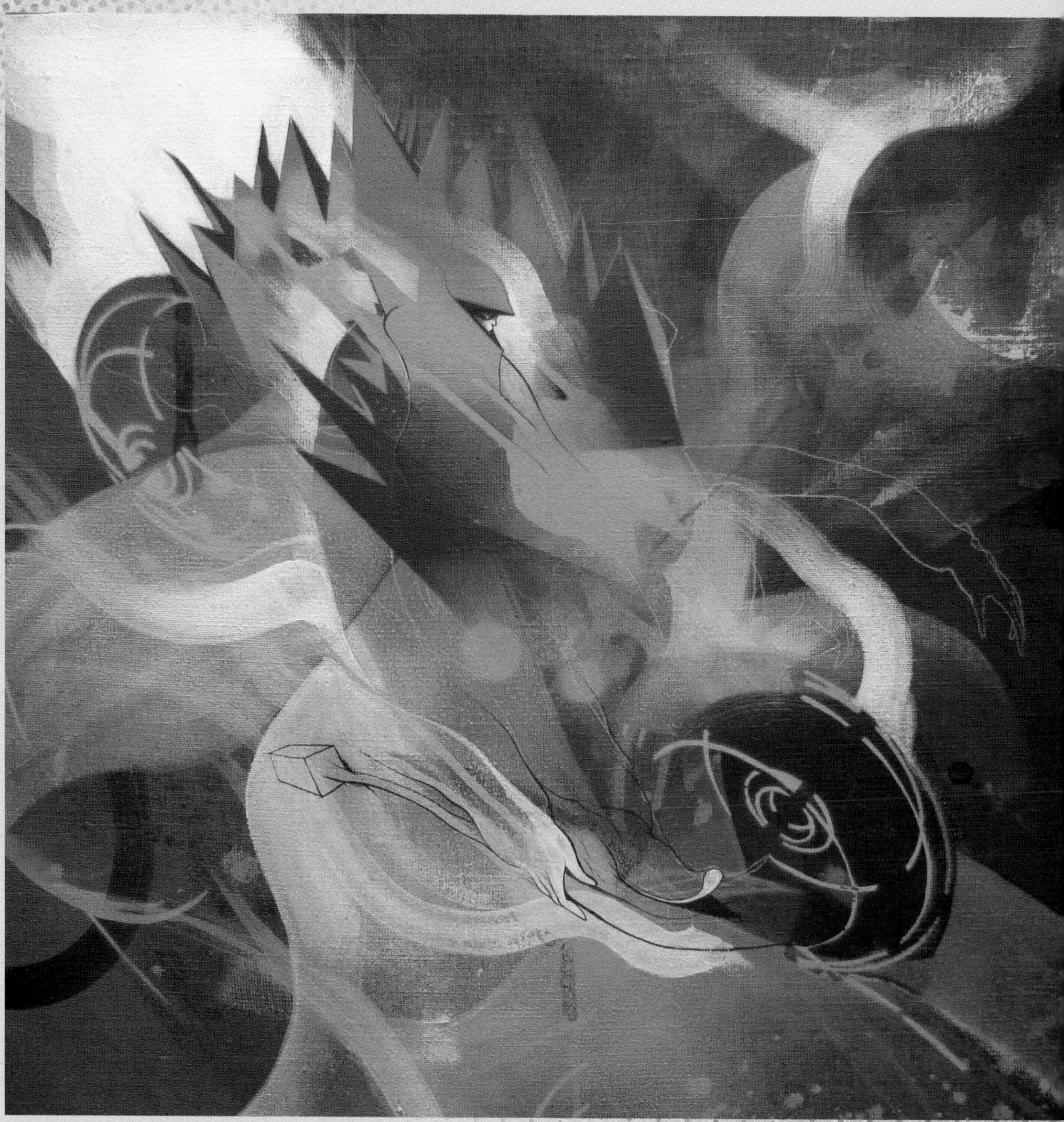

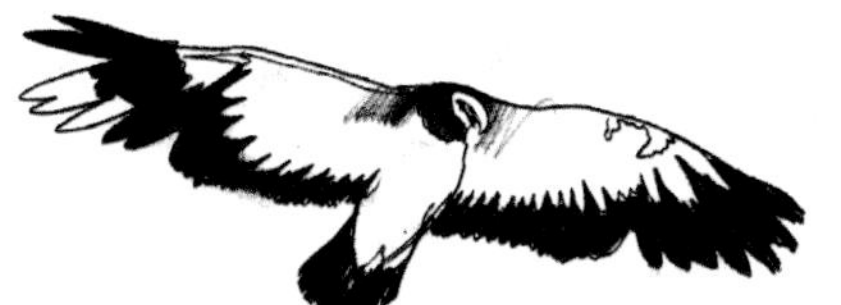

FAR LEFT: ***Heathen.***
Acrylic and spray paint on canvas.

LEFT: ***Eagle.***
Pencil on paper.

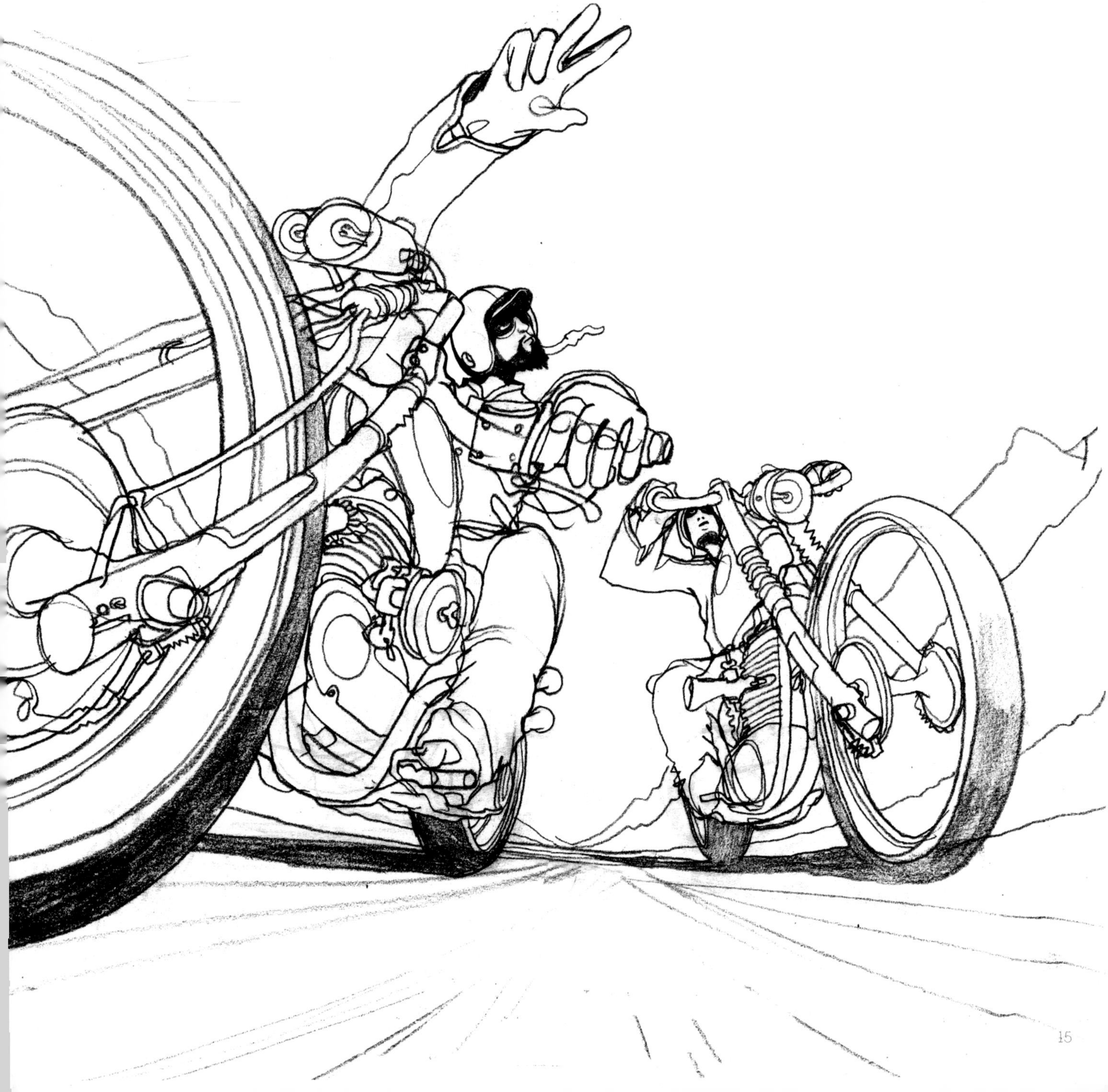

RIGHT: ***Say Something Good To Me.***
Acrylic and spray paint on canvas.

BELOW: ***Bad Clown on Monkey Bike.***
Acrylic and spray paint on canvas.

FAR RIGHT: ***Passengers.***
Acrylic and spray paint on canvas.

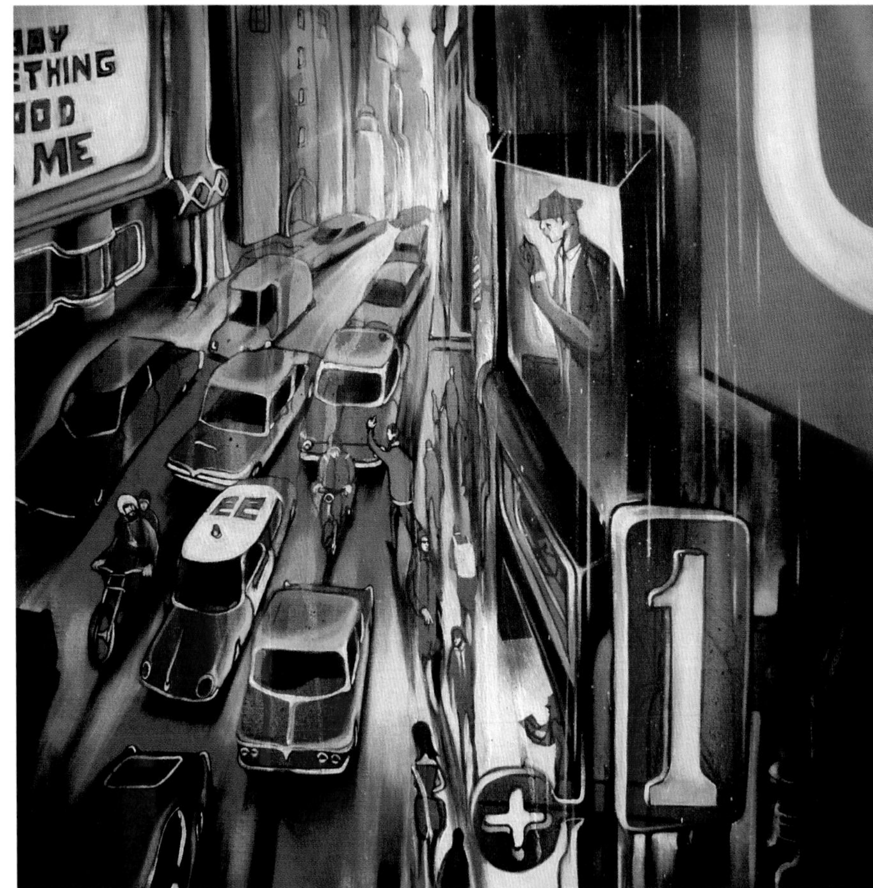

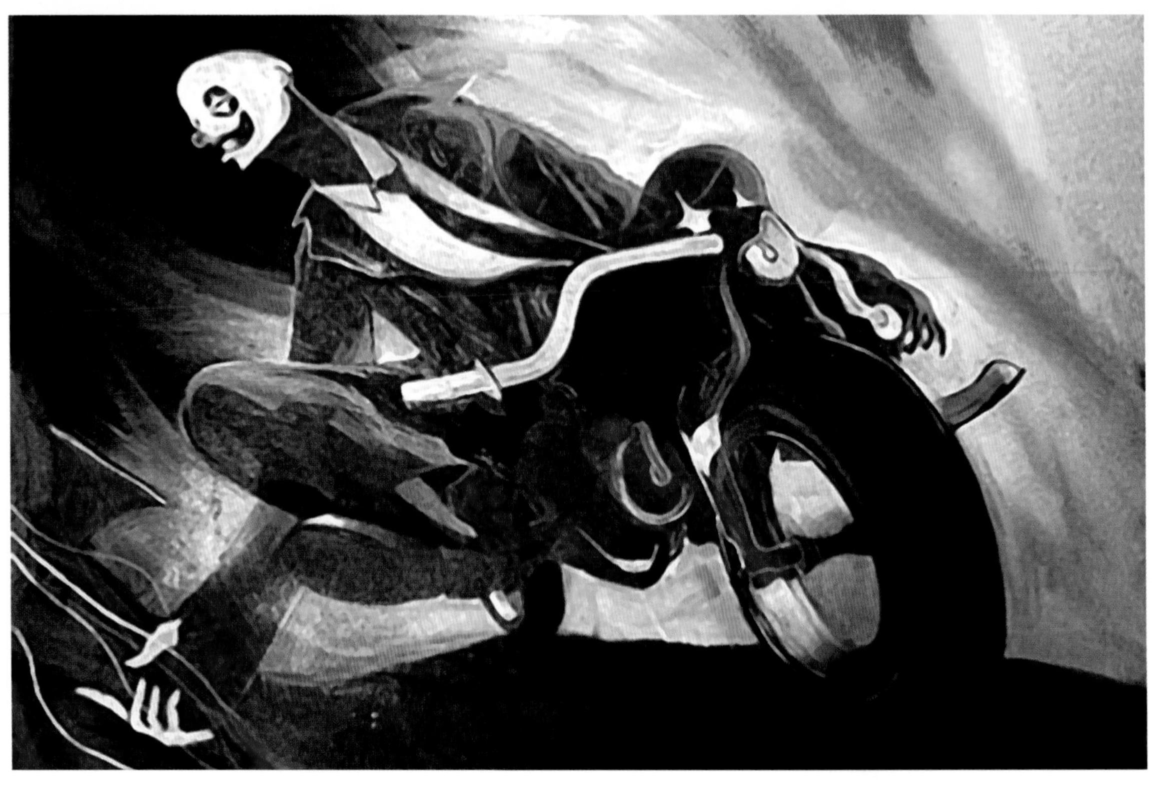

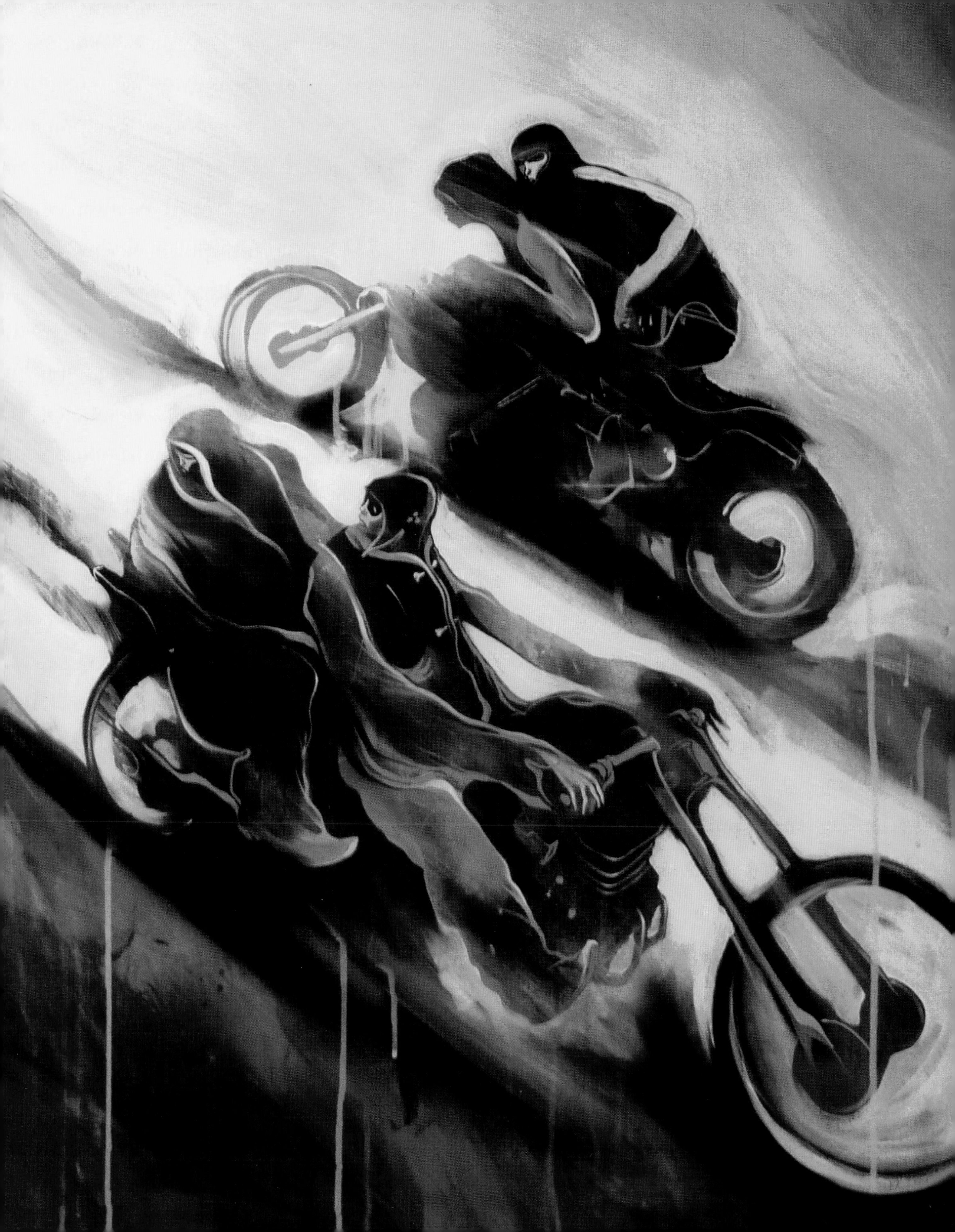

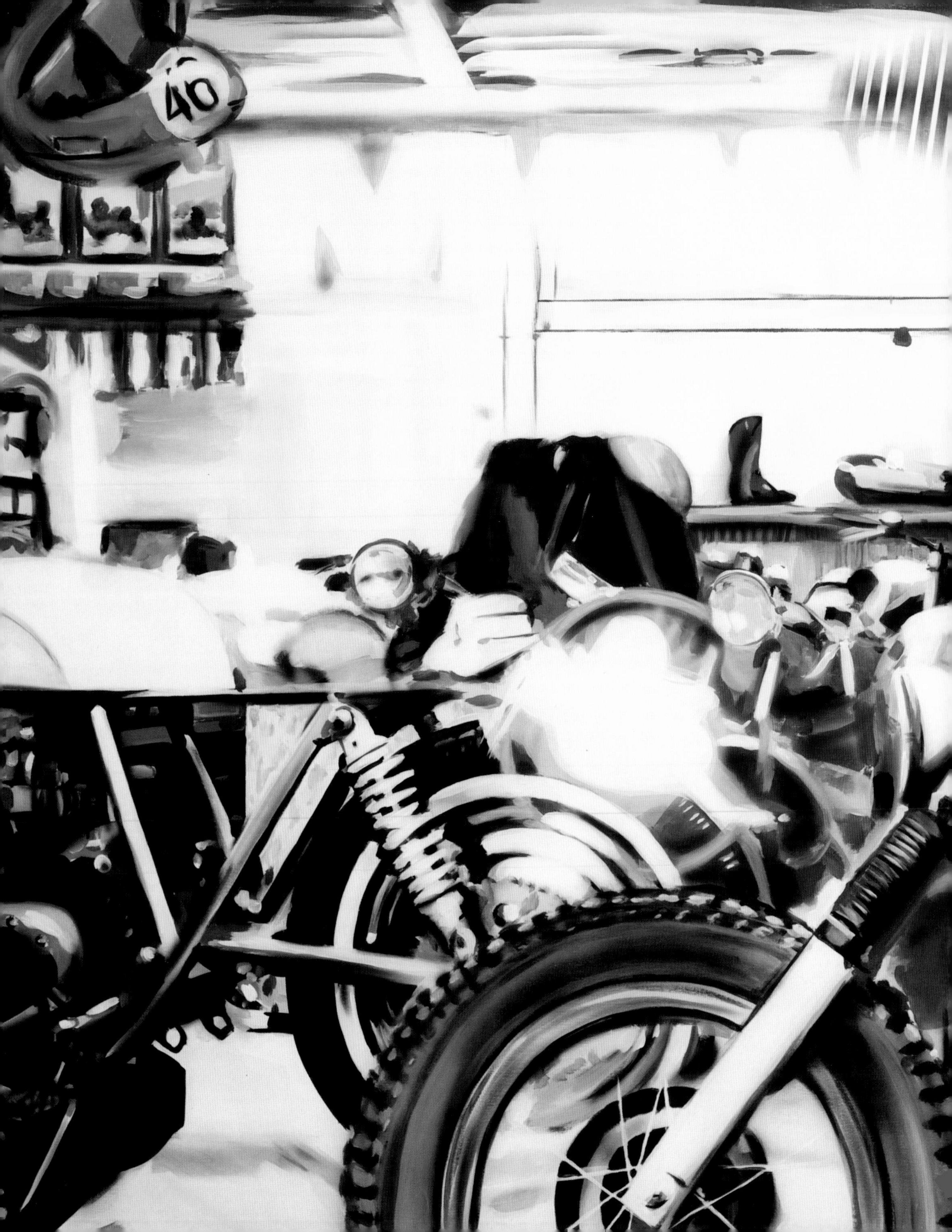
40

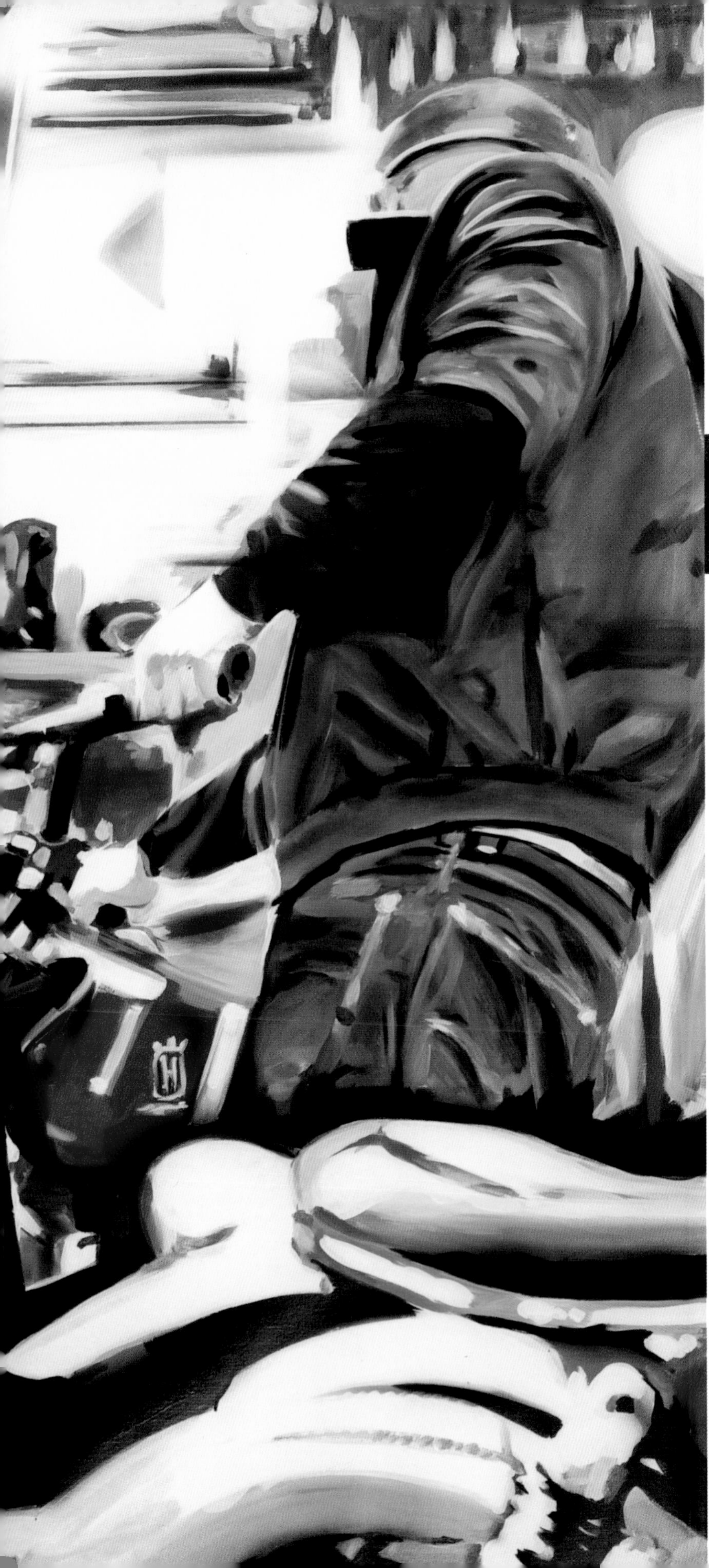

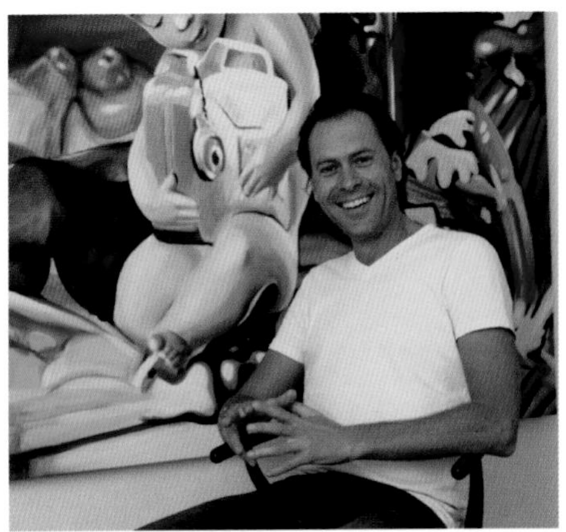

CAY BRØNDUM

"My large scale paintings are acrylic and oil on canvas. The mixed media and illustrations are mostly ink and watercolour combined with collage, but I don't really have one way to do stuff," says Copenhagen-based Cay. "I love new challenges, finding new ways to create and use my ideas, drawing and painting skills." True to his word, Cay has worked as a professional illustrator, a cartoon animator, a sign painter, a tattooist and has painted graffiti, pinstriped cars and airbrushed motorcycle gas tanks. "If, one day, someone wants me to decorate a spaceship, I'll be honoured," he adds. Cay has always been into bikes. "I've lost count of how many bikes I've had, but the last one was a Harley-Davidson Panhead. I started with a bare wishbone frame, and hunted parts all over the world. Slowly I build a Hydra bobber exactly the way I wanted it. It was a fantastic project with great help from my garage buddies." Cay's art subjects vary massively. Still, he often returns to two wheels. "Some of my first drawings as a kid were car and motorcycle-related. And my first sweater, hand-knitted by my mum, had a bike on it - need I say more?"

LEFT: *Garage.* Acrylic and oil on canvas.

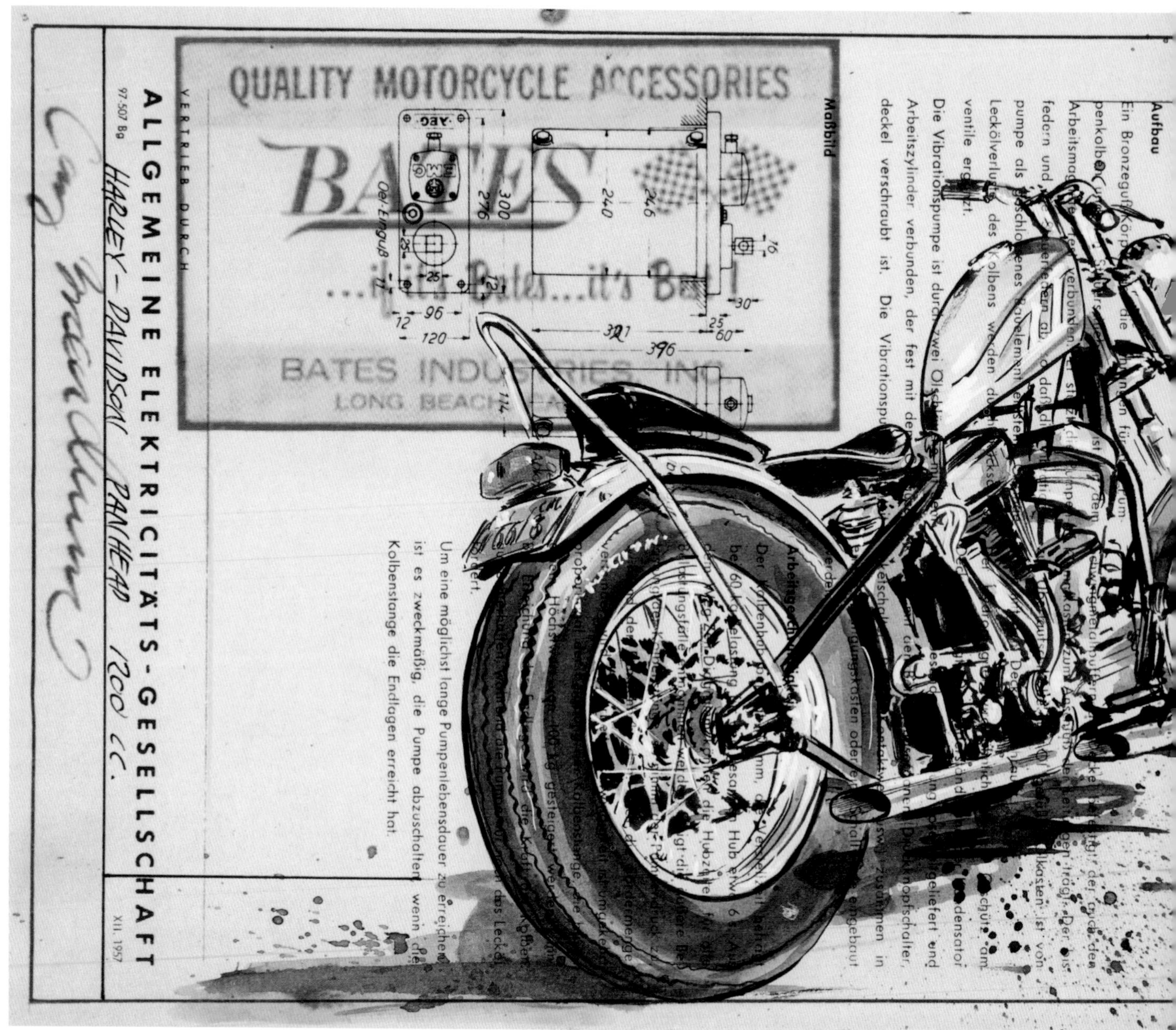

ABOVE: ***Panhead.***
Ink and watercolour on vintage paper.

ABOVE RIGHT: ***Matchless.***
Ink and watercolour on vintage paper.

RIGHT: ***Knucklehead.***
Ink and watercolour on vintage paper.

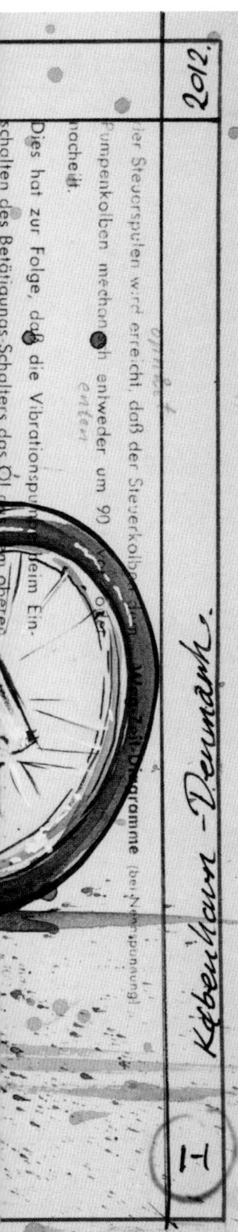

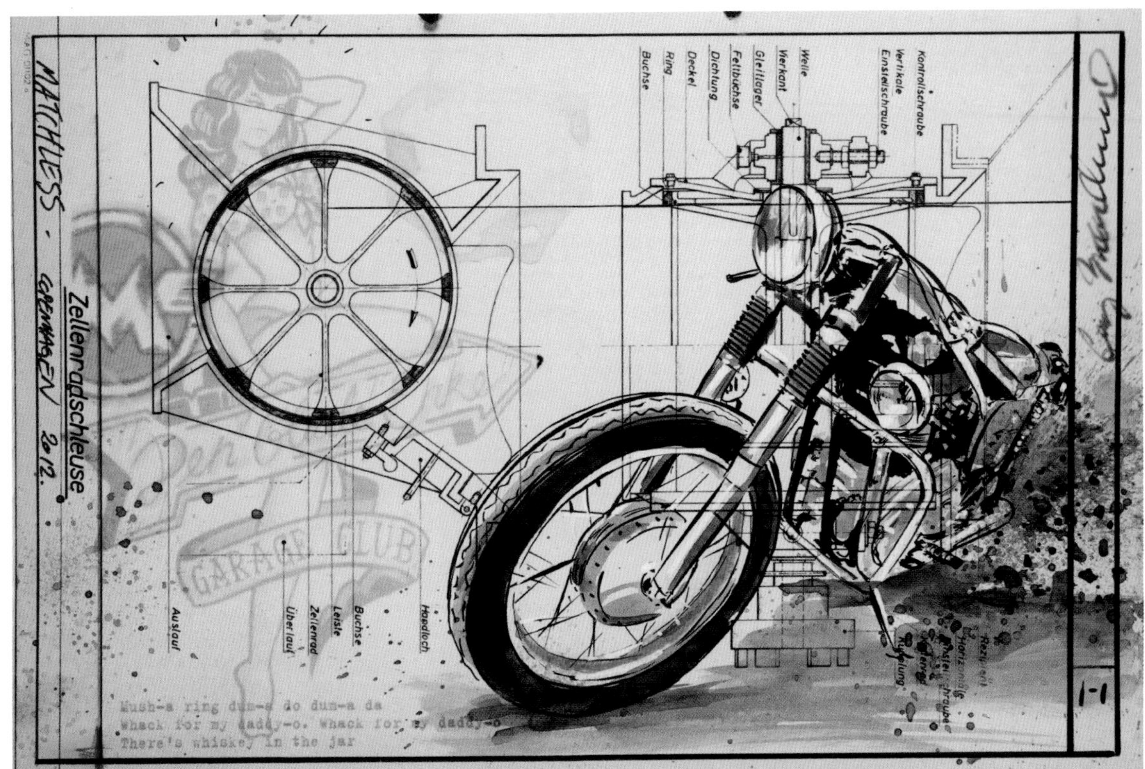
Mush-a ring dum-a do dum-a da
Whack for my daddy-o. Whack for my daddy-o
There's whiskey in the jar

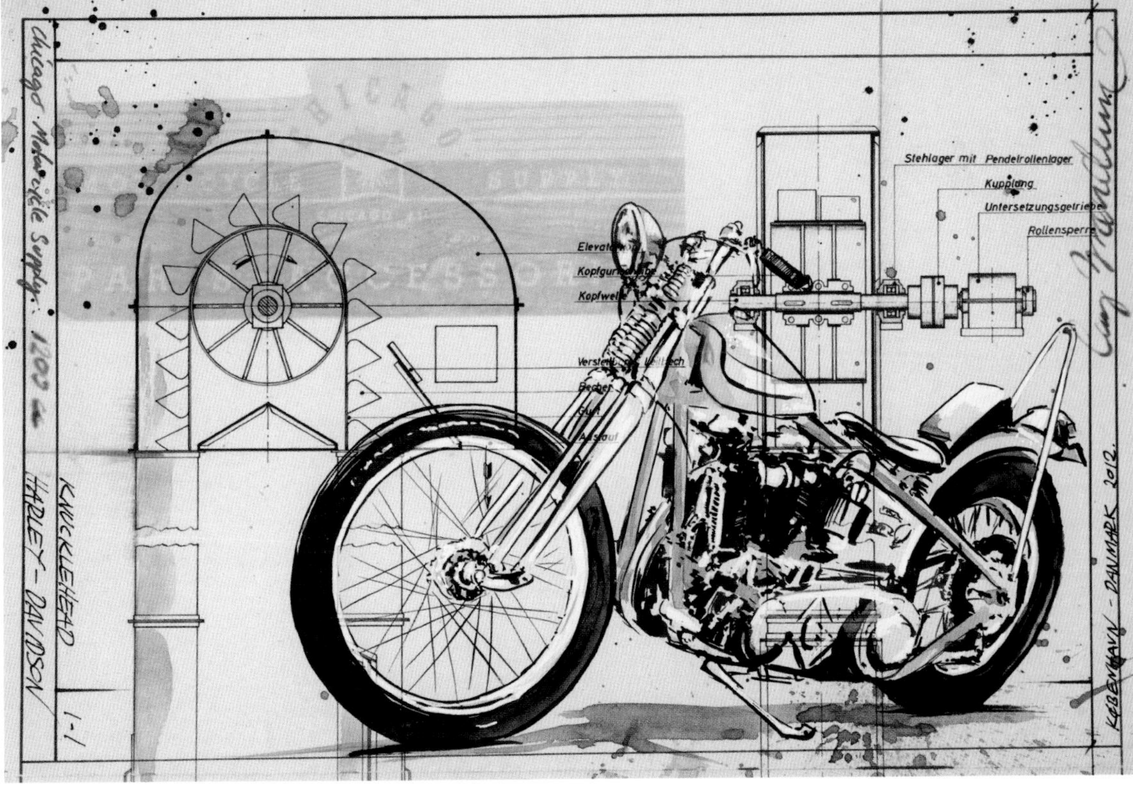
Stehlager mit Pendelrollenlager
Kupplung
Untersetzungsgetriebe

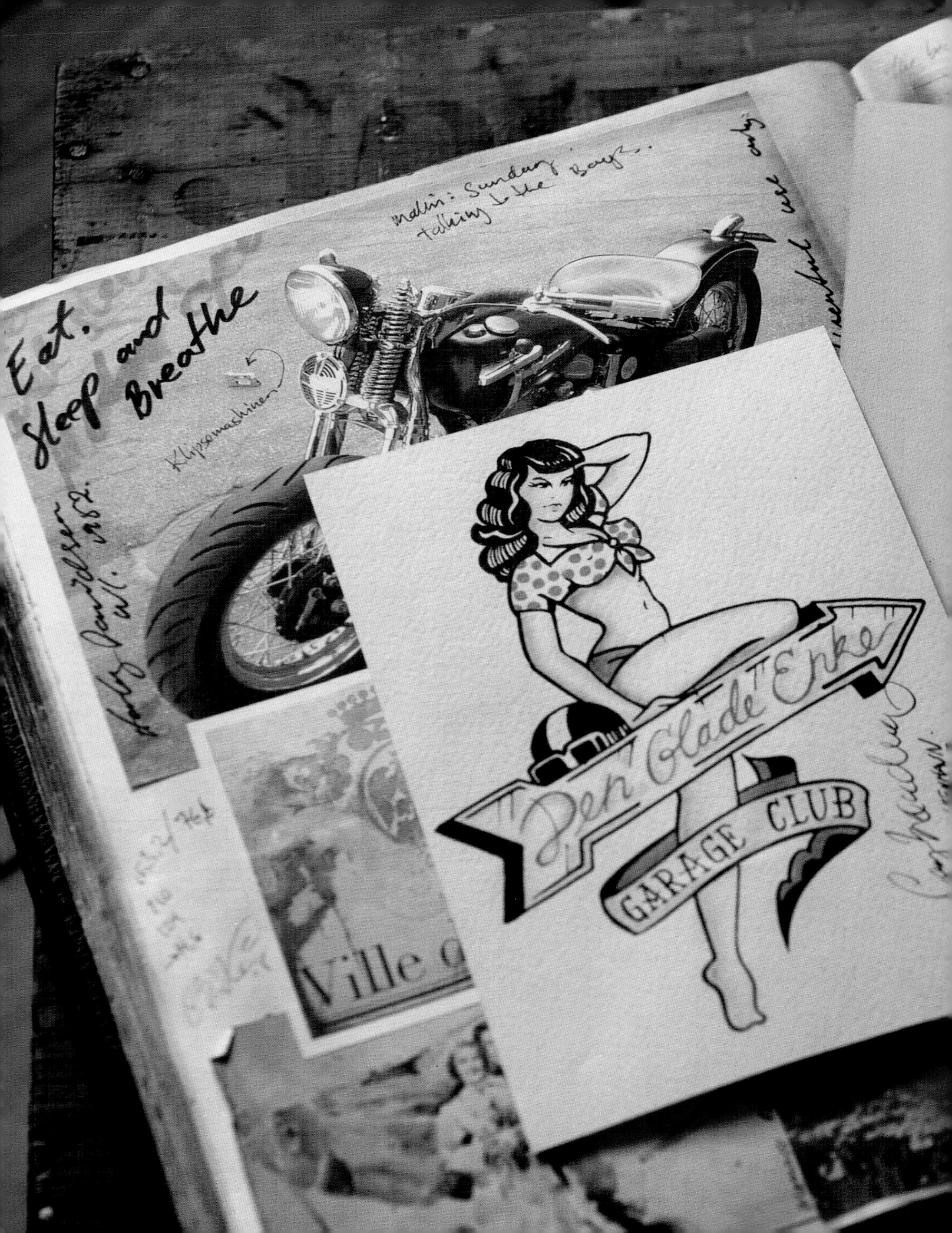
Eat, Sleep and Breathe
Malin: Sunday talking to the Boys.
Den Glade Enke
GARAGE CLUB
Ville

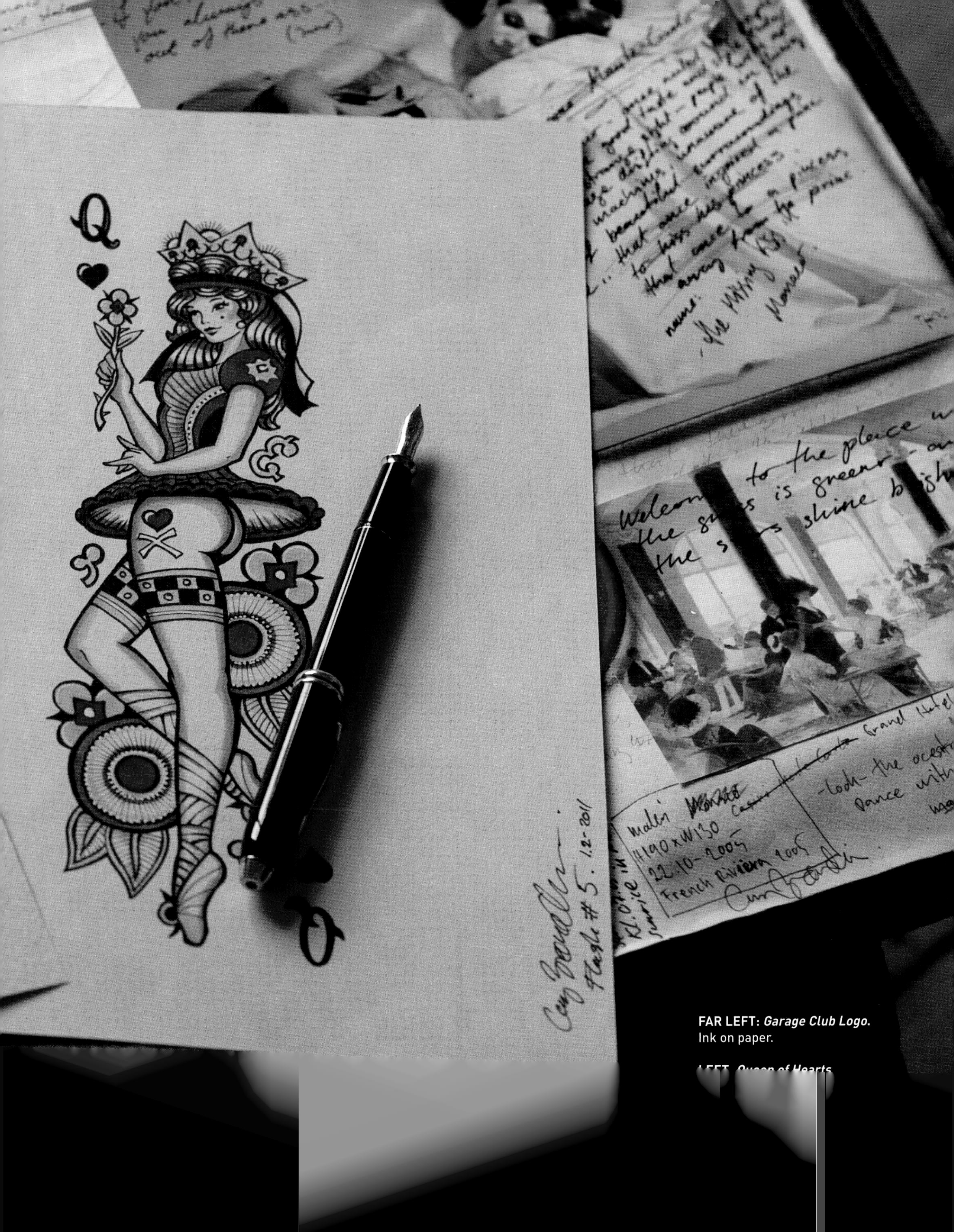

FAR LEFT: ***Garage Club Logo.***
Ink on paper.

LEFT: ***Queen of Hearts***

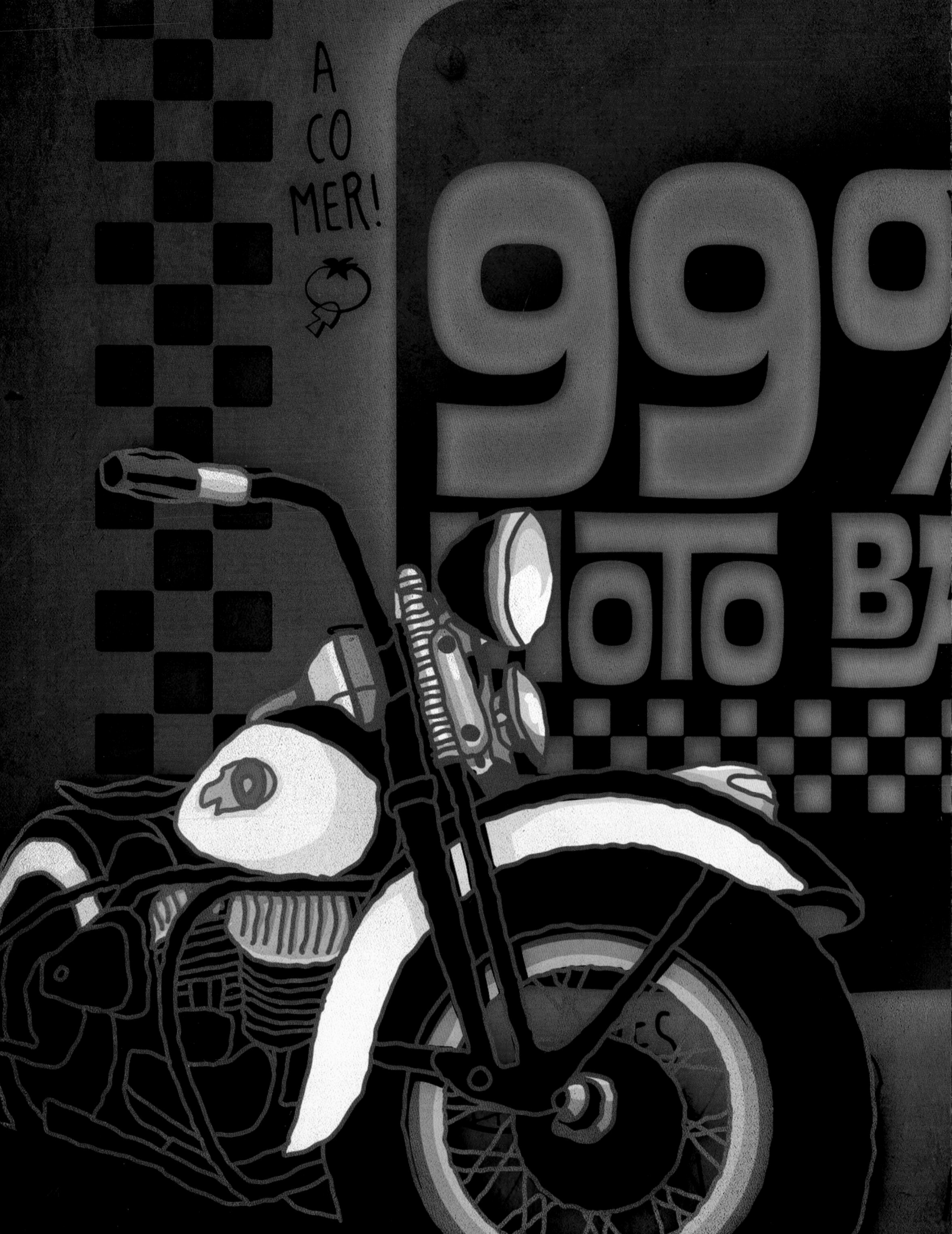
A
CO
MER!

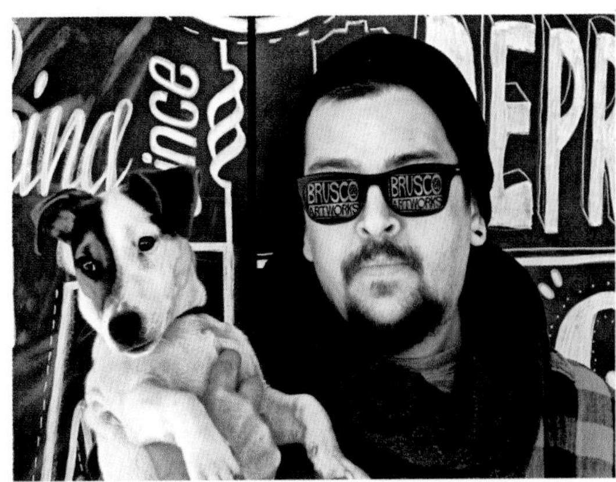

BRUSCO

The son of hippie parents, Hugo Jose Maria Corral (a.k.a. Brusco) grew up in a small town on Spain's Mediterranean coast, surrounded by dogs and bicycles that he'd strip and rebuild when he wasn't chalking pavements. At the age of ten, he moved to Barcelona, where he is still based. "Barcelona is a motorcycle city with an amazing cultural and artistic environment. It's a place that loves design." Despite studying art for four years and working as a full-time illustrator, Hugo doesn't consider himself an artist: "I'm a graphical communicator or scribble professional. My inspiration comes from all around me: movies, comics, tattoos and books... and, above all, other artists that I follow online. I try to find new techniques to bring to my own work." Today Hugo works almost exclusively with digital. "I love Photoshop, Flash and Illustrator. I'm completely self-taught in this area. I used to always sketch and draw directly in Flash, using my Wacom tablet. Recently I've tried drawing directly in Photoshop or I sketch on paper and then finish in Photoshop." When switching off, Hugo rides his Harley or Yamaha SR250.

LEFT: ***99% MotoBar Brand & Bike.***
Vector sketching, digital colours and texture.

RIGHT: 99% MotoBar WC signs.
Vector illustrations.

FAR RIGHT: ***Biker Topics by Brusco: el Chungo.***
Vector sketching, digital colours and textures.

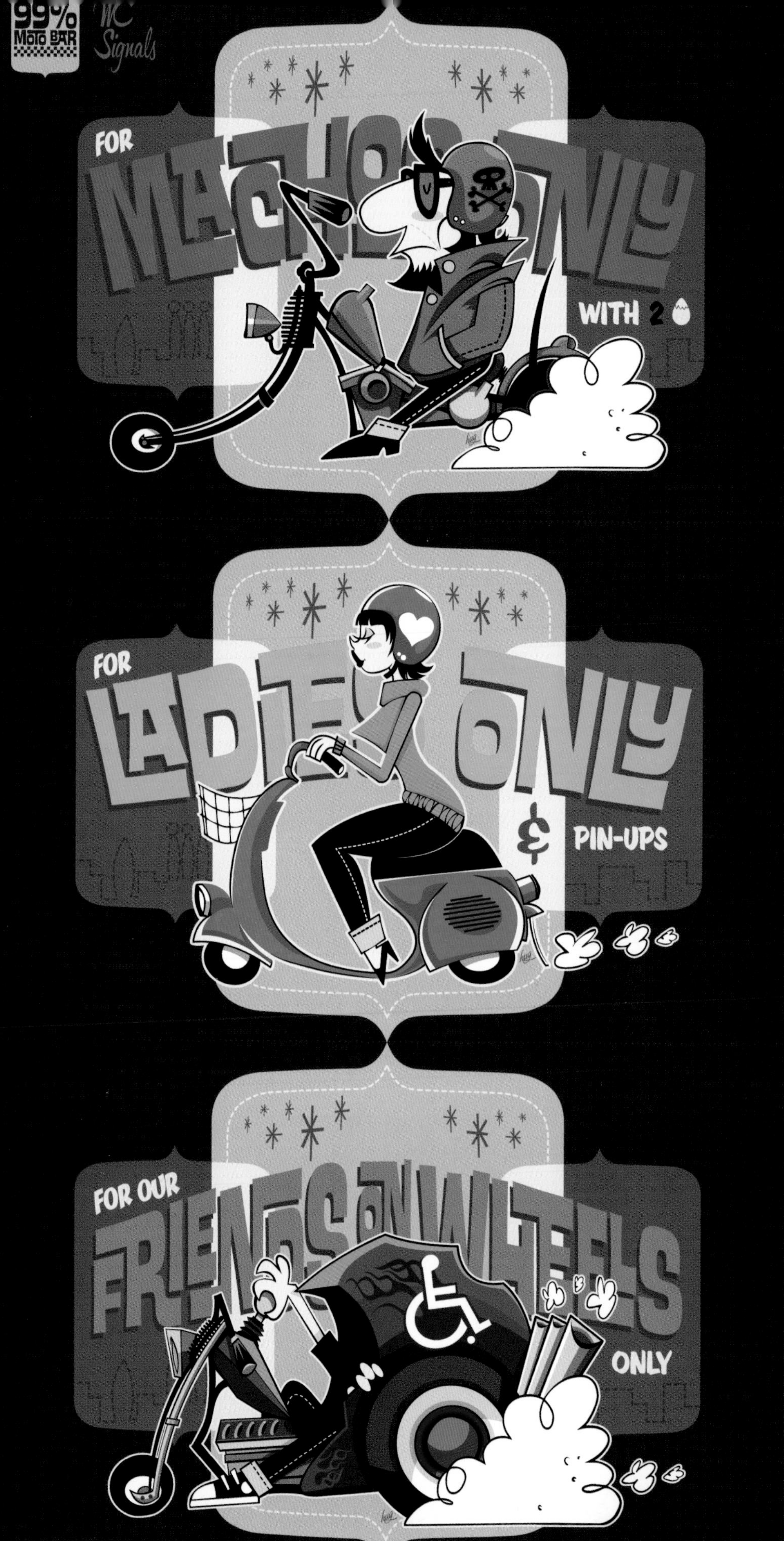

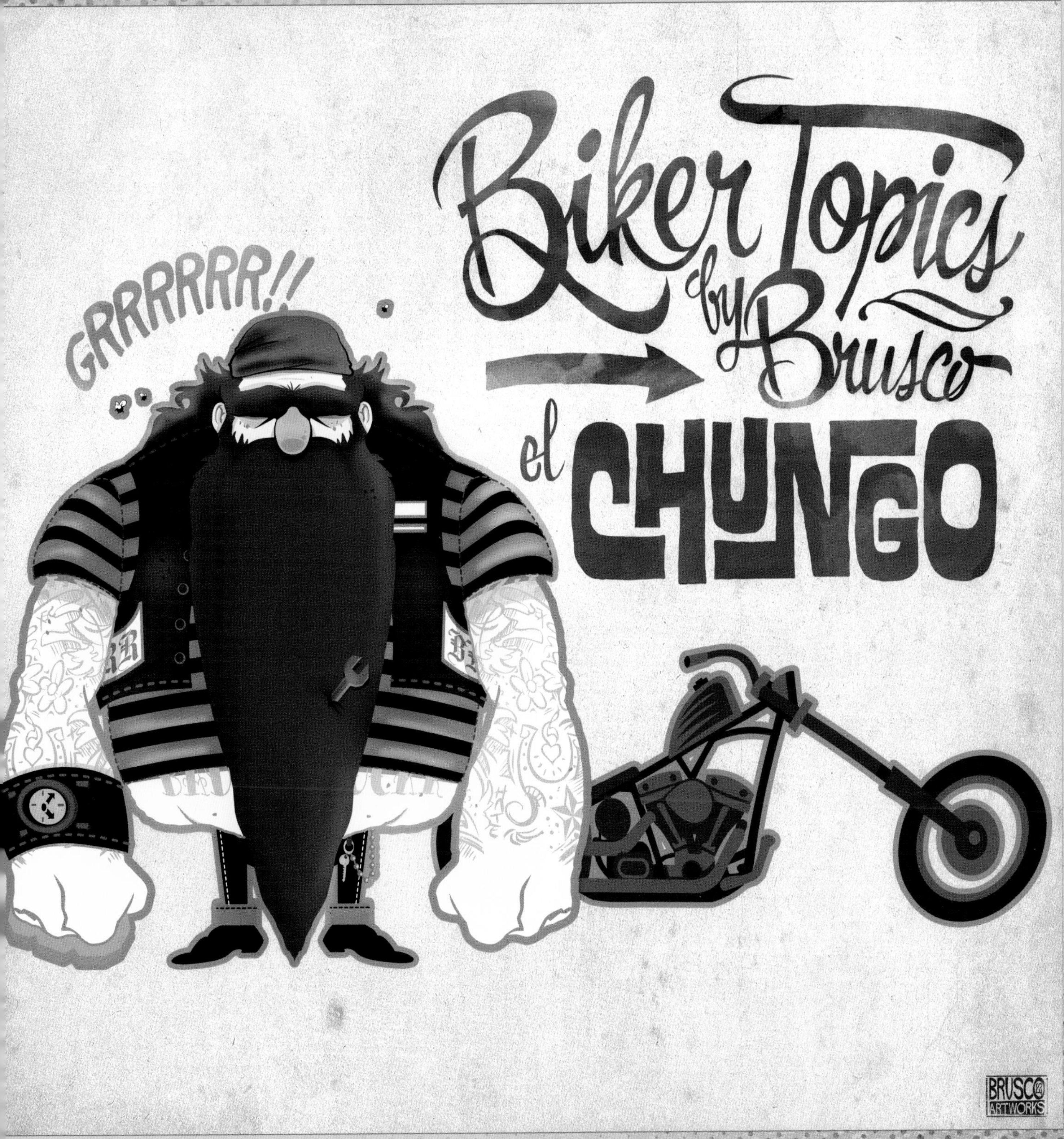

Biker Topics by Brusco

el CHUNGO

GRRRRRR!!

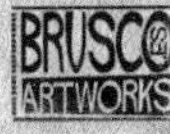

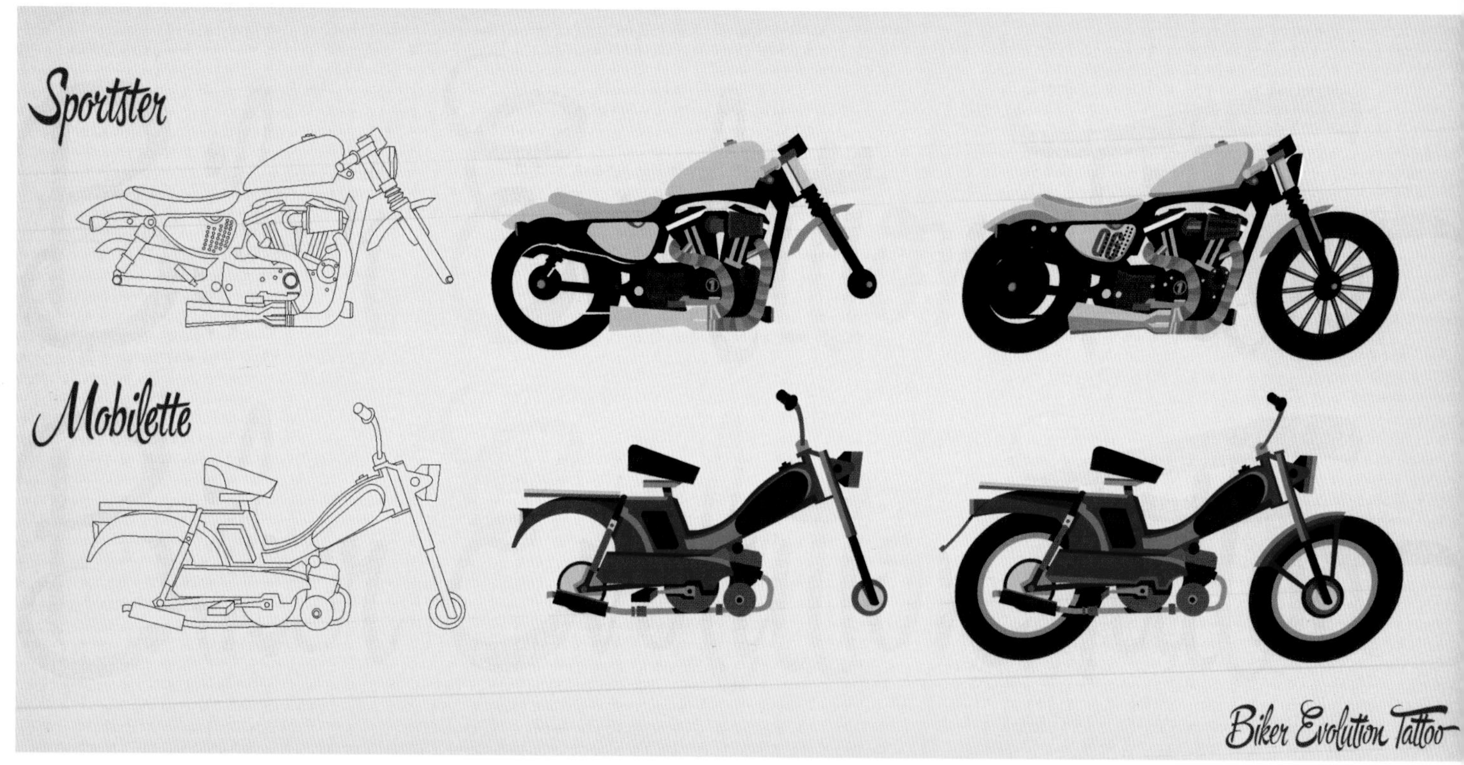

ABOVE: ***Biker Evolution Tattoo (process).***
Vector illustration.

RIGHT: ***Born To Be Wild.*** Digital Art.

we were born

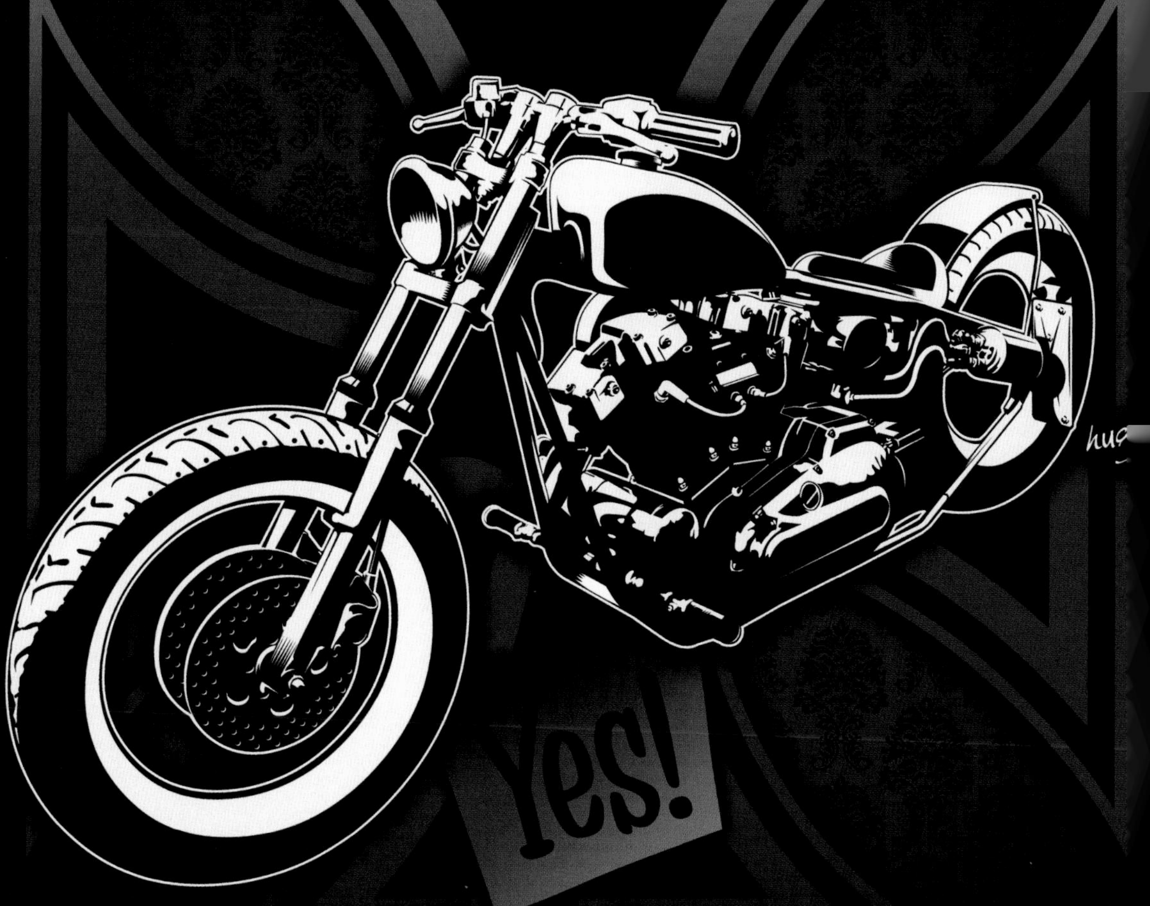

born to be wild

BELOW: ***Sideburn 11 Launch Party at Kiddo.***
Vector sketching, digital colours and textures.

BELOW RIGHT: A&K Wedding invitation design.
Vector sketching, digital colours and textures.

FAR RIGHT: ***Super Motor Barcelona.***
Digital illustration.

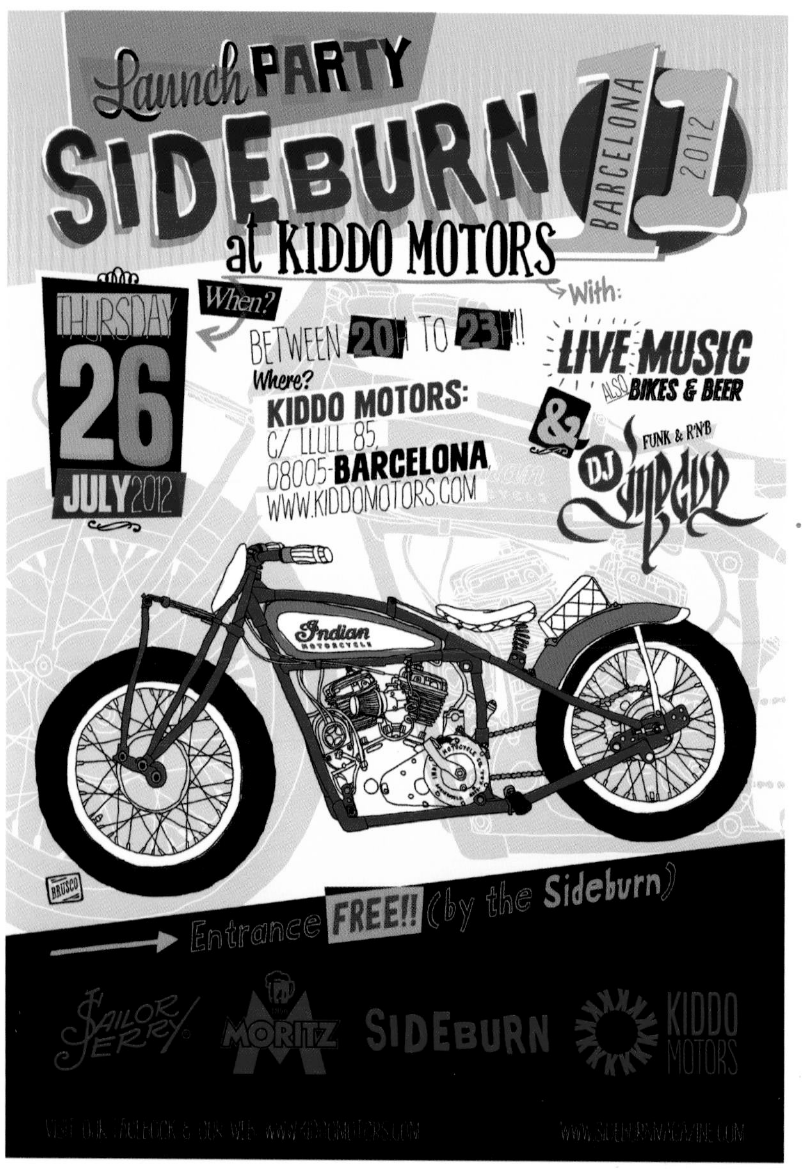

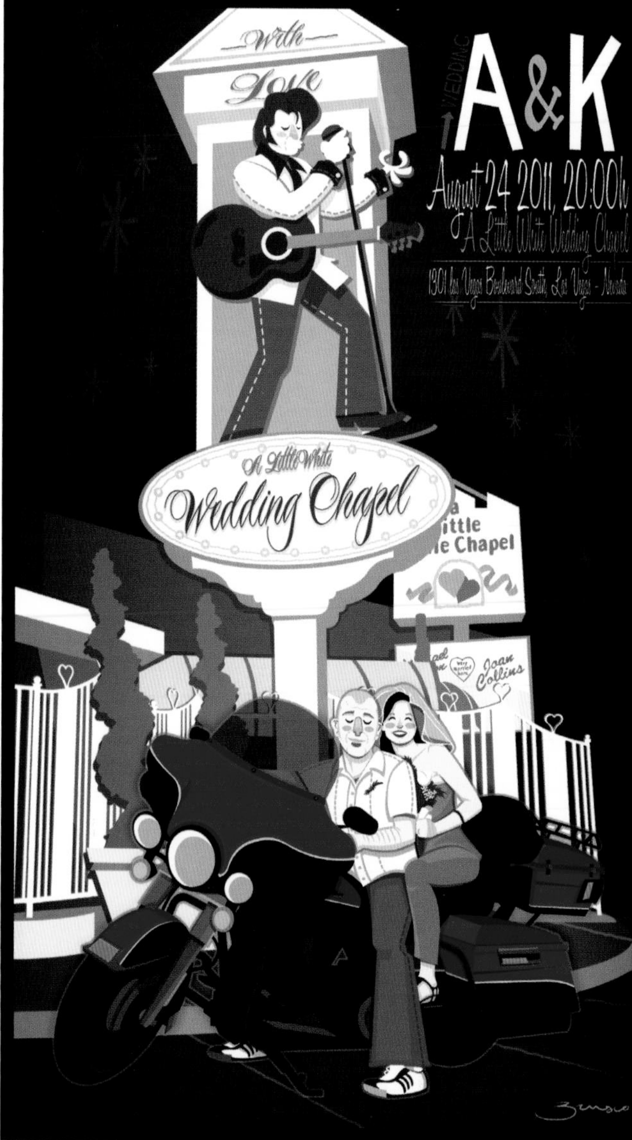

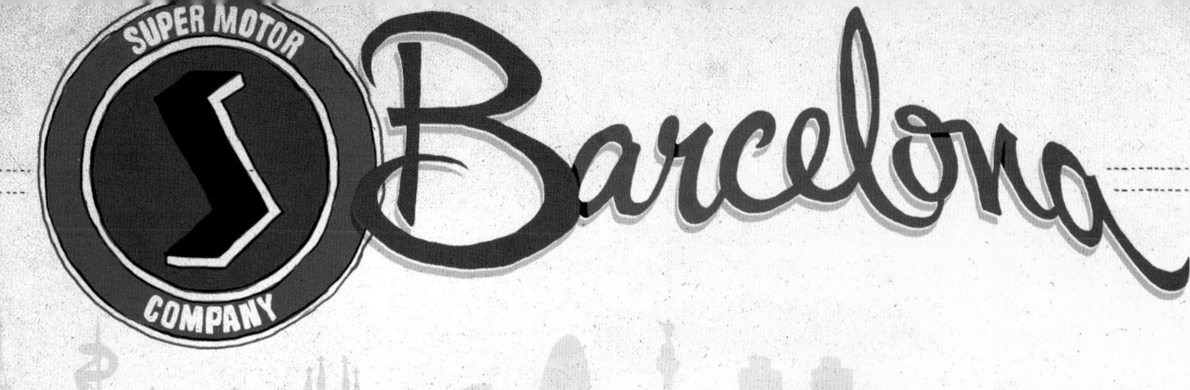

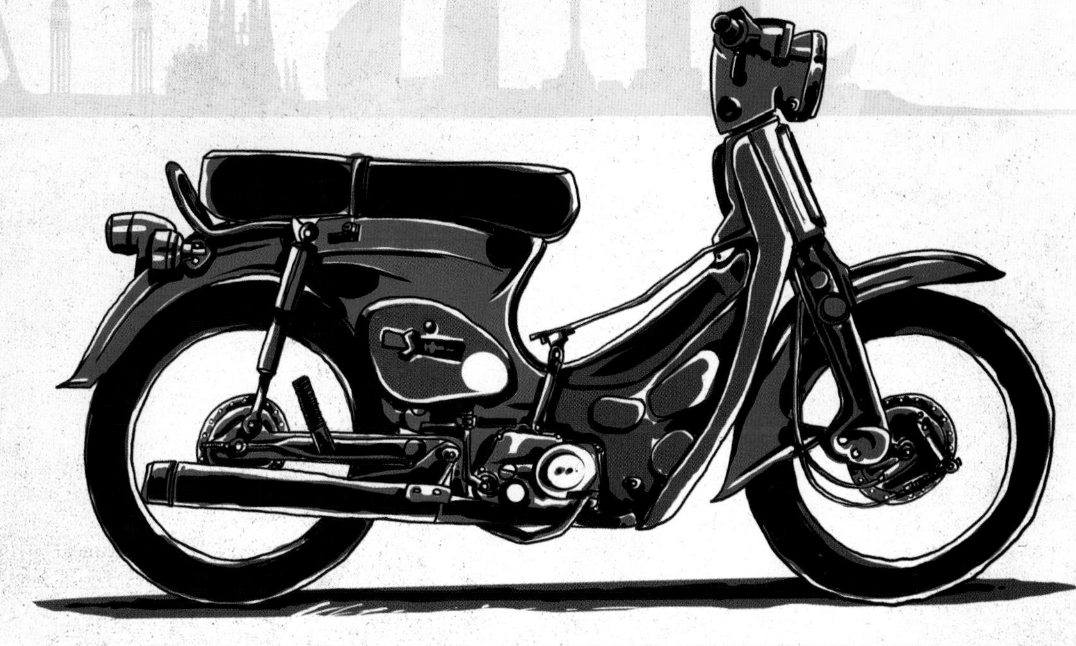

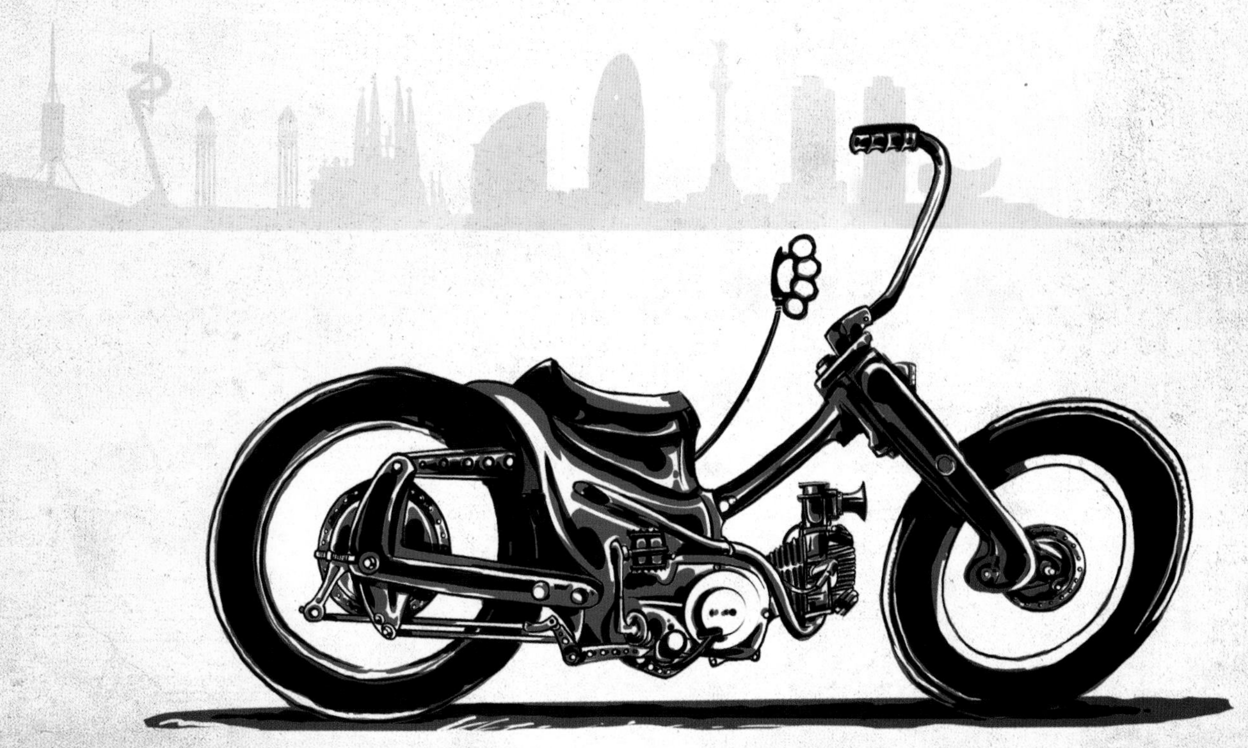

FTW Customize! BRUSCO ARTWORKS

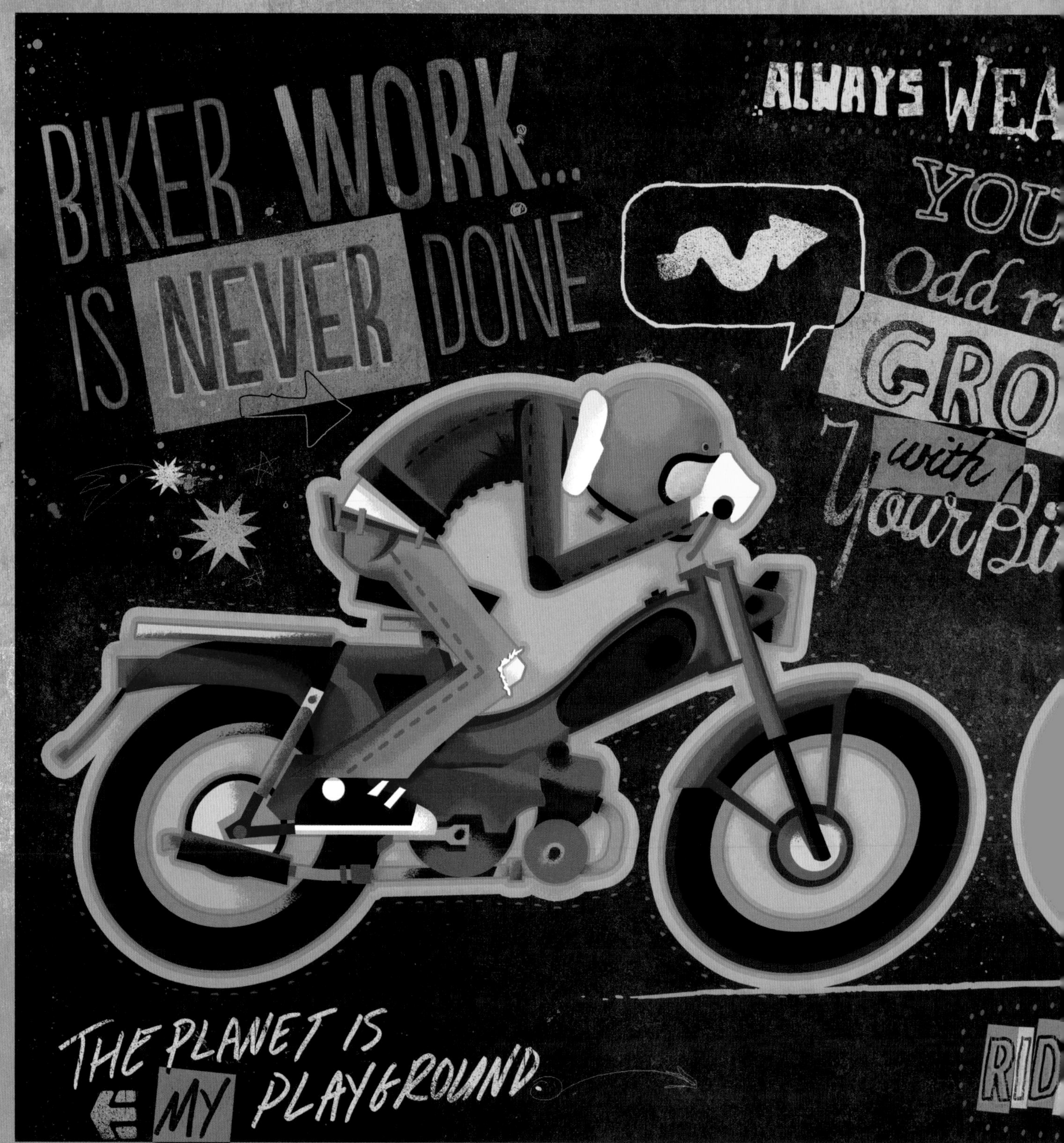

ABOVE: ***Biker Evolution.***
Vector sketching, digital colours and textures.

UR Wayfarer

RIDE MuthaFucka

it's What's inside THAT COUNTS... OR NOT?

ST IS A horizontal FALL

BRUSCO ARTWORKS 2012

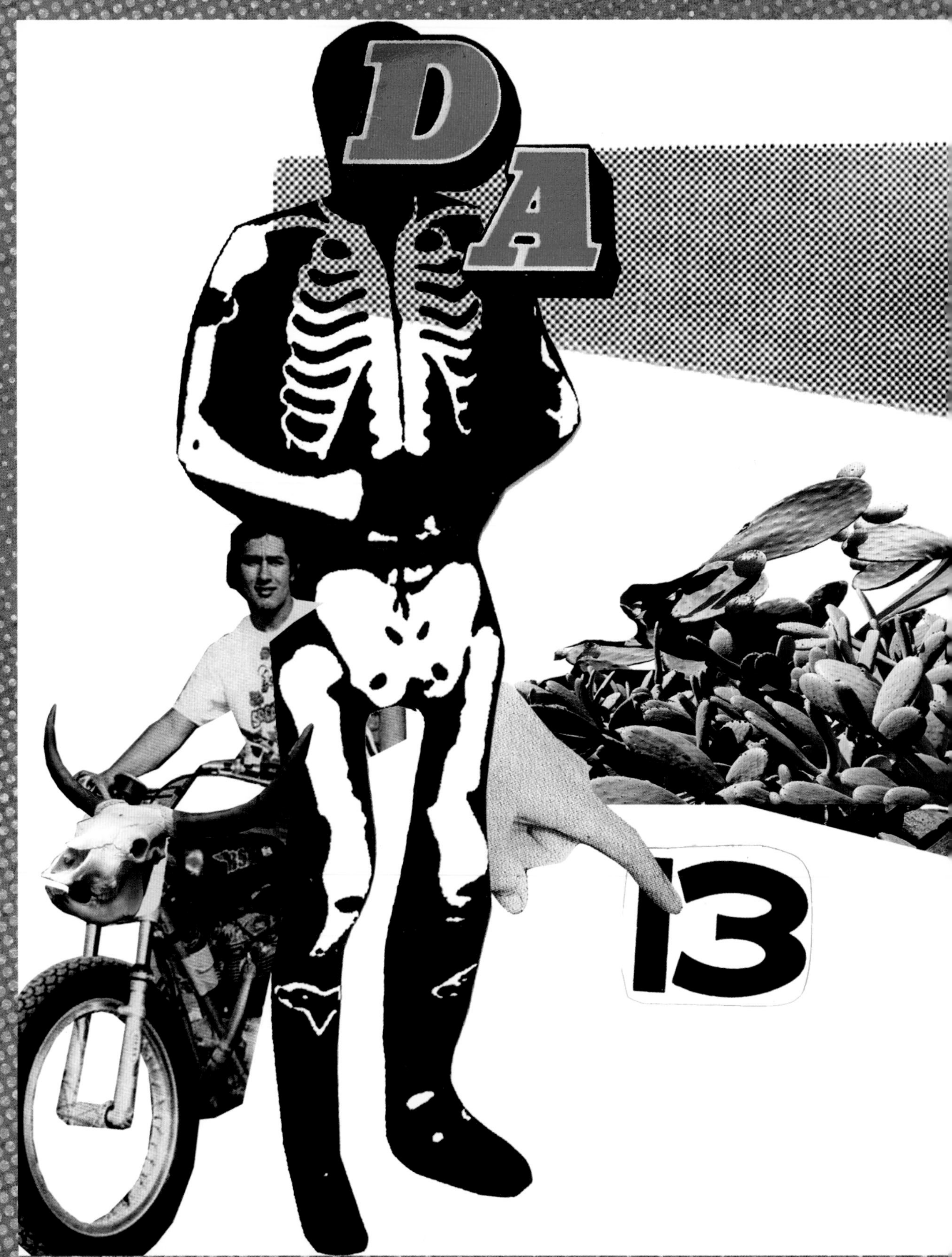
DA
13

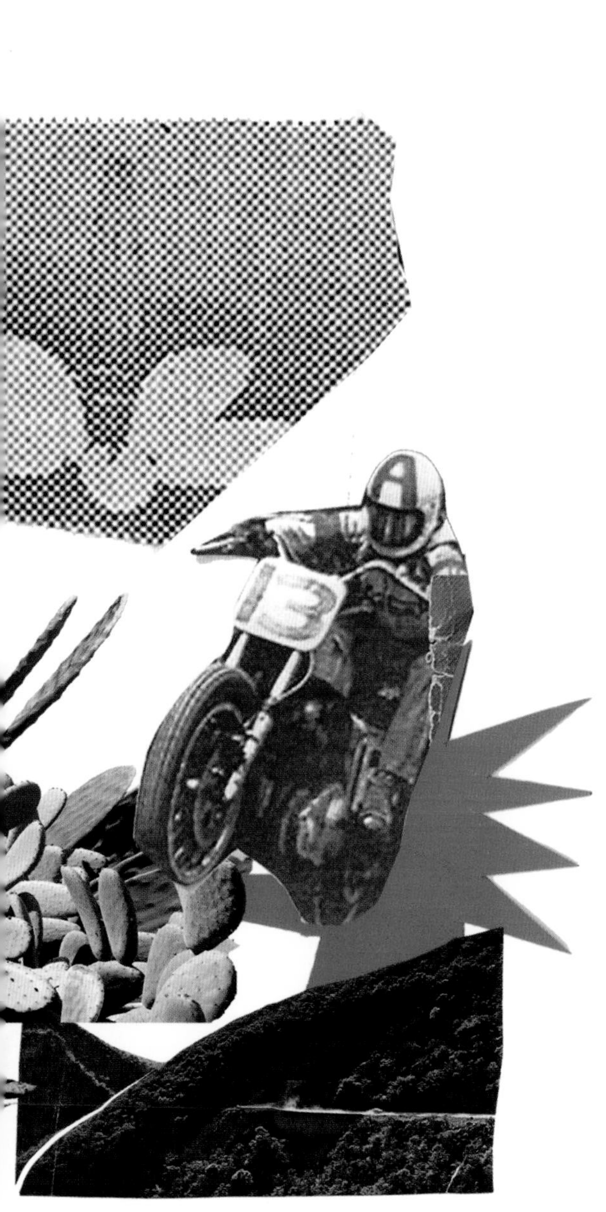

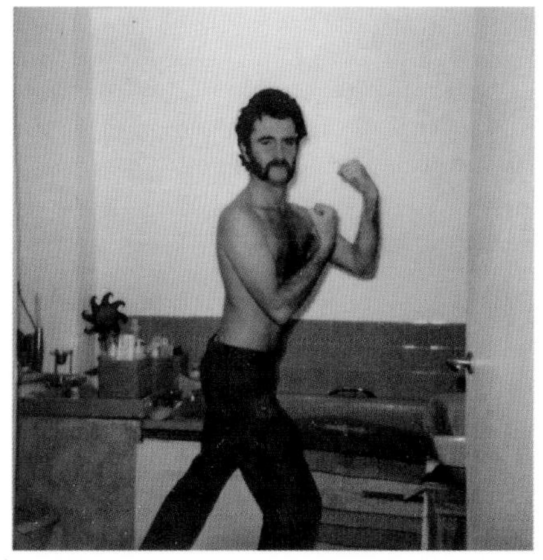

JAMES CHAPPELL

"My work is collage-based using old magazines and coloured paper. To this I might add paint, pencil and old Letraset that I stole from college," says Londoner James Chappell. He first decided to start producing art with motorcycles at the core because he didn't know anything about them and enjoyed the challenge.

"I can't drive or ride, but I did steal a moped while working on a building site in Germany many moons ago. I went riding around the countryside with a Nazi helmet on my head."

Both the reality and two-wheeled dreams that fill Chappell's mind are like one of his collages.

"My dream bike is a BSA Bantam and I would ride it wearing 1940s clothing and take Salma Hayek for a cocktail across the English South Downs, while being chased by Nazis."

LEFT: *D.A. 13.*
Multimedia collage.

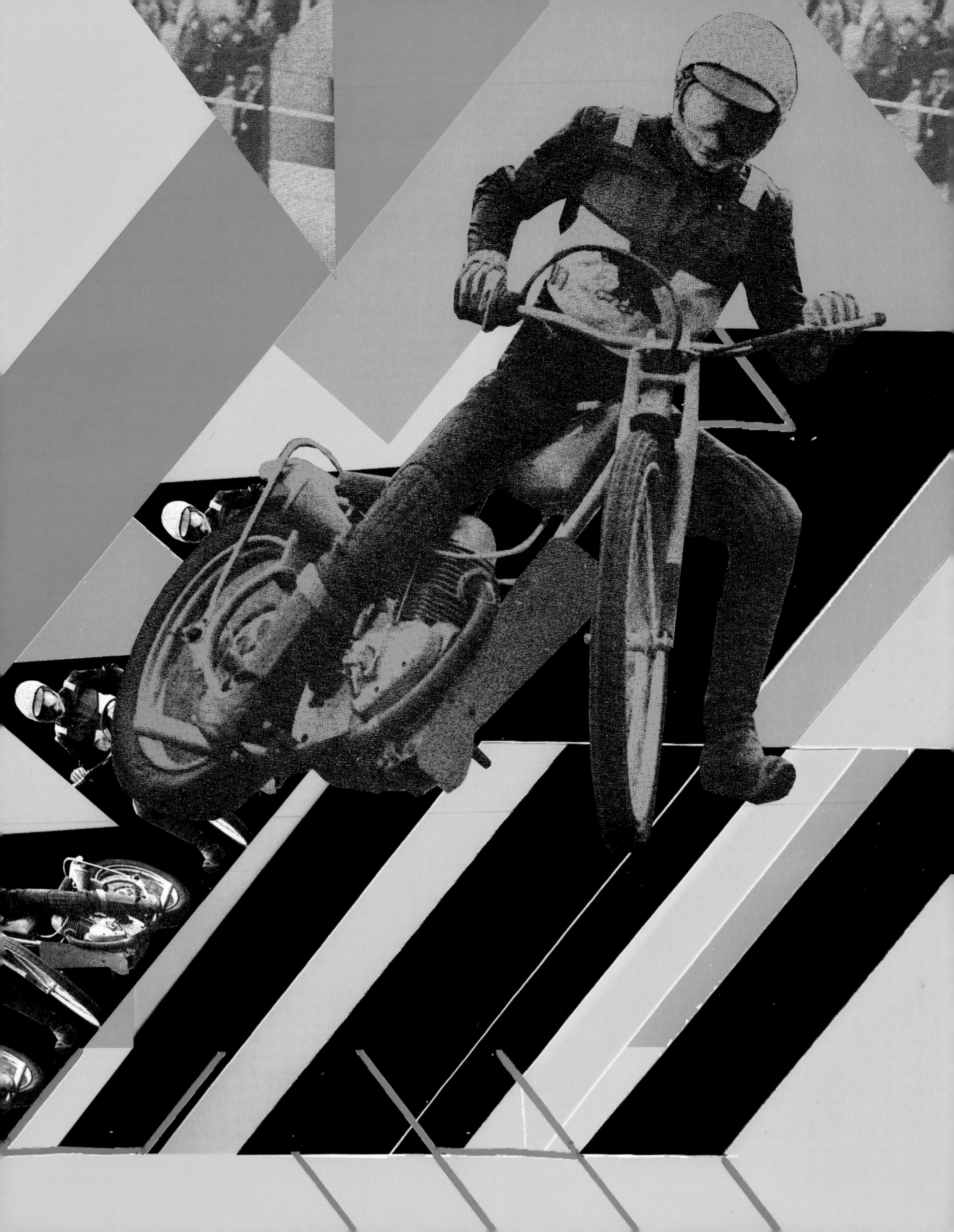

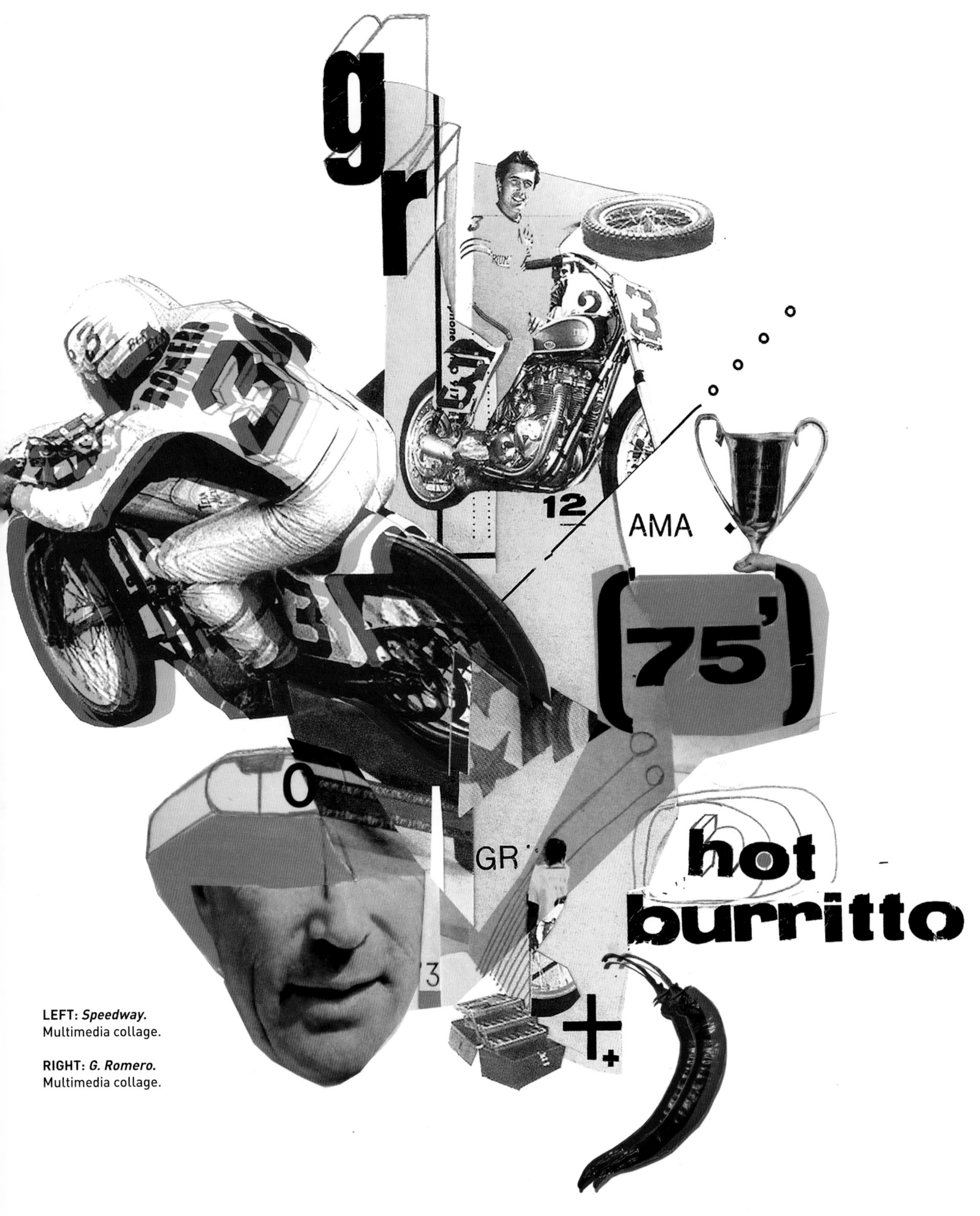

LEFT: *Speedway.*
Multimedia collage.

RIGHT: *G. Romero.*
Multimedia collage.

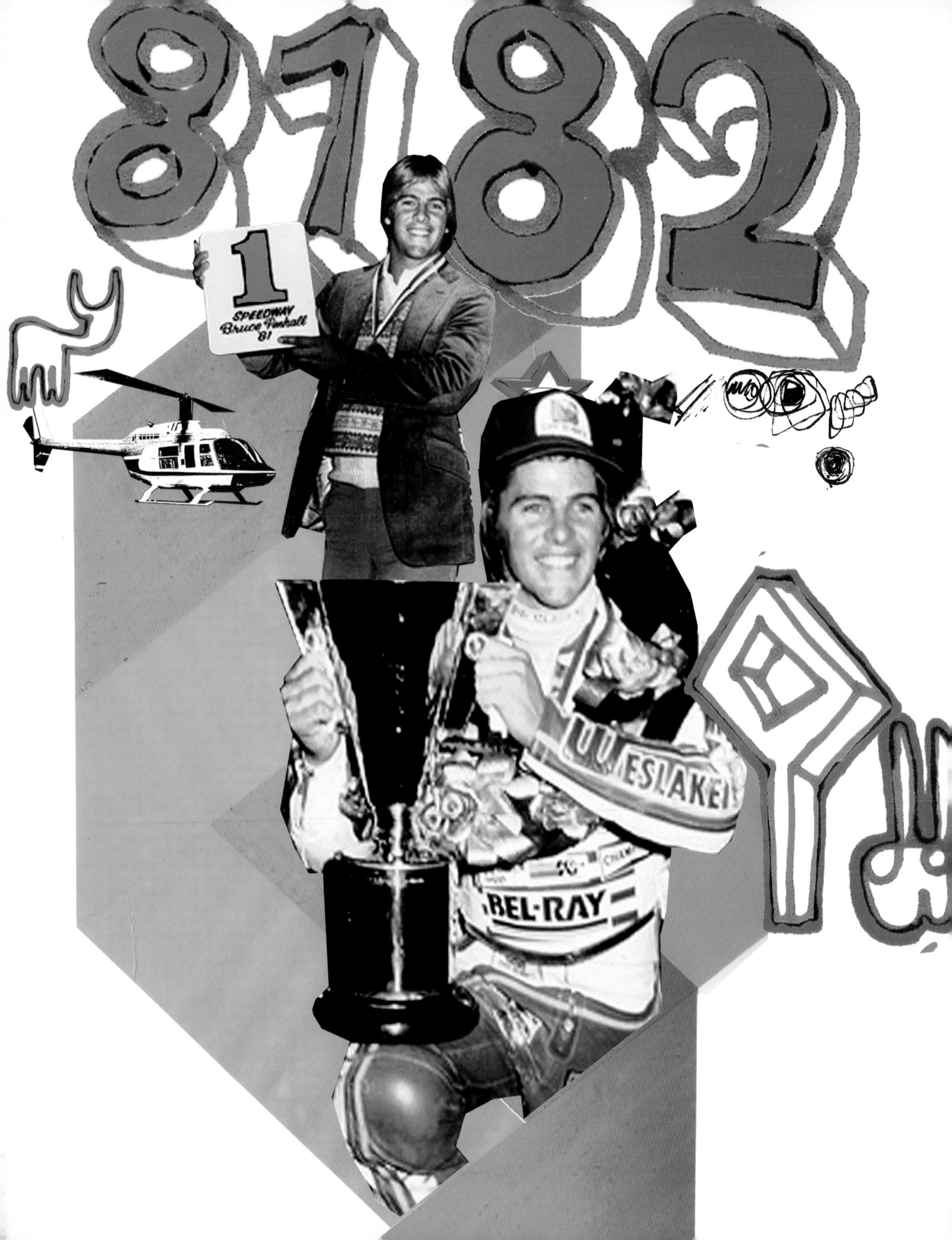

81 82
1
SPEEDWAY
Bruce
81
ESLAKE
BEL-RAY

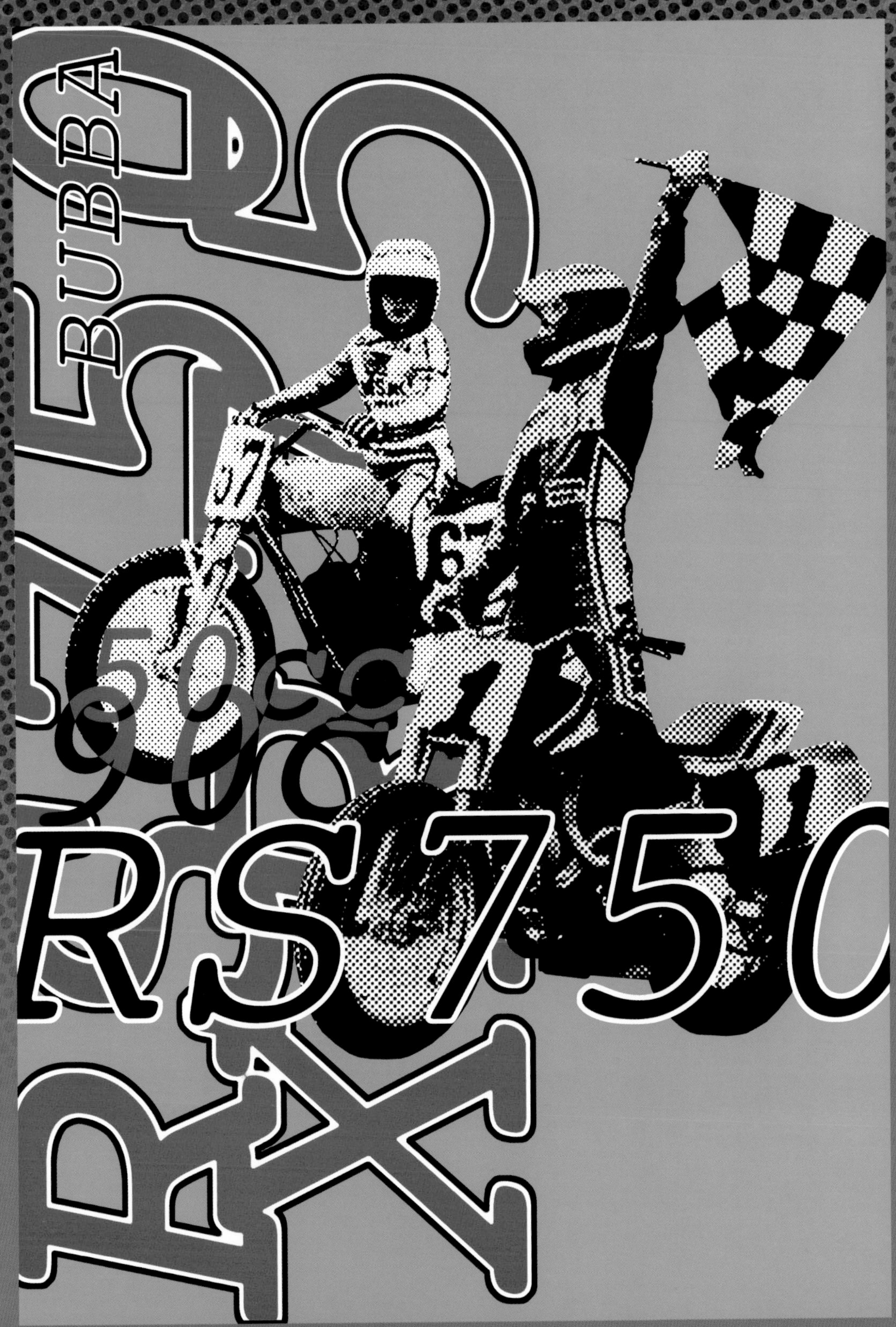

LEFT: ***Bubba S.***
Multimedia collage.

FAR LEFT: ***Bruce P.***
Multimedia collage.

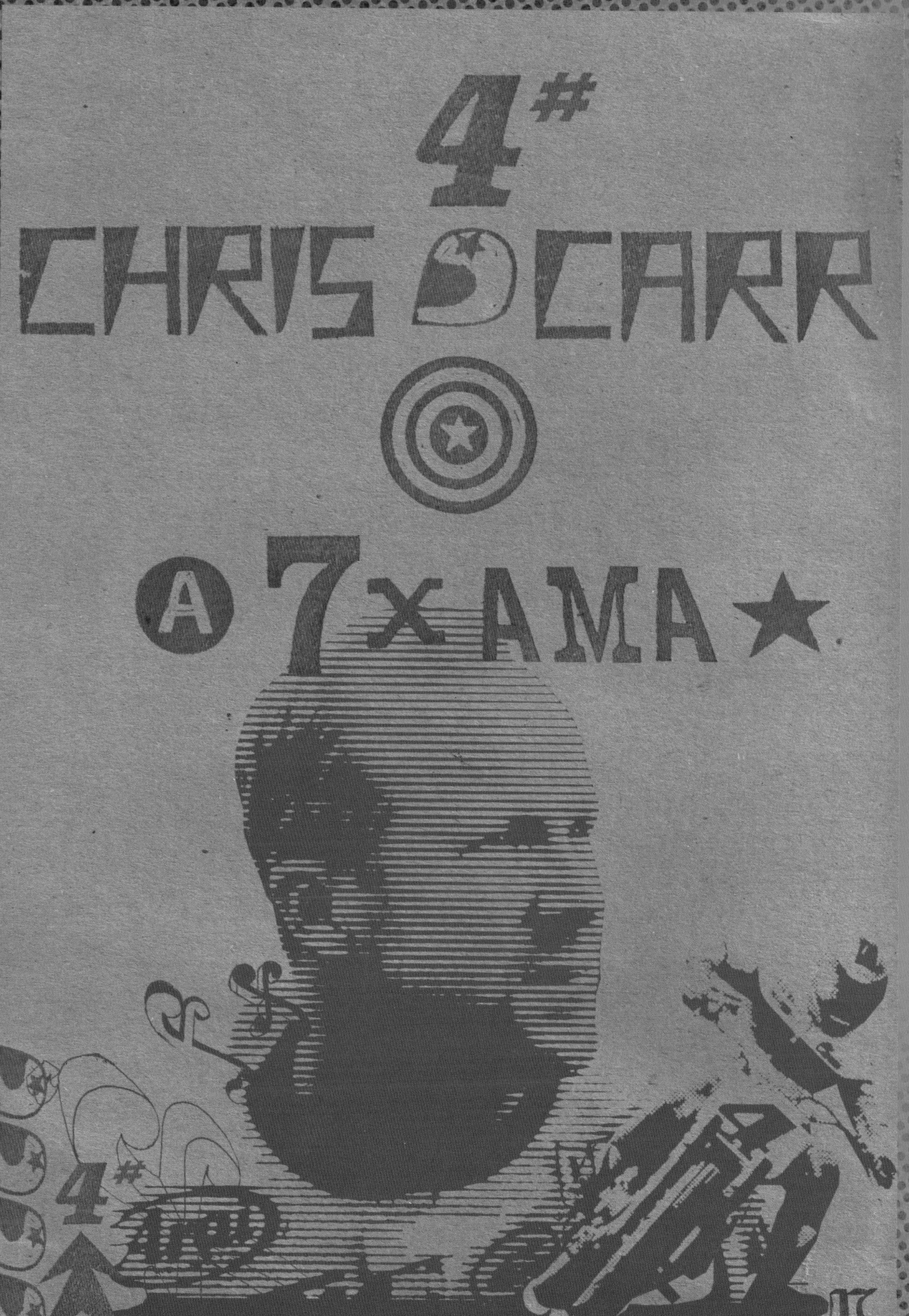

4#

CHRIS CARR

A 7 x AMA ★

4#

BELOW: ***Eddie Lawson.***
Multimedia collage.

FAR LEFT: ***Chris Carr.***
Multimedia collage.

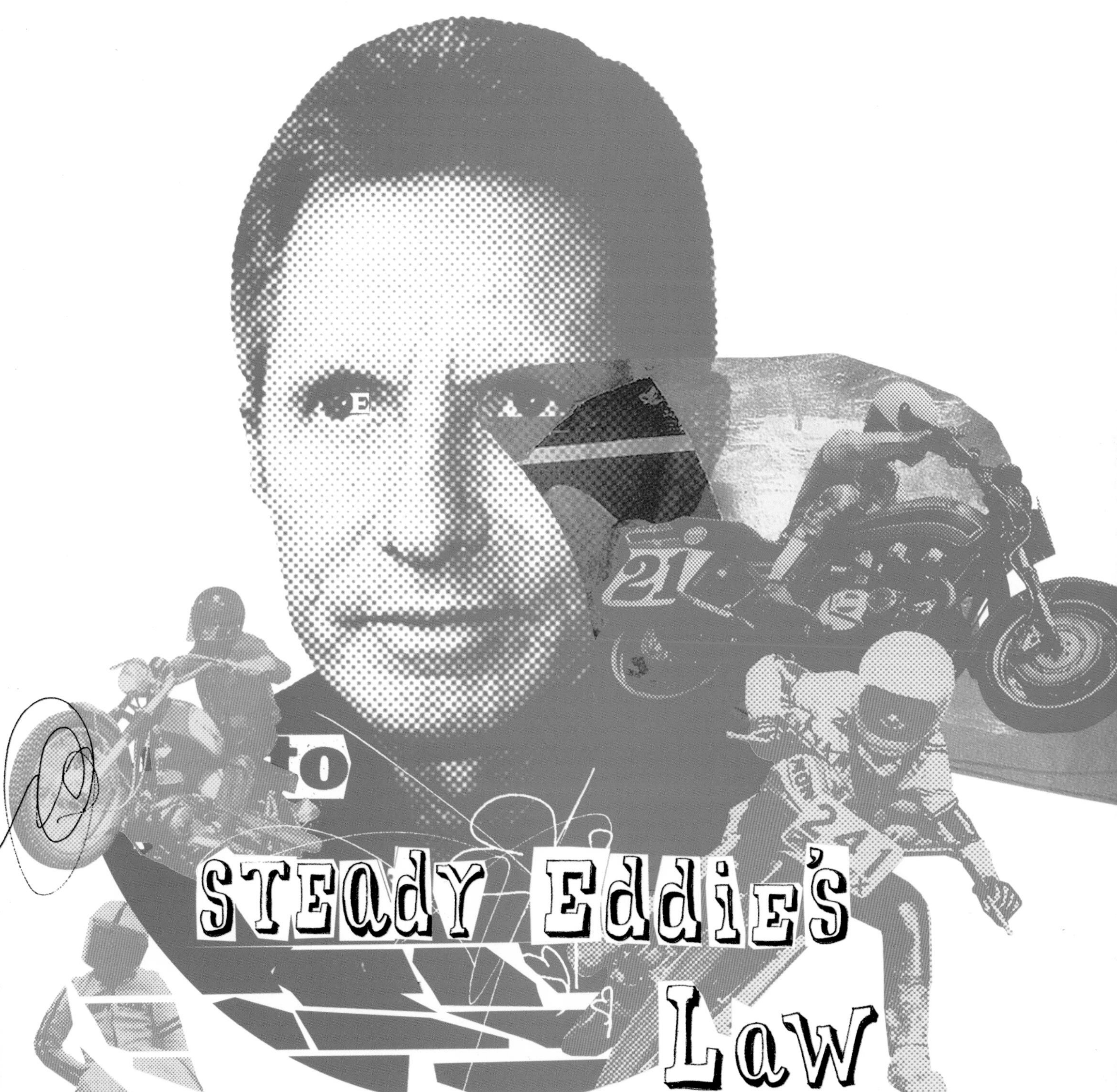

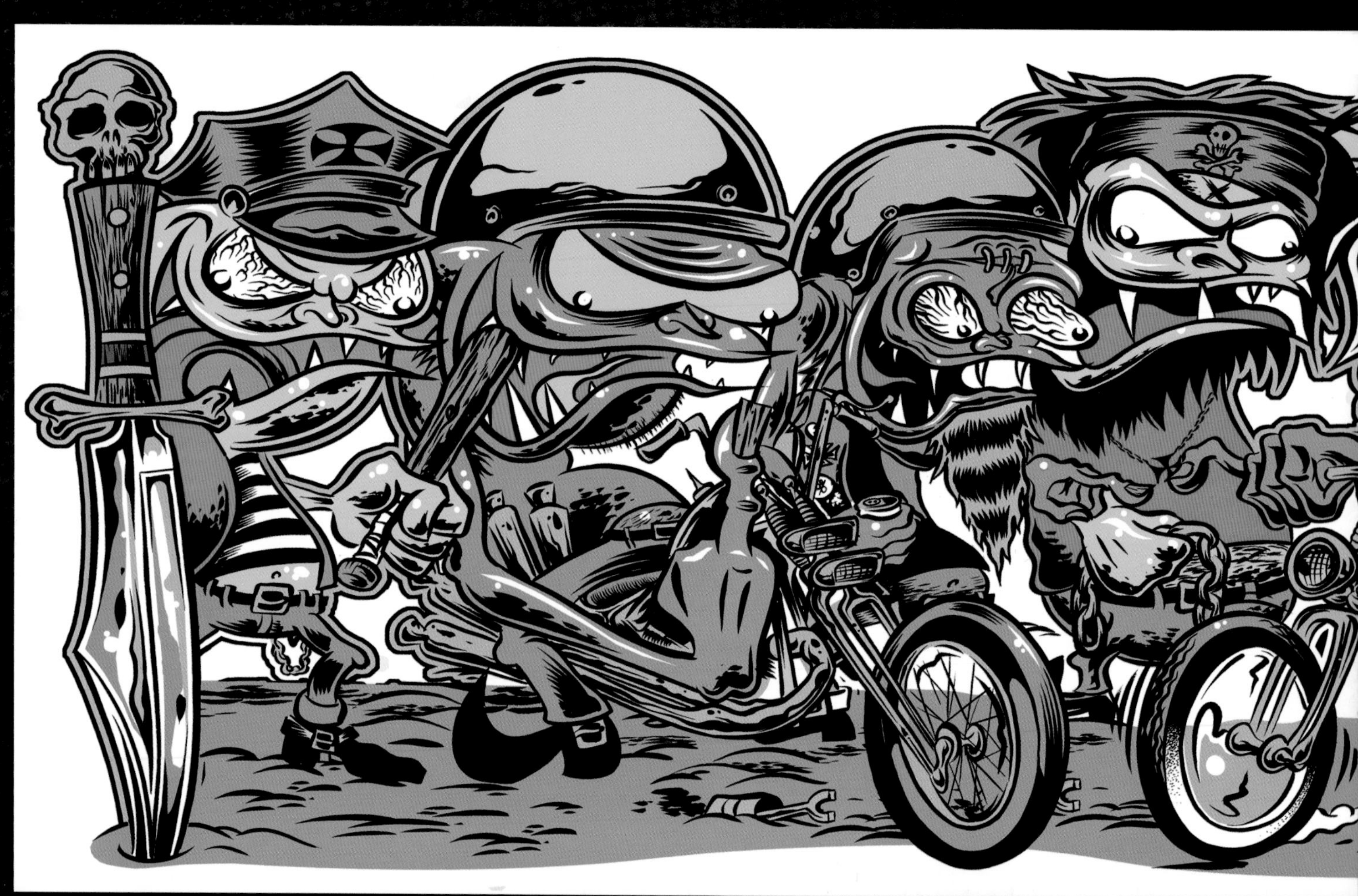

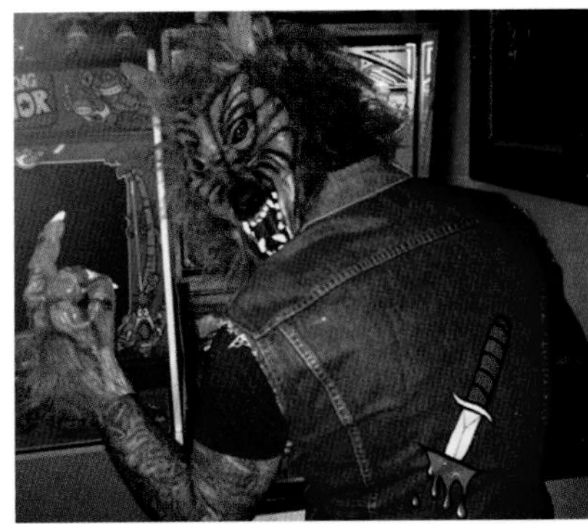

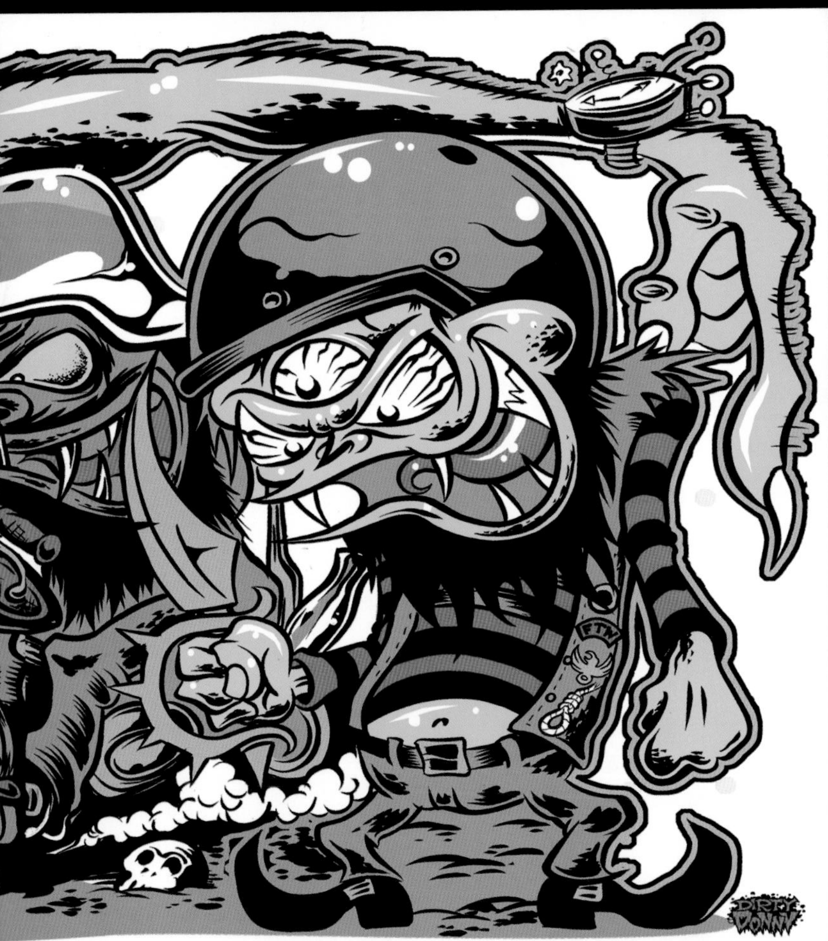

DIRTY DONNY

Dirty Donny's art crosses boundaries like few others of his generation, as the intro of Monster Revolt! The Art of Dirty Donny, explains, "... guitar picks and skateboard decks, sandwich boards on the sidewalks and recording studio walls. Helmets and record album covers. Decals and posters. Vinyl toys and canvases, cigar store Indians and pinball machines. Chopper gas tanks and wristwatches." When it seems as though he couldn't possibly find another surface his characters might live on, Donny discovers another medium that suits them just fine.

The Canadian-born, San Francisco-based artist keeps it simple when it comes to explaining his motivations, "I've dug cars, bikes, comic books, music and art since I was a little kid. I'm attracted to loud fast, what else can I say?"

ABOVE LEFT: ***Goon Patrol.***
Ink on paper.

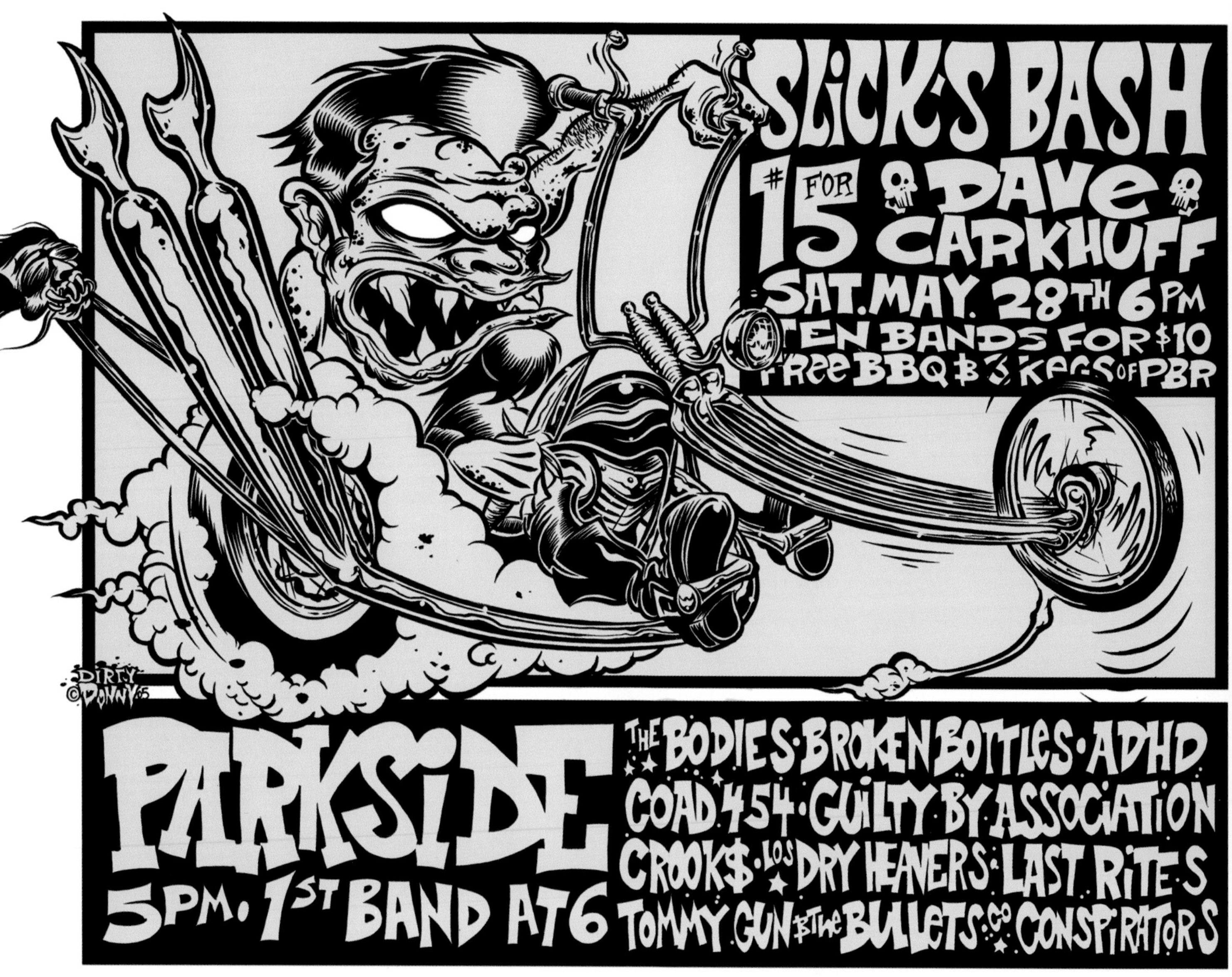

ABOVE: ***Slick's Bash Poster.***
Ink on paper.

RIGHT: ***Minibiker.***
Ink on paper.

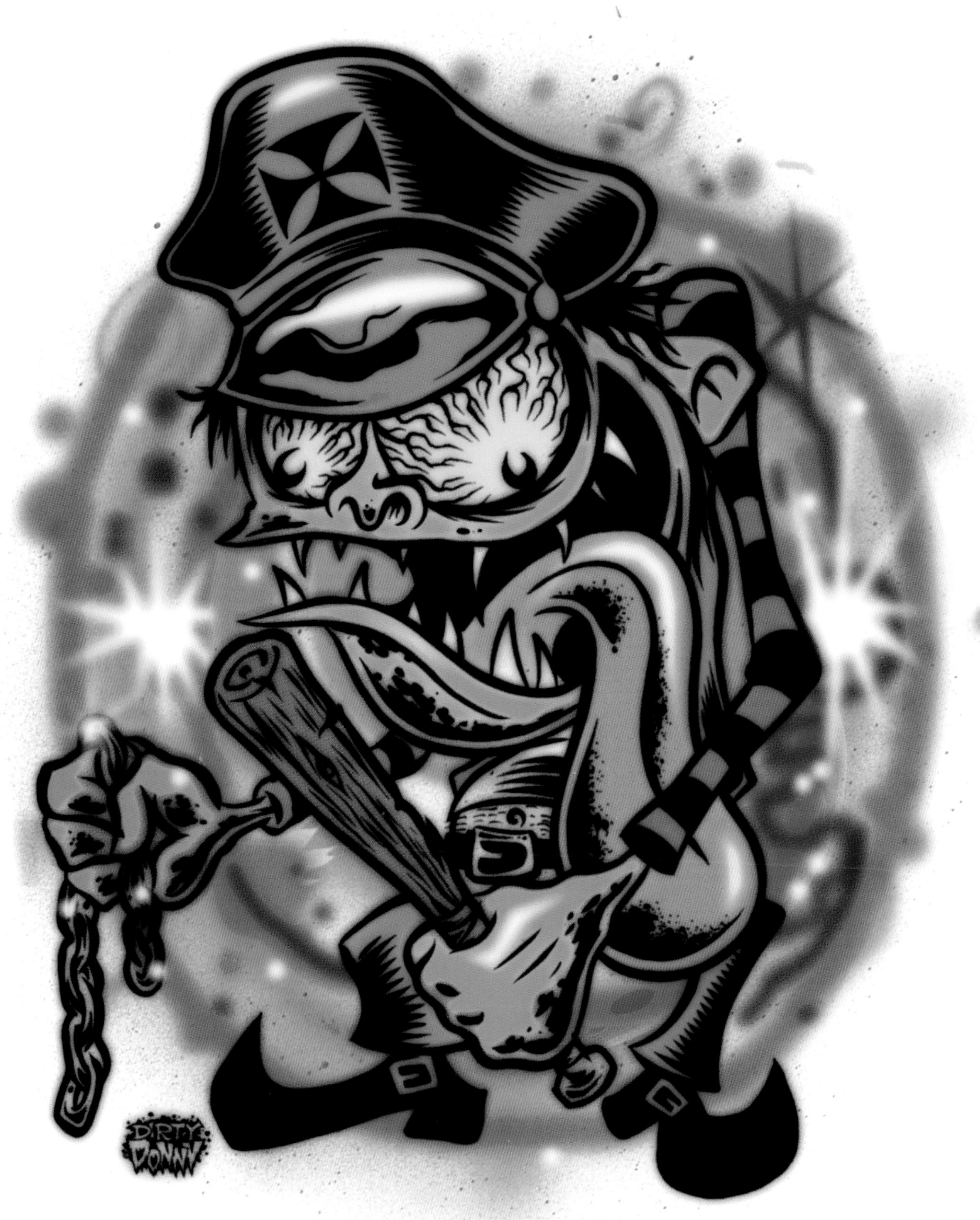
DIRTY DONNY

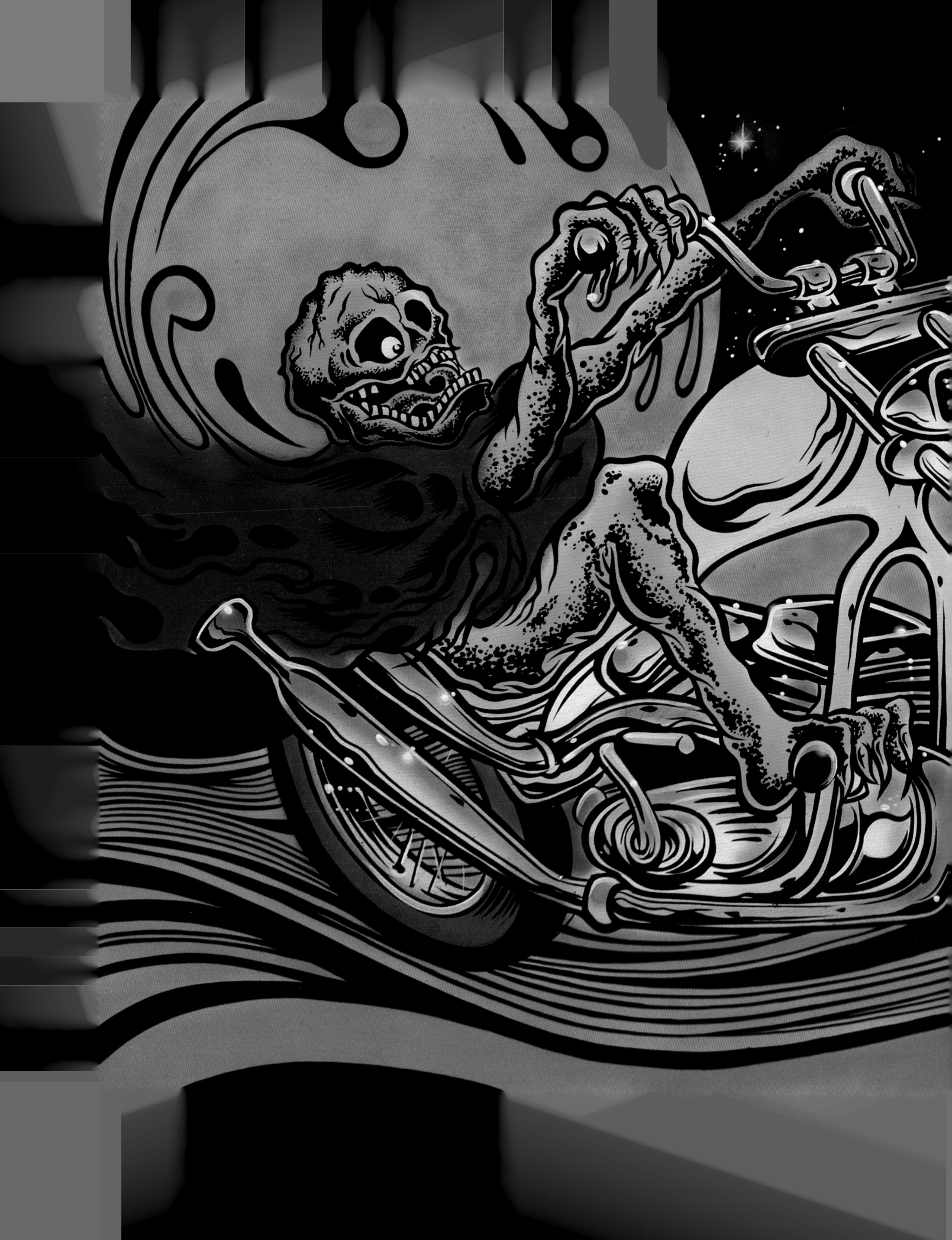

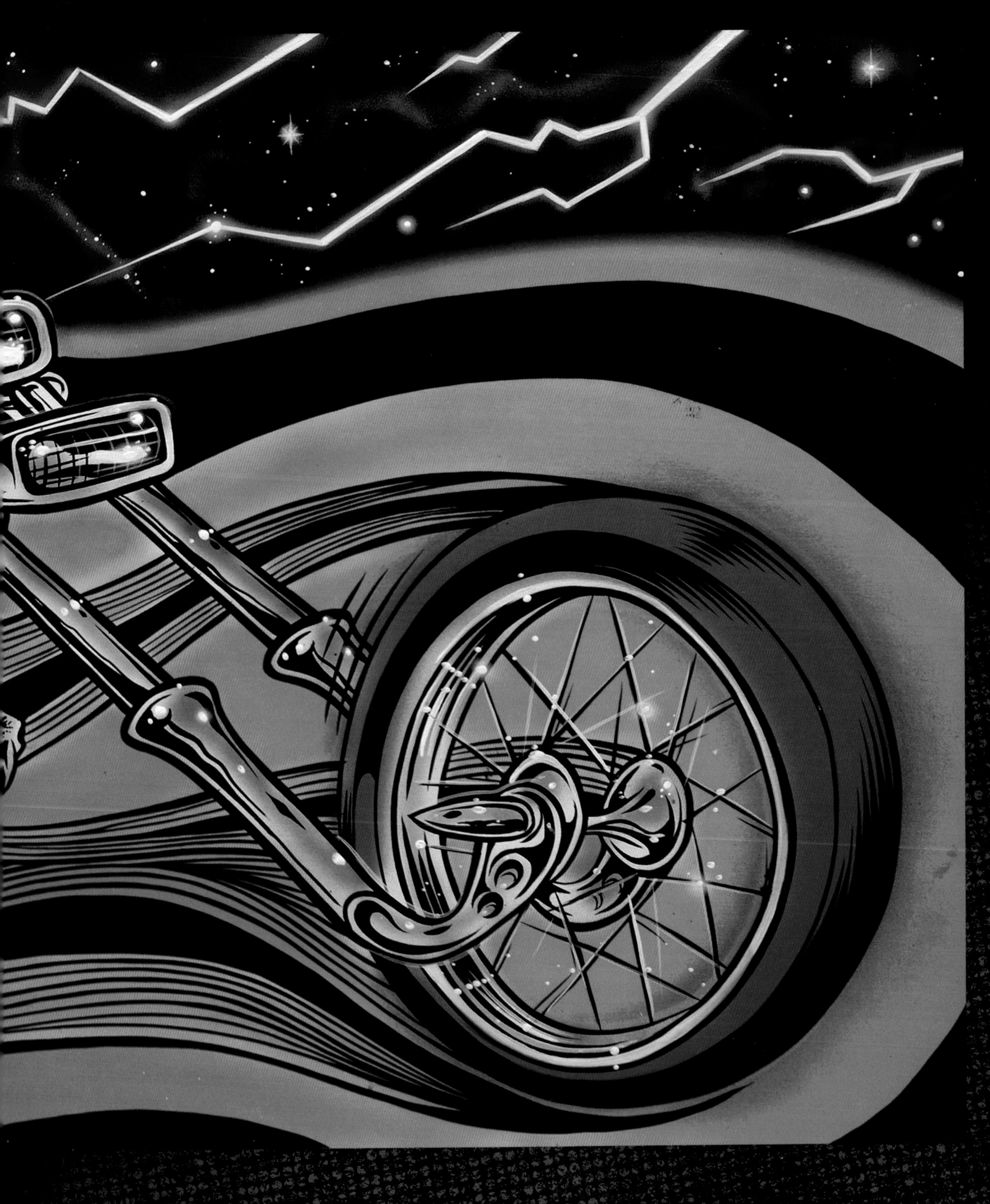

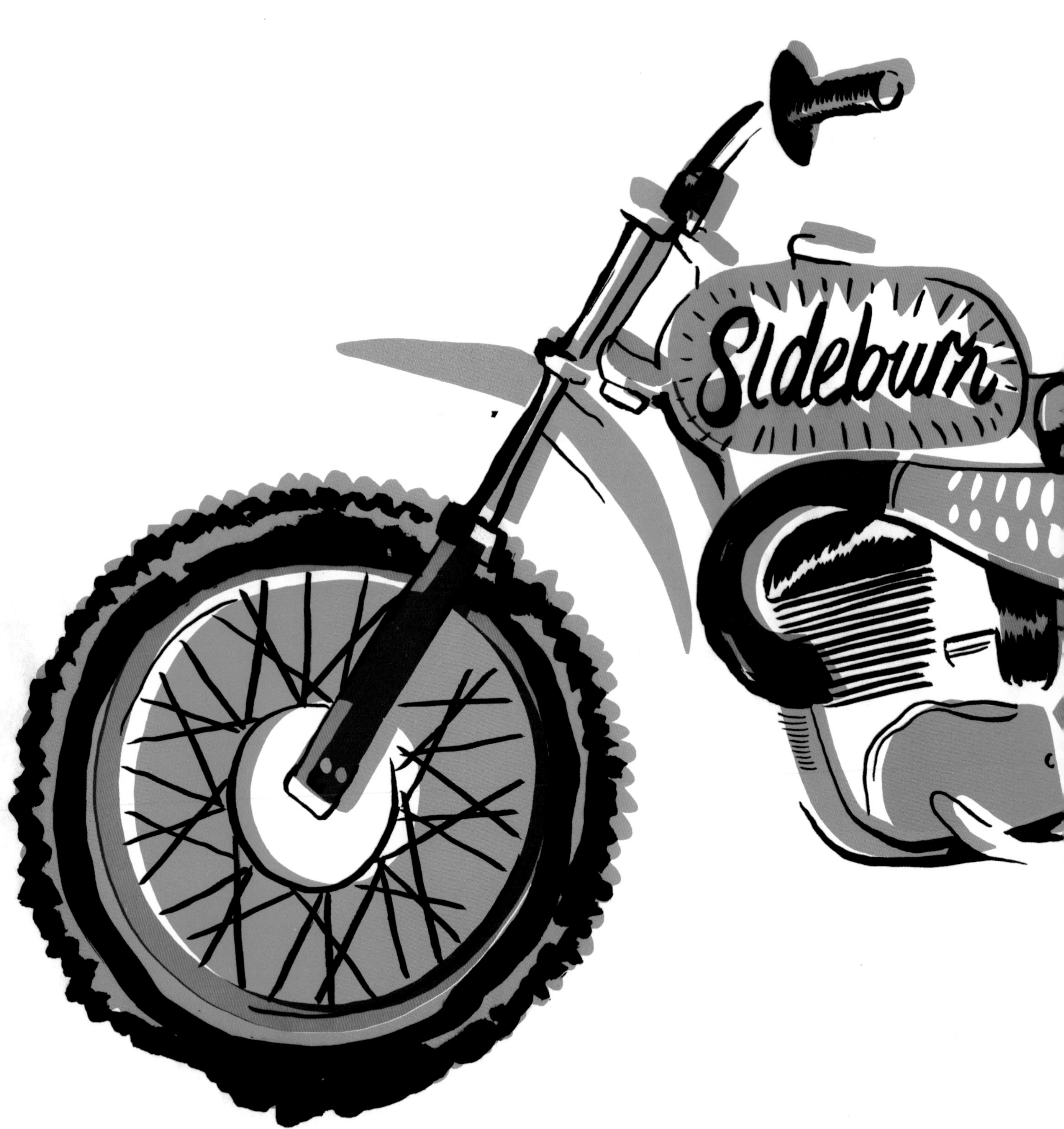
Sideburn

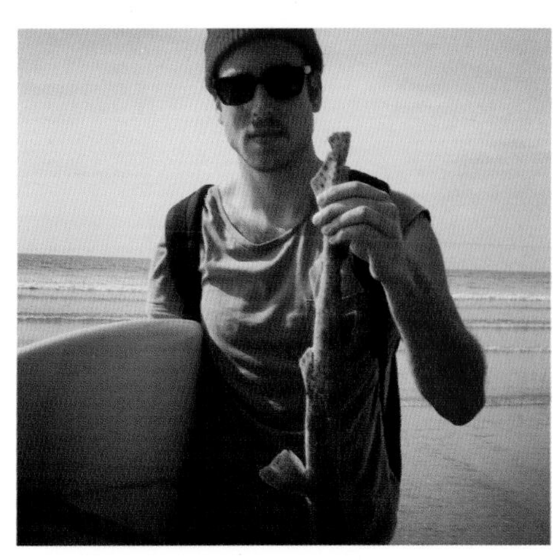

STEVIE GEE

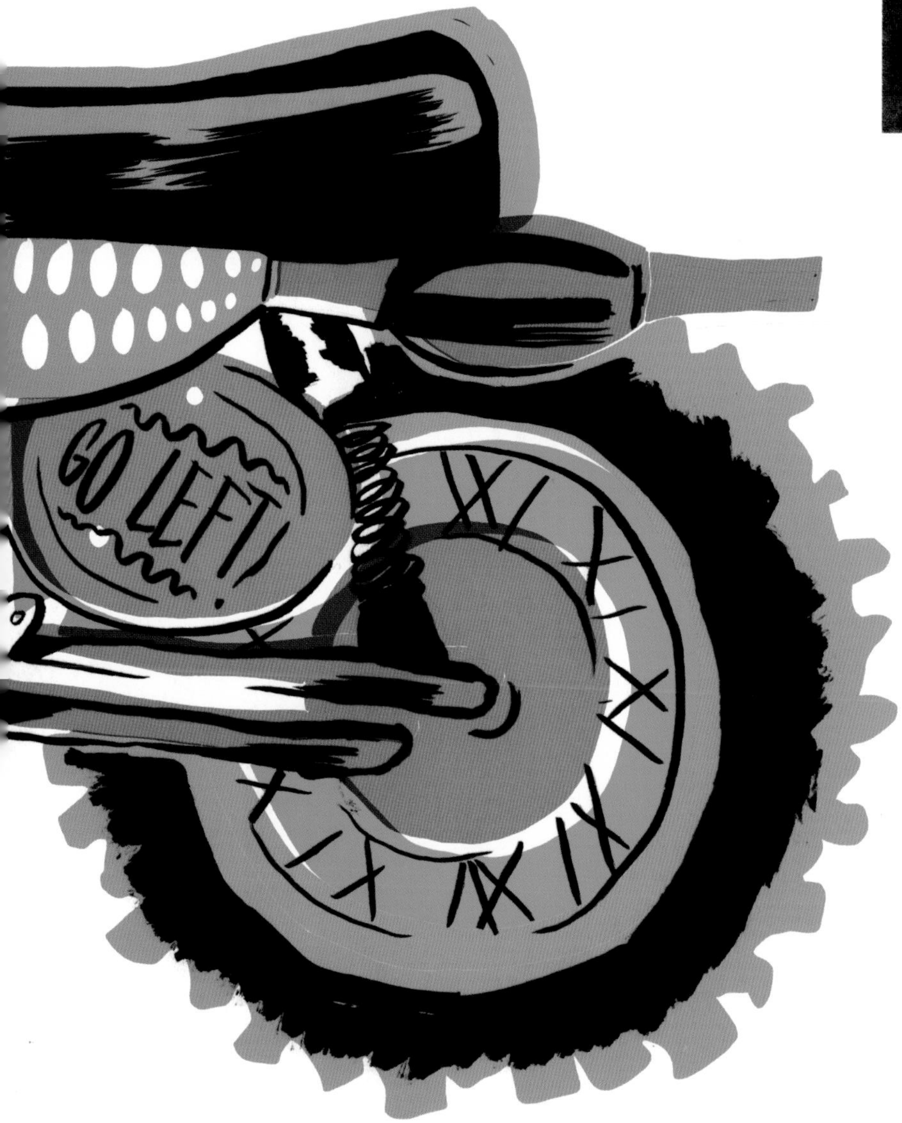

"I was kicked out of the Royal Marines for being too hardcore; drawing was my only other skill," says Stevie Gee, from his North London bunker, explaining how he became an in-demand artist. "I have lived in or around London all my life, except for the year I spent working on an Indian trawler. I'm in Muswell Hill now because it's where The Kinks started out, but I really want to live near the sea." That's so he can spend more time with his feckless surf gang, The Dead Clams. "The freedom you experience riding bikes is second only to surfing and making love. There is a connection you feel to the world around you, details that are easy to miss when you are caged in a box looking out. Motorbikes are an iconic symbol of freedom and rebellion, even if the police also ride them." Stevie has an extensive range of clients, including Deus Ex Machina, Paul Smith, *Sideburn*, Nike, Beams Japan, Lacoste, Adidas, Death Spray Custom, Parlophone, the BBC and Penguin Books. He lives his life by three simple rules: "Dance like you don't need money, work like you've never been hurt and make love like no-one's watching."

LEFT: ***McQueen's Huskie.***
Ink on paper.

BELOW: ***Rogue.***
Ink on paper.

RIGHT: ***Deeds Not Words.***
Ink on paper.

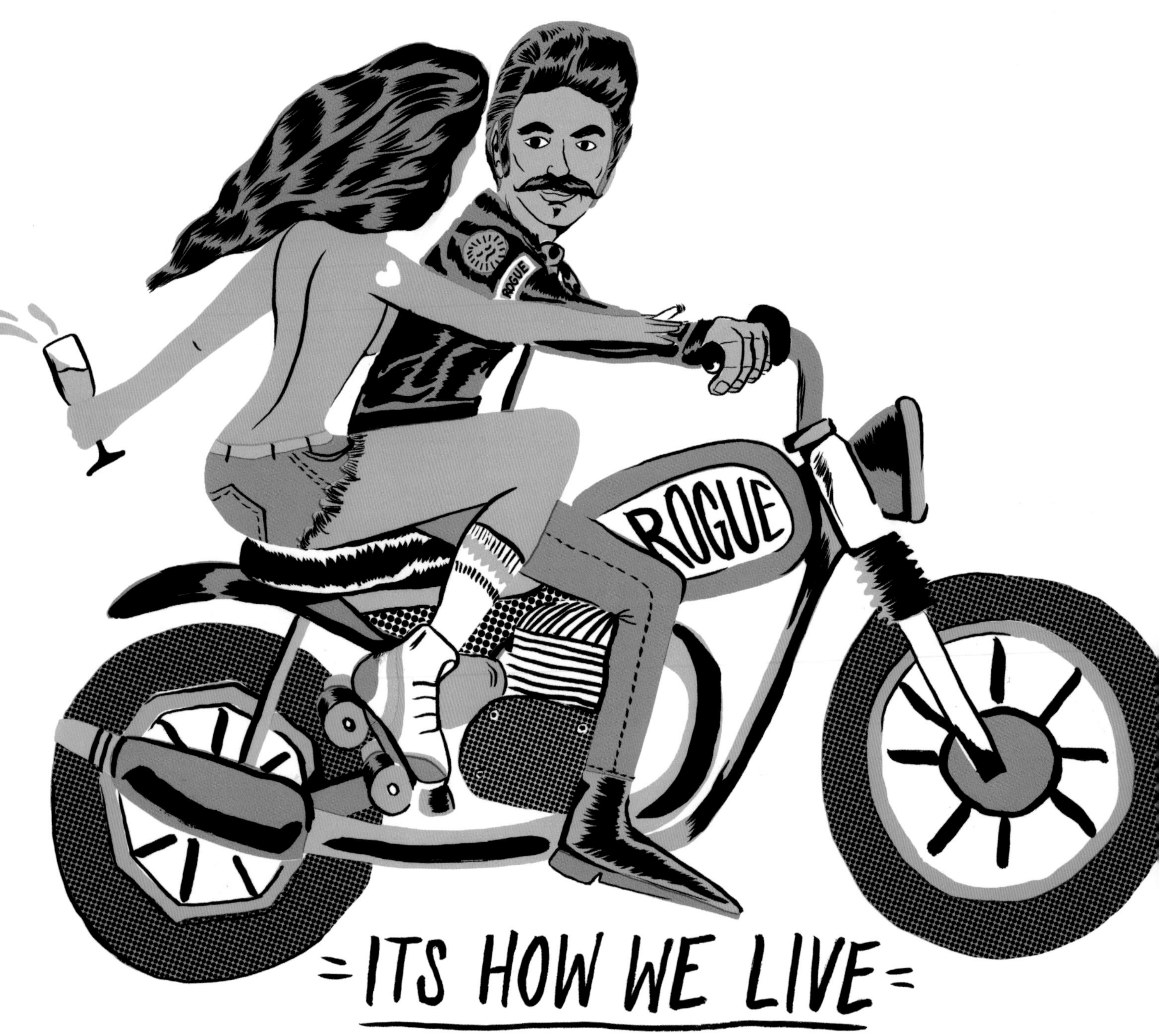

THE DEUS GALLERY PRESENTS

Stevie Gee.

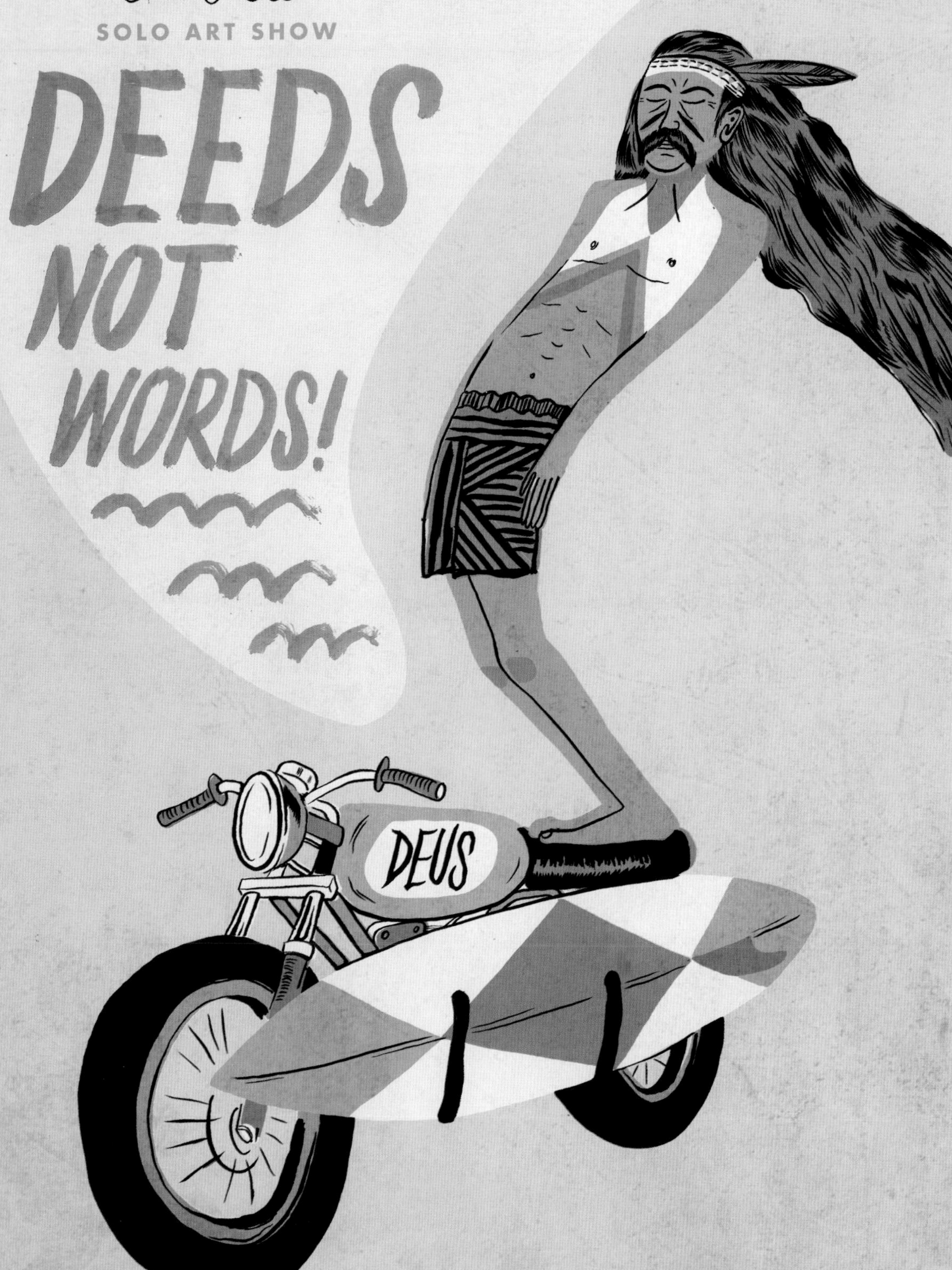

Deus Ex Machina®

**7PM SUNDAY 16TH OCTOBER, DEUS TEMPLE OF ENTHUSIASM,
BATU MEJAN NO.8, CANGGU, BALI, INDONESIA**

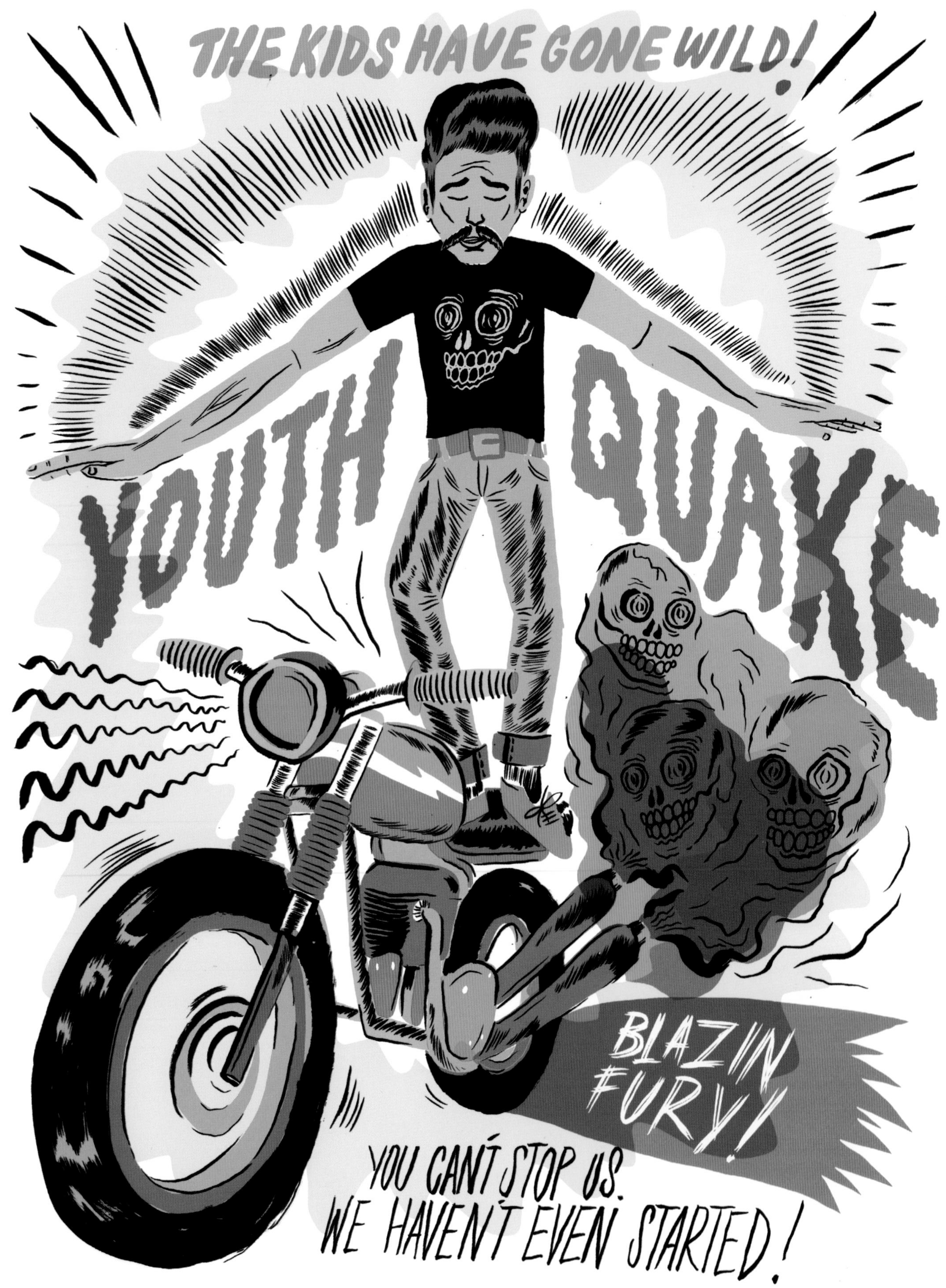
THE KIDS HAVE GONE WILD!
YOUTH QUAKE
BLAZIN FURY!
YOU CAN'T STOP US.
WE HAVEN'T EVEN STARTED!

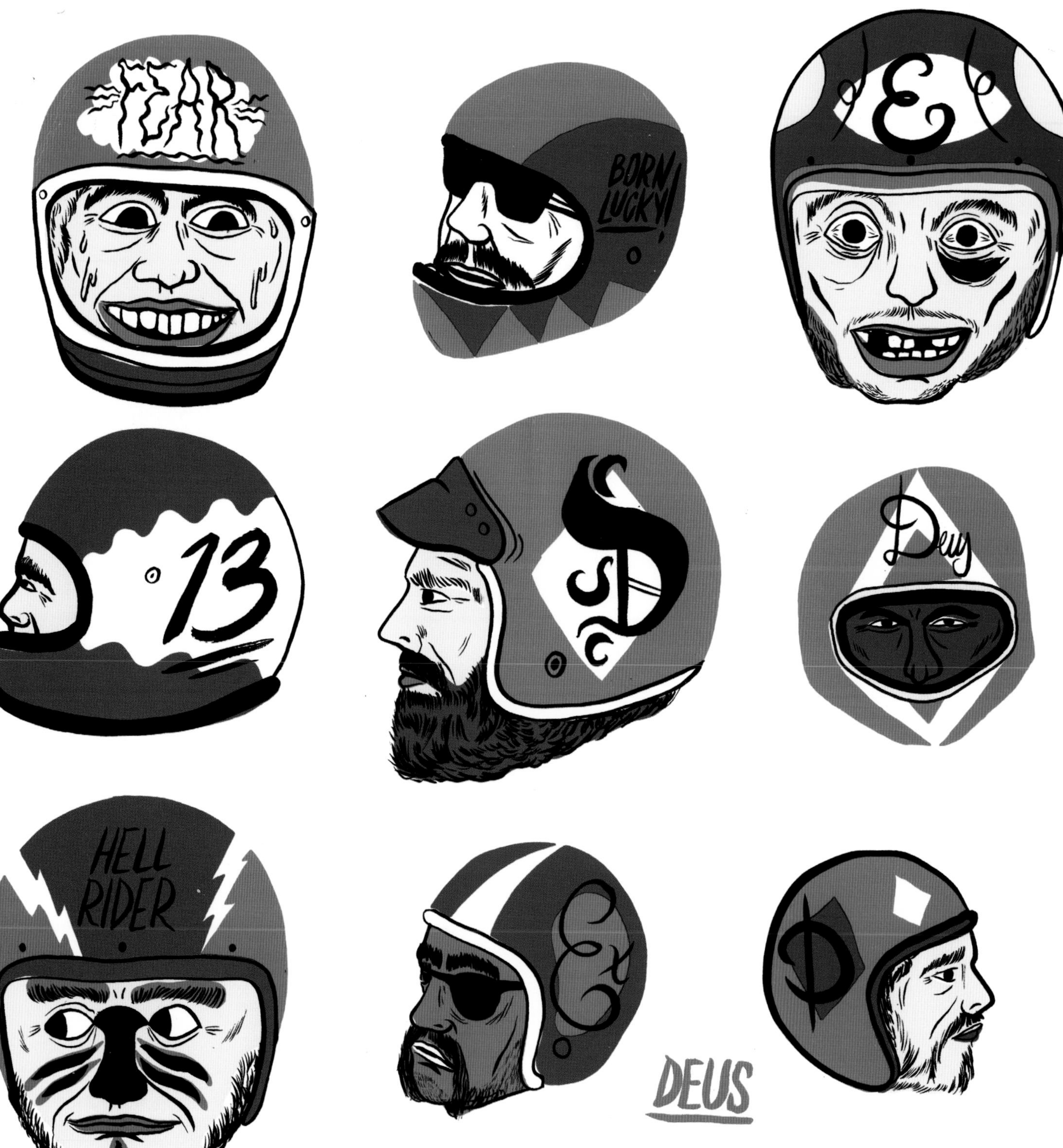

ABOVE: ***The Deus Helmet Krew.***
Ink on paper.

LEFT: ***Youth Quake.***
Ink on paper.

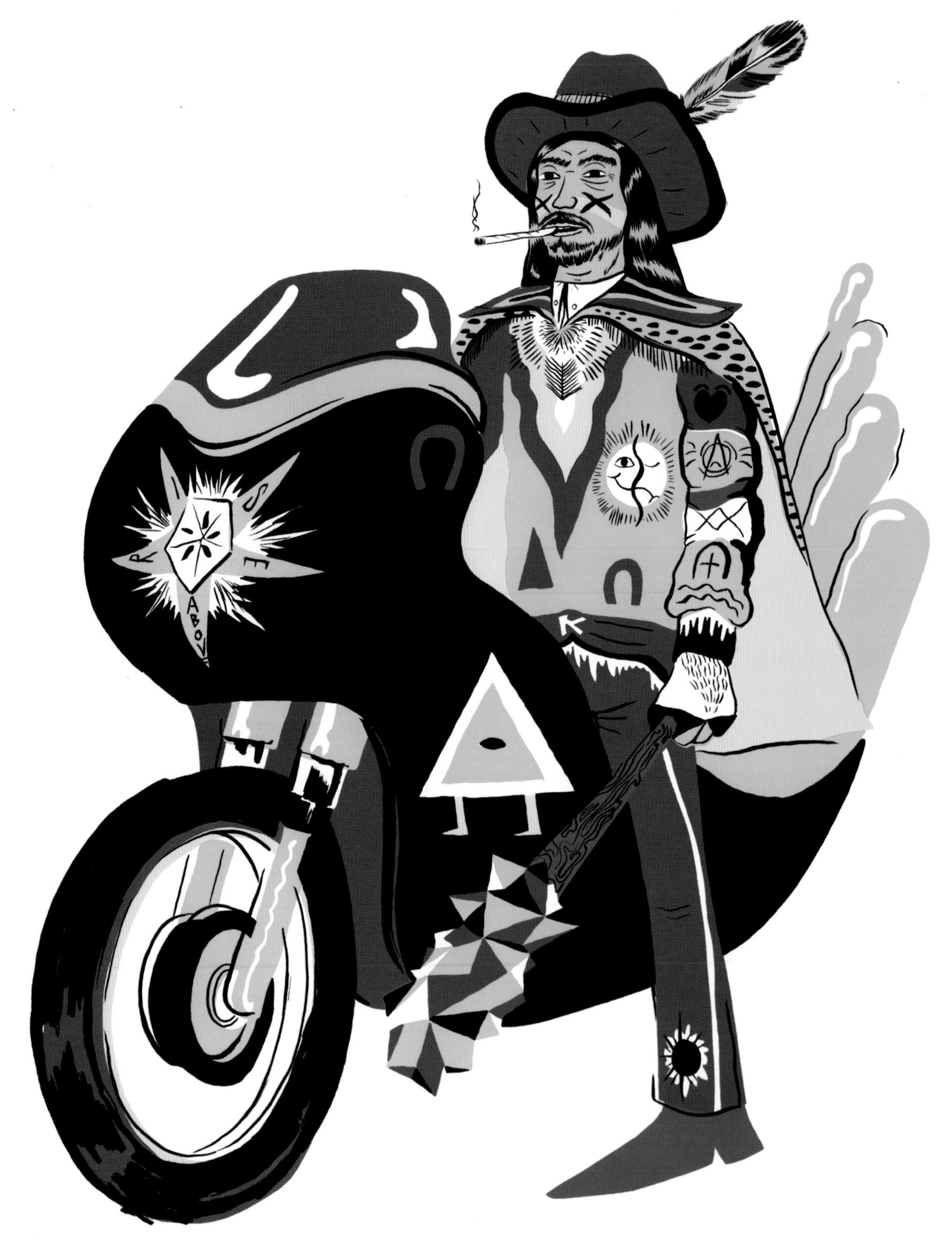

HEADS WILL ROLL!

BELOW: ***Cafe Racer.***
Ink on paper.

LEFT: ***Heads Will Roll.***
Ink on paper.

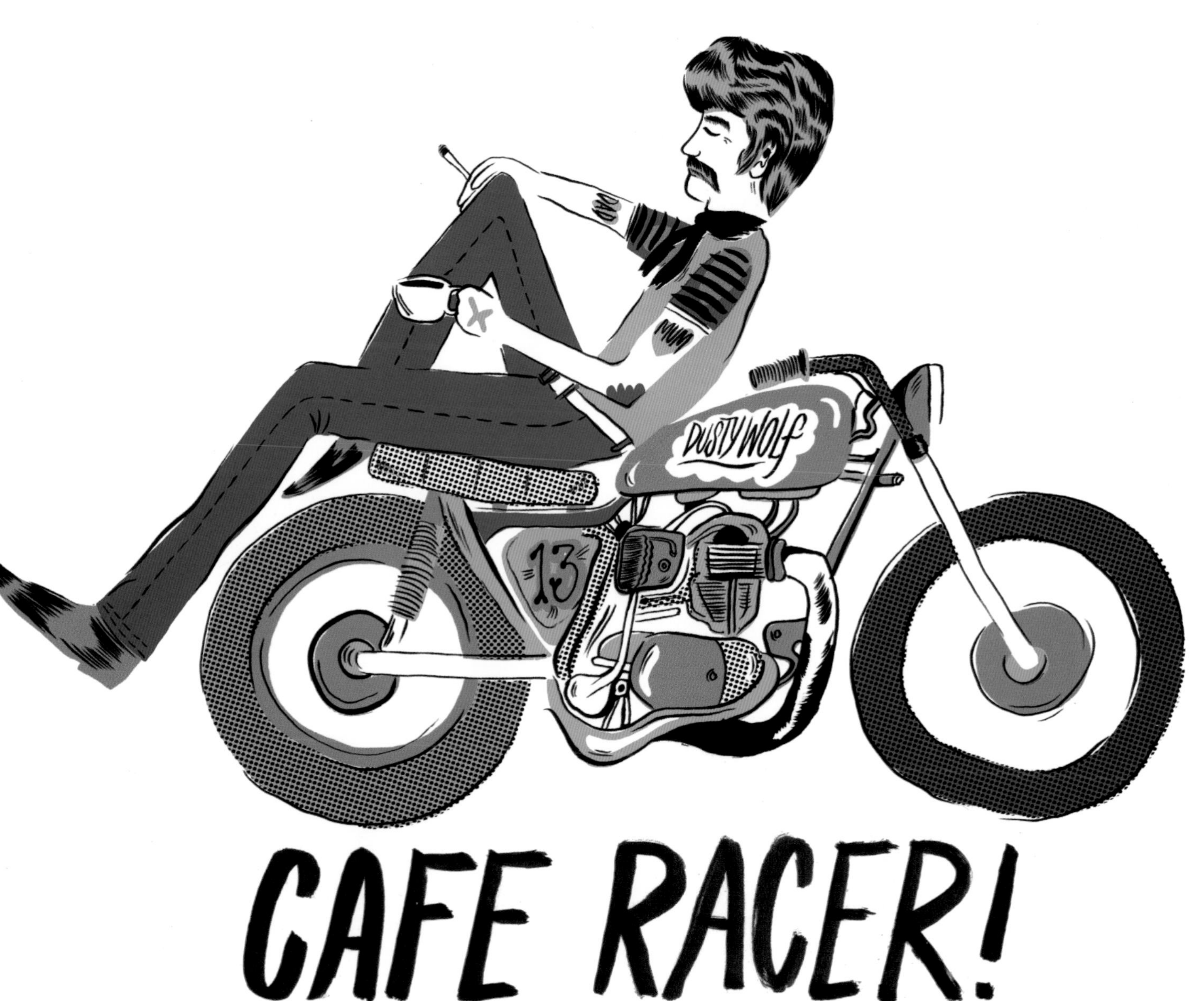

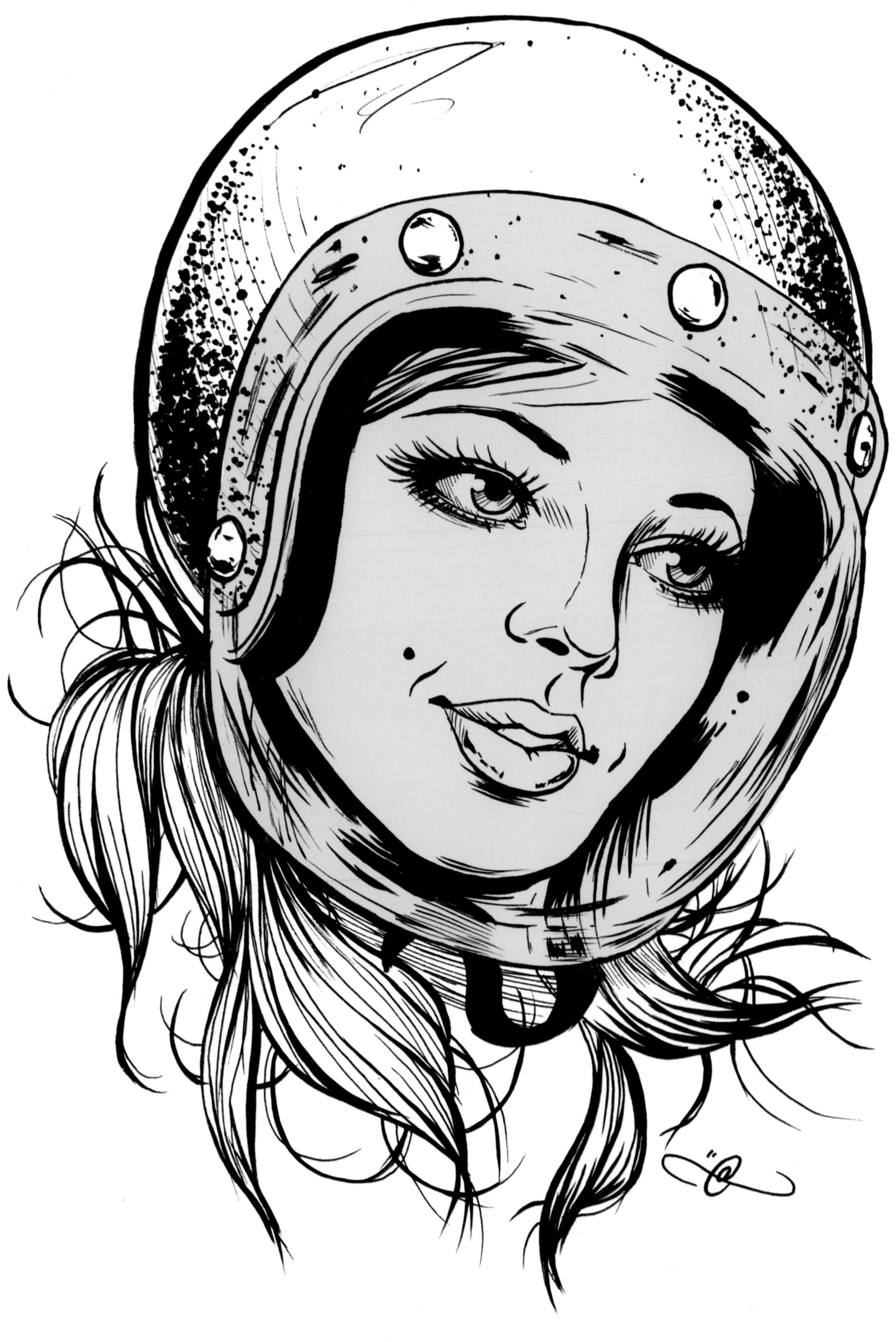

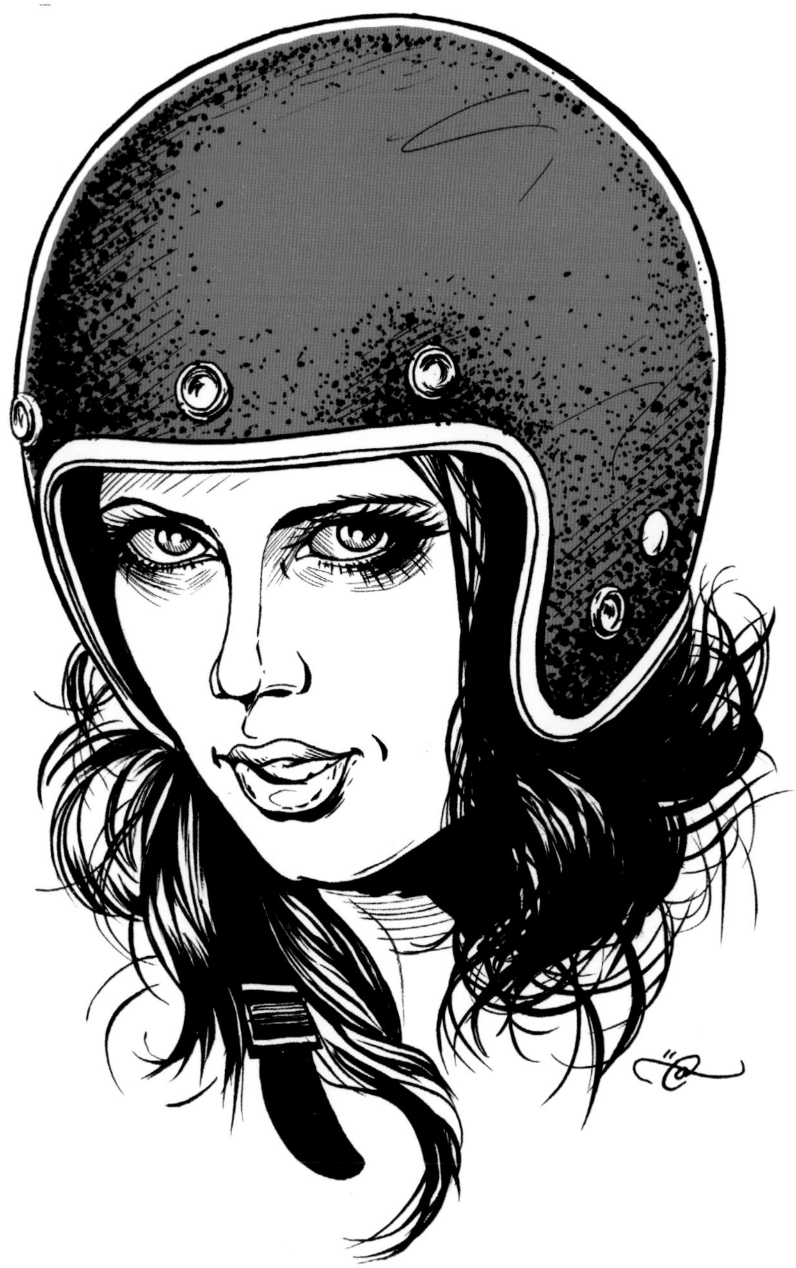

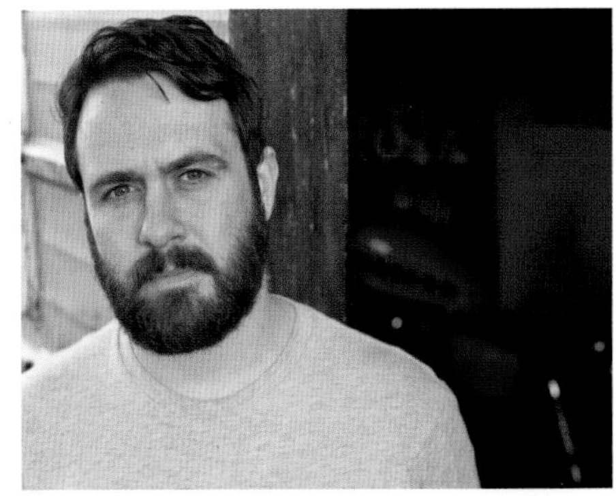

ADI GILBERT

A failed eye test meant Adi couldn't follow his lifetime dream of being an RAF pilot. "The rejection drove me to skateboarding, BMX, drinking, chasing girls and heavy metal. In turn, those things sent me down the path to a more creative, less regimented way of earning money." He had always been good at drawing, so decided to get a job doing graphics to see where it would lead. He brushed up on his design and Mac skills and got his foot in the door of a media agency in London specialising in films and TV programmes on surfing, mountain bikes, graffiti, BMX and skateboarding. "I started off in marketing," says Adi, "and wormed my way into the design department. In my spare time I did a lot of freelance illustration work, especially for BMX brands and magazines." Adi's recent clients have included BMX brands, motorcycle builders Co-Built, Gaymers Cider and Nokia. He has also illustrated for *Bike* magazine and *Sideburn*. "Bikes to motorbikes has been a natural progression," he says, "and there will be a lot more motorcycle work to come." Based in Bristol, Adi is also busy building a 1976 Yamaha XS650 and developing his own brand, Folklore. Reflecting on his career he adds: "I'm still gutted I never got to join up and fly though."

LEFT and ABOVE: ***Chester Belter Girls.***
Indian ink on paper and digital.

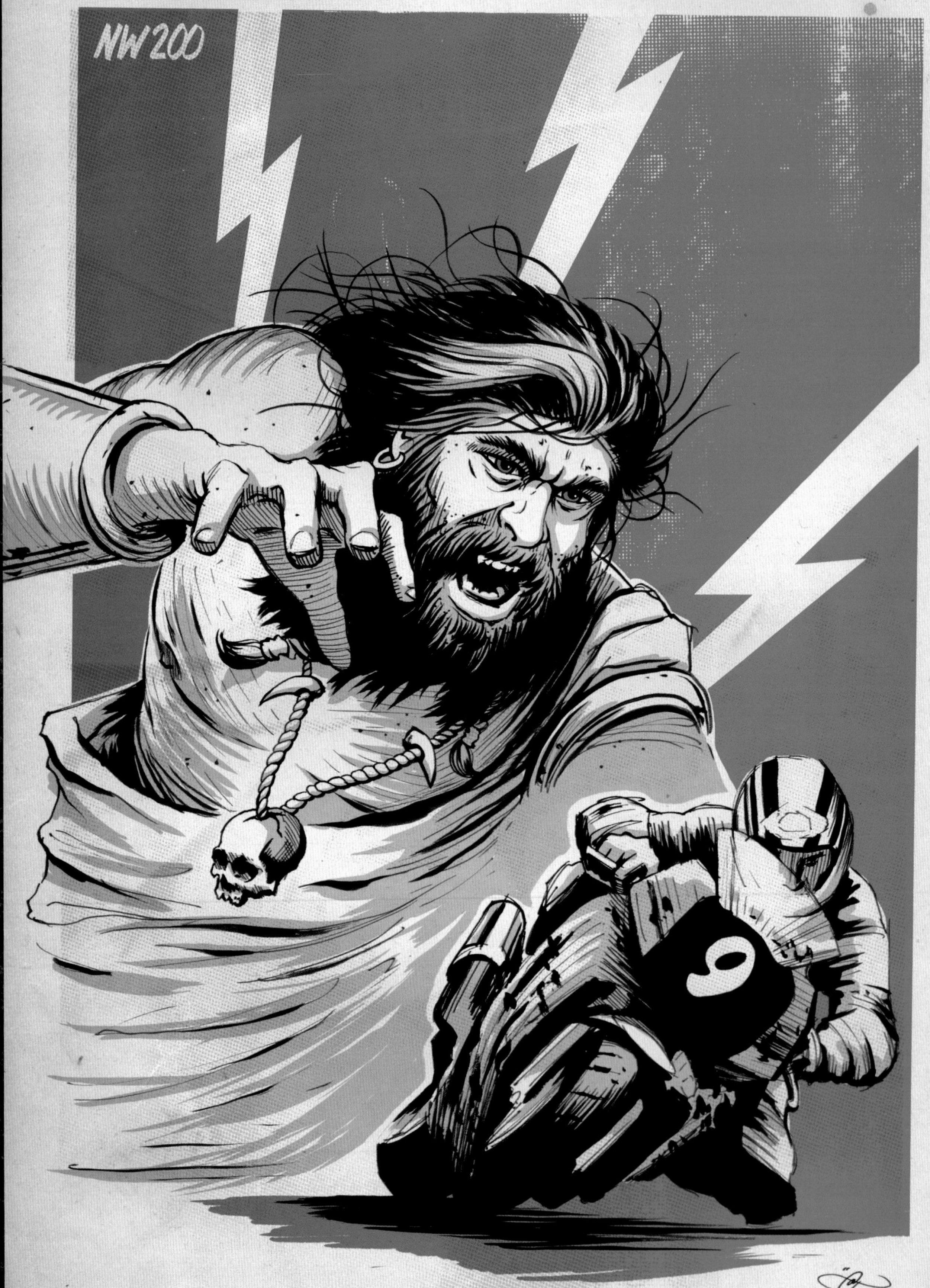
NW200
9

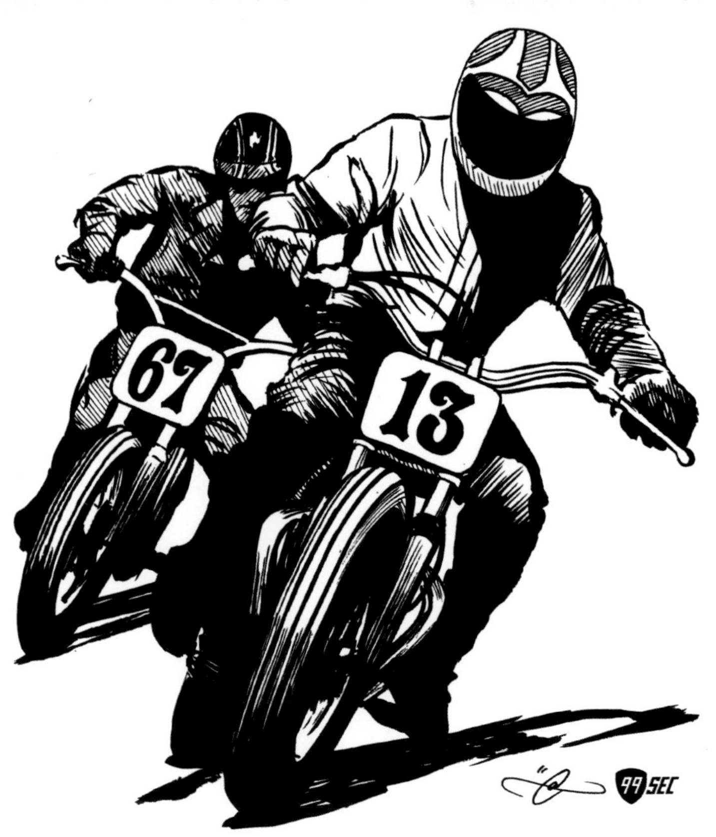

FAR LEFT: ***NW200 Celts.***
Indian ink on paper, digital art and texture.

LEFT: ***Racers.***
Indian ink on paper.

BELOW: ***Dirt Quake Flat Tracker.***
Indian ink on paper and digital.

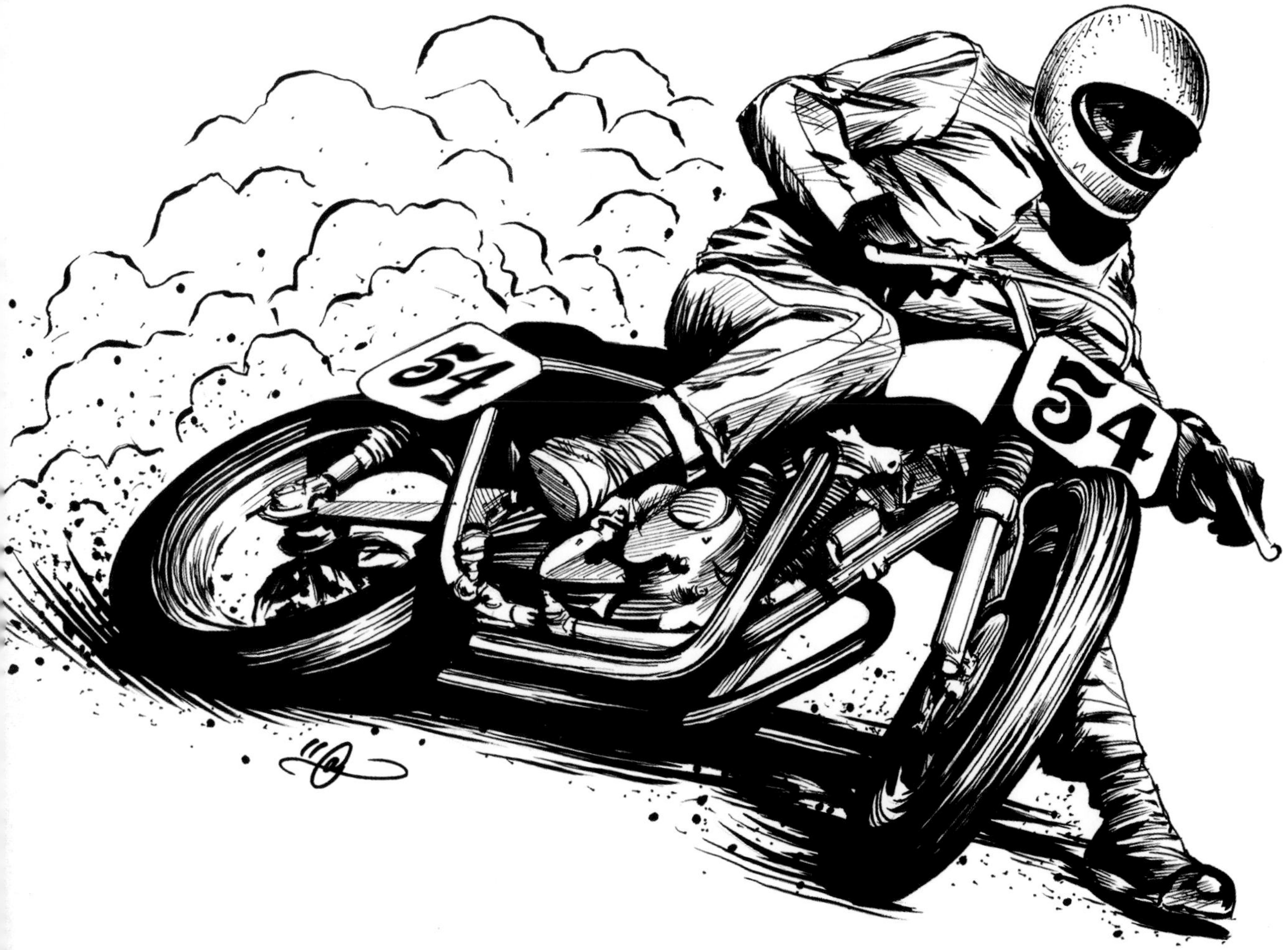

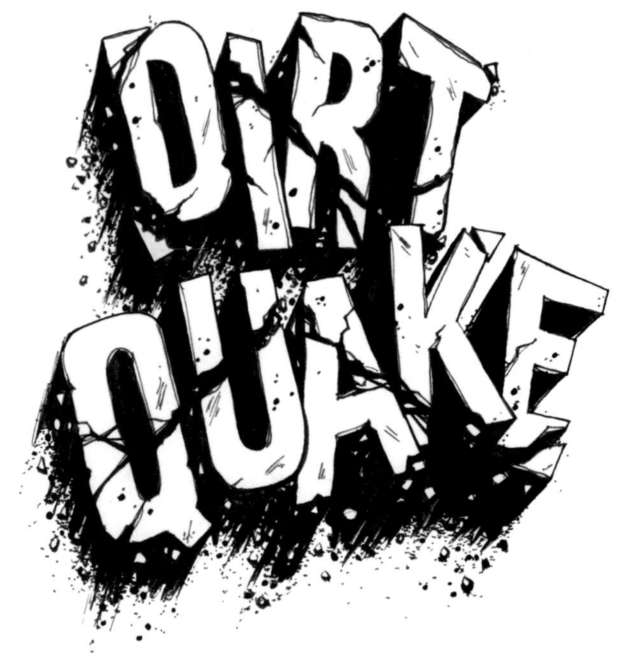

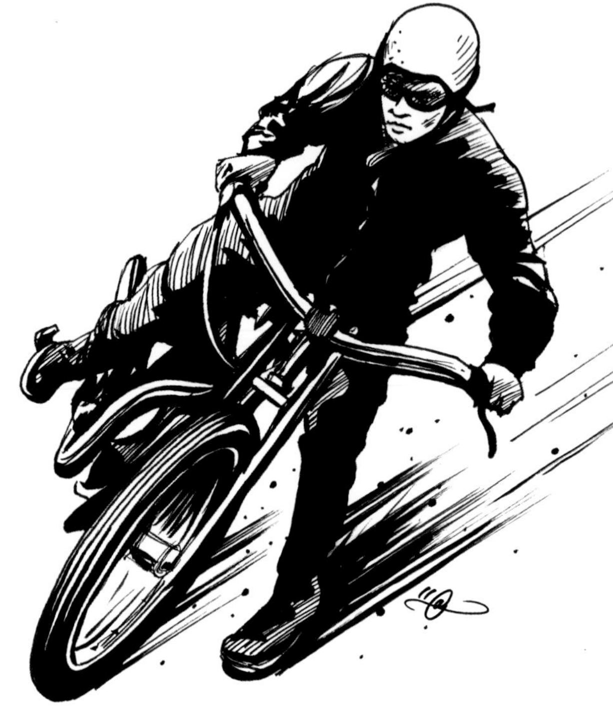

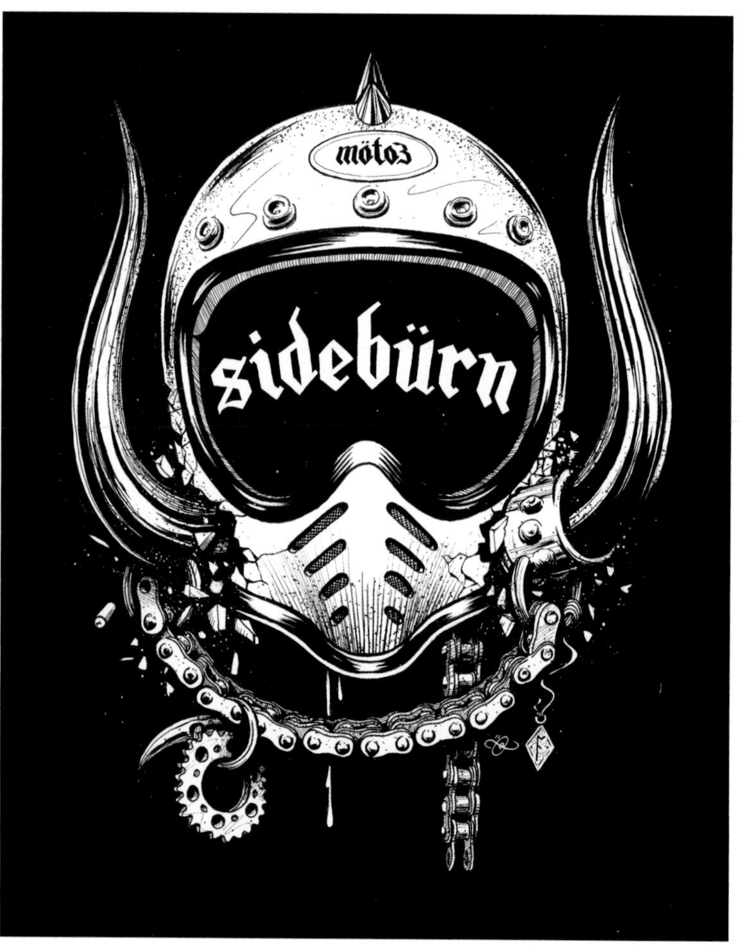

LEFT: ***Möto3.***
Indian ink on paper.

ABOVE LEFT: ***Dirt Quake.***
Indian ink on paper and digital.

ABOVE: ***Dirt Quake Speedway Rider.***
Indian ink on paper and digital.

RIGHT: ***Dungeness.***
Indian ink on paper, digital art and textures.

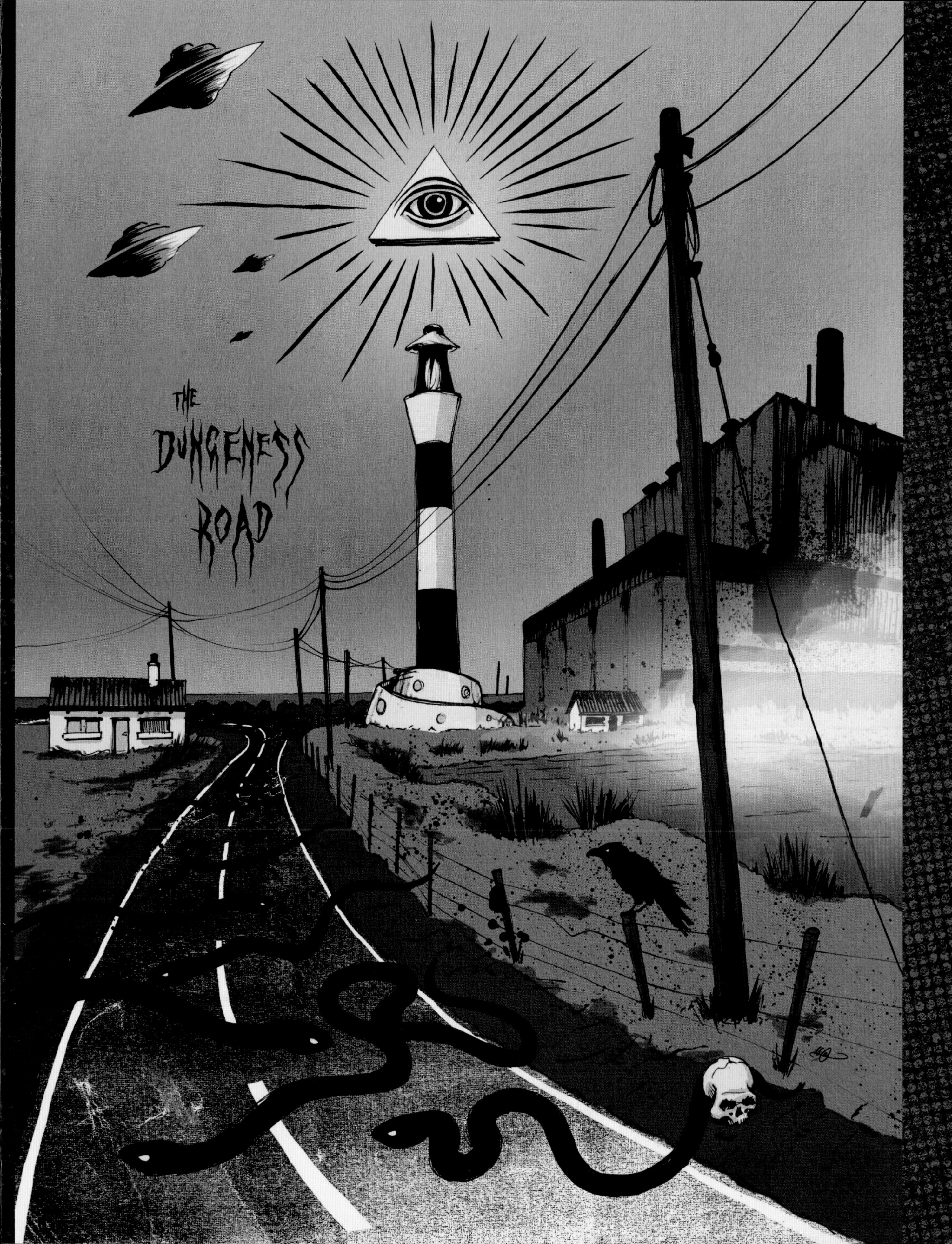
THE
DUNGENESS
ROAD

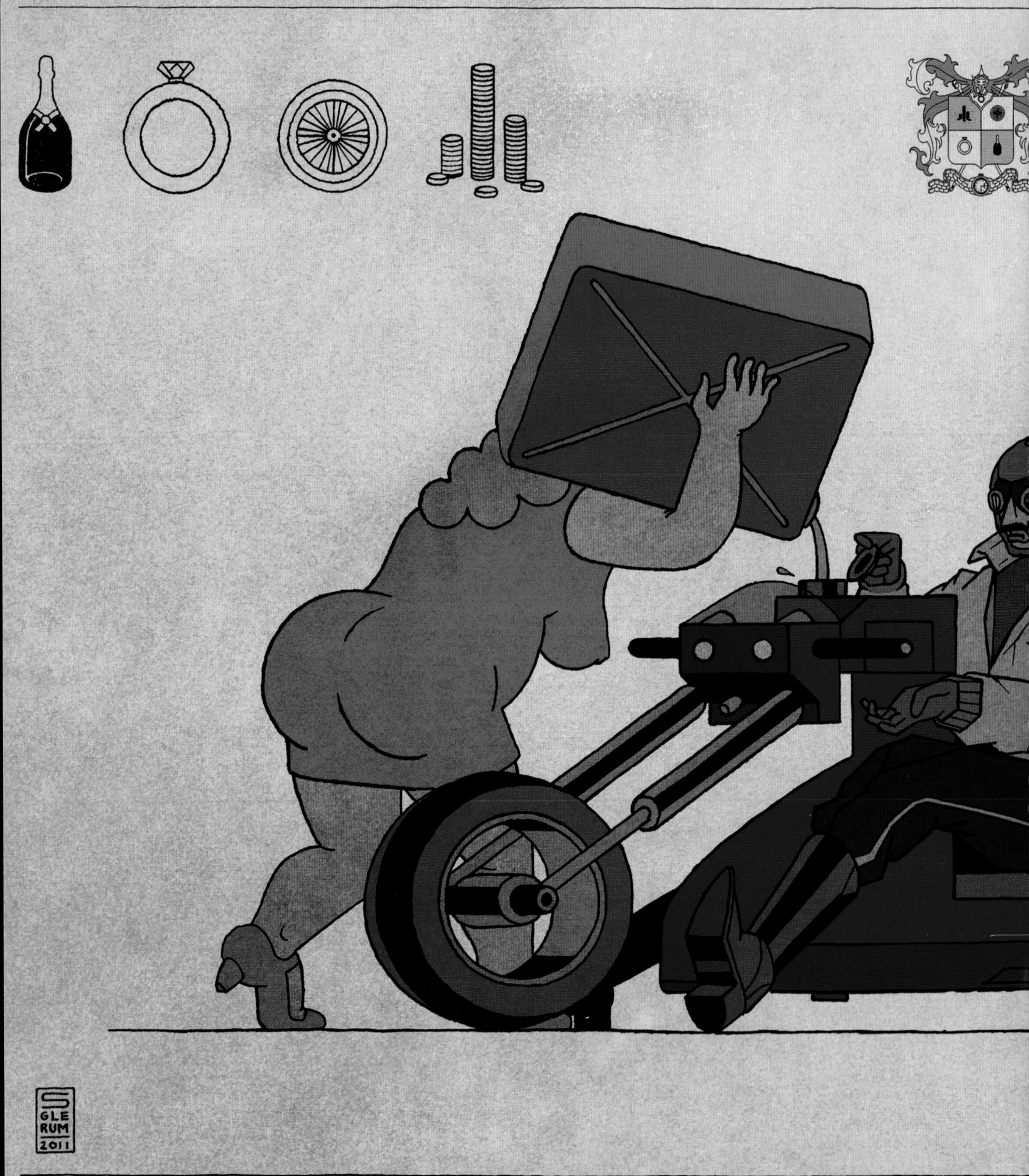

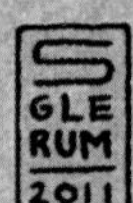
S
GLE
RUM
2011

IGH ROLLERS ONLY

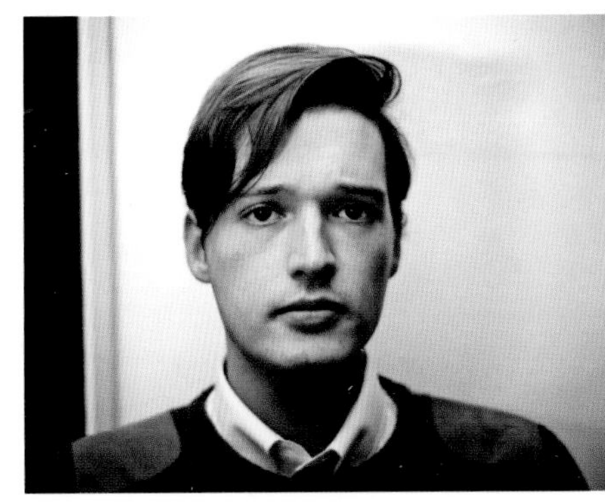

STEFAN GLERUM

"I like motorcycles because they are technical. Anything with speeding wheels appeals to me on a boyish level. It makes me think of making model kits as a kid. I also like particular designs of motorcycles purely for their aesthetics," says Stefan Glerum. The Amsterdam-based artist apprenticed with world-famous cartoonist and architect, Joost Swarte, before studying illustration at the Academy St. Joost. Glerum is plainly influenced by the 'ligne claire' style favoured by his early mentor. His artworks always start with drawing by hand. "I sketch out my illustrations with pencil, rulers and a compass. After that, I ink the lines with either a dipping pen and India ink or Rotring pen. For my free work I use acrylics for colour, for most commissioned work I colour by computer." His illustrious client list includes Pirelli, Duvel, Adidas, Jameson and *GQ*. Despite both recognisable and mutant bikes appearing in his work, Stefan admits he's never ridden a motorcycle. If he ever does buy one, he knows what he wants it to look like: "The bike in *Akira* that Kaneda rides."

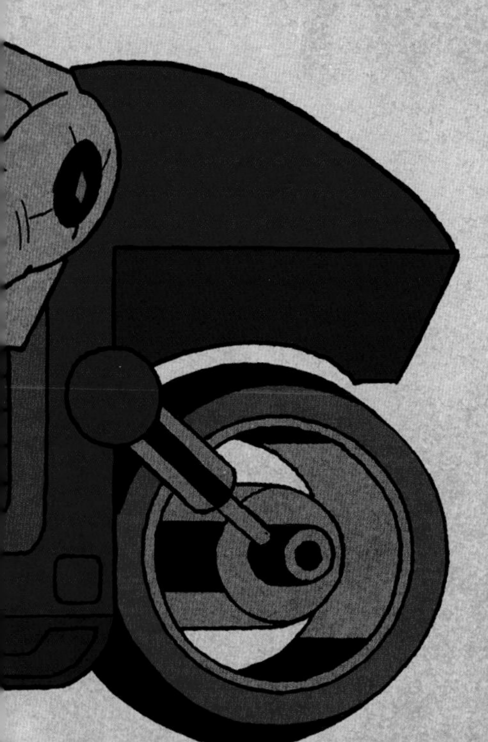

LEFT: *HRO Pitstop.*
Indian ink on paper, digital colours.

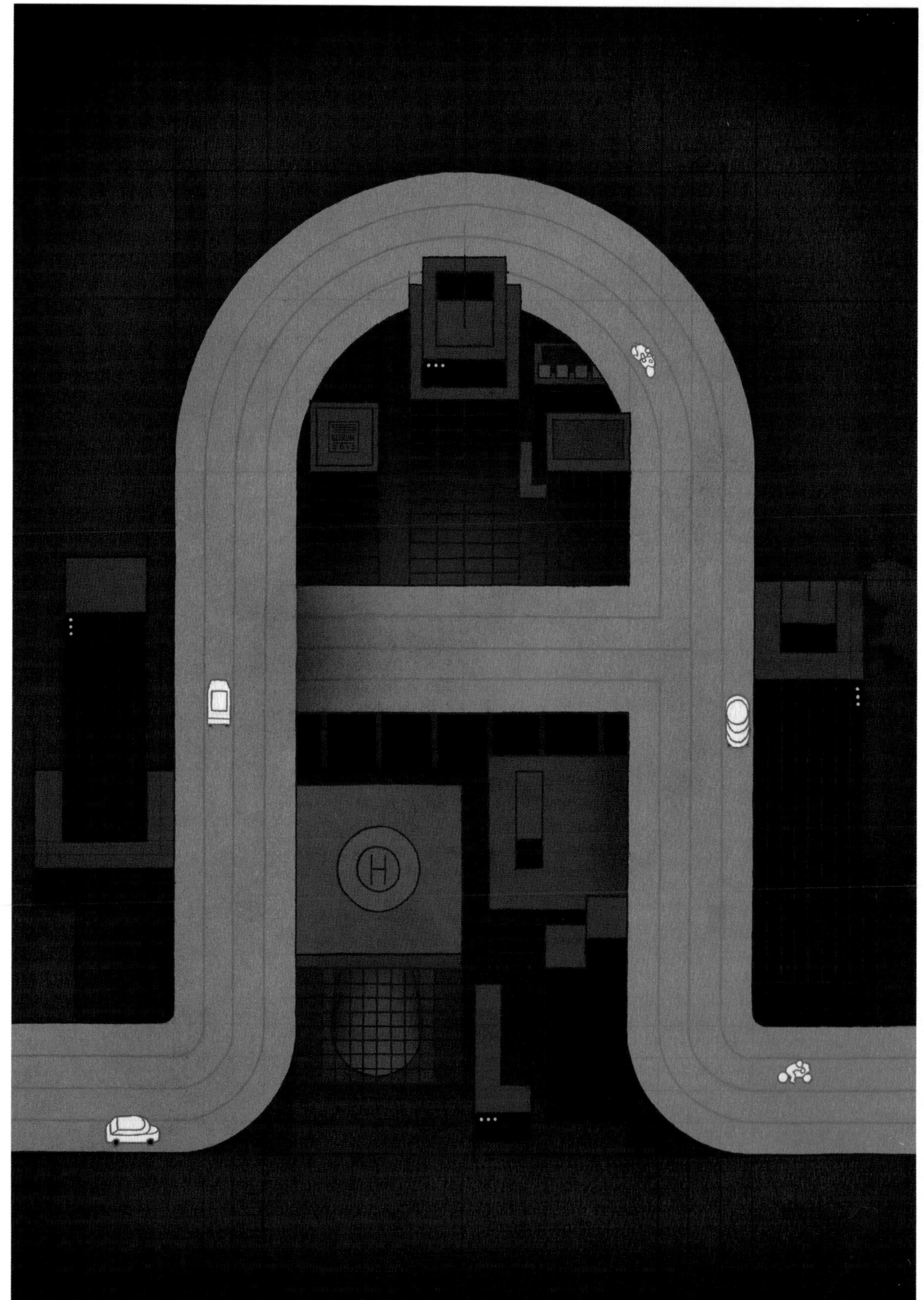

RIGHT: ***A Cover.***
Design for Pirelli.
Indian ink on paper, digital colours.

FAR RIGHT: ***Speed.***
Design for Pirelli.
Indian ink on paper, digital colours.

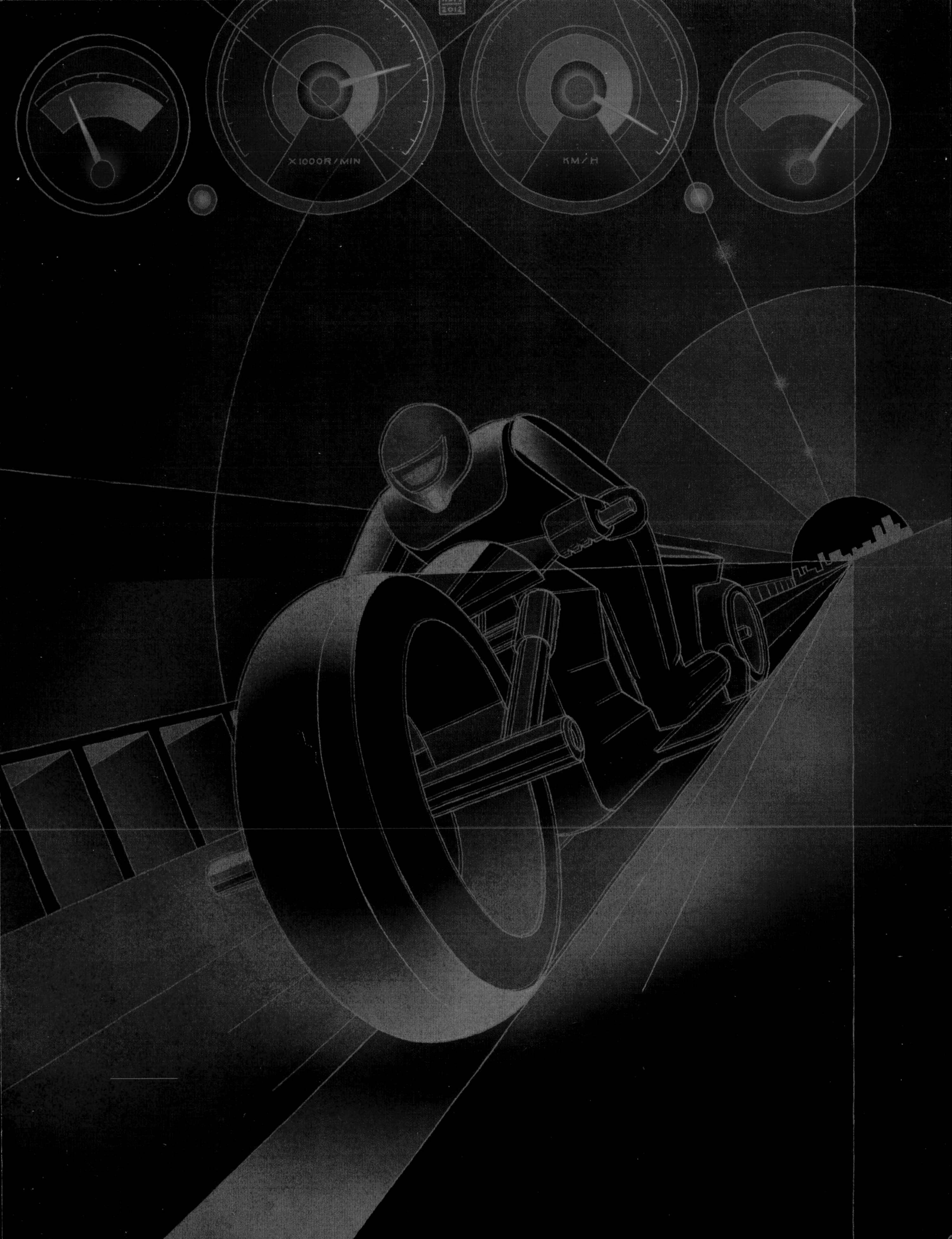
X1000R/MIN
KM/H

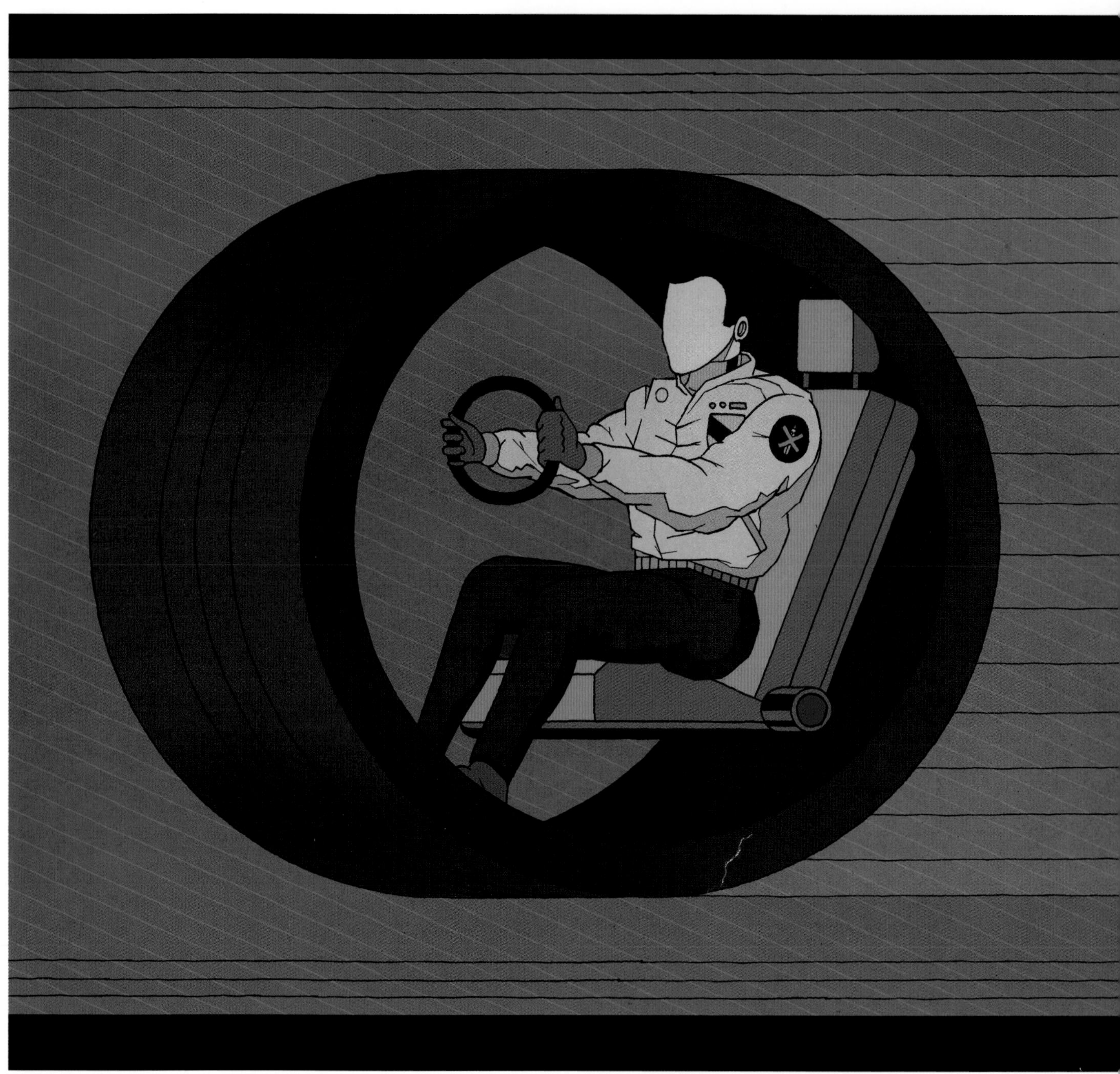

ABOVE: ***Pirelli Experience*****. Design for Pirelli.**
Indian ink on paper, digital colours.

RIGHT: ***Obey 1950s.***
Indian ink on paper, digital colours.

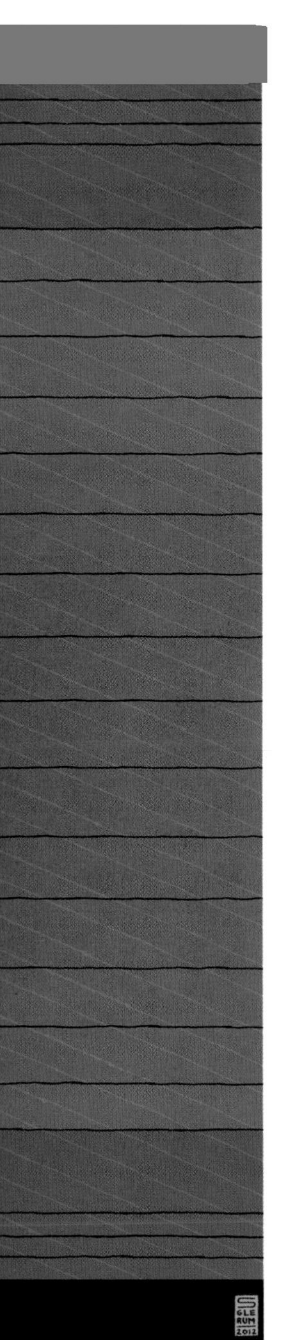

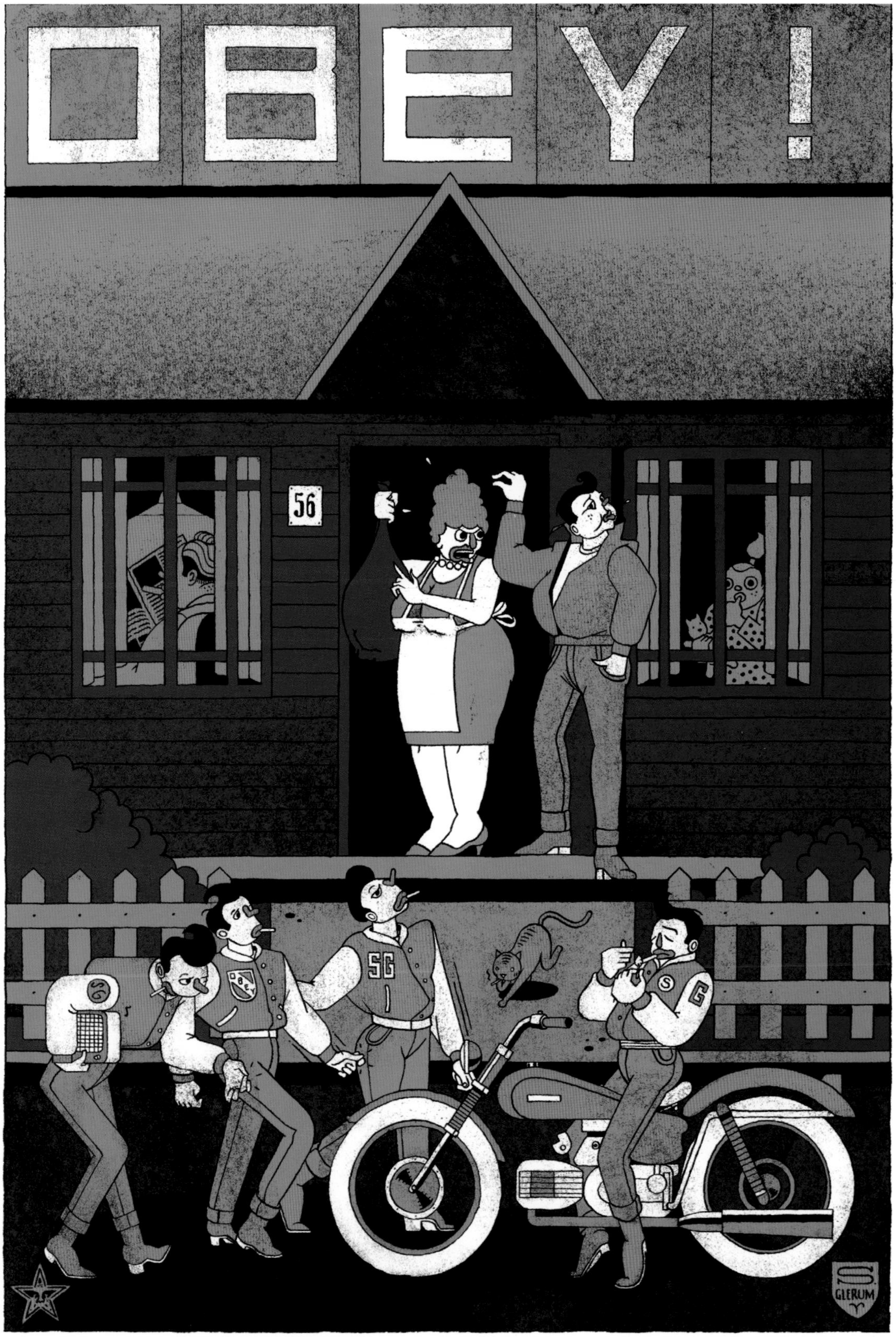

OBEY !

56

SG

S. GLERUM

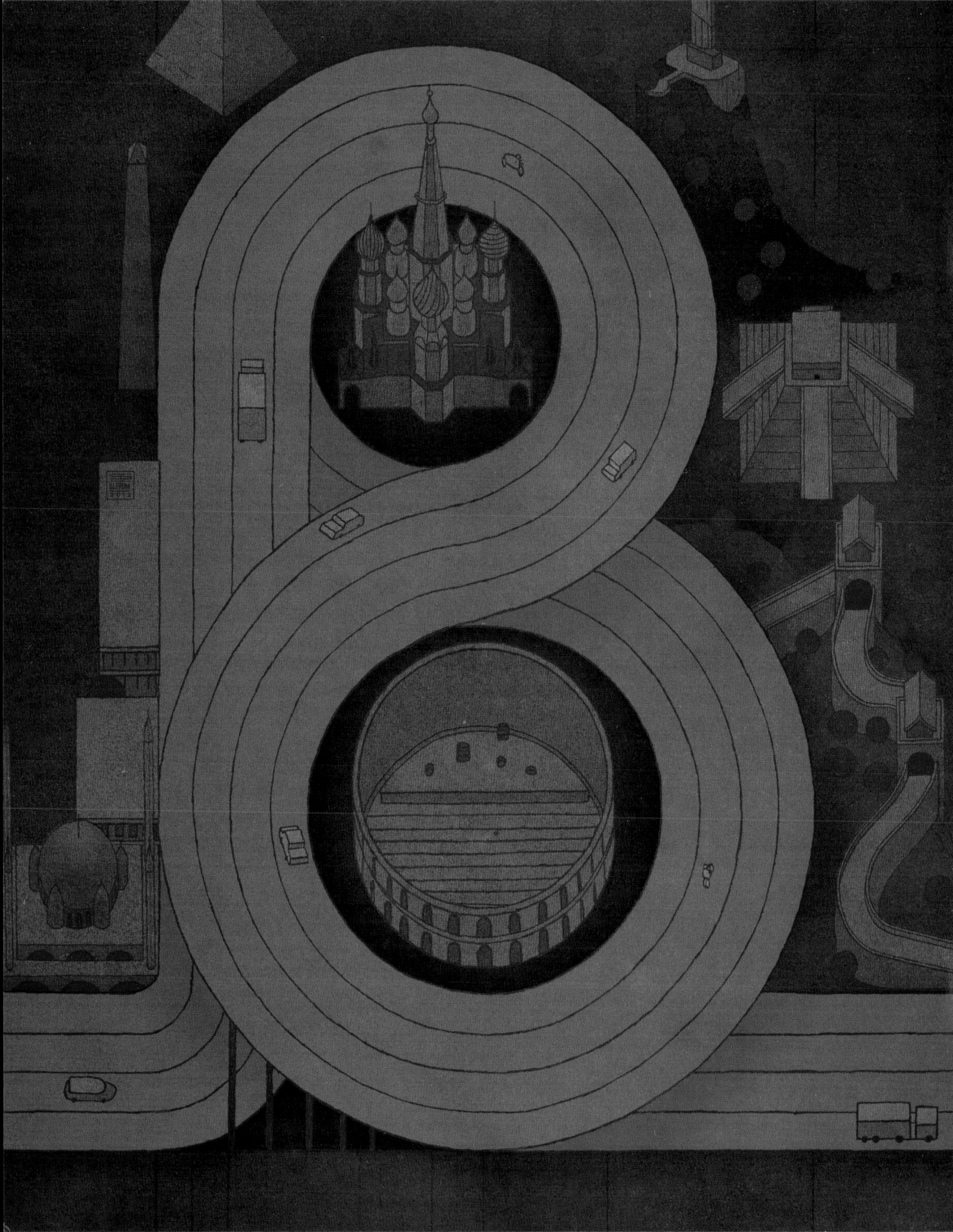

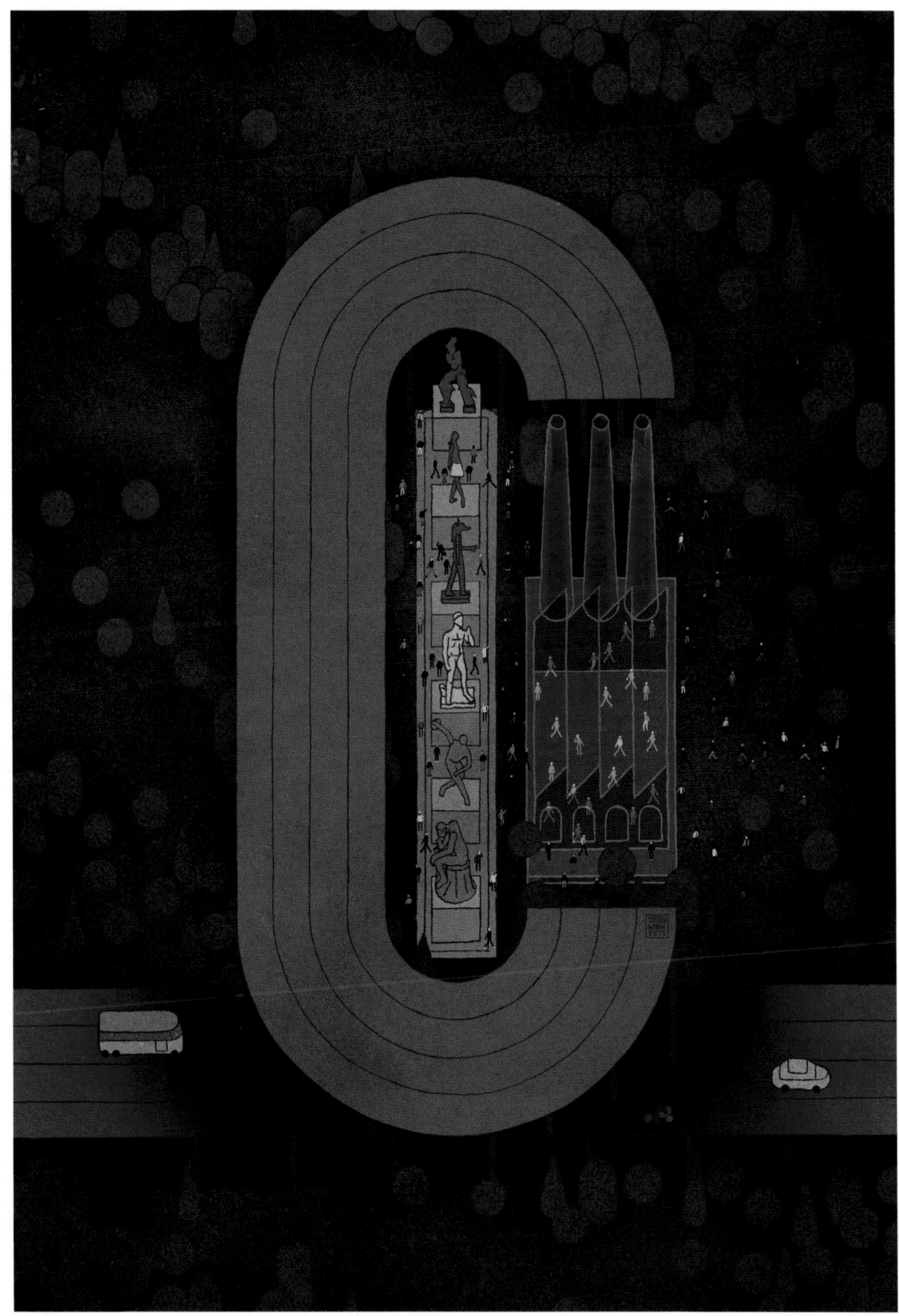

LEFT: *C Cover.* Design for Pirelli.
Indian ink on paper, digital colours.

FAR LEFT: *B Cover.* Design for Pirelli.
Indian ink on paper, digital colours.

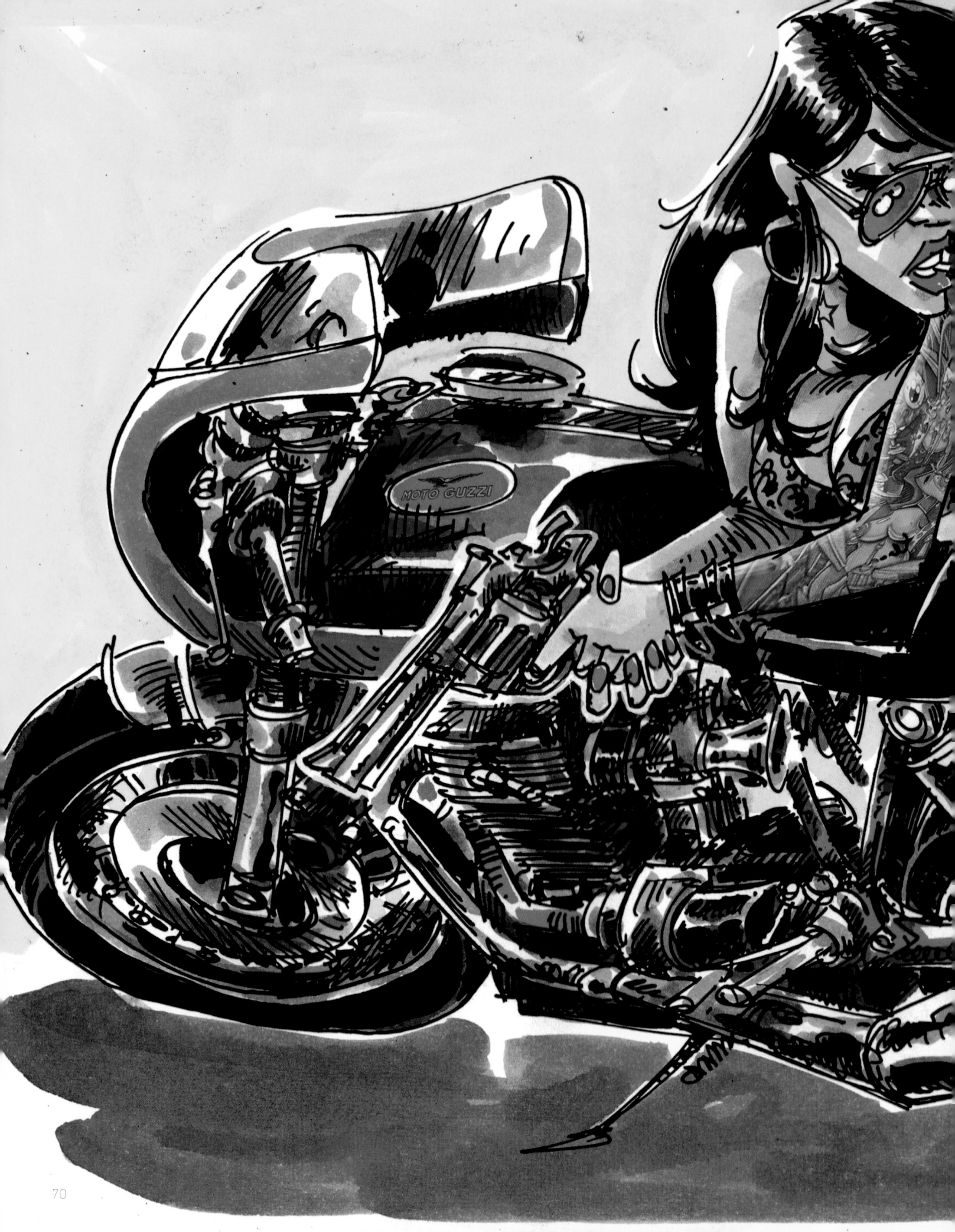
MOTO GUZZI

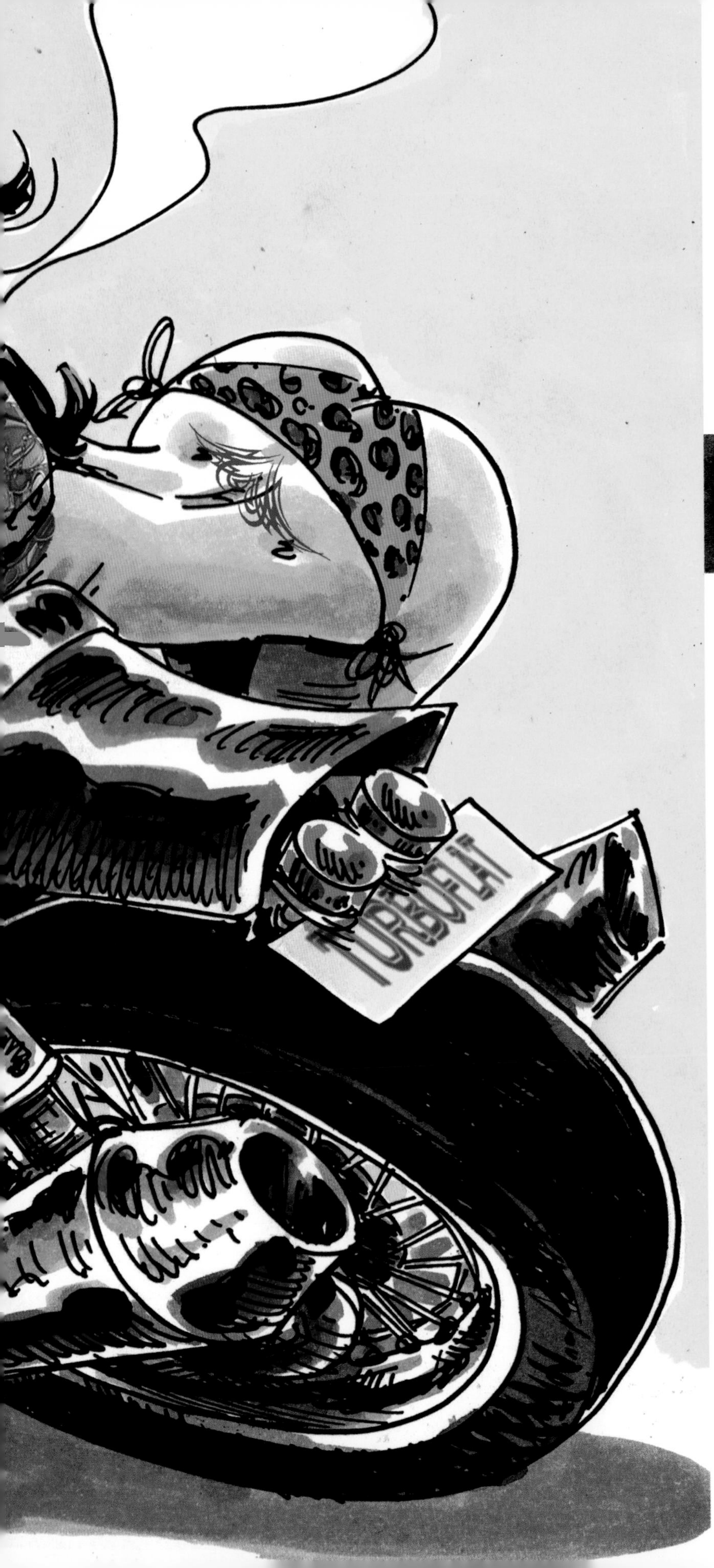

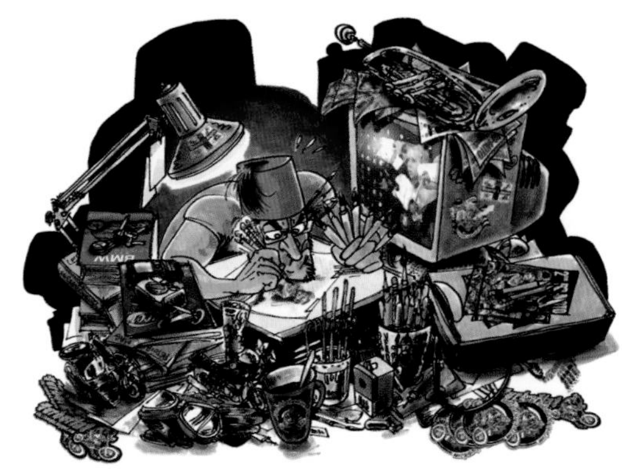

PHILIPPE GÜREL

"I was born in Paris but grew up in Nogent sur Marne, in the eastern suburbs," says Philippe Gürel. "As a teenager, I used to ride my moped and race any scooter or bicycle I could see. I had to be the fastest. I was also fascinated by my father's drawing table - he was an architect. I would look at him work for hours. He is the one who taught me about perspective in drawings." Gürel studied at the European School of Visual Art, Angoulême – "To learn more about the 'how-to' of comics" – then went on to study at the Gobelins École de L'Image, where he learned how to make stop-motion animated films. "I usually draw quite fast. The way the drawing comes out of my pen on the first draft is usually the way it will look in the end, with some improvements, of course, but I like that raw, instinctive feel." Even though no one in his family was a motorcyclist, Gürel has always been attracted to motorcycles. "Some passions you can't explain, they just happen. It quickly turned into a passion for classic motorcycles." Gürel currently owns two BMWs and a Kawasaki Z1100. "I have had wonderful experiences and encounters while riding. And I never use a GPS because taking a wrong turn can prove to be a great discovery."

LEFT: ***Guzzi Girl.***
Watercolour, coloured ink, coloured pencils and digital.

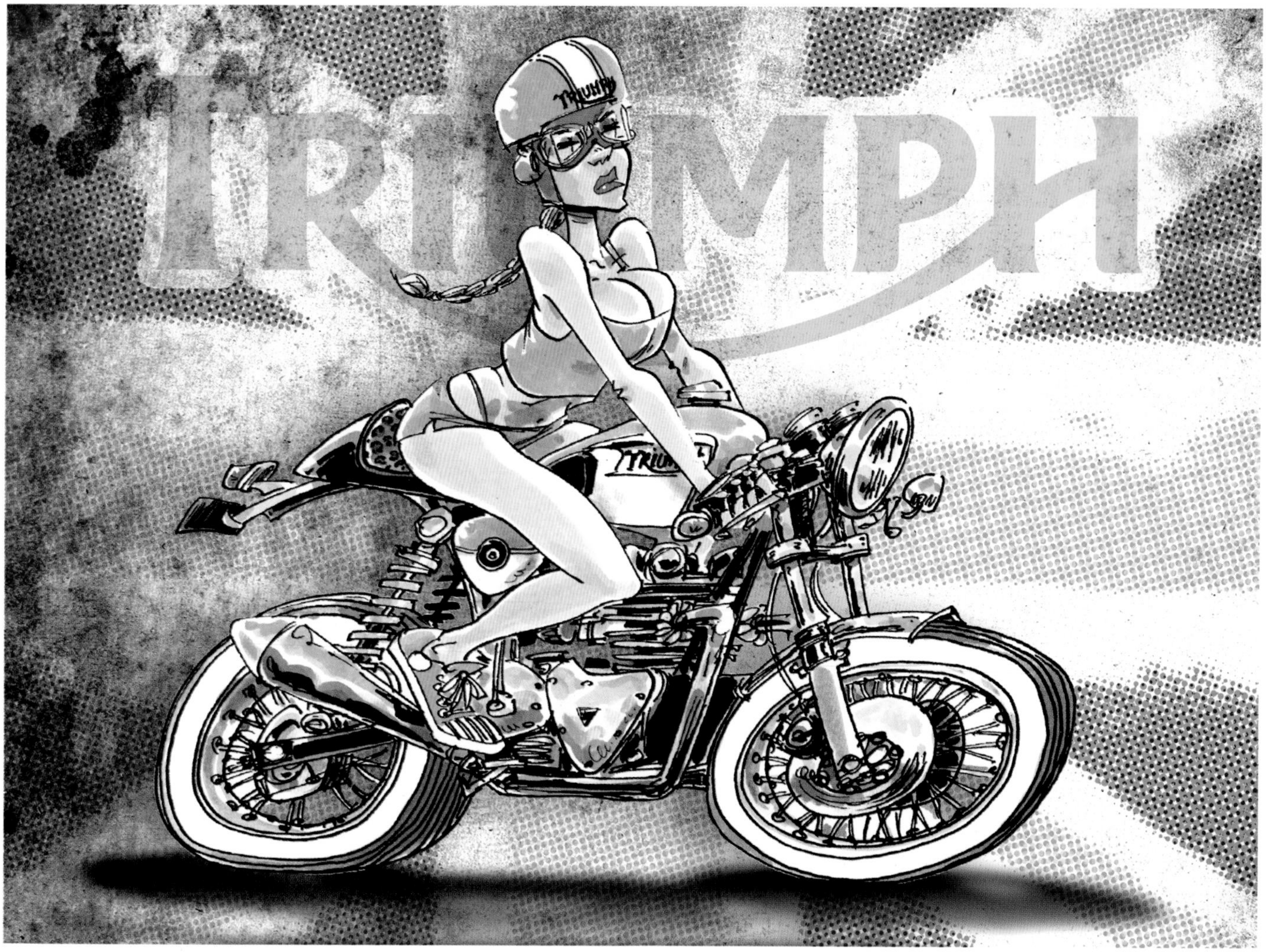

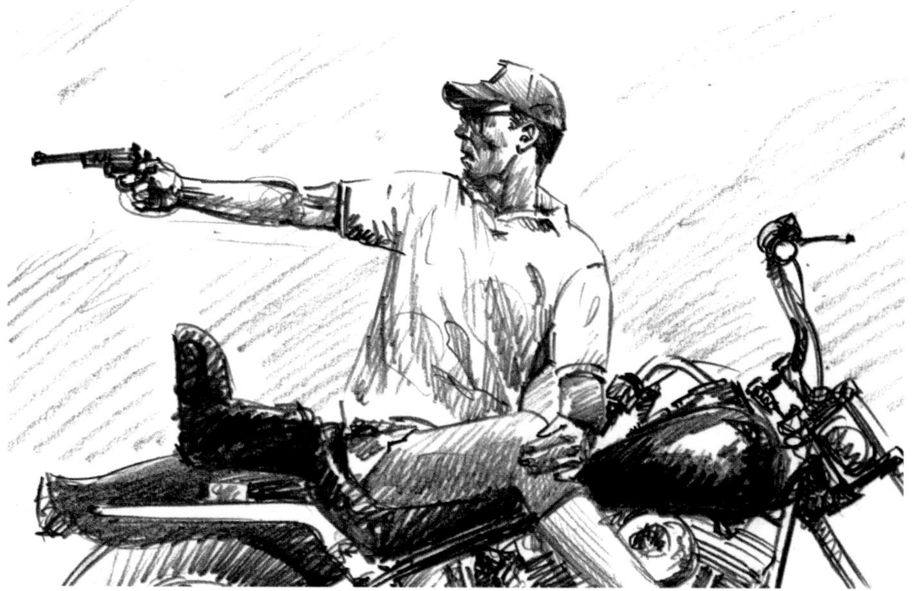

ABOVE: ***Pink Bonnie.***
Watercolour, coloured ink and digital.

LEFT: ***Hunter S. Thompson.***
Pencil on paper.

RIGHT: ***Turbofrotte.***
Ballpoint pen, ink and digital.

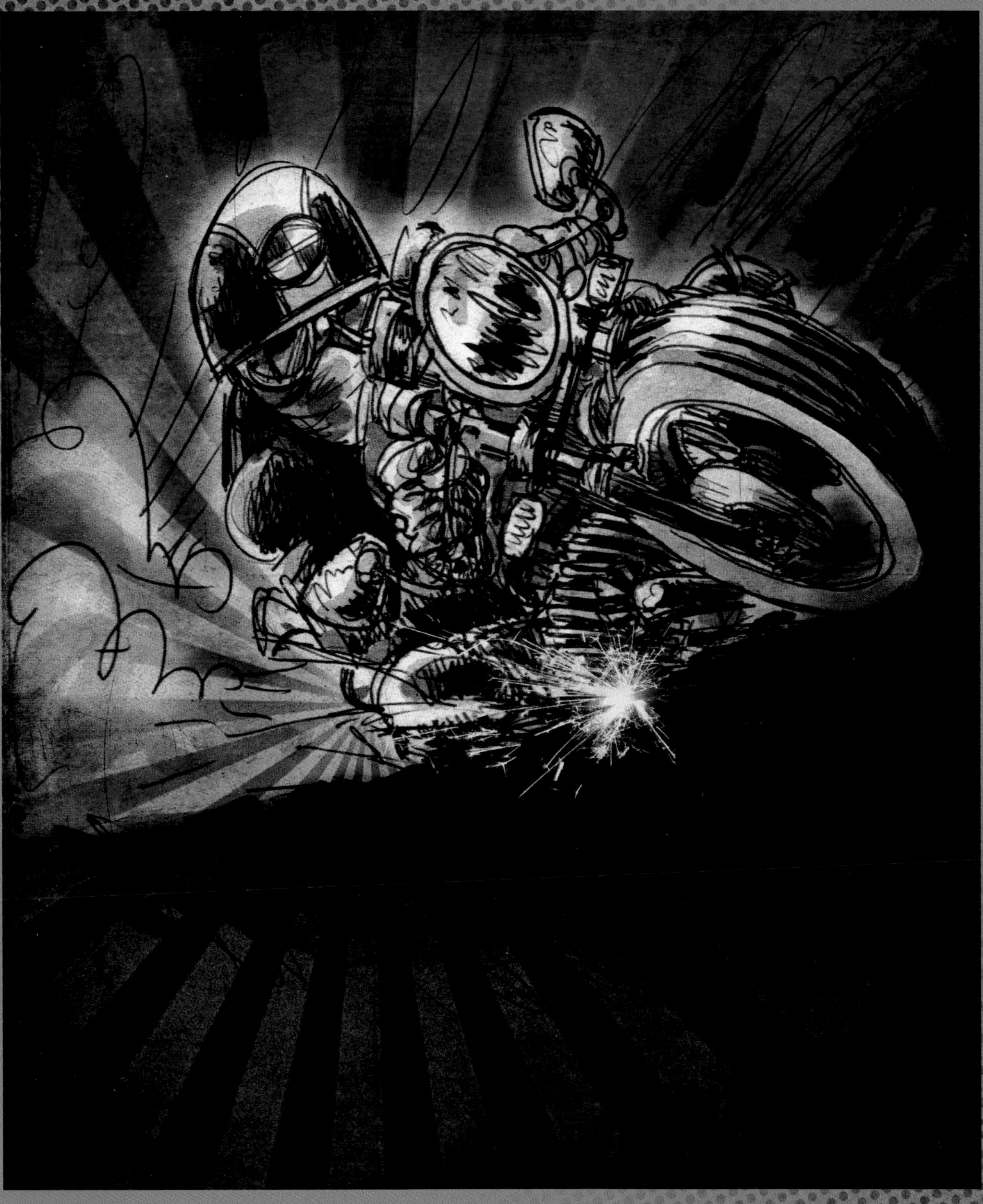

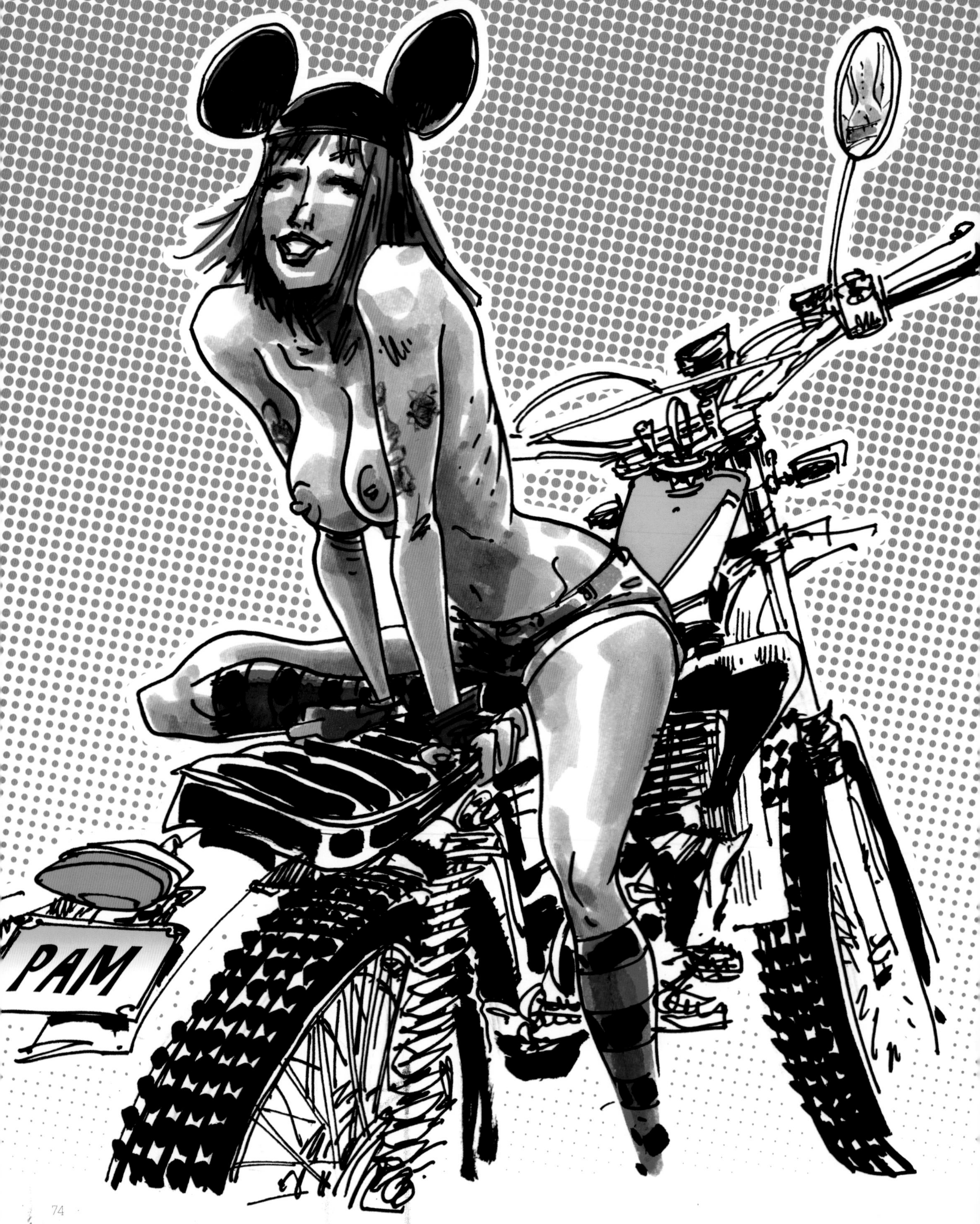
PAM

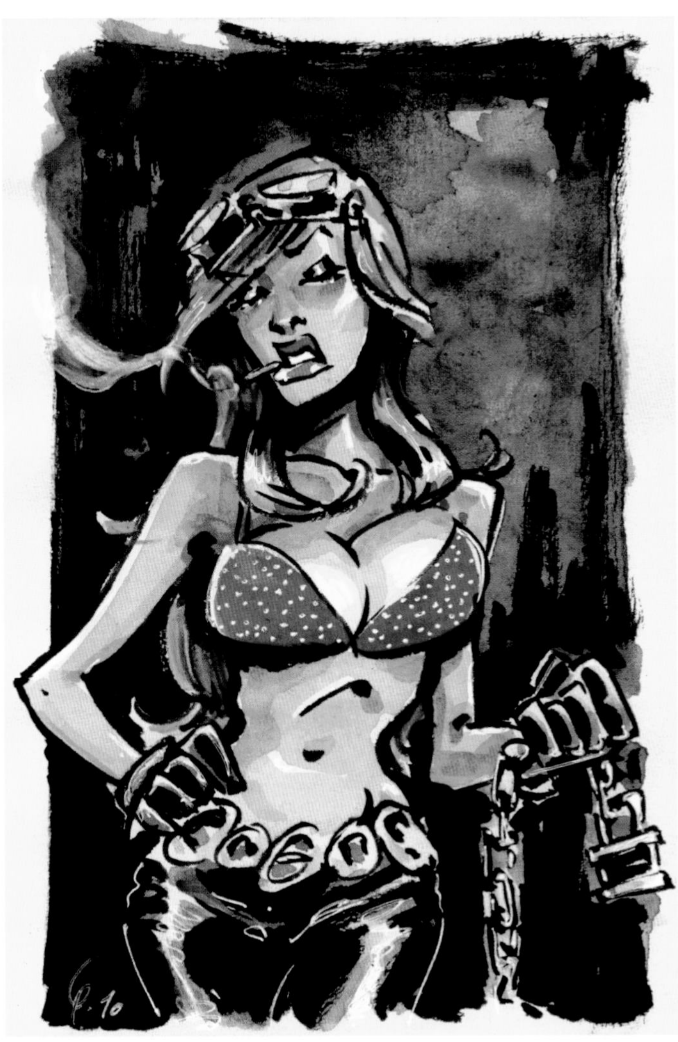

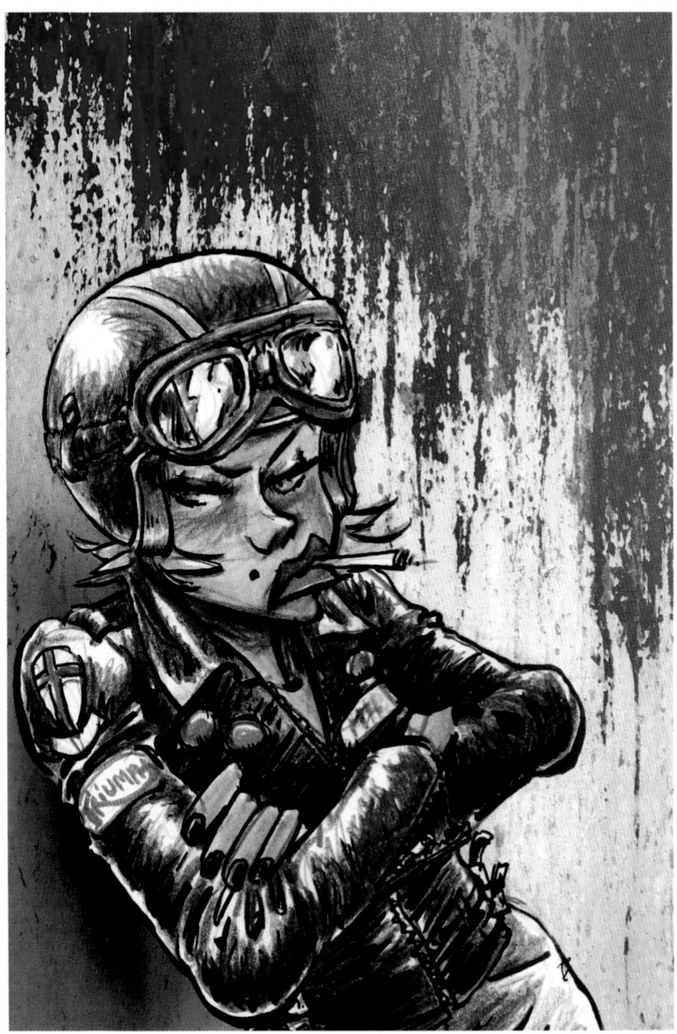

ABOVE: ***Girls On The Loose.*** Watercolour, coloured ink and gouache.

ABOVE RIGHT: ***Motarde.*** Coloured pencil and digital.

RIGHT: ***Triumph Hurricane.*** Pencil, coloured pencil and watercolour.

LEFT: ***The Paminator.*** Watercolour, coloured ink, felt pen and digital.

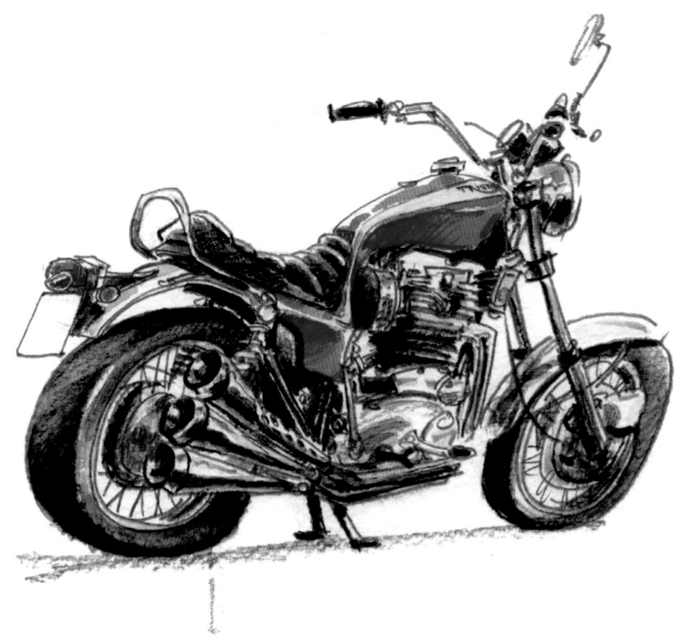

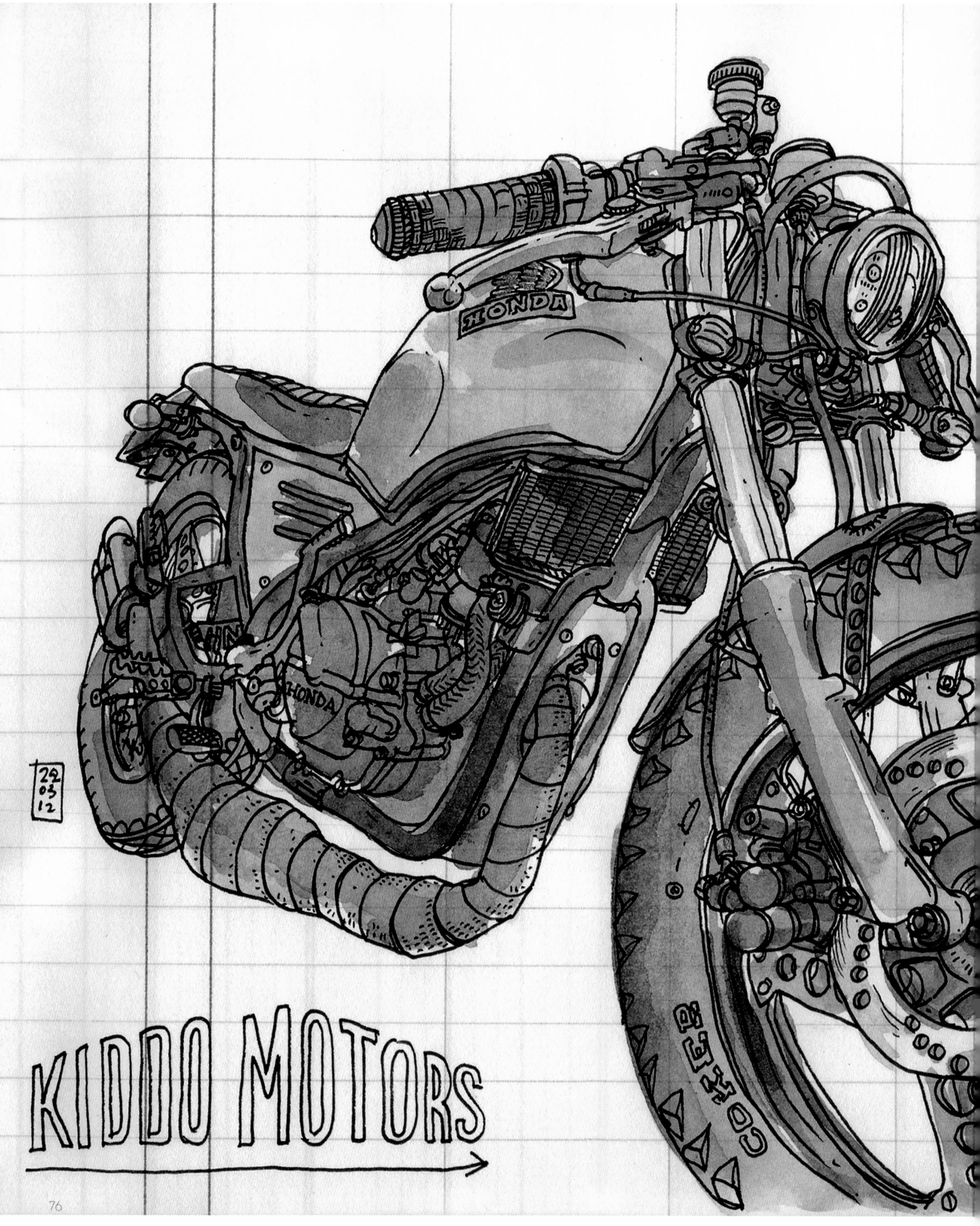
HONDA
HONDA
29
03
12
KIDDO MOTORS

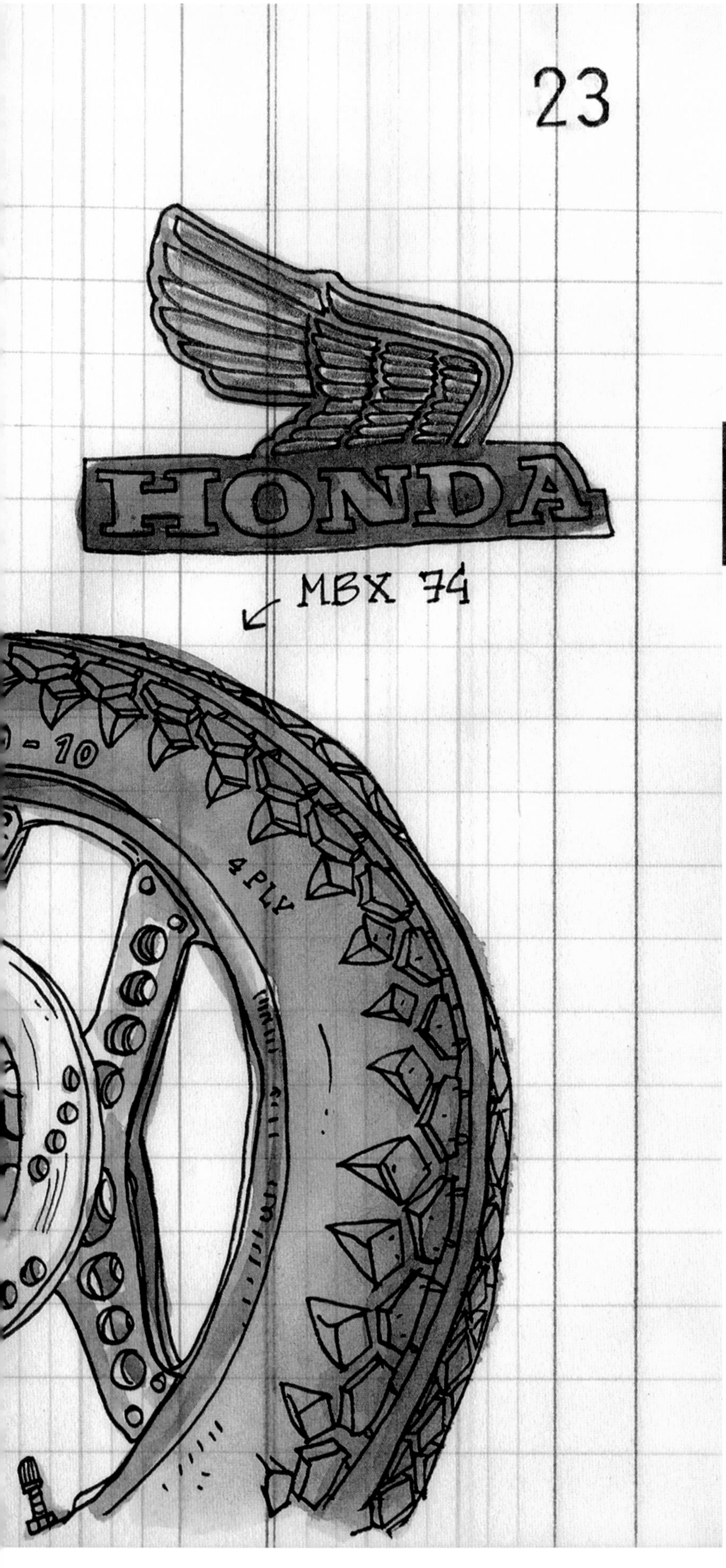

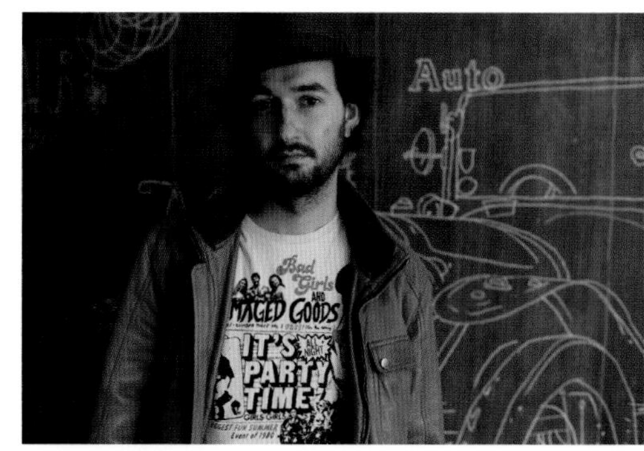

LAPIN

"Why are the wheels always such a nightmare to sketch?" wonders French-born, Barcelona-based sketch supremo Lapin. Lapin grew up next to a small airport where his father worked. "Quite naturally," he explains, "I received my flight license. That's when my attraction for mechanical engines was born; at the time I also invested any spare cash on flying lessons, so I never passed my driving test." Lapin studied in what he calls "an old-fashioned, disciplined art school" in Nantes, France. "I learned all the traditional techniques, perspective, anatomy, hyperrealism, painting... It was where I developed my addiction for sketching." He works with a black ink pen (a Uni Pin 0.1mm) and then colours with pens and pencils. For sketchbooks he uses secondhand account books, from the 1940s to '70s, which he finds in flea markets. His client list includes the likes of Porsche, but away from professional commissions he still sketches compulsively, "especially if I see a neglected, broken or decomposing bike on the street, which is why I always have one of those sketchbooks on me."

LEFT: ***Honda.***
Ink, watercolour and colouring pencils on vintage paper.

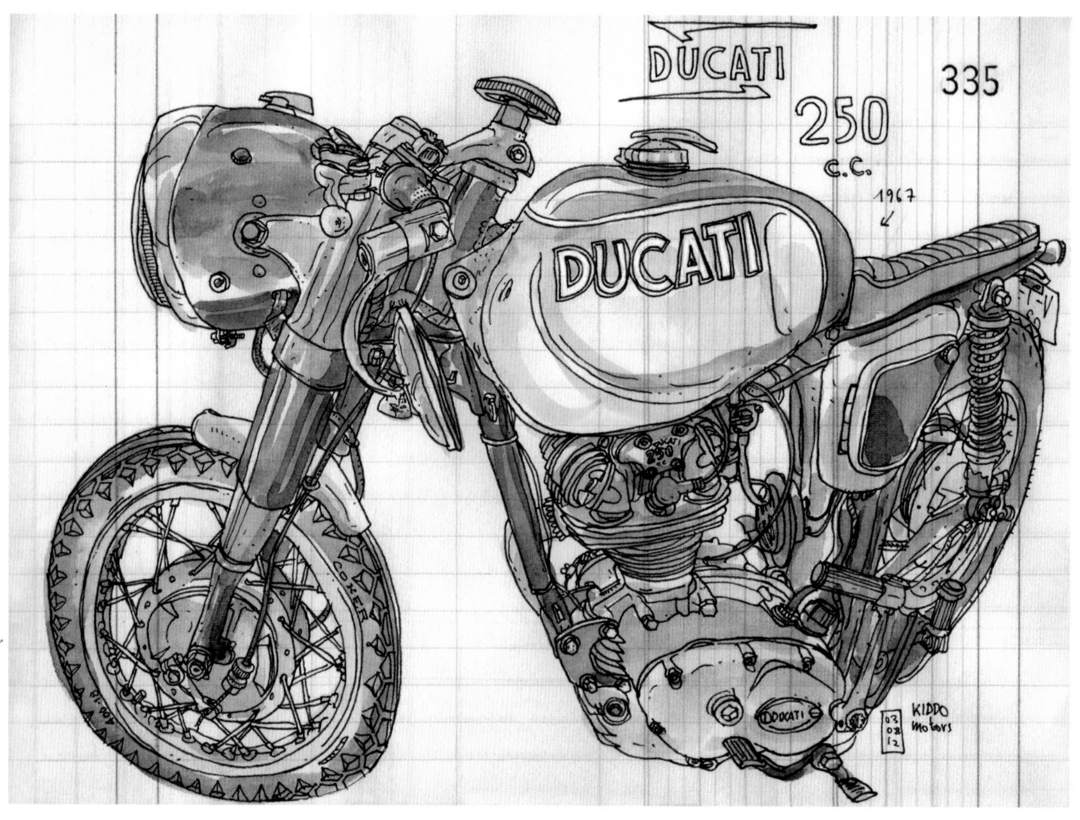

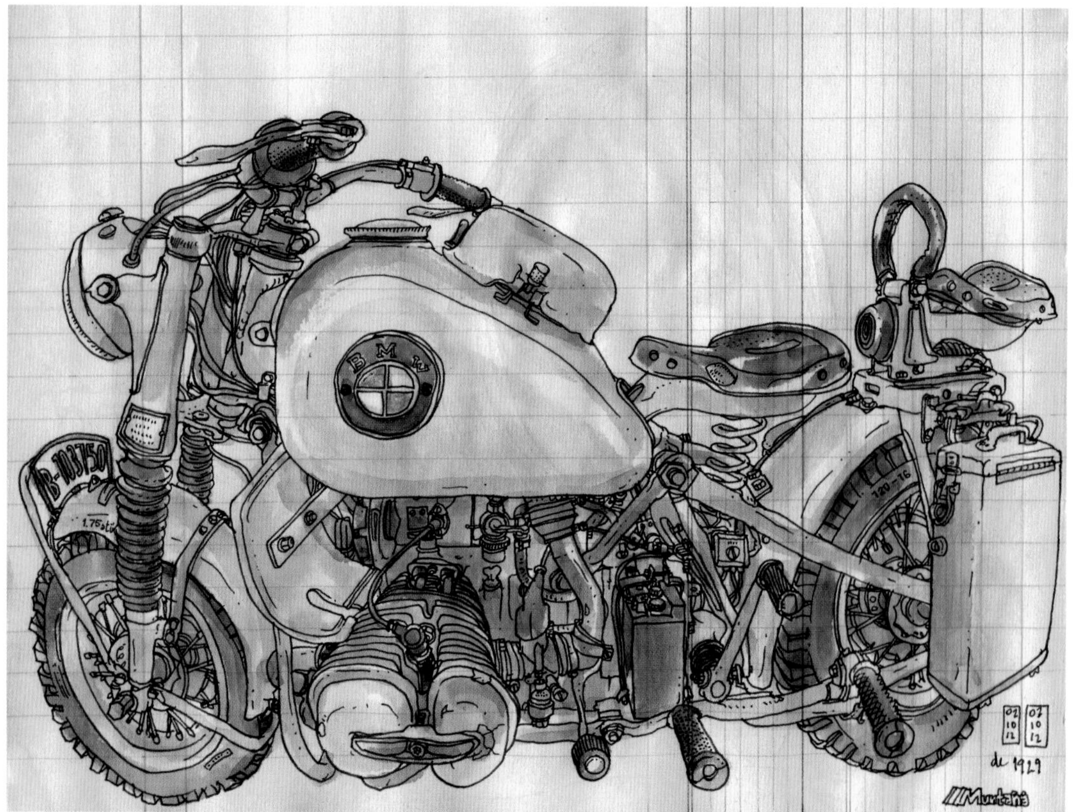

ABOVE: ***Ducati.***
Ink, watercolour and colouring pencils on vintage paper.

LEFT: ***BMW.***
Ink, watercolour and colouring pencils on vintage paper.

RIGHT: ***Bultaco.***
Ink, watercolour and colouring pencils on vintage paper.

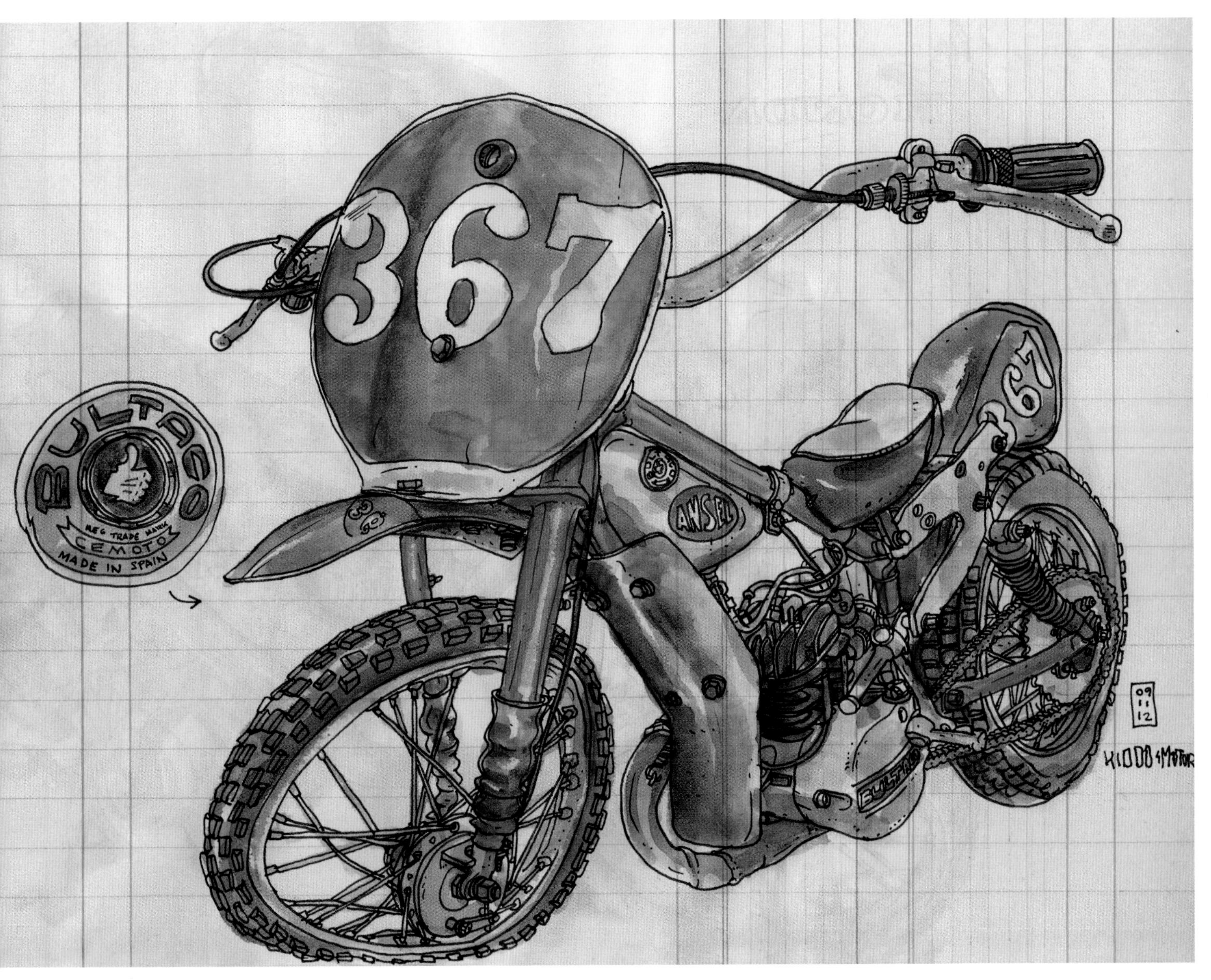
367
BULTACO
REG TRADE MARK
CEMOTO
MADE IN SPAIN
ANSEL
BULTACO
09 11 12
KIODOS MOTOR

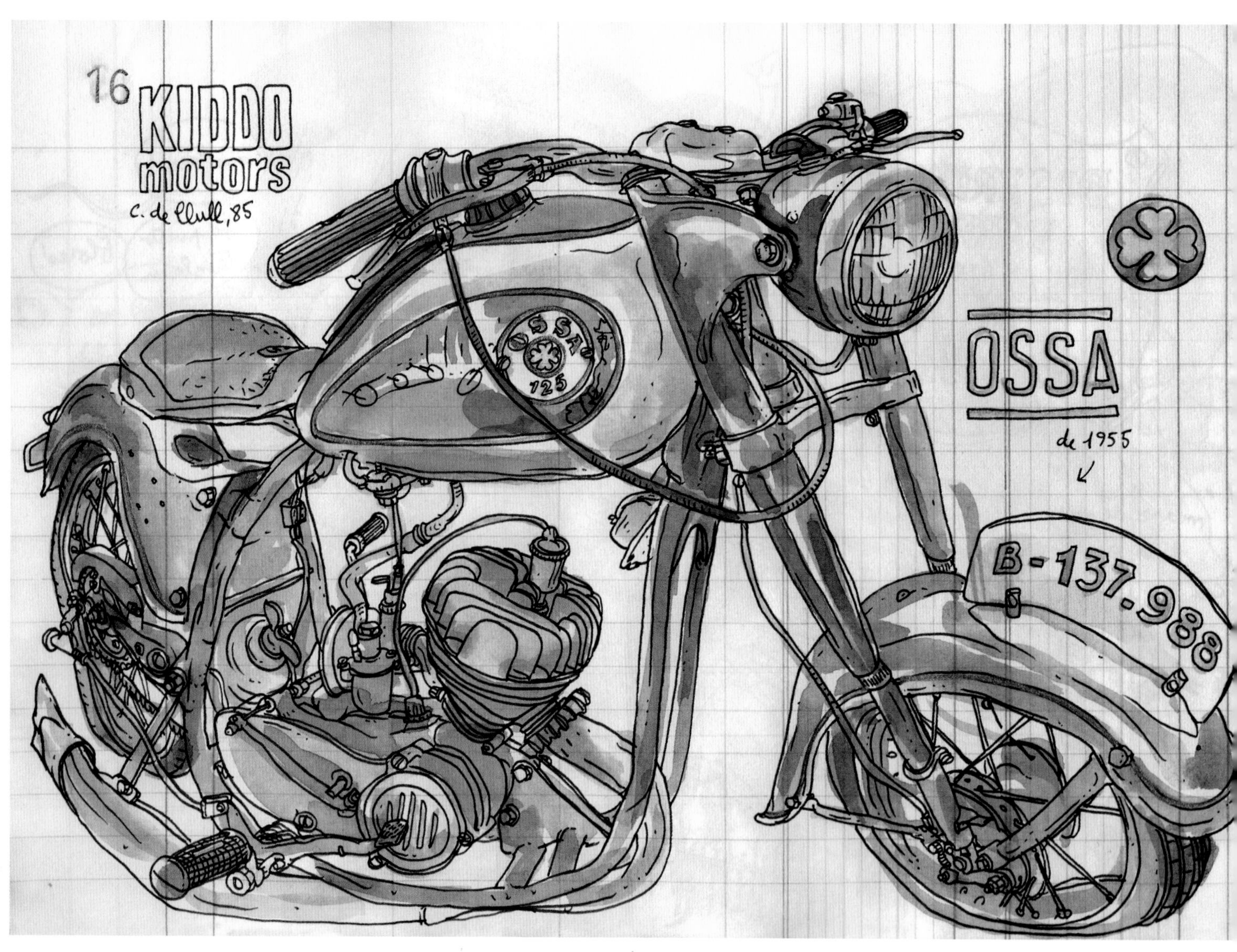
16 KIDDO motors
c. de Llull, 85
OSSA 125
OSSA
de 1955
B-137.988

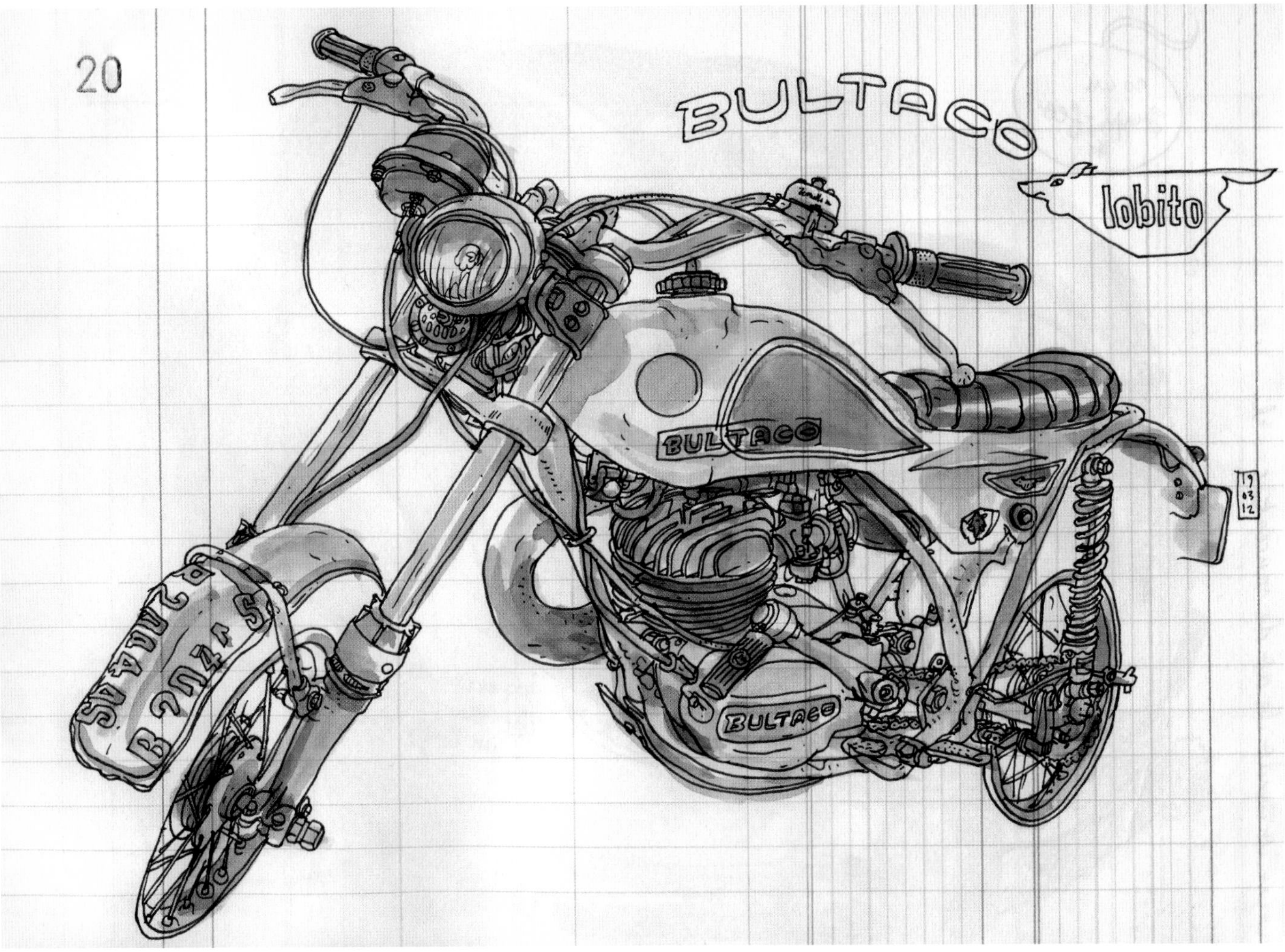

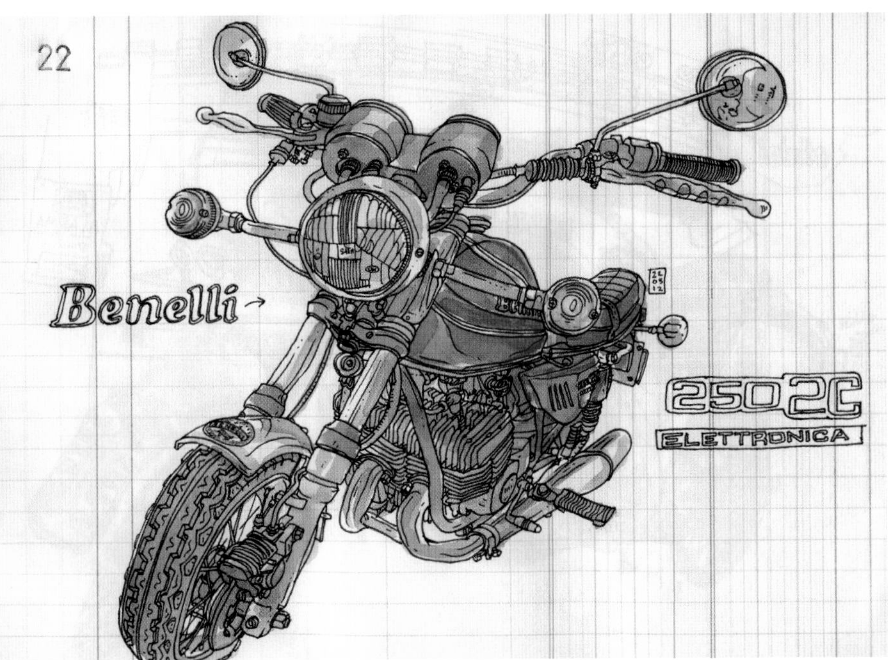

ABOVE: ***Bultaco.***
Ink, watercolour and colouring pencils on vintage paper.

LEFT: ***Benelli.***
Ink, watercolour and colouring pencils on vintage paper.

FAR LEFT: ***Ossa.***
Ink, watercolour and colouring pencils on vintage paper.

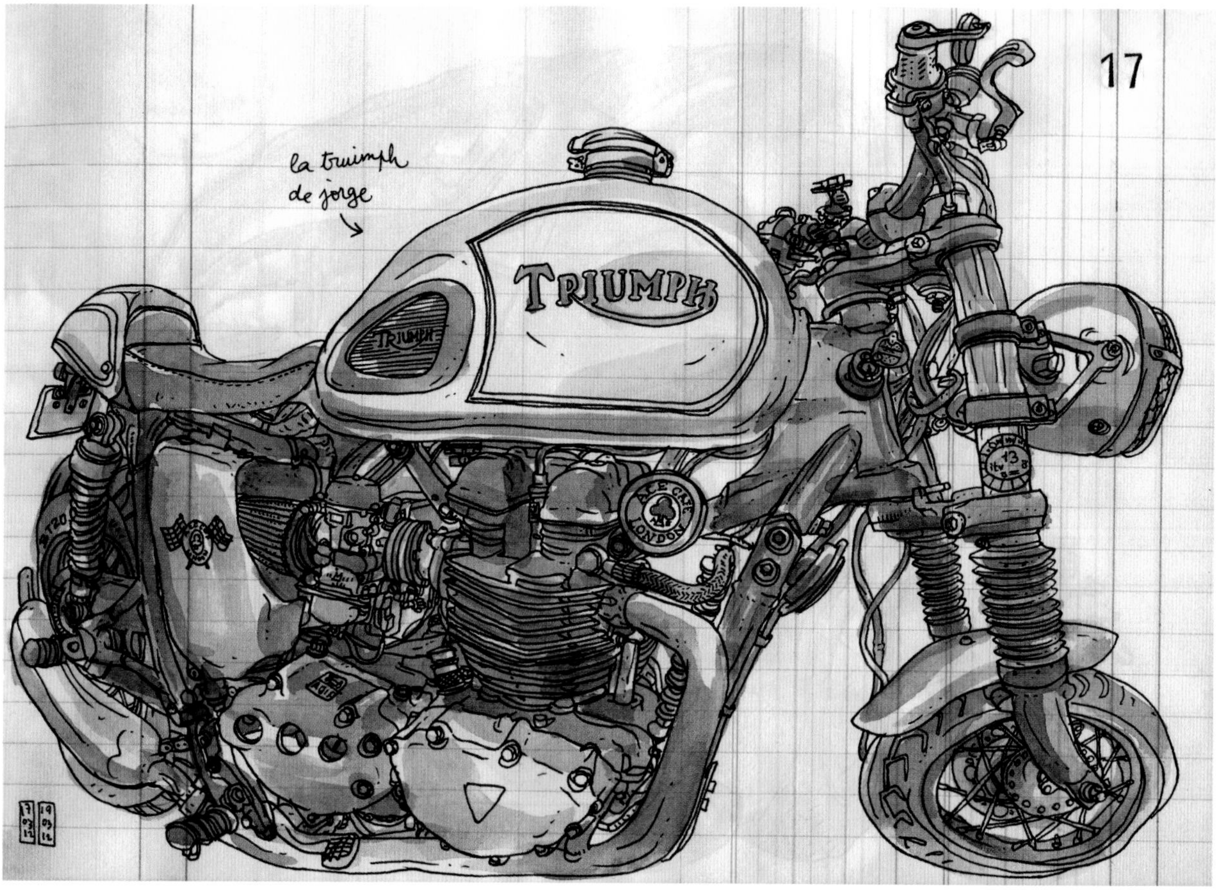

ABOVE: ***Triumph.*** Ink, watercolour and colouring pencils on vintage paper.

RIGHT: ***Peugeot.*** Ink, watercolour and colouring pencils on vintage paper.

FAR RIGHT: ***Wrenchmonkees.*** Ink, watercolour and colouring pencils on vintage paper.

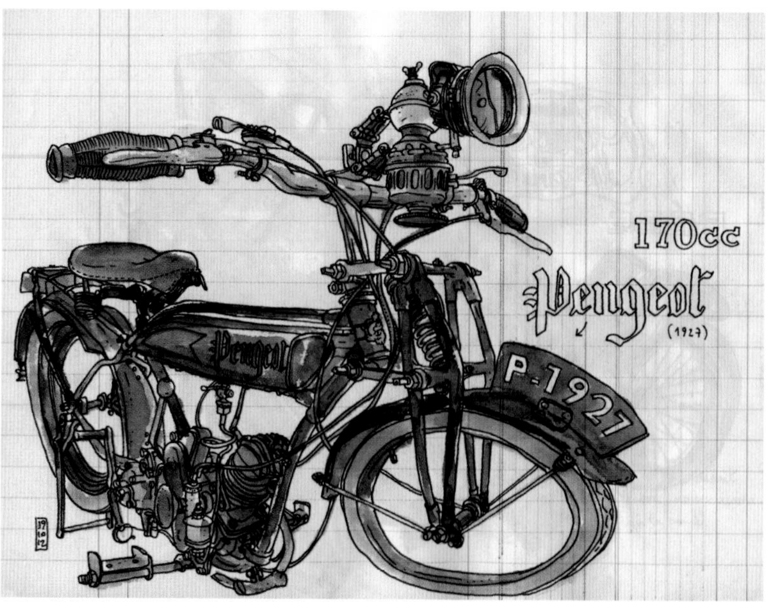

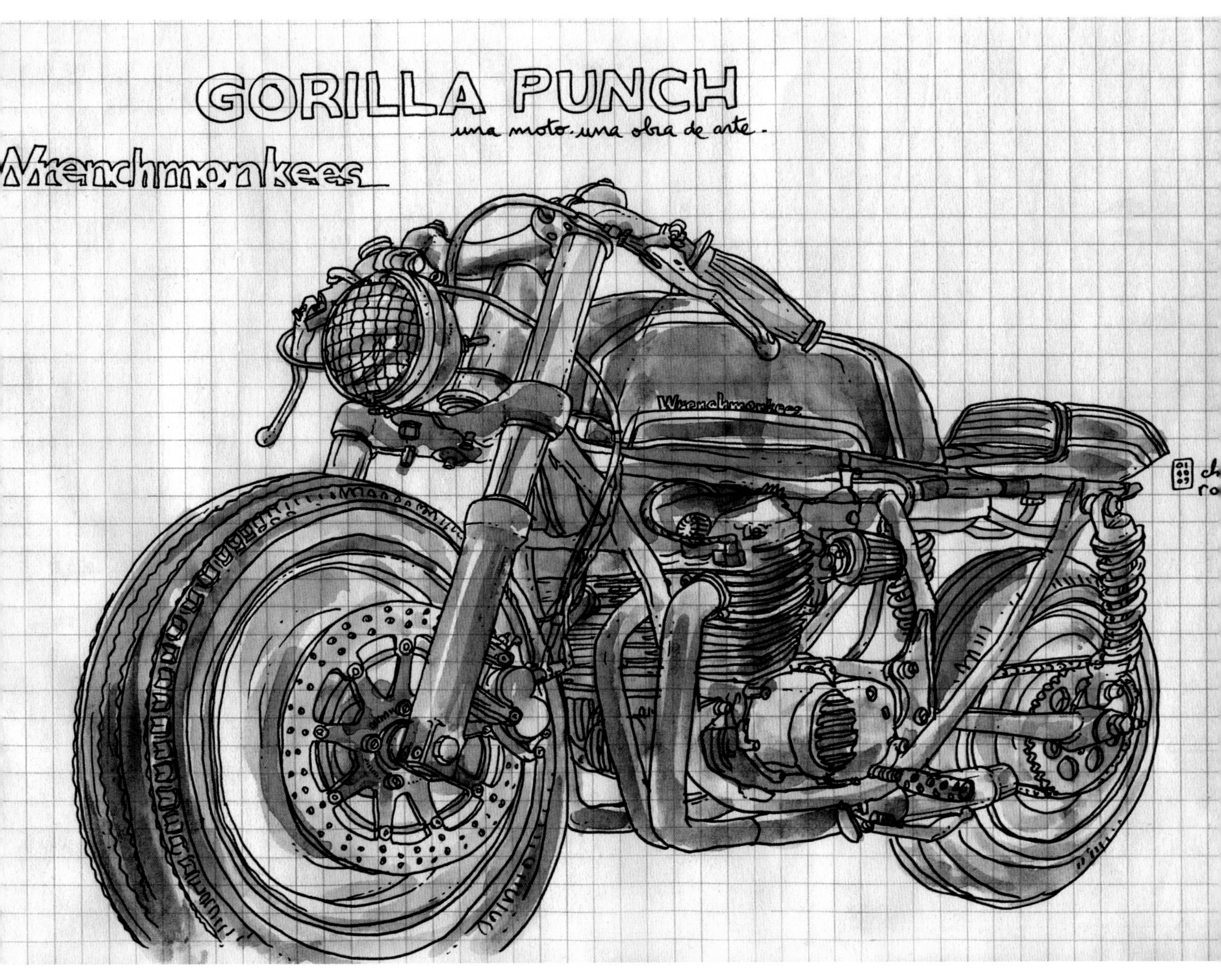
GORILLA PUNCH
una moto. una obra de arte.
Wrenchmonkees
Wrenchmonkees

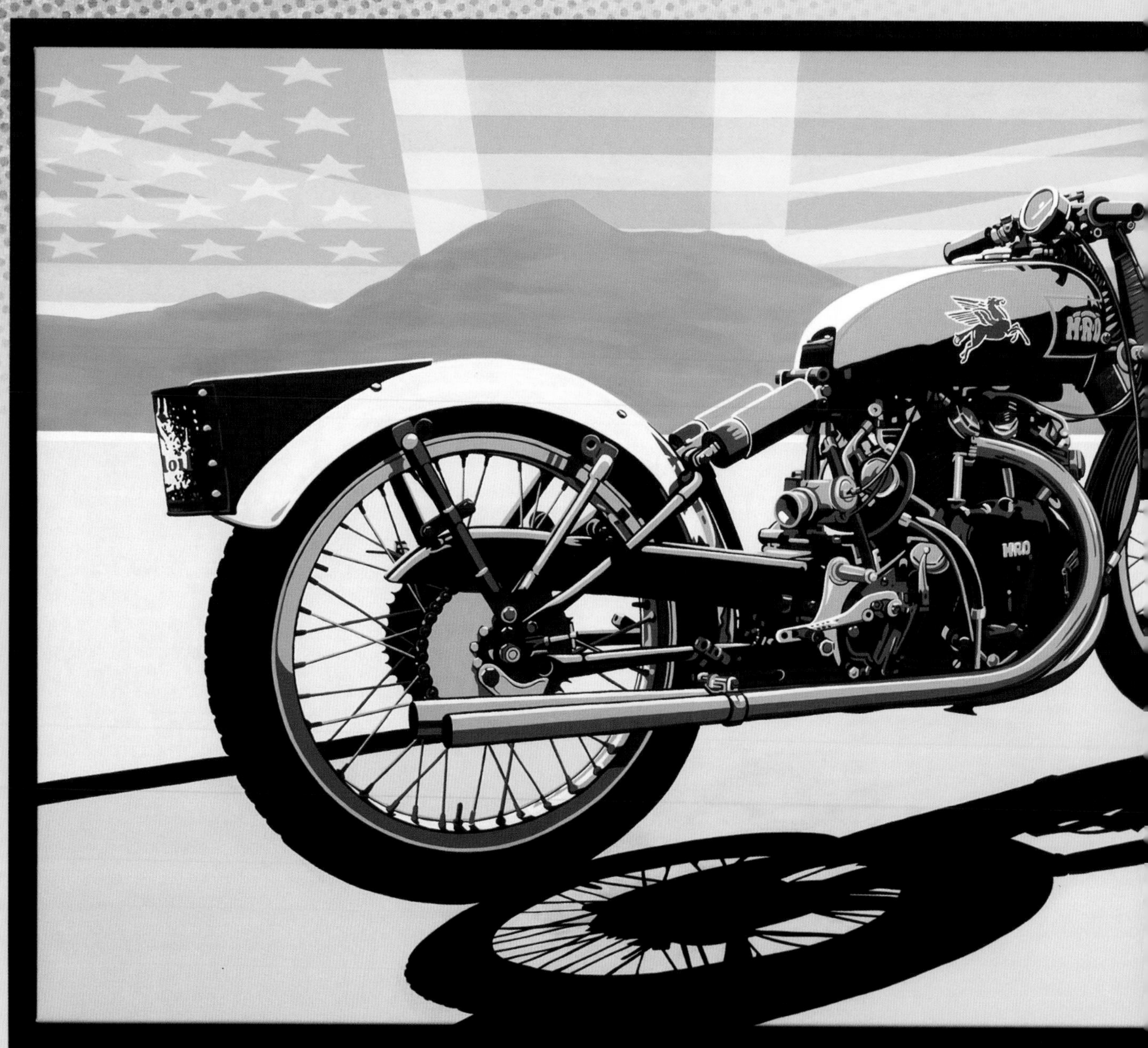
HRD
HRD

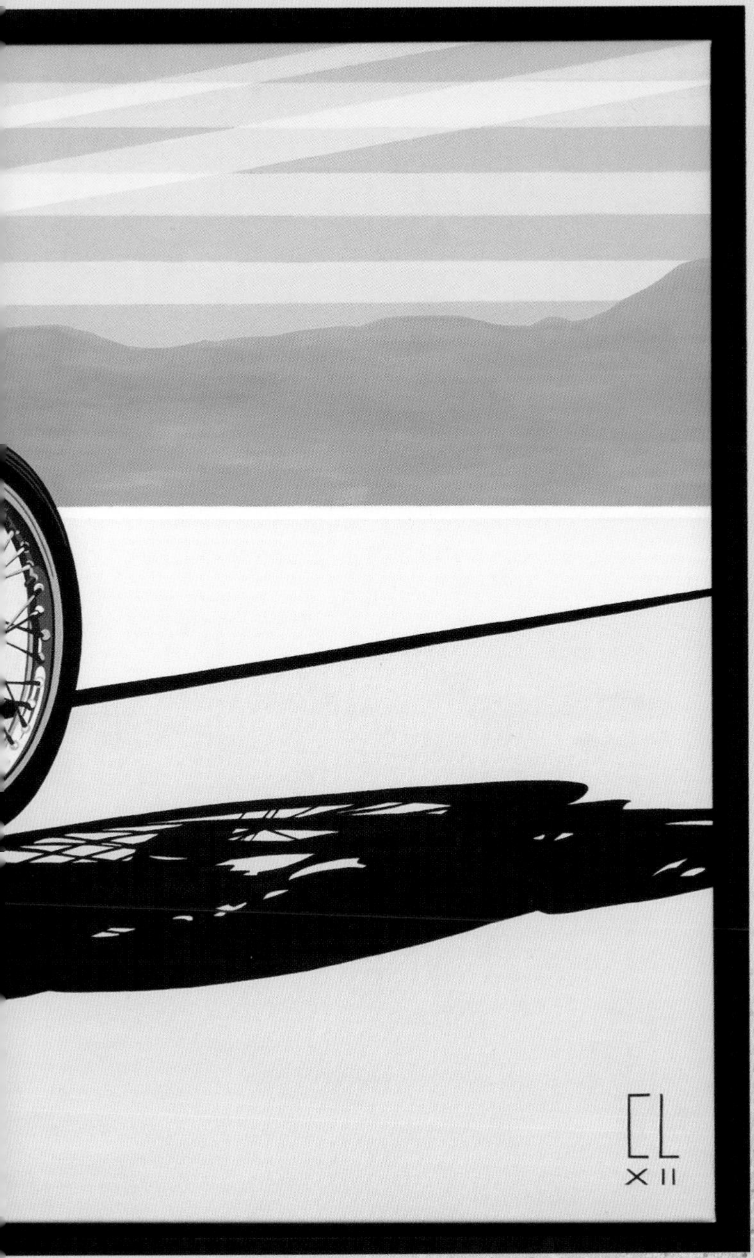

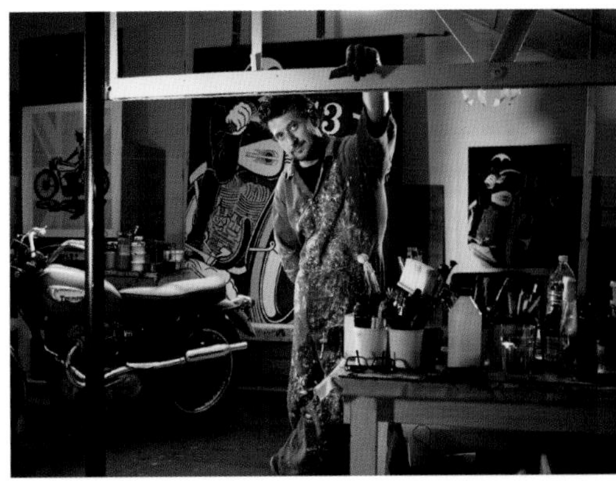

CONRAD LEACH

"I've always been driven to make paintings and drawings," says London-based Conrad. "It was instinctive." He has been obsessed with motorcycles since he was a boy, but is also keen to point out he doesn't just paint moto-related art. "I'm not a motorcycle artist, but even when I'm painting I'm thinking, how am I going to find time to repair the blown top-end of my Panhead? Motorcycles are never out of my thoughts." Conrad sees the very concept of motorbikes running parallel with art: "They are flicking absolutely the same switches. I remember, aged 12, being offered the chance to ride an FS1E – my first chance to ride a motorcycle ever. I knew exactly how to ride it: pull the clutch in, put it in gear, give it a few revs. I rode it up and down, got off it and that was it. It was like someone had just put a huge needle in my veins." After art school, Leach worked in the fashion industry for 15 years before becoming a full-time painter. He works in a very particular way. "I have a certain size in my mind and the only way to get that is to make the canvas myself. That's a very important part of the process for me. The image is fairly fully formed in my head. I work with a pop aesthetic. The size of the images comes from cinema. When I'm making big paintings, with bright flat colours, that's what I'm referencing. Then it becomes a technical exercise in getting the colour onto the canvas as brightly and smoothly as possible. I'm anal about it. I paint with a very particular acrylic, that I've researched and developed over ten years. I'm not going to tell you what it is, it's my secret ingredient."

LEFT: ***Lost in Space.***
Acrylic on canvas.

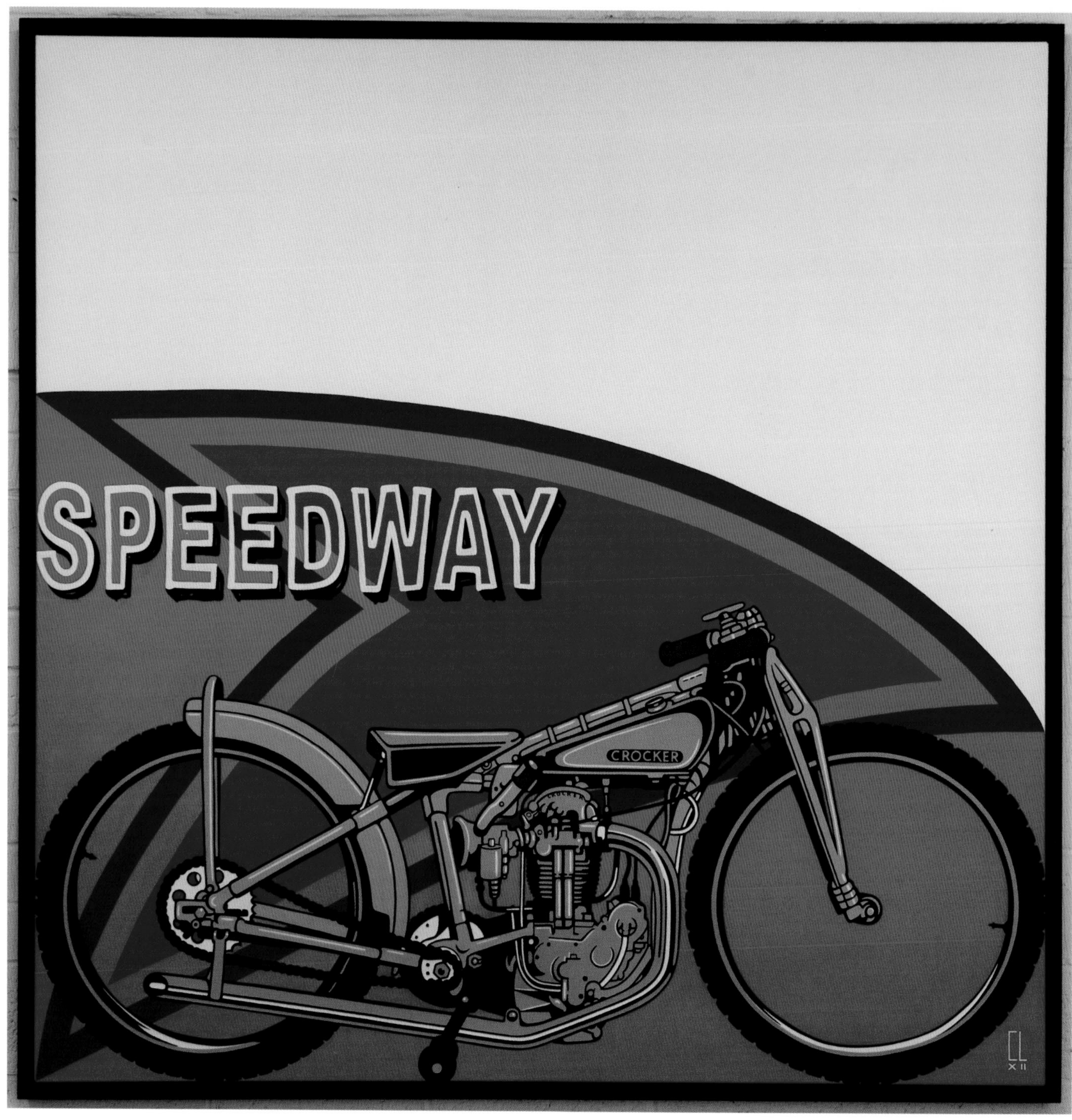

ABOVE: ***Speedway.***
Acrylic on canvas.

RIGHT: ***American Tan.***
Acrylic on canvas.

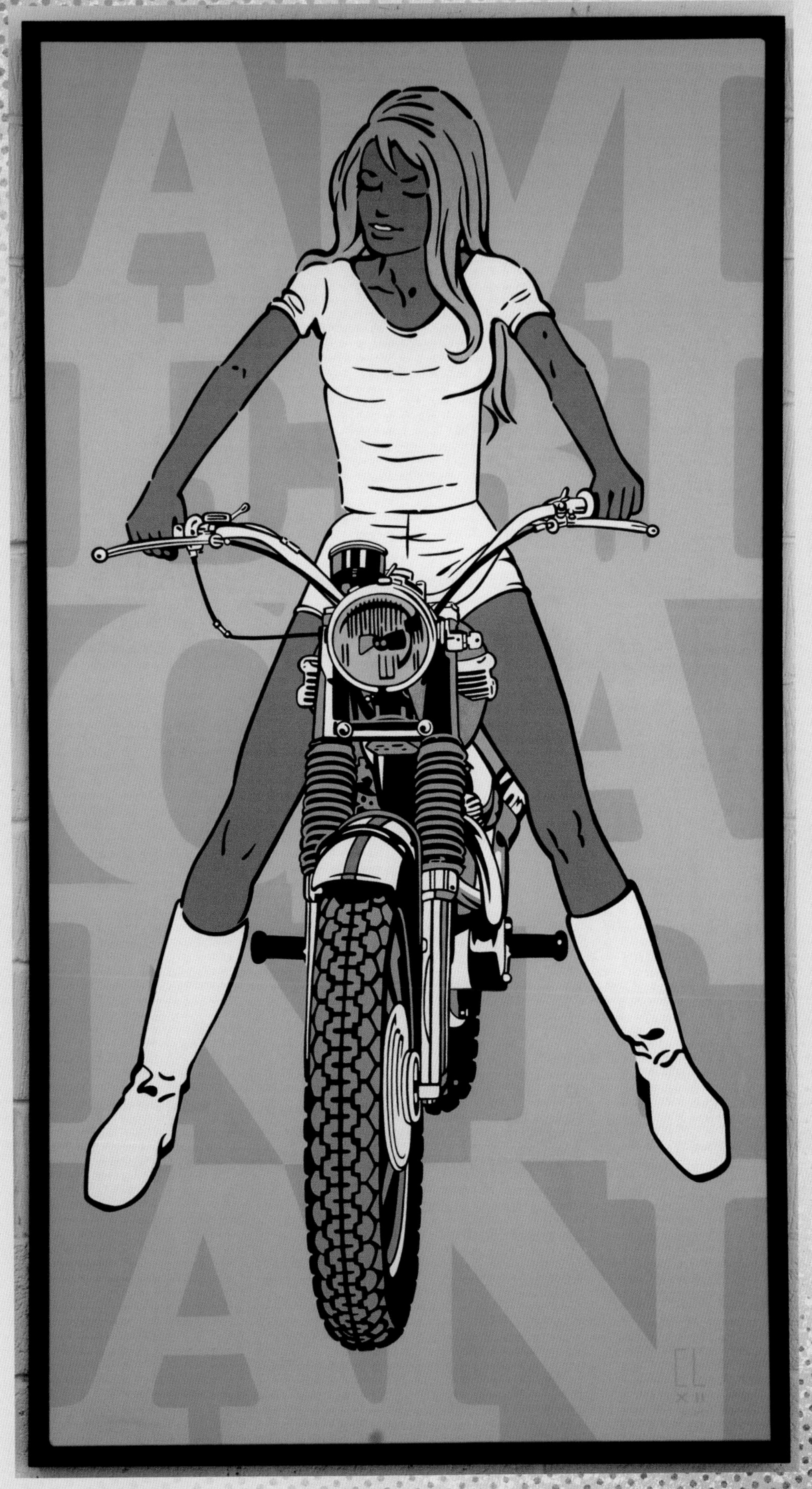

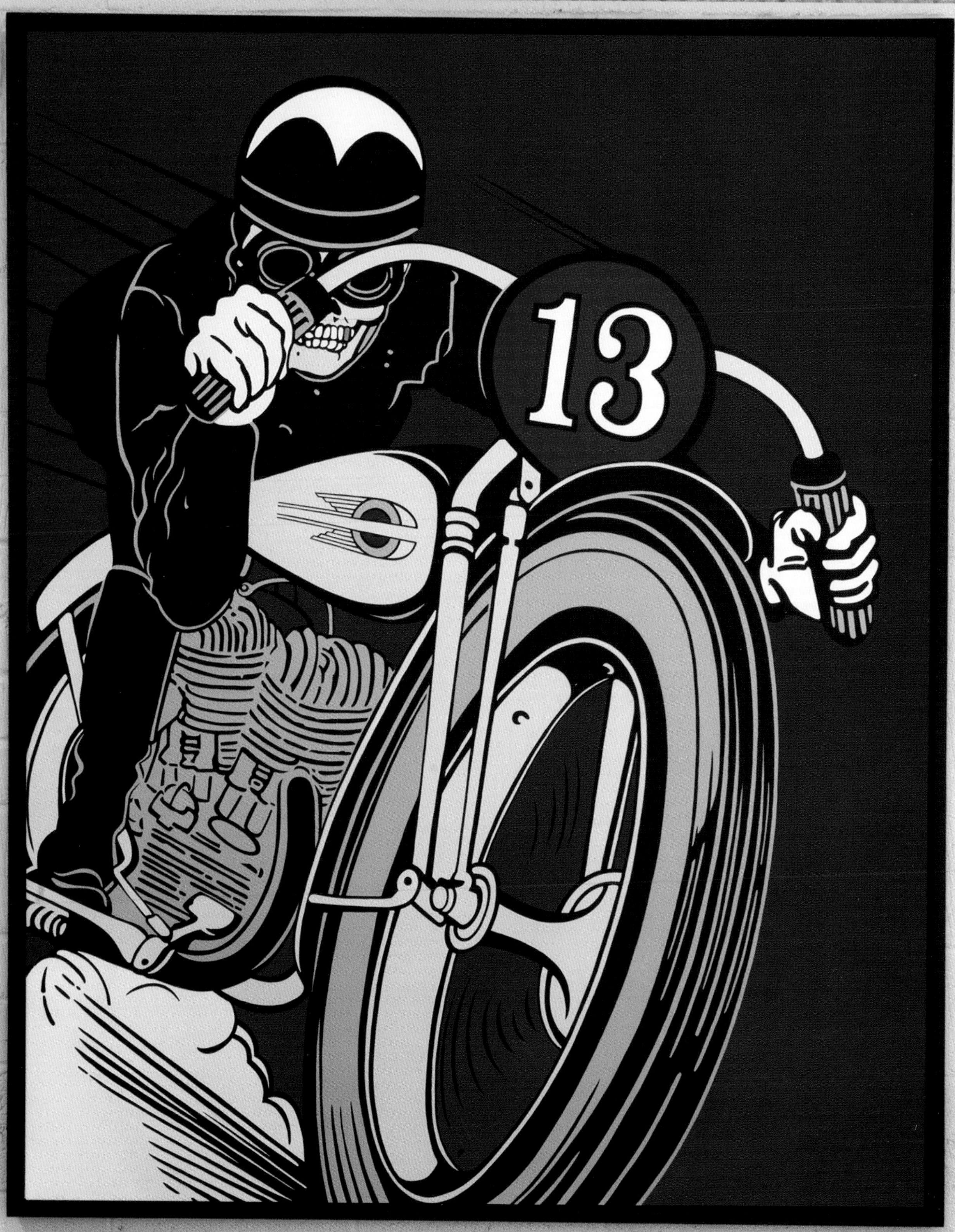

ABOVE: *Lucky 13.*
Acrylic on canvas.

RIGHT: *Pack Animal.*
Acrylic on canvas.

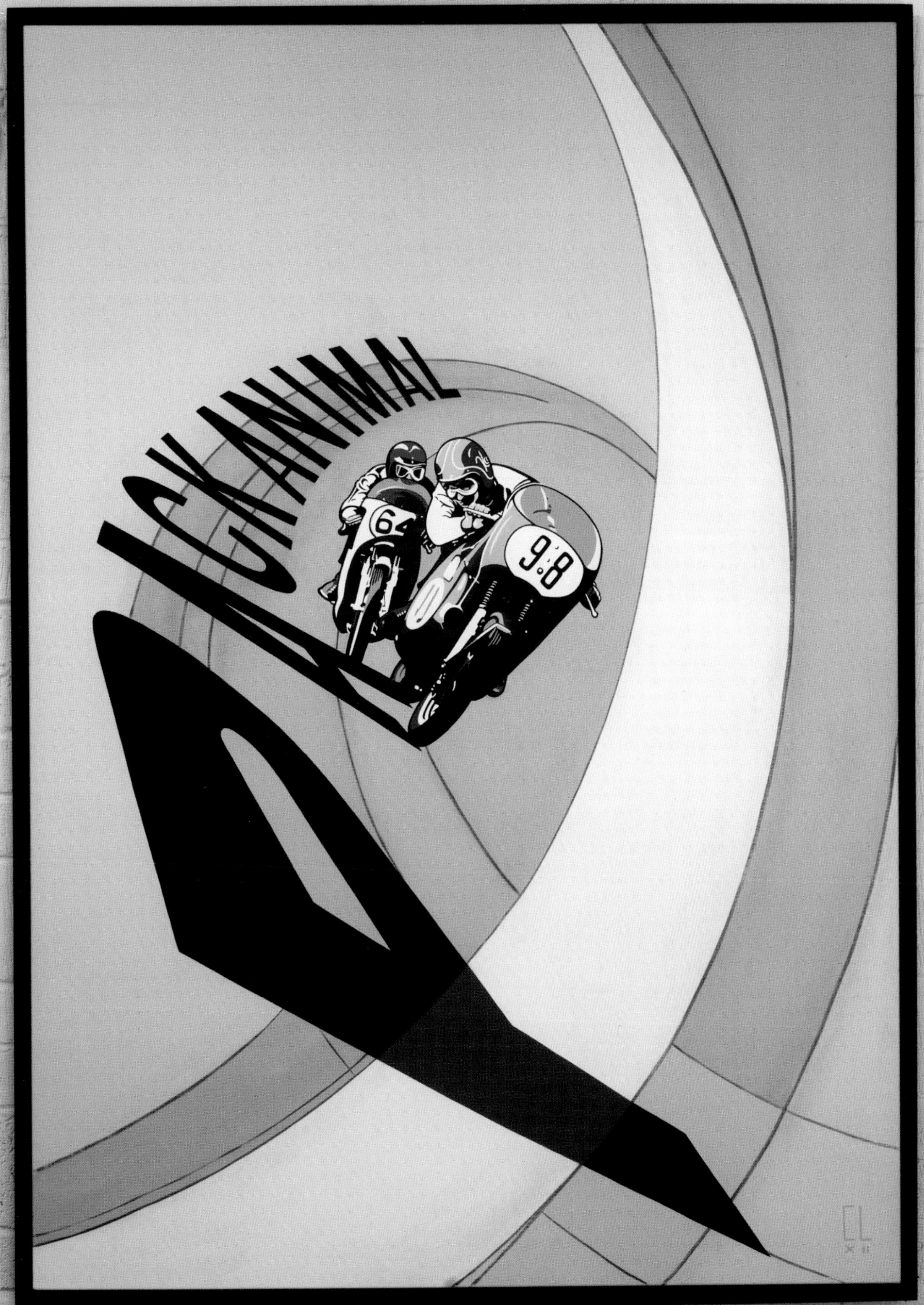

CK ANIMAL
64
98

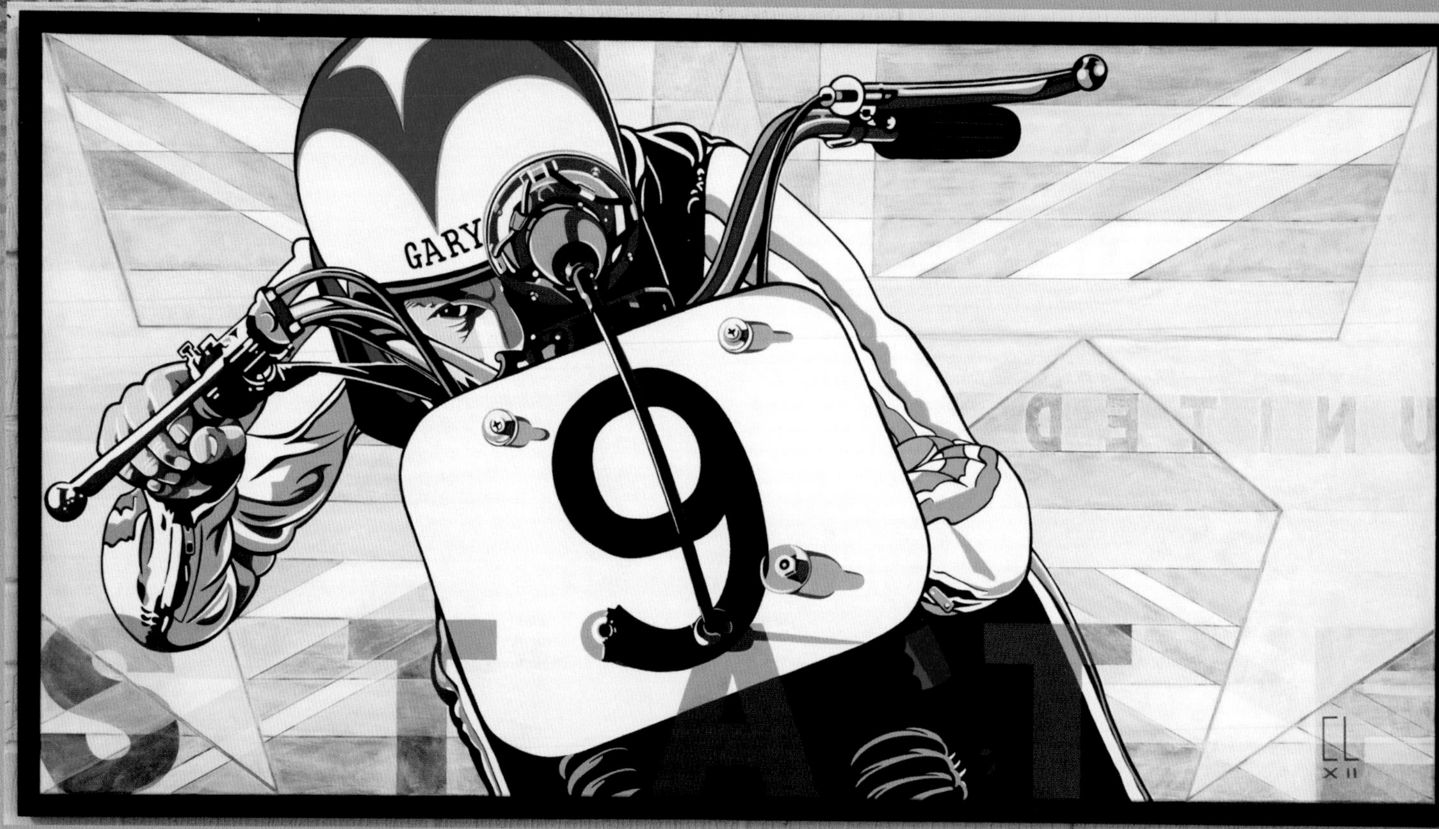

ABOVE: ***United State.***
Acrylic on canvas.

RIGHT: ***Norton Duke.***
Acrylic on canvas.

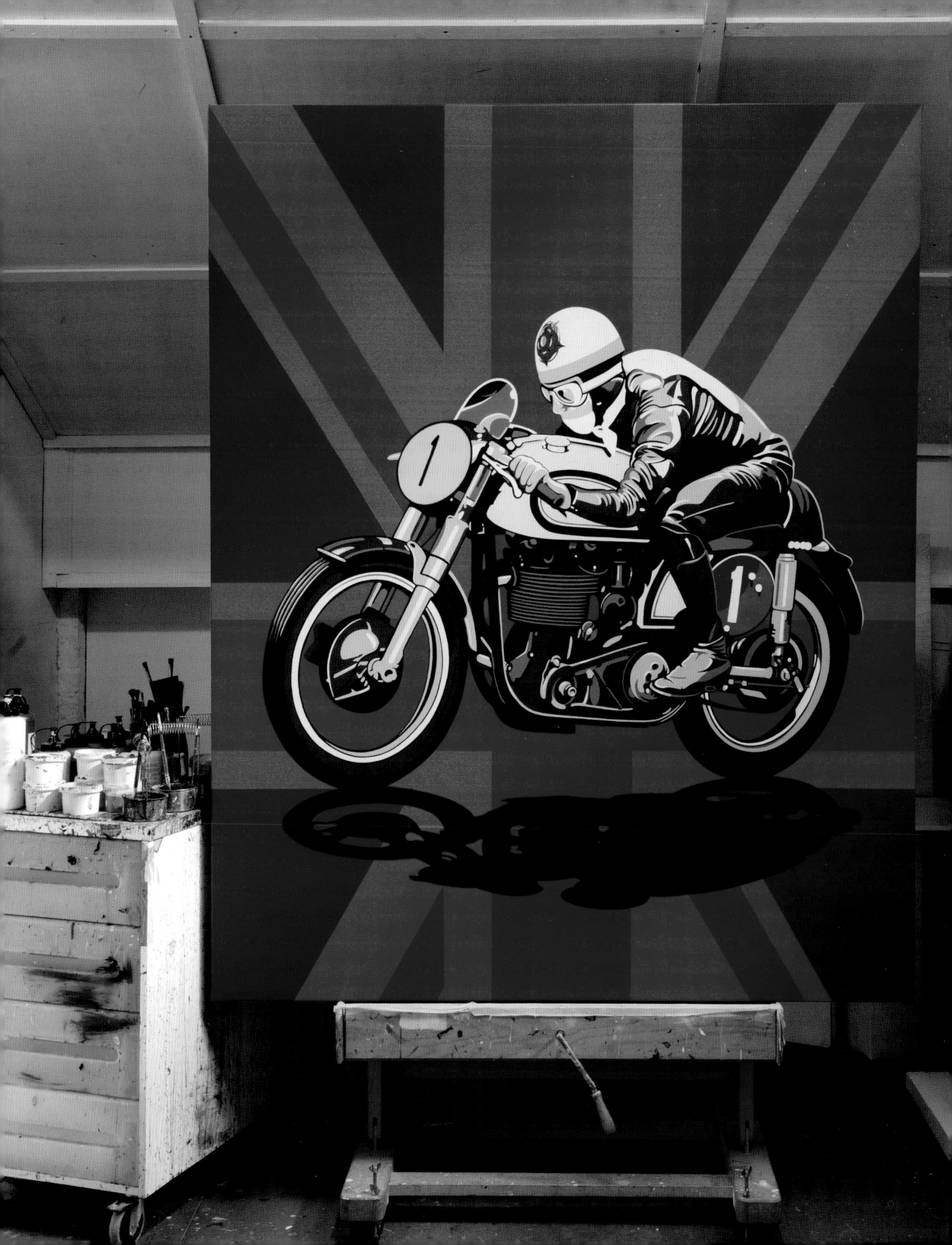

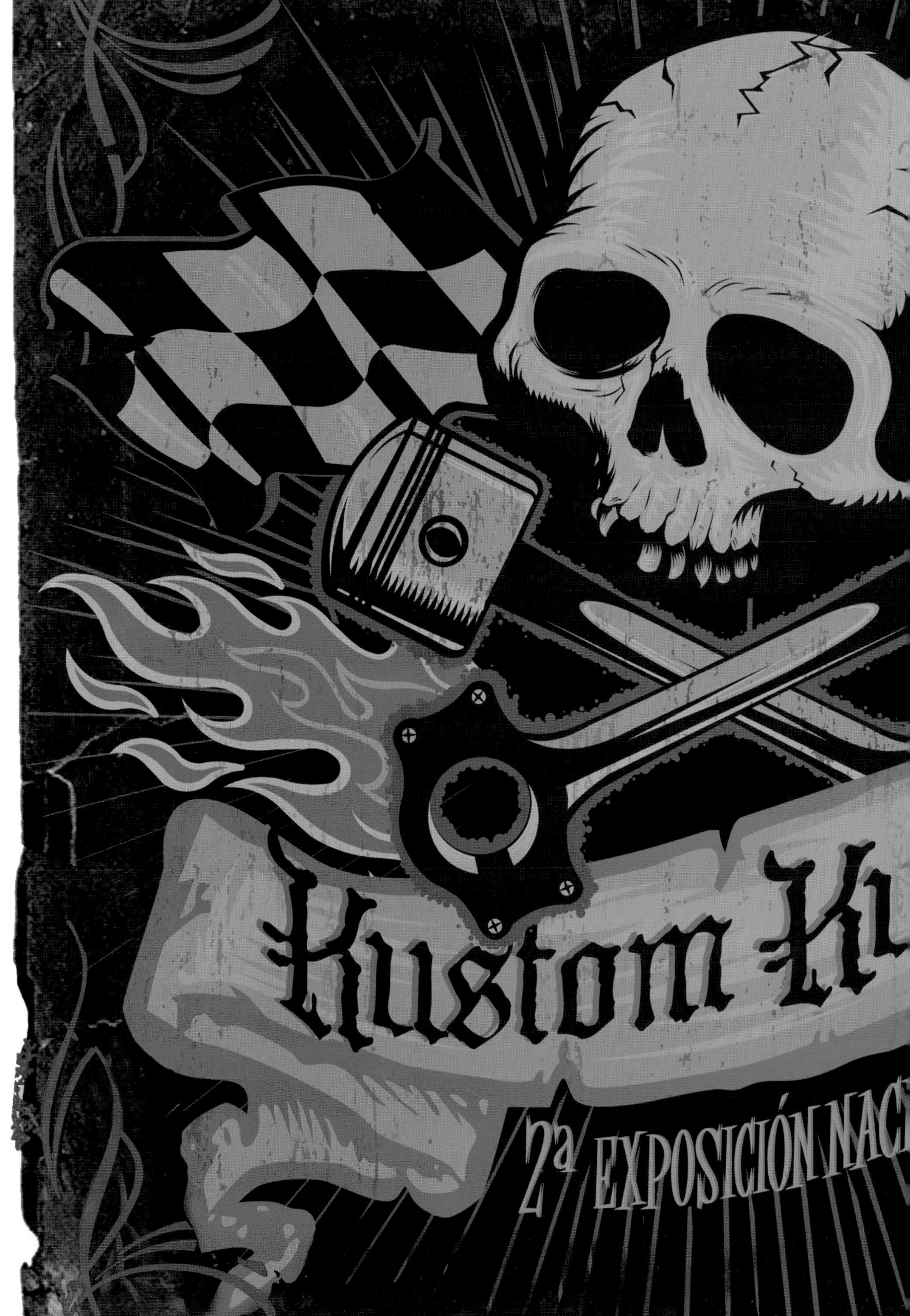
Kustom Ku
2ª EXPOSICIÓN NAC

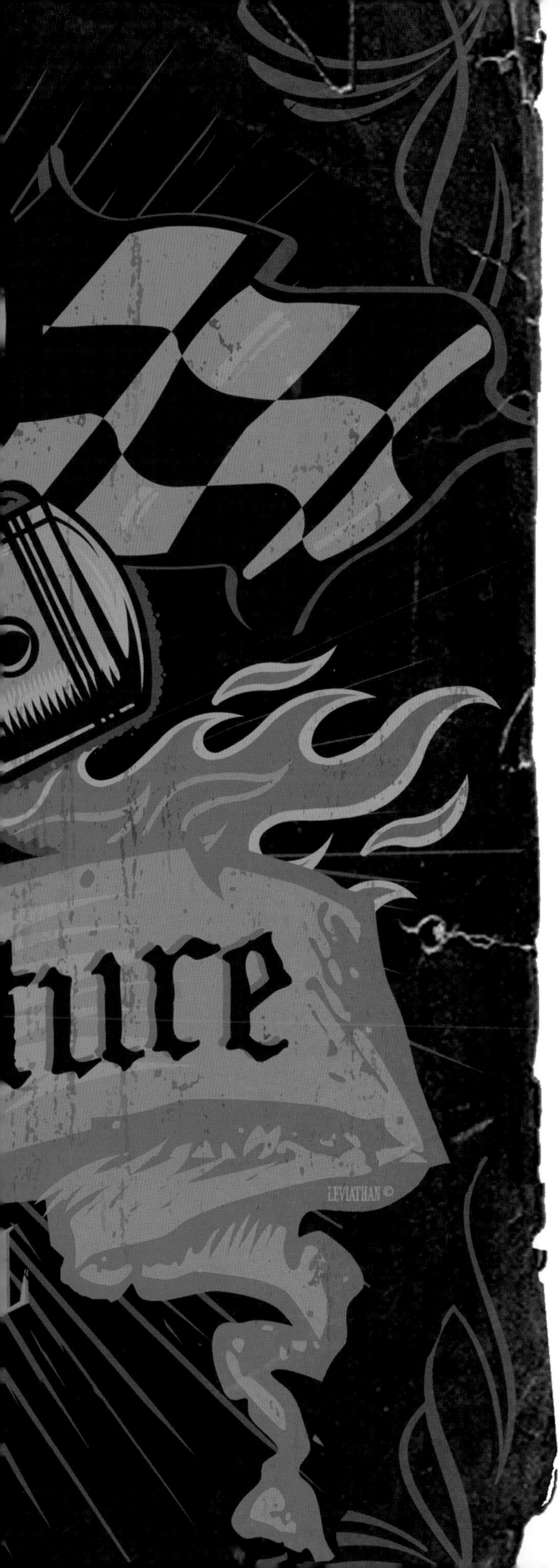

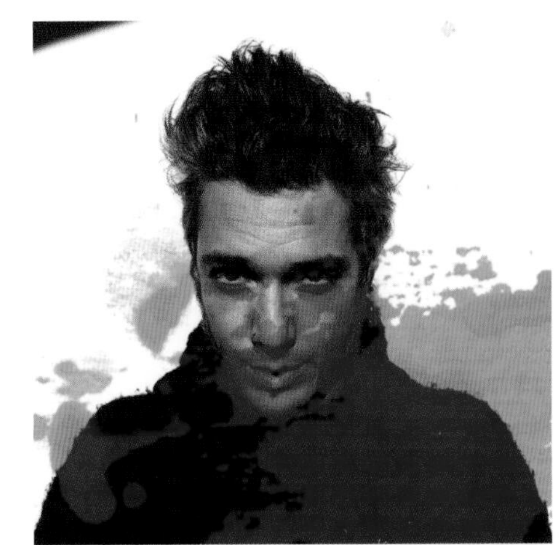

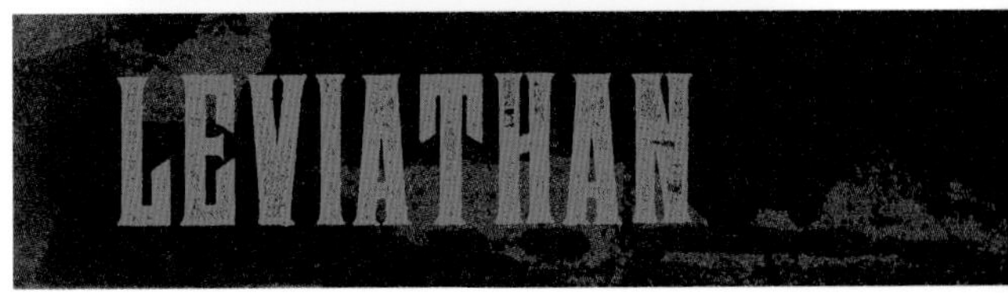

LEVIATHAN

From his Spanish base, Manuel 'Leviathan' LaVey has garnered a global following for his t-shirt and poster designs in 18 years as a professional artist. When asked why motorcycles feature in his work so often, he sums up the attraction succinctly: "I like two wheels." His parents are painters, photographers and advertisers. "They gave me the interest for art since I was really young." His great-grandmother was a cabaret dancer, too, and he began, at an early age, airbrushing motorcycles, then leather, before moving to canvas. All these early influences regularly feature in his work. "I've been riding motorbikes for about 18 years now. I always loved it. Right now I have a Harley-Davidson Fat Boy that I have transformed into a rat-style bobber. My bike appears in my drawings many times." His prodigious output includes the artwork, year after year, for many festivals, including the Burlesque Festival of New Orleans, the Las Vegas Shakedown festival, Freakland, Crossroad and Kustom Navacerrada Day. He is also much in demand for bands such as The Stray Cats, The Misfits, Zen Guerrilla, Willy DeVille, Buddy Guy, The Lords of the New Church and The Dictators, and for artists as diverse as Raimundo Amador and Little Richard.

LEFT: *Kustom Kulture.*
Digital art.

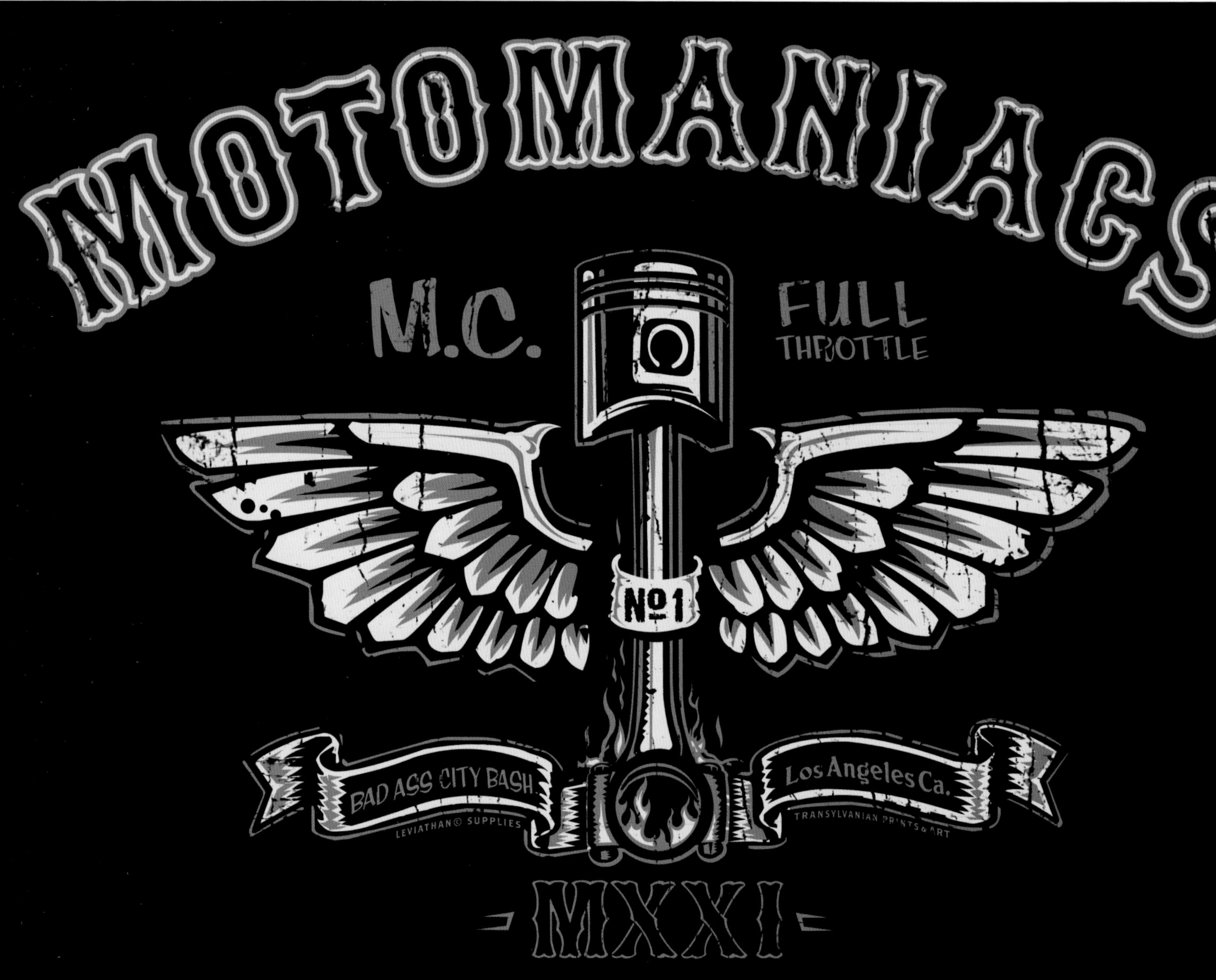

ABOVE: ***Motomaniacs.***
Digital art.

RIGHT: ***Biker and Hot Rod Meeting, Letur 2011.***
Digital art.

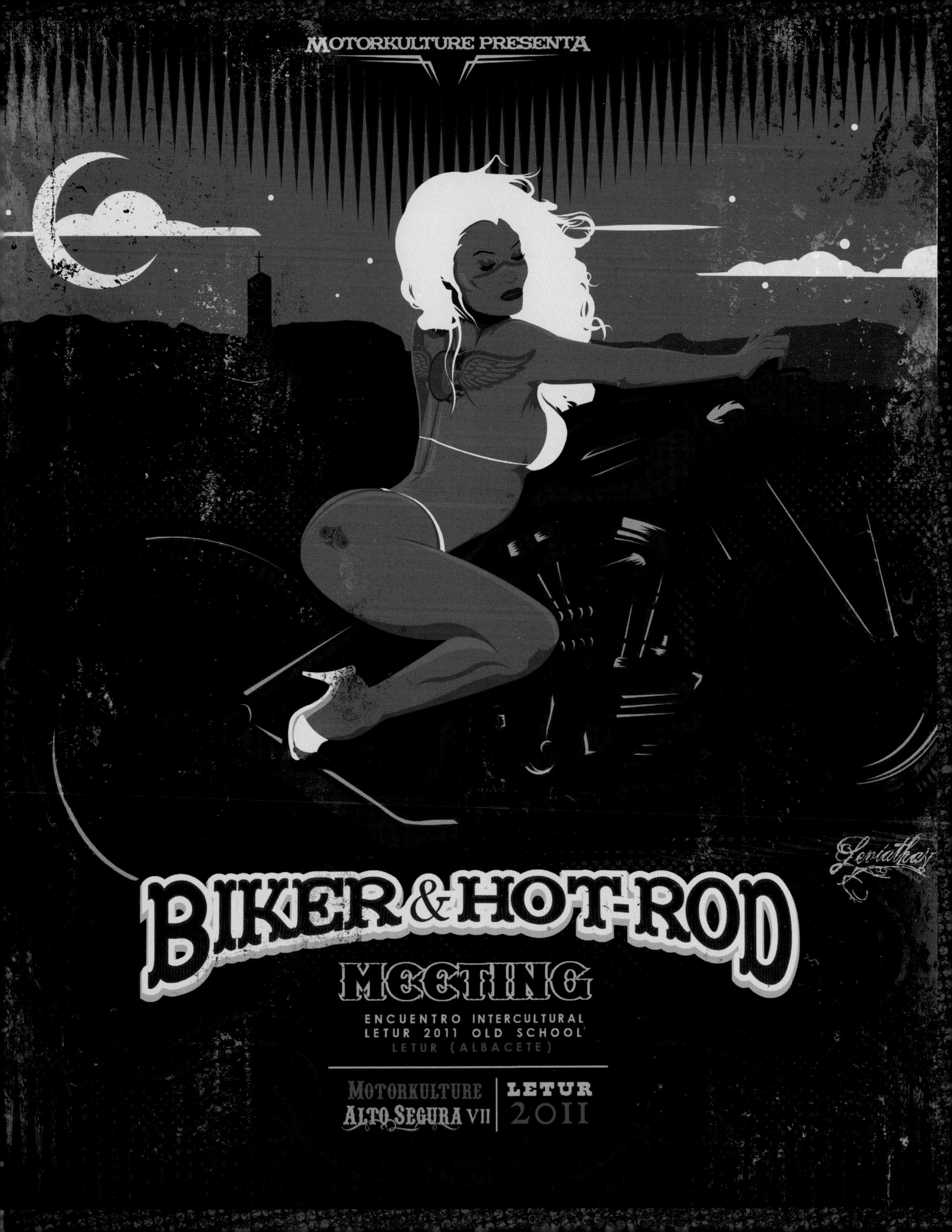

MOTORKULTURE PRESENTA

BIKER & HOT-ROD
MEETING

ENCUENTRO INTERCULTURAL
LETUR 2011 OLD SCHOOL
LETUR (ALBACETE)

MOTORKULTURE
ALTO SEGURA VII

LETUR
2011

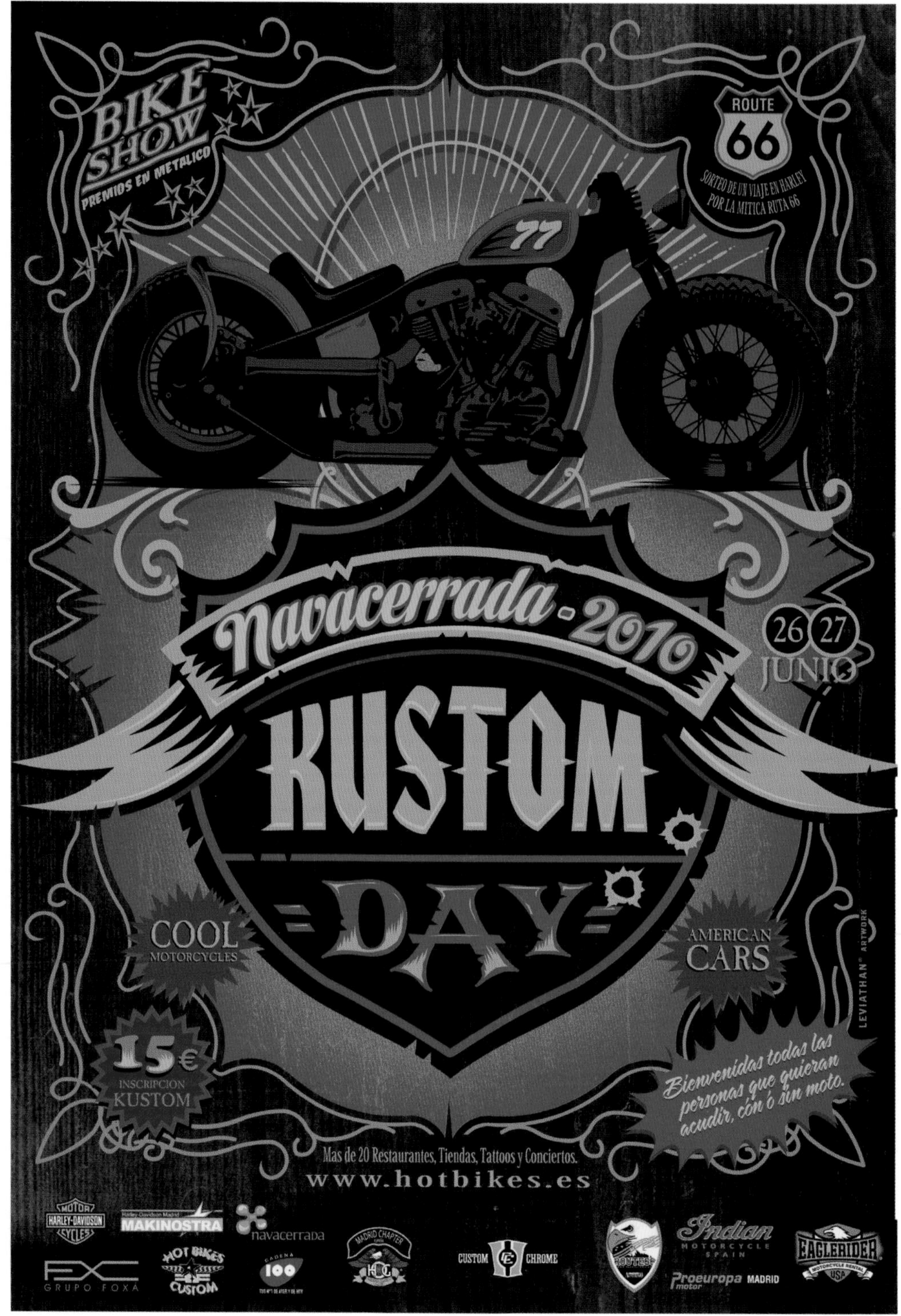

RIGHT: ***Kustom Day, 2010.***
Digital art.

FAR RIGHT: ***Tormento de Amor.***
Digital art.

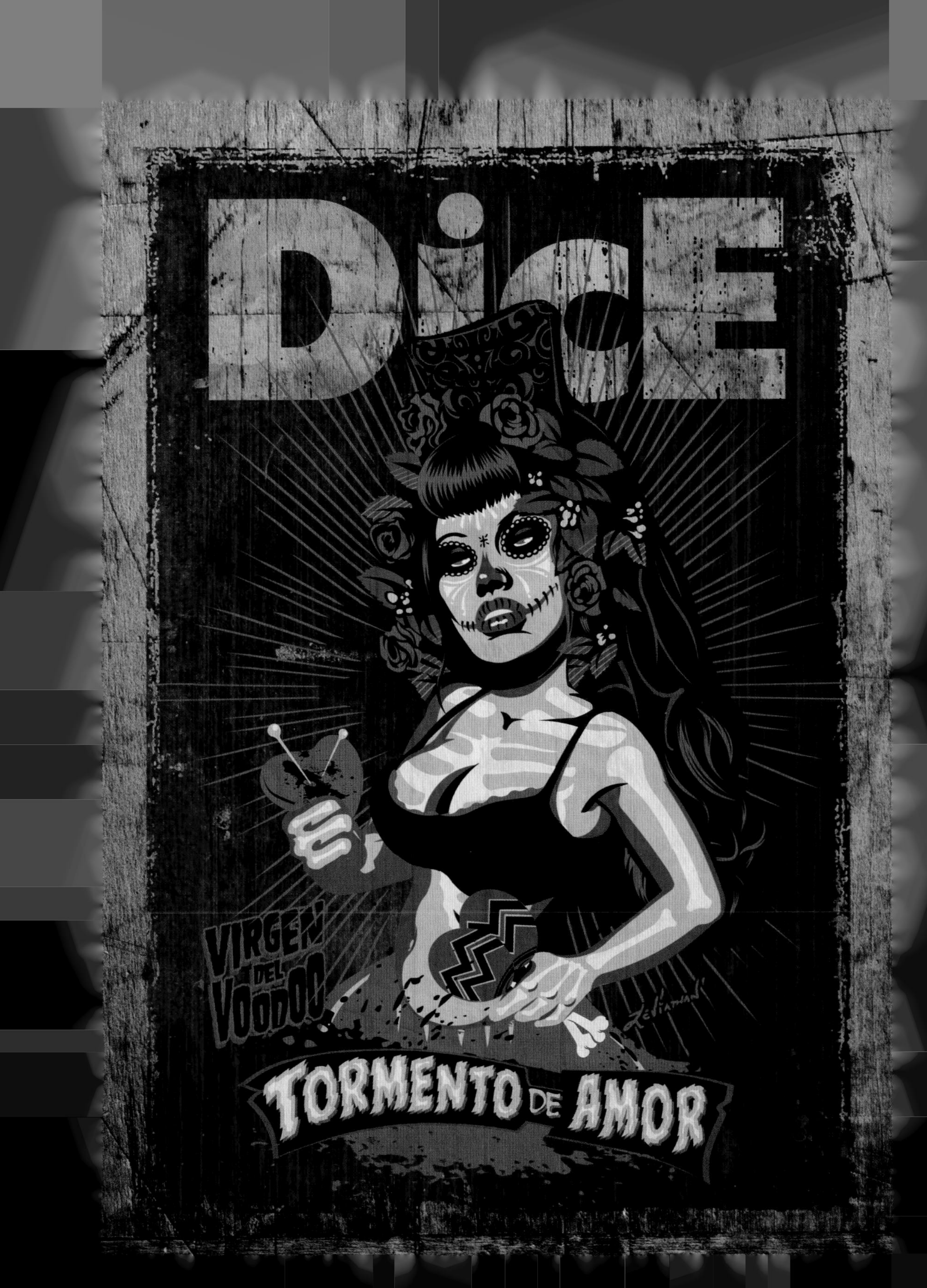
DiCE
VIRGEN DEL VOODOO
TORMENTO DE AMOR

BELOW: ***Bombshell Attack.***
Digital art.

FAR RIGHT: ***Lady Death.***
Digital art.

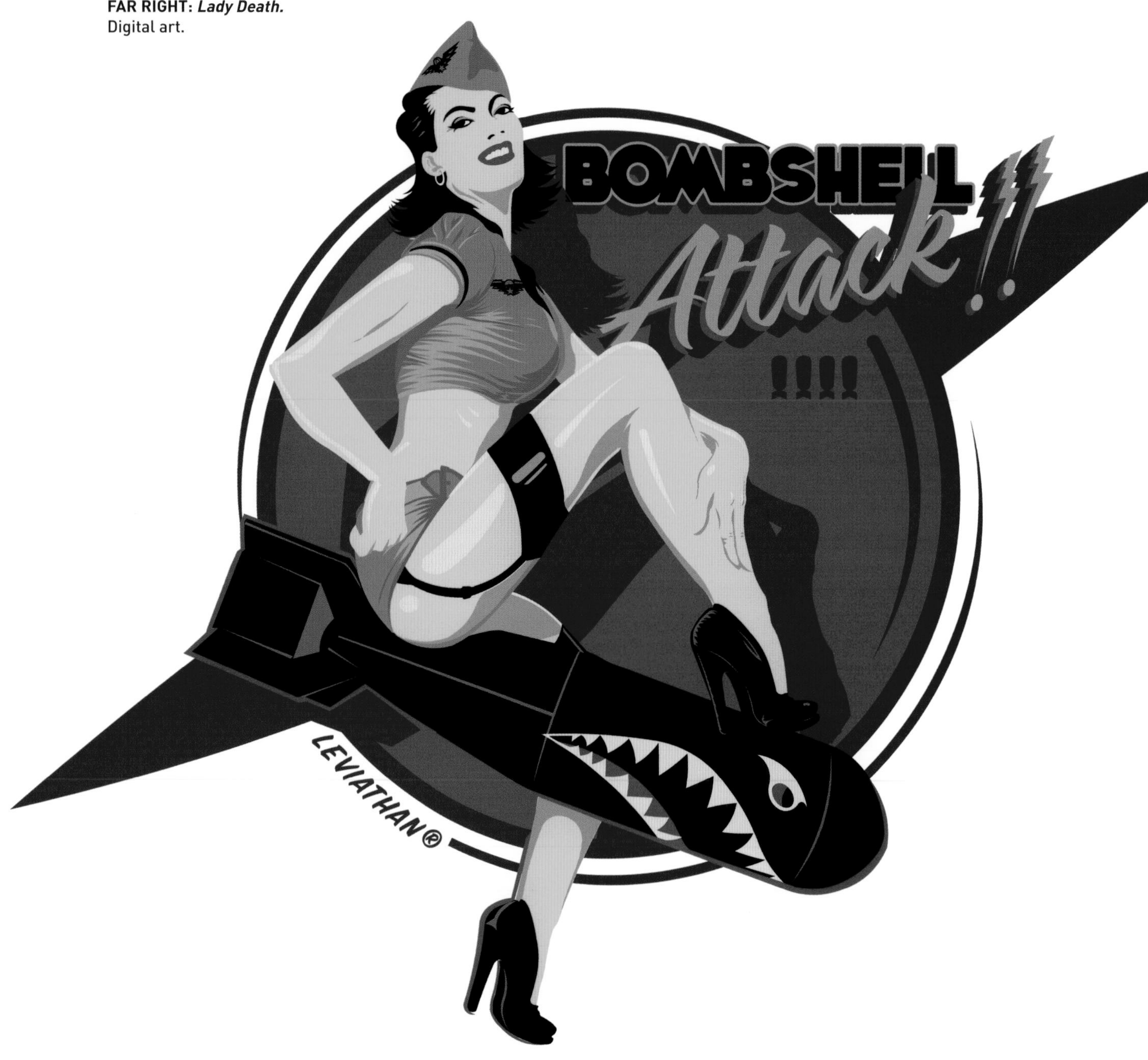

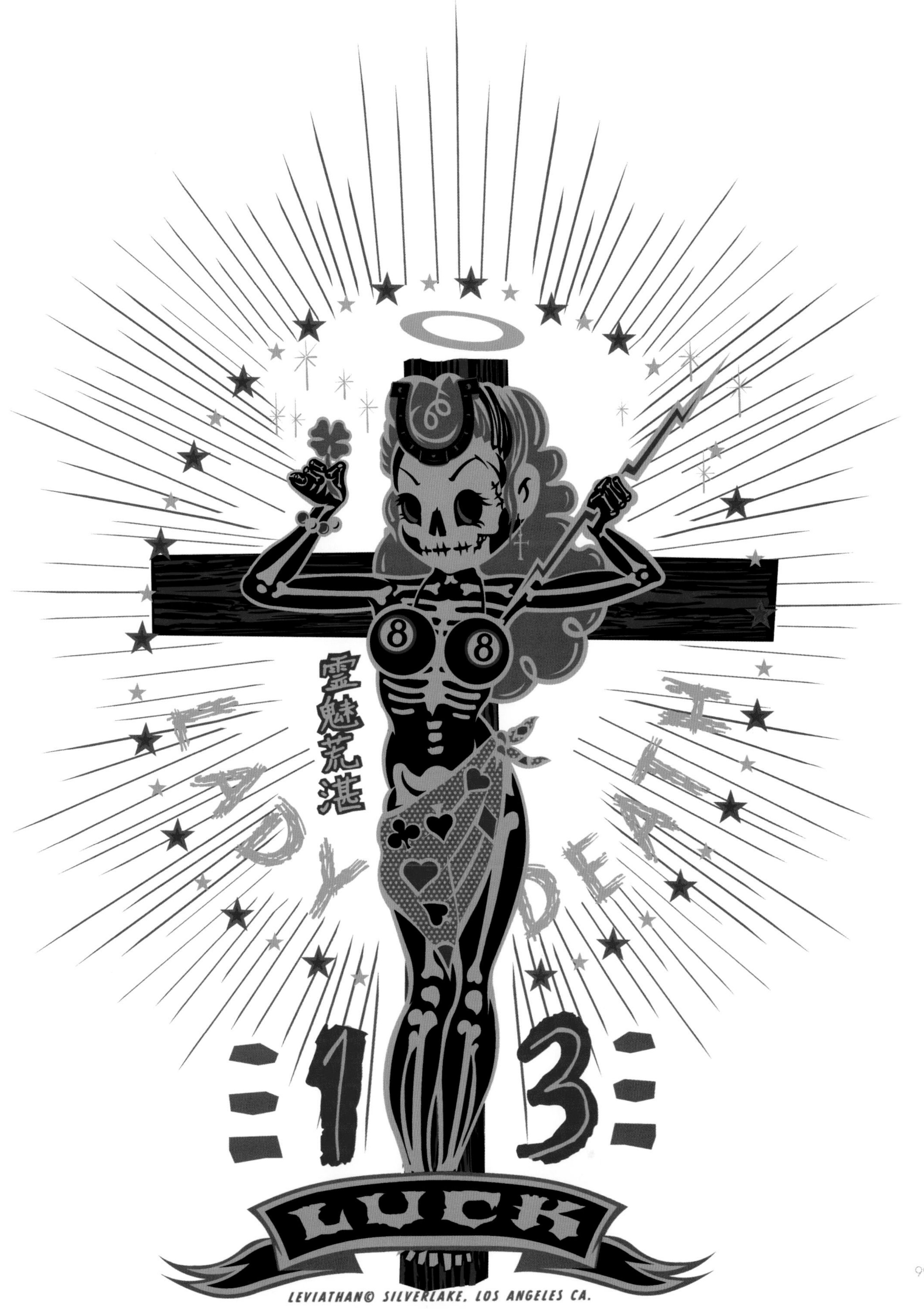
霊魅荒湛
LADY
DEATH
13
LUCK
LEVIATHAN© SILVERLAKE, LOS ANGELES CA.

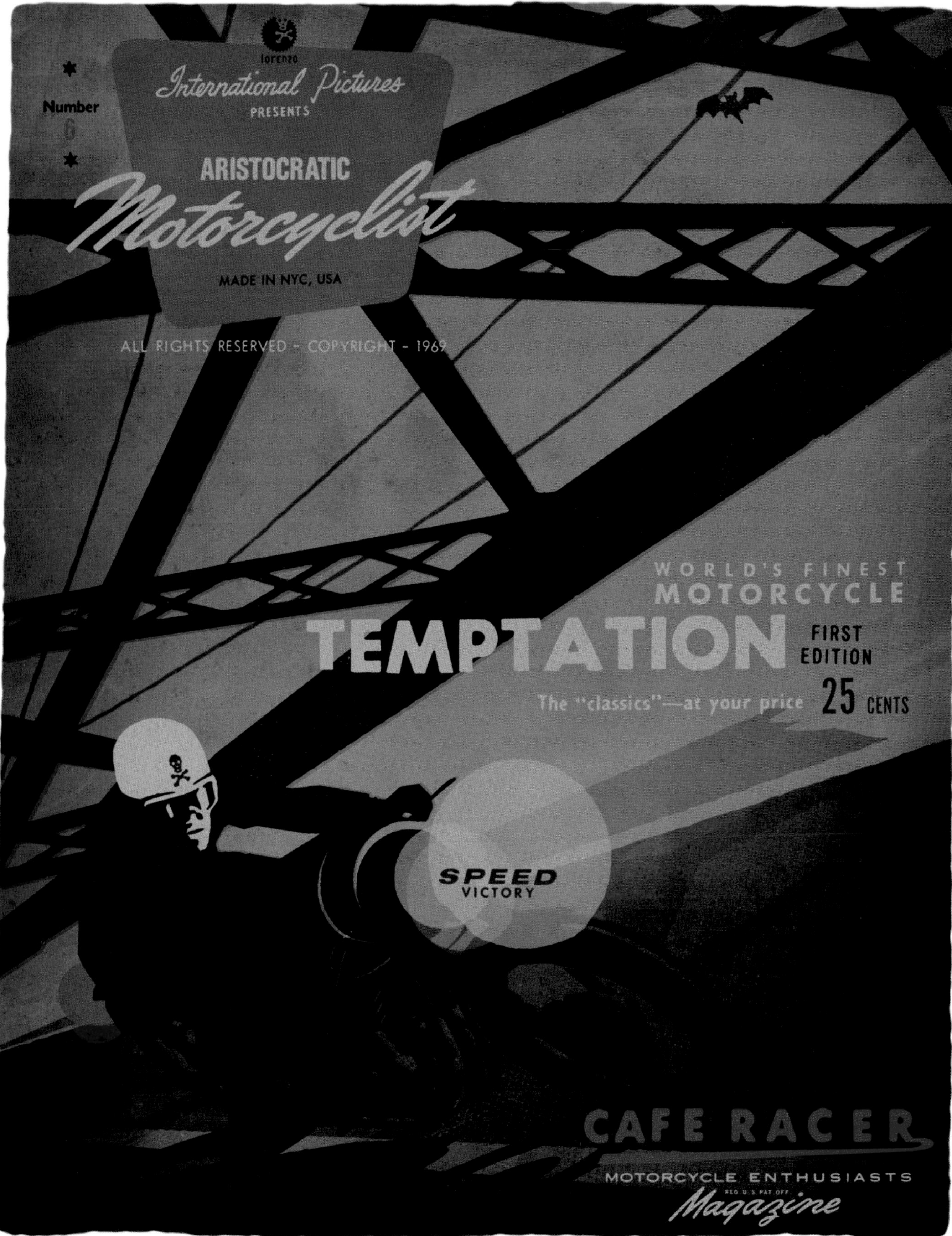
lorenzo
International Pictures
PRESENTS
Number
6
ARISTOCRATIC
Motorcyclist
MADE IN NYC, USA
ALL RIGHTS RESERVED - COPYRIGHT - 1969
WORLD'S FINEST
MOTORCYCLE
TEMPTATION
FIRST
EDITION
The "classics"—at your price
25 CENTS
SPEED
VICTORY
CAFE RACER
MOTORCYCLE ENTHUSIASTS
REG. U.S. PAT. OFF.
Magazine

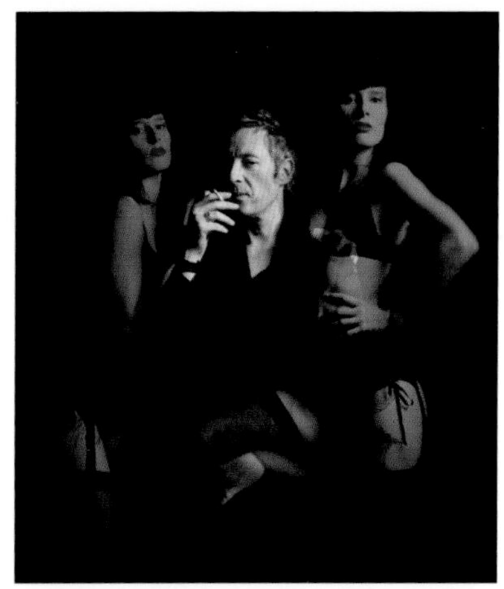

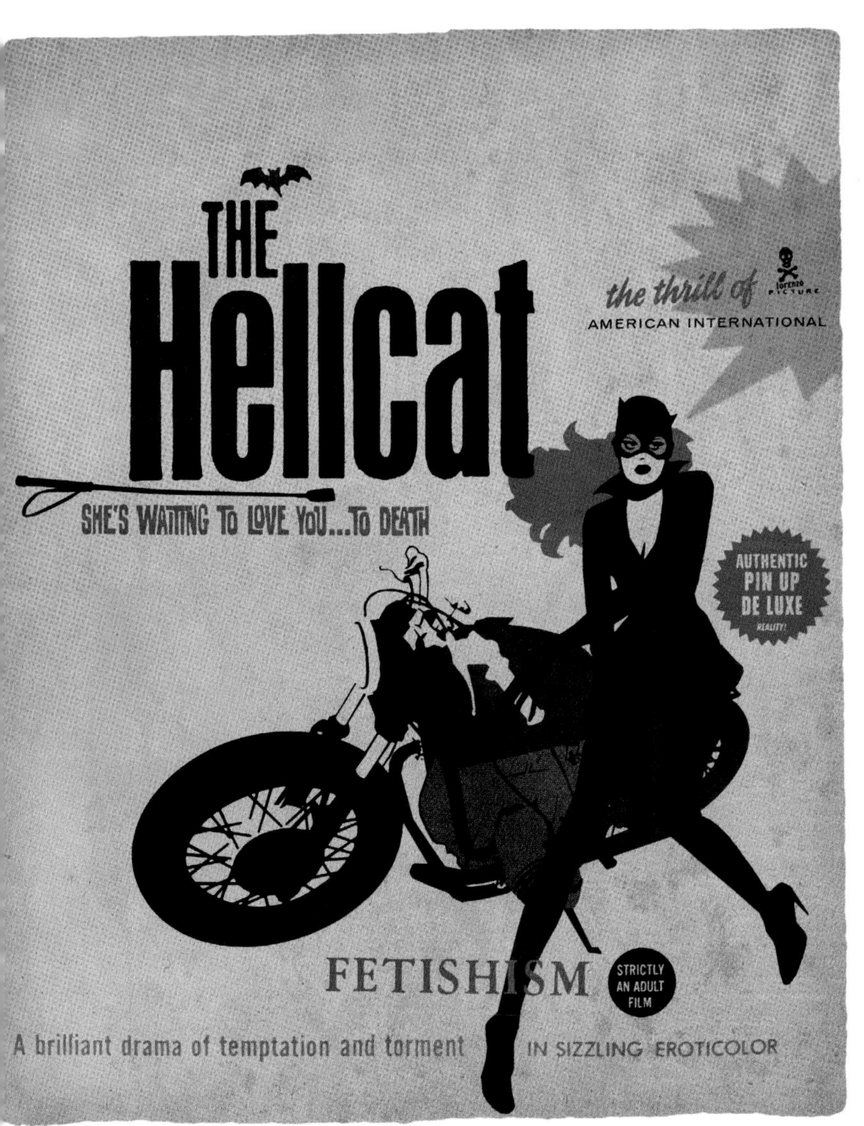

LORENZO

"I'm a poster maker, not a painter or drawer. My work is aimed to be printed in a limited number of copies. The idea of a single piece disturbs me," says Parisian poster perfectionist, Lorenzo. His career, he claims, was determined by a wizard, "When I was a child, this weird old man with a long, white beard said to my family:'This boy will become a great artist...' The prophecy played an important role in my life. I do my best to comply to the prophecy of this noble, old wizard." He works under the name Lorenzo Eroticolor, and explains, "I immerse myself in my work, when I am not studying the Sacred Texts... or riding, or trying to fix my damn, evil motorcycle." Sometimes his artwork is accompanied by stories, under the banner of The Aristocratic Motorcyclist. "For me there are only two categories: the gentlemen and the others. The aristocratic motorcyclist, alone in the storm, and the rest of the world, driving in Ugly Family Van to go on holidays!"

Lorenzo has advice for aspiring aristocratic motorcyclists. "Take to the road and ride, maybe something will happen to you, maybe you will feel life running inside you. But we will never be heroes, none of us. That time is over. Modern life killed that spirit. Hell is the destination, believe me!"

ABOVE: ***Hellcat.***
Ink and mixed media.

LEFT: ***Temptation.***
Ink and mixed media.

THE *Greatest* OF THEM ALL

THE MODERN MOTORCYCLE

we have never relaxed our efforts to provide all that is best in motor cycle design

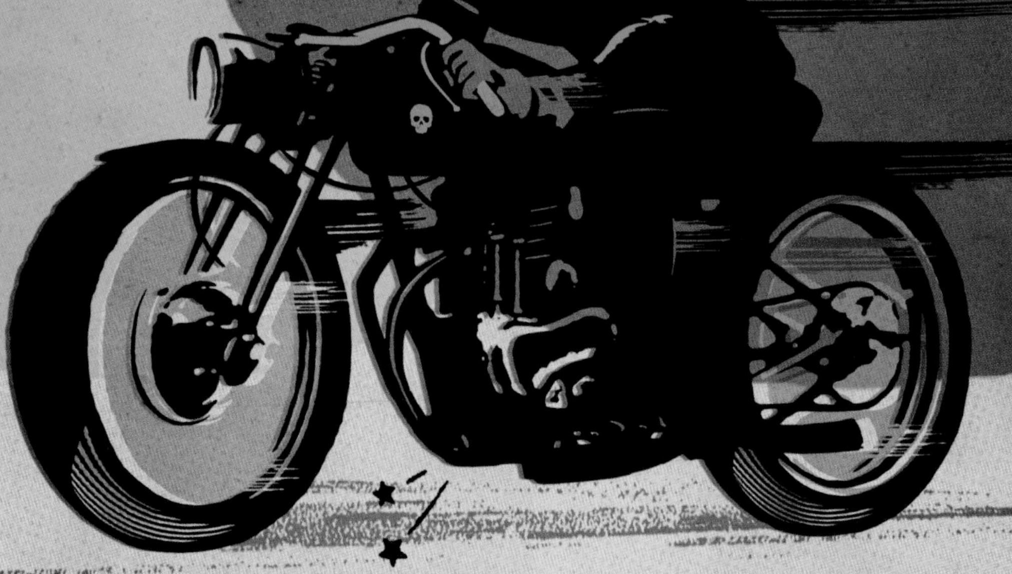

Number 7

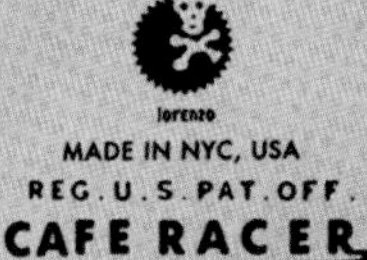

ARISTOCRATIC *Motorcyclist*

Exclusive features that make all the difference

LEFT: ***The Modern Motorcycle.***
Ink and mixed media.

BELOW: ***Porcupine.***
Ink and mixed media.

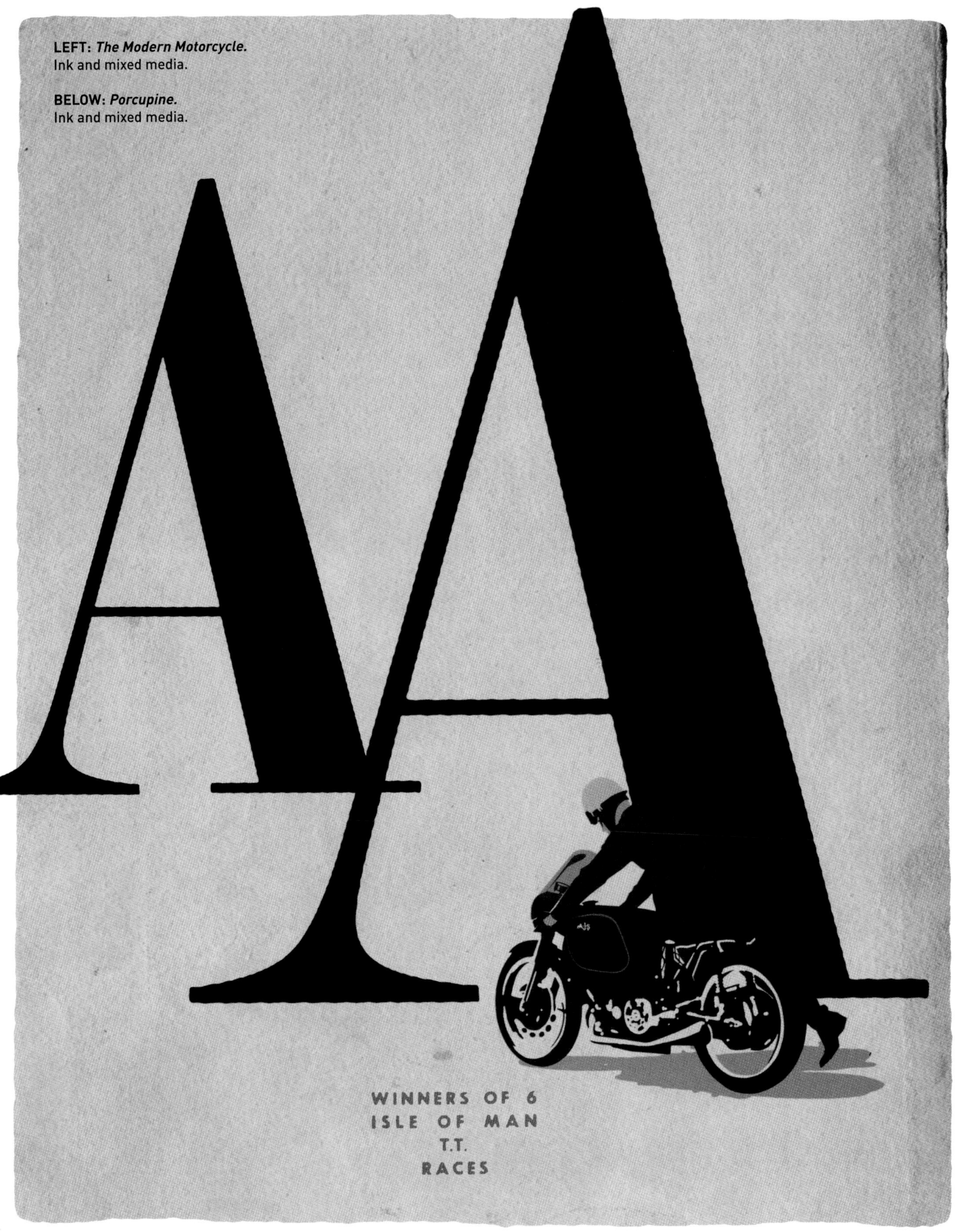

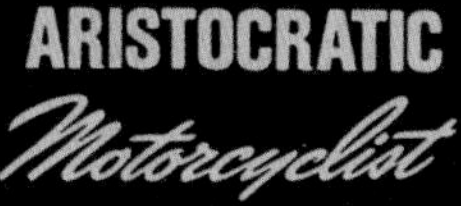

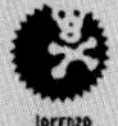

MADE IN NYC, USA
REG. U. S. PAT. OFF.

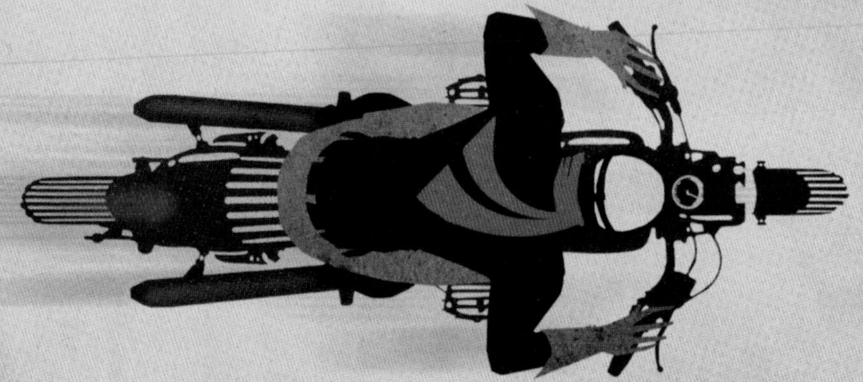

The machine for **BUSINESS, PLEASURE** or **SPORT.** Perfect control. Reliable. Durable.

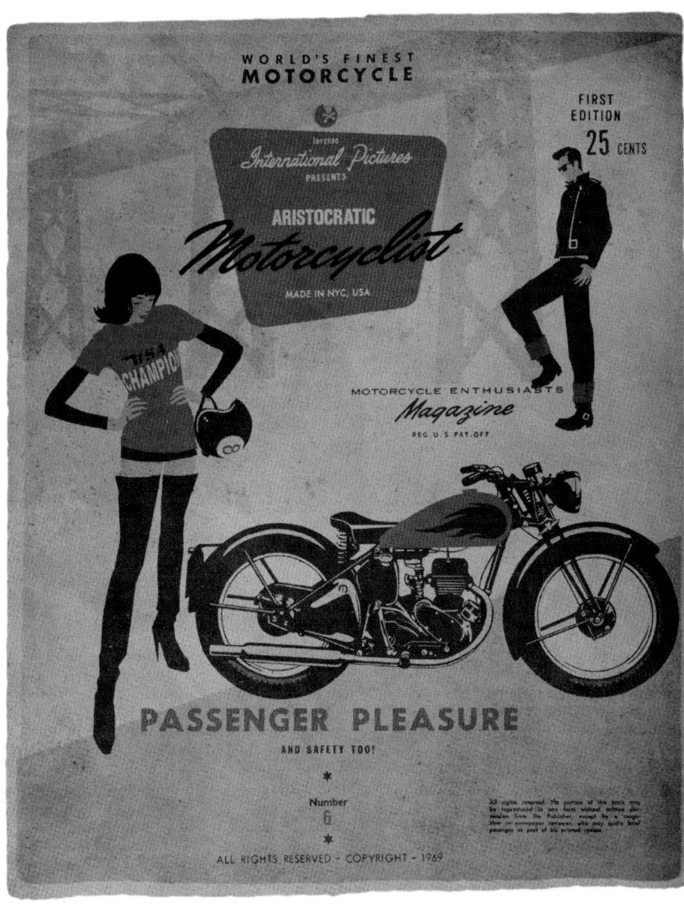

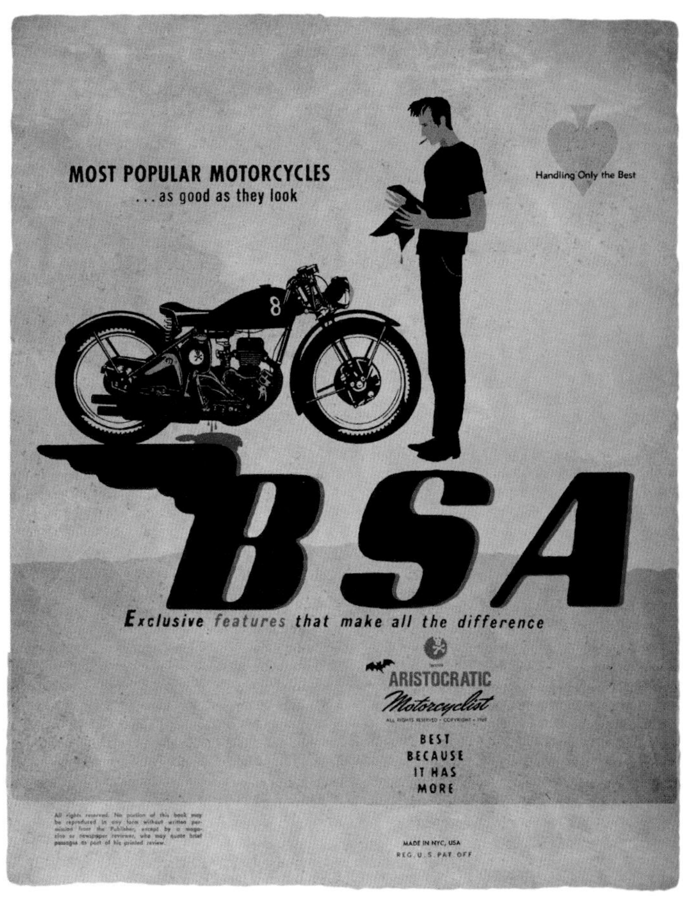

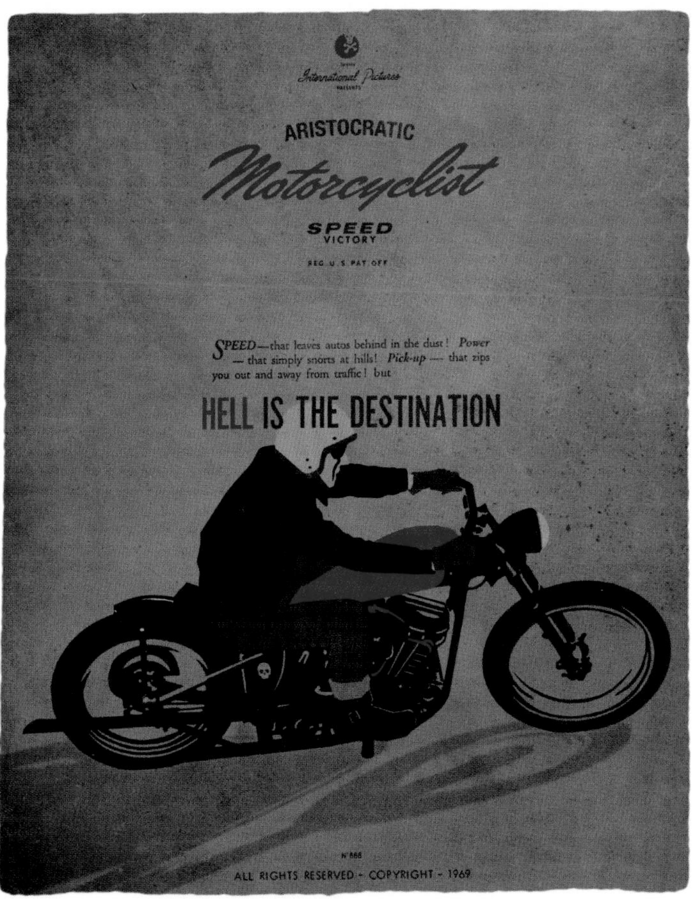

ABOVE LEFT: ***Passenger Pleasure.***
Ink and mixed media.

ABOVE: ***Most Popular.***
Ink and mixed media.

LEFT: ***Hell is the Destination.***
Ink and mixed media.

FAR LEFT: ***Business, Pleasure or Sport.***
Ink and mixed media.

BELOW: ***Motorcycle Enthusiast.***
Ink and mixed media.

RIGHT: ***Naked Under Leather.***
Ink and mixed media.

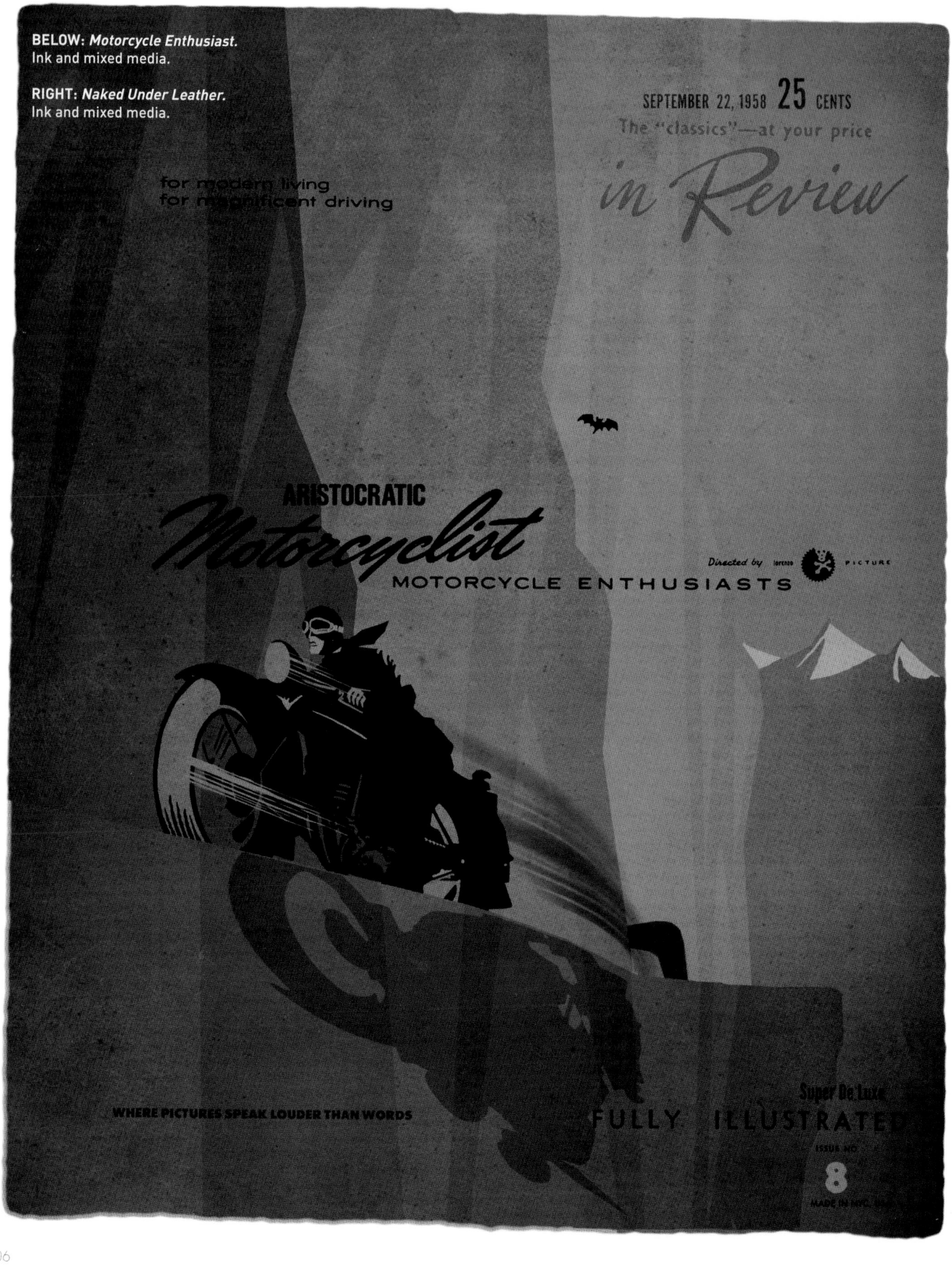

SEPTEMBER 22, 1958 25 CENTS
The "classics"—at your price
in Review

for modern living
for magnificent driving

ARISTOCRATIC
Motorcyclist
MOTORCYCLE ENTHUSIASTS

WHERE PICTURES SPEAK LOUDER THAN WORDS

Super De Luxe
FULLY ILLUSTRATED
ISSUE NO
8

NAKED
UNDER
LEATHER

THE
GIRL ON
THE MOTORCYCLE

REAL
LIFE-LIKE
FULL COLOR
PRINTS

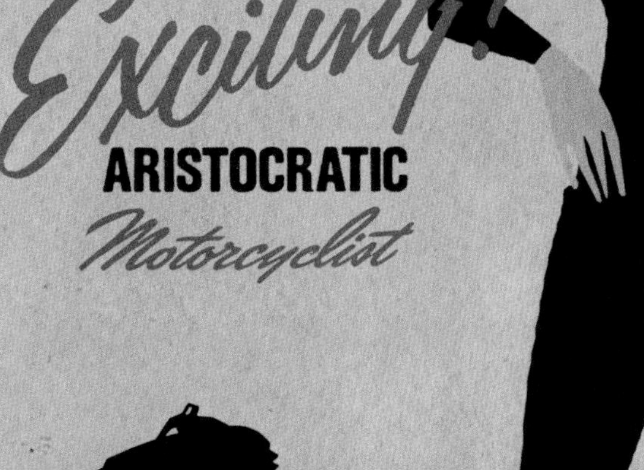

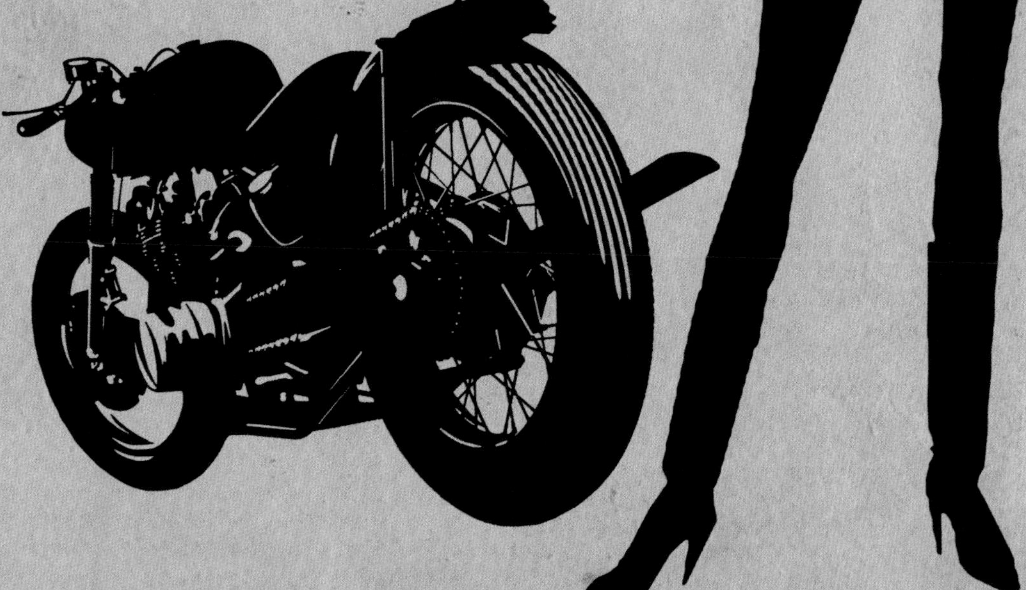

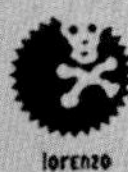

LIKE NOTHING IN THIS WORLD YOU'VE EVER THRILLED TO BEFORE!

MADE IN NYC, USA
REG. U. S. PAT. OFF.

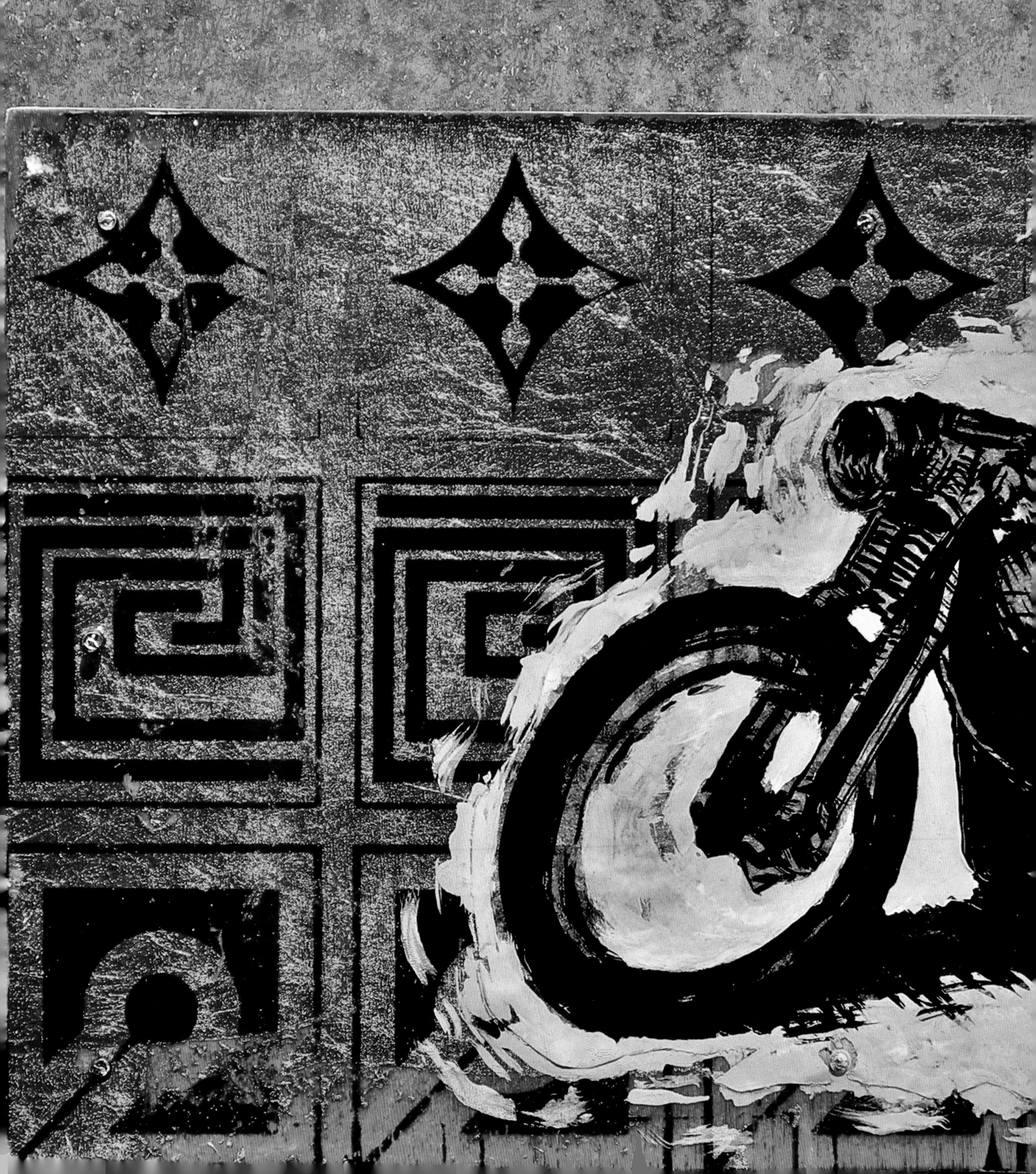

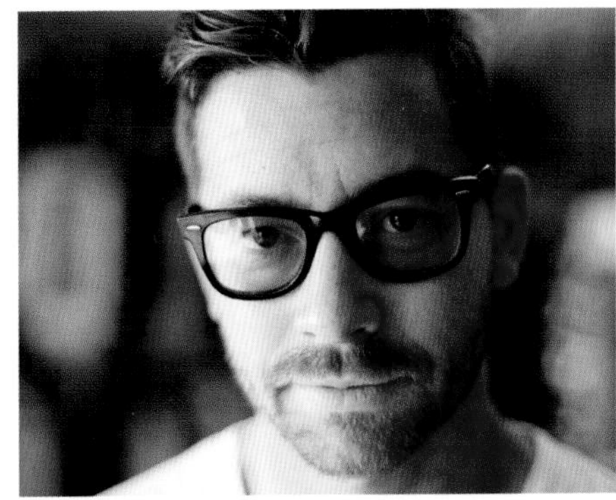

SHAWN MCKINNEY

"I don't know if one thing inspired me to be an artist," explains Shawn McKinney, "but it was something I just had to do." Shawn grew up on an Ohio cow farm. "It was a case of long hours, little gratitude and a lot of grime all over me by the end of the day. Not much has changed." Shawn attended The Art Institute of Pittsburgh, majoring in Industrial Design, minoring in Special Effects, and became engulfed in the 3-D design world, exploring materials and processes. "I feel my work continues to unite my background of both fine and applied art."

He now lives in Southern California, where he acquired his first motorbike, a 1984 Yamaha that he traded for some paintings. "I have been building, trading and riding ever since. I currently have several Harleys. Motorcycles and the culture that defines them, to me, has always represented a free lifestyle, much like that of an artist. It's a way of not subscribing to the standard social constructs that rule most peoples' lives."

LEFT: ***Joe Davis.***
Oil and ink on wood.

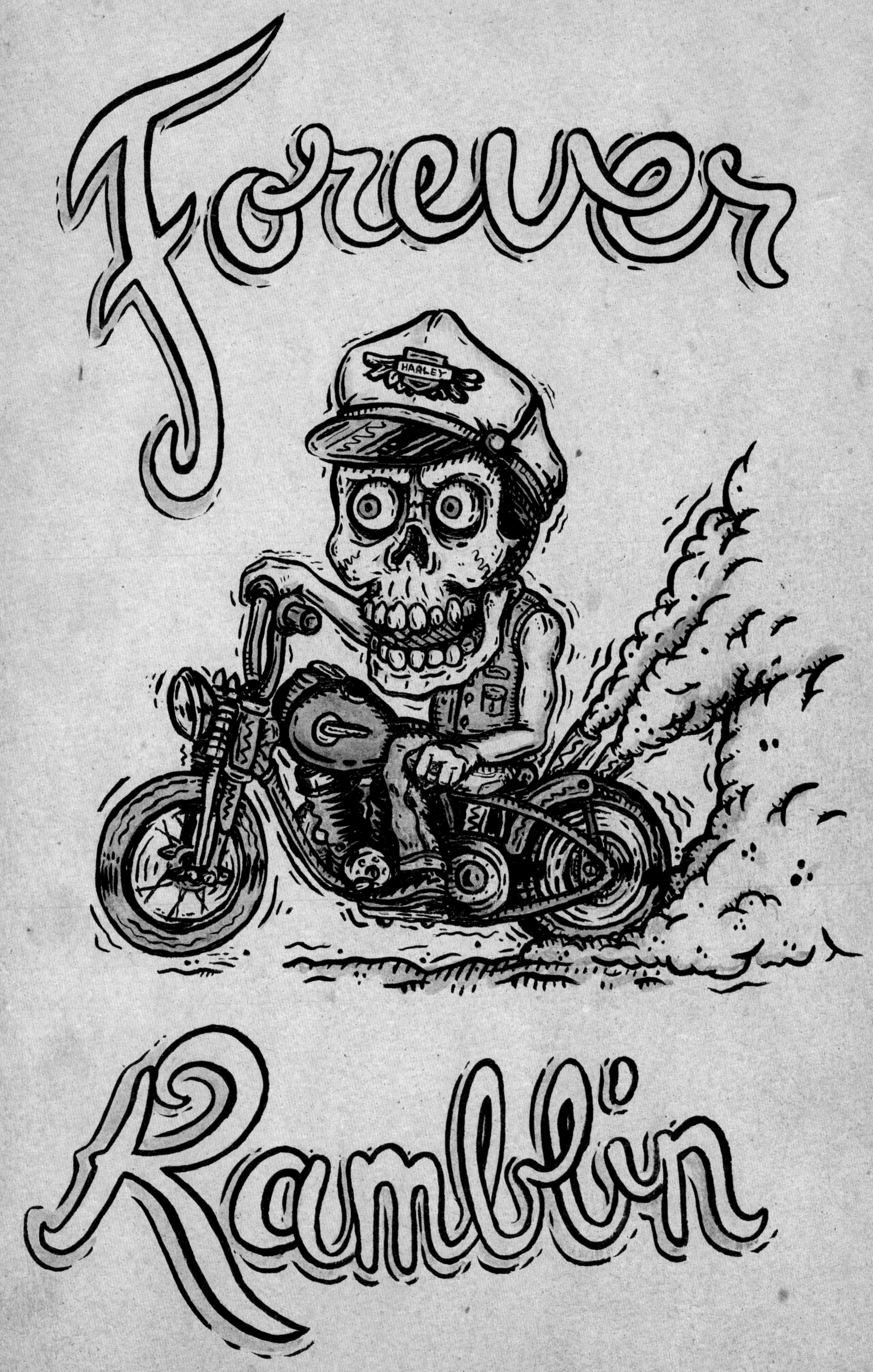
Forever
HARLEY
Ramblin

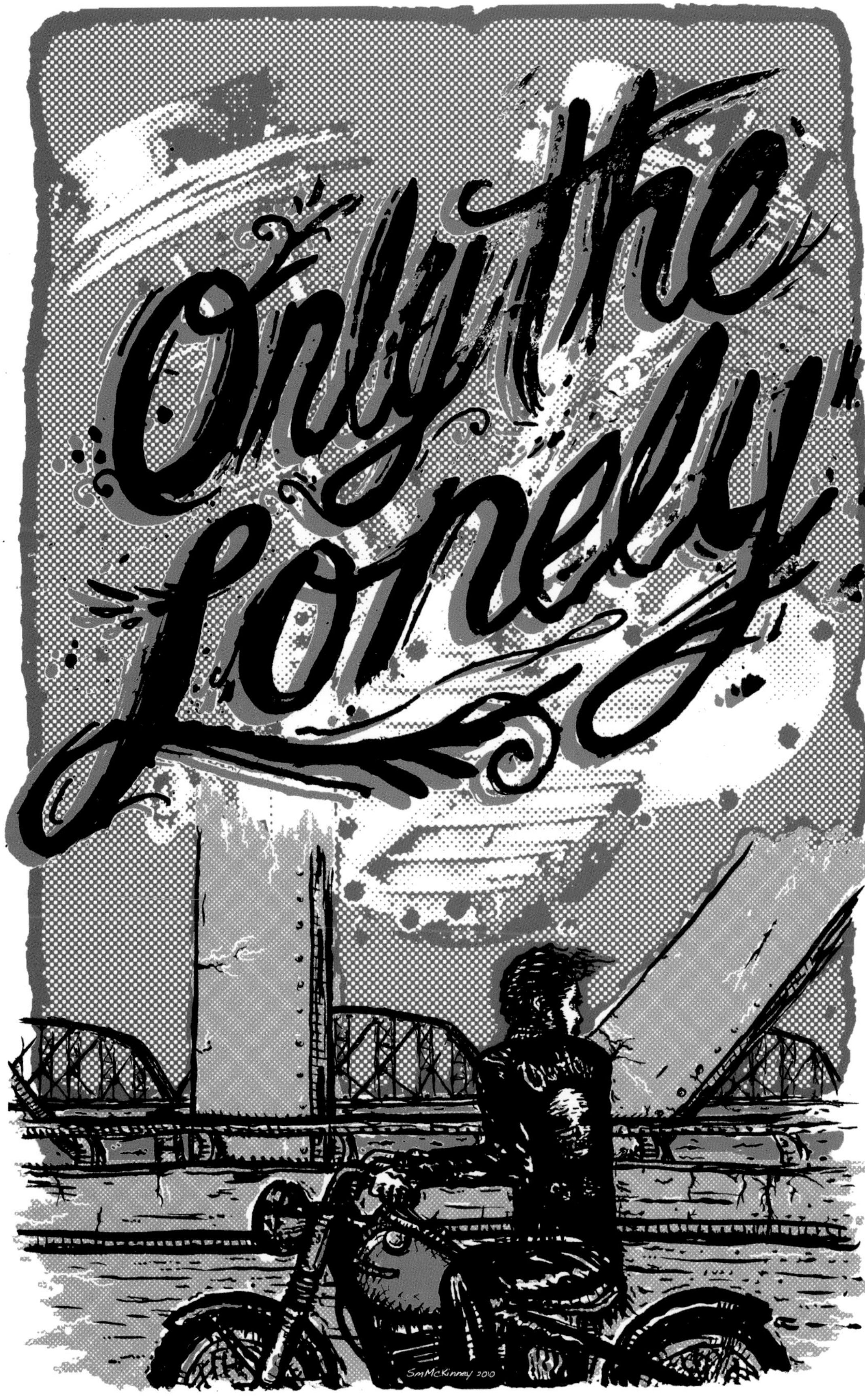

FAR LEFT: ***Ramblin'.***
Ink on paper.

LEFT: ***Only Outlaws are Lonely.***
Ink on paper and digital.

BELOW: ***Jesus Died So You Can Ride.***
Ink on paper.

FAR RIGHT: ***Chopper Fever.***
Oil and ink on wood.

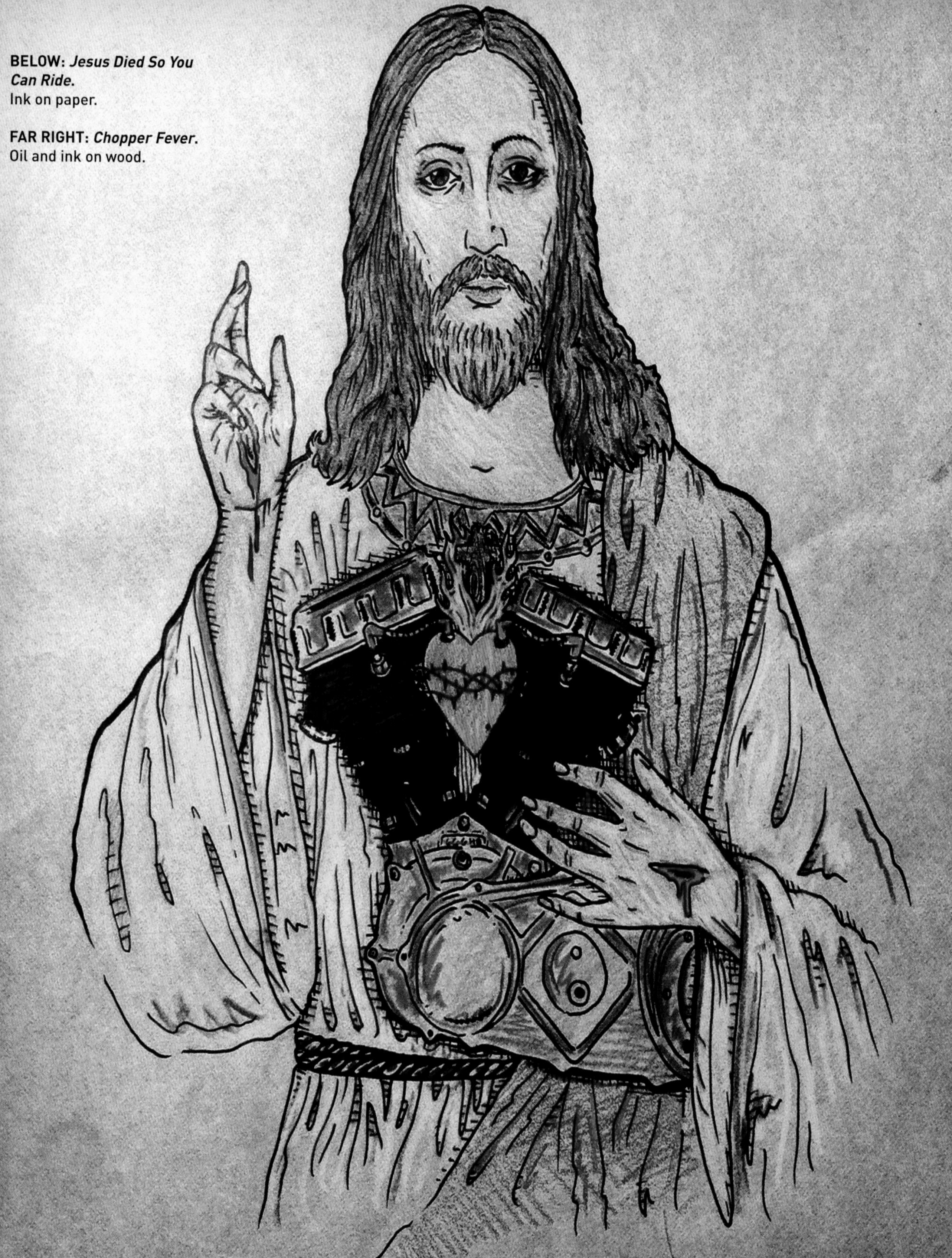

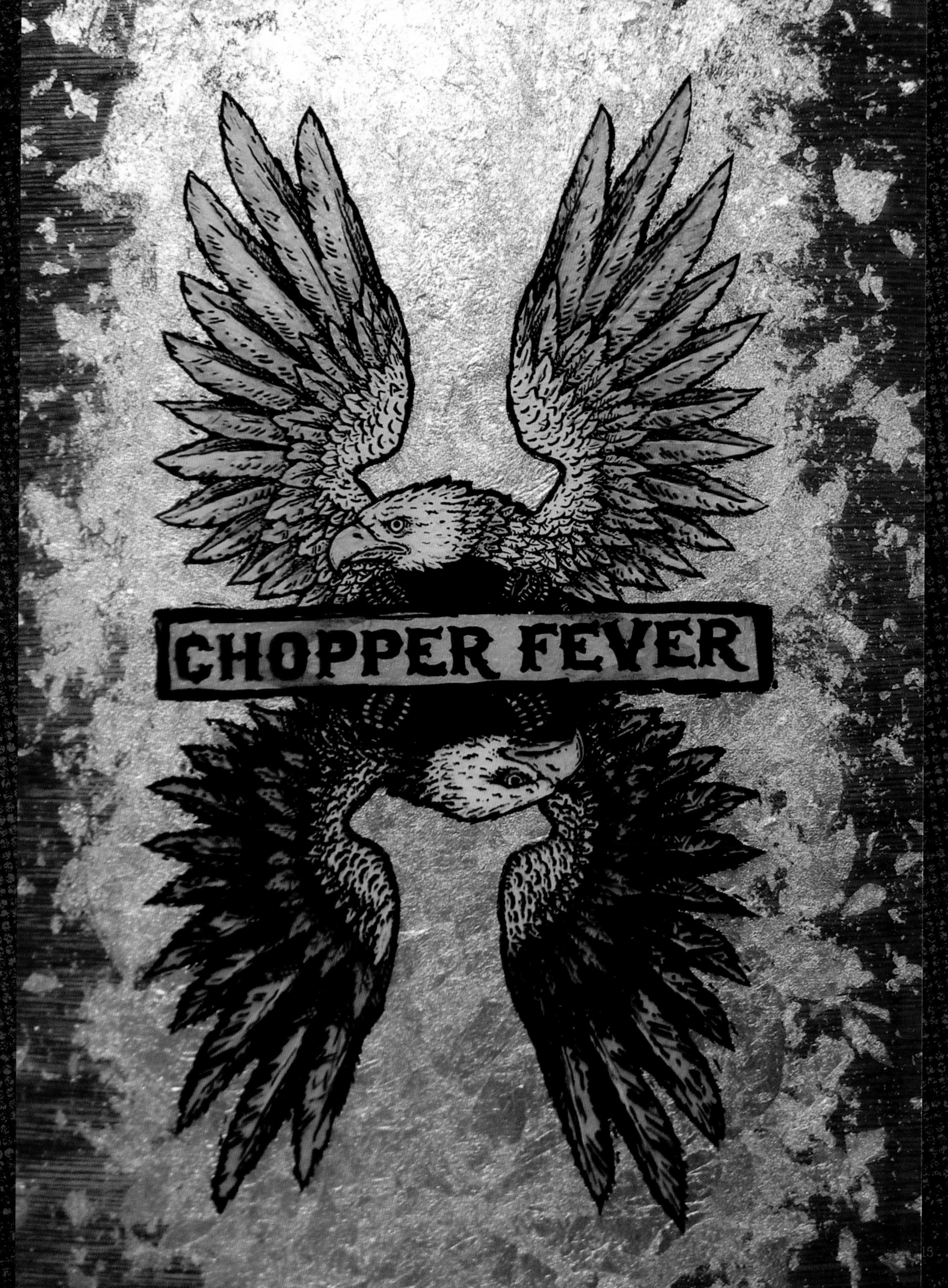
CHOPPER FEVER

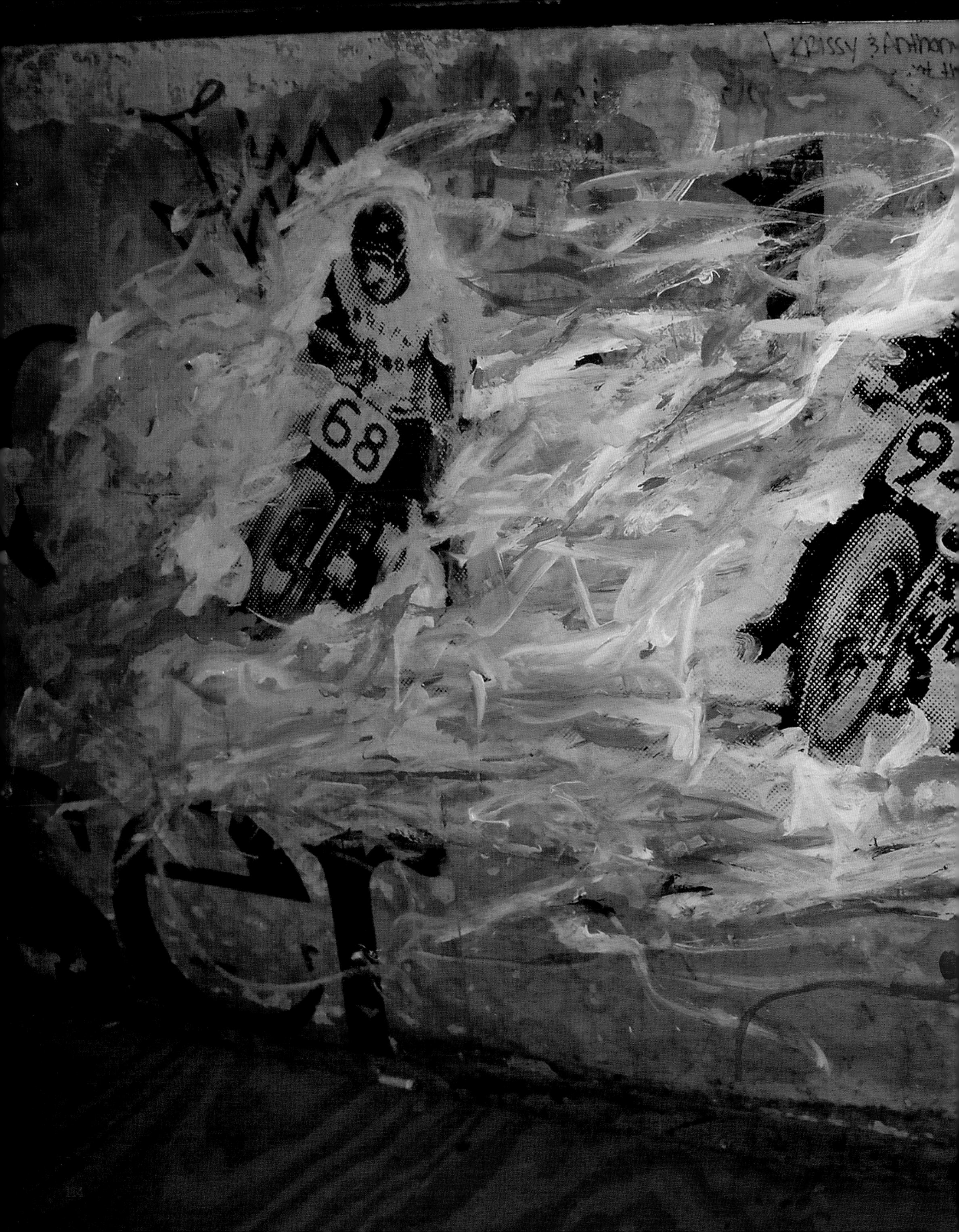
68

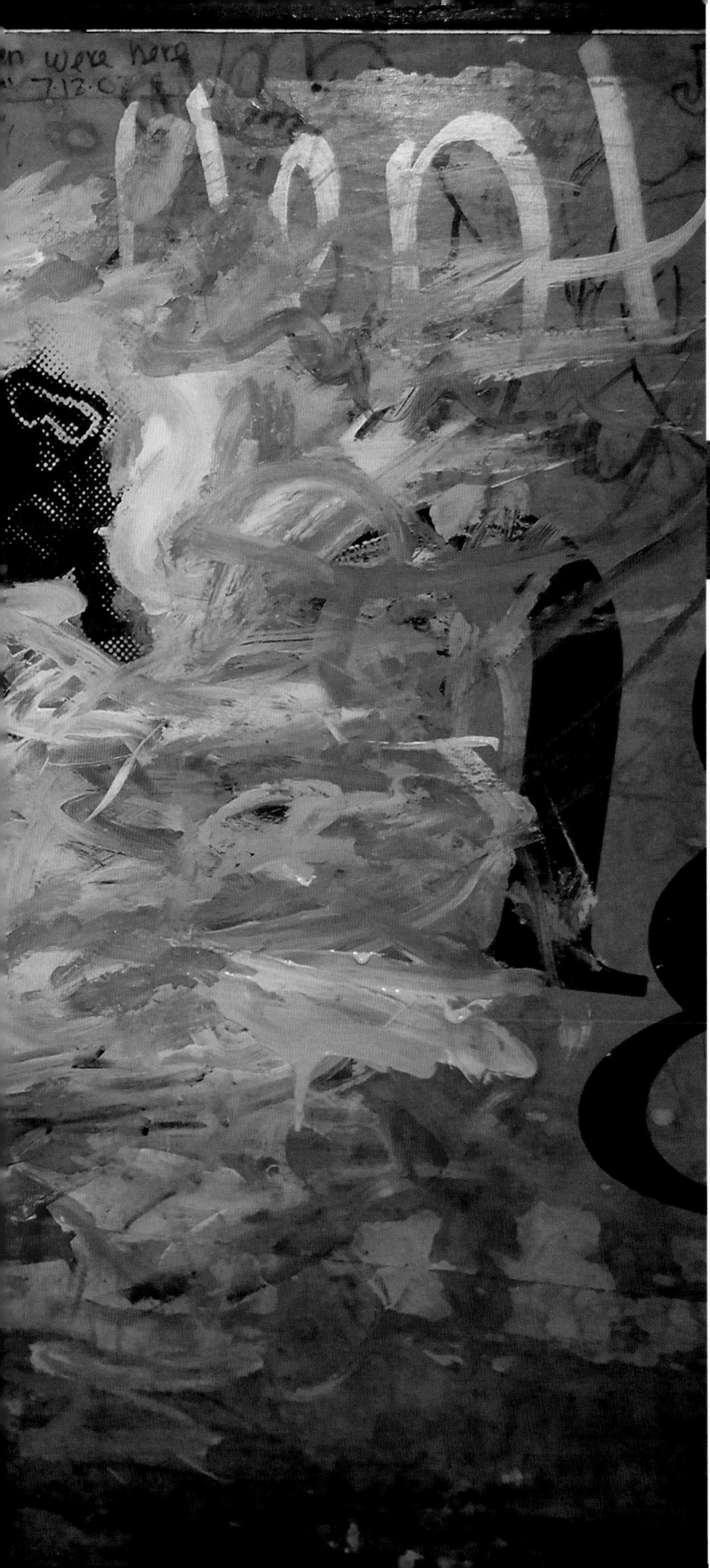

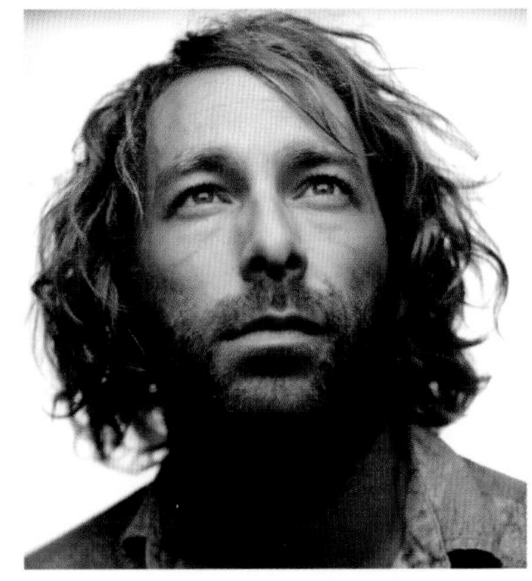

BRANDON MCLEAN

Brandon McLean's path into art was more traumatic than most. "I suffered a right brain stroke when I was 18, and I sometimes credit it as one reason that art became so important to my life. I hadn't been overly interested in art previously, but after the stroke it became an everyday thought." Coming across *Art and Life,* a book detailing the work of Robert Rauschenberg, had a big impact. "I fell in love with some aspects of his aesthetics, and started creating my own collage and mixed media works." Based in Orlando, Florida, Brandon specializes in both art forms. "I mainly use paper, acrylic paint, and photocopy transfers. Along the way a composition I can live with appears." Brandon doesn't own or ride a motorcycle. "I originally became interested in motorcycle culture when a friend gave me a stack of her dad's old *Motorcycle Enthusiast* magazines. I remember falling in love with the contrast dot-styled print images of flat track racers. Recently I have become interested in aspects of manhood, and all that goes along with being a man: being good enough, providing, competition, and expectations; some of the motorcycle images I use in my artworks are all part of that investigation."

Left: *Untitled: Booth Piece.*
Wheatpaste and acrylic on wall.

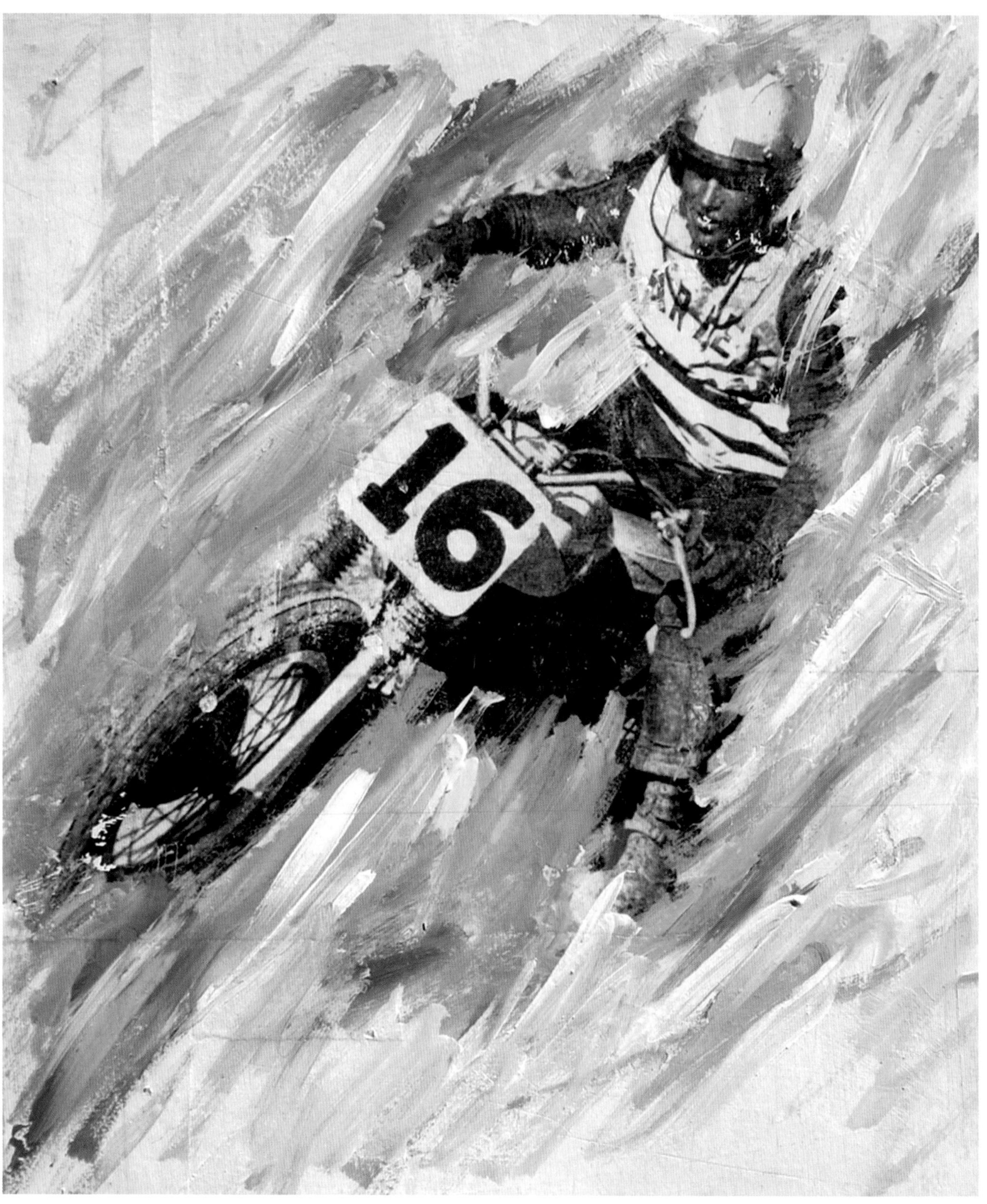
16

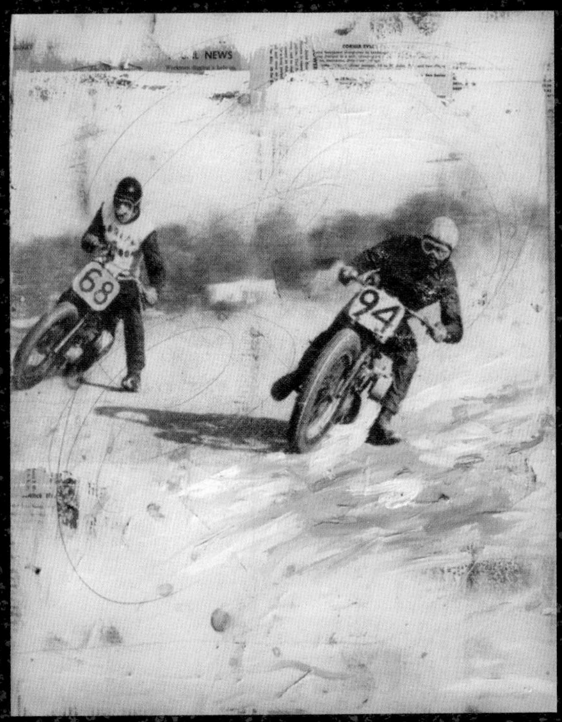

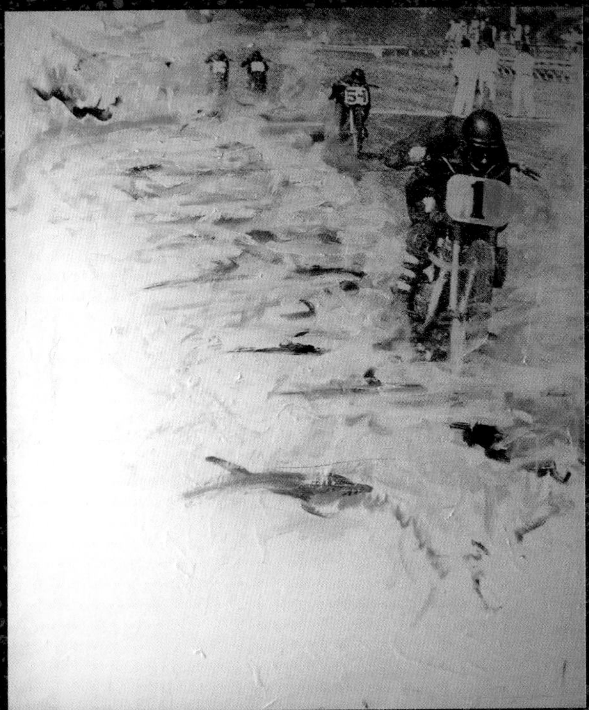

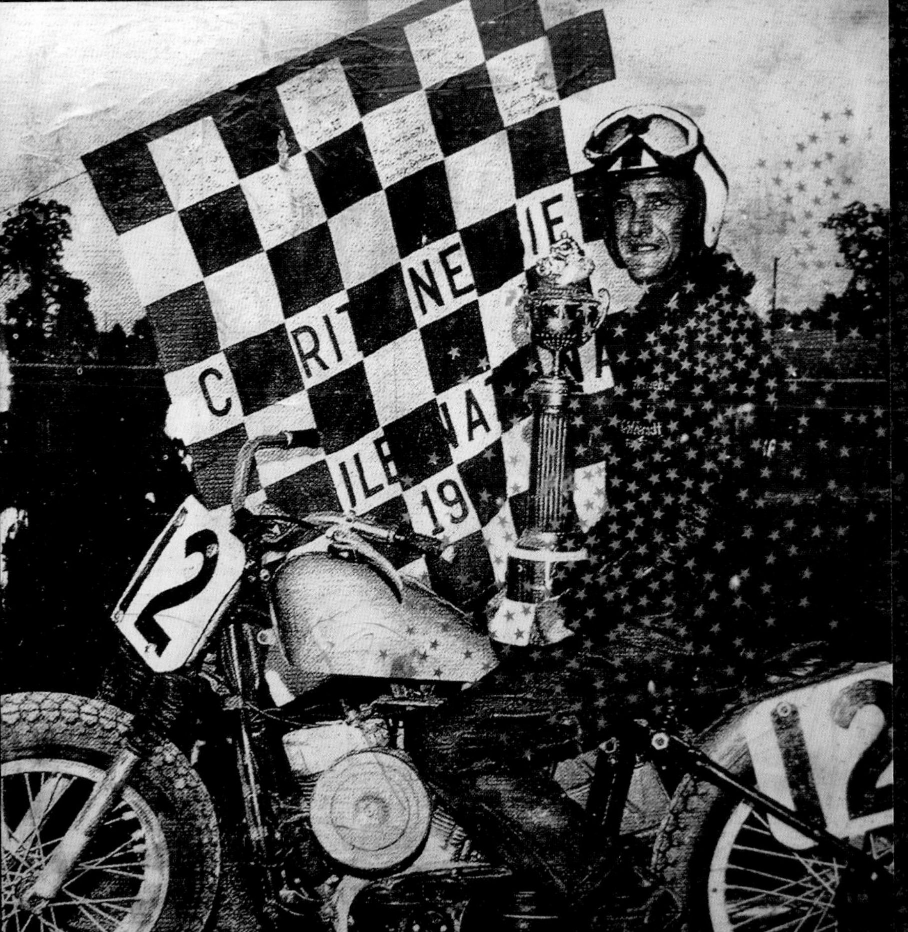

Above Left: ***No 68.***
Gel transfer, paper and acrylic on canvas.

Above Right: ***Numero Uno.***
Gel transfer, paper and acrylic on canvas.

Left: ***Bert.***
Gel transfer, paper and acrylic on canvas.

Far Left: ***Hammered.***
Gel transfer, paper and acrylic on wood.

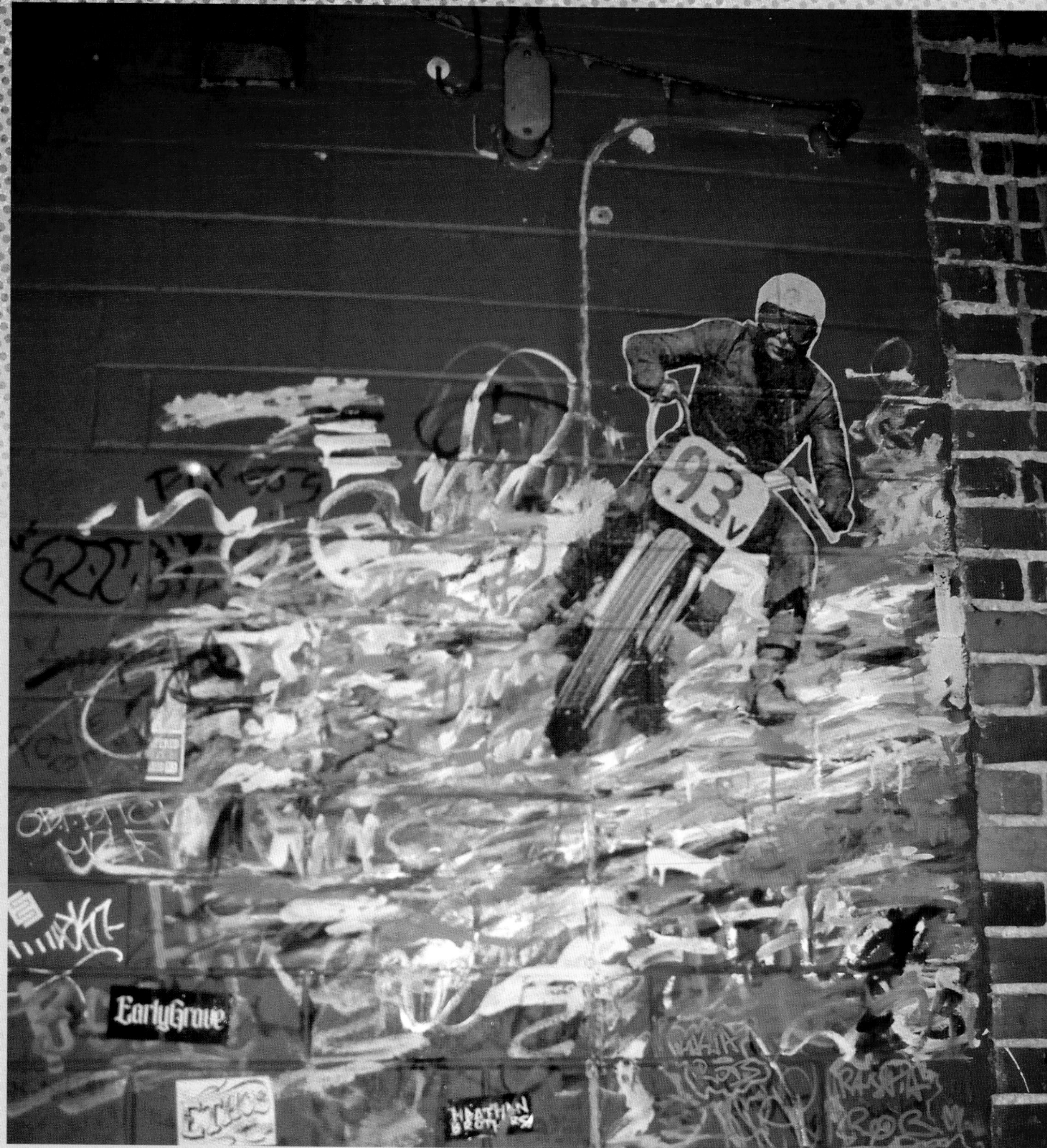

ABOVE: ***No 93.***
Wheatpaste and acrylic on wall.

RIGHT: ***Somehow That Doesn't Help At All.***
Collage on paper.

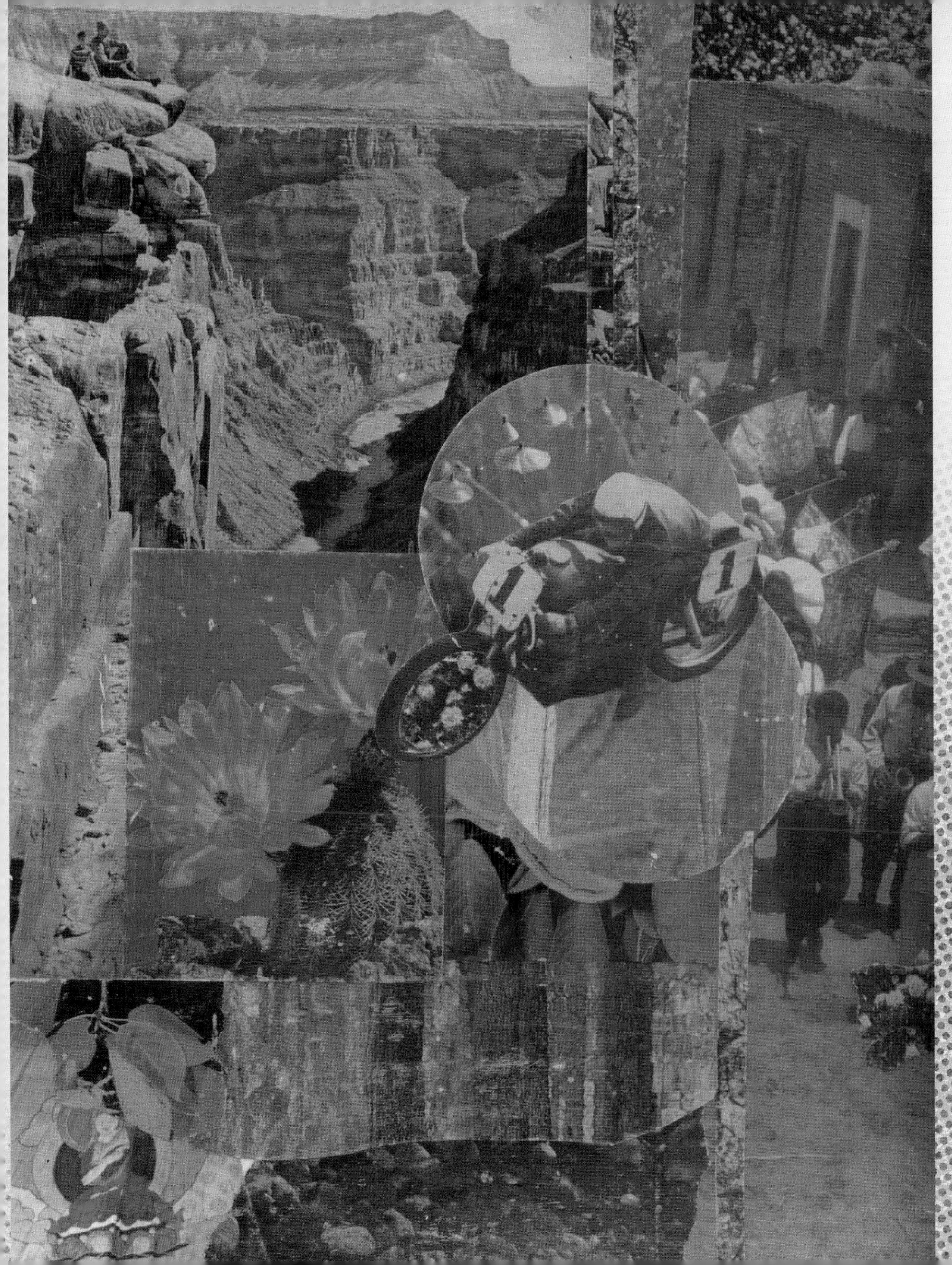

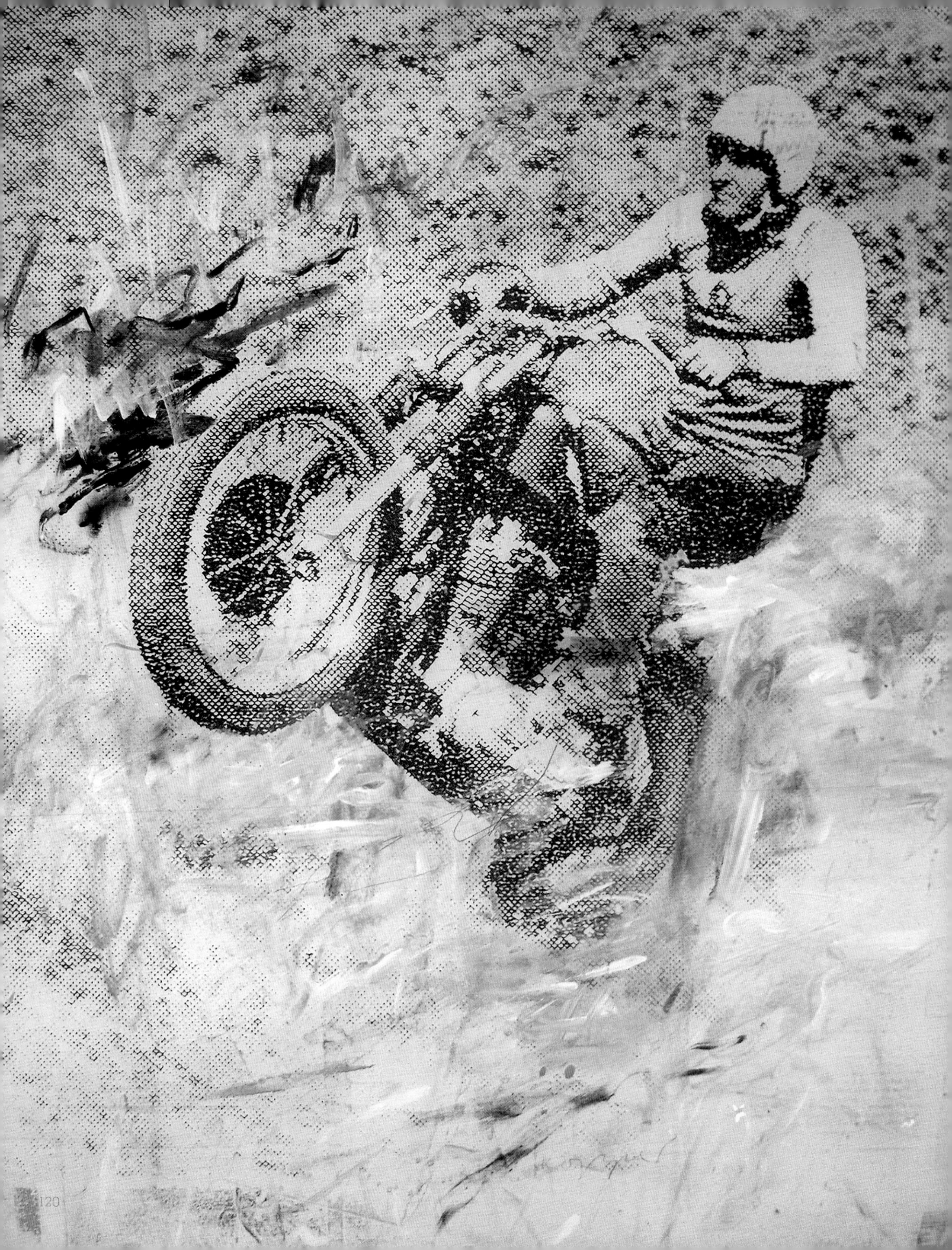

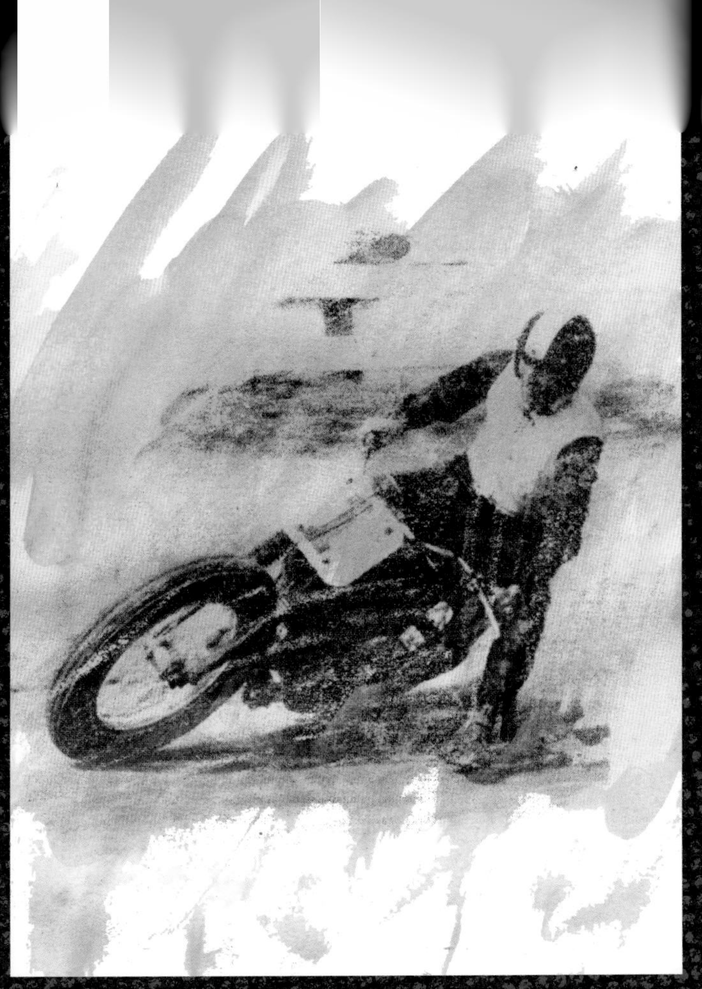

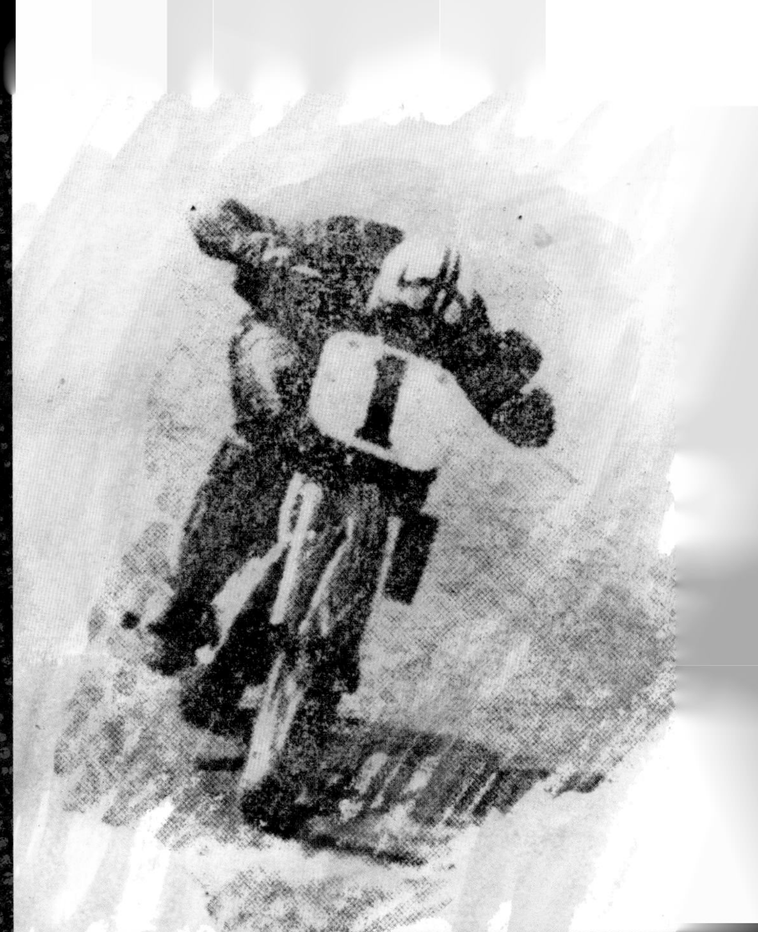

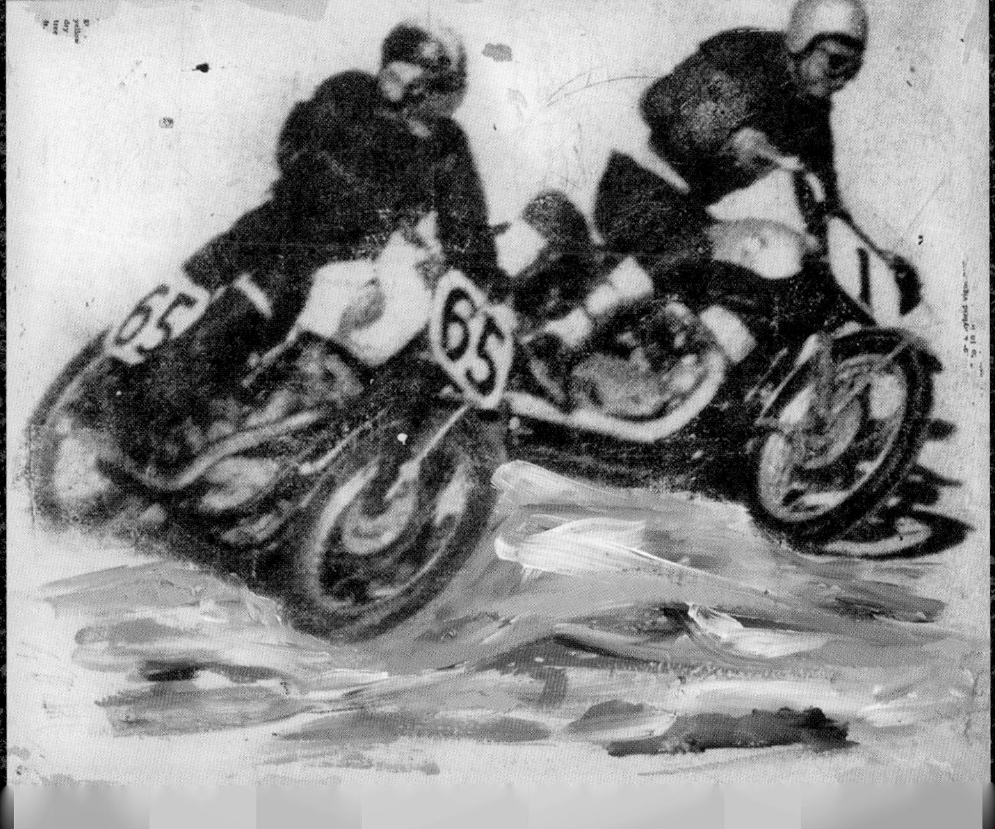

ABOVE LEFT: ***Ride One.*** Solvent transfer and watercolour on paper.

ABOVE: ***Race One.*** Solvent transfer and watercolour on paper.

LEFT: ***No 65.*** Gel transfer, paper and acrylic on canvas.

FAR LEFT: ***Grasshopper.*** Gel transfer, paper and acrylic on canvas.

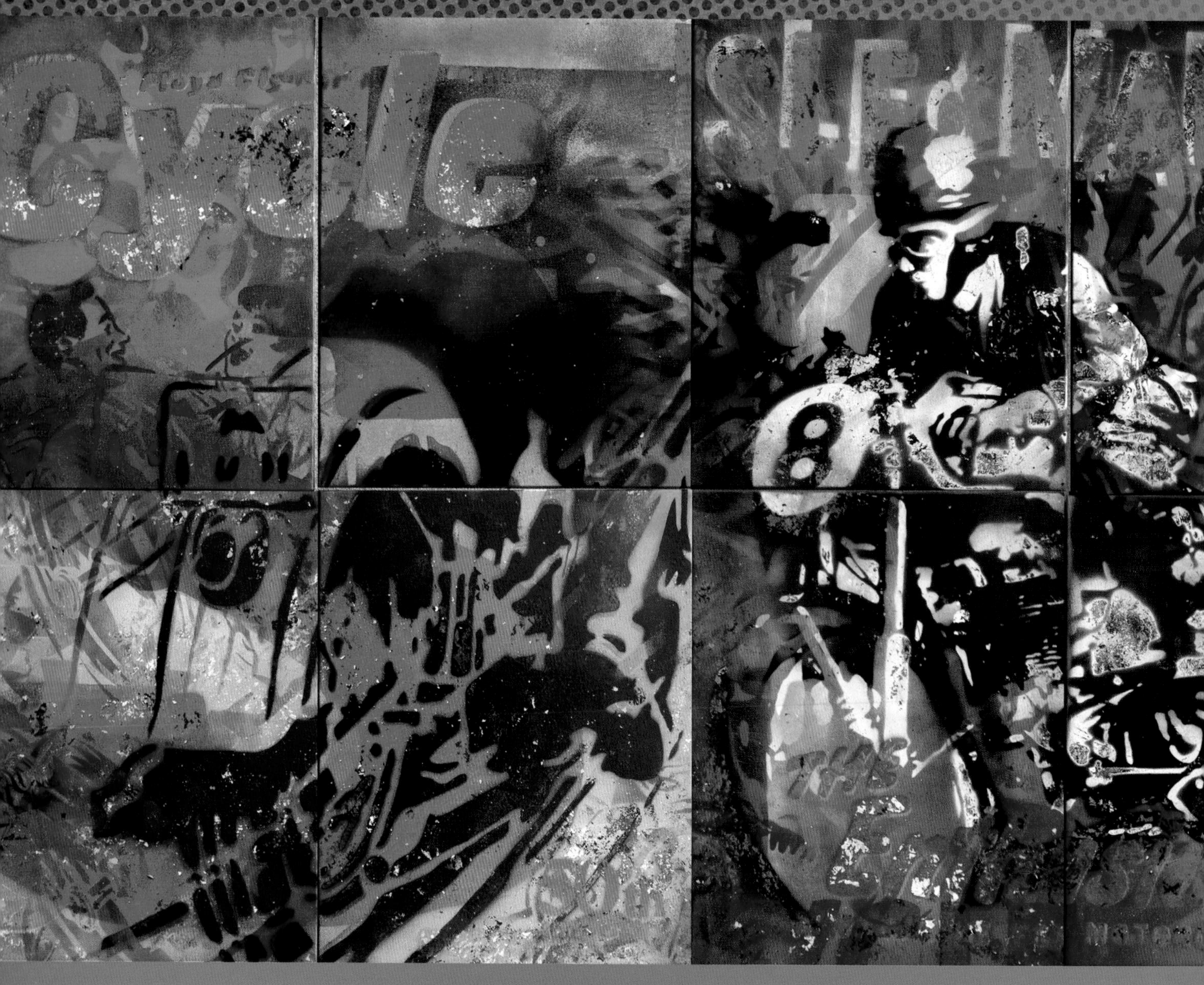

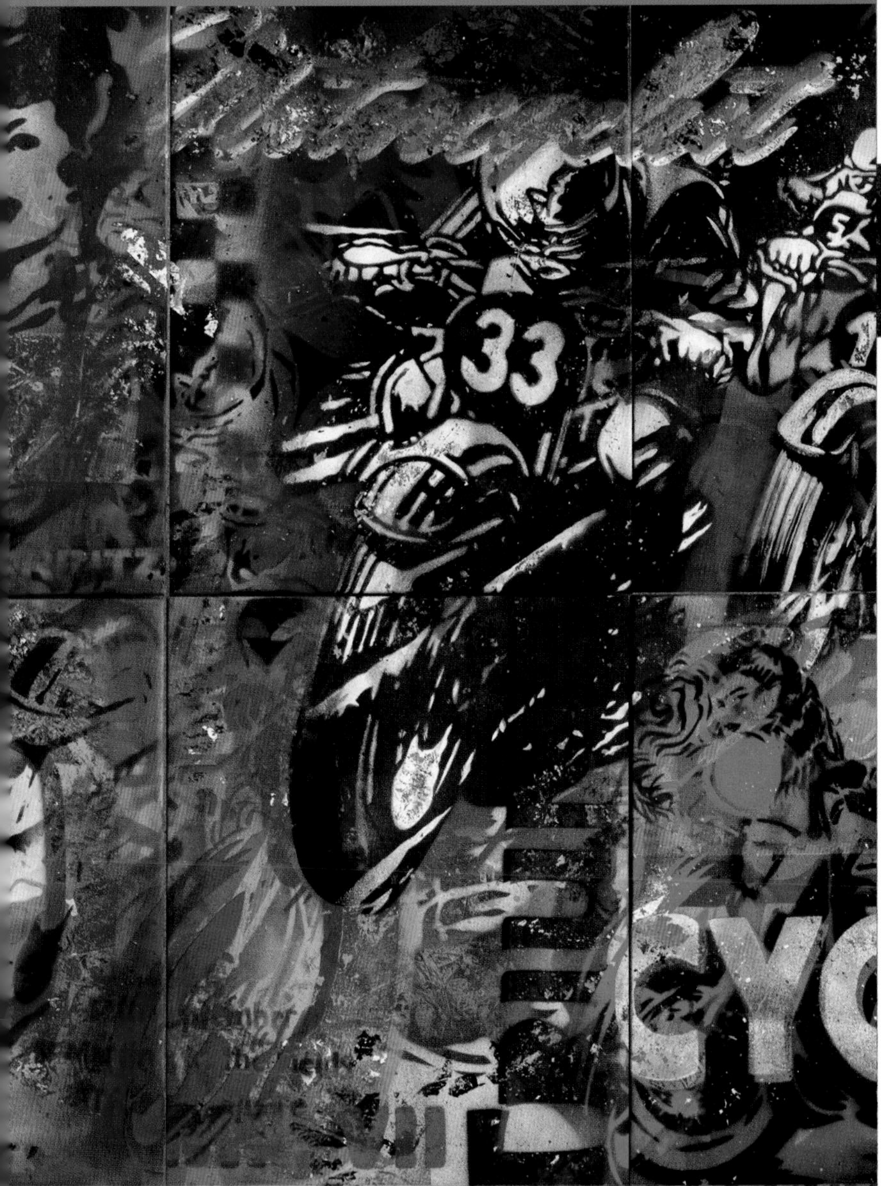

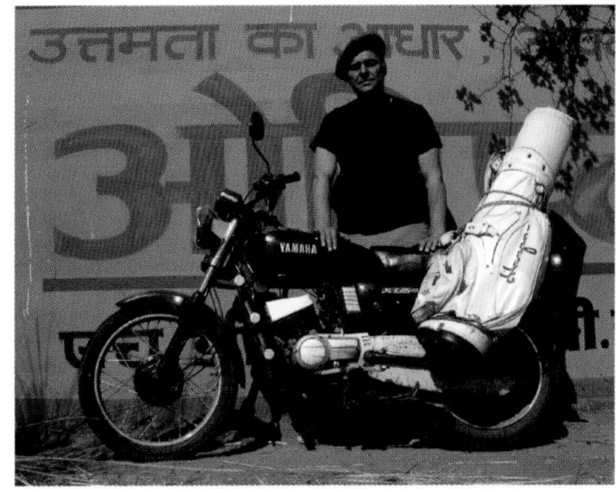

ANTONIO MERINERO

Antonio Merinero's love of bike culture fits perfectly with his passion for travel: he has biked through India, Nepal, Thailand, Vietnam, Indonesia, Morocco and much of Europe, the latter on his 1972 Harley Electra Glide. As a boy growing up in Madrid, a city with which he has a love/hate relationship, Antonio was surrounded by bikes and art. "My father had a bike; I rode to school everyday on a scooter; our house was literally next to the Prado museum; the Reina Sofia museum was a five-minute walk away. I grew up seeing exhibitions. As a child I imagined a colourful parallel world, an invented world. I still do." His main technique is paper collage. "I began using collage when making travel diaries in places like Bombay, New York, Salvador de Bahia (Brazil), Lisbon, Berlin... The collages were made with locally found graphic material: soap wrappers, matchboxes, tourist maps, metro tickets, pictures and stamps that I assembled and arranged to tell something about the trip." Today he works with series and 'free' collages. "I find and store graphic material in my studio and I dig it out when I have found its perfect match. So, an Indian matchbox collected in 1992 could tell a story, together with, say, a Portuguese poster from 2000."

LEFT: Cycle.
Spray paint on canvas.

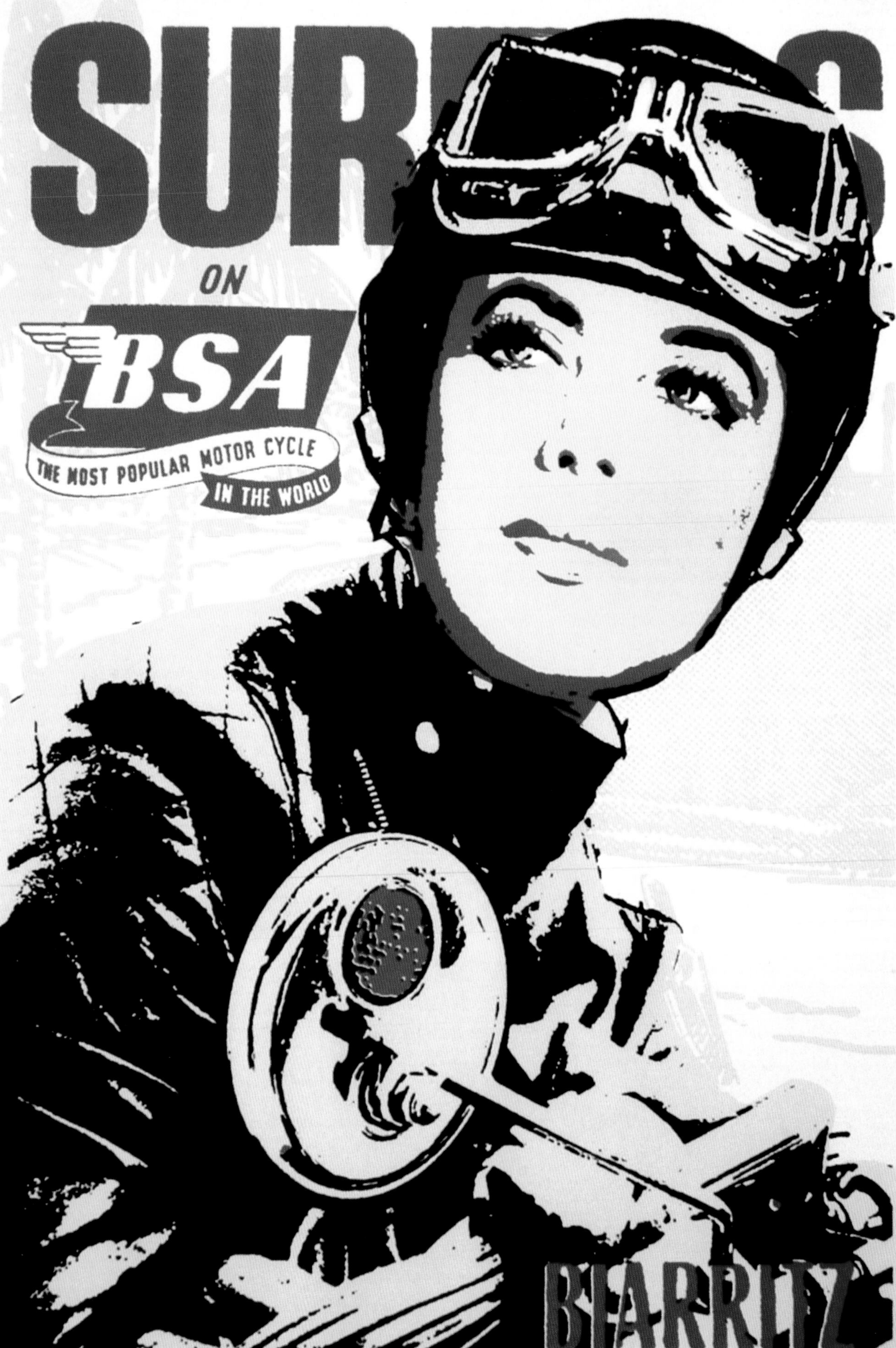
SUR
ON
BSA
THE MOST POPULAR MOTOR CYCLE
IN THE WORLD
BIARRITZ

LEFT: **Surfers.**
Screen print on paper.

RIGHT: Wheels & Waves.
Spray paint on paper.

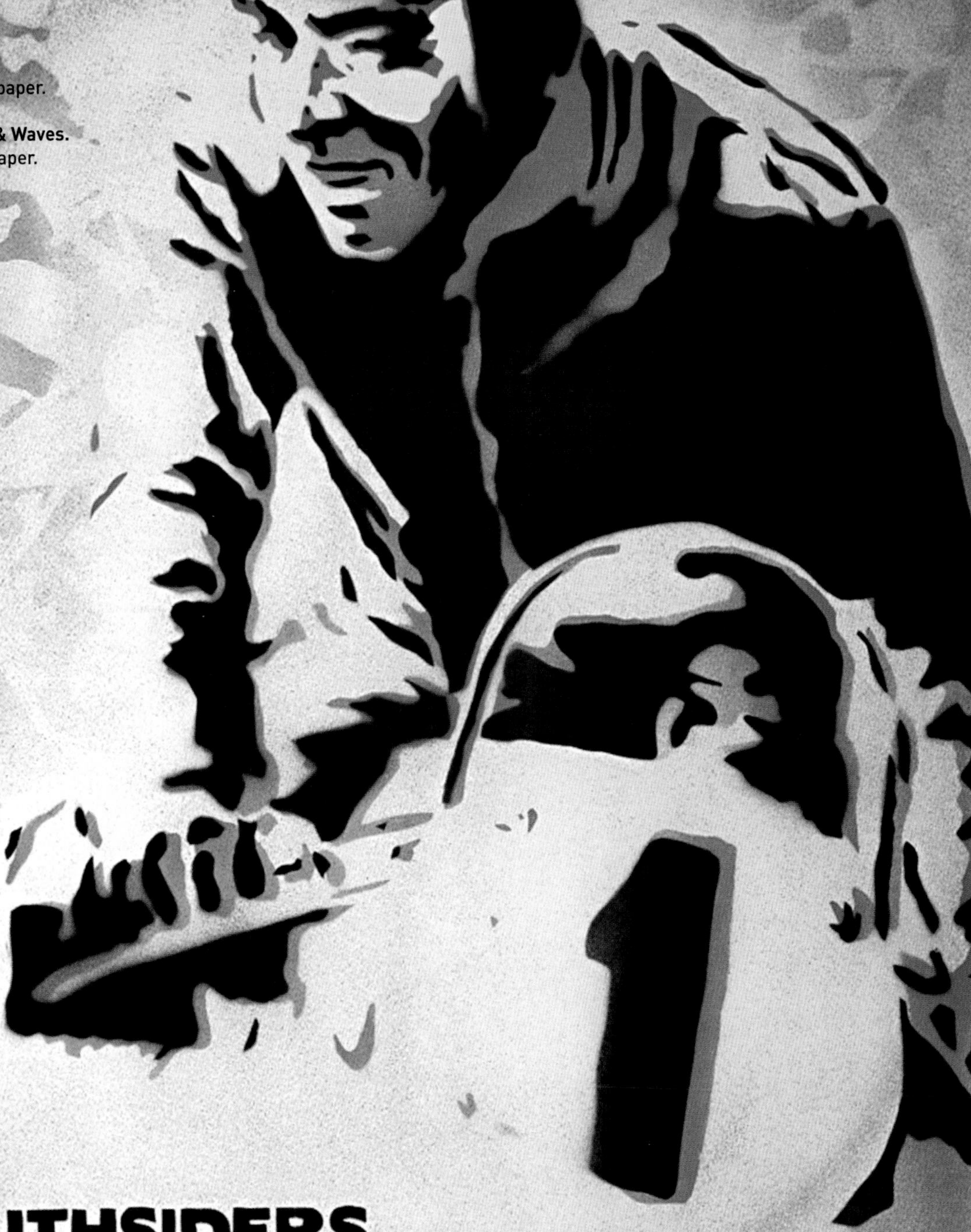

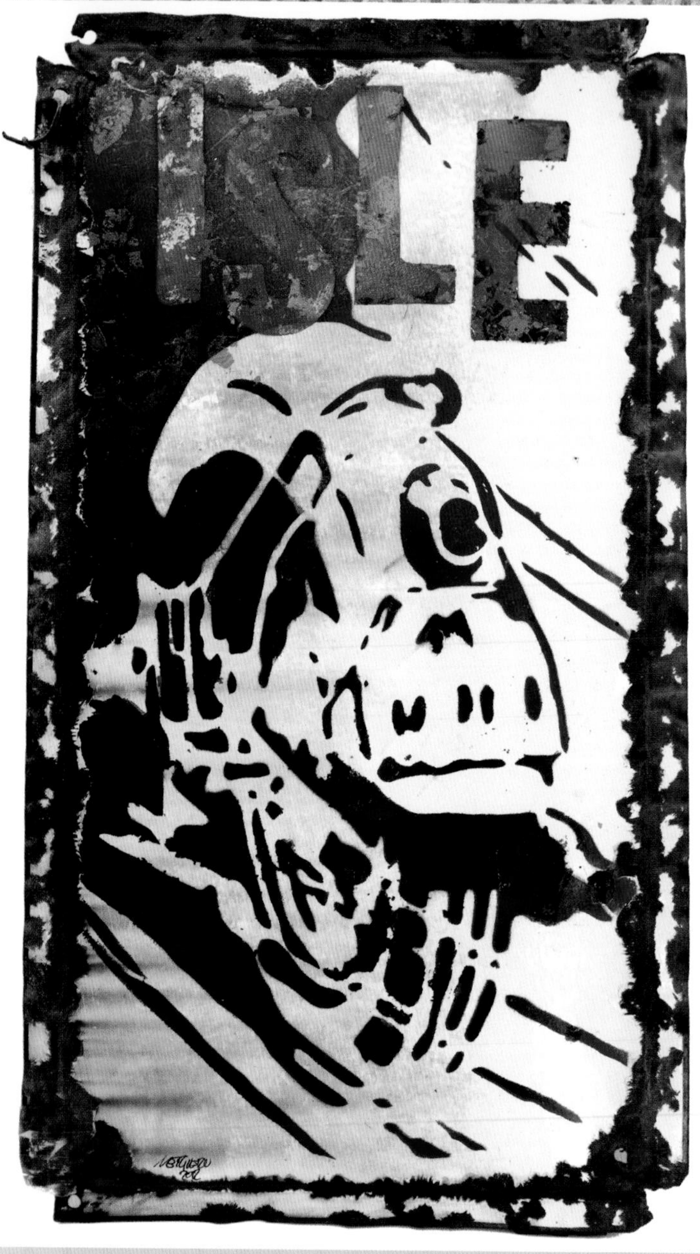

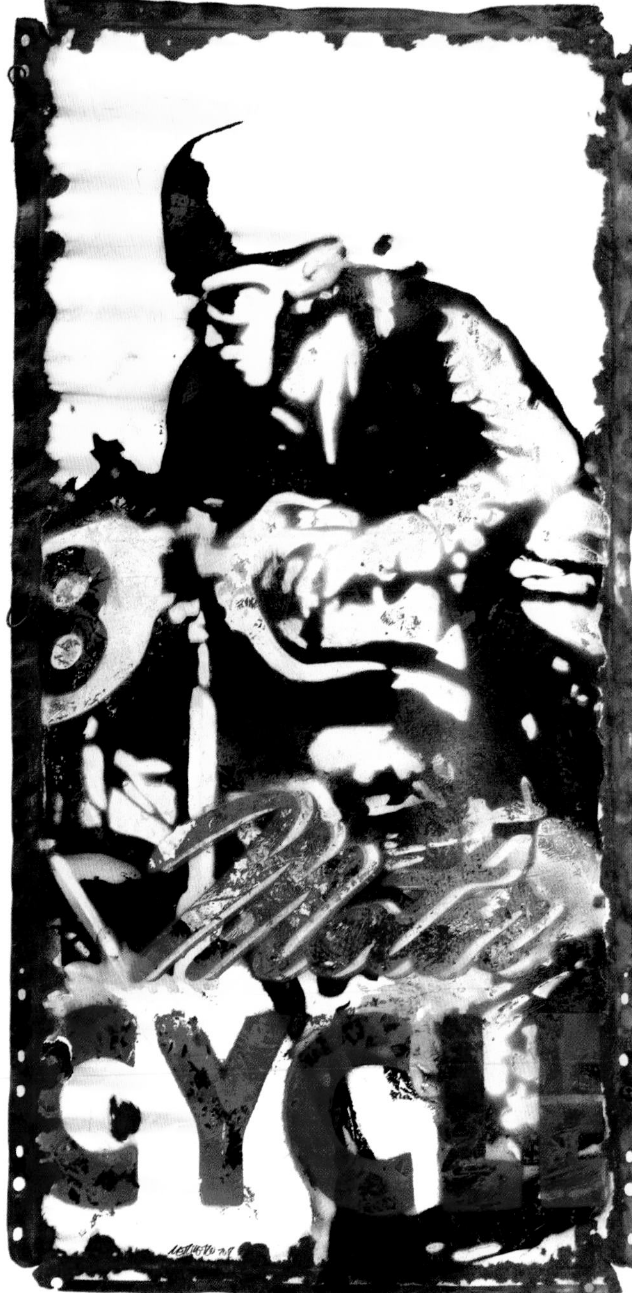

ABOVE: ***Isle.***
Spray paint on scrap metal.

ABOVE RIGHT: ***Motor Cycle.***
Spray paint on scrap metal.

FAR **RIGHT:** ***Chopper On.***
Spray paint on paper.

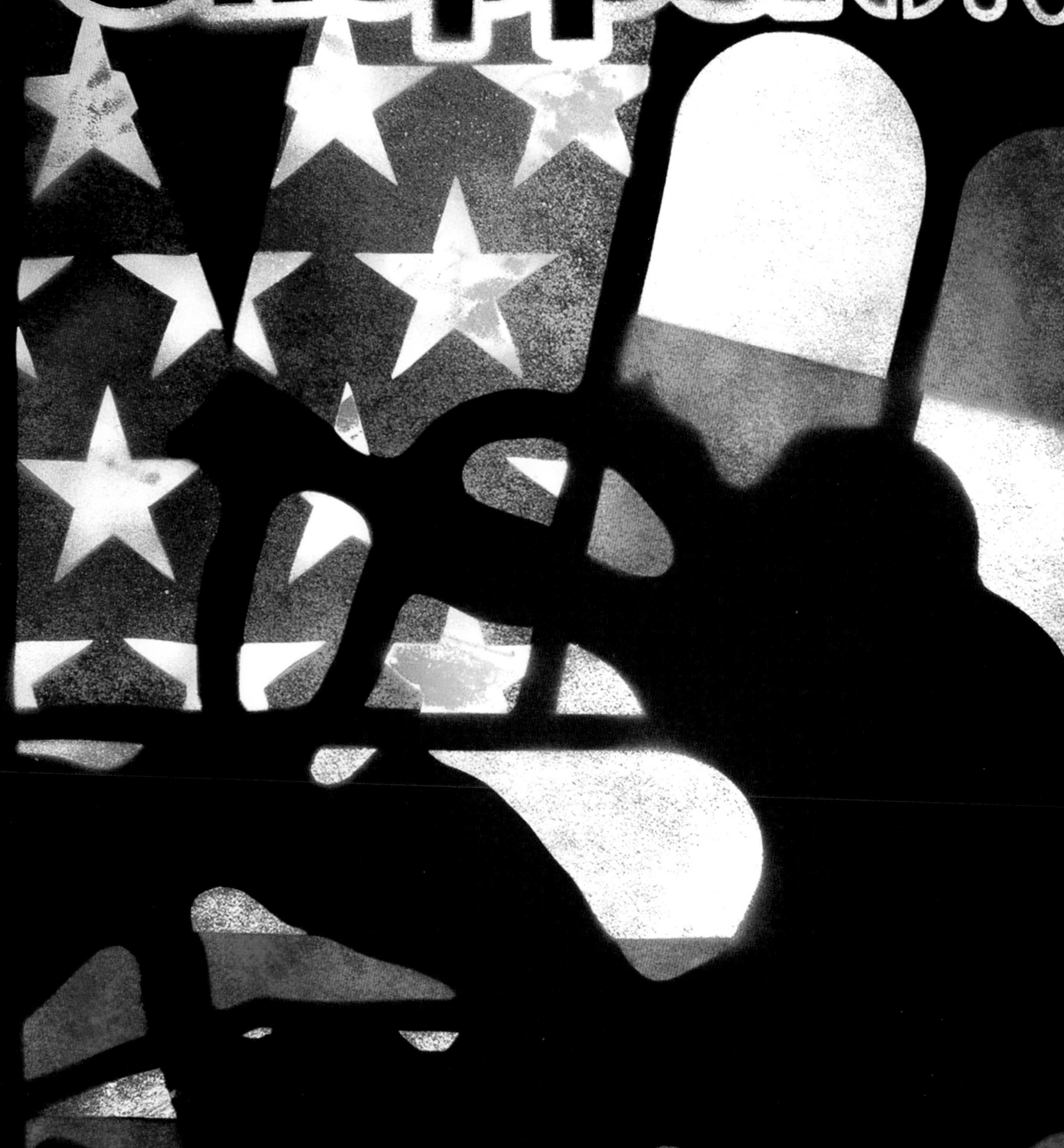
ChopperON

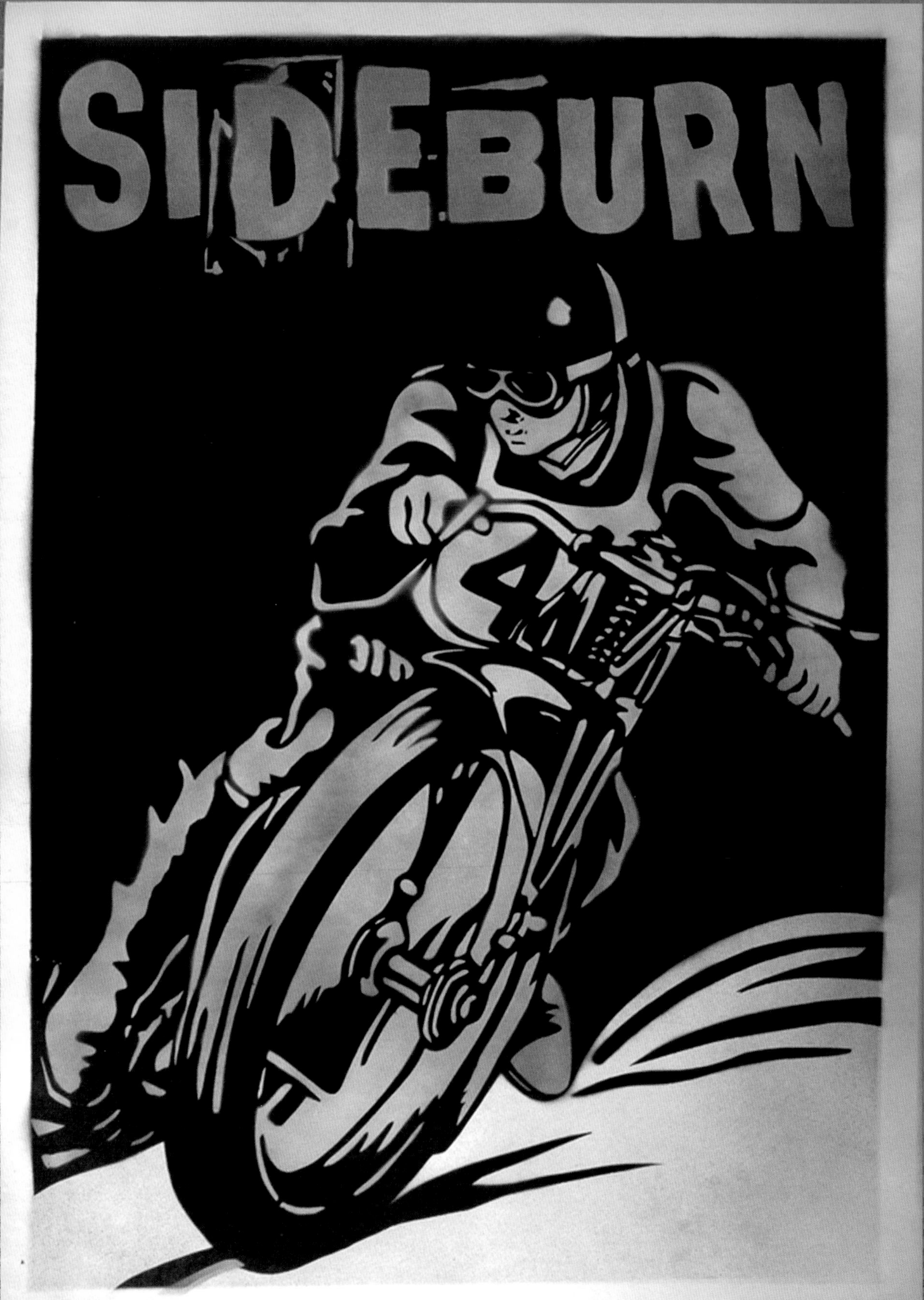

SIDEBURN

4

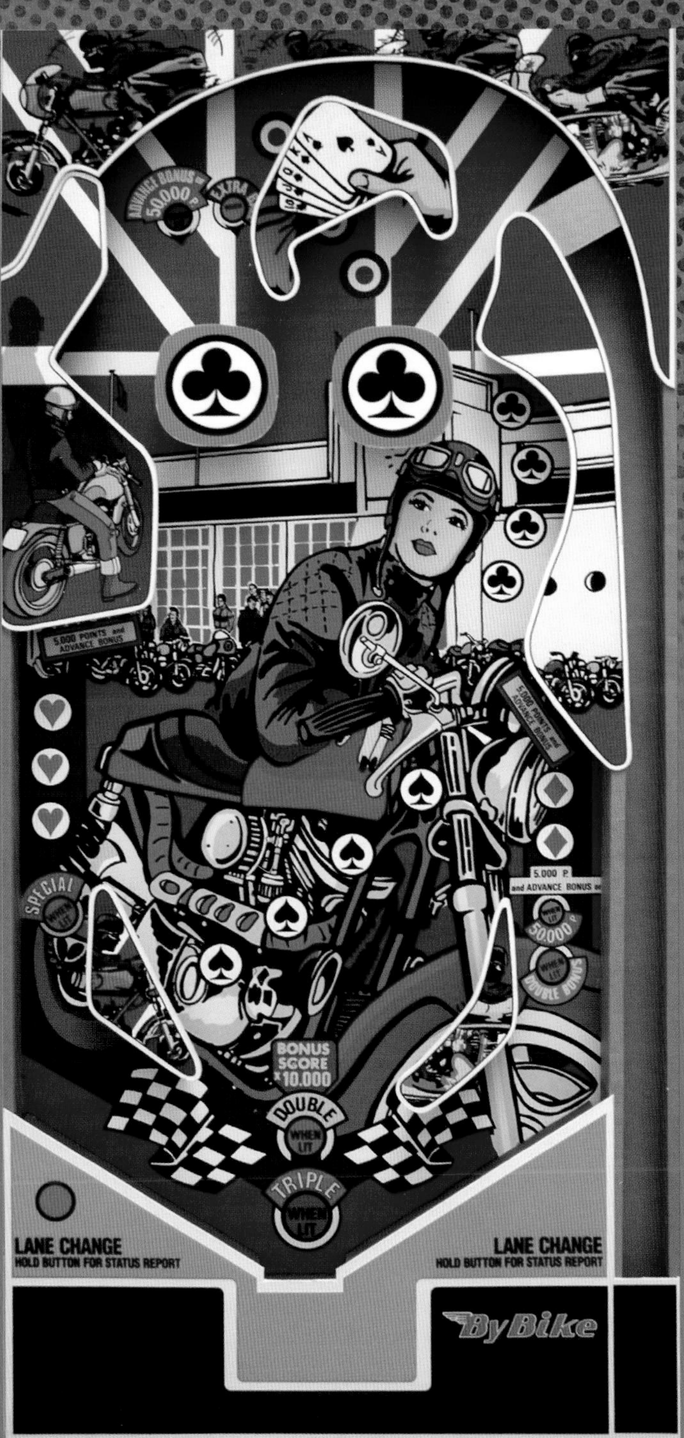

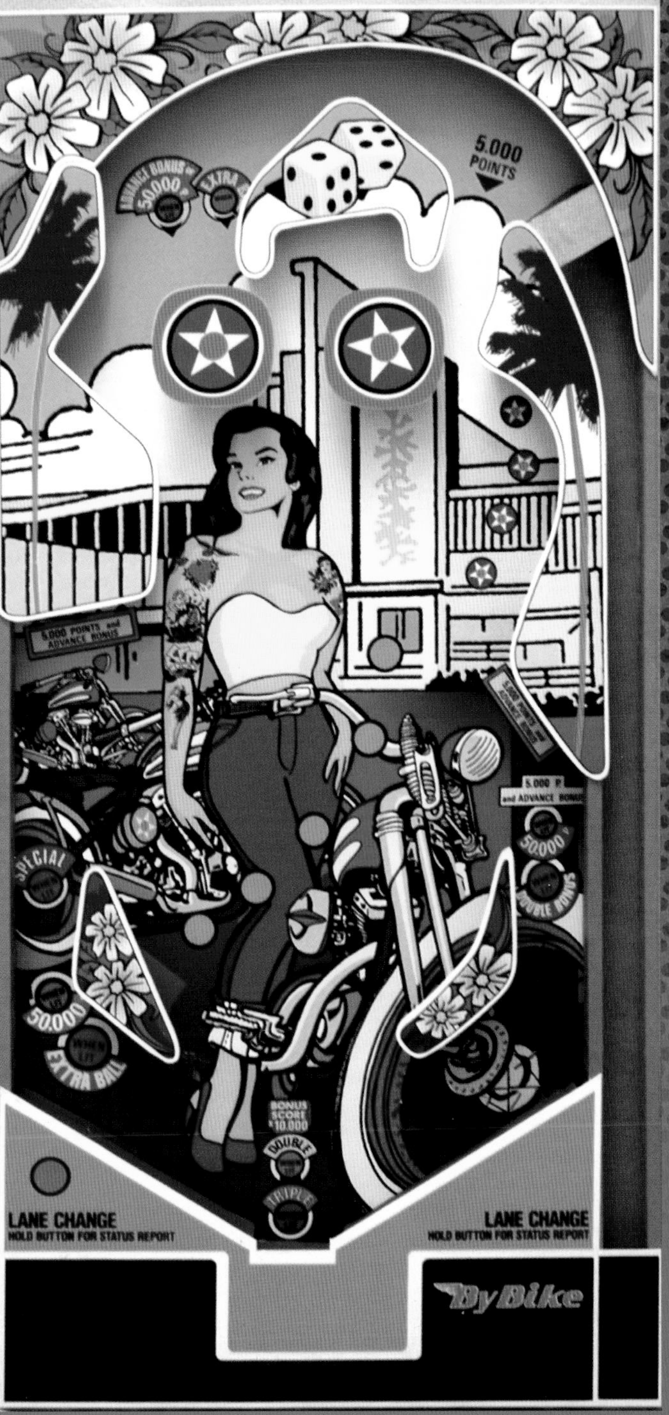

LEFT: ***Sideburn.***
Spray paint on paper.

ABOVE: ***Ace Café.***
Pen and ink and digital colours on paper (in the form of a pinball table).

ABOVE RIGHT: ***Bobber.***
Pen and ink and digital colours on paper (in the form of a pinball table).

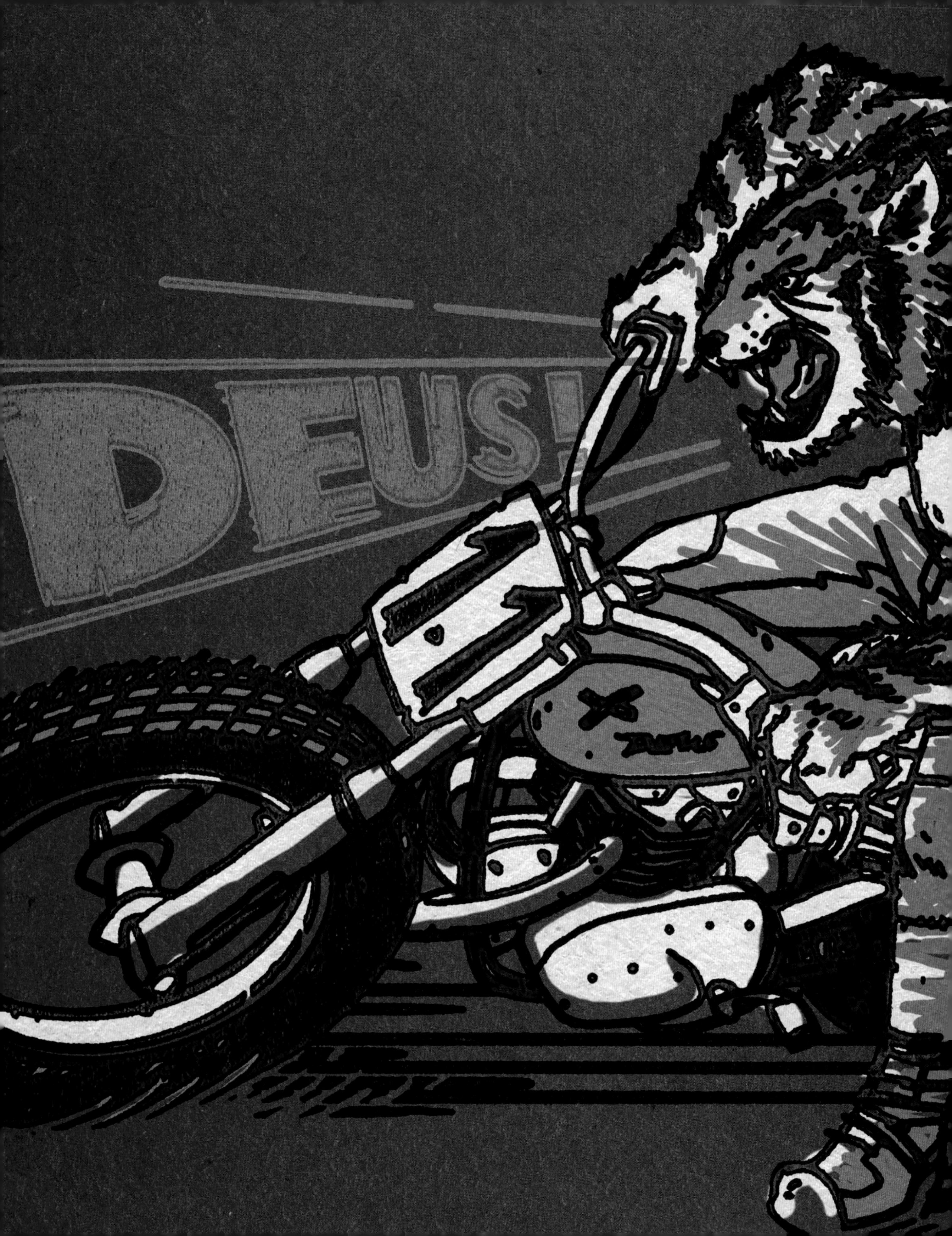
DEUS!

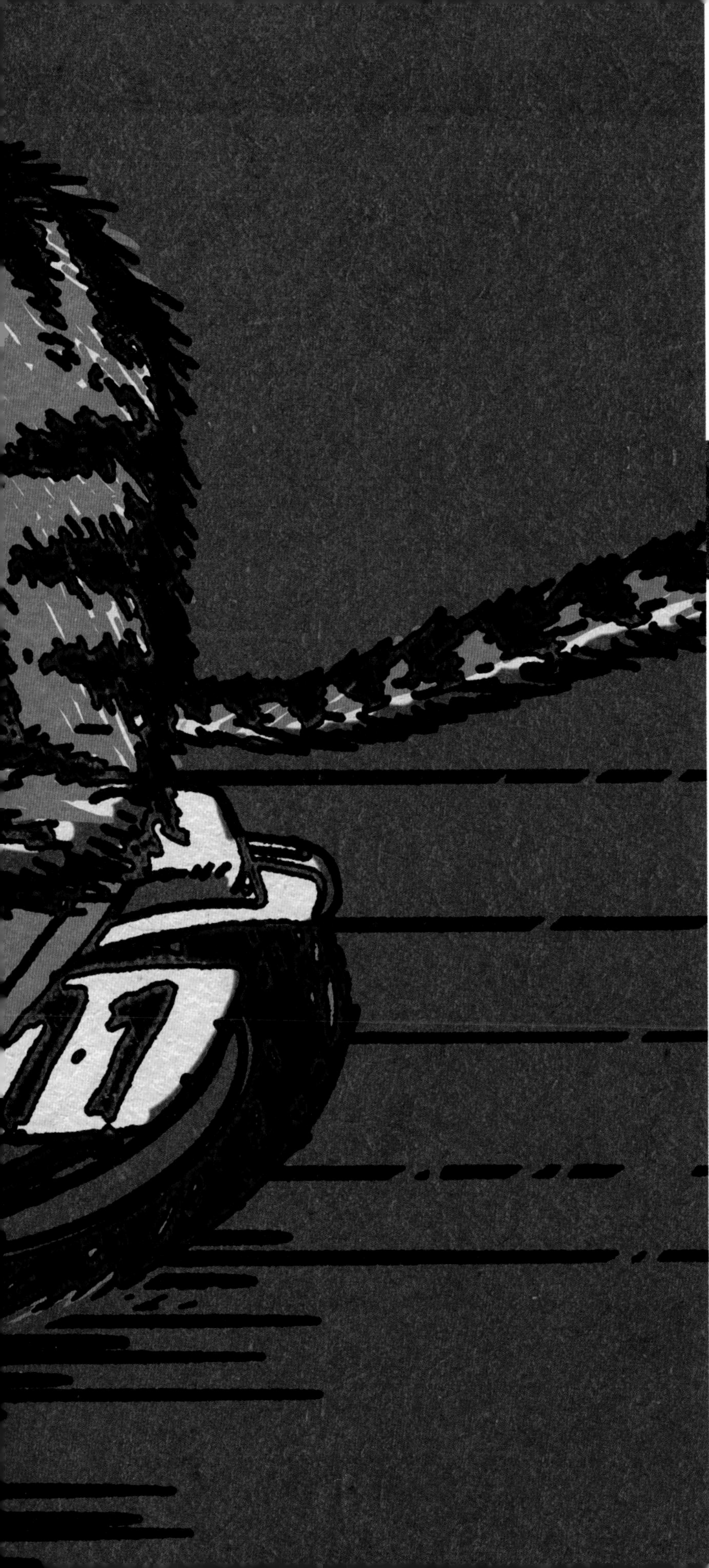

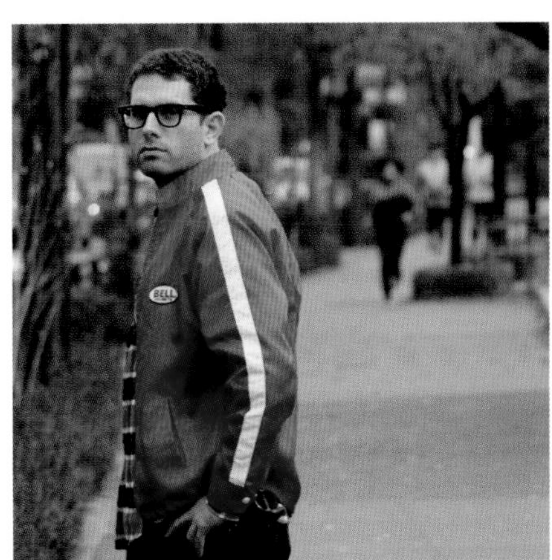

ADAM NICKEL

Despite living on the Sunshine Coast in Queensland, Australia, "Where you can ride a motorcycle every day of the year," it still took Adam Nickel a long time to acquire his first bike."I started riding in 2008. I spent about four years before that being obsessed with vintage bikes and choppers but just thinking they were too dangerous. It took me a little while to realize that some things are worth the risk." He now owns a '55 Thunderbird Triumph. "It's currently in a drag bike sort of style, but it's always changing. I need to work on it more often, but there's always something else that needs doing." That something is working for clients such as *The Daily Telegraph*, Random House, *The Guardian*, *New Scientist*, *Popular Mechanics* and Stereo Skateboards. In the motorcycling world he has produced illustrations for Born Loser, Honrio Cham (Throttle), *Dice Magazine* and Deus Ex Machina. "As far back as I can remember I would draw stuff I thought was cool. I grew up near a train line and so I spent a lot of the mid-'80s drawing graffiti that I saw." Today Adam works mostly in digital. Of bikes he says:"I like building them, and seeing them as art, and I like creating art that involves motorcycles. It's the combination of art and function that works for me."

LEFT: *Flat-track Feline.*
Digital illustration.

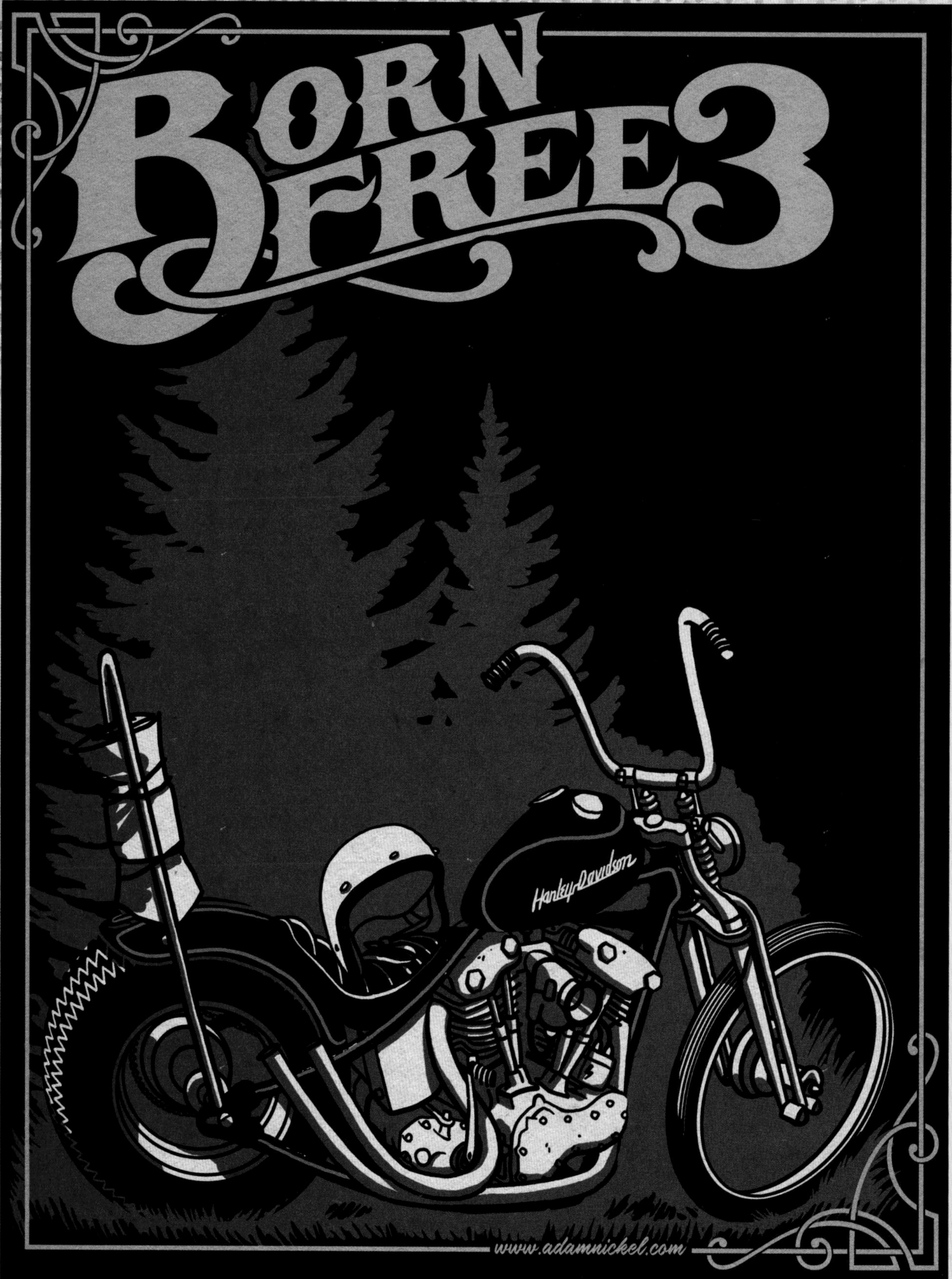
BORN FREE 3
Harley-Davidson
www.adamnickel.com

BELOW: ***Motorcycle Restyling.***
Digital illustration.

LEFT: ***Born Free 3.***
Digital illustration.

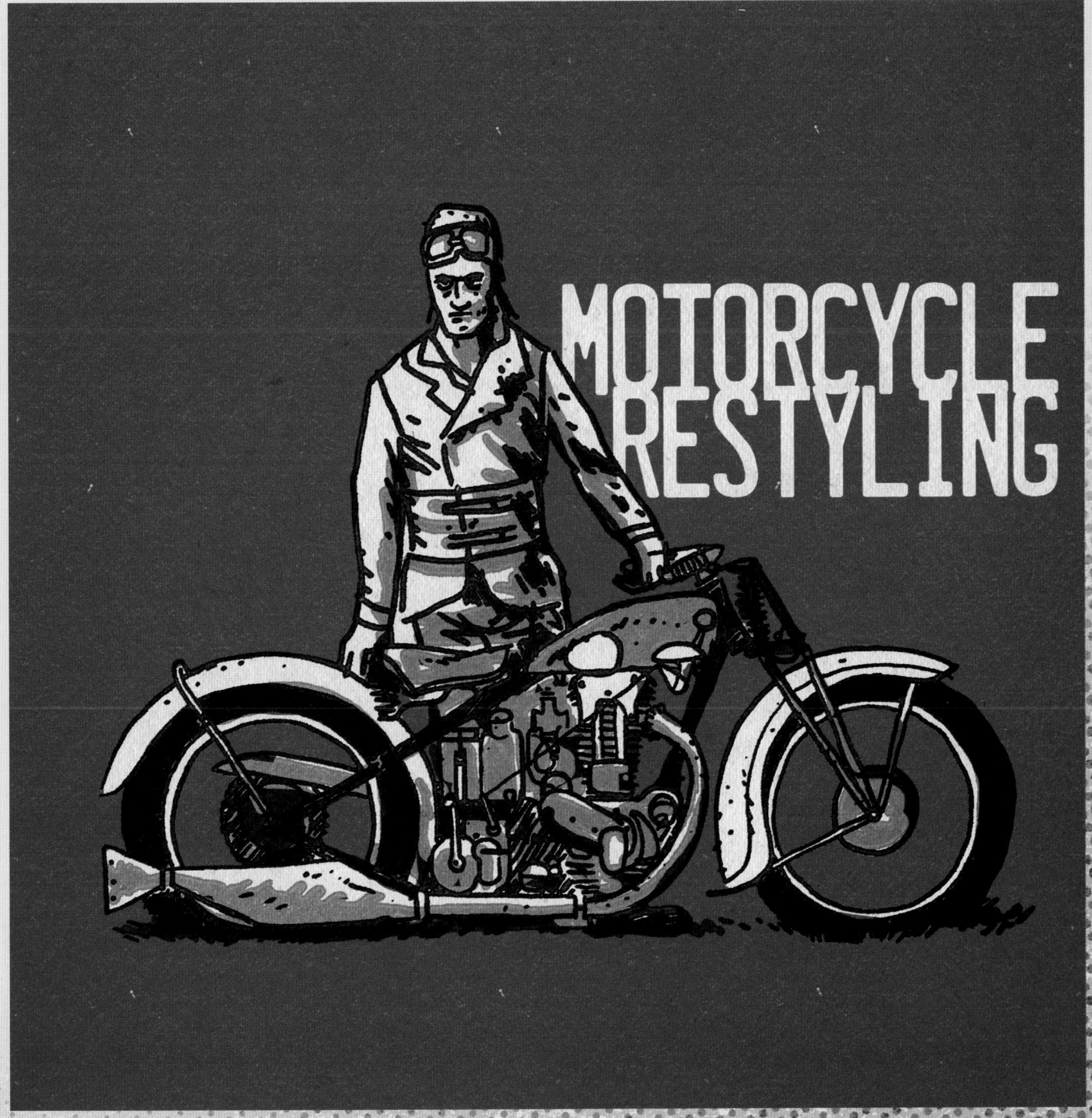

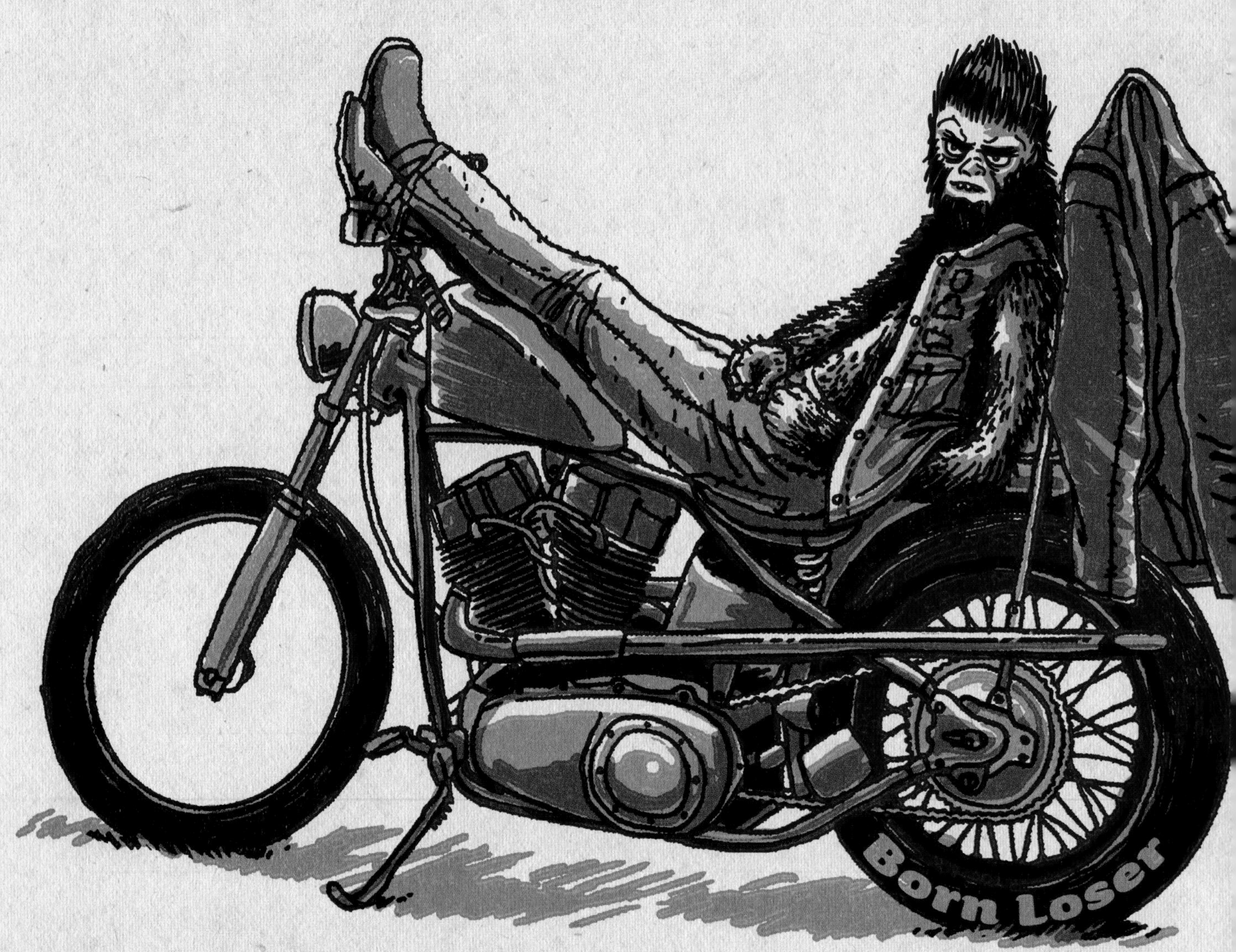

ABOVE: ***Wolfman.***
Digital illustration.

ABOVE RIGHT: ***Wolfman Wheelie.***
Digital illustration.

RIGHT: ***The Wolf and the Switchblade.***
Digital illustration.

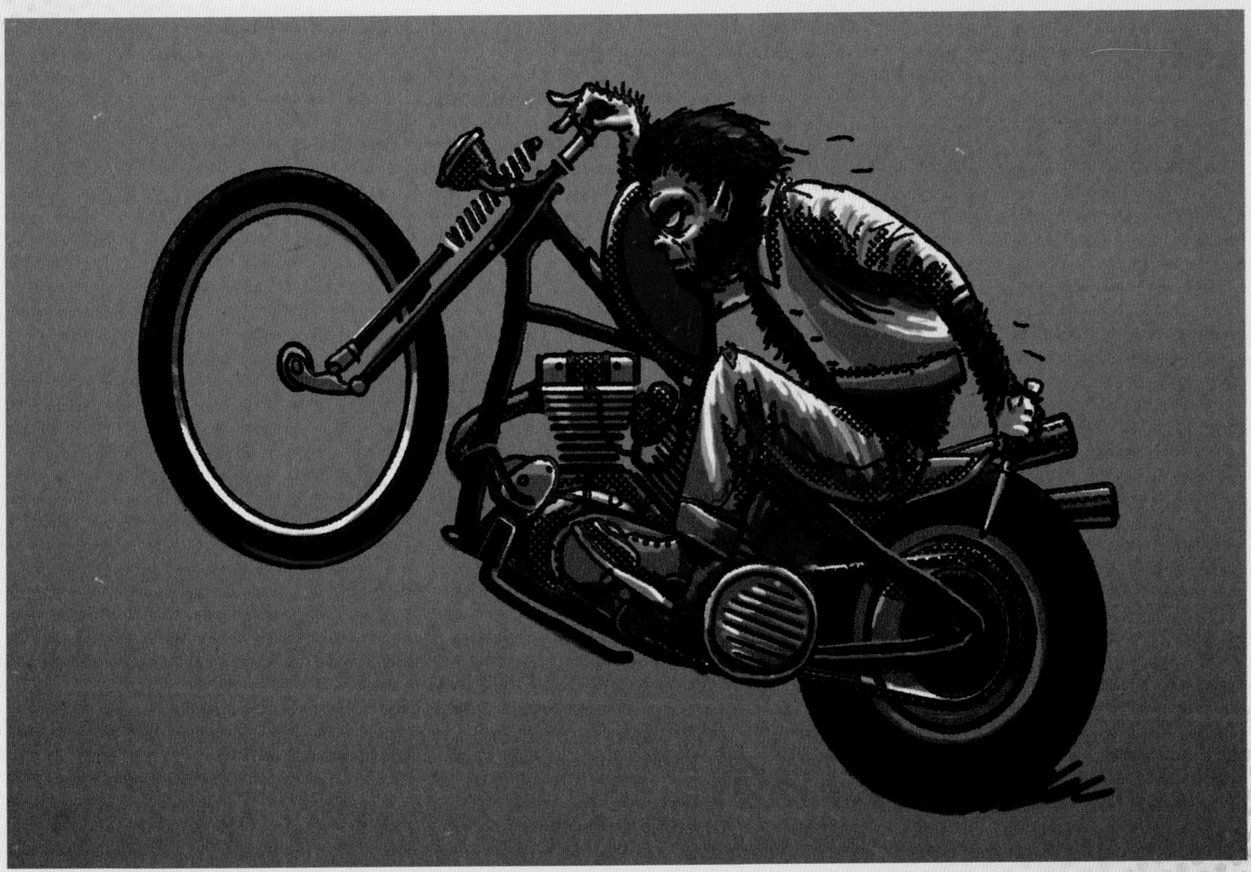

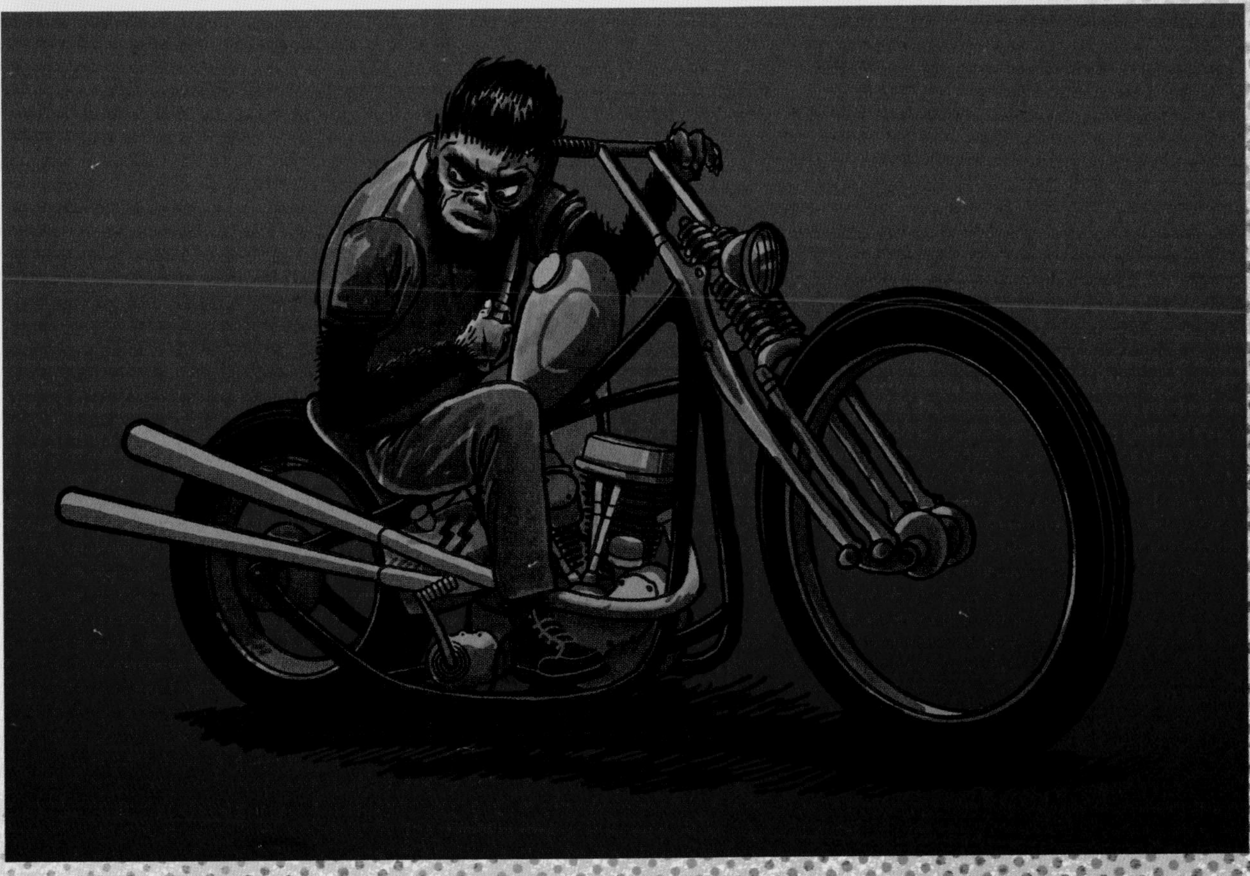

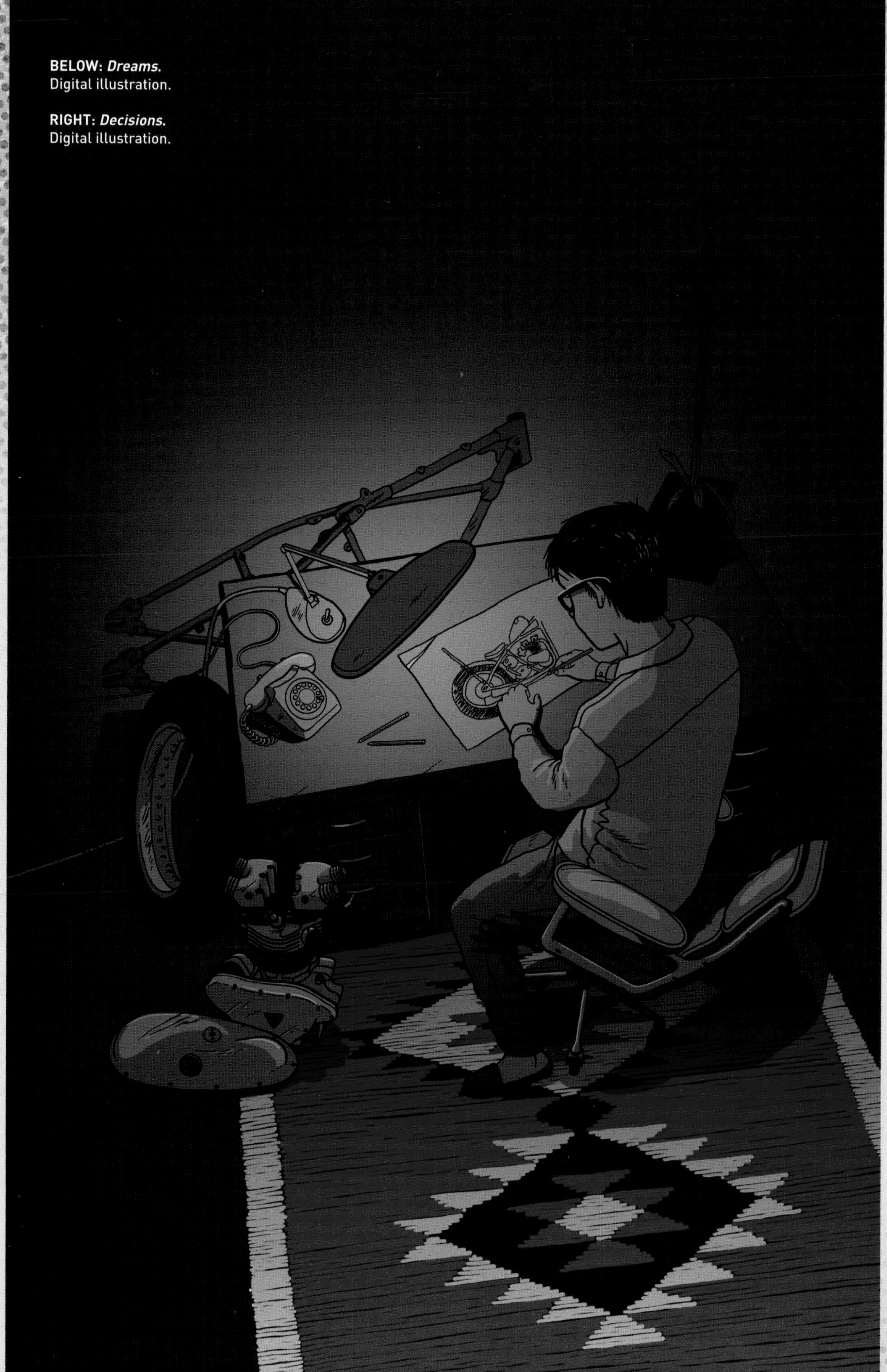

BELOW: ***Dreams.***
Digital illustration.

RIGHT: ***Decisions.***
Digital illustration.

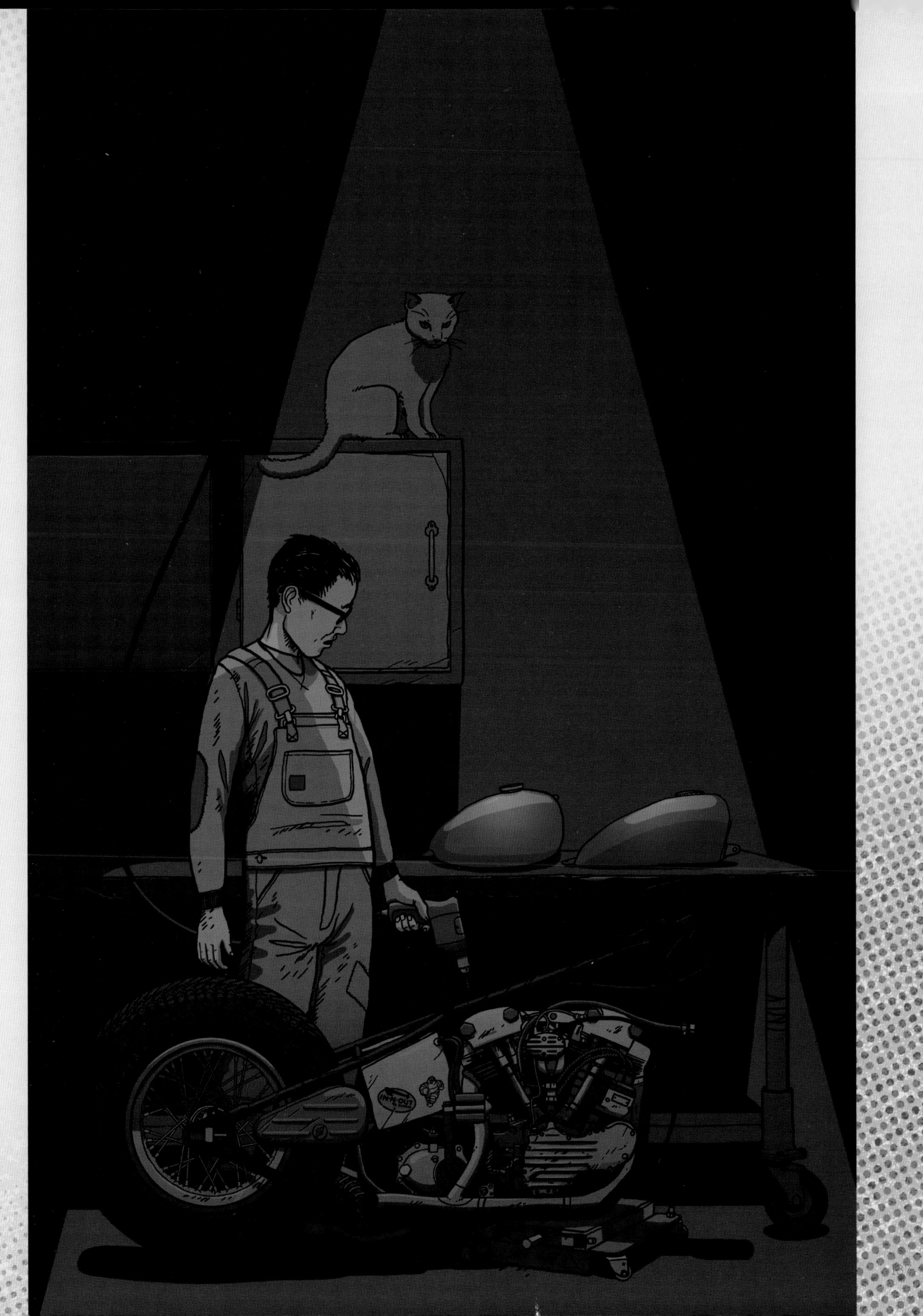
IN-N-OUT

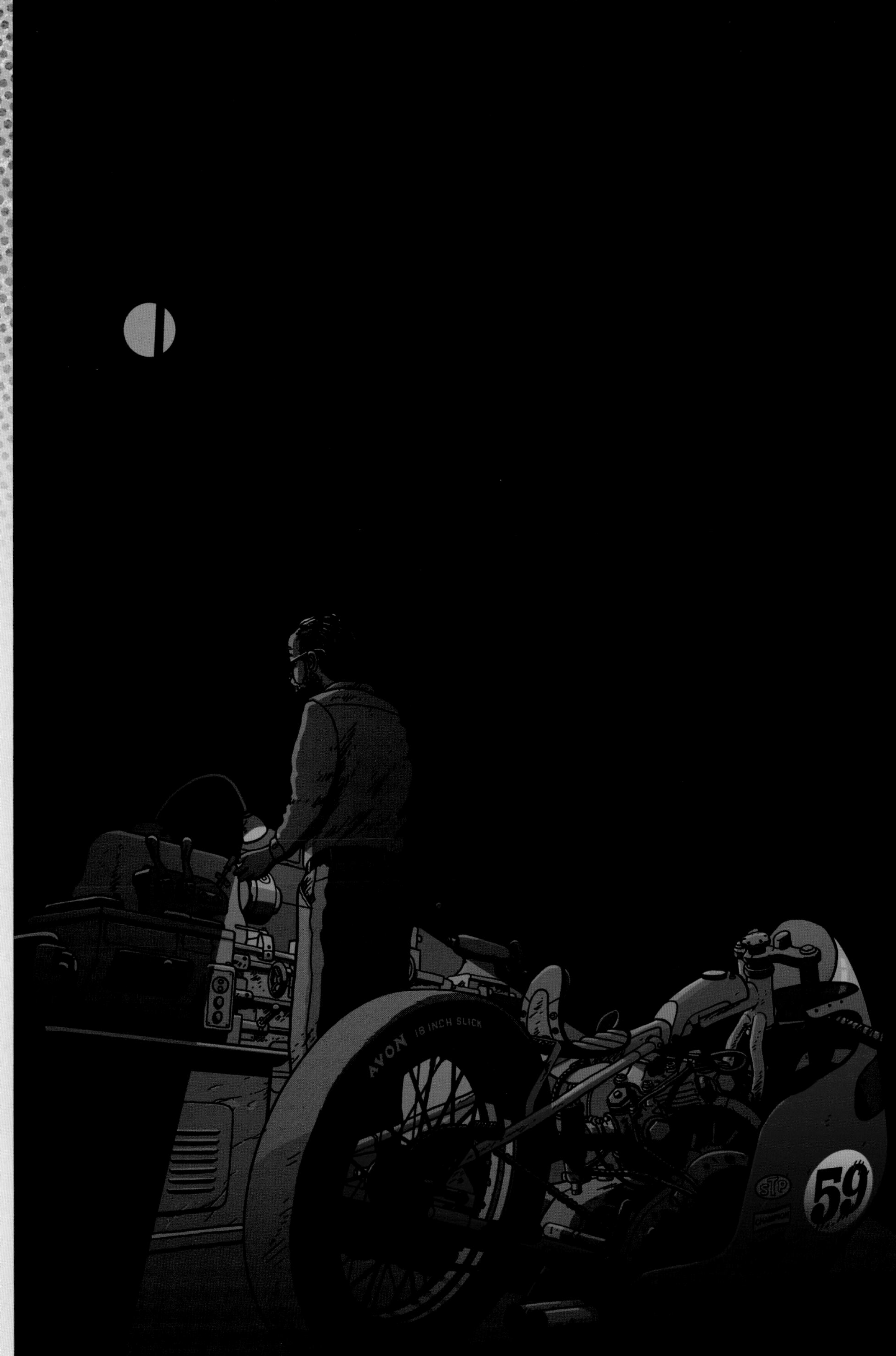
AVON 18 INCH SLICK
STP
59

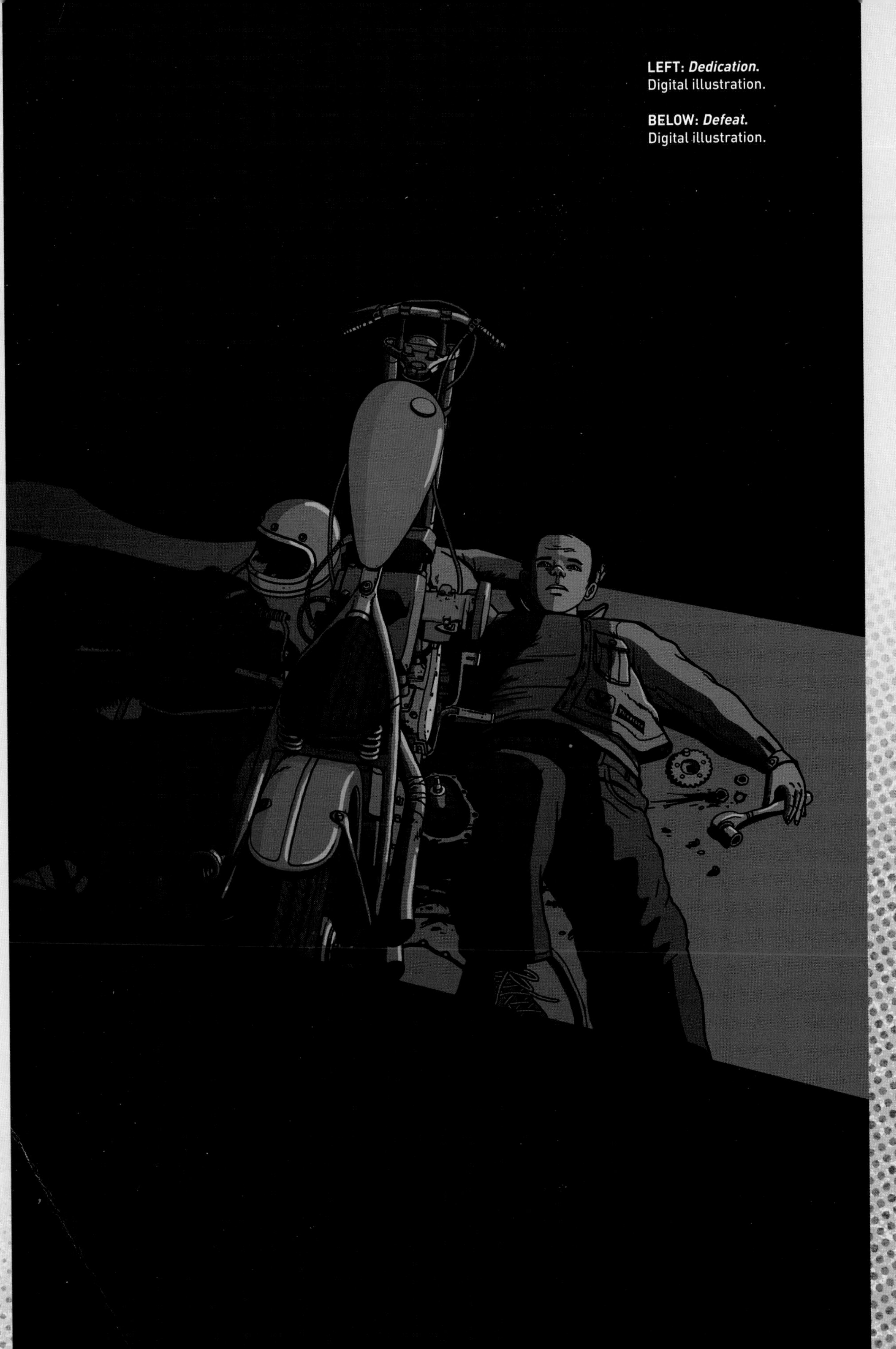

LEFT: ***Dedication.***
Digital illustration.

BELOW: ***Defeat.***
Digital illustration.

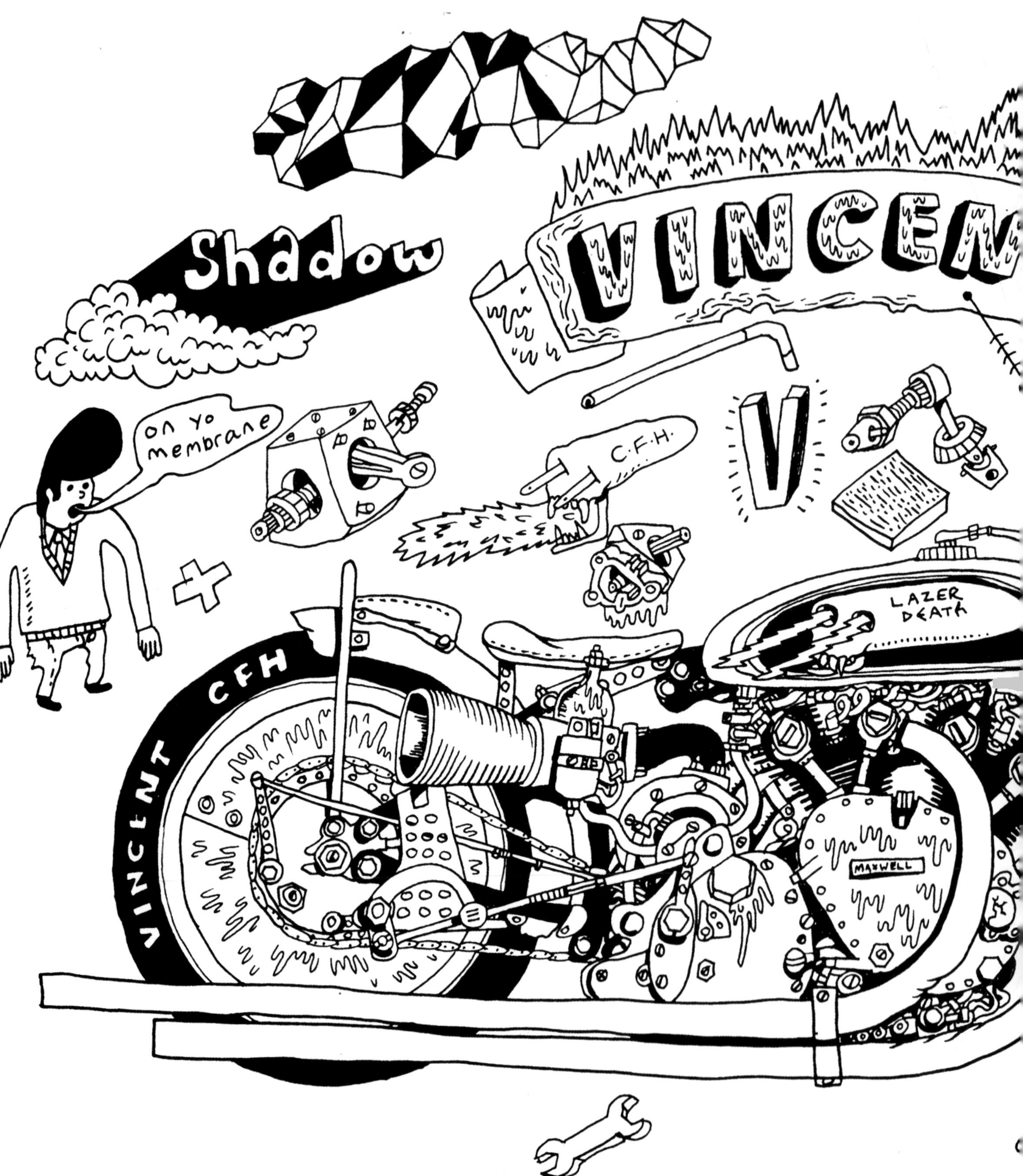
Shadow
VINCEN
on yo membrane
C.F.H.
V
LAZER DEATH
CFH
VINCENT
MAXWELL

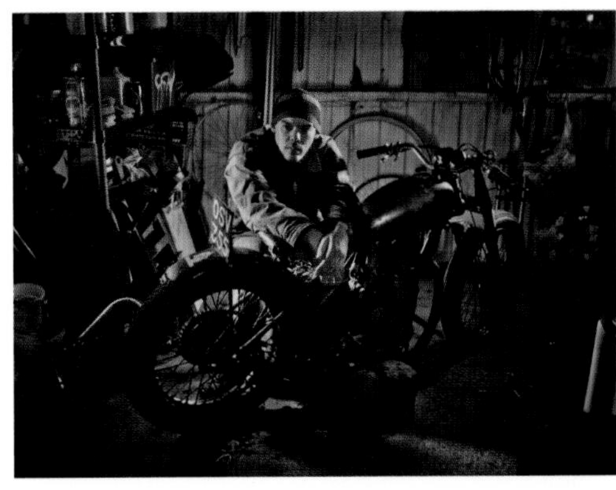

MAXWELL PATERNOSTER

Born in Ipswich, in Suffolk, England, Maxwell was raised in rural countryside, "...Driving cars and riding motorbikes while being surrounded by large bits of farm machinery that were juxtaposed against flat natural surroundings." Riding on tractors and driving cars and motorbikes as a child sparked his interest in the mechanical, technological aspect of the world. He was also exposed to the realities of meat production. "Being taken to the pig-rearing unit that my father ran, I saw slurry, silage, vomit, excrement, guts, gore and more. Also I saw pits full of decaying animal bodies of the weaker pigs that never survived." These biomechanical mental montages have worked their way into much of Maxwell's phantasmagorical art. His technique is simple – thin black pen and ink, colouring on computer. "Art was always fun and drawing pictures of weird things is fun, not boring like maths," he explains. "I just had to do it, much the same as now." Today Maxwell is also the *de facto* leader of the Corpses From Hell Motorcycle Gang and rides his self-built, rigid BSA M33 around the UK and much of Europe, meeting kindred spirits on the way.

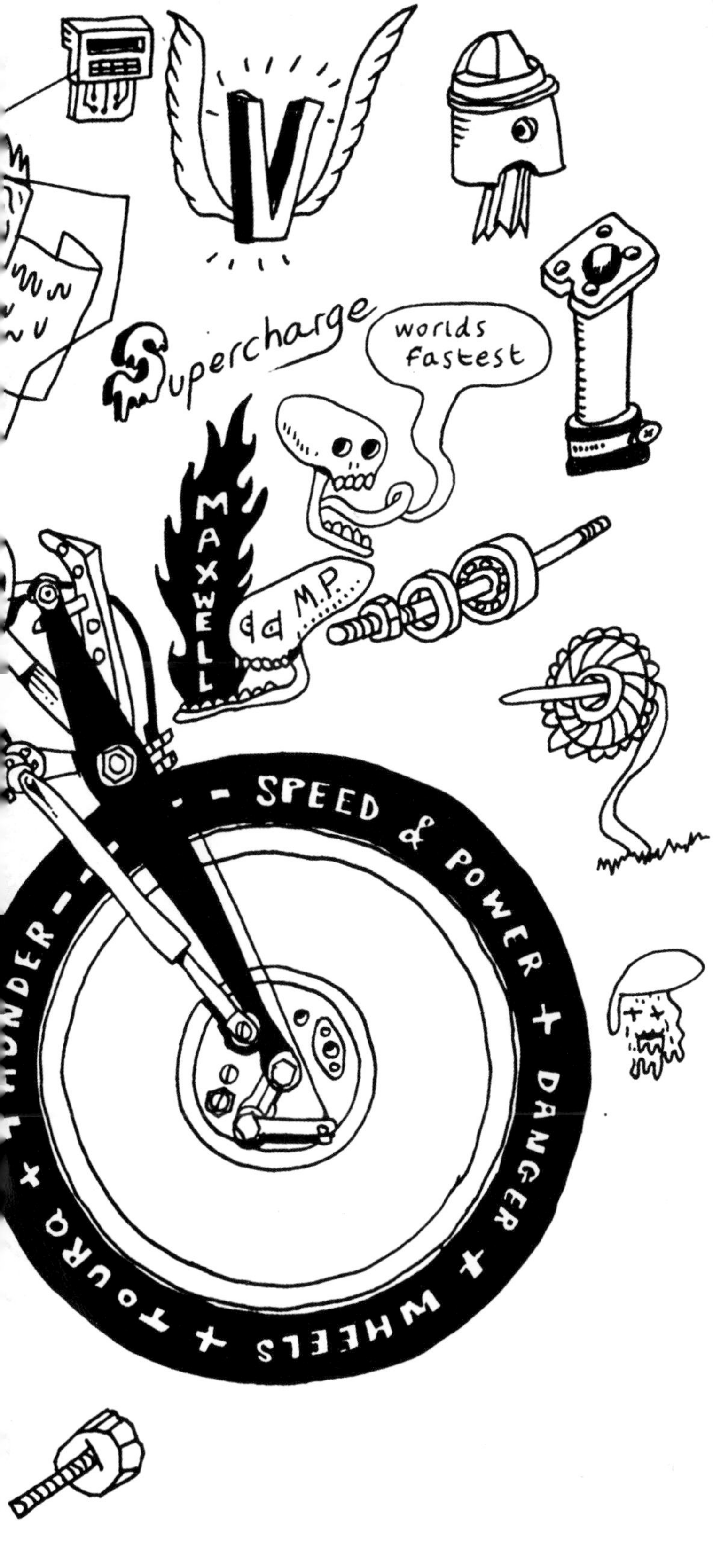

LEFT: *Sumf.*
Ink on paper.

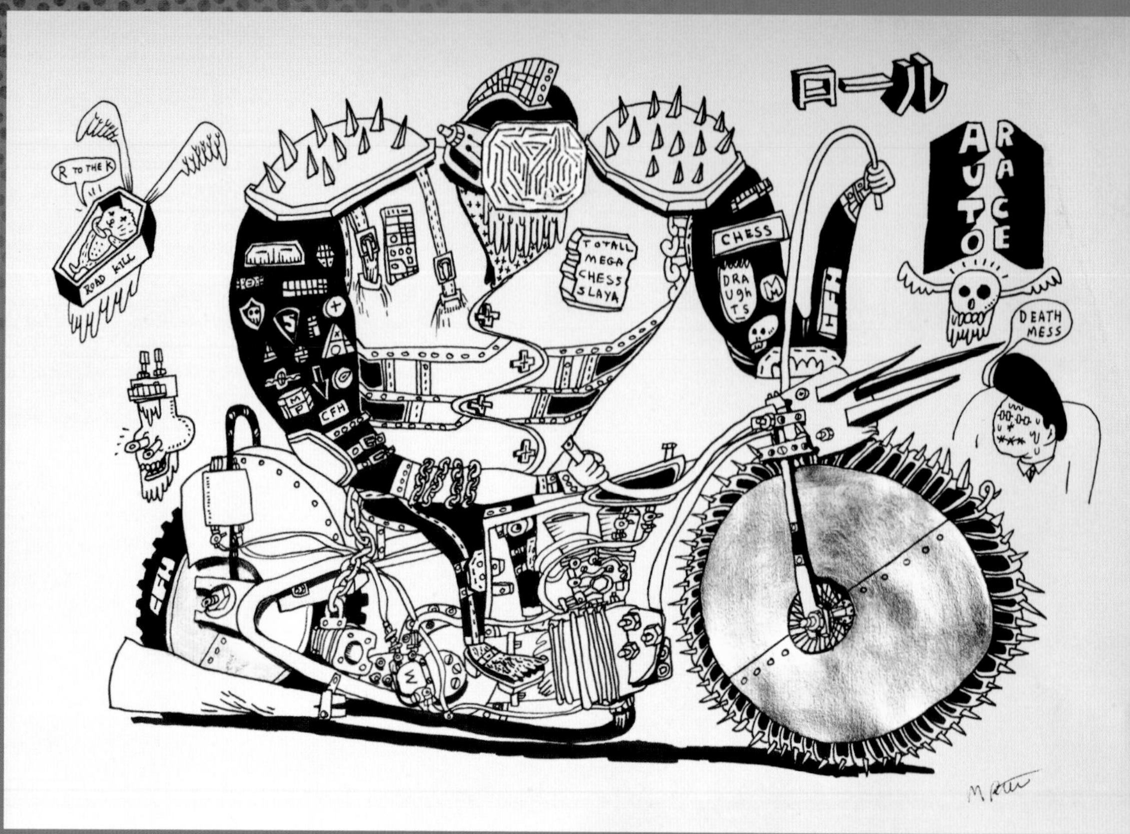

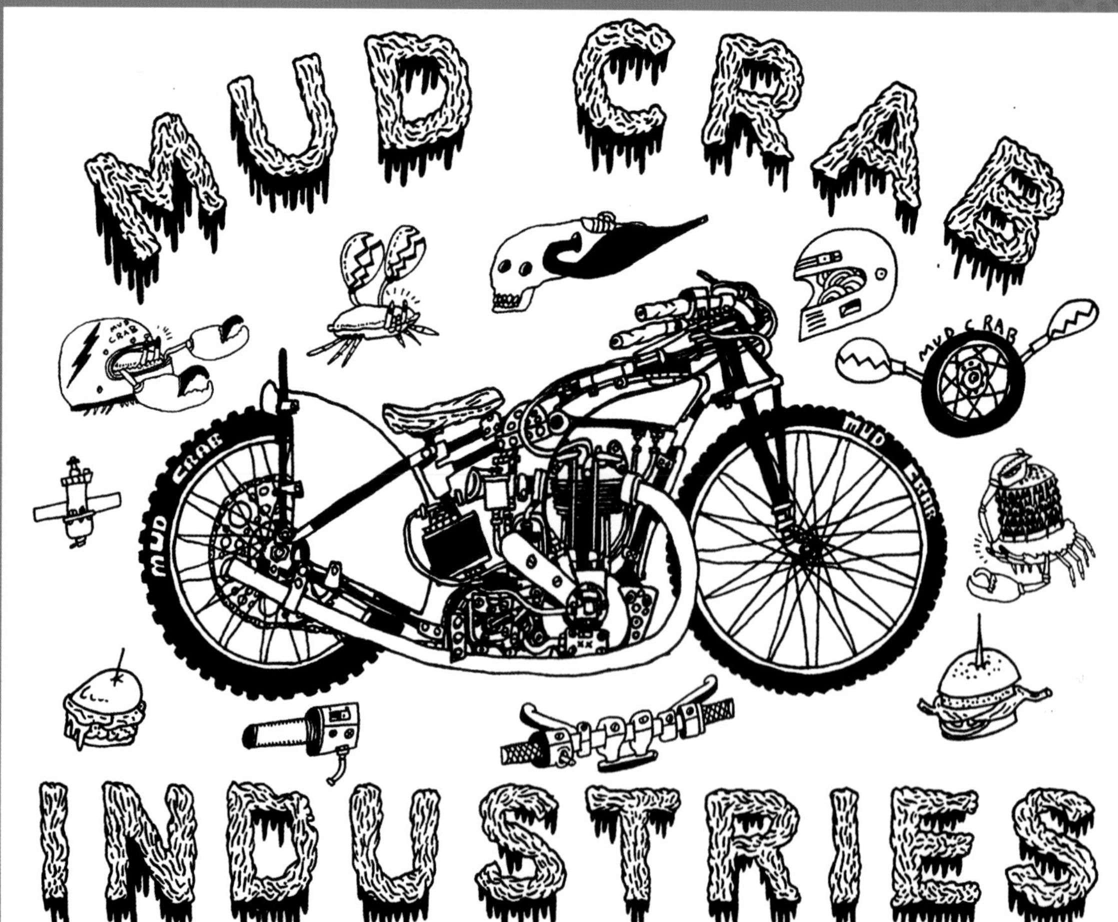

ABOVE: ***Autoerase.***
Ink on paper.

RIGHT: ***Mud Crab Industries.***
Ink on paper.

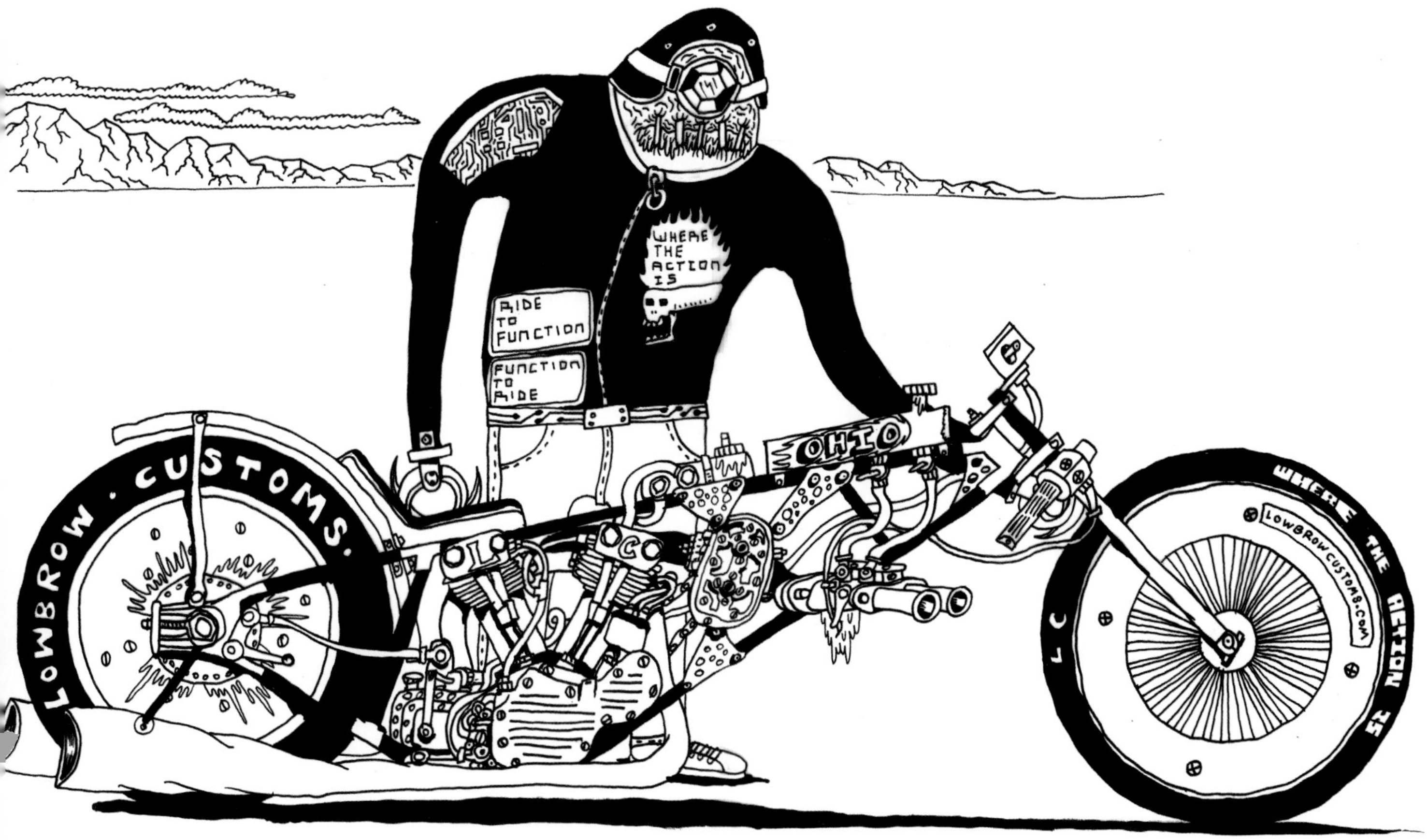

ABOVE: *Salt Lizard.*
Ink on paper.

RIGHT: *Toad Inferno.*
Ink on paper.

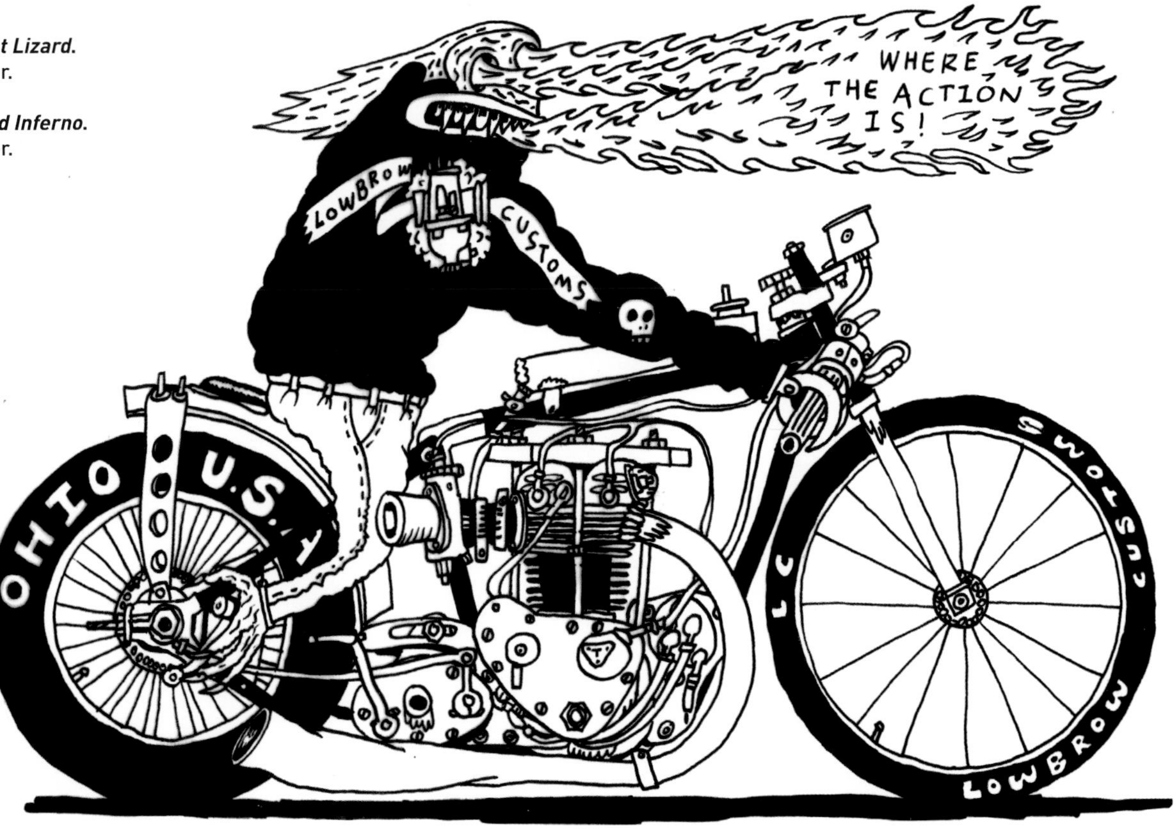

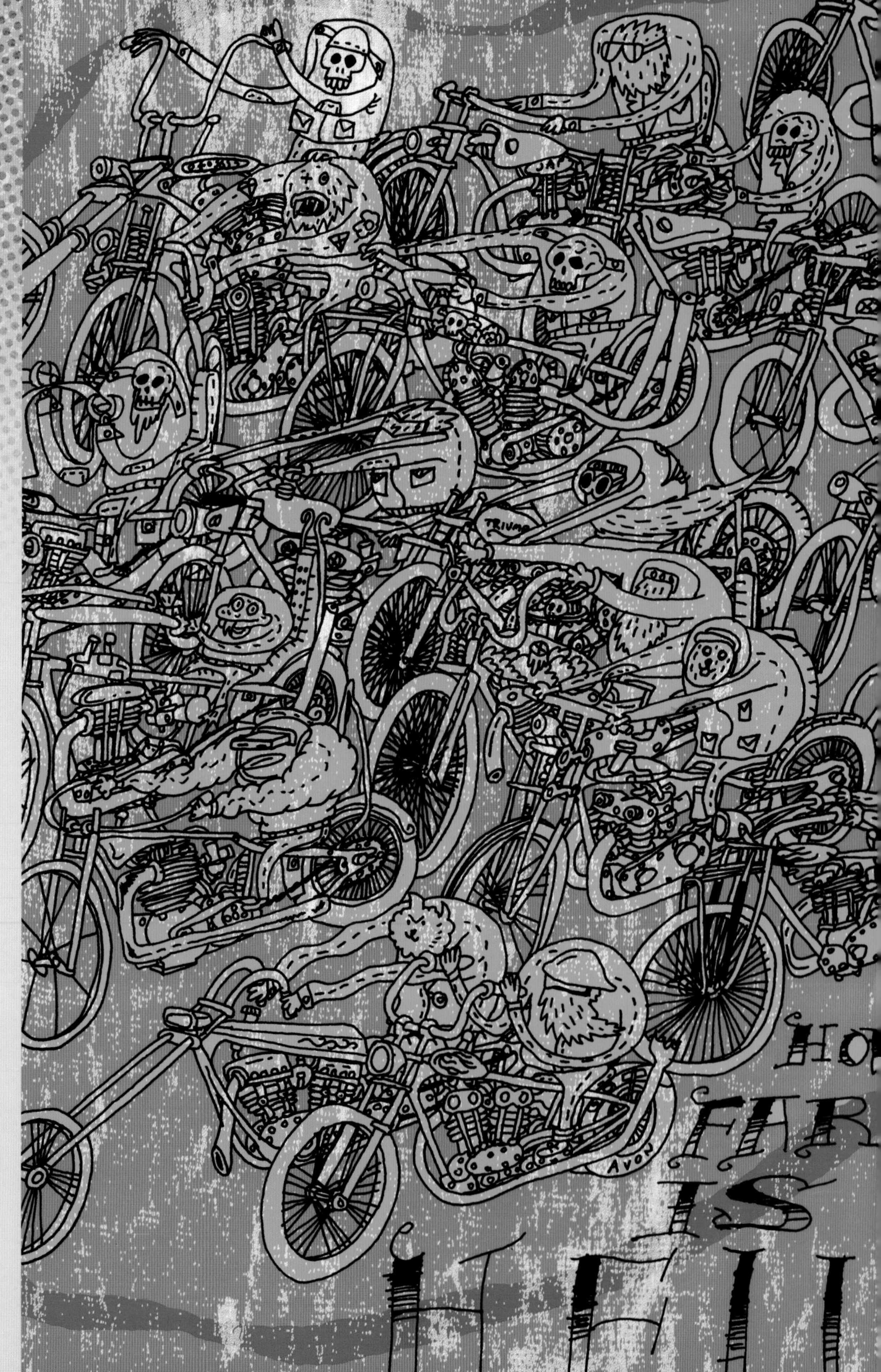

RIGHT:
Biker Gang.
Ink on paper, digital colours.

FAR RIGHT:
Wall of Death.
Ink on paper, digital colours.

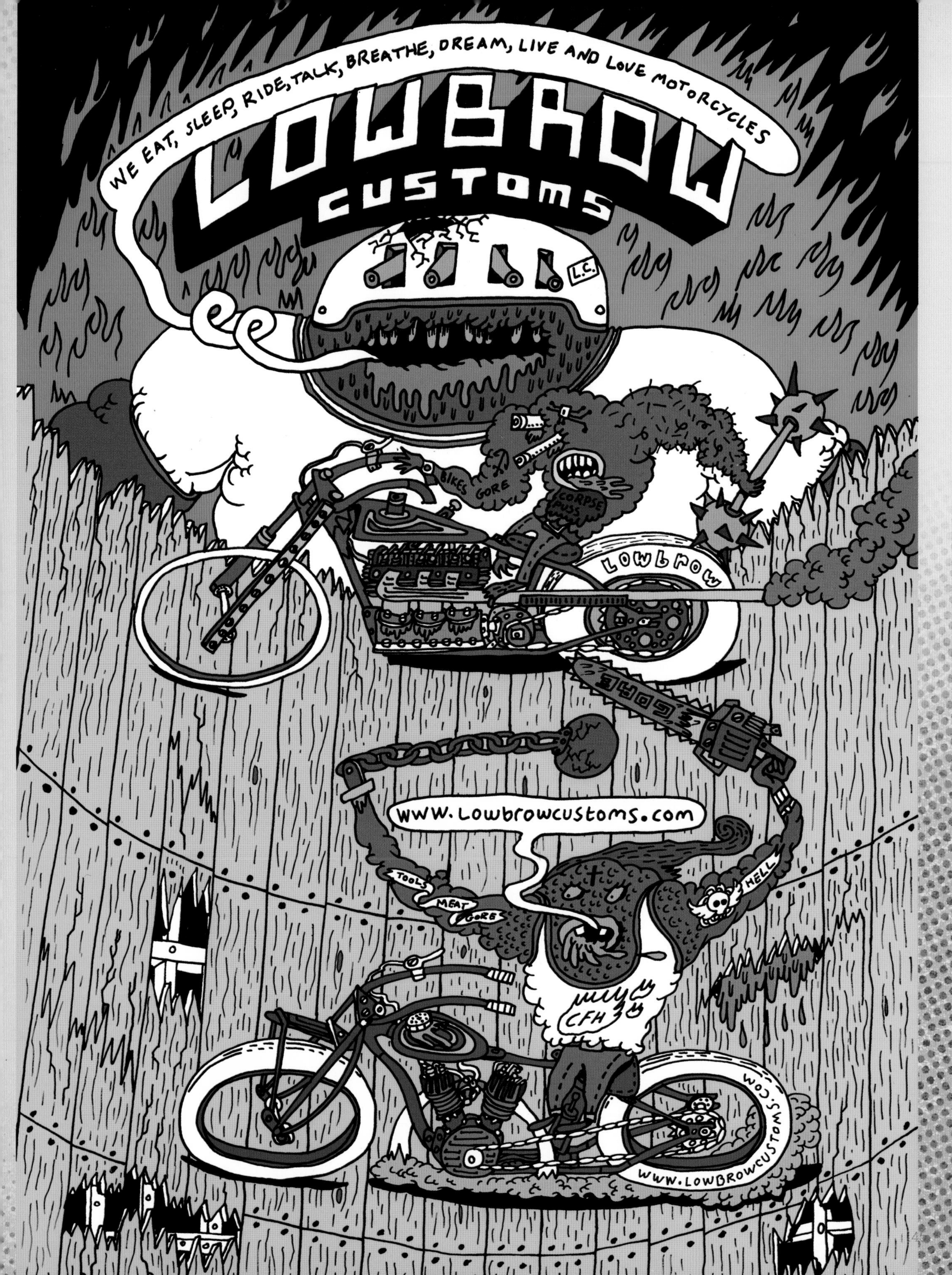

WE EAT, SLEEP, RIDE, TALK, BREATHE, DREAM, LIVE AND LOVE MOTORCYCLES
LOWBROW CUSTOMS
L.C.
BIKES GORE
CORPSE PUSS
LOWBROW
GORE
www.lowbrowcustoms.com
TOOLS
MEAT
GORE
HELL
CFH
WWW.LOWBROWCUSTOMS.COM

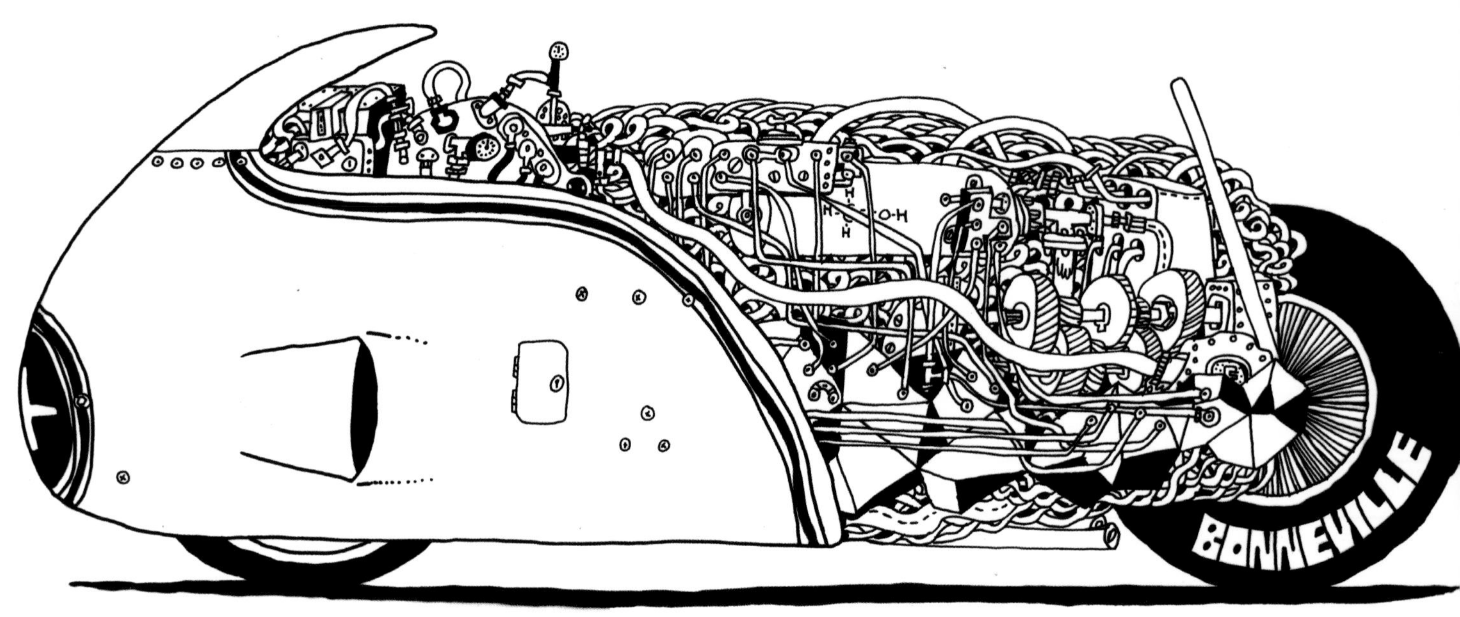

ABOVE: ***Impossible Team.***
Ink on paper.

BELOW: ***Dirt Tracker.***
Ink on paper.

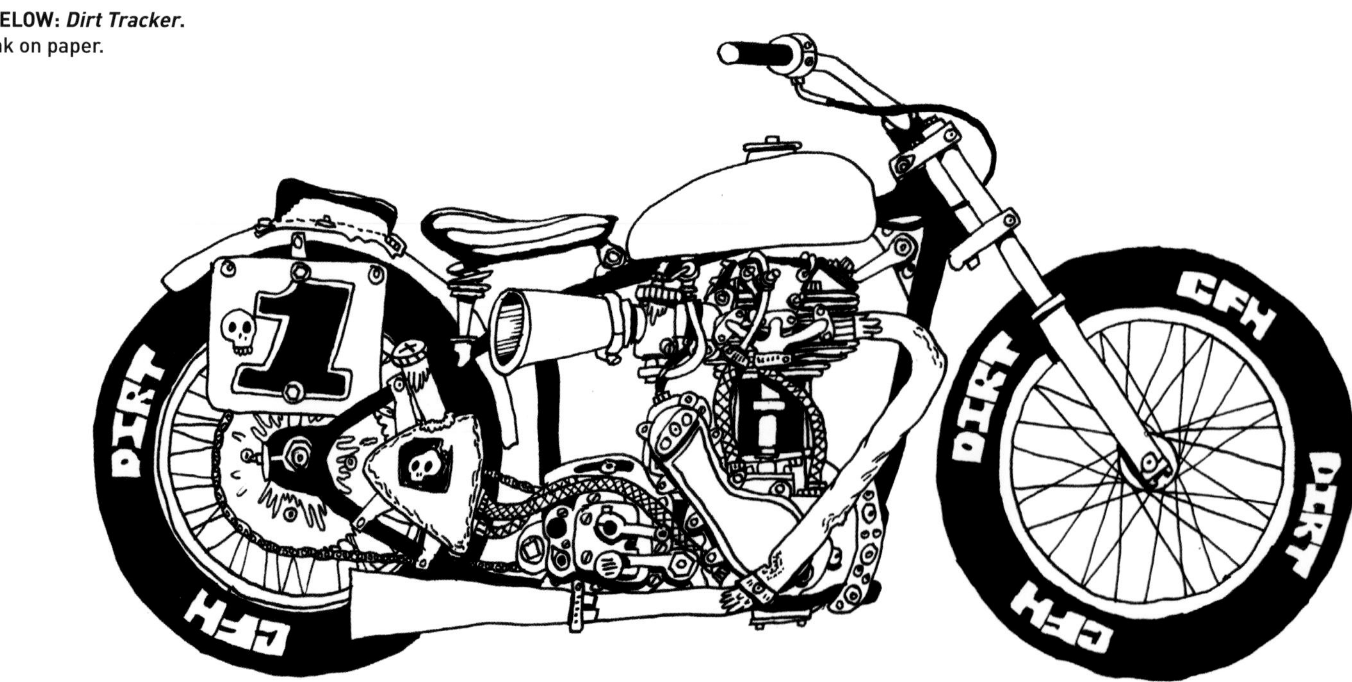

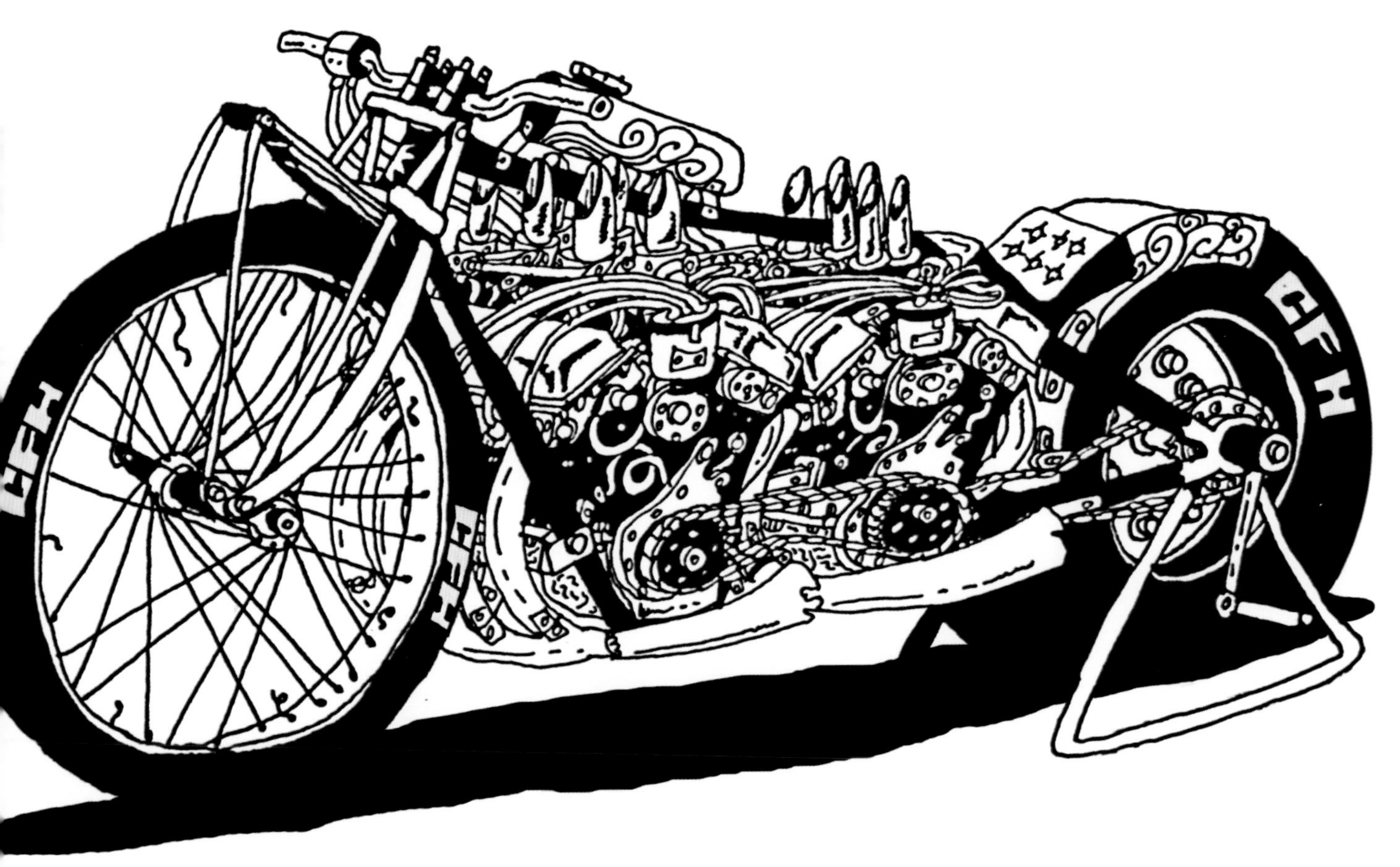

ABOVE: ***Drag V8.***
Ink on paper.

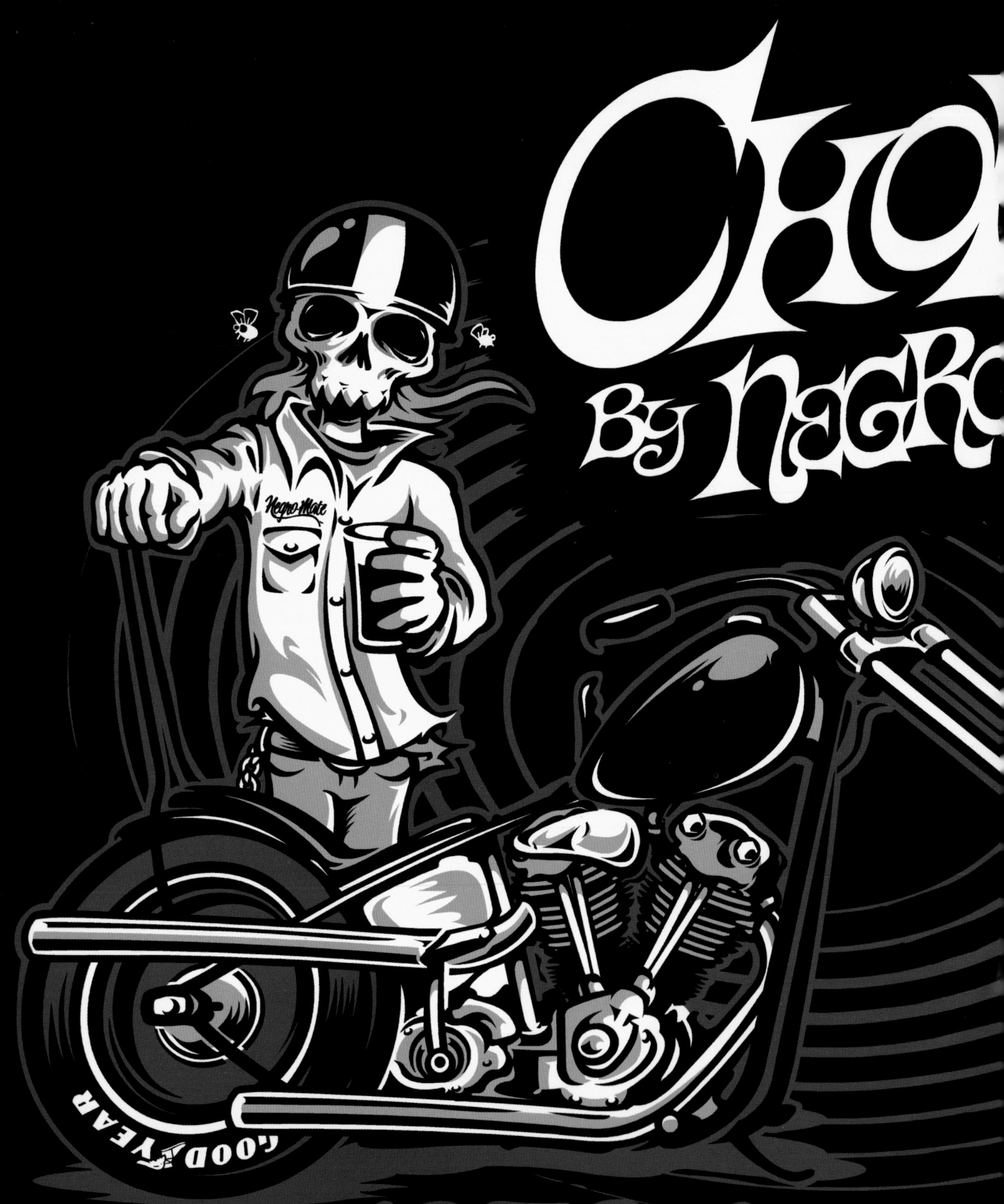
By
Negro-Mate
GOODYEAR
1972
Swedish
KNUCKLEHEAD

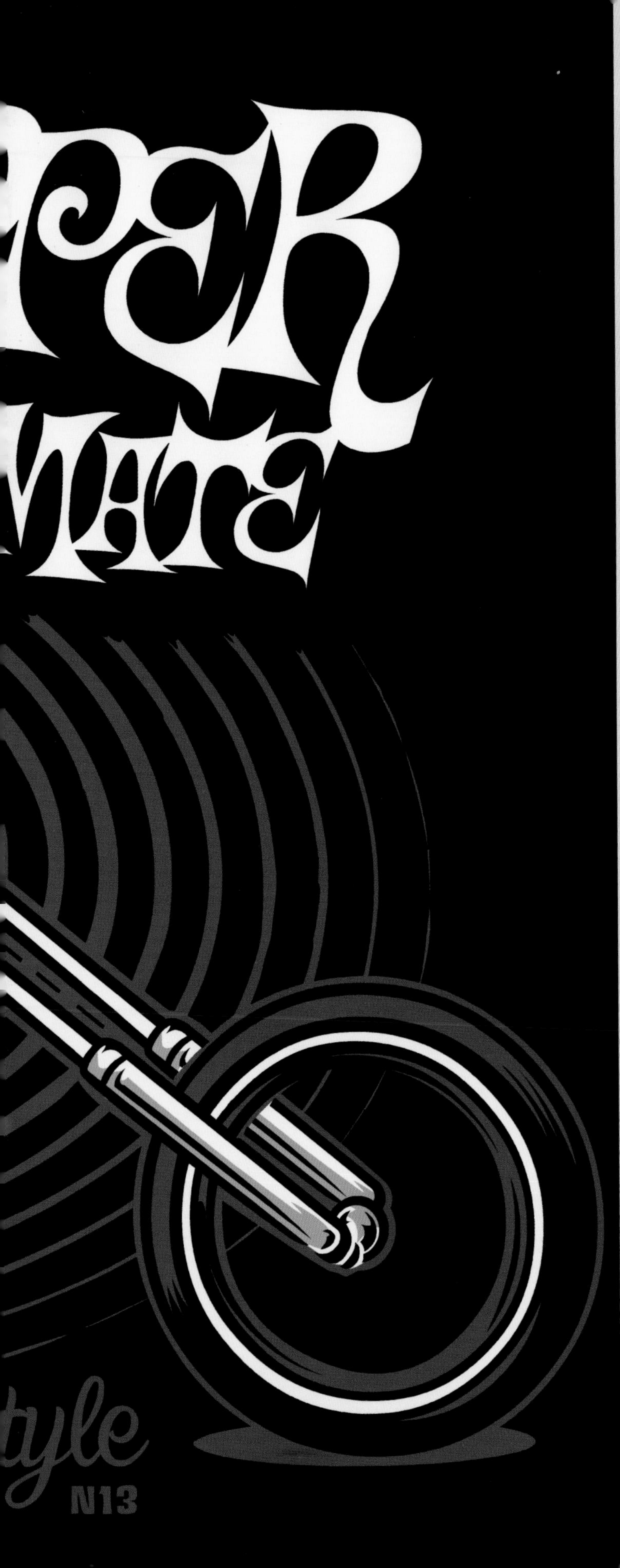

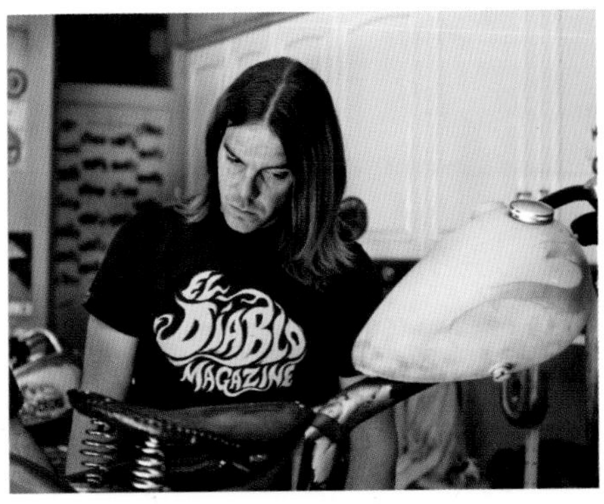

ALEX PATROCINIO

The creative force behind BurnClan Kustom Graphics and the online kustom kulture magazine, *El Diablo,* Alex Patrocinio grew up in and around Barcelona. He studied at the best comic college in Spain, Escola Joso Cómic, before joining the Spanish Army. "Now I live back in Corbera de Llobregat, near Barcelona. I love the mountains and I have my best friends, wife and my two sons here." His inspirations are a familiar roll call of skateboard graphics, heavy metal music, comic books, Tarantino films, hot rods, his tutors and motorcycles. "Motorcycles are my life, my passion. Motorcycles are dangerous, they have only two wheels and they are the evolution of horses. I've ridden since I was 16 and all the bikes I've owned have been custom bikes. It's my favourite style of bike."

Alex's work is much in demand. He has produced commissions for Negro Mate Clothing, Jesse James' West Coast Choppers, the former MotoGP racer Sete Gibernau, *El Diablo Magazine*, Andy's Body Electric Tattoo, *Sideburn* magazine, Barcelona Harley Days and Dirk Behlau...to name only a few.

LEFT: *Chopper by Negro-Mate.*
Pencil on paper and digital.

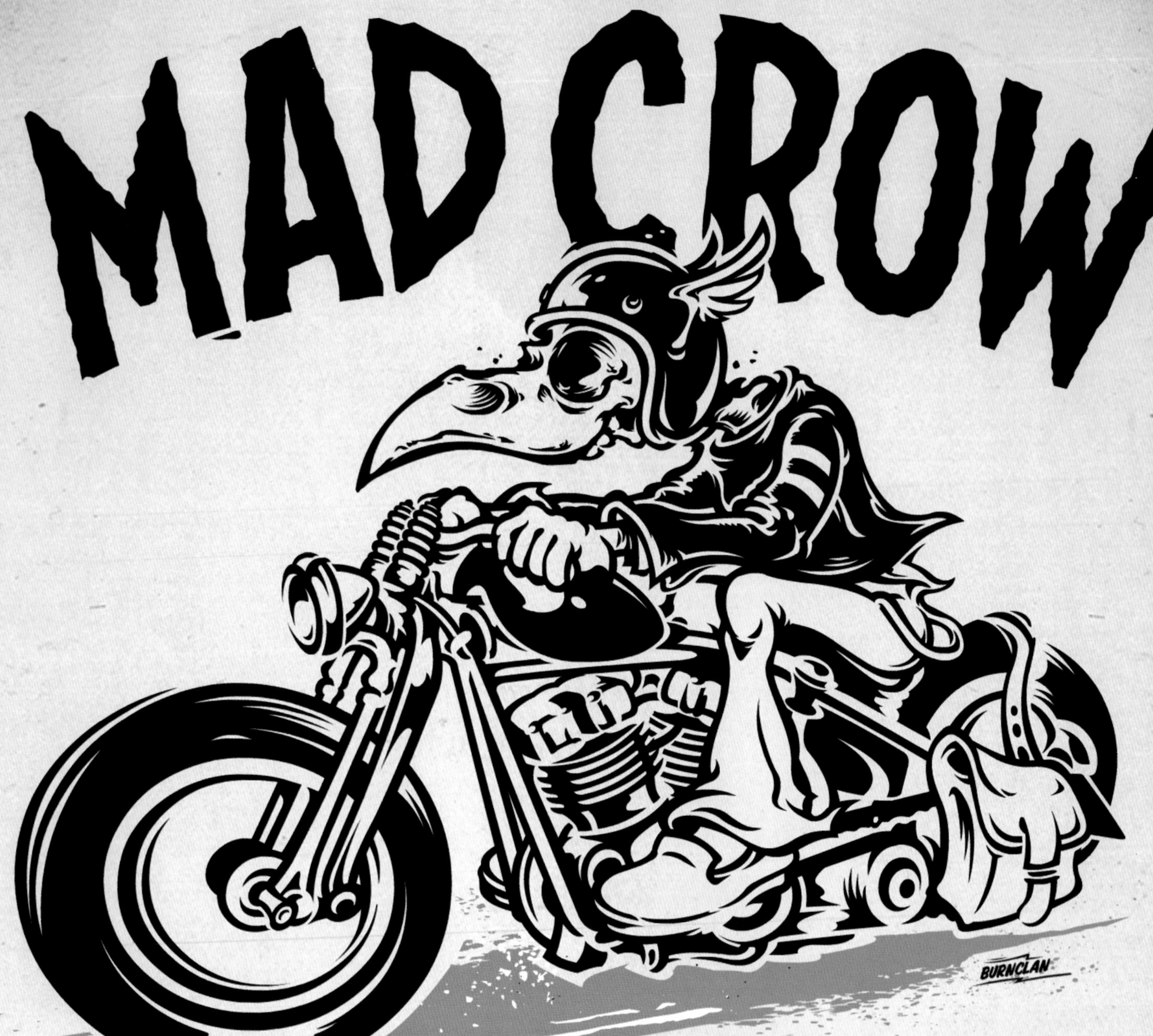
MAD CROW
BURNCLAN
GARAGE

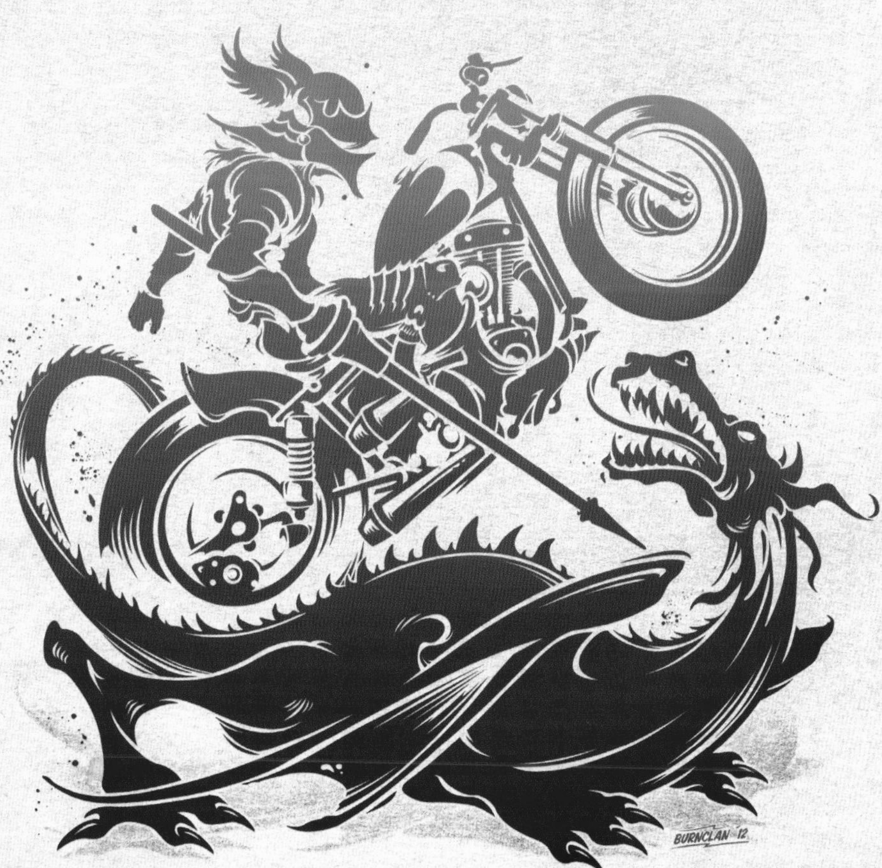

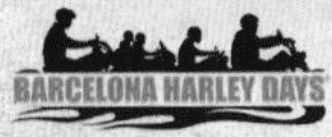

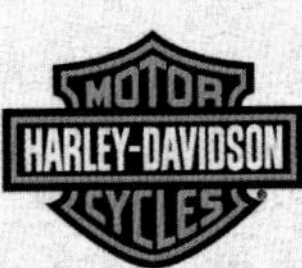

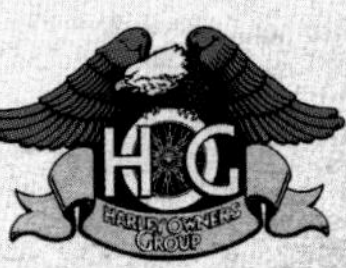

LEFT: ***Harley Days, Barcelona 2012.*** Pencil on paper and digital.

FAR LEFT: ***Madcrow Garage Samurai Bobber.*** Pencil on paper and digital.

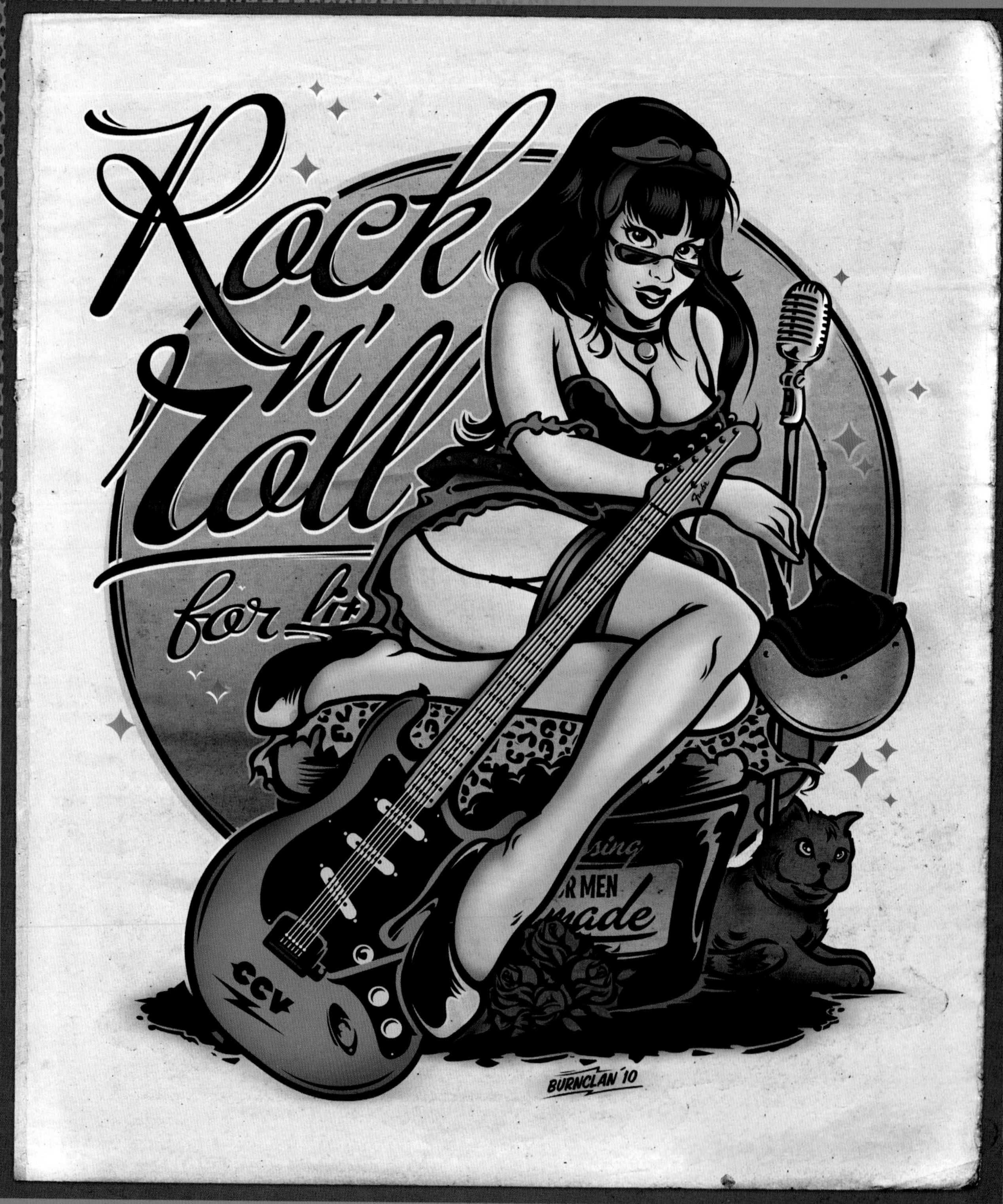

ABOVE: ***Camil Valls Rock Strato Girl.***
Pencil on paper and digital.

RIGHT: ***Boardtrack 1912.***
Pencil on paper and digital.

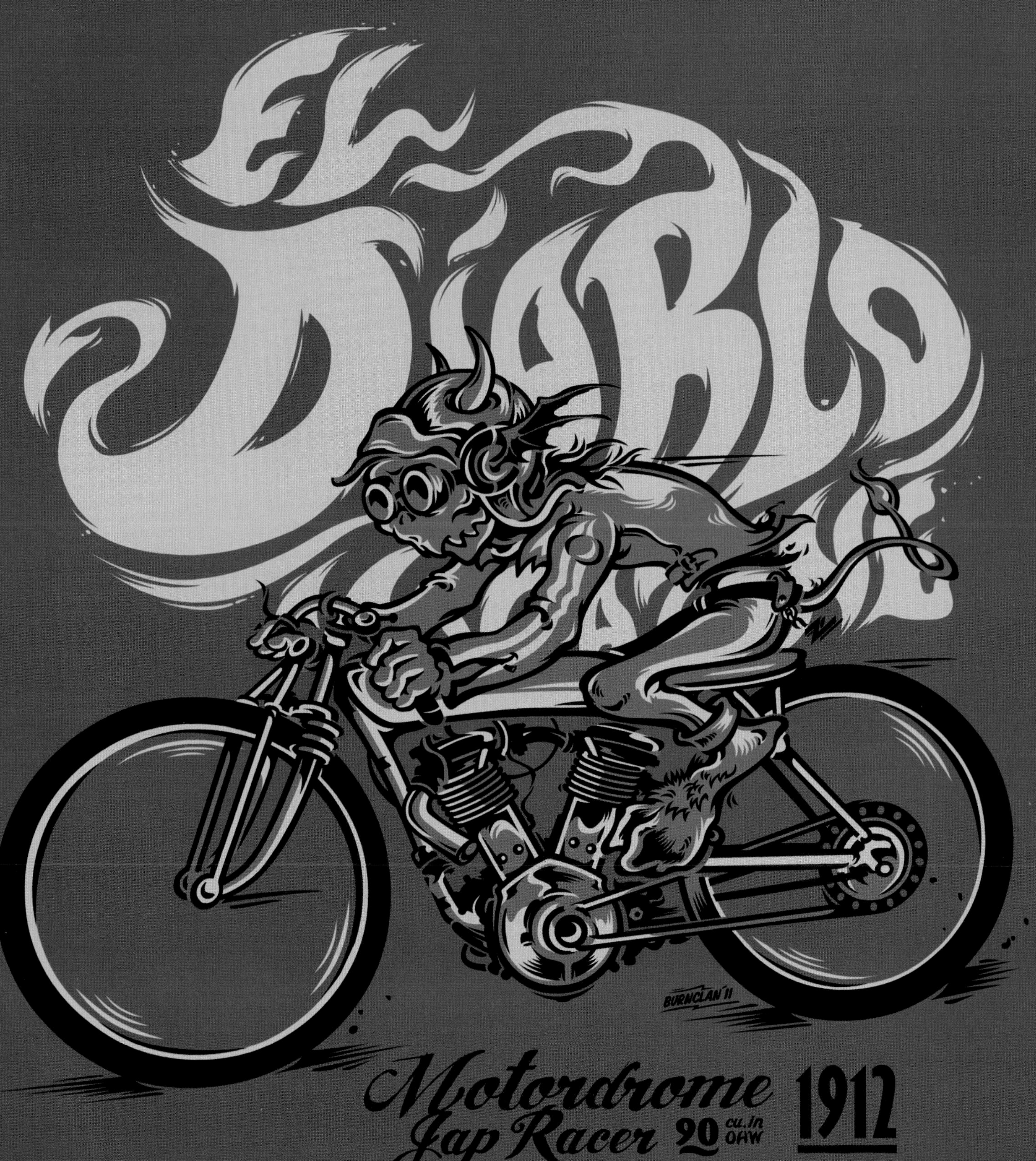
El Diablo
BURNCLAN '11
Motordrome
Jap Racer
90 cu.in OHV
1912

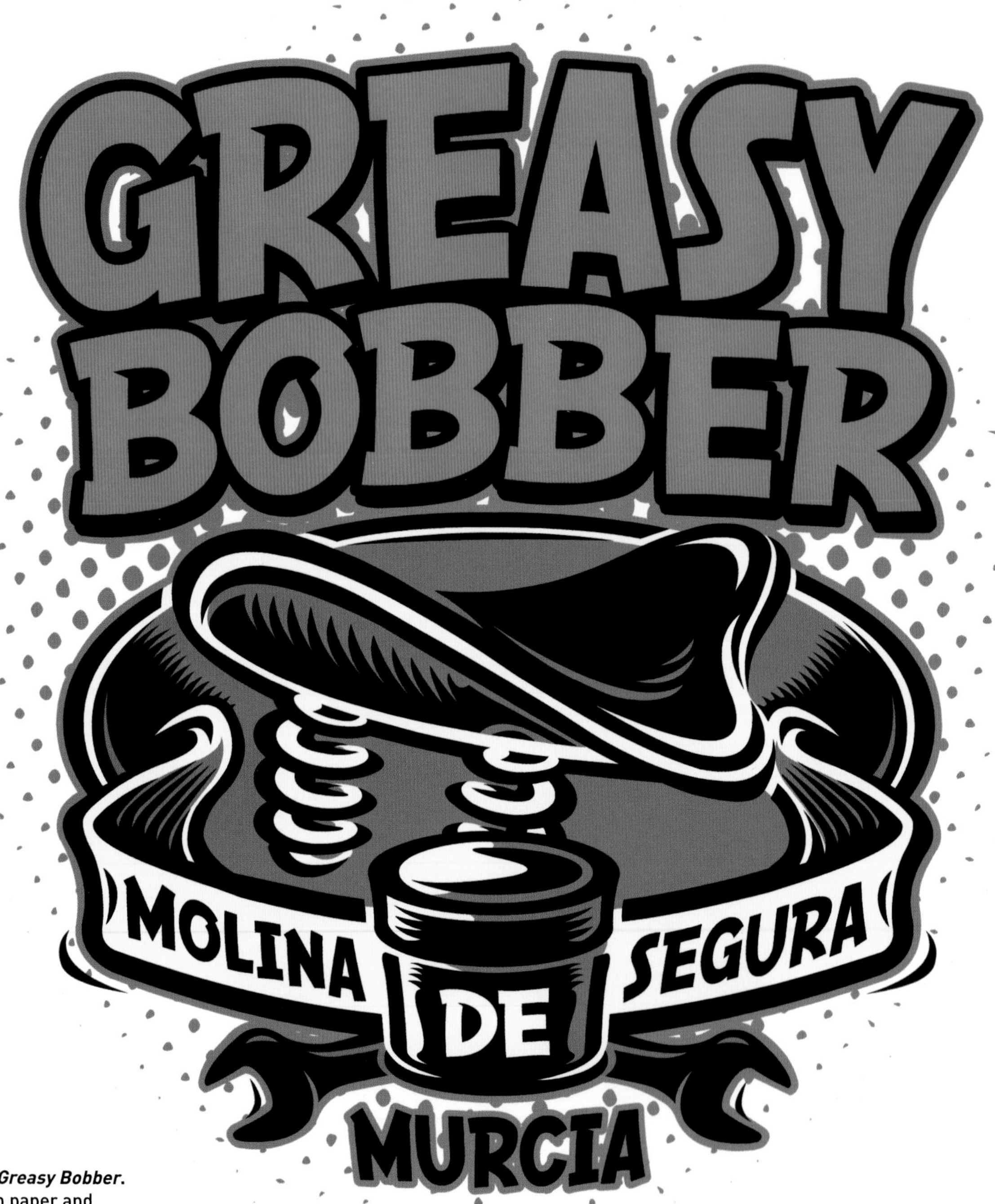

ABOVE: ***Greasy Bobber*****.** Pencil on paper and digital.

FAR RIGHT: Logo design for Sete Gibernau. Pencil on paper and digital.

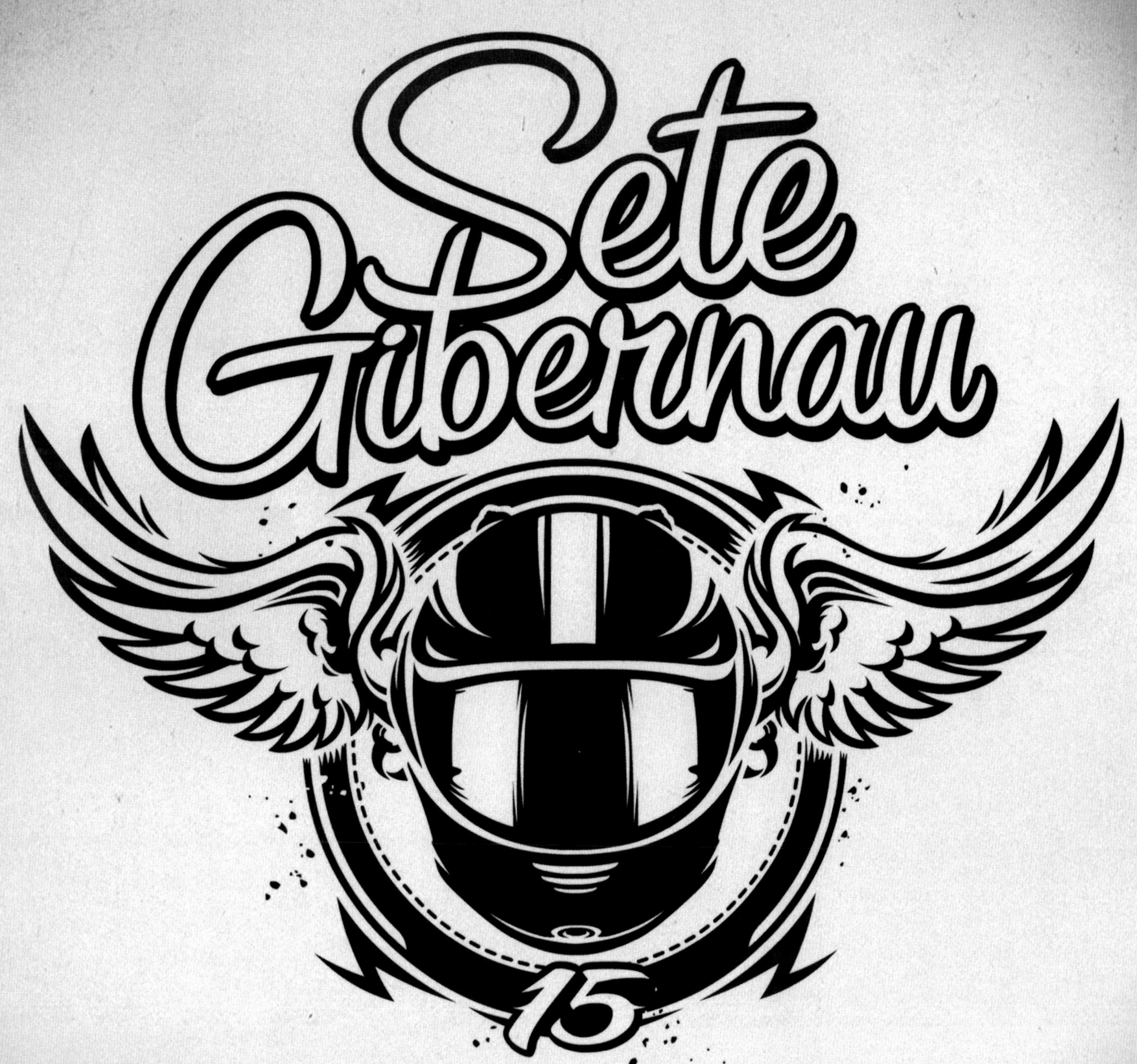
Sete
Gibernau
15

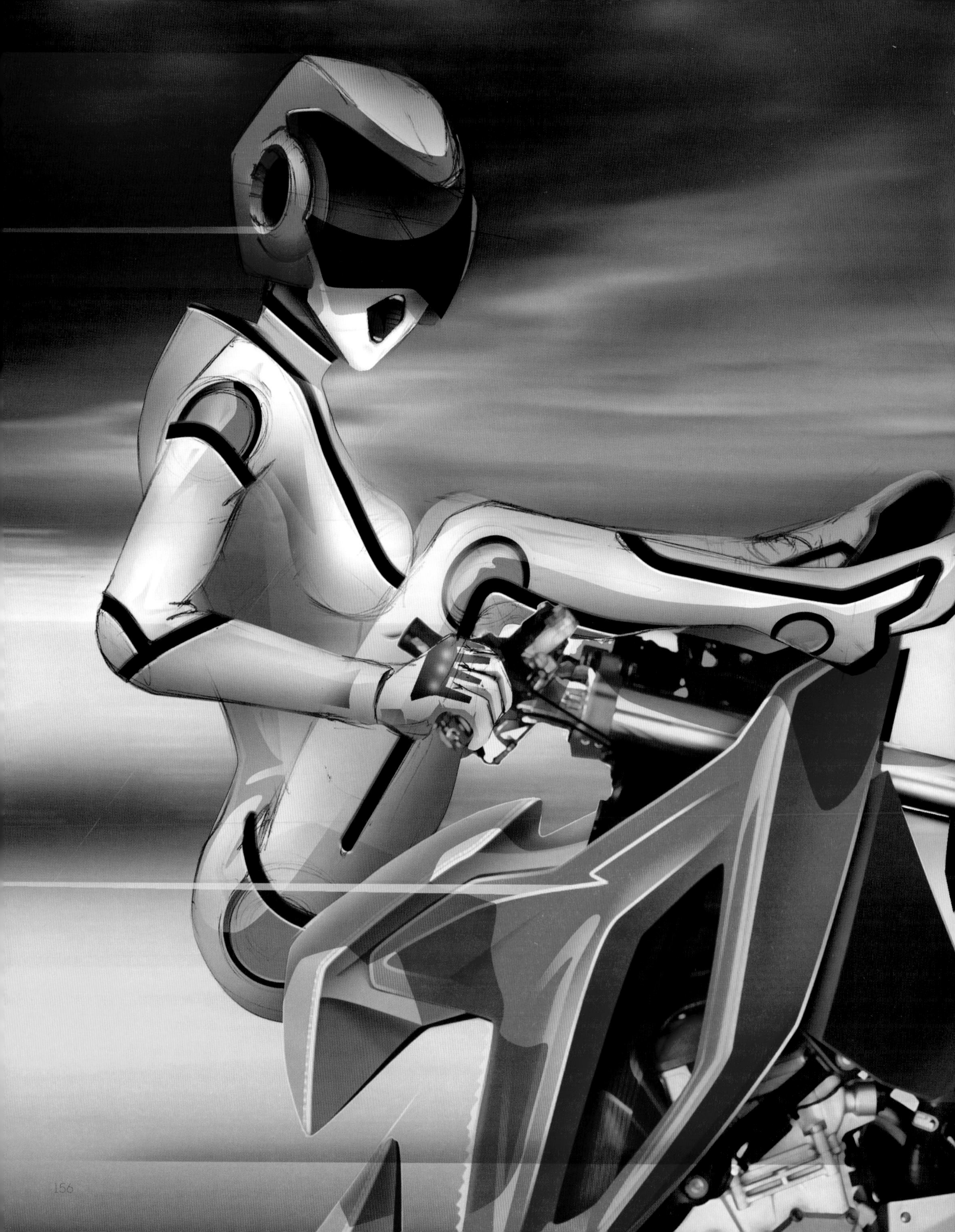

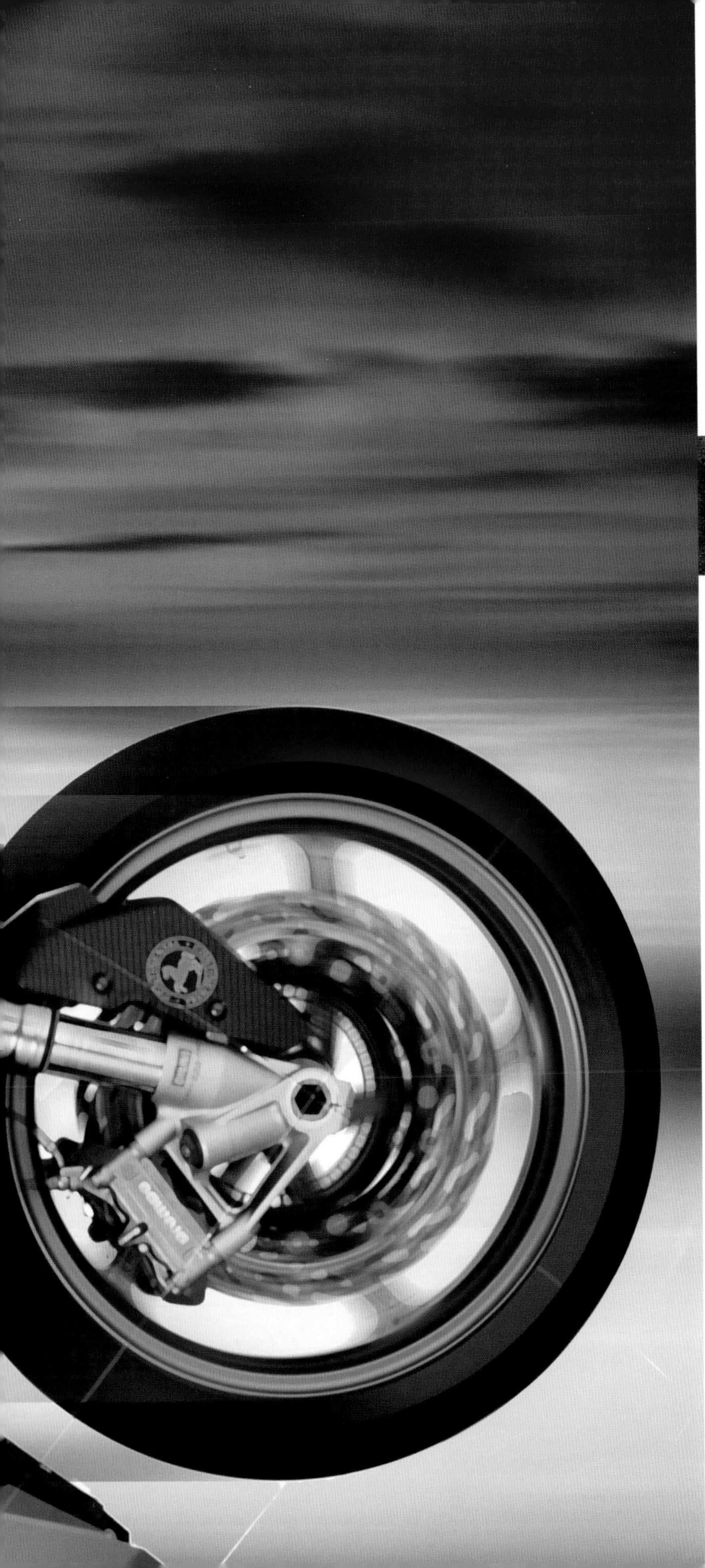

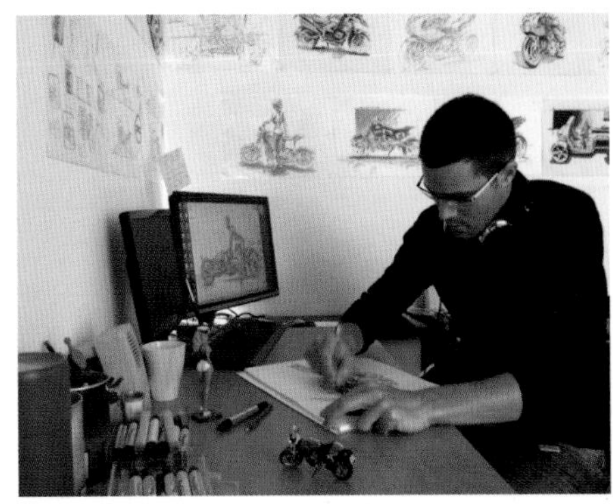

NICOLAS PETIT

The son of a BMW motorcyle dealer, young Nicolas Petit was never a fan of the German machinery. "I always found these motorcycles totally ugly," says the Frenchman. "When I would get back from school to the family garage, I loved to imagine them with the other, sexier forms. I began to draw with a typical cartoon style because I always read comic strips. It is probably why I often put a sexy girl on a project. A bike is always more alive with a character."

Today Nicolas is a freelance designer working within the motorcycle industry and creates his concept art to develop ideas. He works with pen and ink, but also makes composites with 3D modelling programs like Alias Autodesk.

"I work with pencil, roller pen and twin-tip marker to begin a project, as I look for ideas or for a style..."

And he owns a BMW now...

LEFT: *Girl in Fenwick- Husqvarna 1000R.*
Pencil base, digital colours.

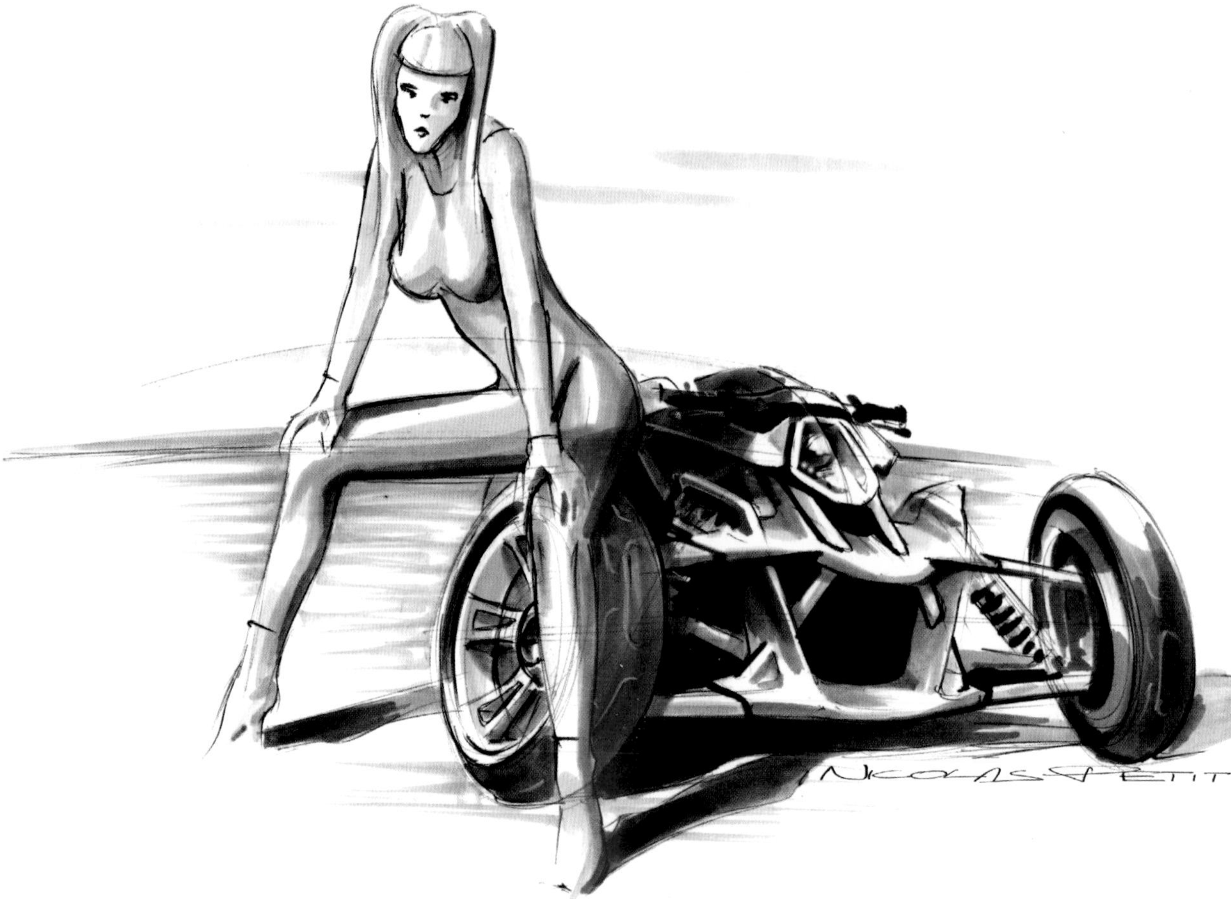

ABOVE: ***Pinup on 3-Wheeler – Ducati Desmosedici.***
Black pen, cold grey marker and white pencil on layout paper.

RIGHT: ***Happy New Year 2012.***
Black pen, cold grey and coloured markers and white pencil on layout paper.

FAR RIGHT: ***Midnight Tokyo – Yamaha Shenron and Girl Rider.***
Black pen base, digital colours.

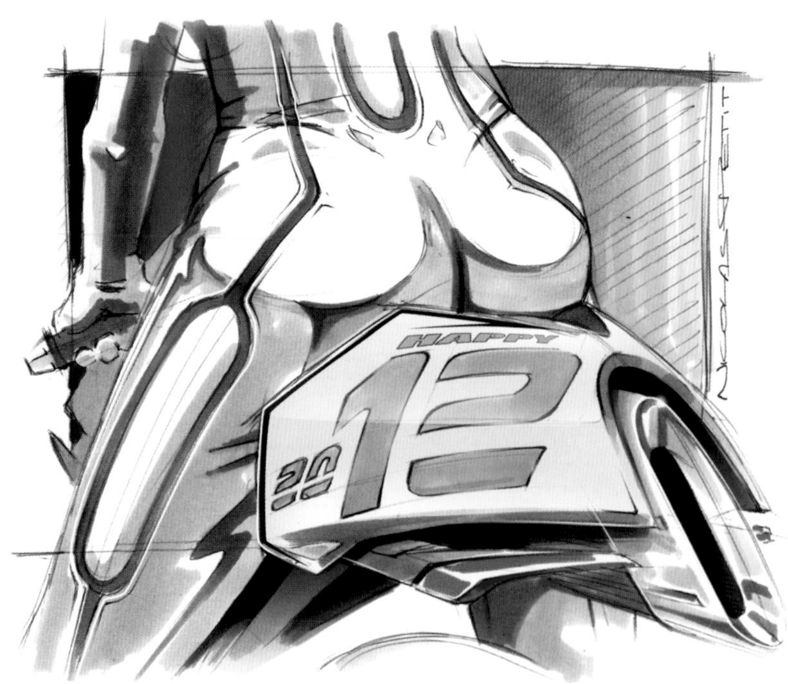

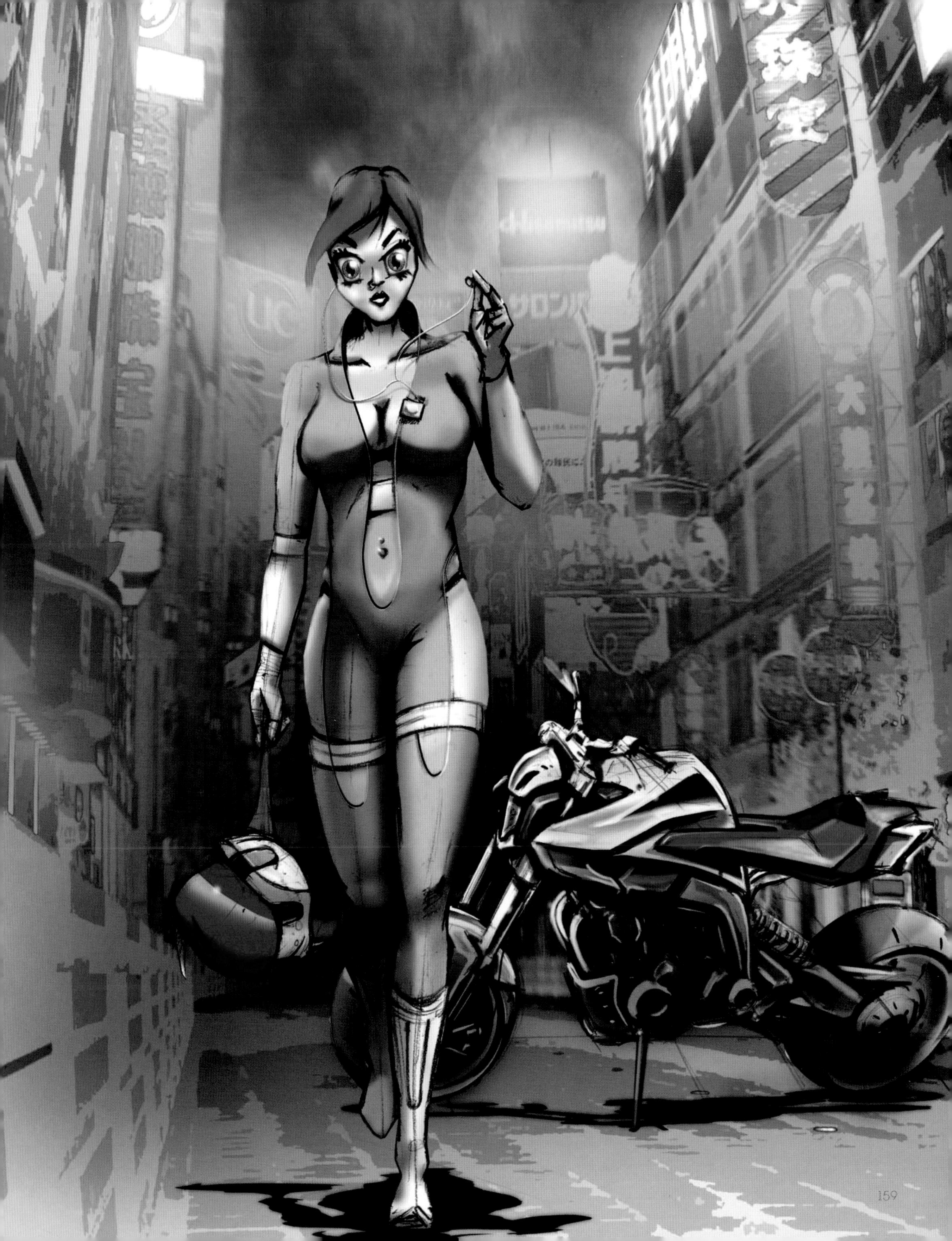

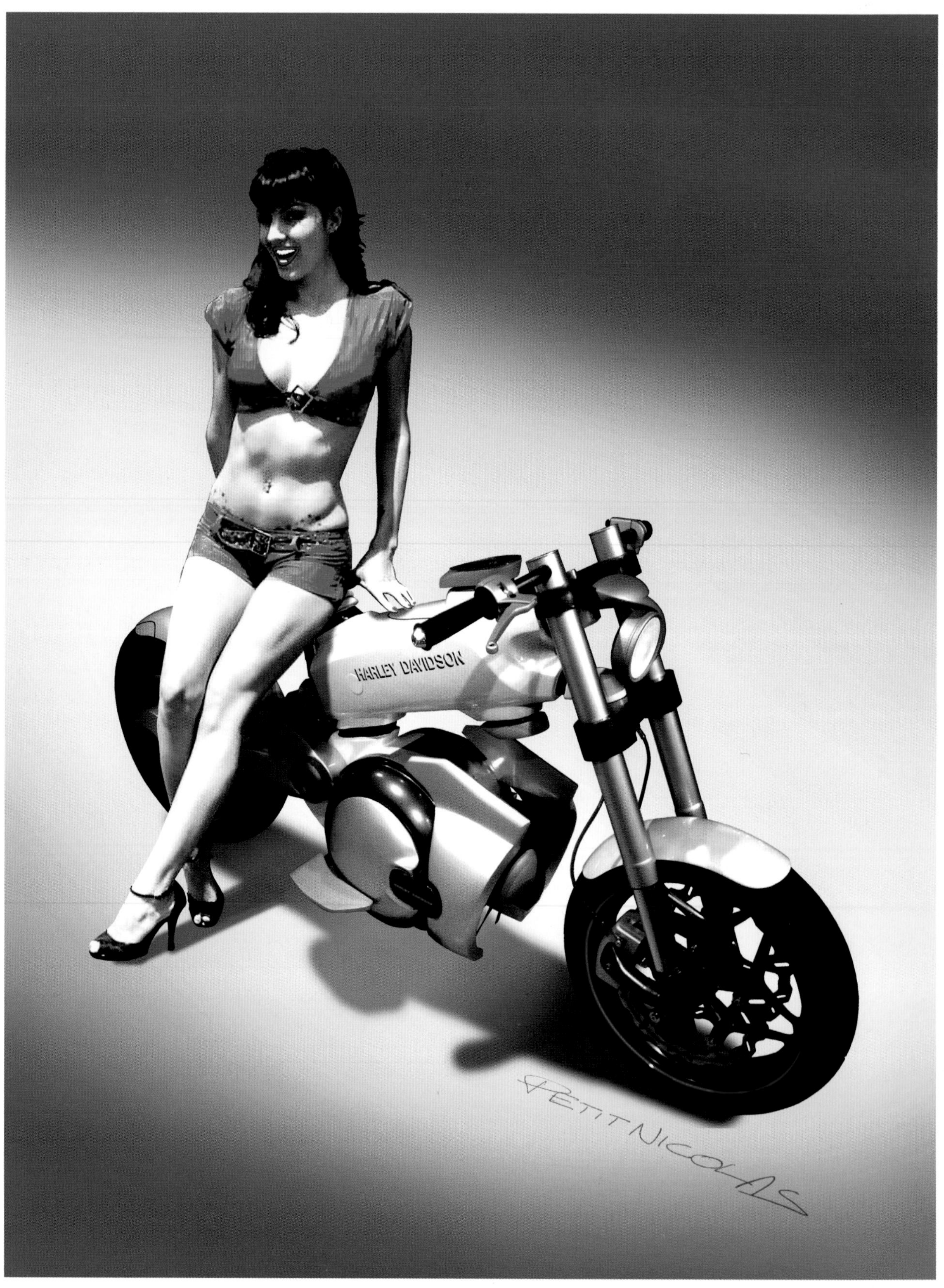
HARLEY DAVIDSON
PETIT NICOLAS

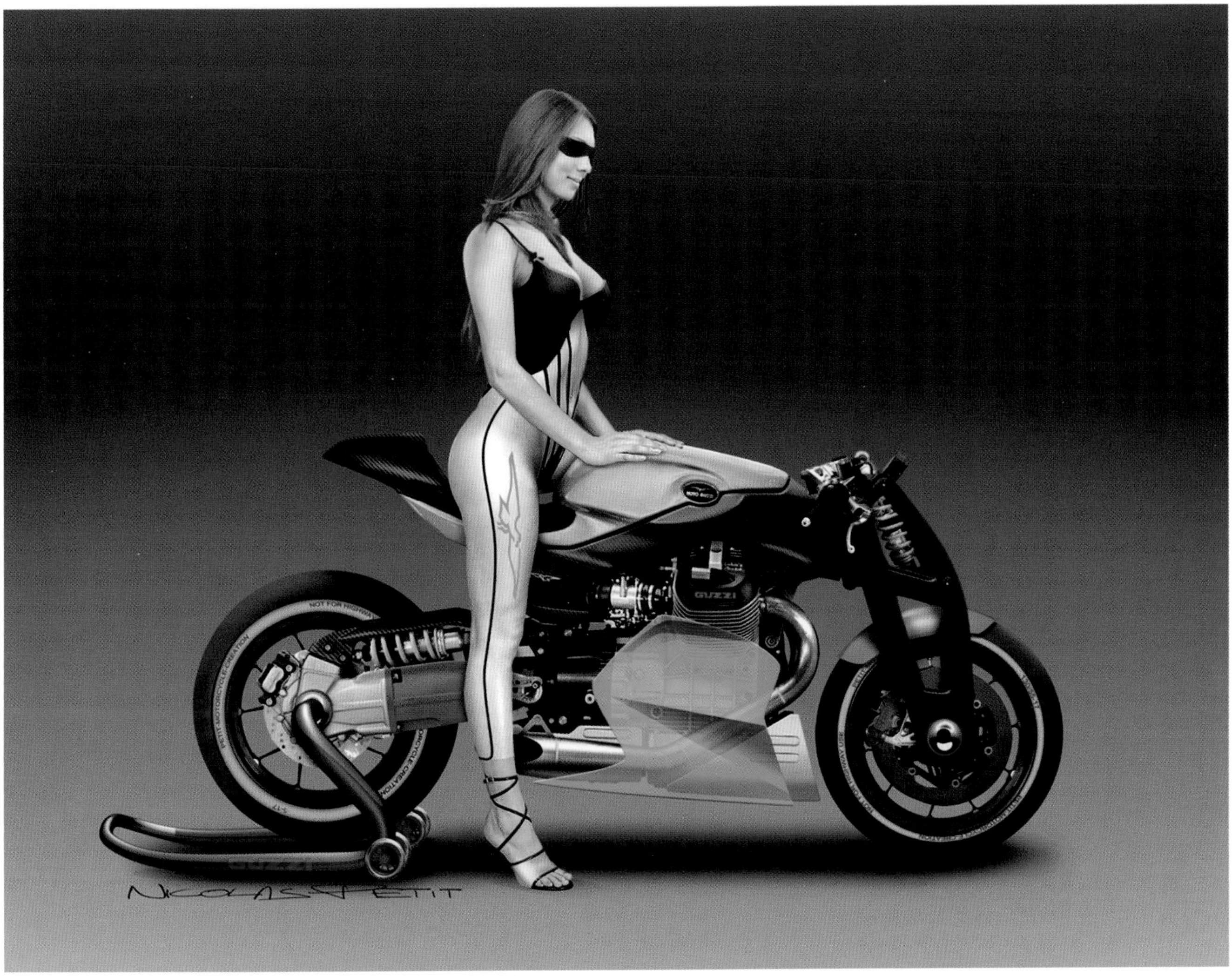

ABOVE: ***Guzzi Big Twin Naked.***
Digital art, 3D render, digital photography.

RIGHT: ***Kawasaki Drag - Enginatural Creation.***
Black pen, cold grey and coloured markers and white pencil on layout paper, digital retouch.

LEFT: ***Trunk Harley Davidson – Ecologique Creation.***
Digital rendering from the prototype 1:1 scale model and digital photography.

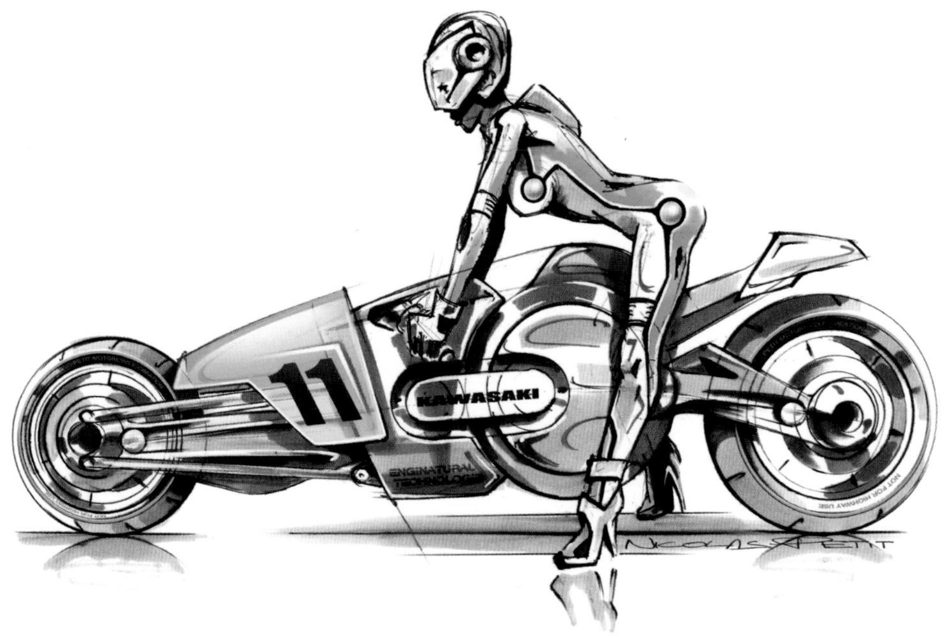

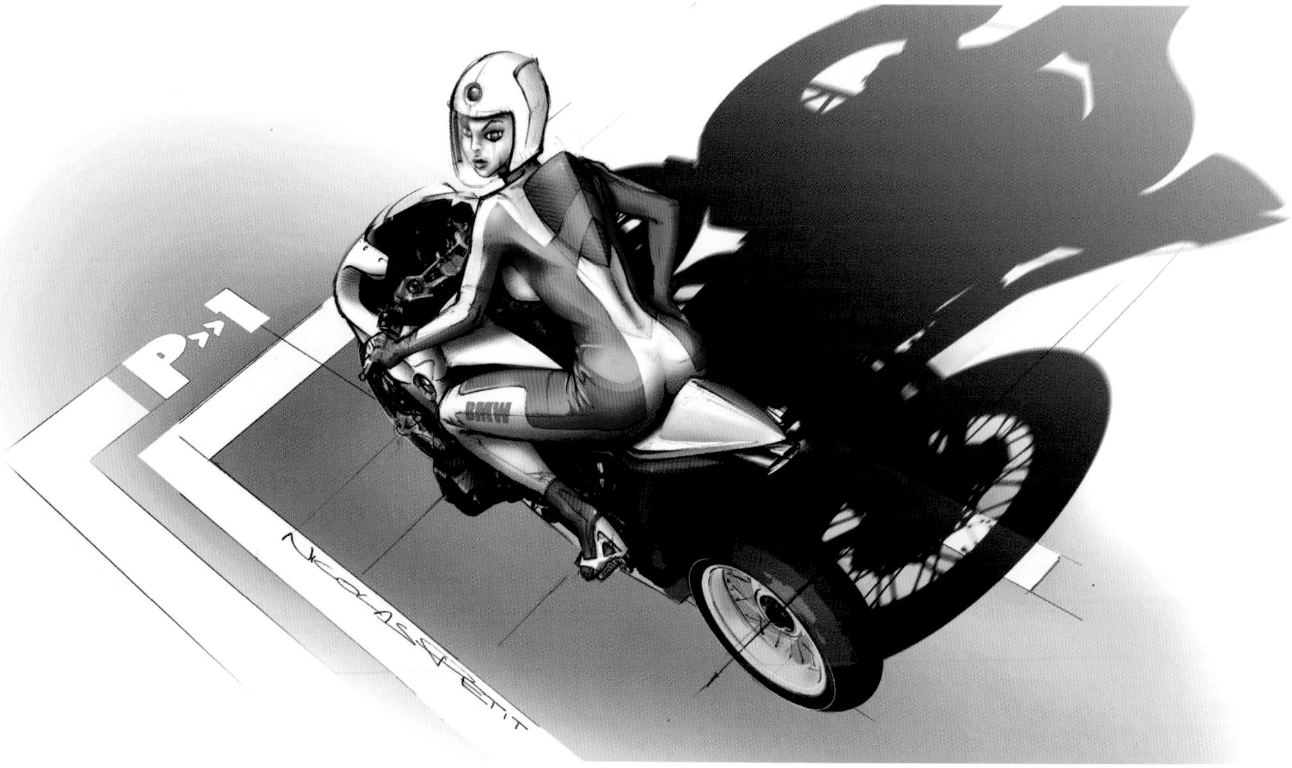

ABOVE: ***BMW Cafe Racer.***
Black pen, cold grey and coloured markers and white pencil on layout paper, digital retouch.

RIGHT: ***BMW Big Twin Naked.***
Digital art, 3D render and digital photography.

FAR RIGHT: ***Mono and Girl – Speed Research – Enginatural Creation.***
Black pen, cold grey and coloured markers and white pencil on layout paper, digital retouch.

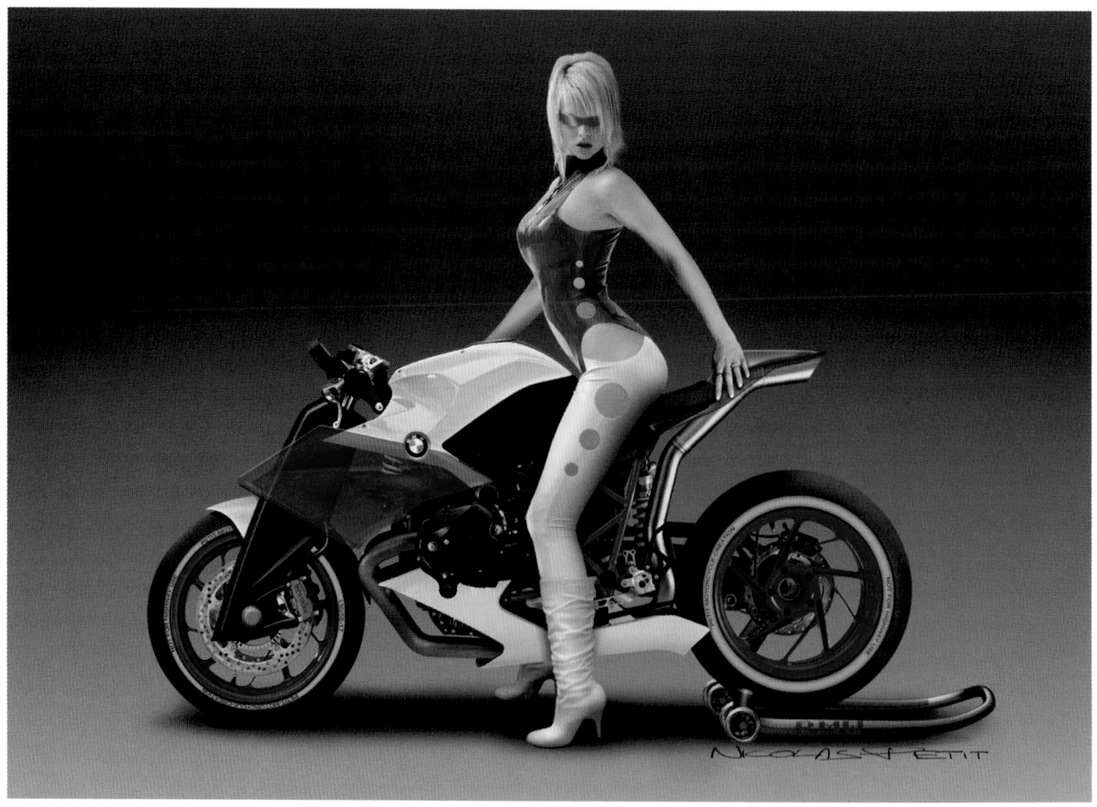

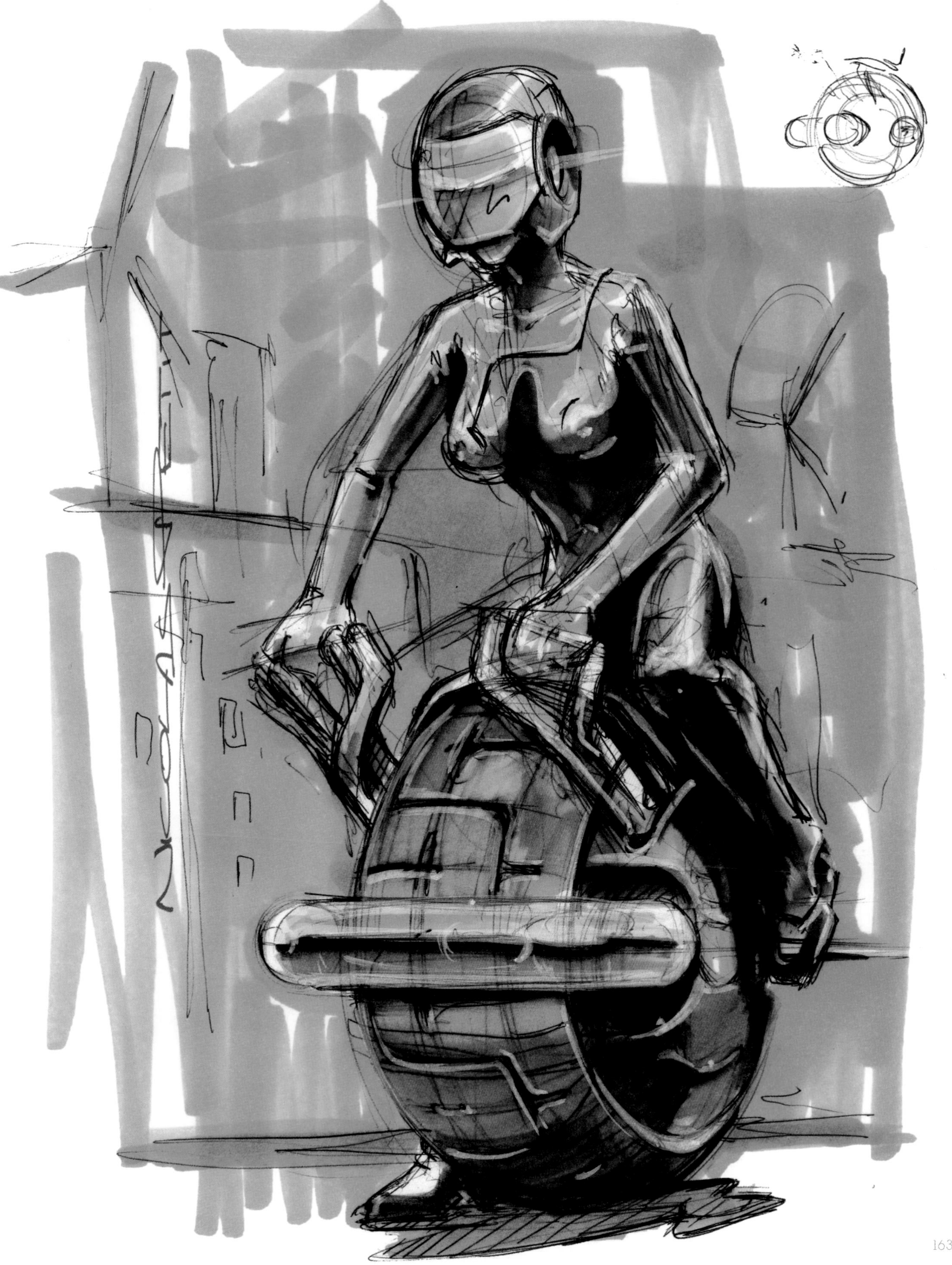

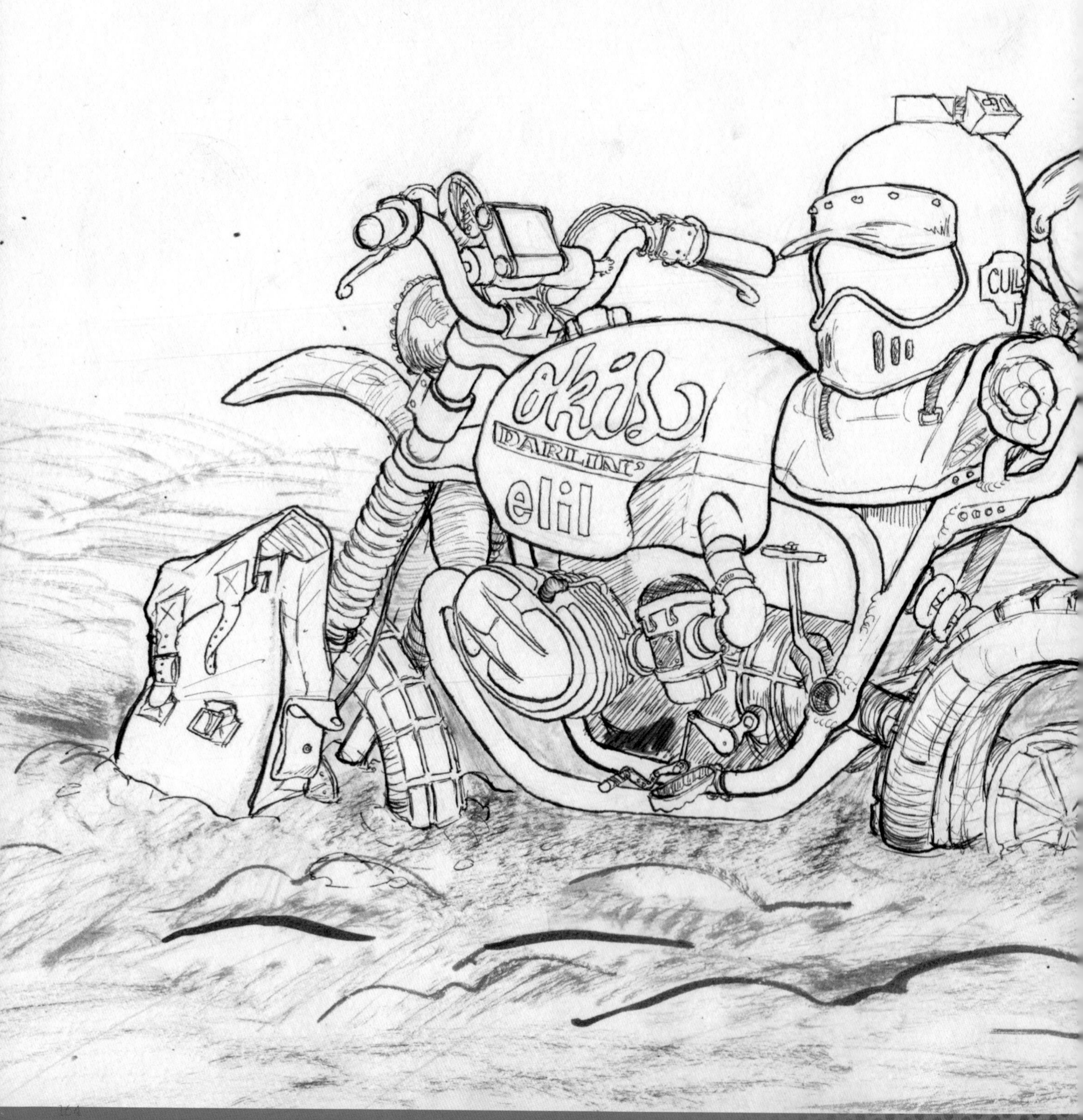
CUL
DARLIN'
elil

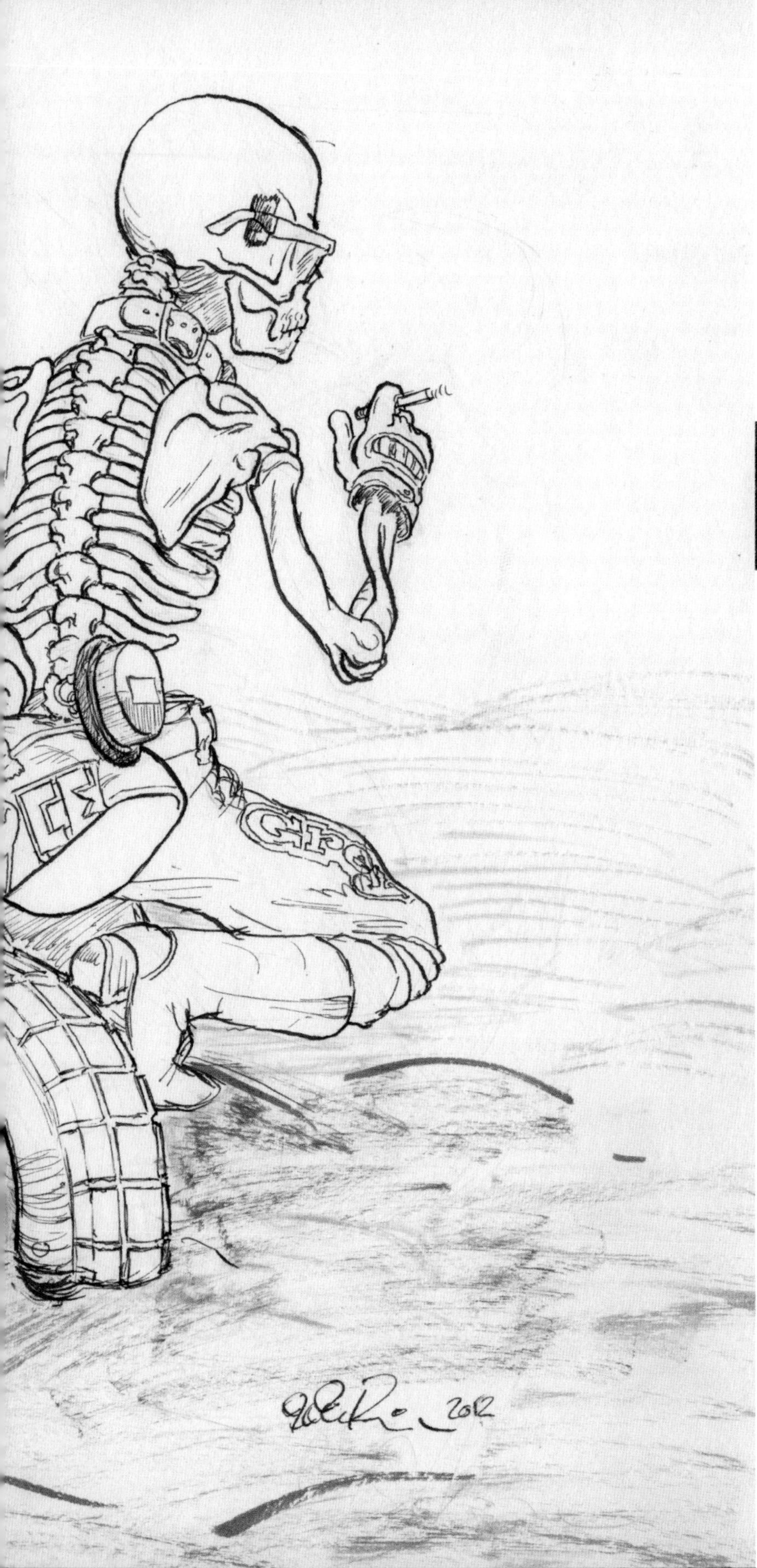

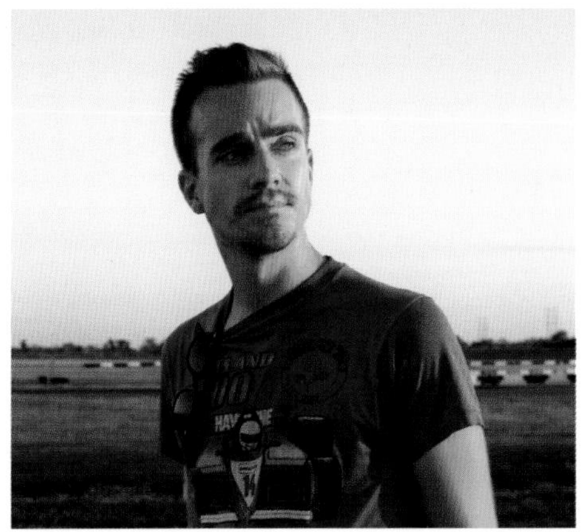

WILL PIERCE

Will Pierce grew up in East Texas with "Lots of diesel thump-rattle, dirt, the open road." Now he lives in Houston because, "You get to feel like NASA and the Astrodome are part of you." Contrary to that first impression, Will reckons, "I've never been a storyteller, but I love narrative. As a kid I loved drawing a single picture and then seeing all the implied drama and character in it; as I got better I stopped trying to figure out what was happening in a piece and then began letting the piece tell me what it wanted to be." When it comes to addressing a range of clients, Will has got the extremes covered. "I designed a patch for a tactical weapons supplier and am in the process of illustrating two childrens' books." He is precise about his sketching technique. "I prefer high-tooth 98 lb paper, switching pencils as much as I can to keep the feeling of the stroke fresh and surprising. For inking, I typically use a Speedball No.107 dip pen, but lately have become entranced with ink brushing. After years of using the 107 it's shocking how fast-smooth-sexy brushwork is." When it comes to motorcycles, Will would prefer to swap fast-smooth-sexy, for basic and versatile. "I lust for efficiency and utility without compromise."

LEFT: *Okis.*
Dip pen with acrylic ink on paper.

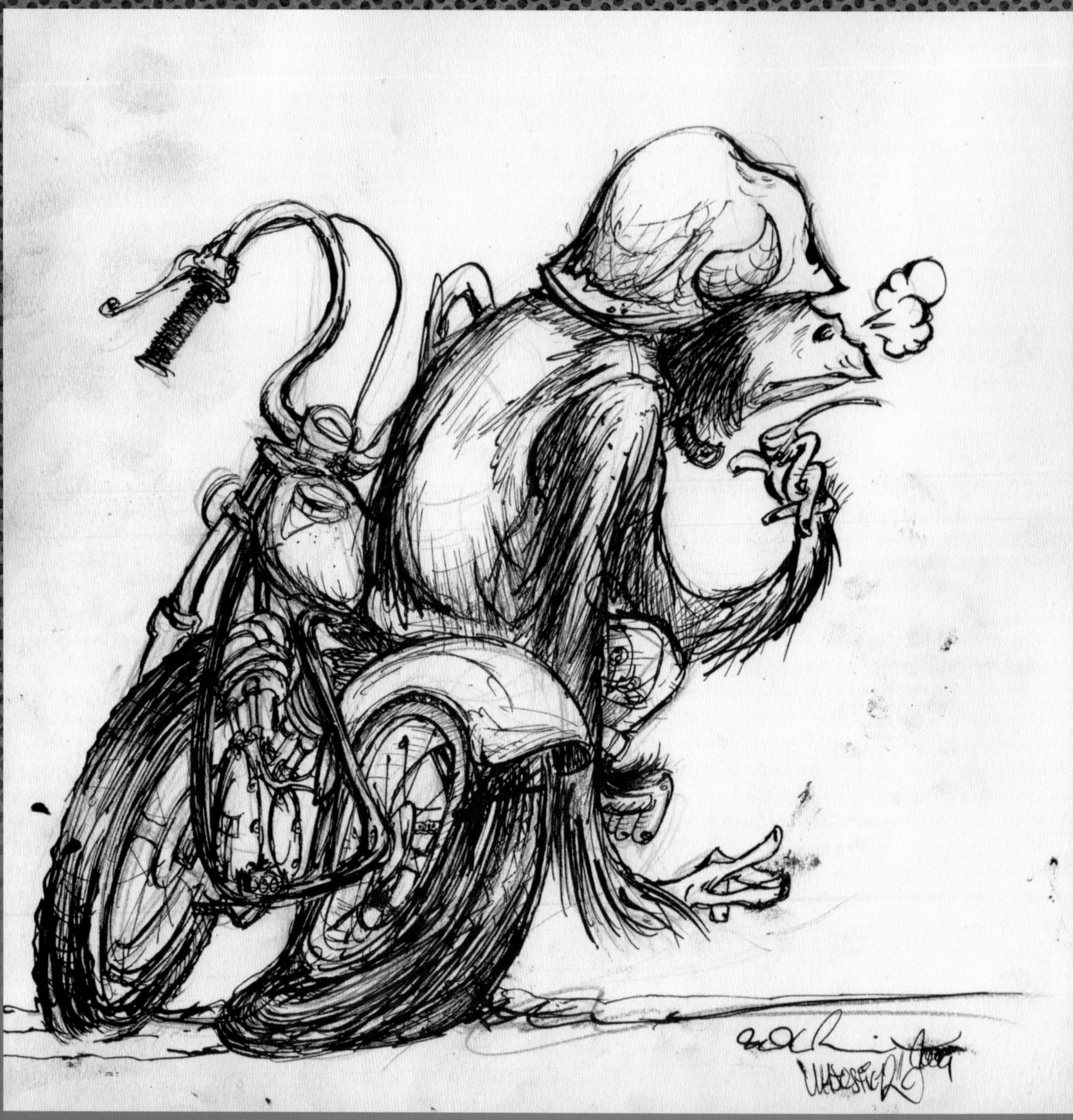

ABOVE: ***Journey to the West.***
Dip pen with acrylic ink on paper.

RIGHT: ***Sarastro.***
Dip pen with acrylic ink on paper.

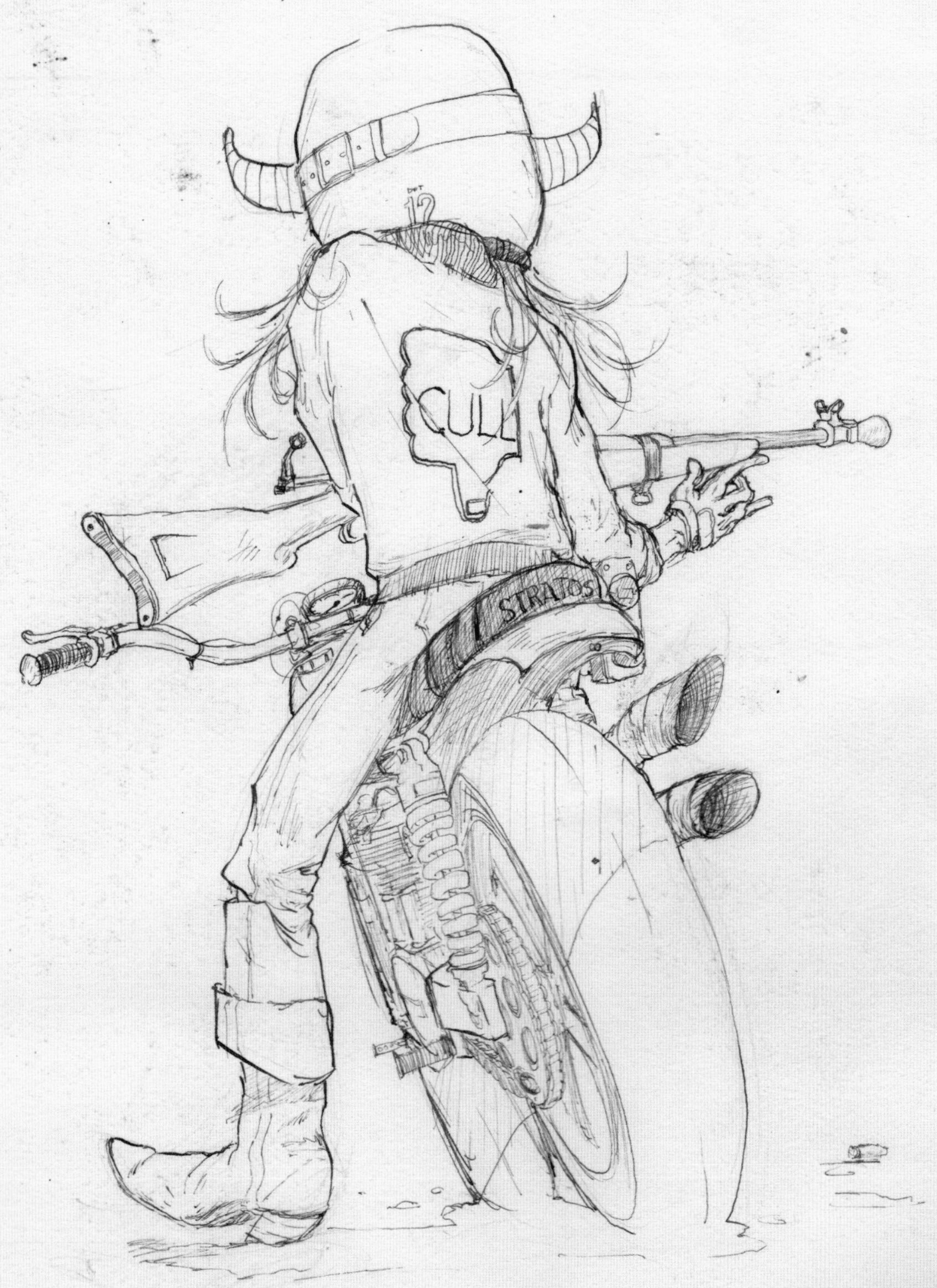
12
CULL
STRATOS

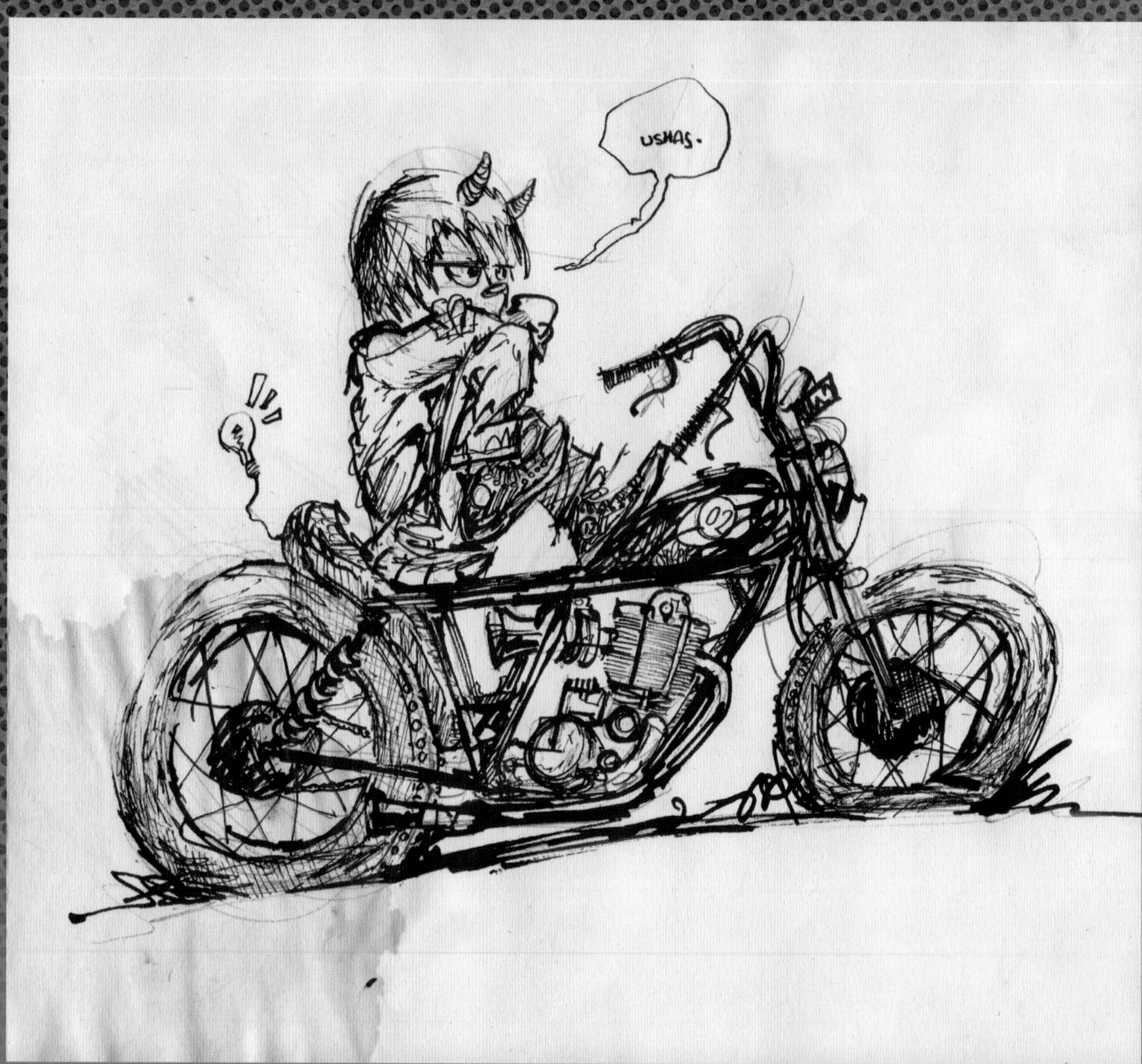

ABOVE: ***Ushas.***
Dip pen with acrylic ink on paper.

RIGHT: ***Born Free.***
Ink on paper.

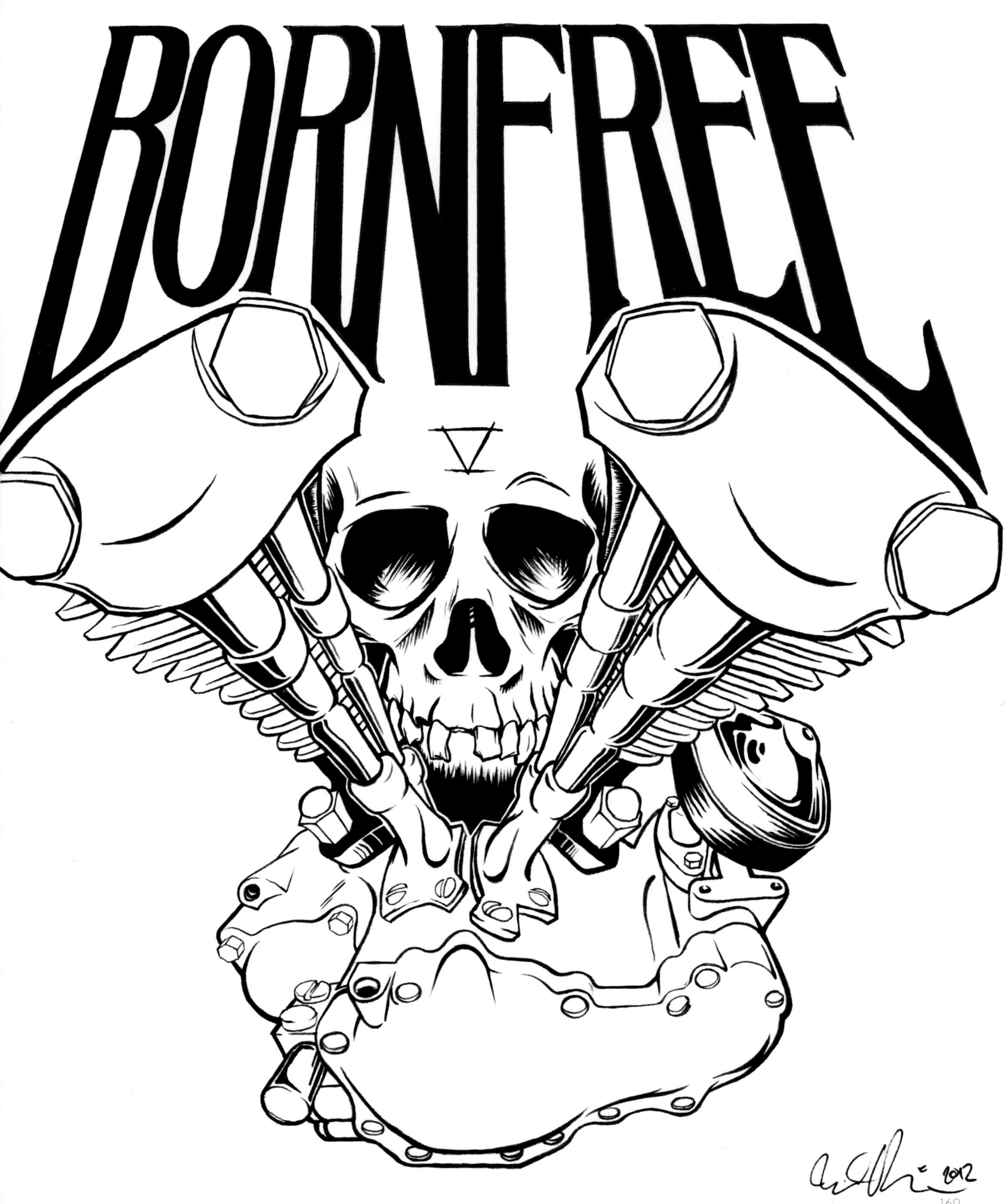
BORNFREE
2012

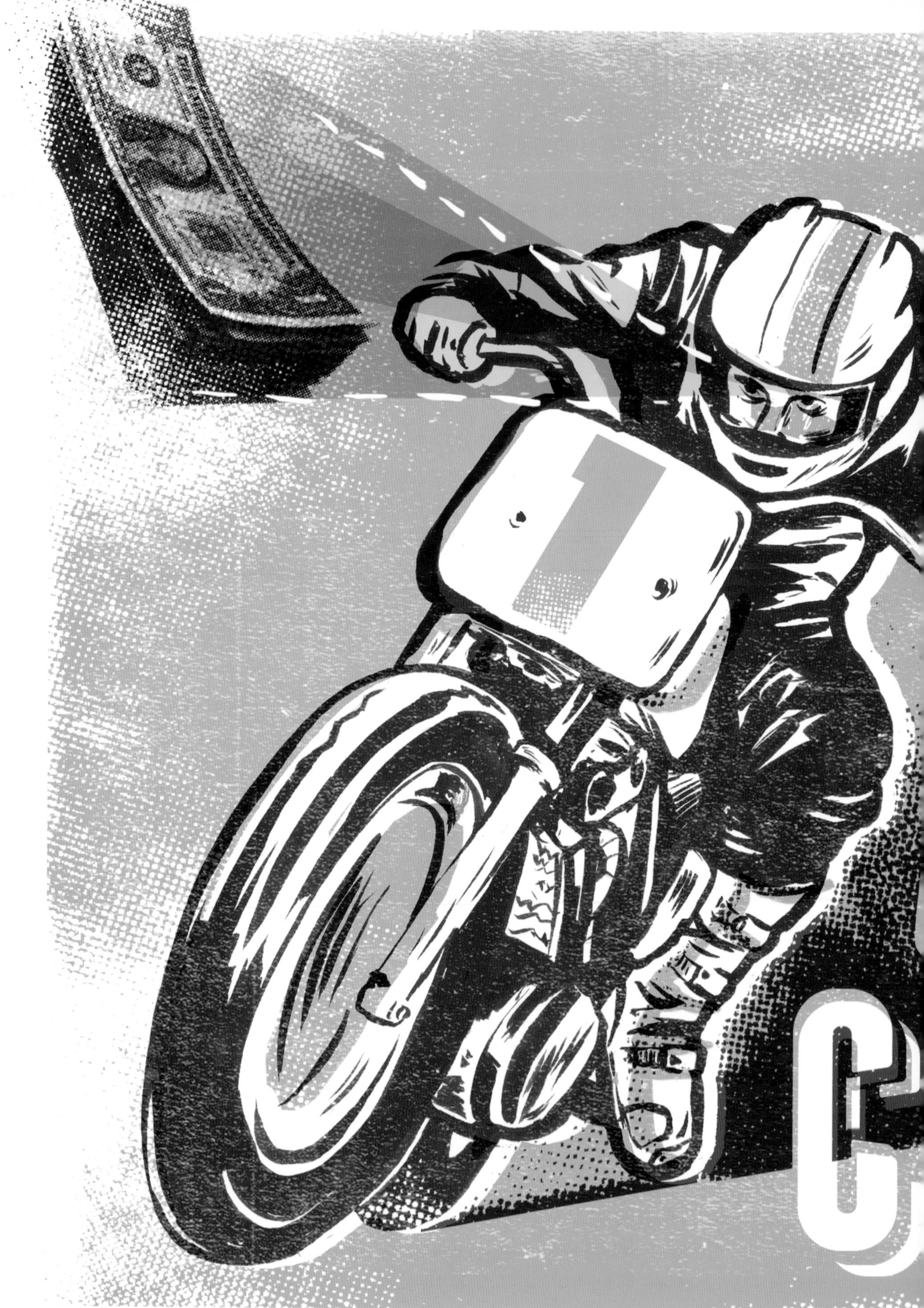

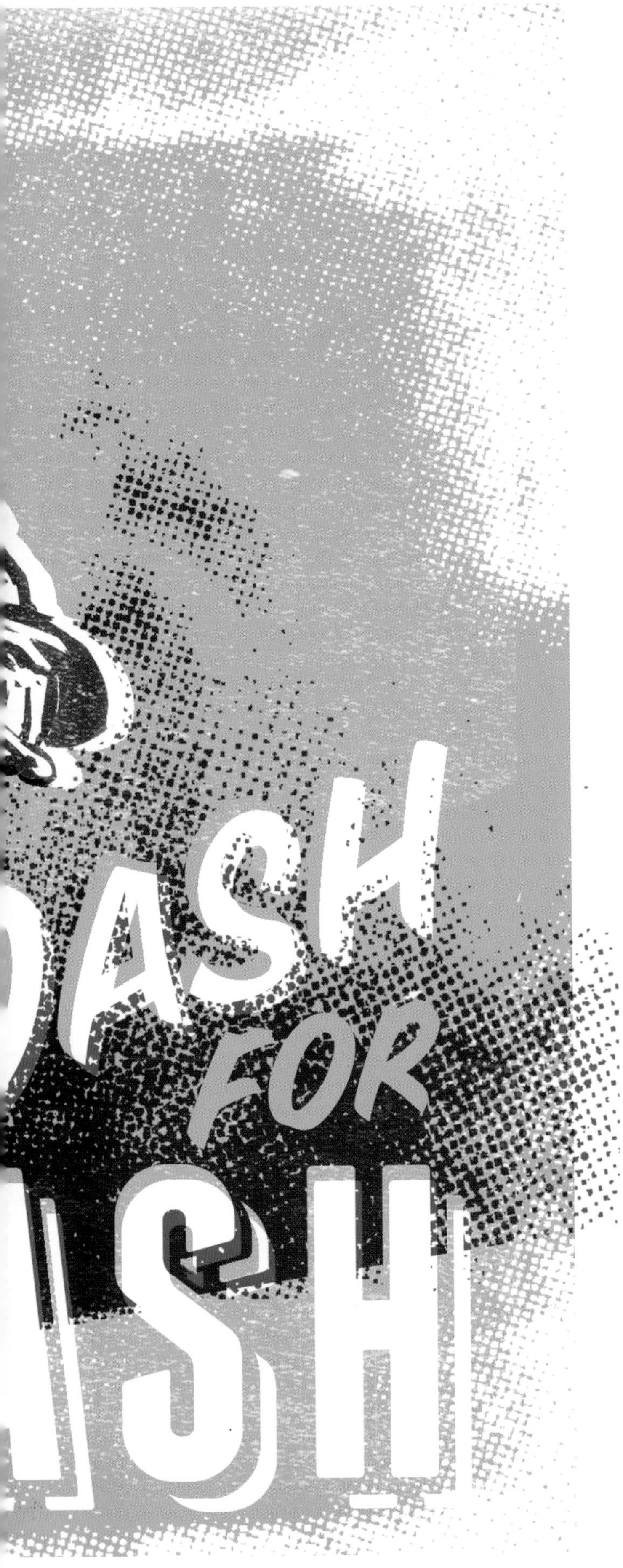

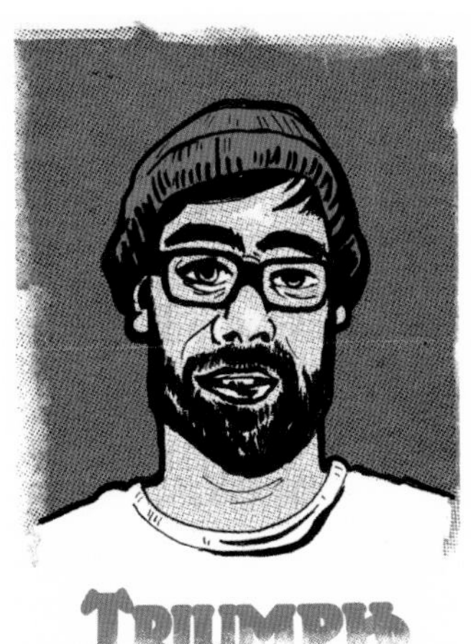

RYAN QUICKFALL

"I knew my injury was bad when the doctor took out his phone and asked if he could take a picture." It was a cold, slimy, British winter's day, the kind that makes people emigrate, and Ryan had just crashed his Yamaha R6 sportsbike on spilt diesel. For some, that would've been the end of bikes, but not Ryan. "Heal yourself then get back onboard, that's the way to deal with it they say. So that's what I did." Quickfall – rather an unfortunate name for a motorcyclist – earns his living creating logos and brand identities for companies around the world. "My most fun job was designing graphics for motocross teams. I got to see a lot of the industry and meet some great people." Today his work is split down the middle: commercial and personal. The commercial is mostly created digitally. The personal stuff "generally undergoes a completely different process, due to fewer restraints." Much of this work is intended to be screenprinted. Ryan is also experimenting with larger format artworks, incorporating mixed media, screenprinting and collage. "My inspiration for these is '50s and '60s advertising and poster art."

LEFT: ***Dash For Cash.***
Brush and ink, digital colours.

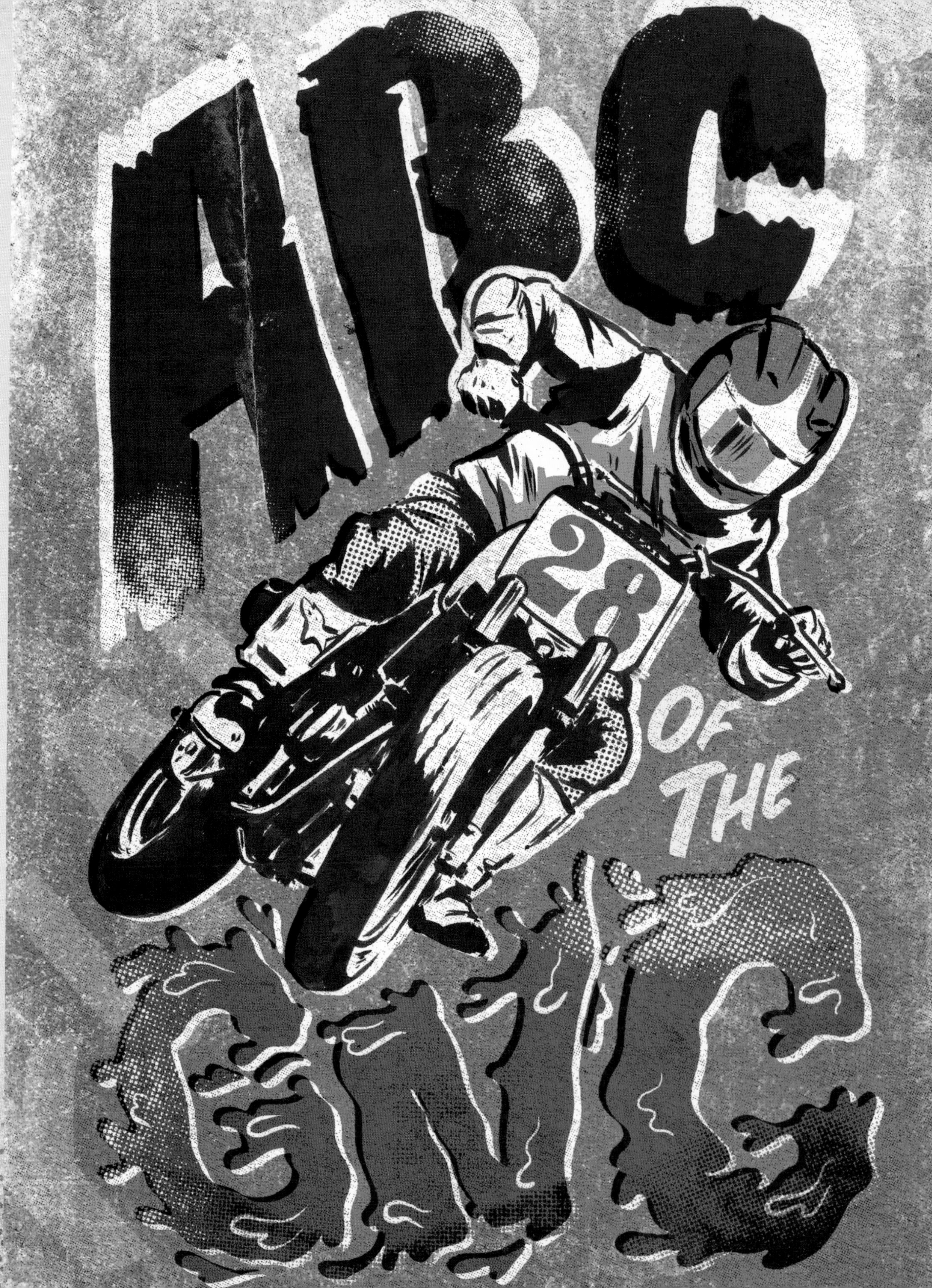
ABC
28
OF
THE

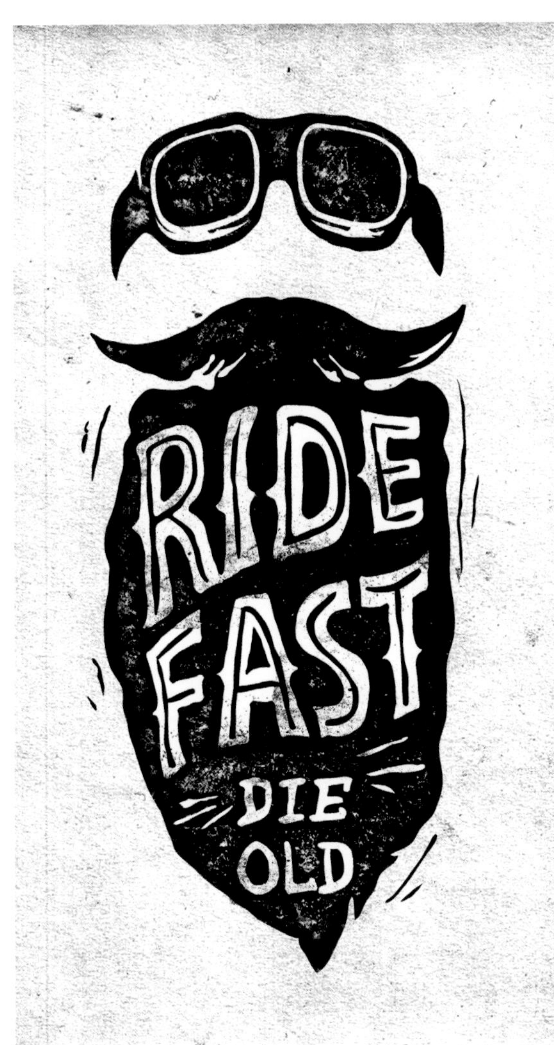

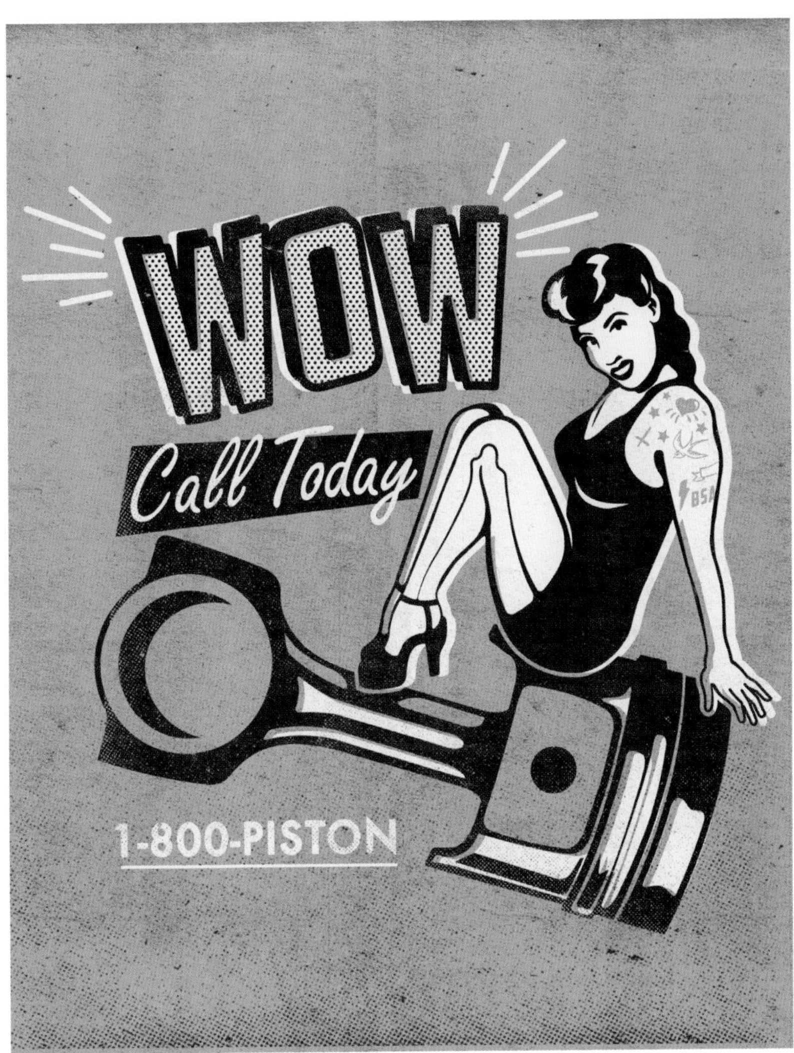

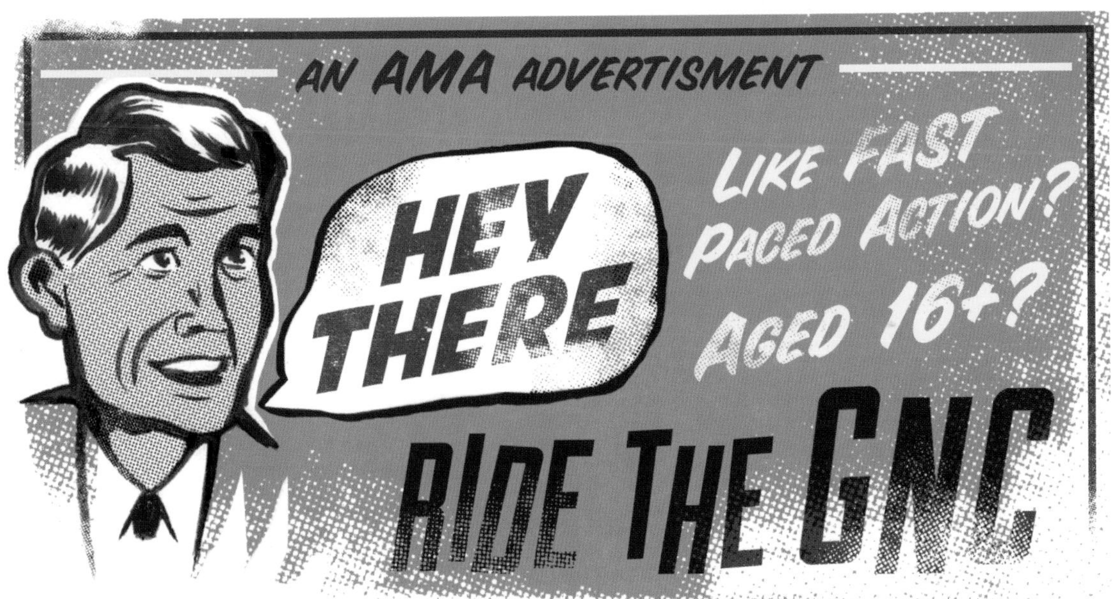

ABOVE LEFT: ***Ride Fast Die Old.***
Ink and digital texture.

ABOVE: ***1-800-Piston.***
Digital artwork.

LEFT: ***Hey There.***
Ink and digital.

FAR LEFT: ***The ABC of GNC.***
Brush and ink, digital colours and texture.

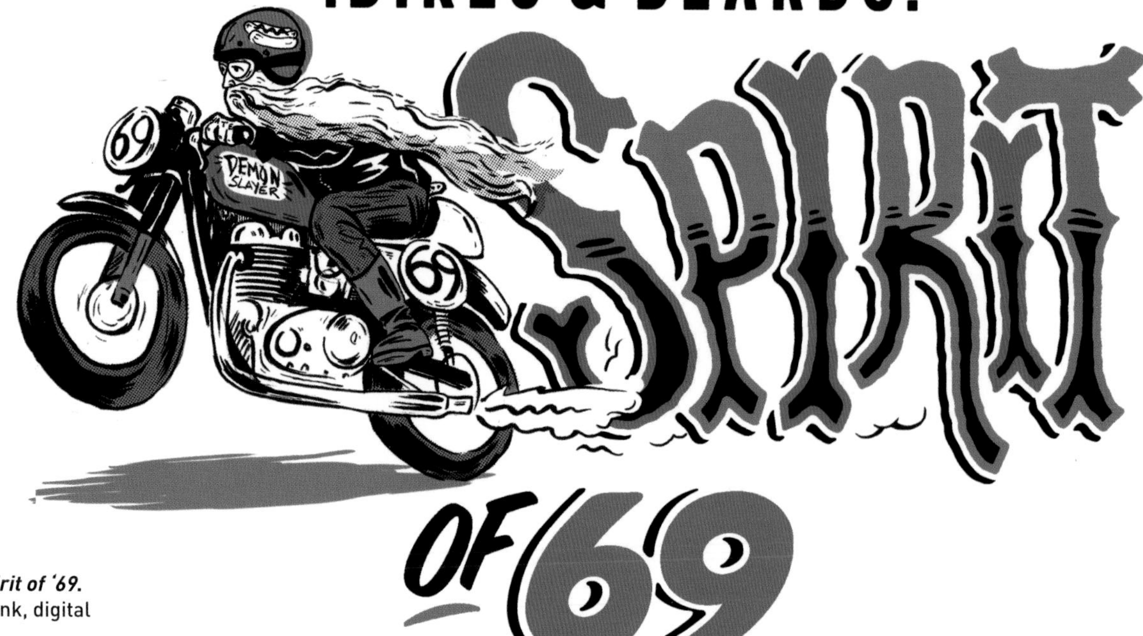

ABOVE: ***Spirit of '69.***
Brush and ink, digital colours.

BELOW: ***Smokin Pipes.***
Ink on paper, digital colours.

FAR RIGHT: ***Vintage Motorcycle.***
Ink and digital.

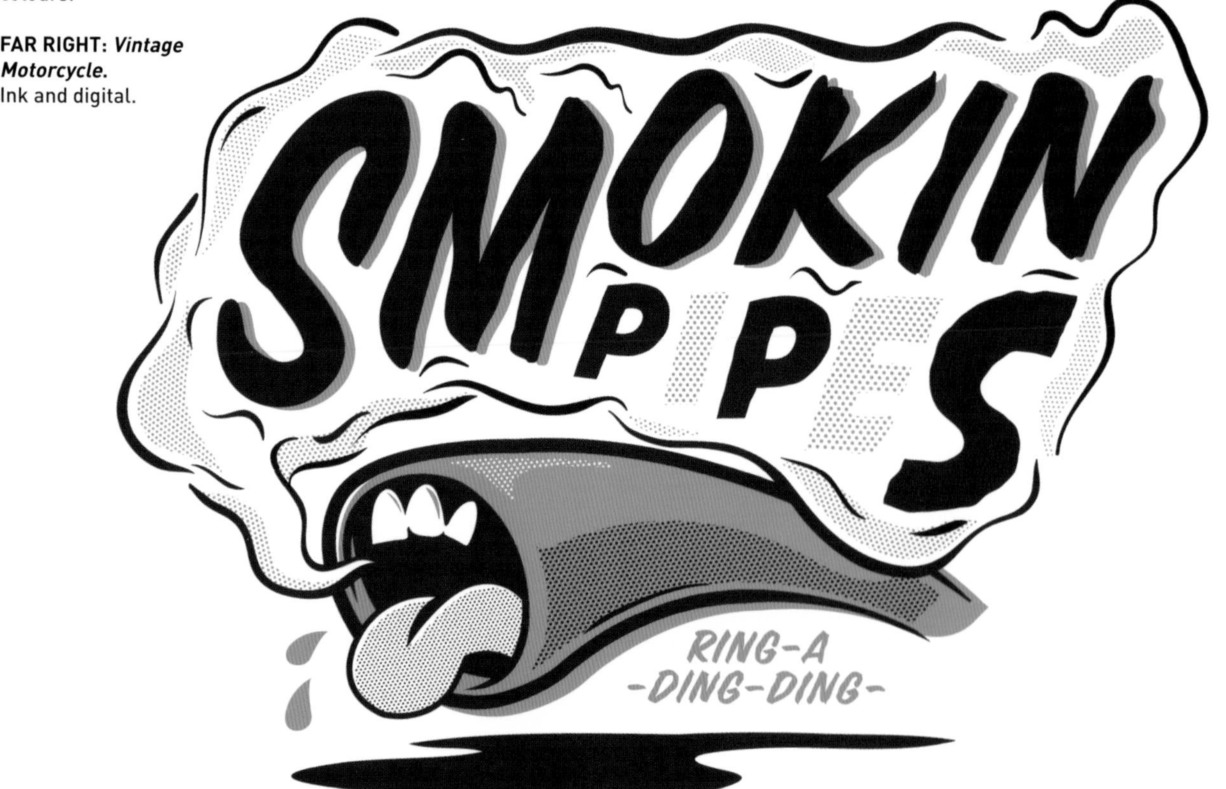

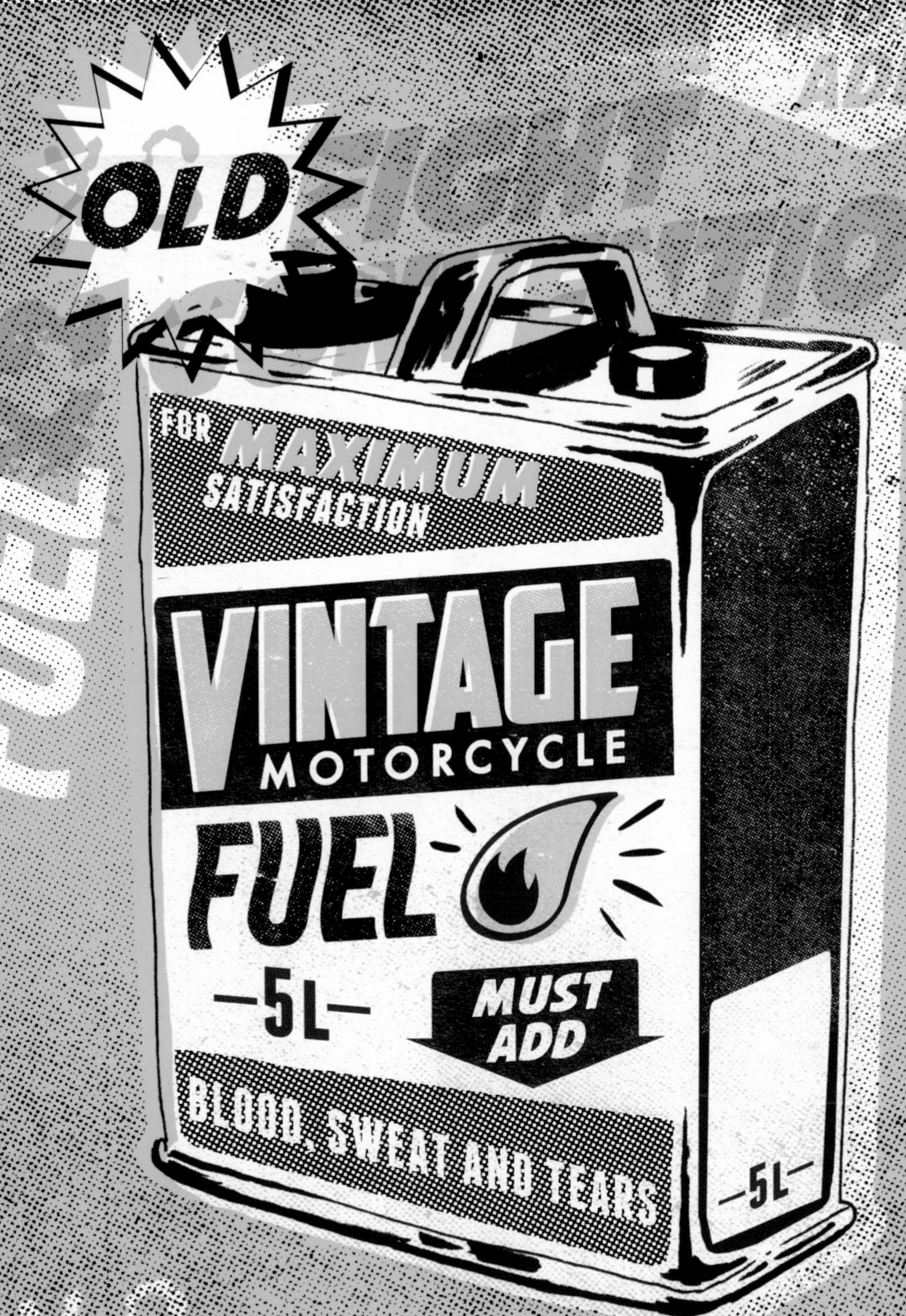
OLD
FOR MAXIMUM SATISFACTION
VINTAGE
MOTORCYCLE
FUEL
—5L—
MUST ADD
BLOOD, SWEAT AND TEARS
—5L—
FOR BEST RESULTS USE WITH BRITISH TWINS

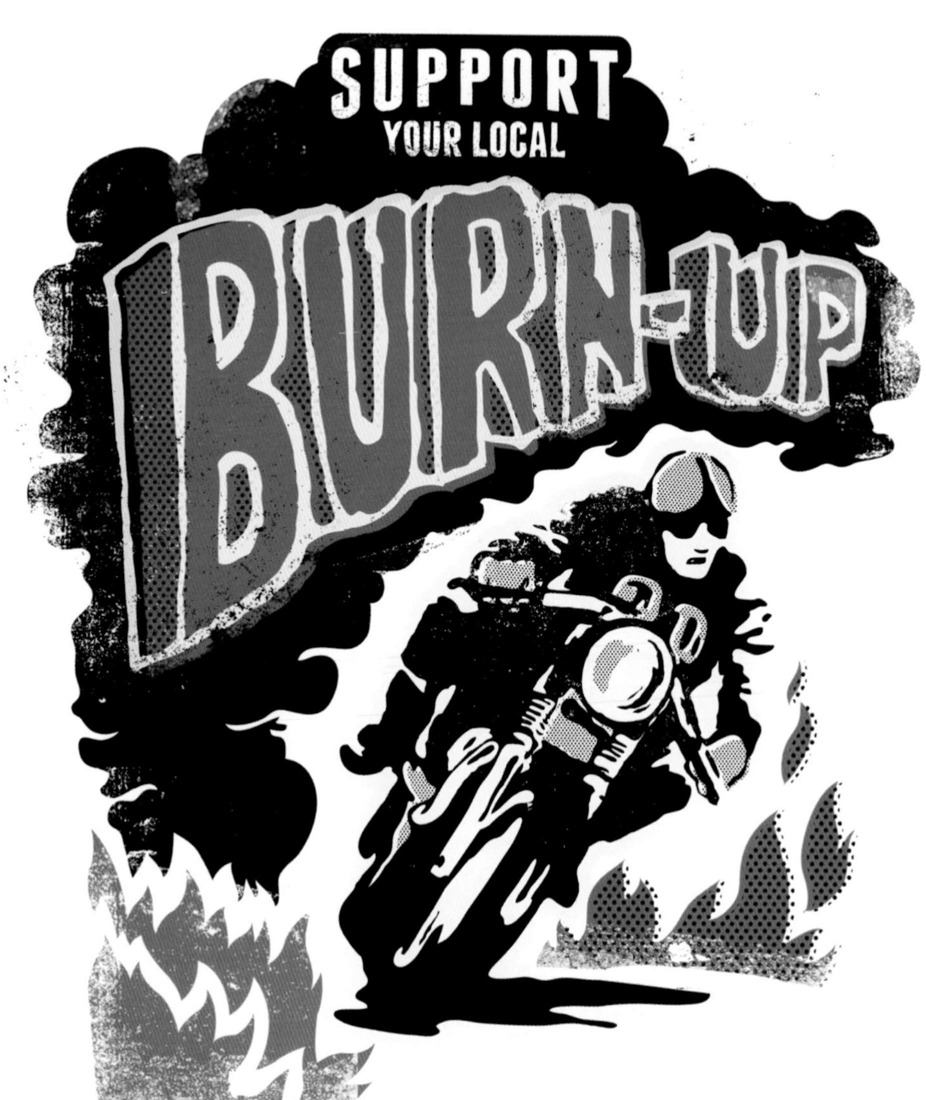

LEFT: ***Burn-Up.***
Brush and ink, digital texture.

BELOW: ***Indy & Peoria.***
Digital artwork.

RIGHT: ***SSBB.***
Pen and digital.

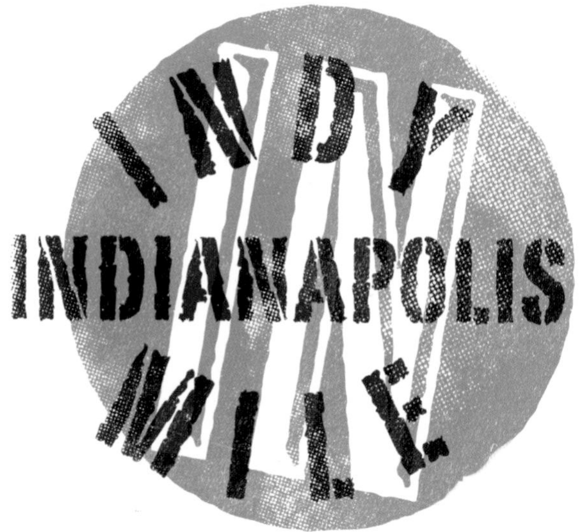

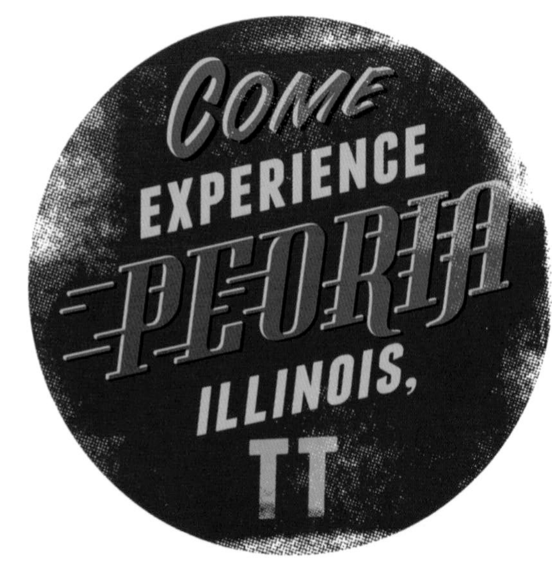

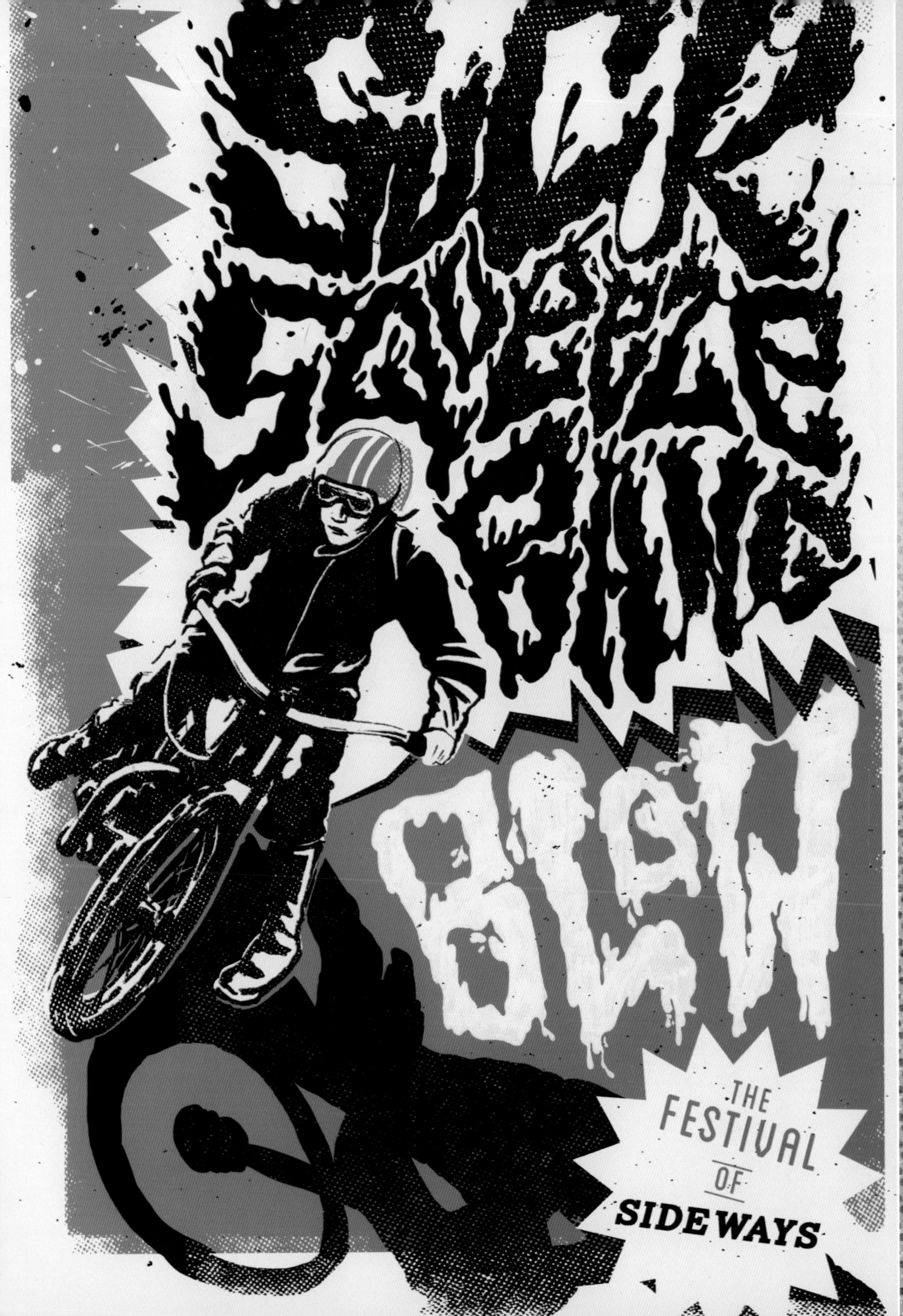
THE
FESTIVAL
OF
SIDEWAYS

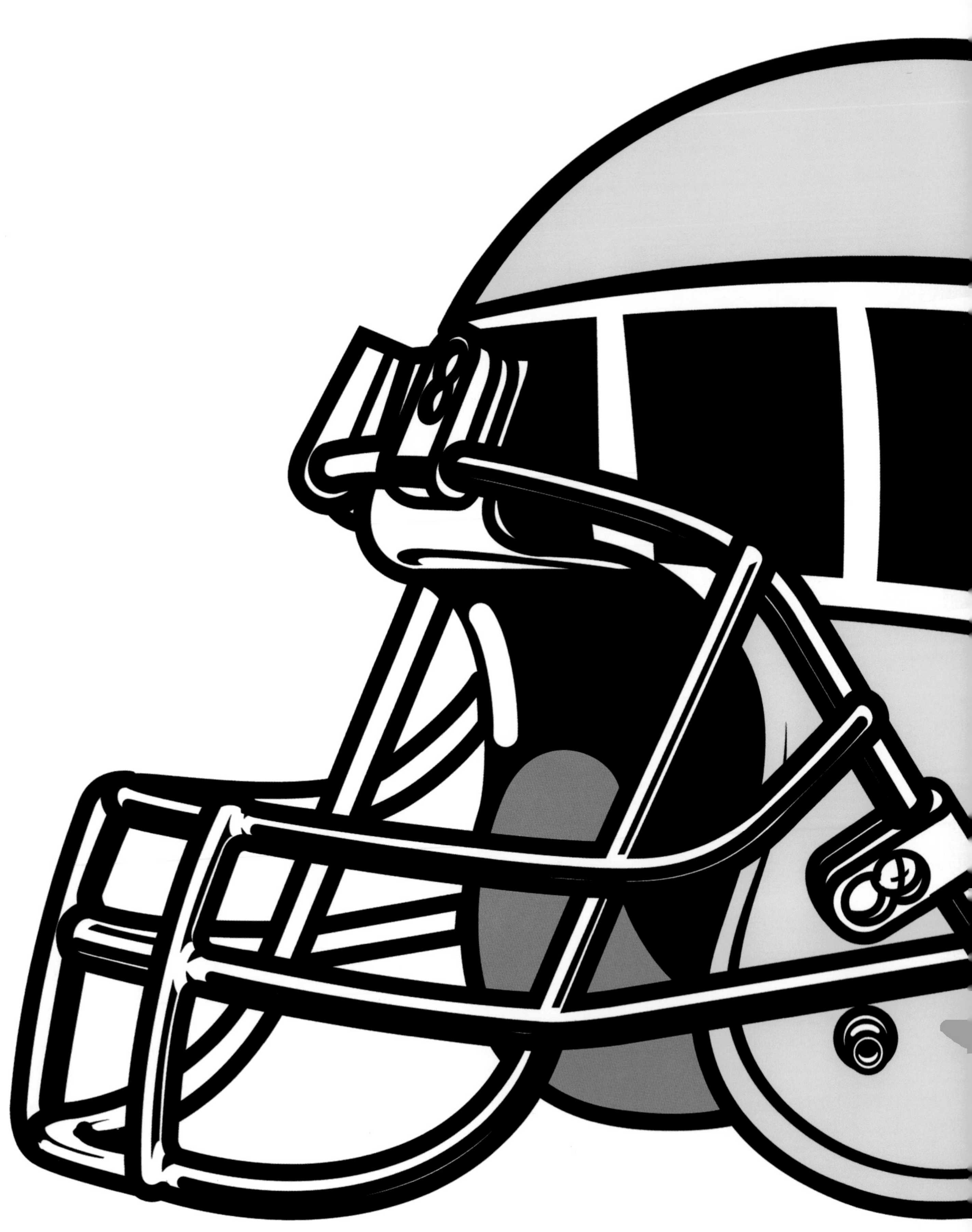

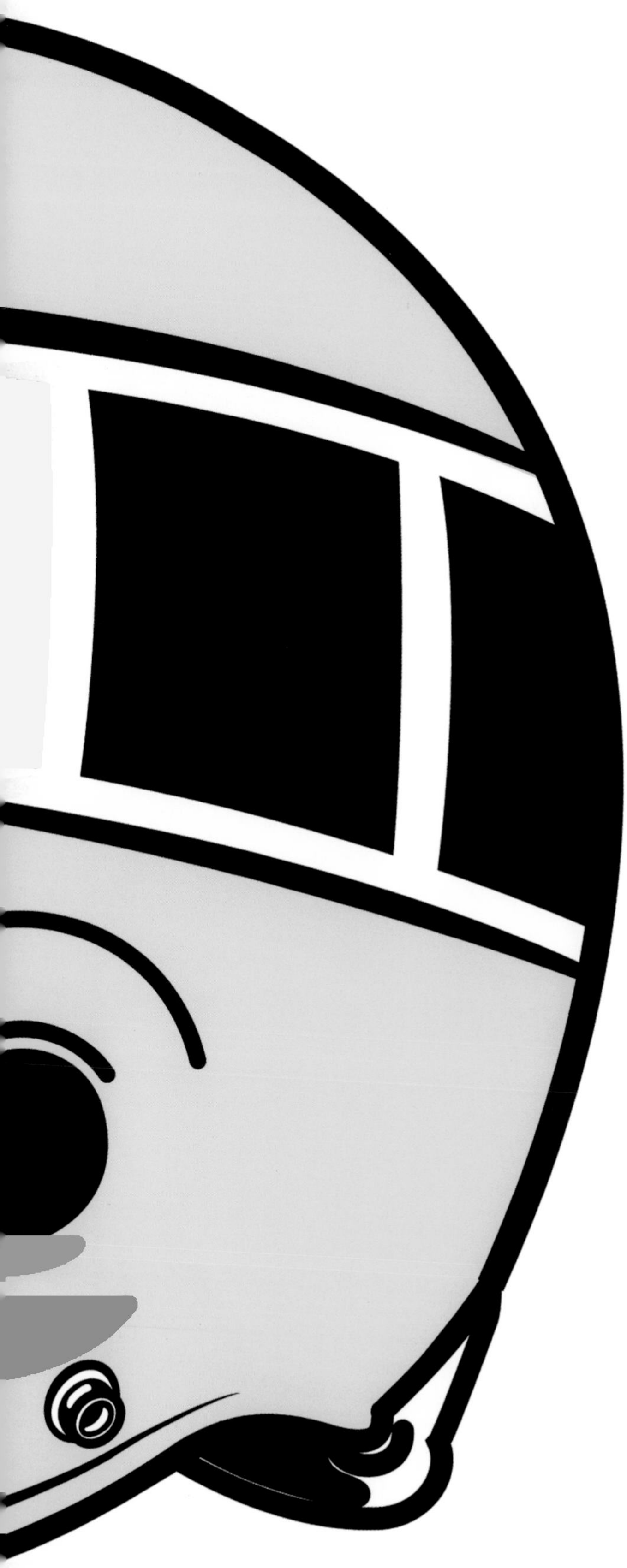

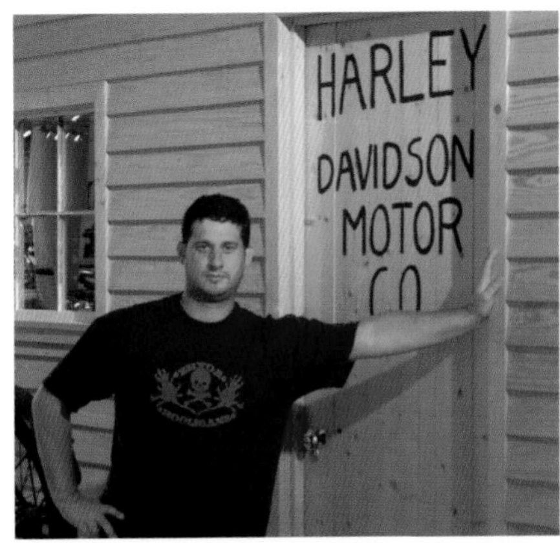

GIANNIS RAGGIAS

Giannis Raggias grew up in Karditsa City, in central Greece. "Back in the '80s I didn't see many bikes, but the ones I did tattooed themselves deeply onto my memory. The '80s in Greece were rebel years. The cops had slow bikes and the kids had fast 750s and 1000s... or even rocked dirt bikes on the street." Giannis then moved to Texas, where he worked for Ducati on one-off bikes, logos and advertising, before moving back to Greece. Today he lives in "a small village 15 miles from my hometown. I wanted to move away from big, noisy cities. This way I'm always relaxed, I enjoy life more and I'm able to ride my bikes 'without being hassled by the man.'" He does get through his bikes, having owned over 60. "I currently have only a few – honestly," says Giannis. "I can't imagine a day without motorcycles. I love all the different biking cultures; although they all use two wheels they are so different." Pretty much all of Giannis's designs start with a sketch. "Sometimes, I feel like a design will look better in watercolours or other media. Other times I scan and work in Photoshop or Illustrator. Some of my logos are done straight in design programmes, but I prefer to see something on paper first."

LEFT: *Yamaha Football Team.*
Digital artwork.

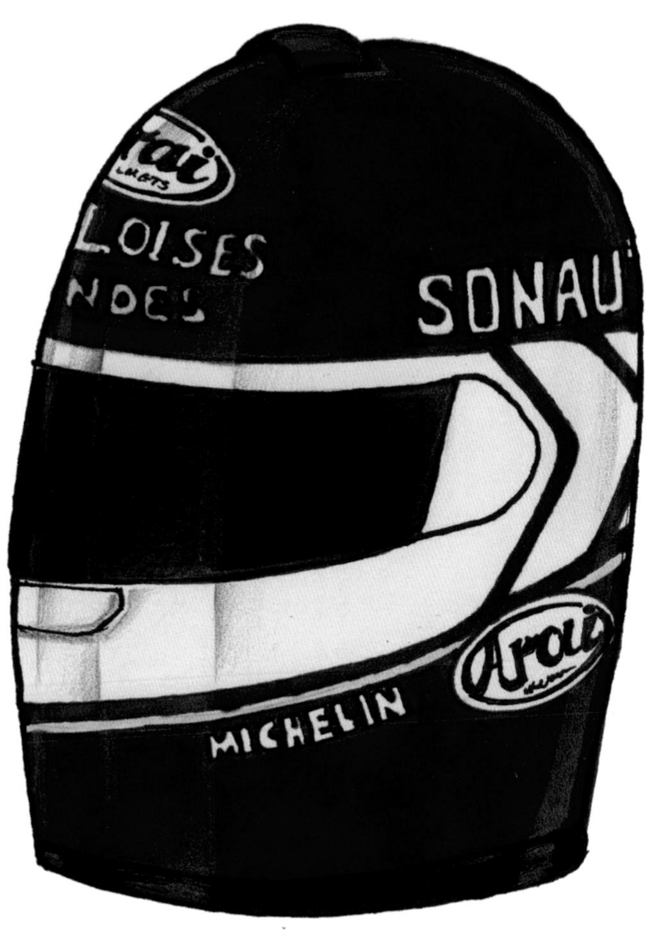

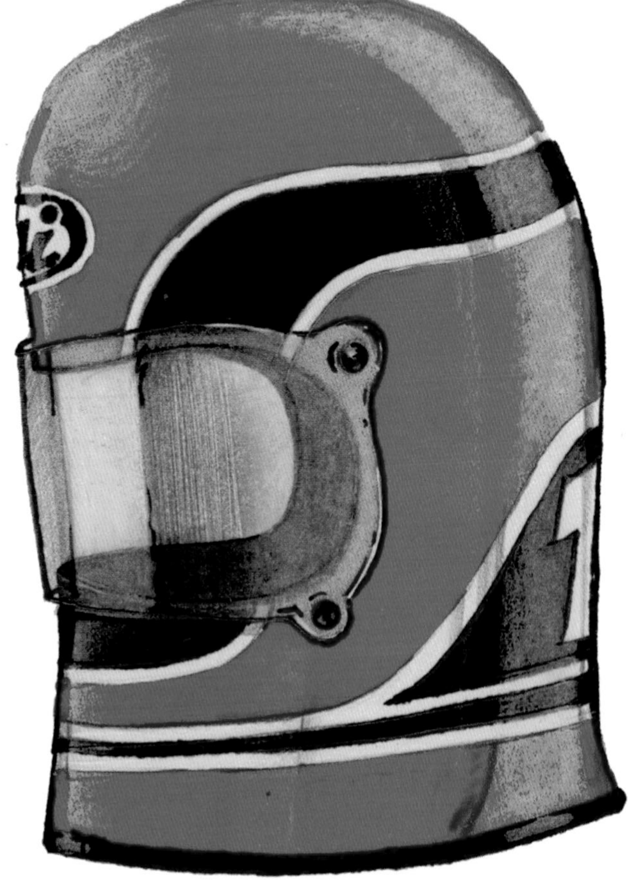

ABOVE: ***Hero Christian Sarron.***
Ink on paper.

RIGHT: ***Hero Randy Mamola.***
Ink on paper.

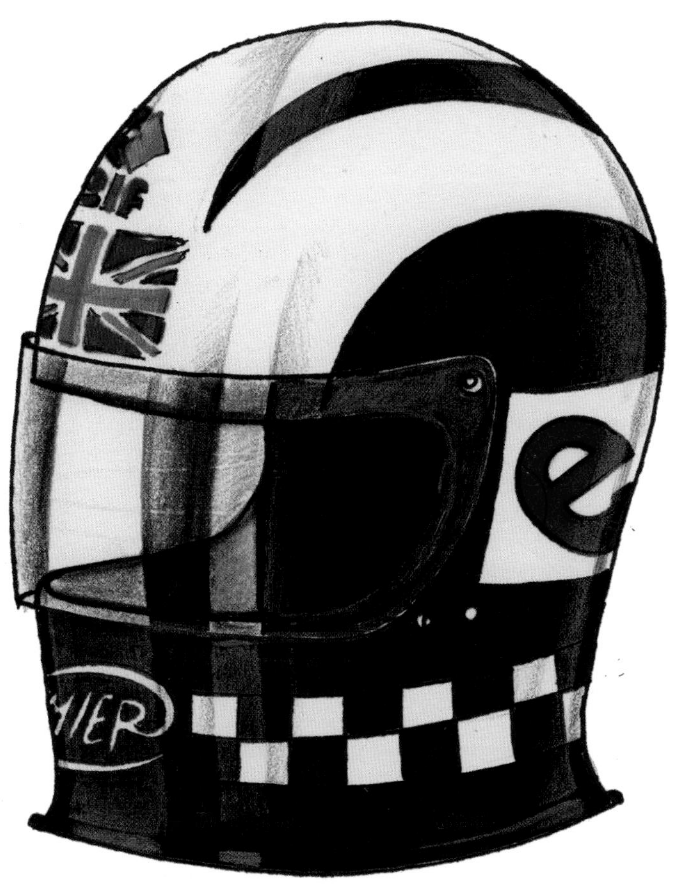

LEFT: ***Hero Phil Read.***
Ink on paper.

BELOW: ***Hero Scott Parker.***
Ink on paper.

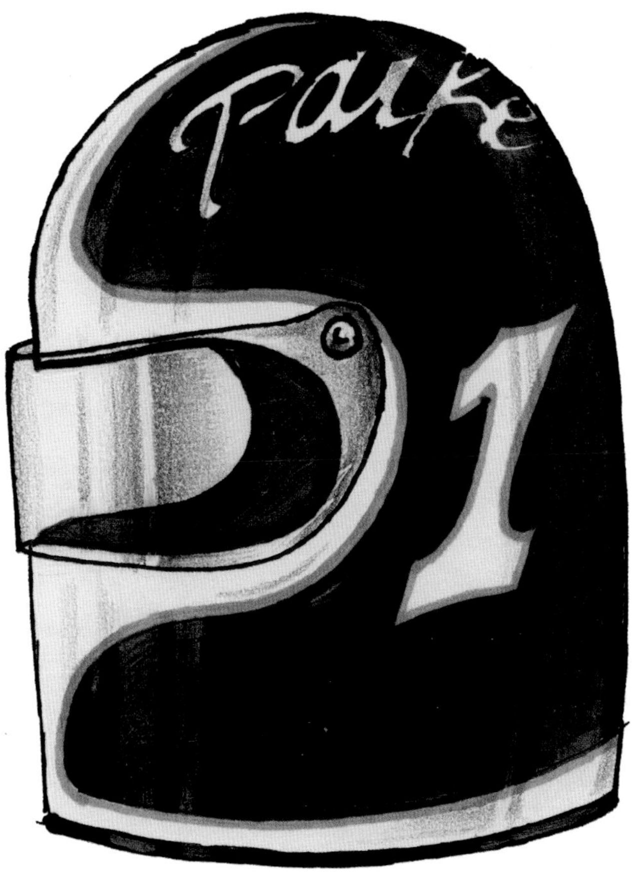

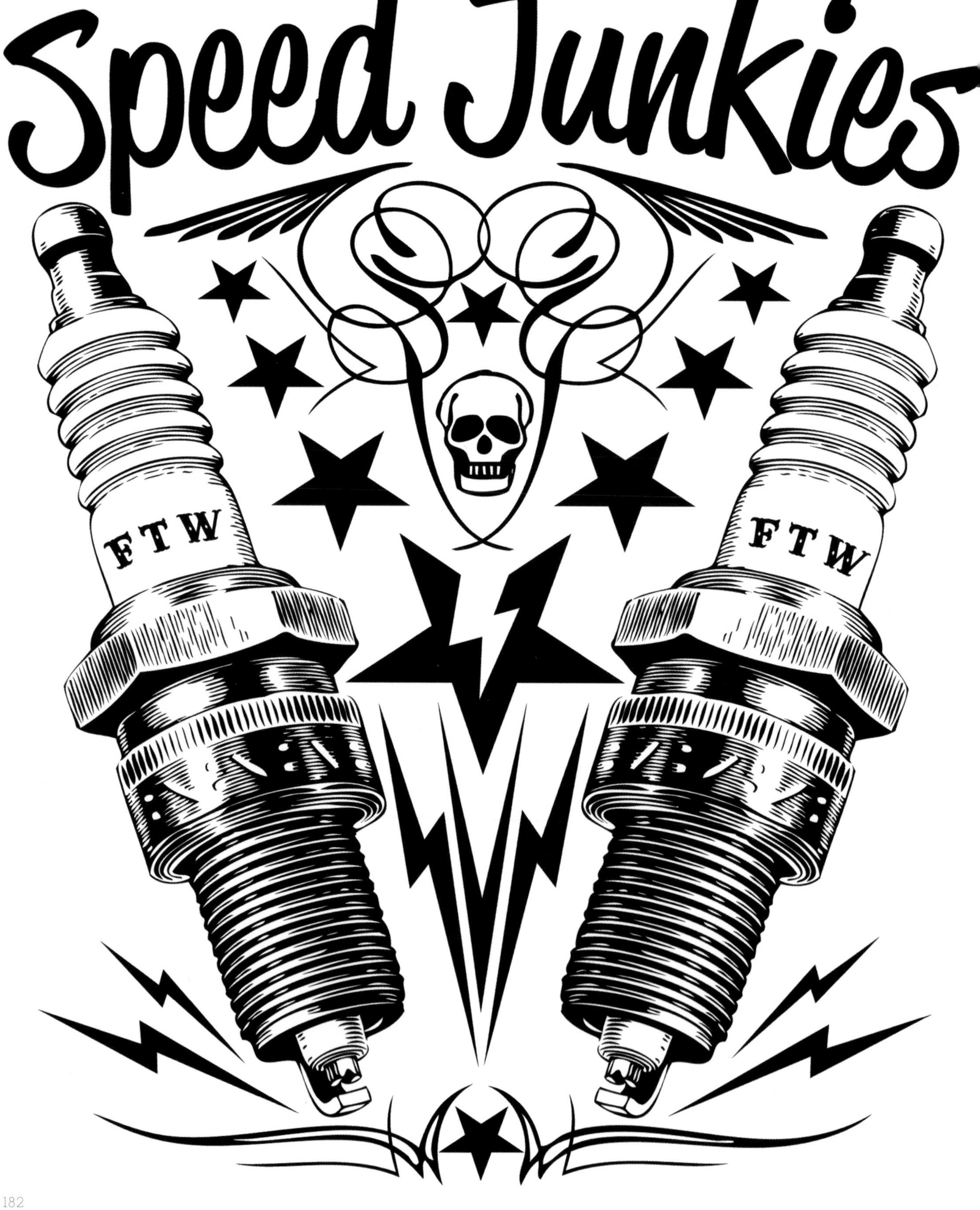

Speed Junkies

FTW

FTW

LEFT: ***Speed Plugs.***
Digital artwork.

RIGHT: ***Cheat Death.***
Digital artwork.

BELOW: ***Love Boso Style.***
Digital artwork.

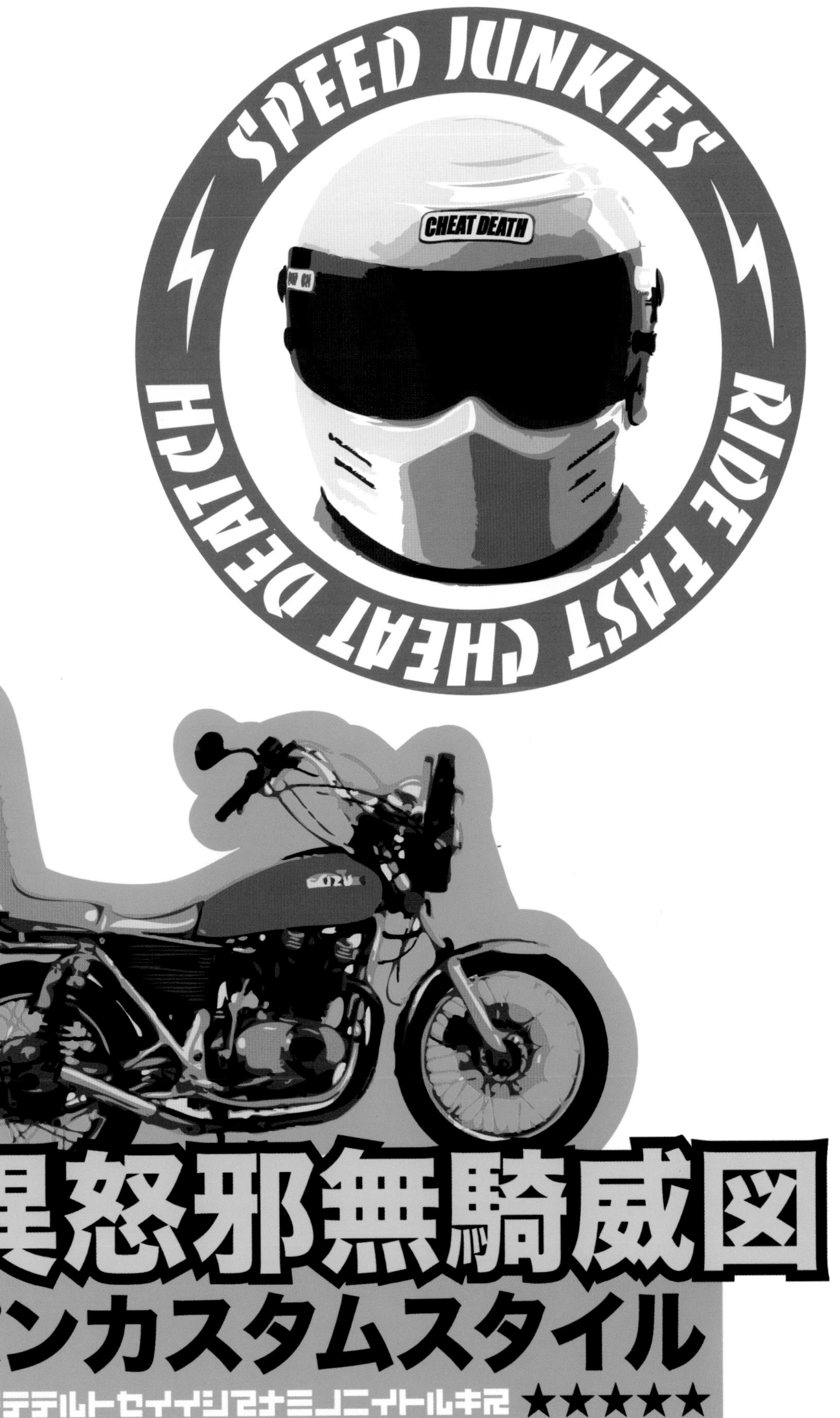

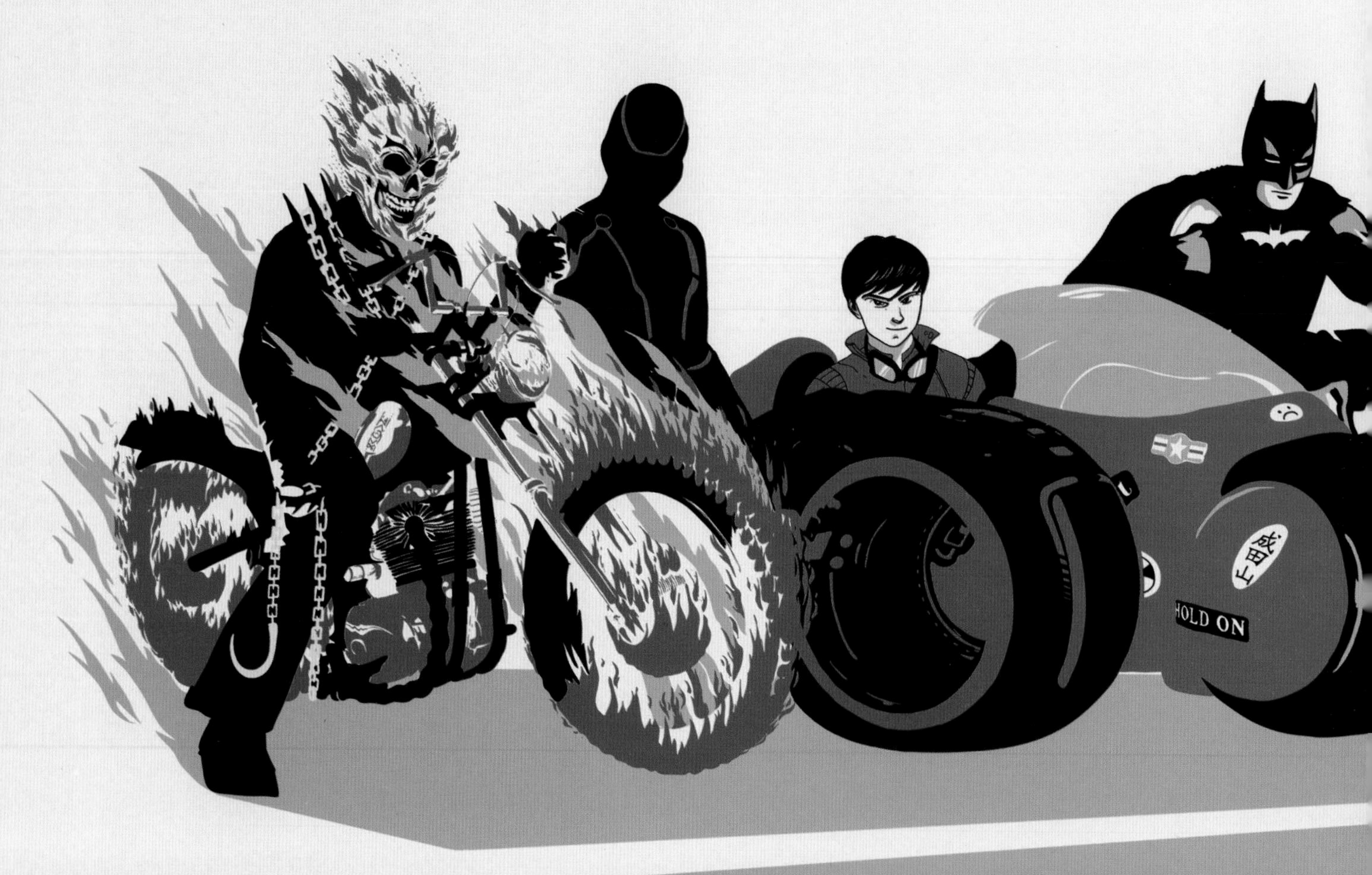
HOLD ON

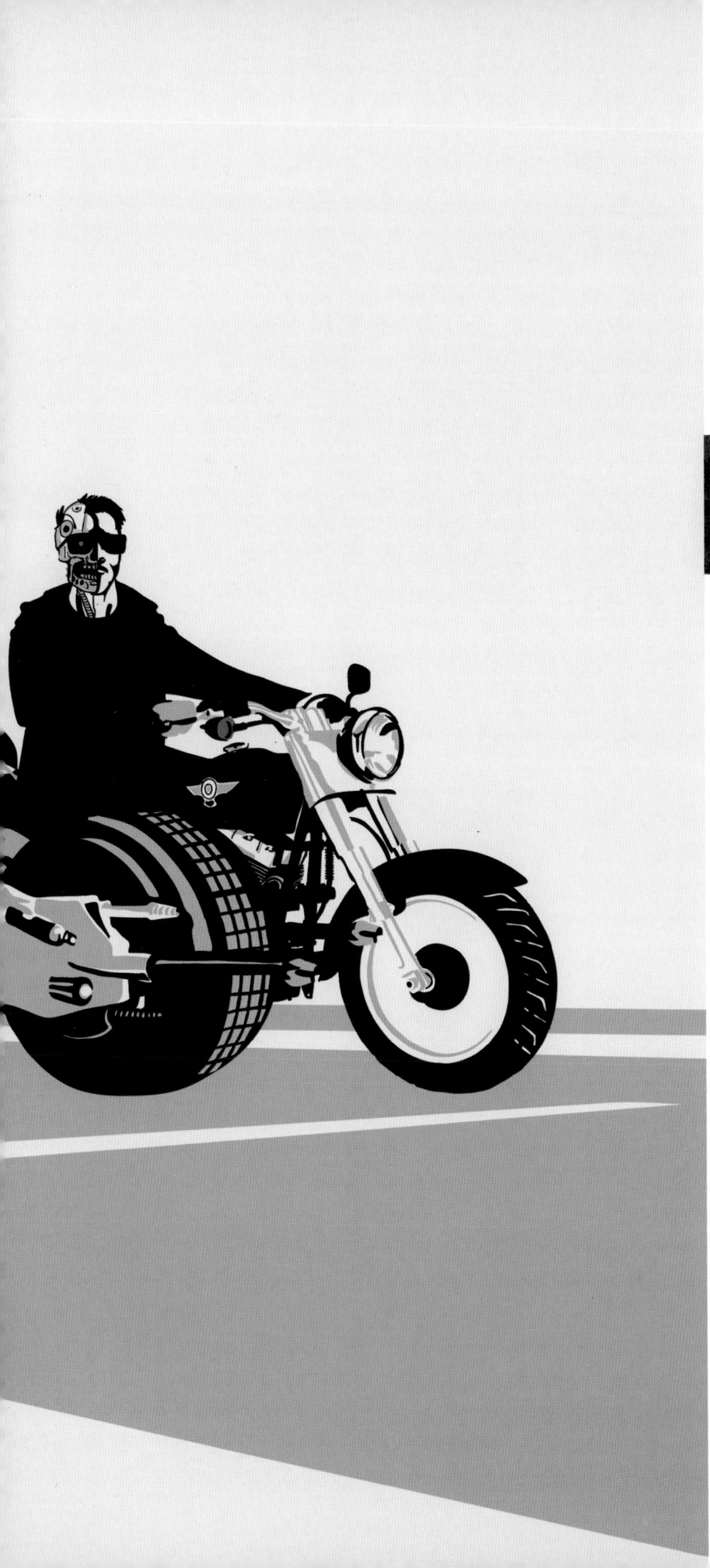

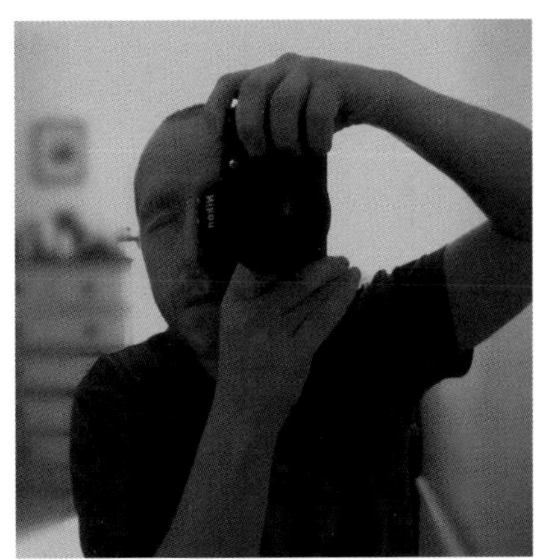

RAID71

"Motorcycles are just lovely to draw, so many shapes and different kinds of surfaces and light reflections to play around with," explains Chris Thornley, a.k.a. Raid71. "Also, they can be quite forgiving. You can leave out details and still capture the shapes; I find no two bikes are the same. Then you add in movement, fashion, culture and status... the list goes on. That's why it's attractive: there's always something new to explore."

As a kid, Chris loved to draw. "Fortunately, I've never grown up, but I work quite hard at getting jobs as an artist." He likes to work with inks, but commercial commissions more often than not mean delivering work digitally, so Chris creates most of this using a Wacom tablet, on a Mac. From his base in Lancashire, England, Raid71 supplies a long and pretty illustrious list of clients, including Dennis Publishing, Hearst Magazines, Gap, Lynx, ESPN, Gola, *NME*, Levi, Threadless, Mercury records, *MacUser*, *Fortean Times*, Hasbro, X-Games, Mercedes and Lego.

LEFT: *Sons of Anarchy*.
Digital artwork.

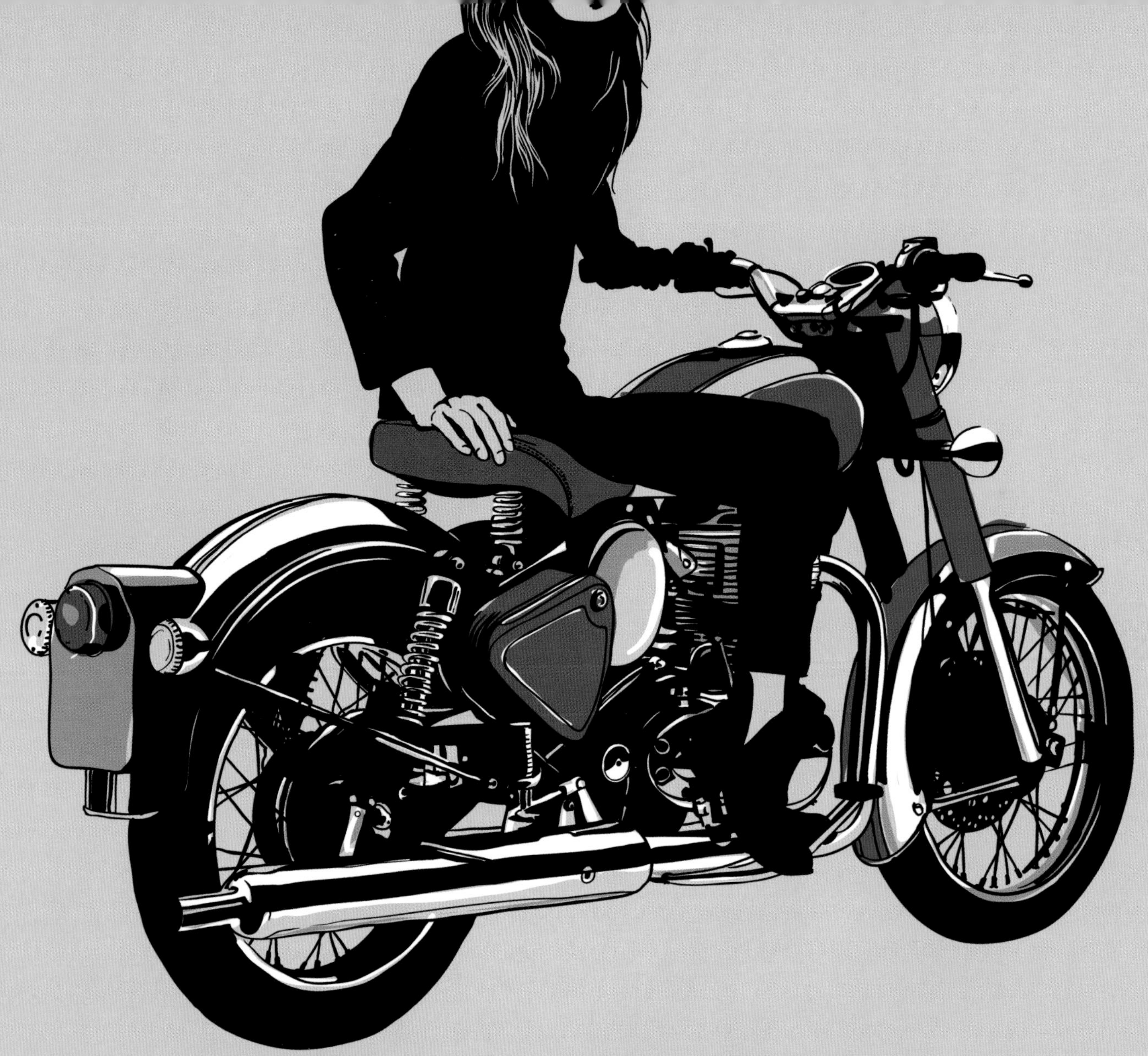

ABOVE: ***Hells Angel.***
Digital artwork.

RIGHT: ***Born Ready?***
Digital artwork.

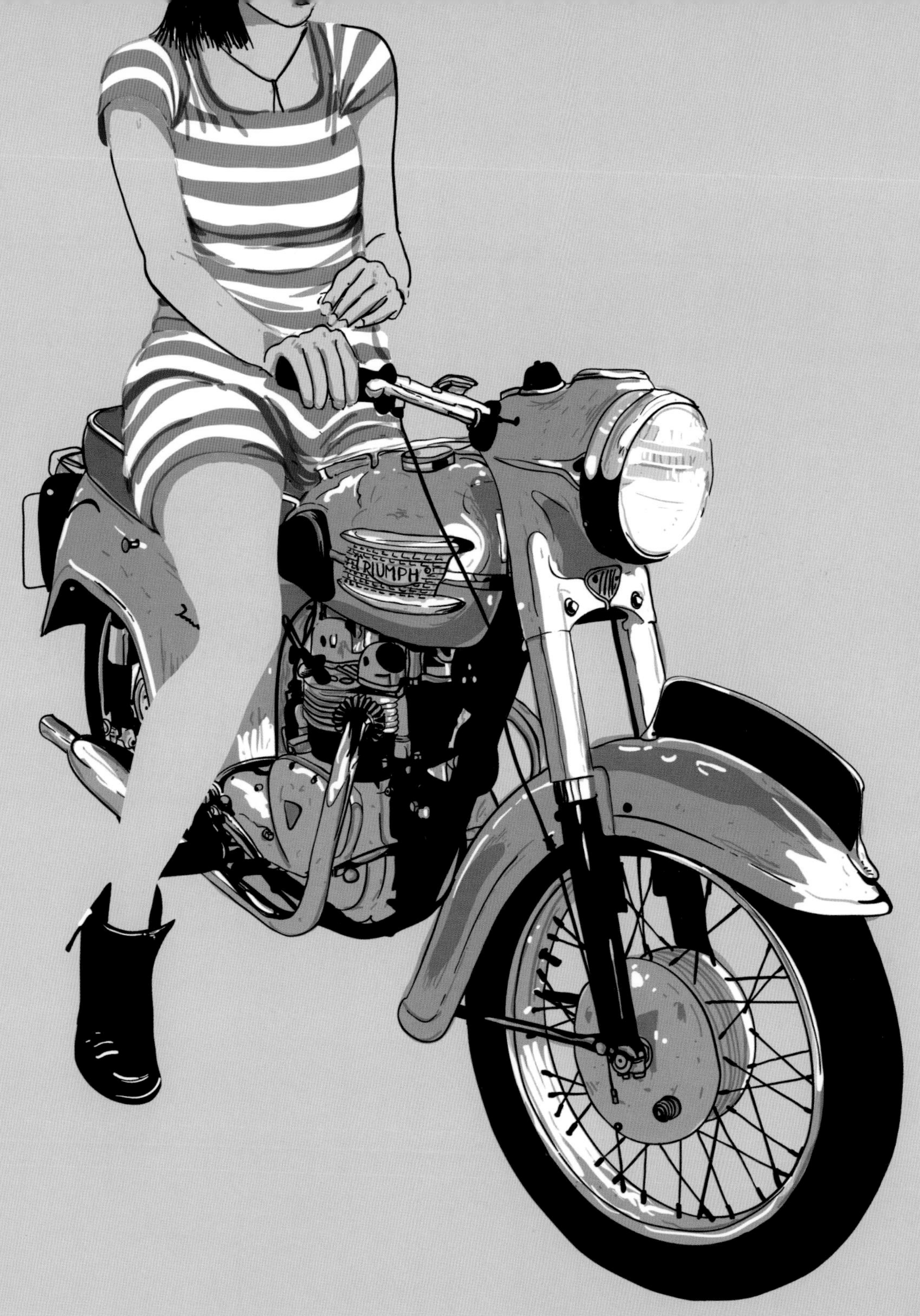
TRIUMPH

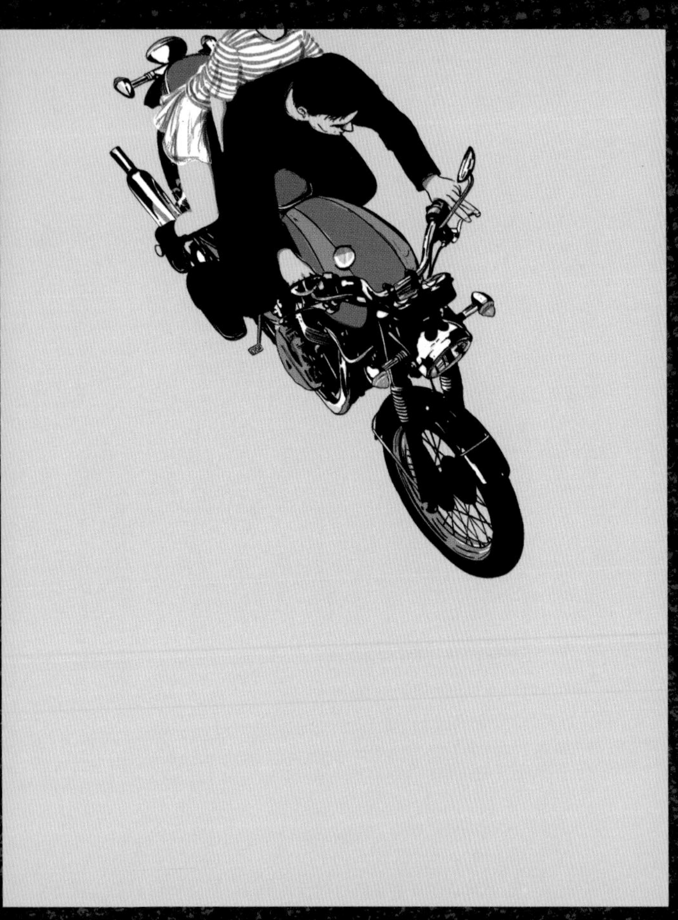

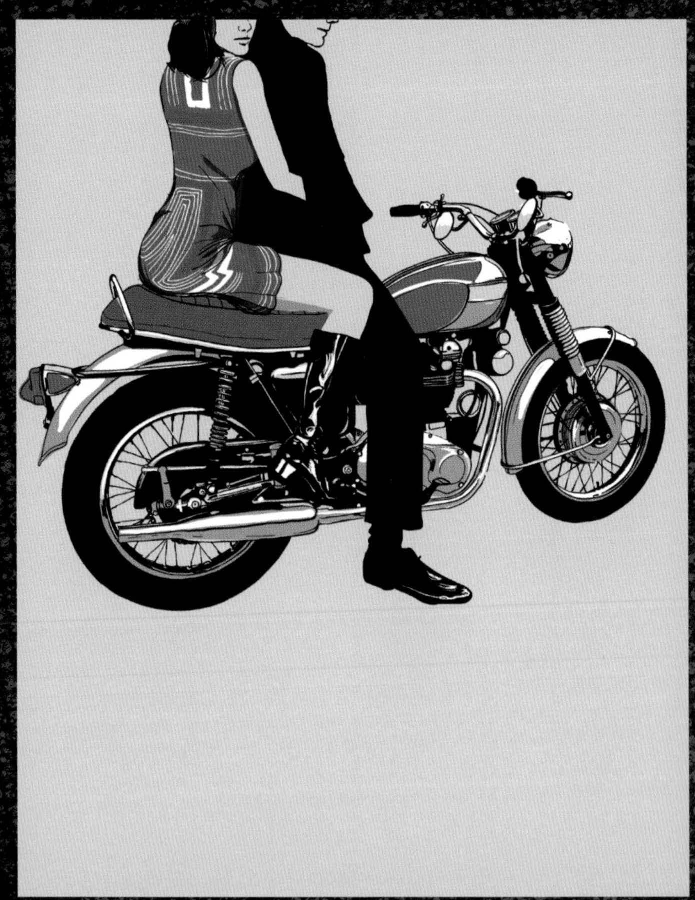

ABOVE: ***Relaxed.***
Digital artwork.

ABOVE RIGHT: ***Ready To Roll.***
Digital artwork.

RIGHT: ***My Heart.***
Digital artwork.

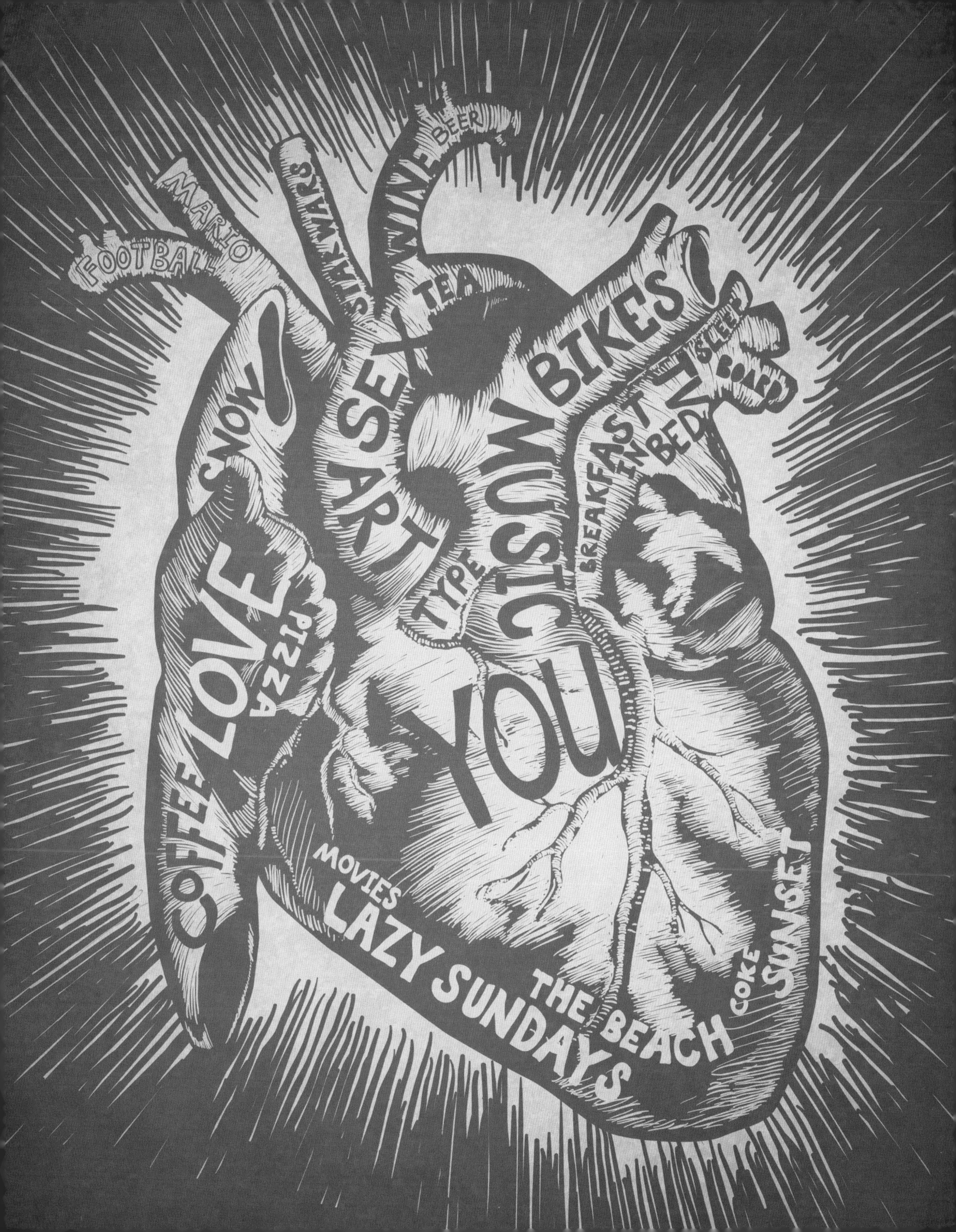
FOOTBALL
MARIO
STAR WARS
WINE
BEER
TEA
SEX
BIKES
SLEEP
BOARD
TV
SNOW
ART
MUSIC
BREAKFAST IN BED
TYPE
COFFEE
LOVE
PIZZA
YOU
MOVIES
LAZY SUNDAYS
THE BEACH
COKE
SUNSET

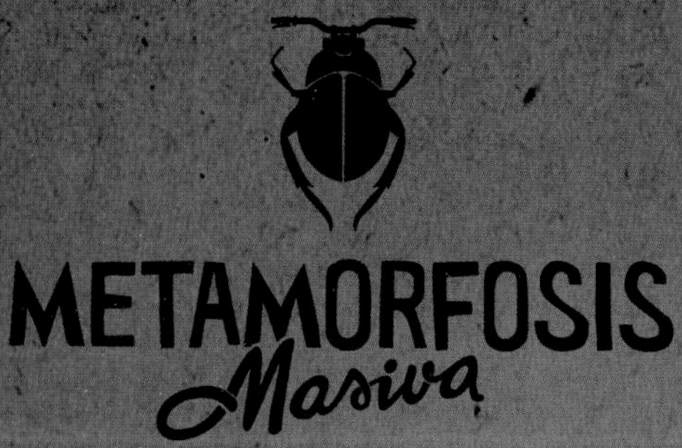
METAMORFOSIS
Masiva

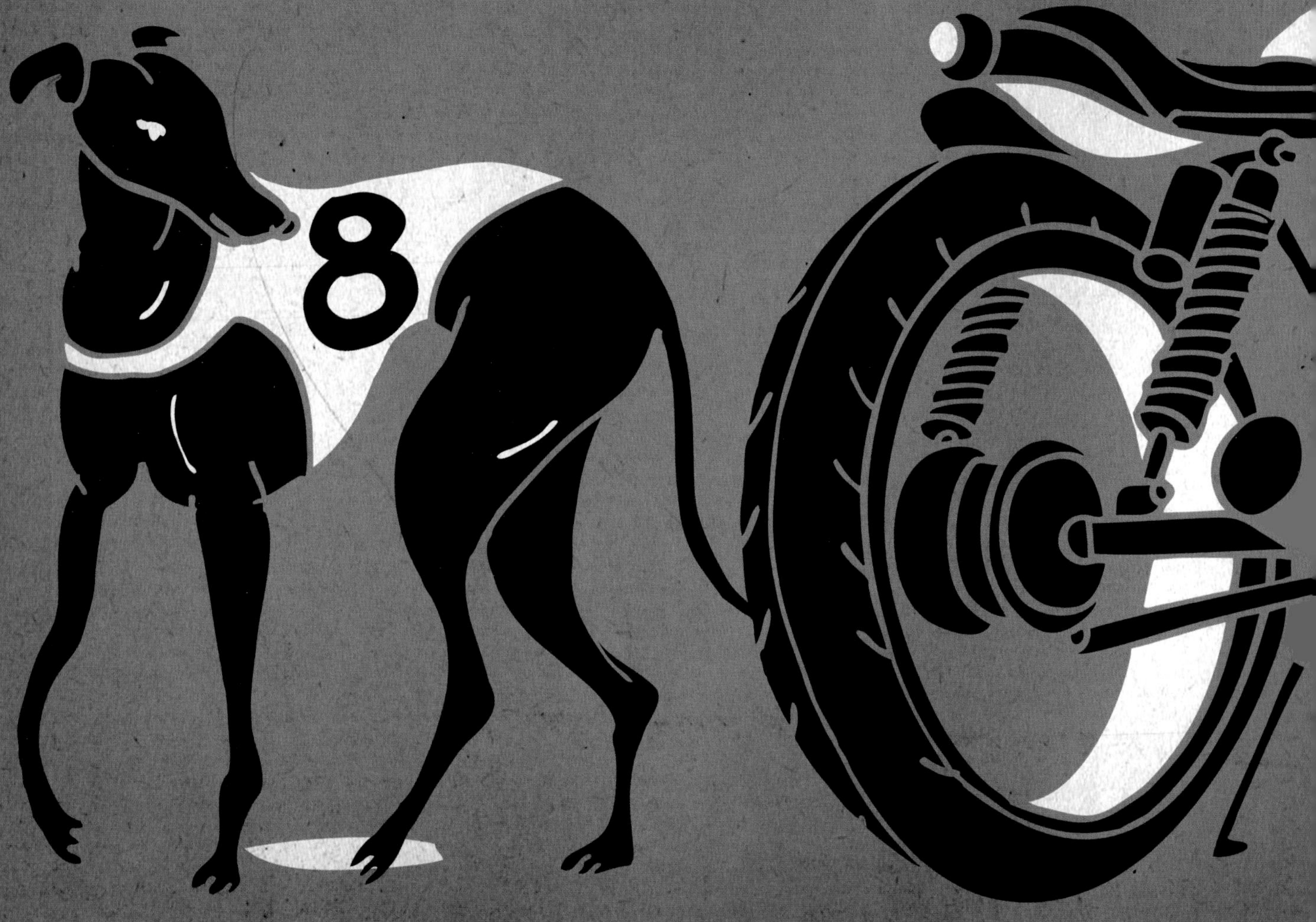

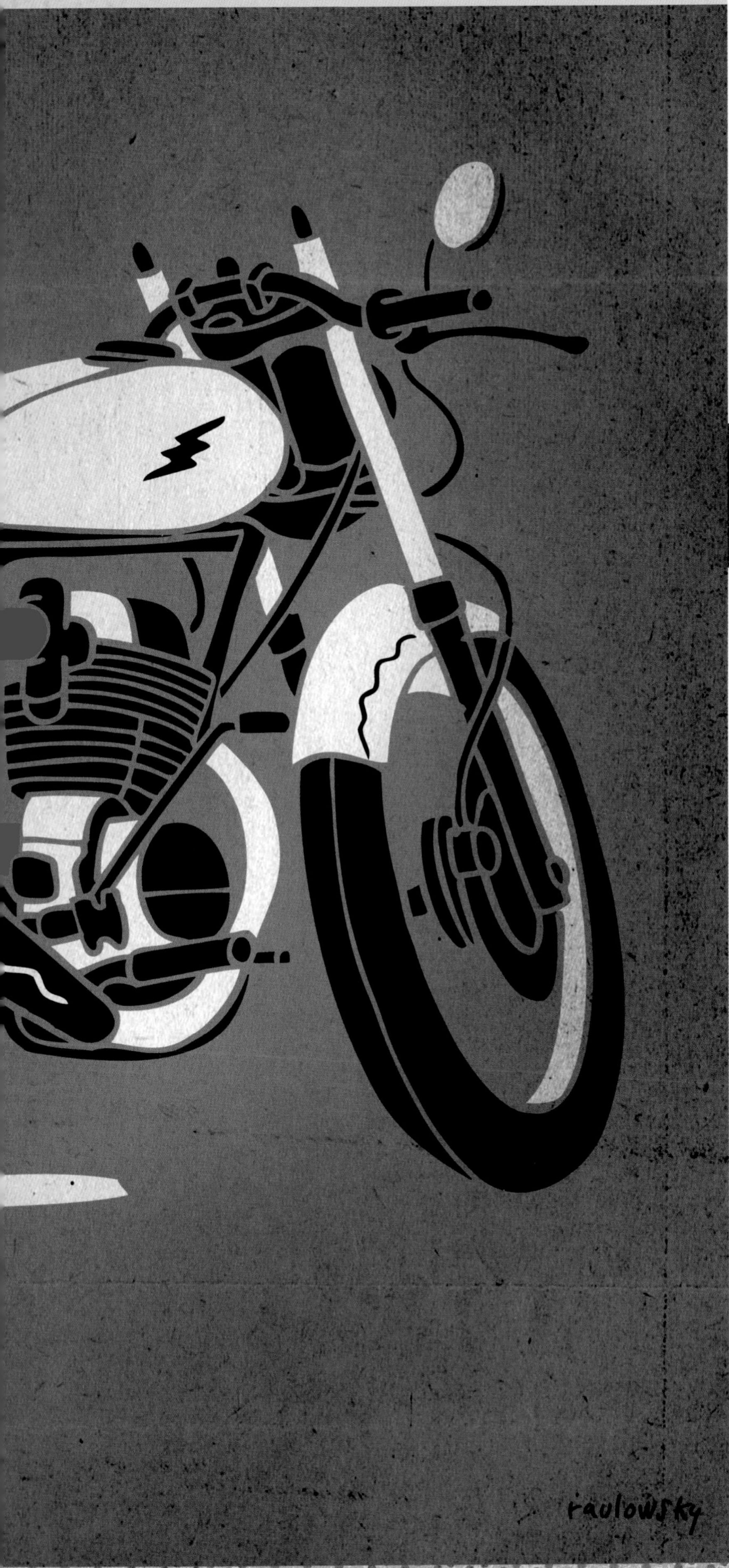

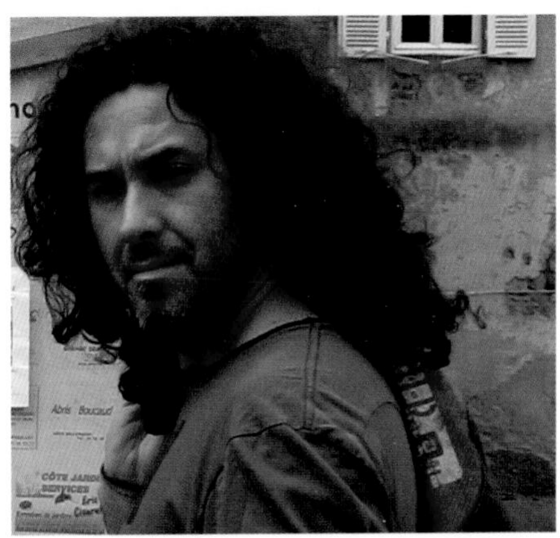

RAULOWSKY

"I enjoyed underground culture in the late '80s and early '90s," says Raulowsky, "when the cultural manifestations were scarce, at least in my town of Badajóz, Spain. We had few resources and had to become inventive; that was a spur to creativity. At that time, Olivetti machines and cutting and pasting were in, a little different from now when almost everything can be achieved using a Mac." Still based in the south of Spain, on the border with Portugal, Raulowsky gives birth to his work on paper with the help of pencils, ink, markers and watercolours. "Then, I digitize the image on my computer, I add some colour and touch it up when necessary. Sometimes I just stick to one instrument, but, in general, I like each technique to leave its own footprint." Raulowsky has been fascinated by motorbikes since childhood. "My dream was to own one and it came true in my teenage years. I have been riding since then. I currently ride my dream bike, a yellow Harley Fat Boy." Sources of inspiration are many: "Motorbike culture, sure that's a major source, but I could also mention music, poetry and long journeys on that Fat Boy."

LEFT: *Inspiración, serie Metamorfosis Masiva.* Ink on paper, digital.

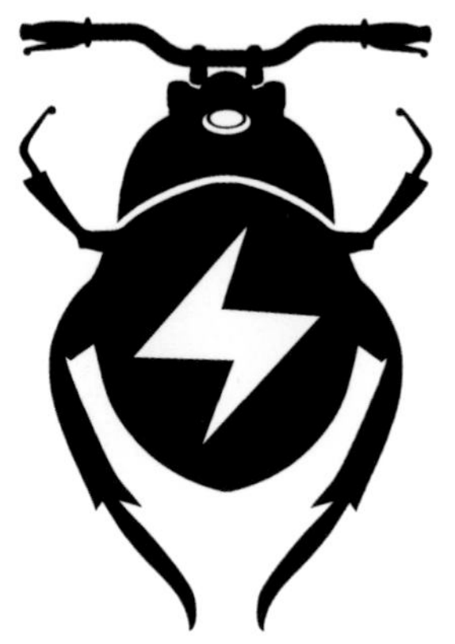

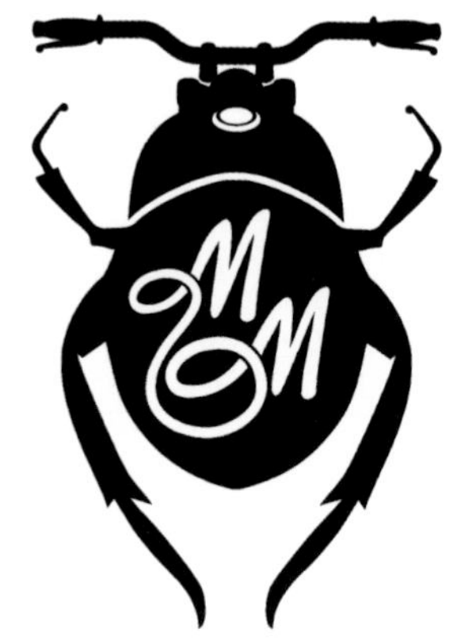

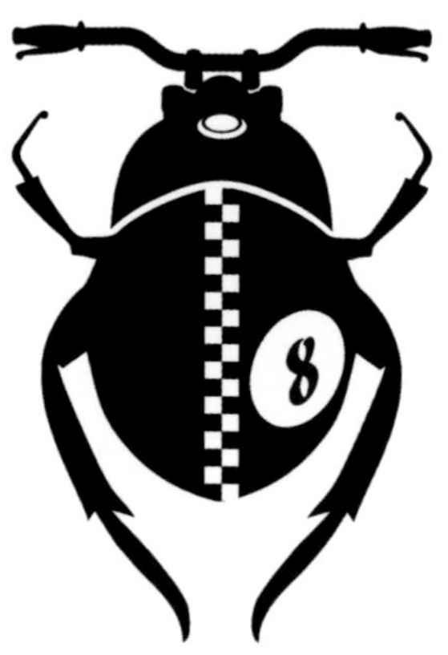

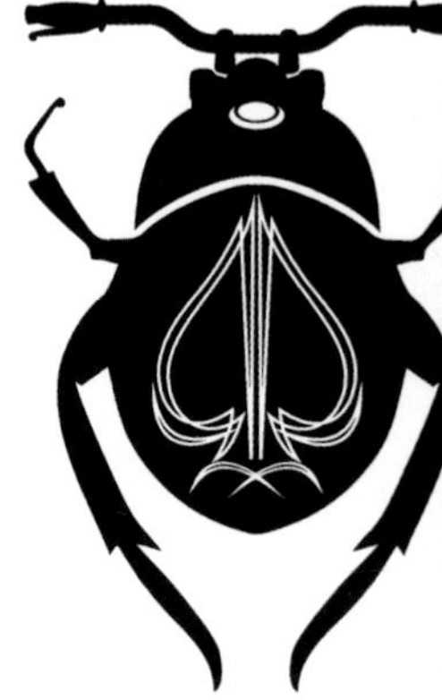

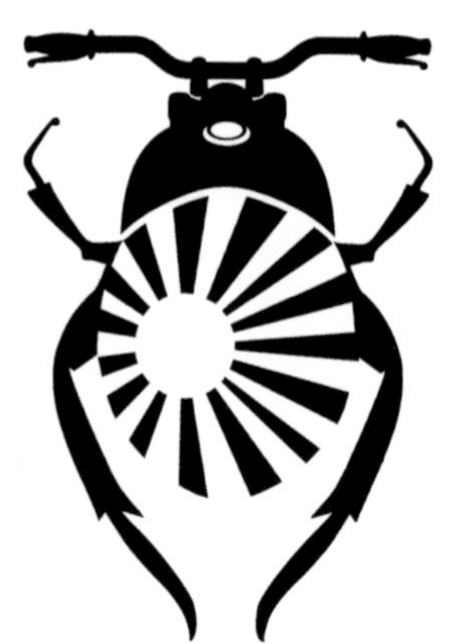

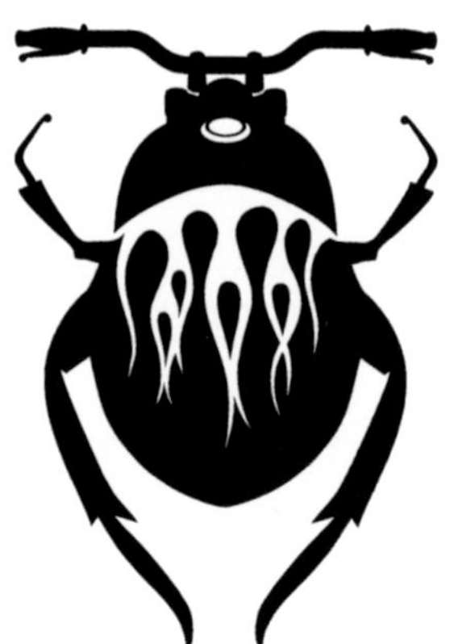

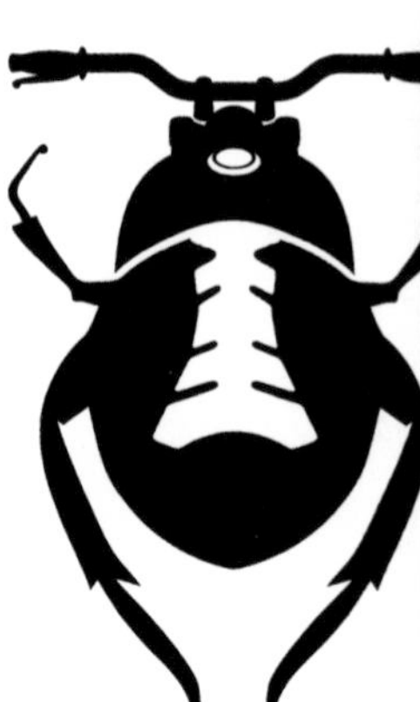

METAMORFOSIS
Masiva

ABOVE: ***Estilos Metamorfosis Masiva.***
Pen and ink.

RIGHT: ***Vieja Escuela Yamaha.***
Collage, watercolour, pencil and ink; digital print.

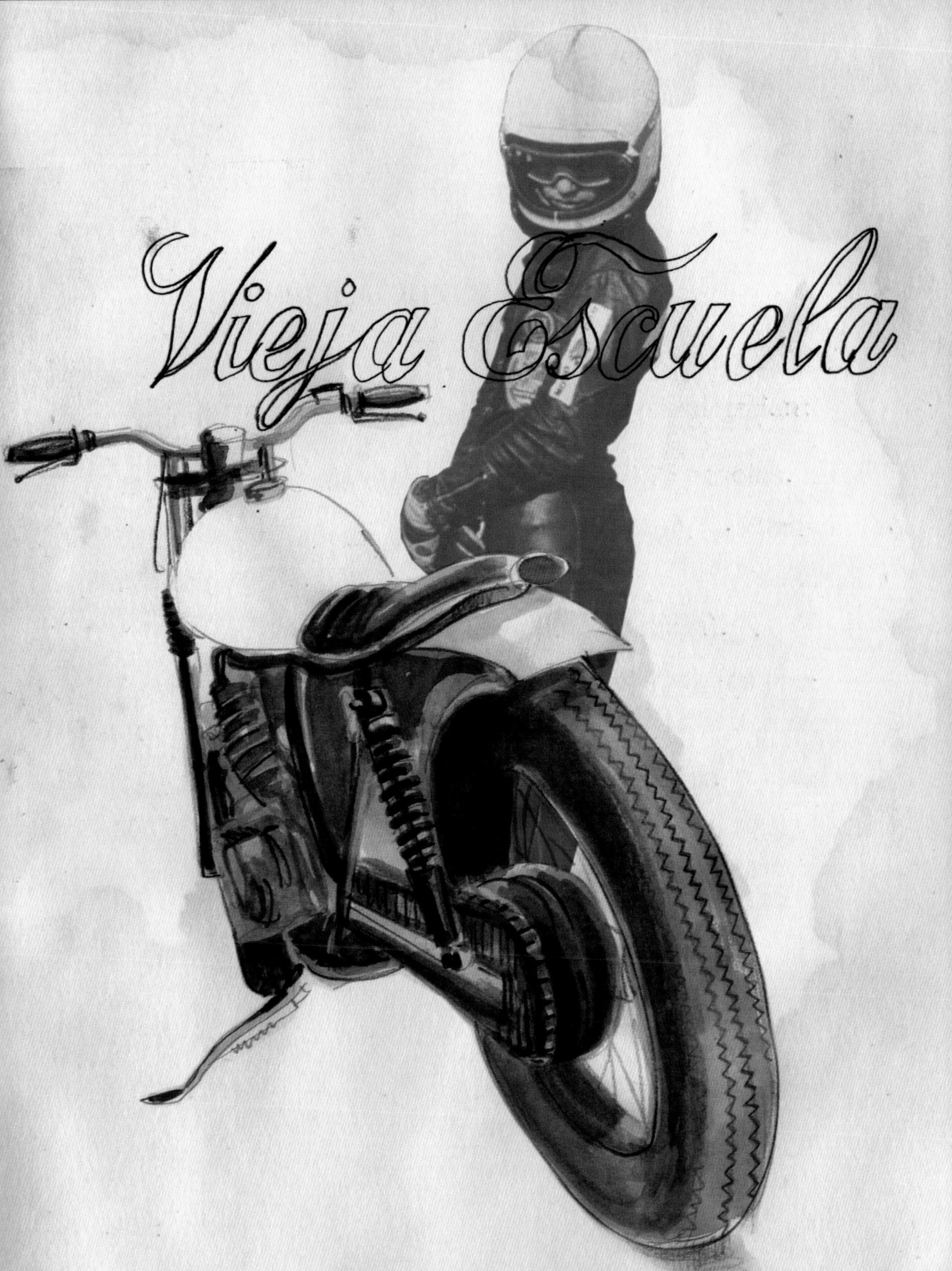
Viejo Escuela
ravlowsky

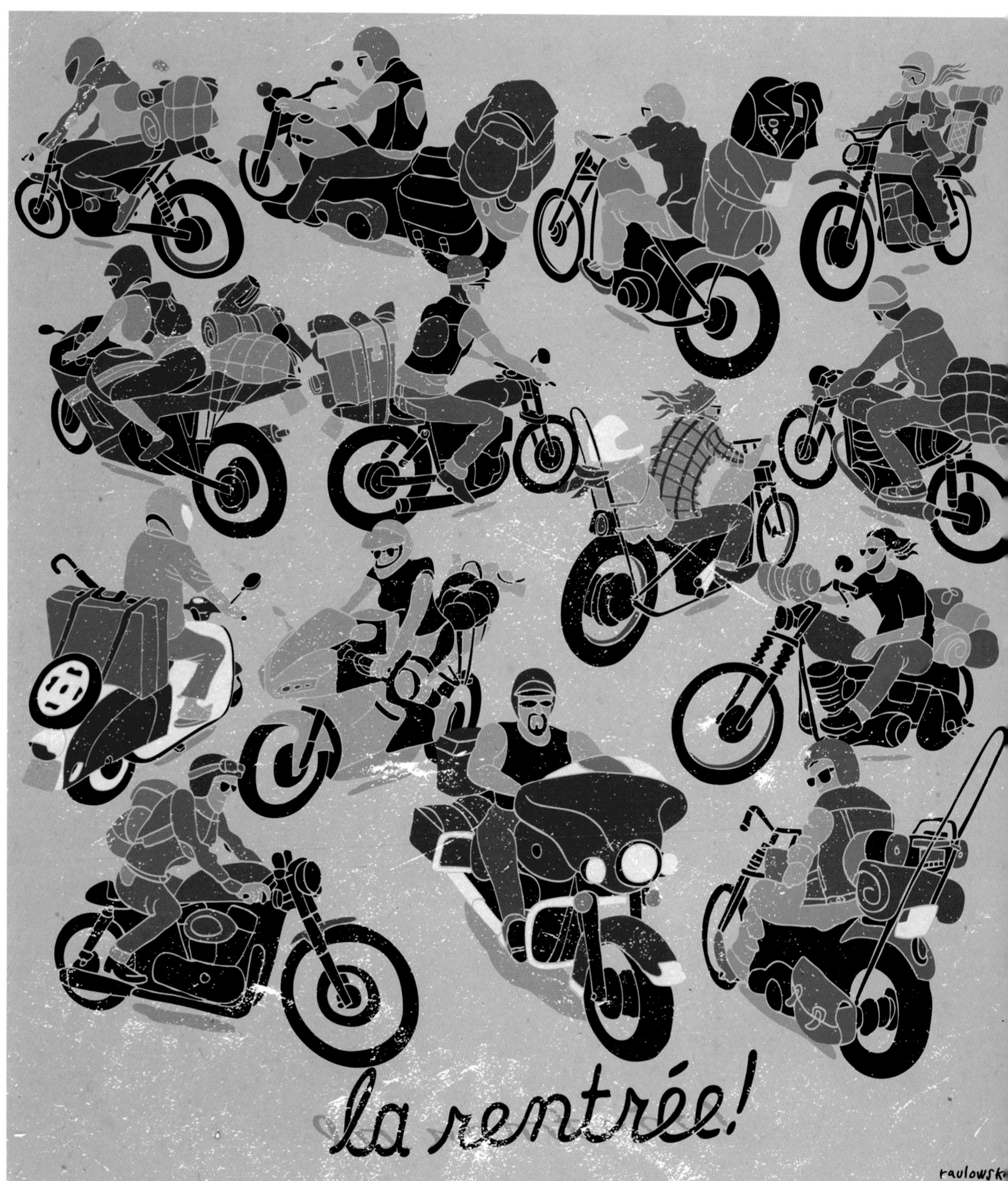
la rentrée!
raulowsk

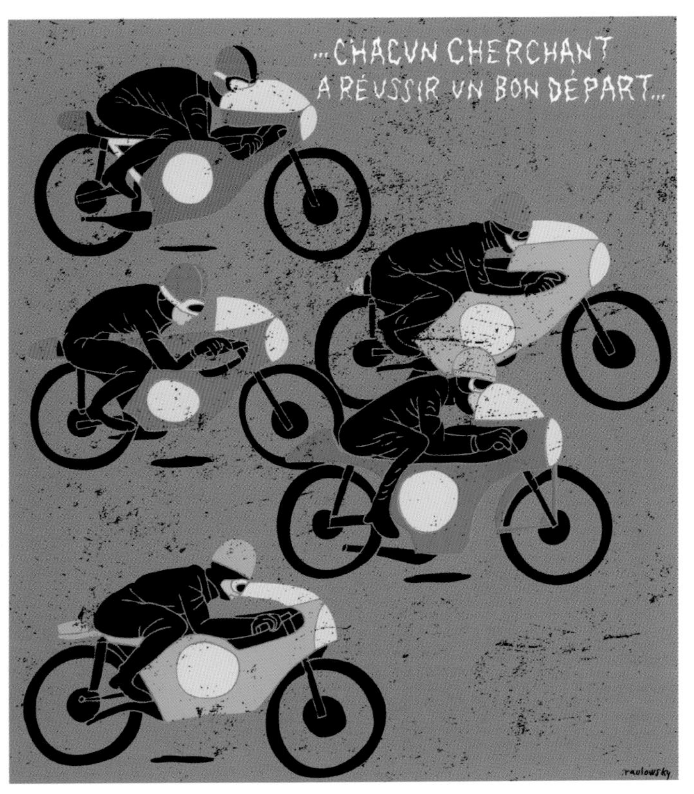

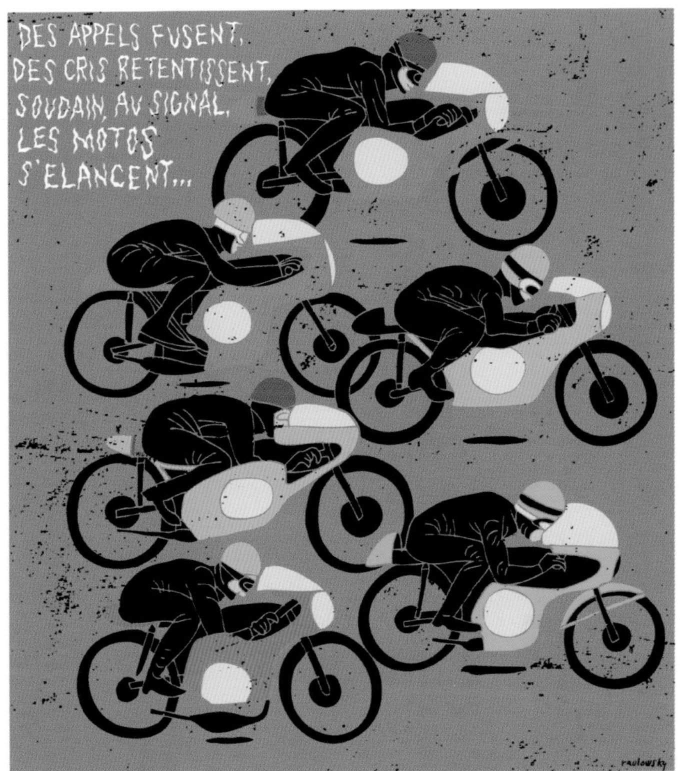

ABOVE: ***Classic 50cc Racer No 1.***
Ink on paper, digital.

ABOVE RIGHT: ***Classic 50cc Racer No 2.***
Ink on paper, digital.

RIGHT: ***Classic 50cc Racer No 3.***
Ink on paper, digital.

LEFT: ***La Rentrée.***
Ink on paper, digital.

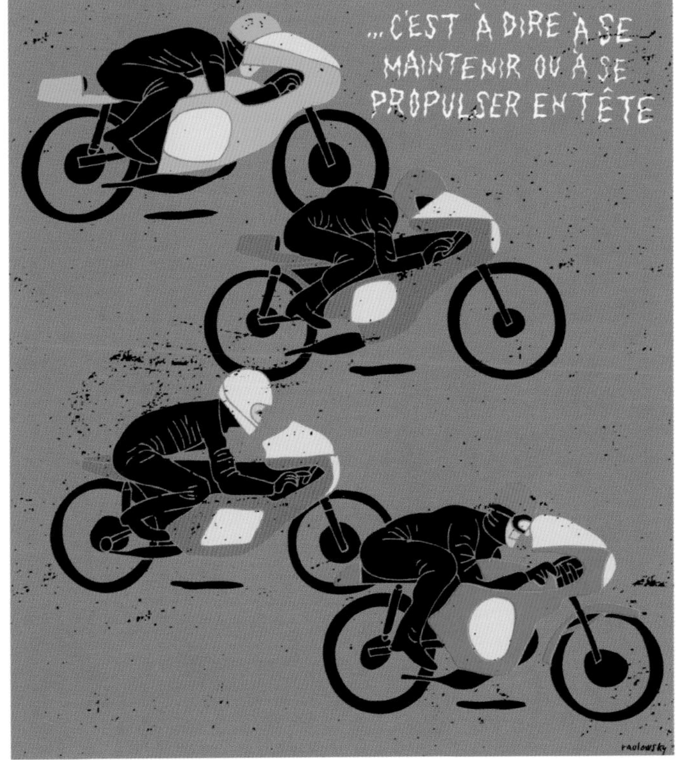

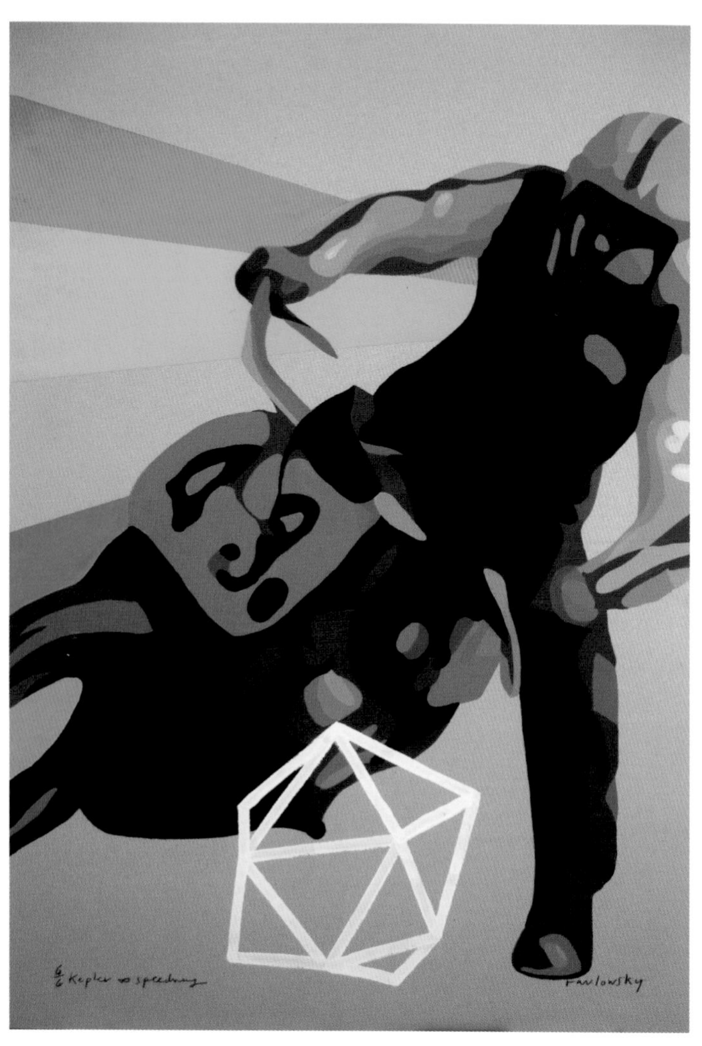

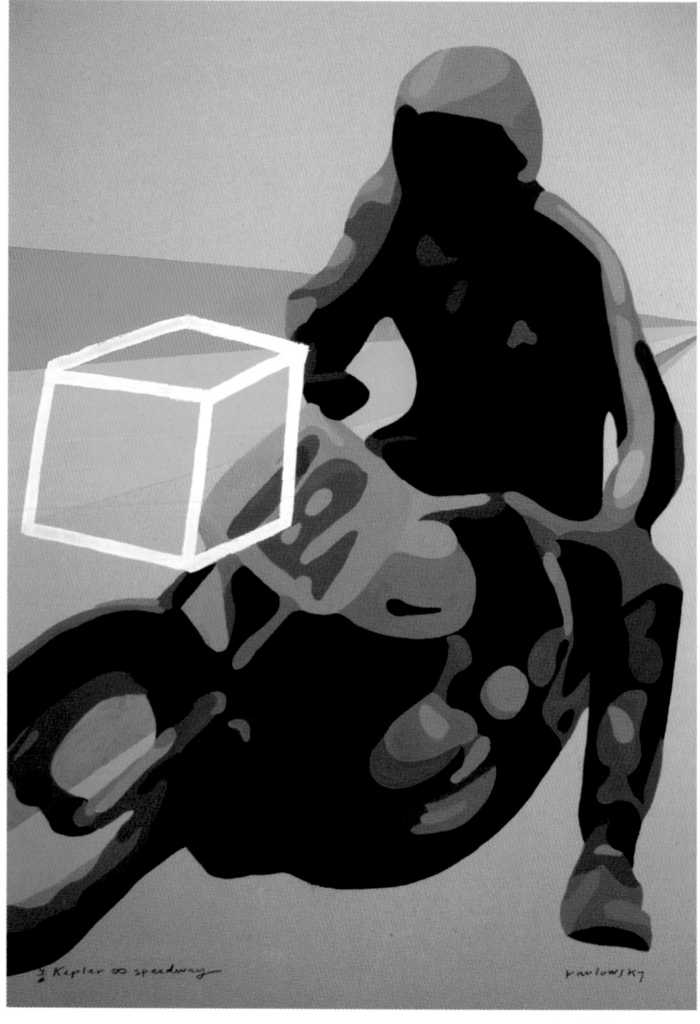

ABOVE: ***Kepler Speedway 4/6.***
Acrylic on cardboard.

ABOVE RIGHT: ***Kepler Speedway 6/6.***
Acrylic on cardboard.

FAR RIGHT: ***Septiembre, Pa Casa (Going Home).***
Digital art.

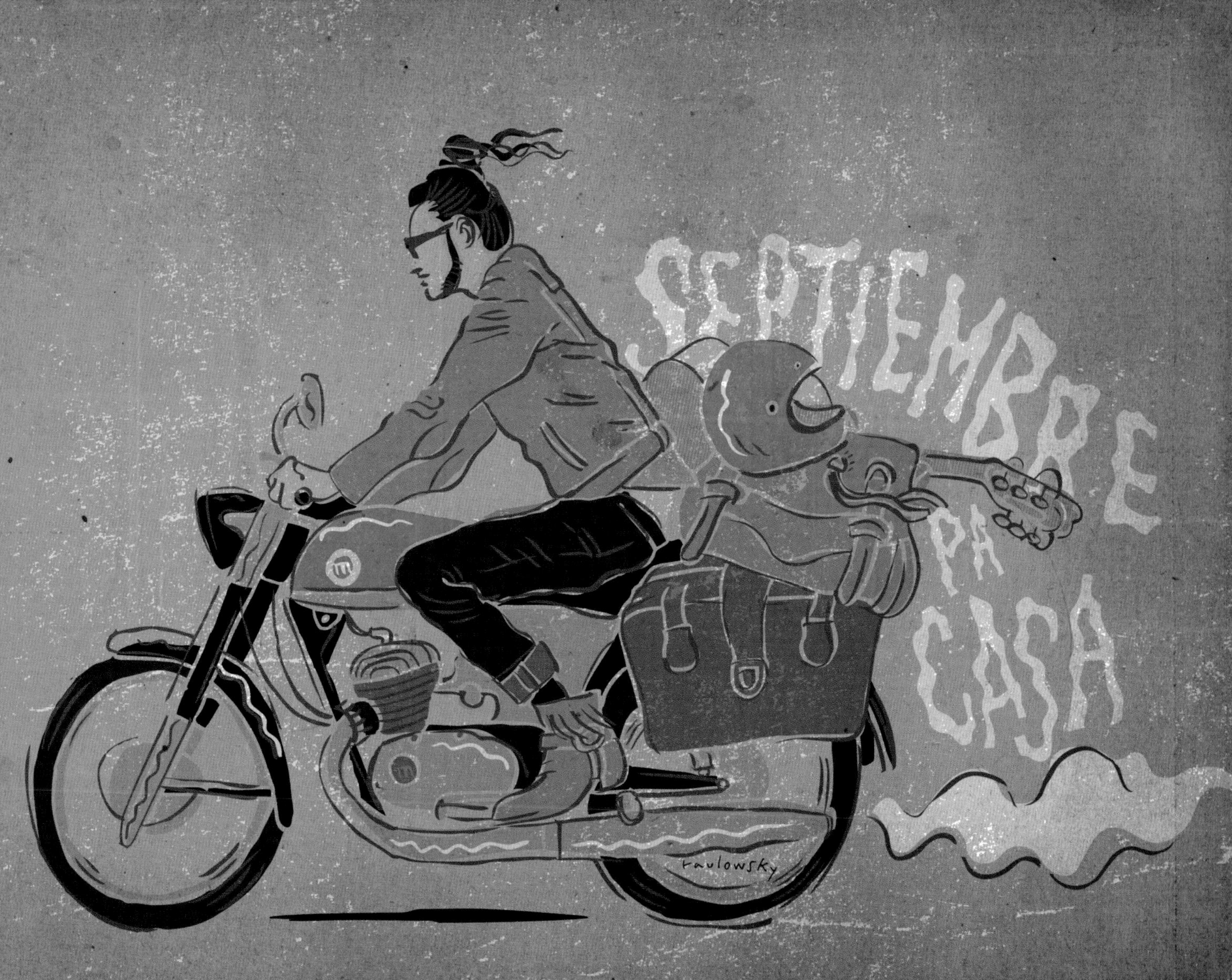
SEPTIEMBRE
PA
CASA
raulowsky

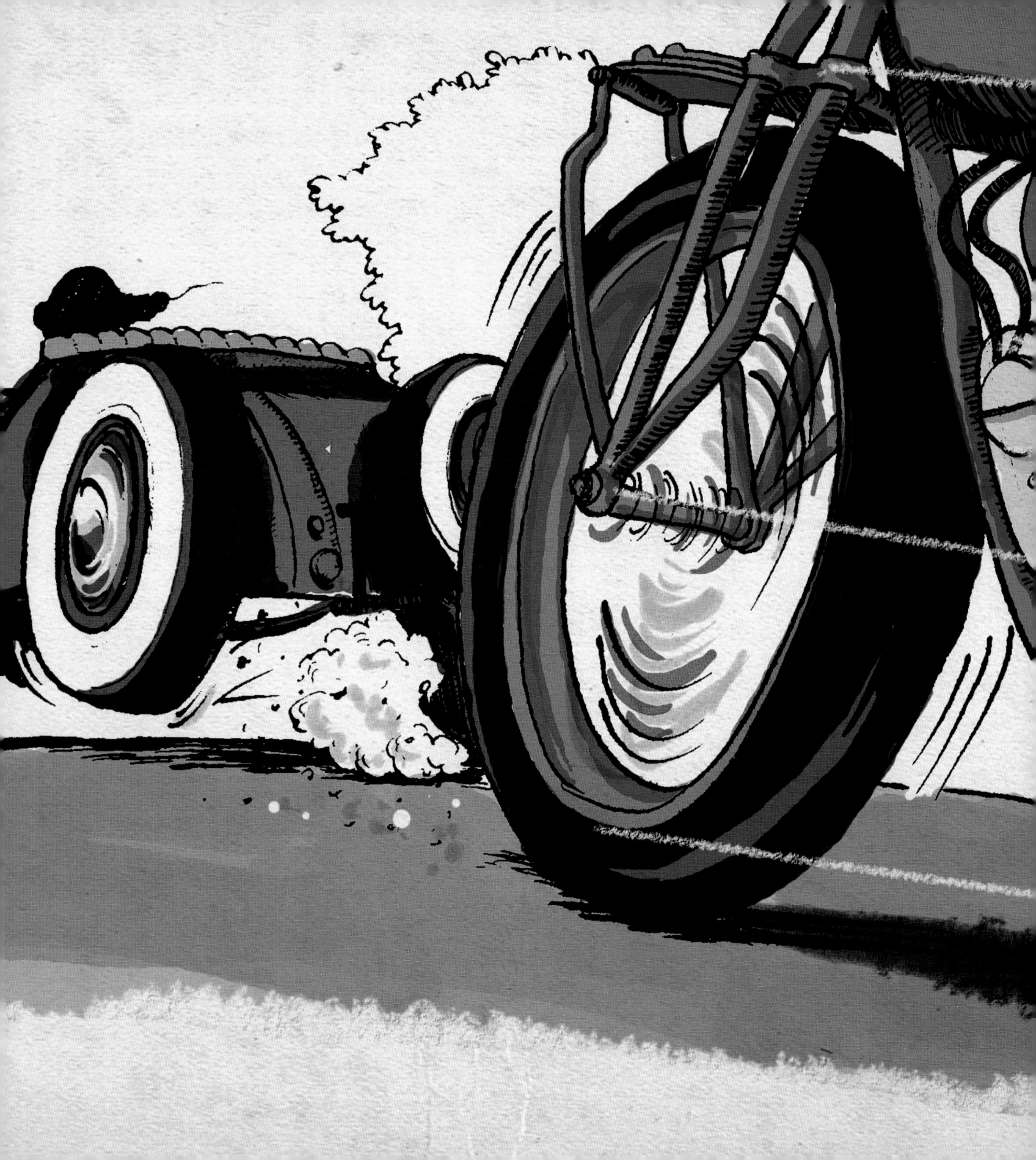

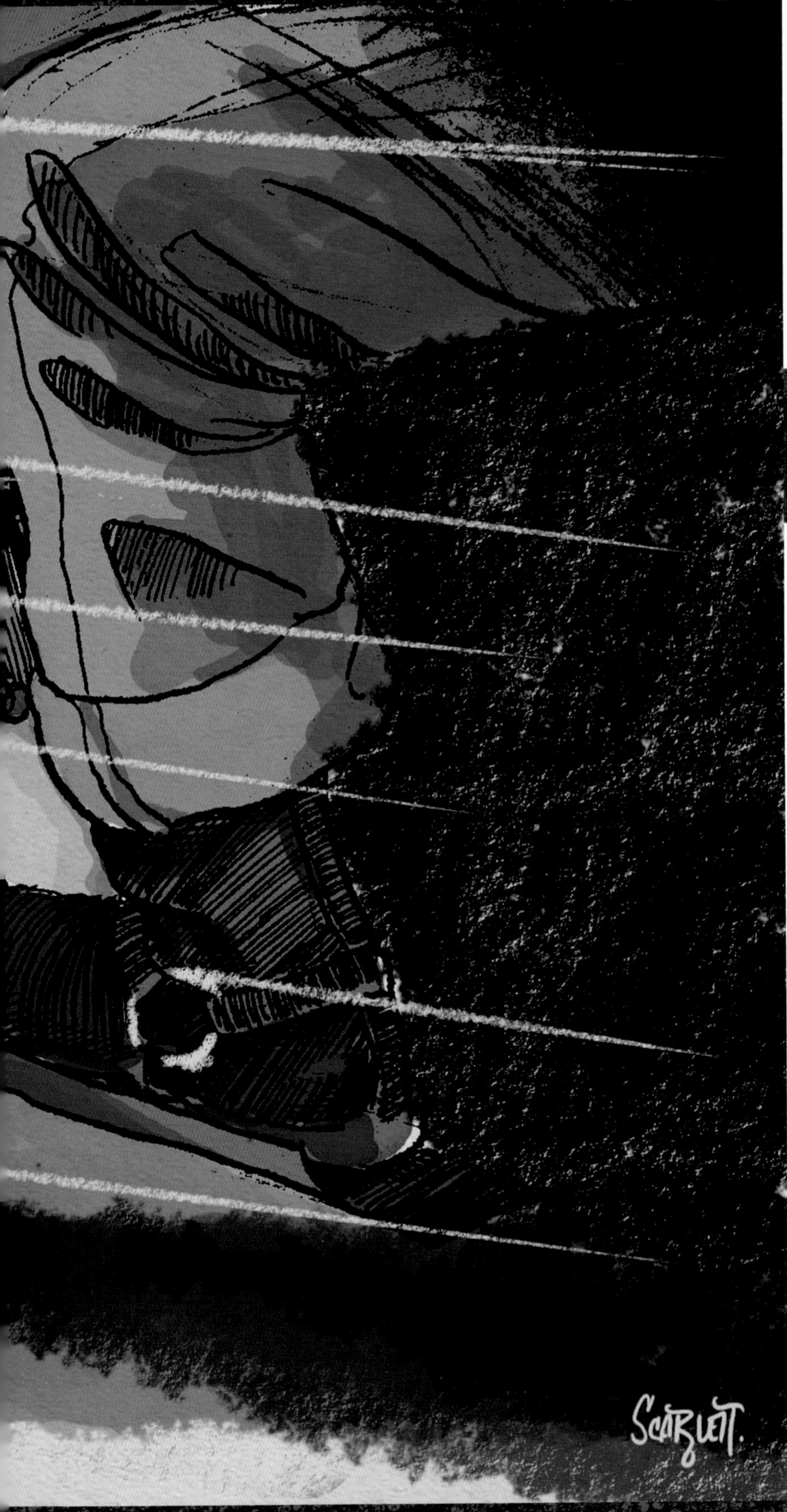

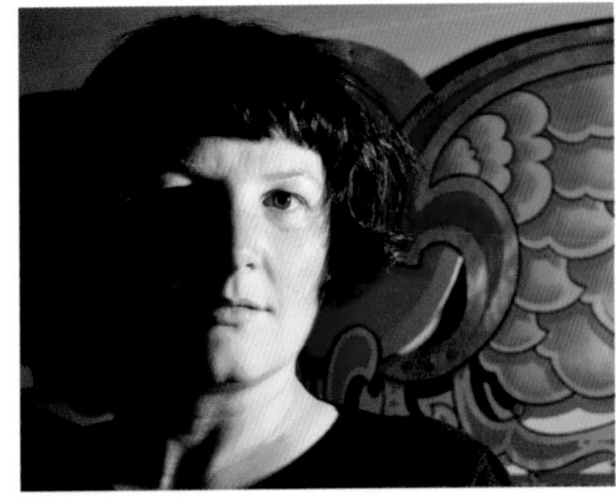

SCARLETT RICKARD

As a young girl, in Lancashire, England, Scarlett found treasure in the local garage, "Ball bearings and spark plugs dug out of the soft, oily floor. That place has been an inspiration throughout my life." The visual diaries of her days rooting around sheds and exploring life led to her becoming a professional illustrator. "I never really decided to become an artist, I suppose I just sort of was one." Scarlett has a love of pre-war bikes, cars, trucks and "other old shit in general." For years she refused to even acknowledge the existence of computers; "I'm more comfortable with Brunel than Berners-Lee, but eventually I decided I couldn't run forever, and it has made my work so much more fun and creative." In addition to sketching on paper and then using the Mac, Scarlett uses vintage dip pens and India ink. "I love the unpredictability of it, the splats and the splutters, and the line thickness is really fluid.' Away from her art, she co-produced an independent magazine called *Dirty* and the Dirty Bobbers website, and plays in a "noisy, oddball, tin-based, avant-garde quartet, The Amusiacs." Scarlett has a Panther in boxes in her kitchen cupboards and a 125cc Villiers Excelsior bobber.

LEFT: *Scouting.*
Pen and Indian ink, digital colours.

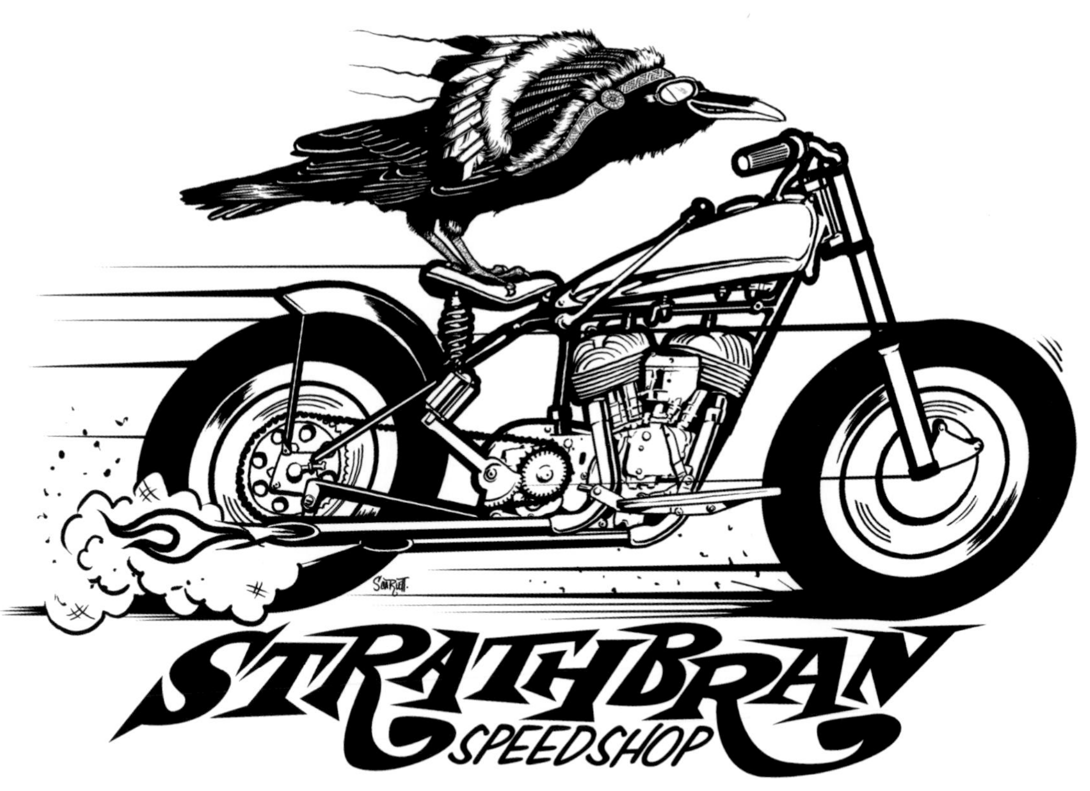

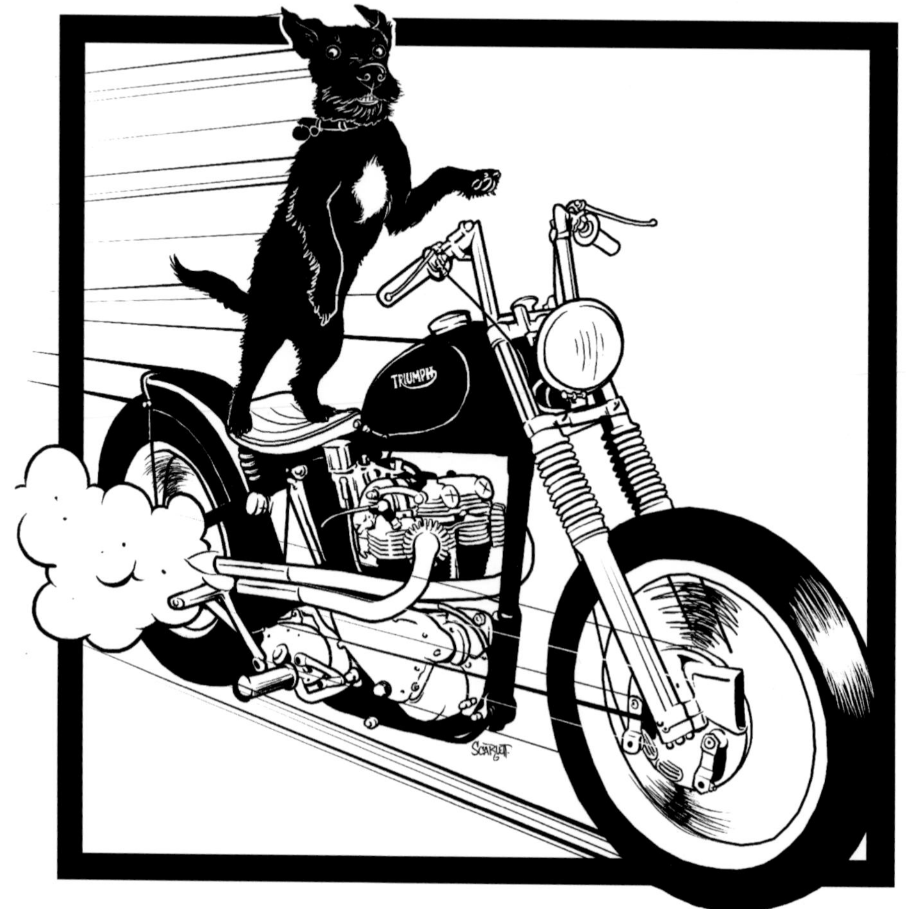

ABOVE: ***Strathbran.***
Digital artwork.

RIGHT: ***Ted.***
Digital artwork.

FAR RIGHT: ***Dirty Bob Wants You.***
Pen and ink, digital colours.

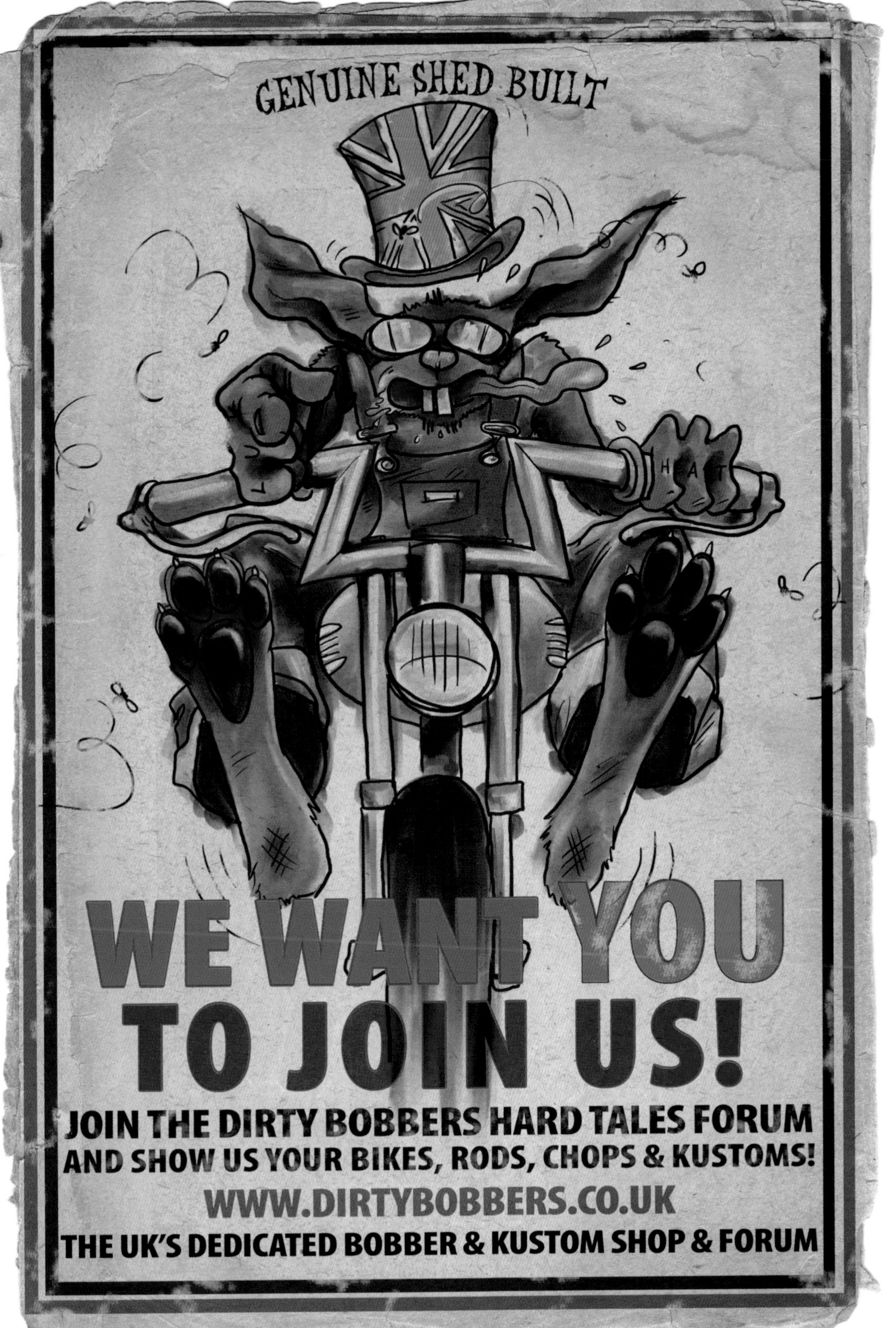
GENUINE SHED BUILT
WE WANT YOU
TO JOIN US!
JOIN THE DIRTY BOBBERS HARD TALES FORUM
AND SHOW US YOUR BIKES, RODS, CHOPS & KUSTOMS!
WWW.DIRTYBOBBERS.CO.UK
THE UK'S DEDICATED BOBBER & KUSTOM SHOP & FORUM

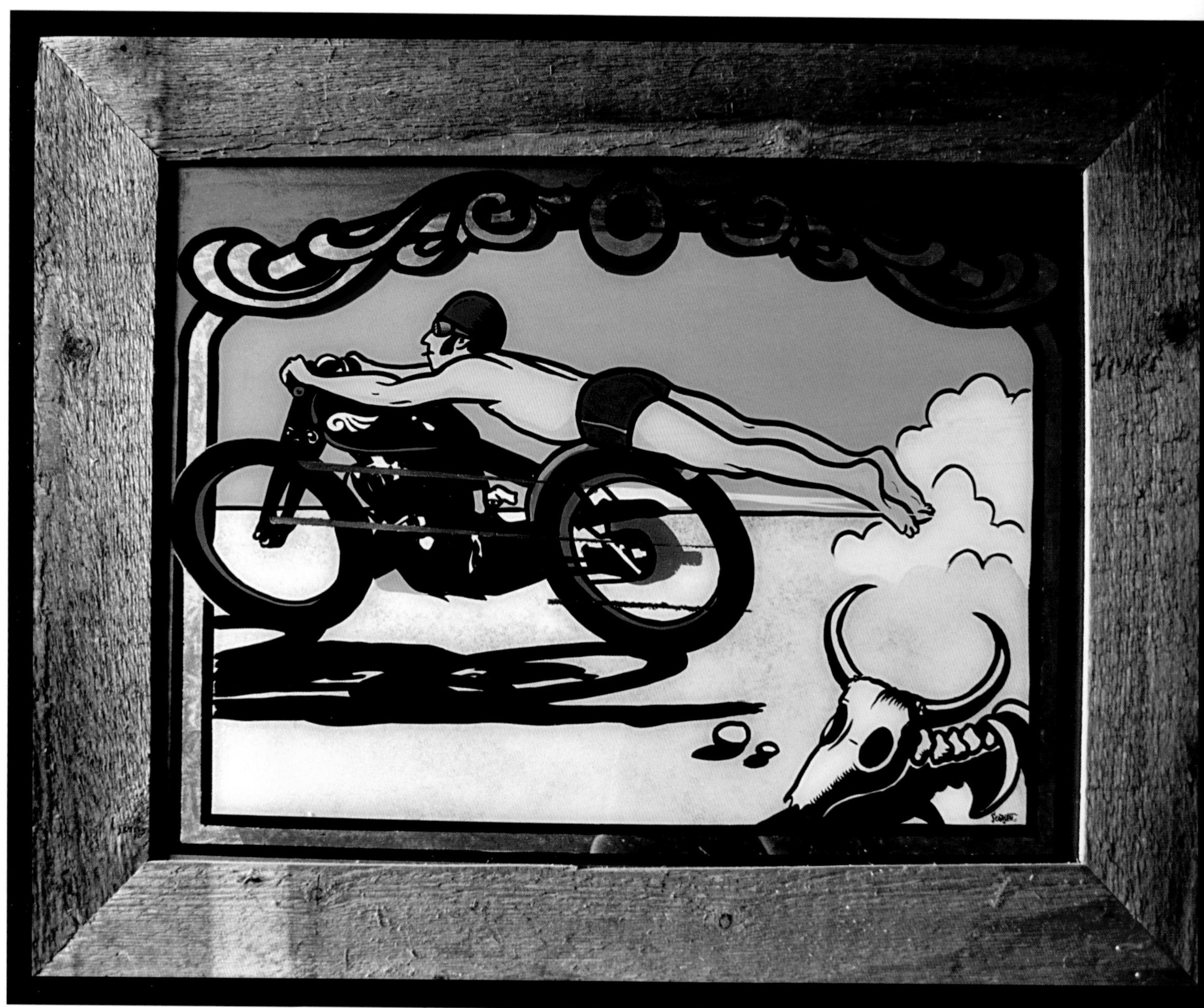

ABOVE: ***Saltflats.***
Enamel, gold leaf and glitter on glass.

RIGHT: ***Boardtracker.***
Enamel, gold leaf and glitter on glass.

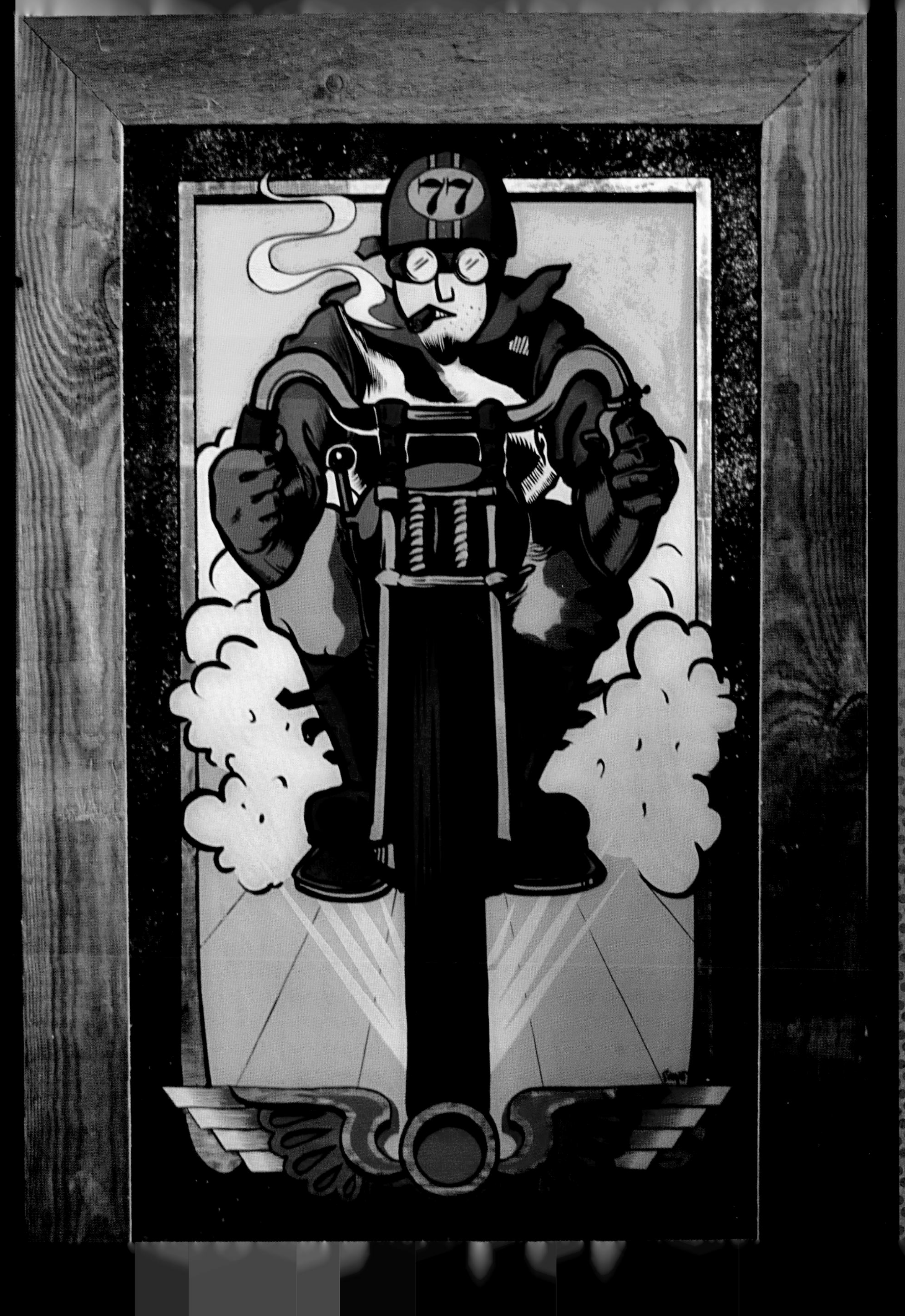
77

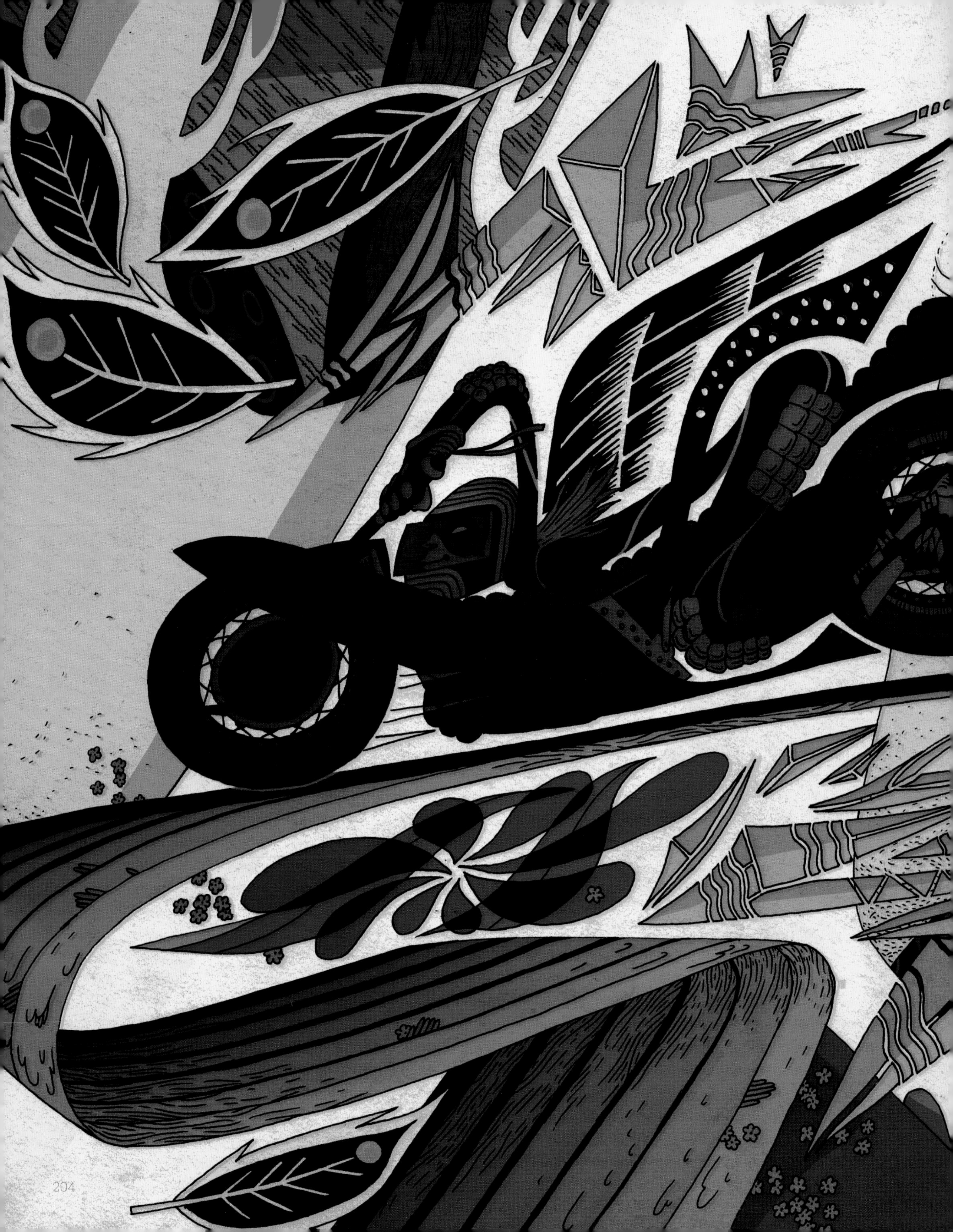

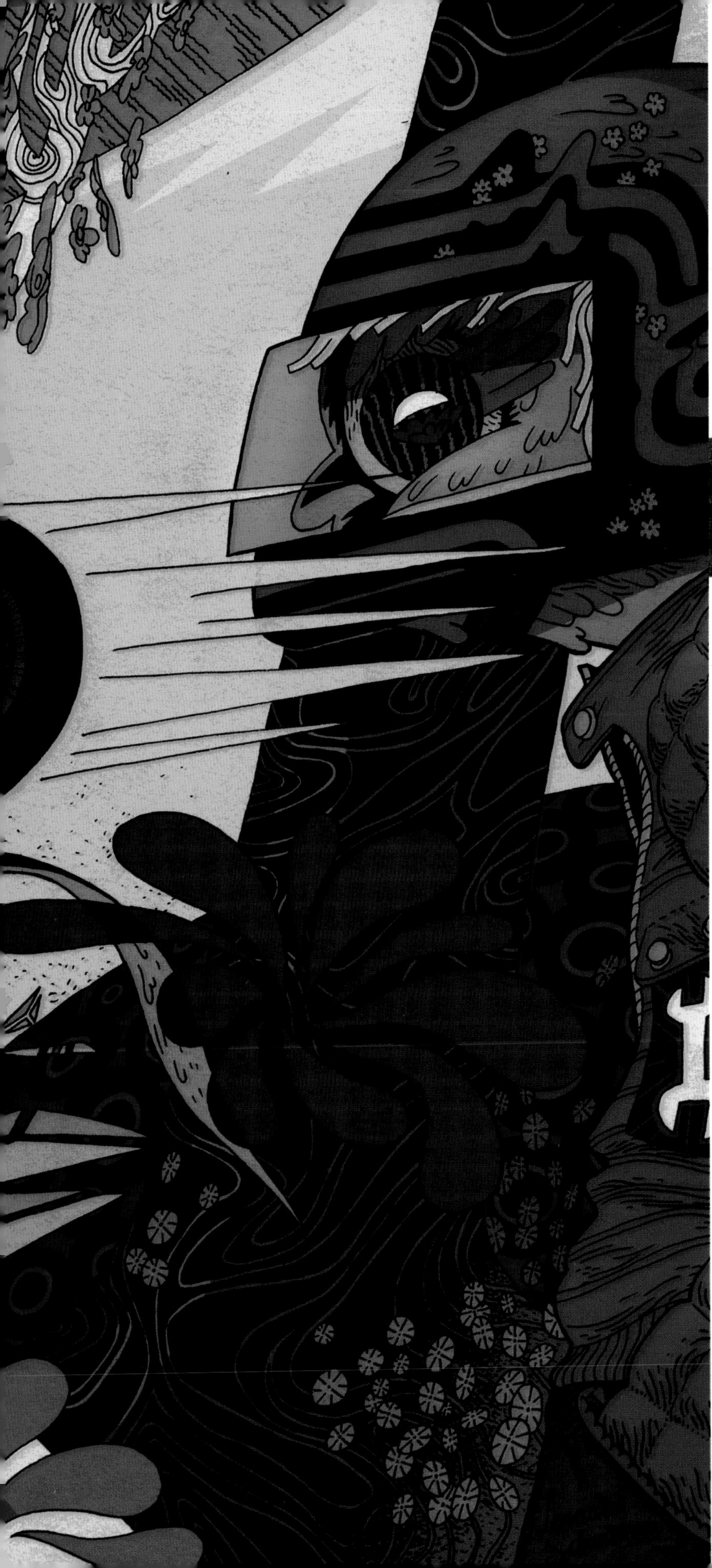

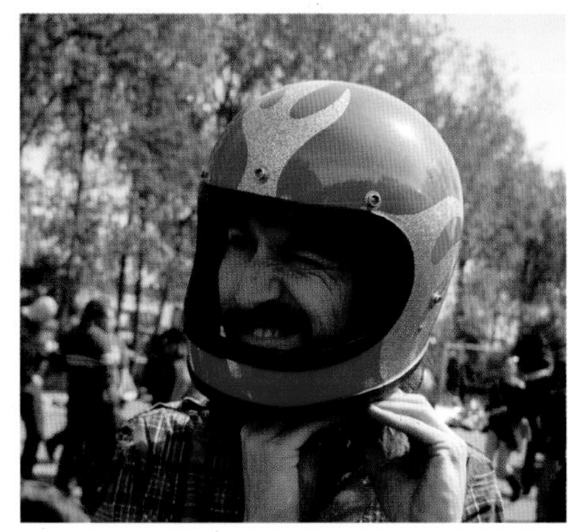

LENNARD SCHUURMANS

So many people say they only ever wanted to be artists, but Lenny Schuurmans admits he dreamed of being a jockey when he was a kid growing up in The Netherlands. Then he decided he'd like to be an architect, "But I was no good at maths." Commercial art beckoned and Lenny found something he could excel at. He has since been commissioned by the likes of Nike and Adidas, has illustrated a children's book and worked for magazines around Europe. Then..."I designed some artist collaboration t-shirts for Levi's and was paid enough to pass my motorcycle test and buy my first bike – a Kawasaki GPz1100. It was an old school streetfighter and way too heavy for a first bike." Since then, Lenny's bikes have got smaller and older. He shares his bike obsession through his *Bubble Visor* blog, and grazing a million other blogs inspires his own art. "I work in pen, then scan the art and add colour with a Wacom tablet on a Mac. I also paint on wood I find. I don't like canvas, it's too soft." Lenny recently started his own brand, Barn Fresh, with products inspired by classic motorcycles and the sub-culture surrounding them.

LEFT: *Ladyspeed.*
Digital art and serigraph on paper.

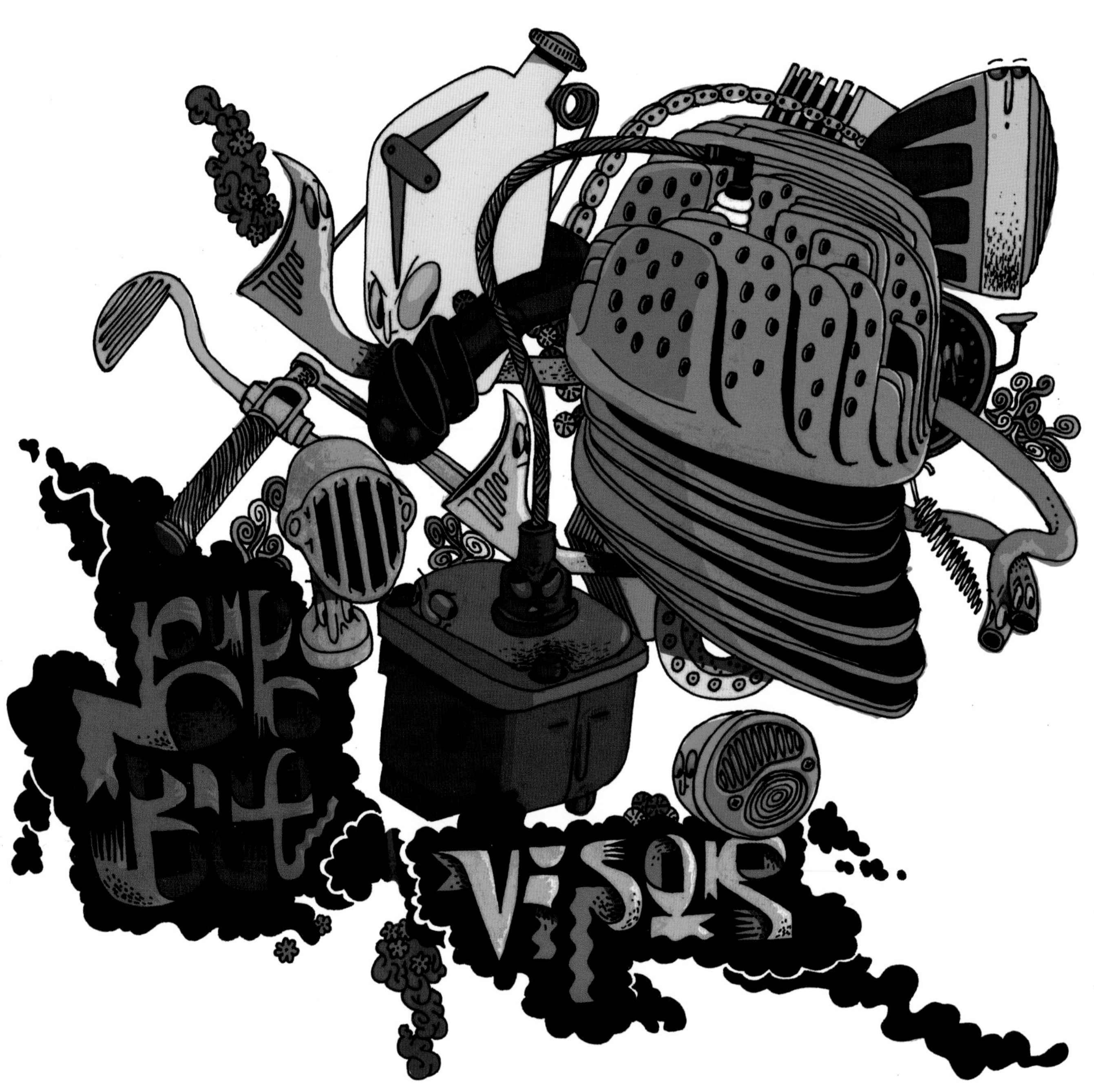

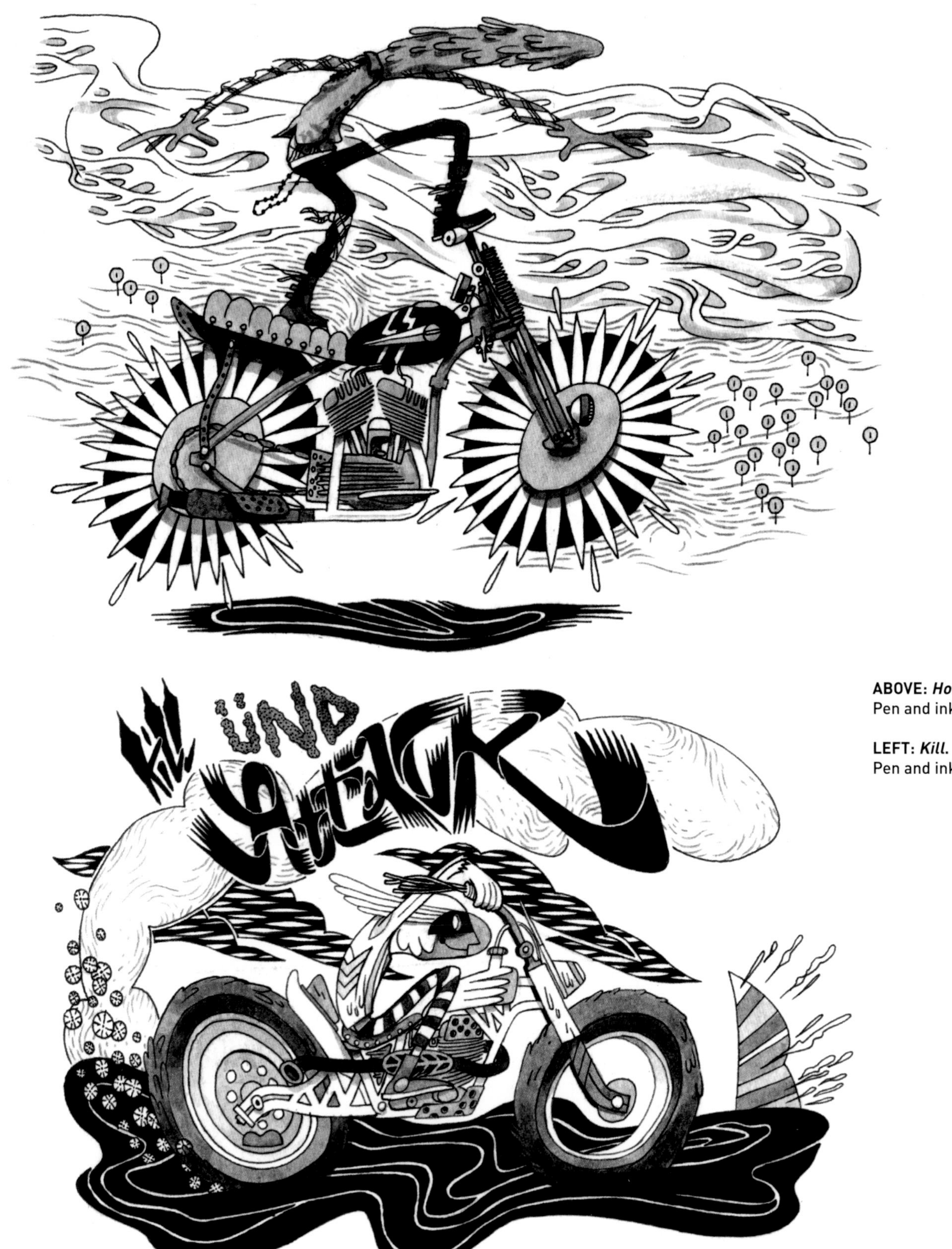

ABOVE: ***Hobo Surf.***
Pen and ink.

LEFT: ***Kill.***
Pen and ink.

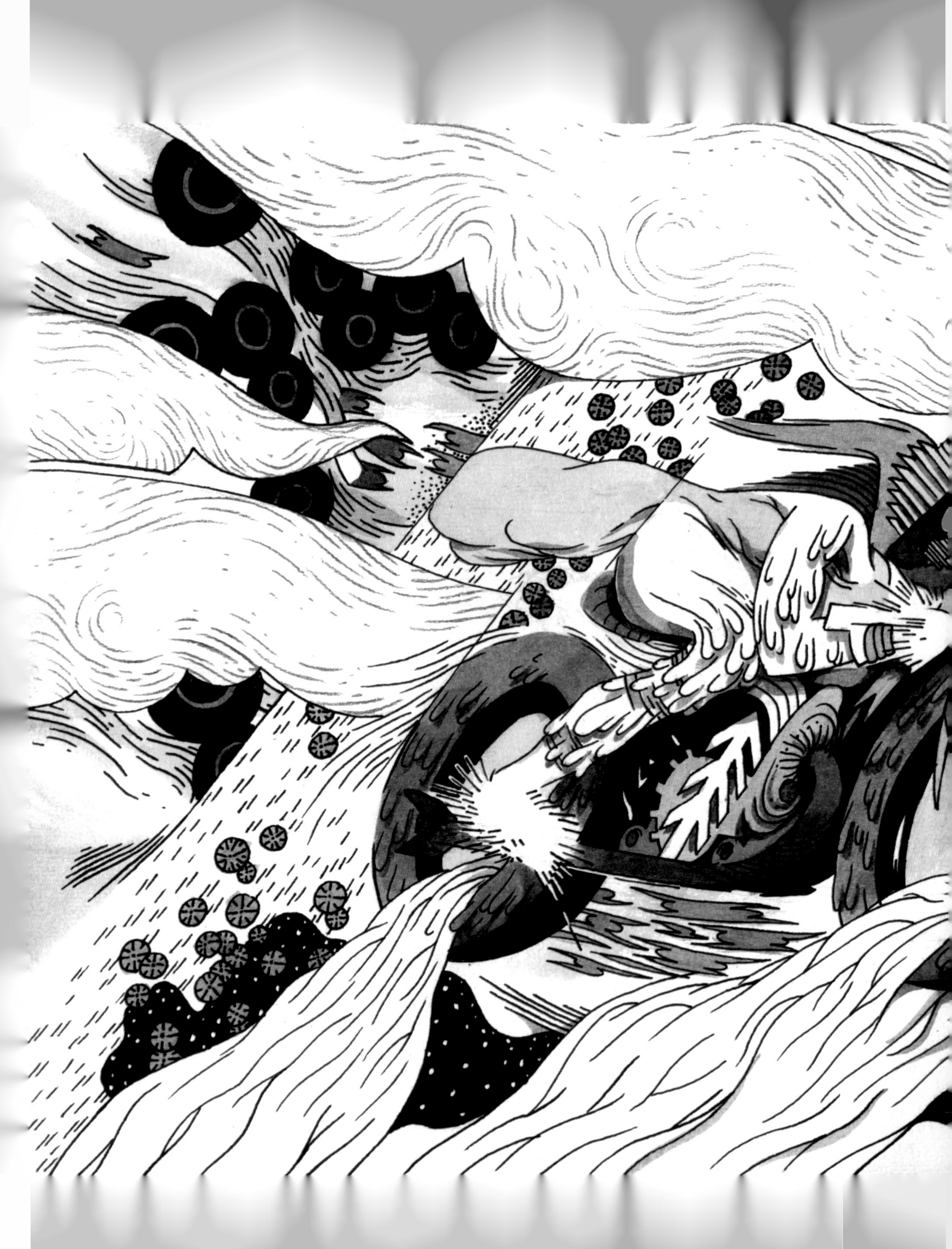

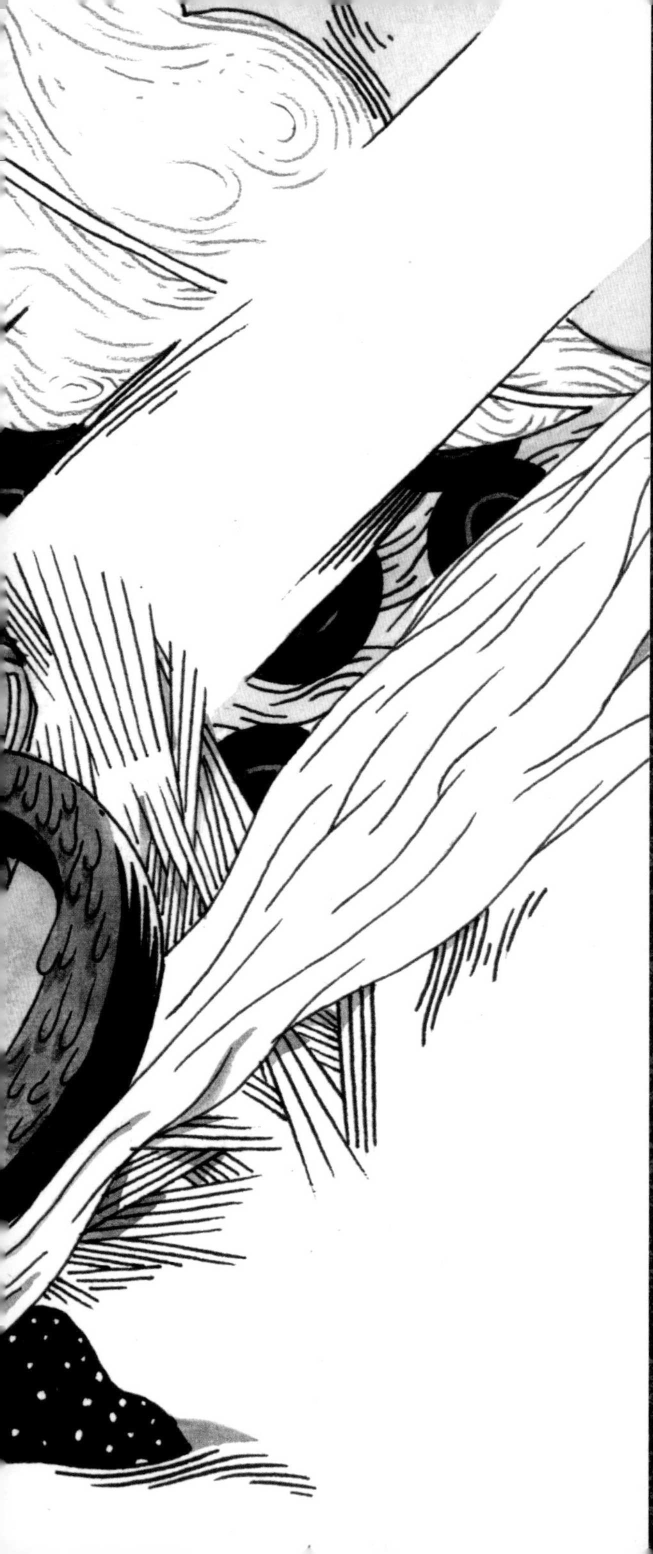

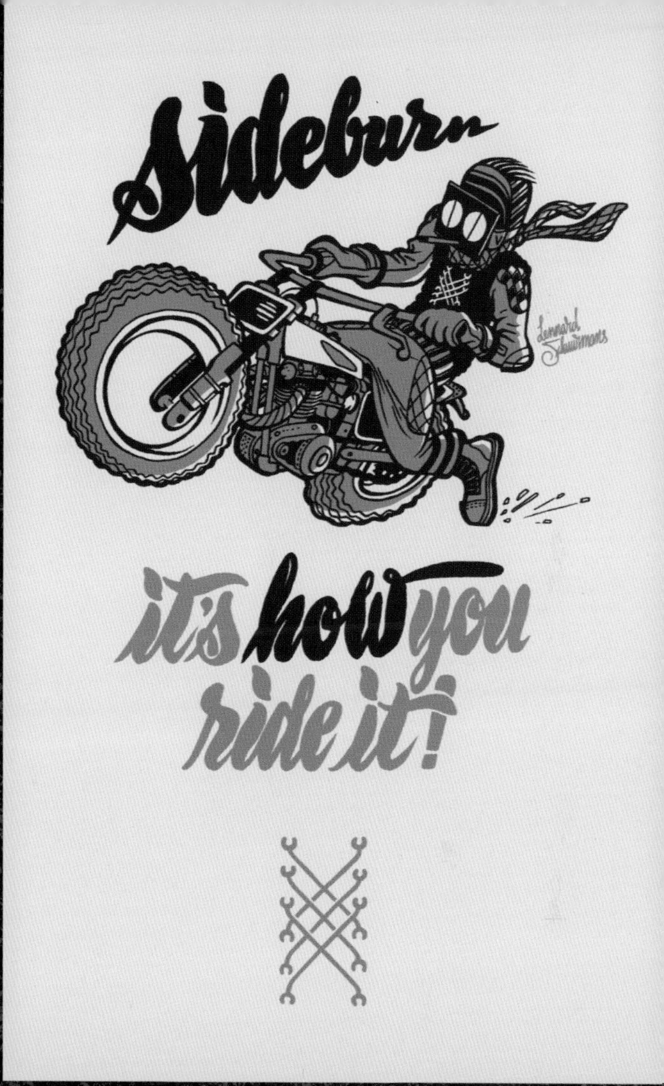

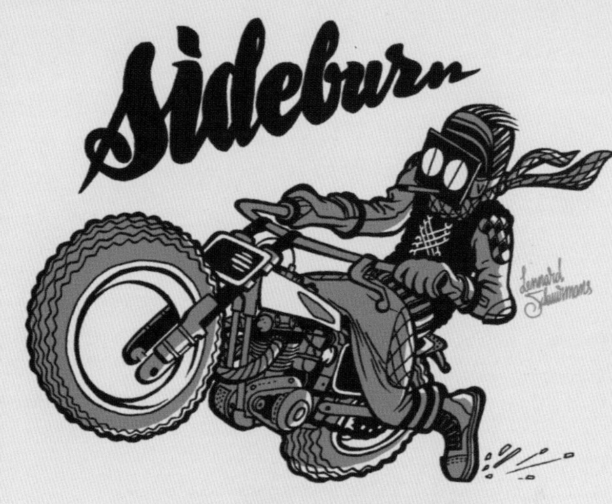

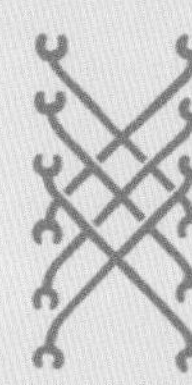

LEFT: ***Deco Dream.***
Pen and ink.

ABOVE: ***Lenny.***
Pen, ink and digital.

RIGHT: *Rusty Gold* Swap *Meet*. Digital art.

FAR RIGHT: *Boys Like Us*. Pen, ink and digital.

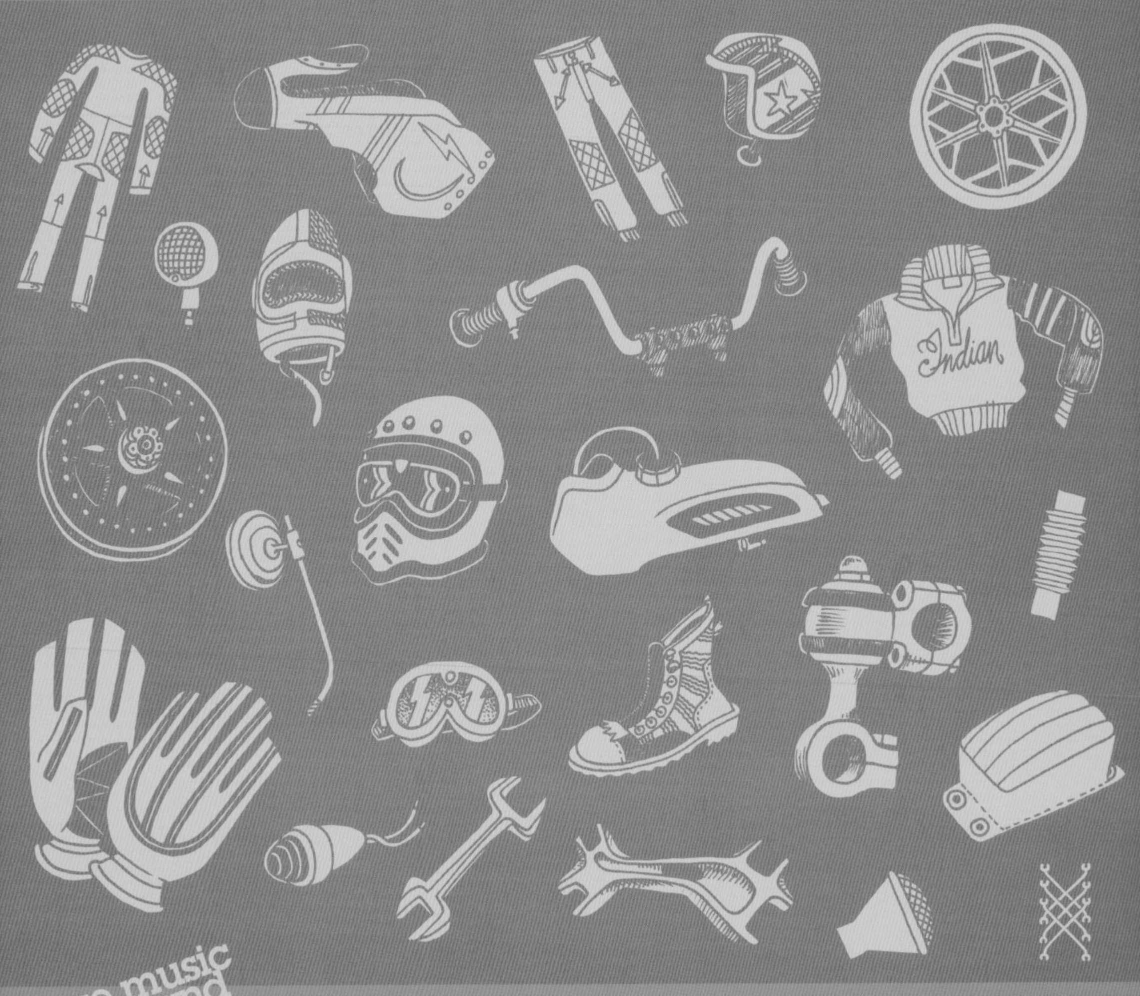

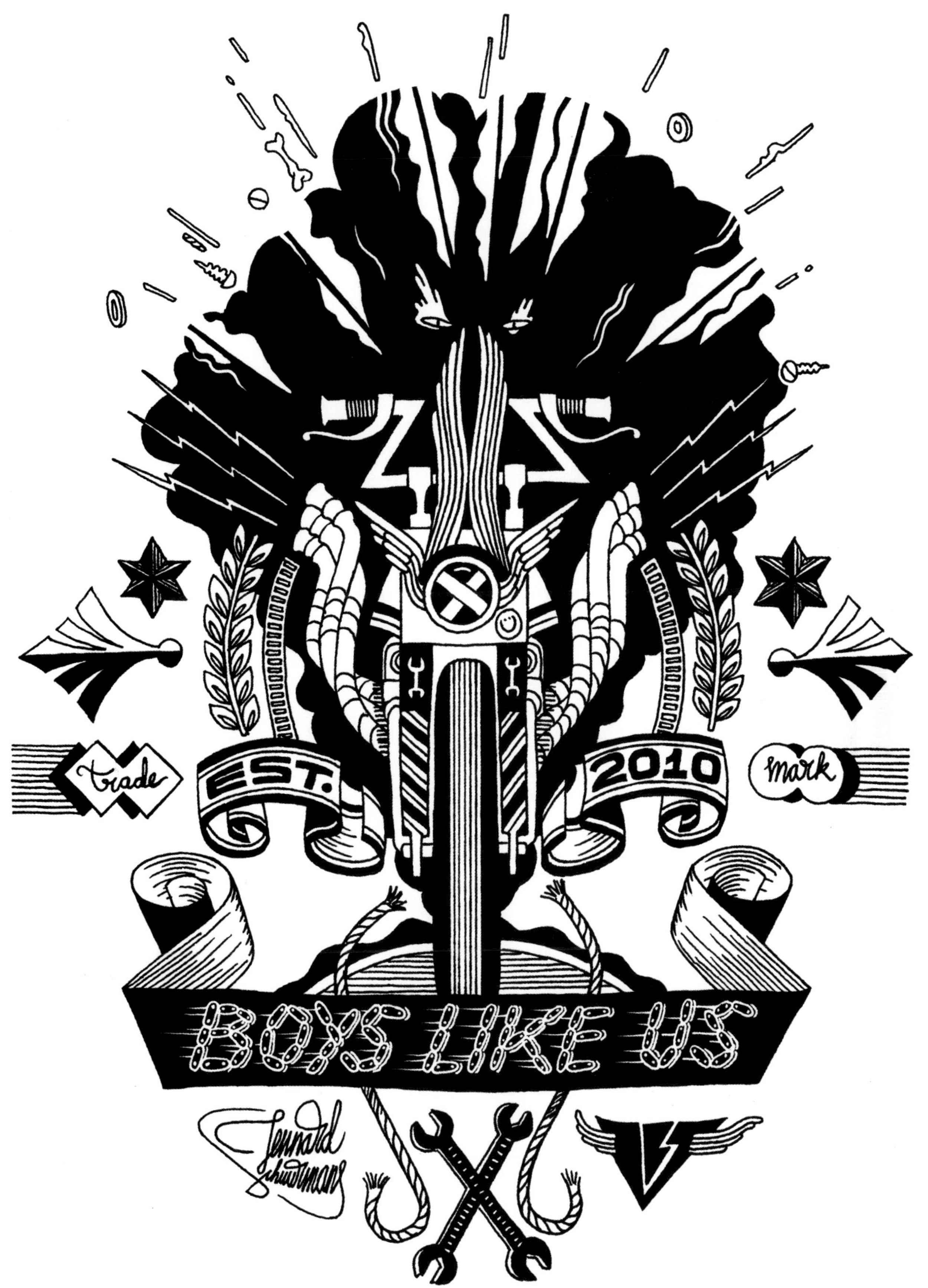
trade
EST.
2010
mark
BOYS LIKE US
Lennard Schuurmans

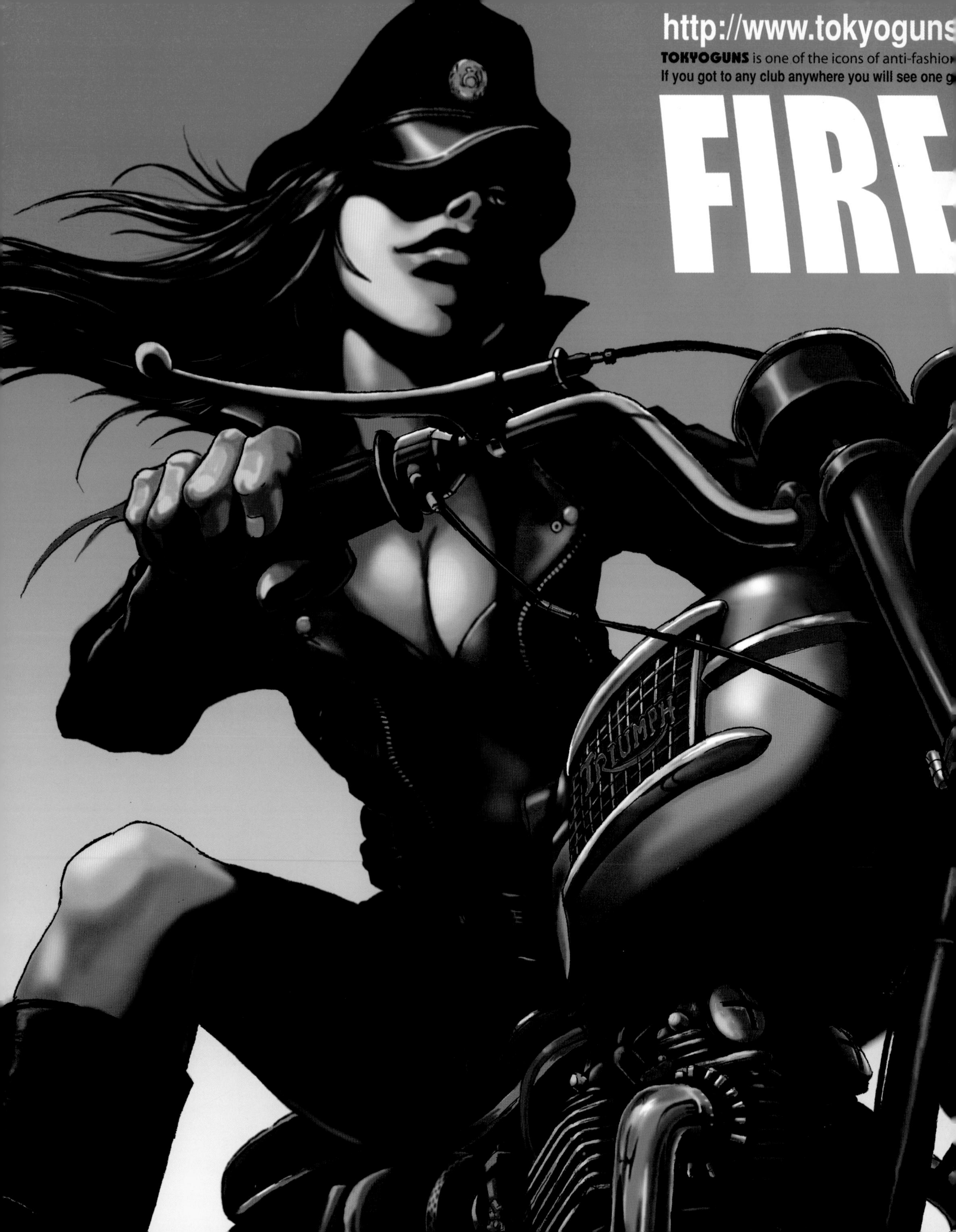
http://www.tokyoguns
TOKYOGUNS is one of the icons of anti-fashio
If you got to any club anywhere you will see one g
FIRE
TRIUMPH

they are an aid to making fashion unfashionable.
he podium dancing who's been influenced by **TOKYOGUNS** ...

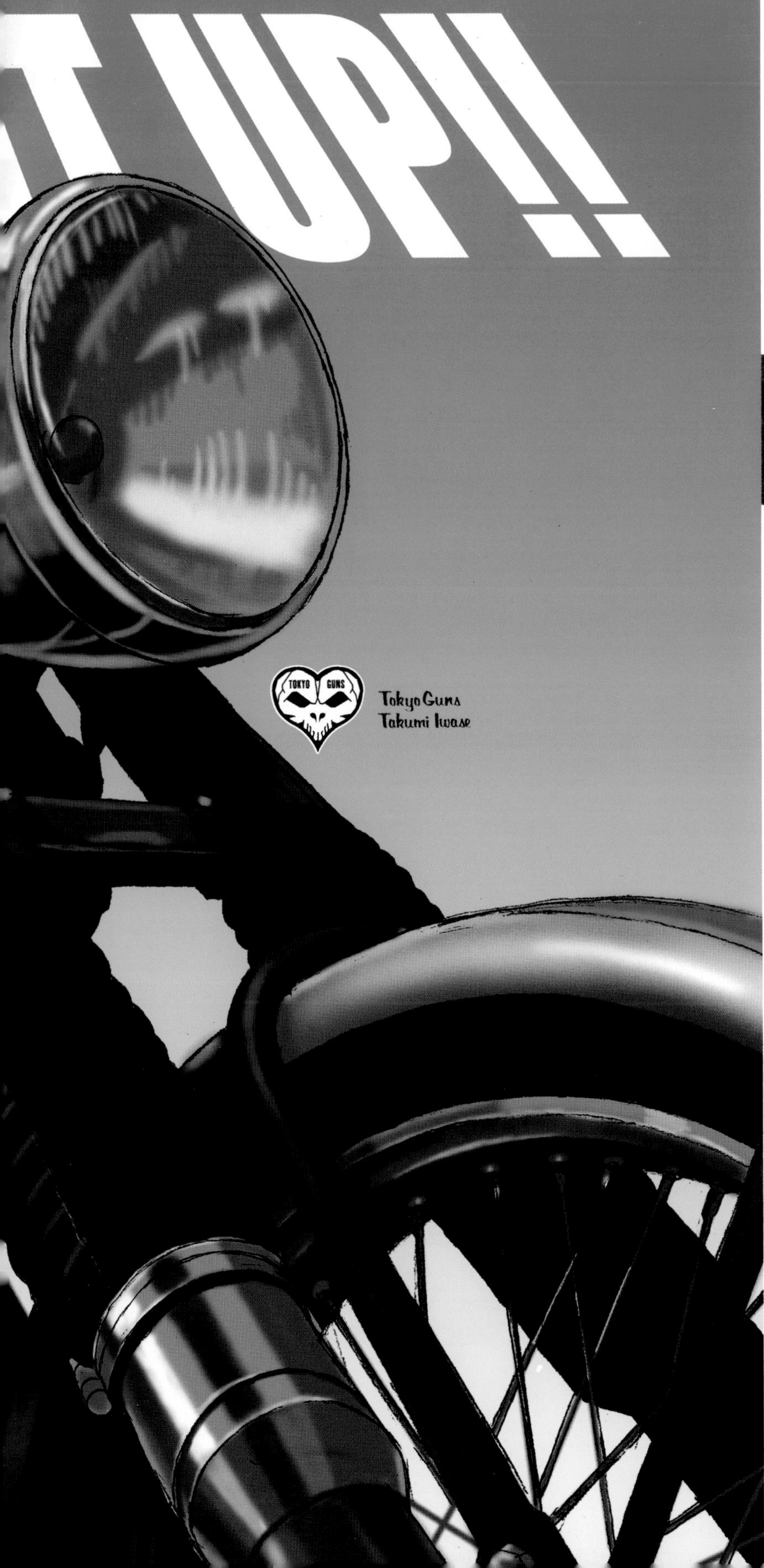

T UP!!

Tokyo Guns
Takumi Iwase

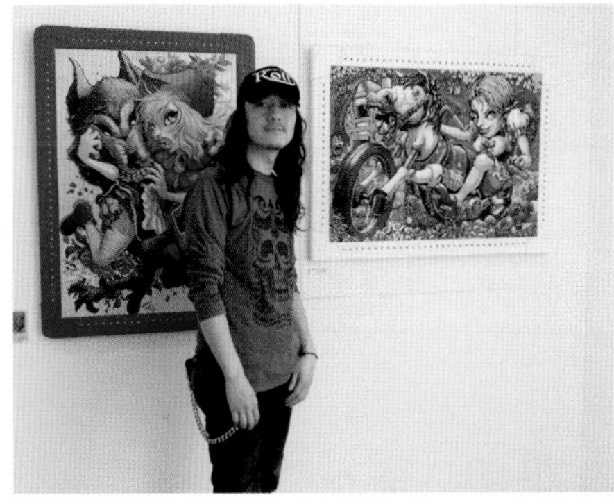

TOKYO GUNS

"I started riding when I was younger because I wanted to be popular with the girls. Then it turned into a pleasure: tweaking the throttle, moving forward and feeling the wind," says Takumi Iwase, a.k.a. the artist Tokyo Guns. "As a teenager, I was fascinated by UK rocker culture and the 'rogueness' of the music. I got into The Stray Cats big time, wore engineer boots and rolled-up my jeans, wore a Stadium helmet and rode a Yamaha SR400. Then I became interested in various types of bike culture. I felt that to draw better illustrations I needed to ride various bikes, so I have owned many." That list includes some all-time classic bikes, like the Harley XLCR and Bonneville T120R. He developed his style at Musashino Art University – where he initially had thoughts of becoming a movie director. His technique is straightforward. "I draw the outline on paper with a pencil or ink, then scan it and colour it on the Mac. I also use acrylic paint on drawing paper." Tokyo Guns is much in demand. Clients include Nike, many toy manufacturers and bands, such as Japanese rock band Shakalabbits. He also creates a centrefold for every issue of cult Japanese motorcycle style magazine, *Street Bikers*.

LEFT: ***Blue Sky.***
Ink on paper, digital colours.

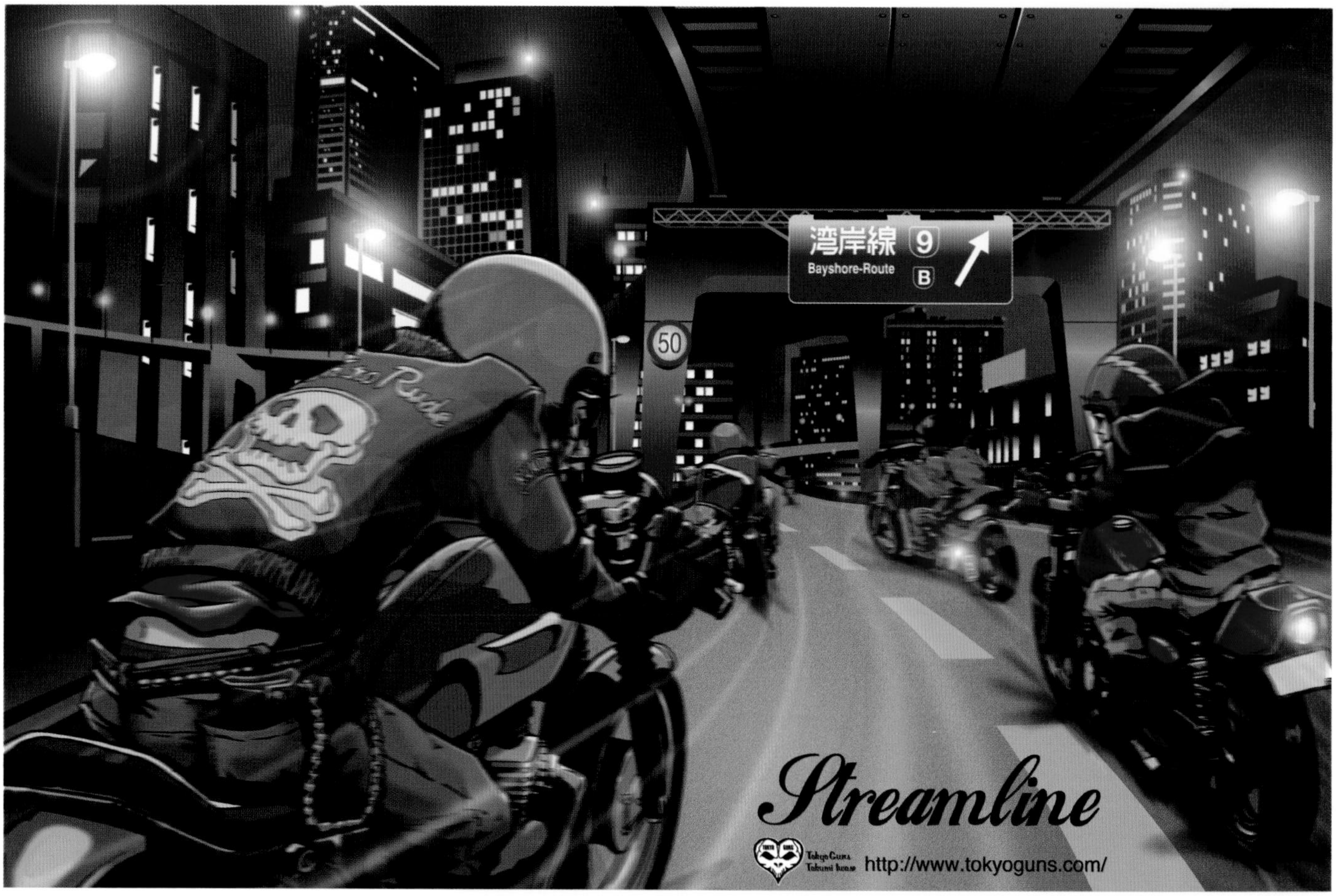

ABOVE: ***Syuto Kousoku.***
Ink on paper, digital colours.

RIGHT: ***Rock On.***
Ink on paper, digital colours.

FAR RIGHT: ***Overkill.***
Ink on paper, digital colours.

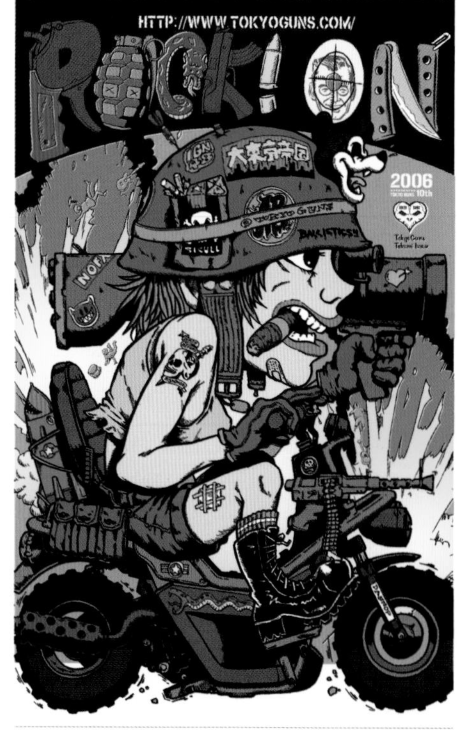

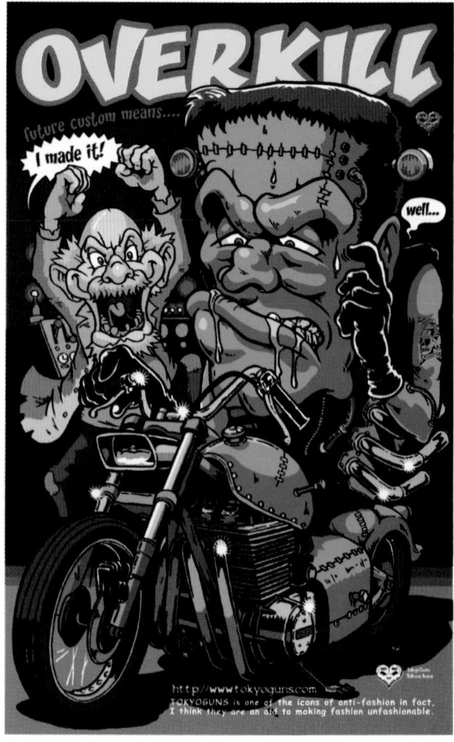

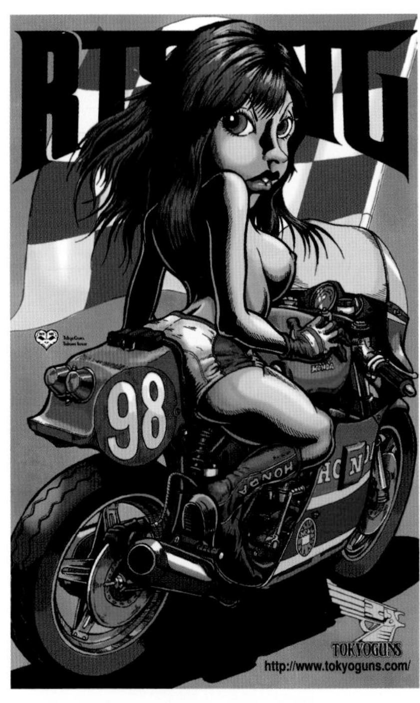

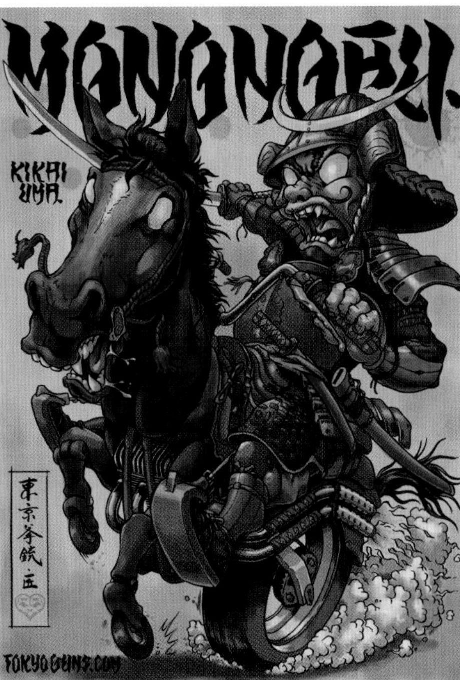

FAR LEFT: ***Honda Glory.***
Ink on paper, digital colours.

LEFT: ***Mononofu.***
Ink on paper, digital colours.

BELOW: ***Märchen.***
Ink on paper, digital colours.

OVERLEAF: ***Outlaw.***
Ink on paper, digital colours.

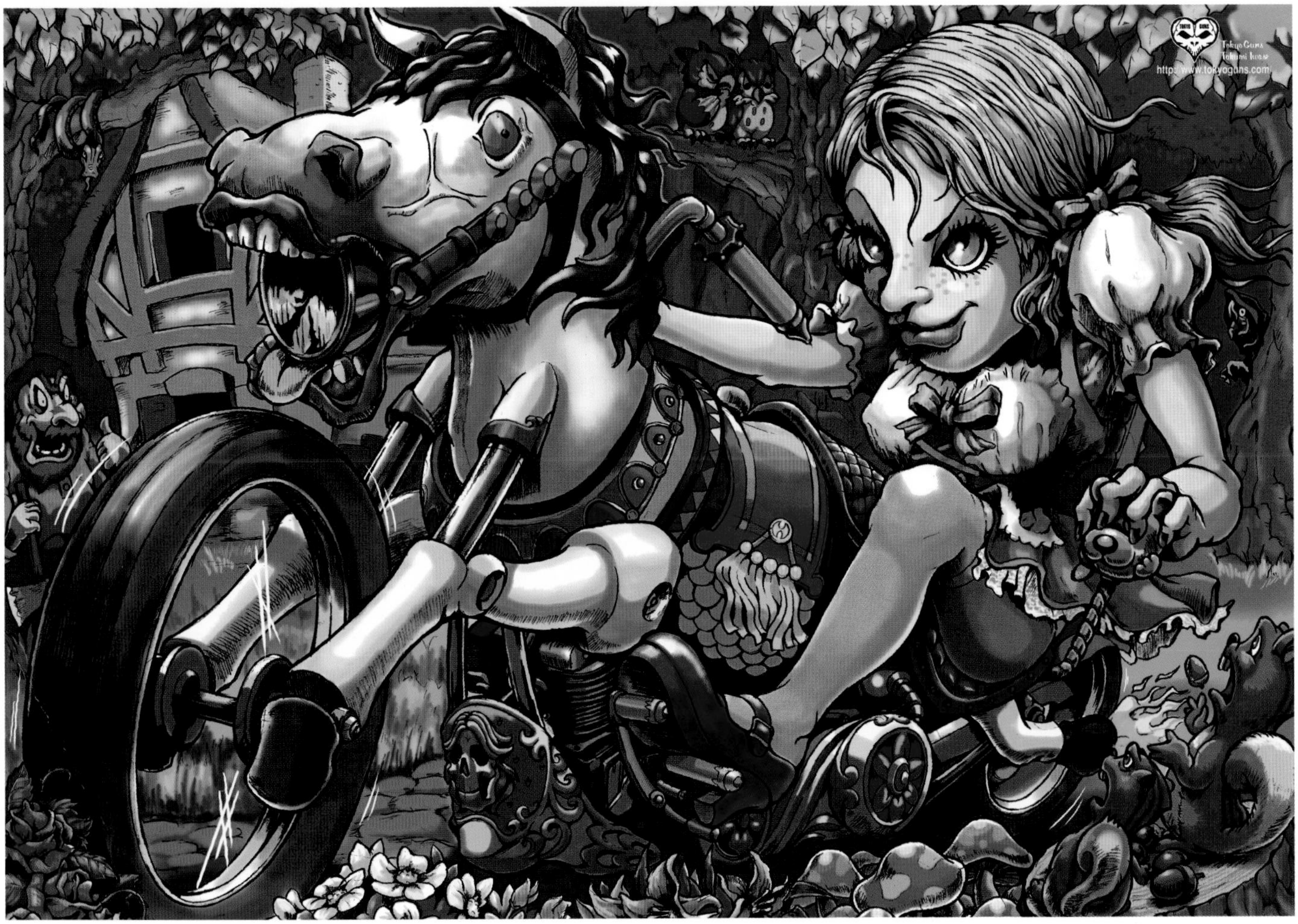

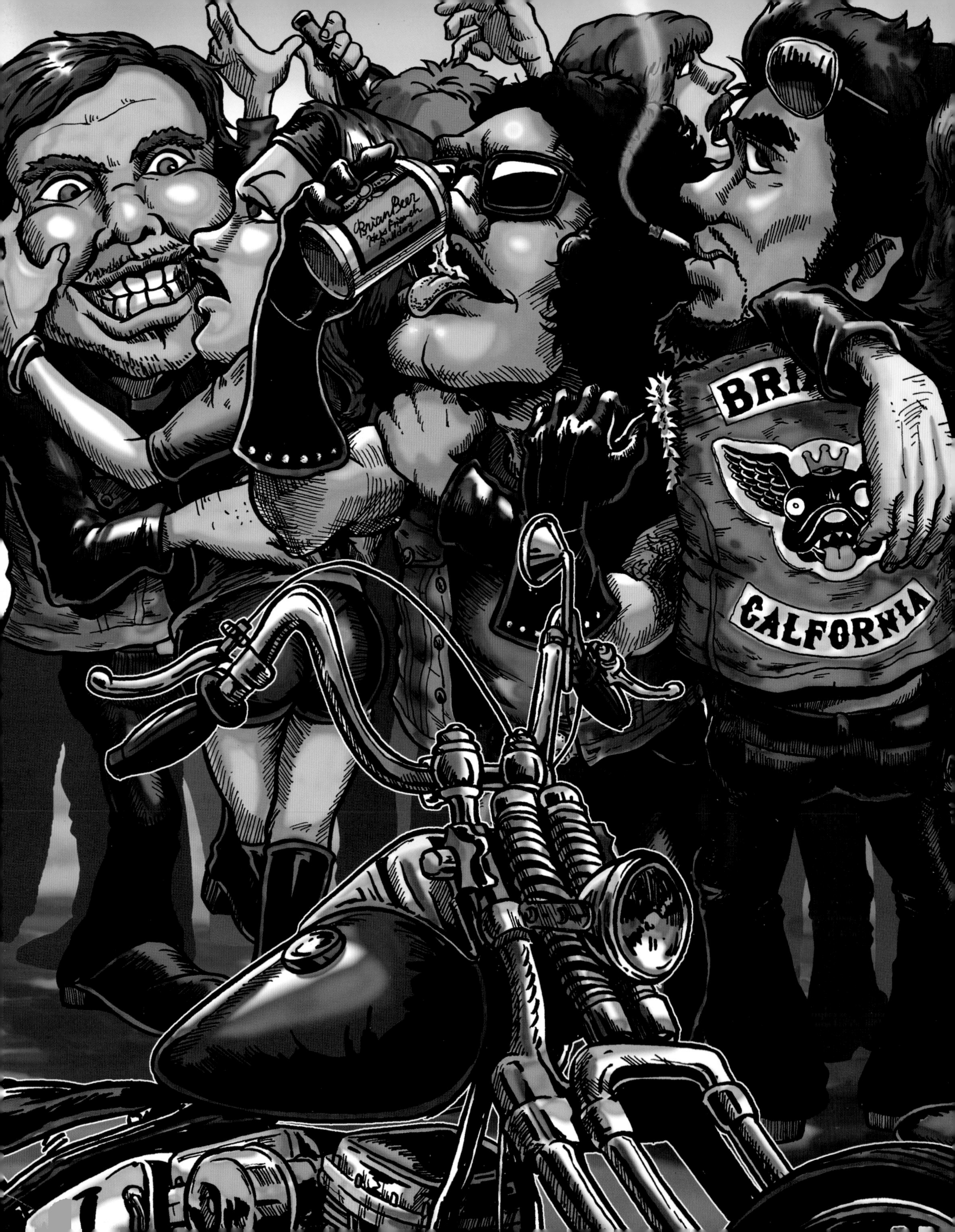
BrianBeer
BRI
CALFORNIA

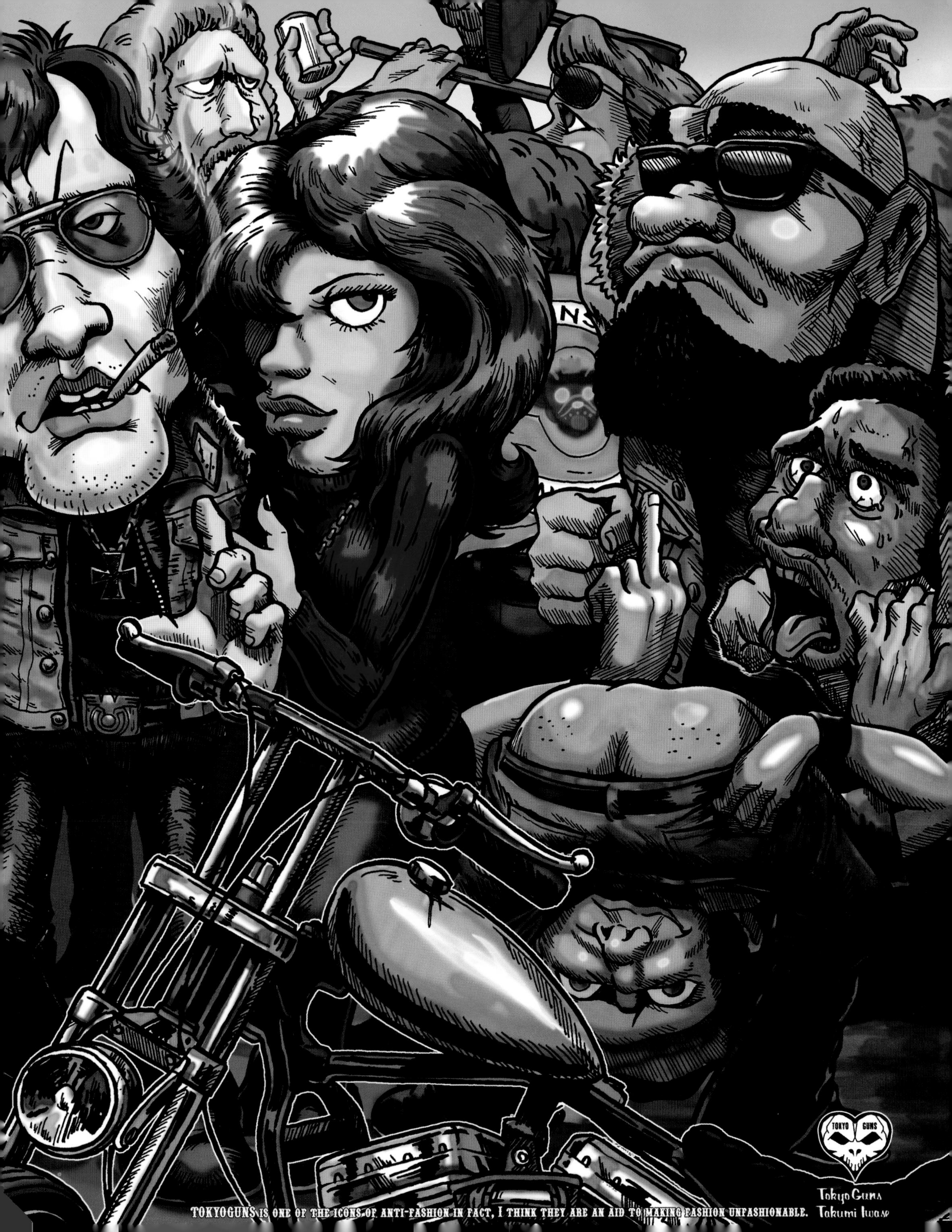
TOKYO GUNS
Tokyo Guns
TOKYOGUNS IS ONE OF THE ICONS OF ANTI-FASHION IN FACT, I THINK THEY ARE AN AID TO MAKING FASHION UNFASHIONABLE.
Takumi Iwase

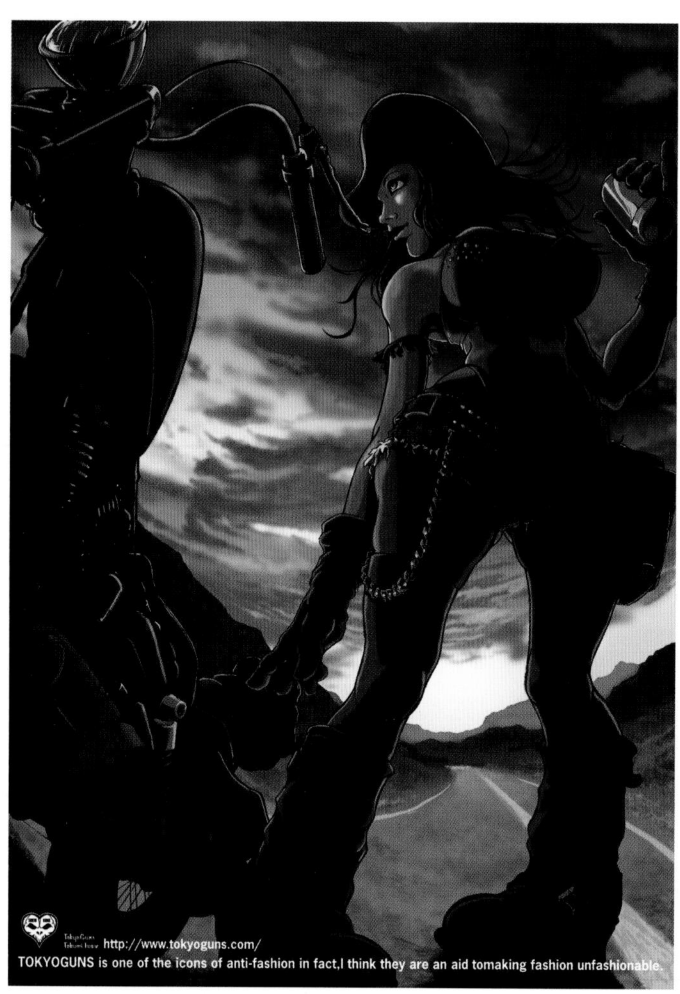

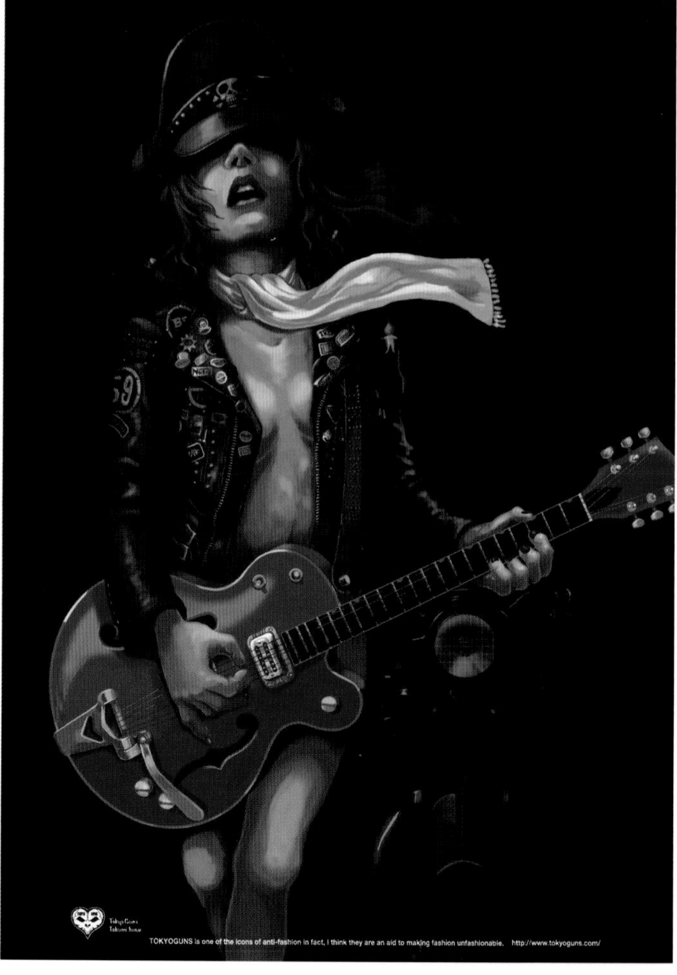

ABOVE: ***Sunset.***
Ink on paper, digital colours.

ABOVE RIGHT: ***Let's Roll.***
Ink on paper, digital colours.

FAR RIGHT: ***Bright.***
Ink on paper, digital colours.

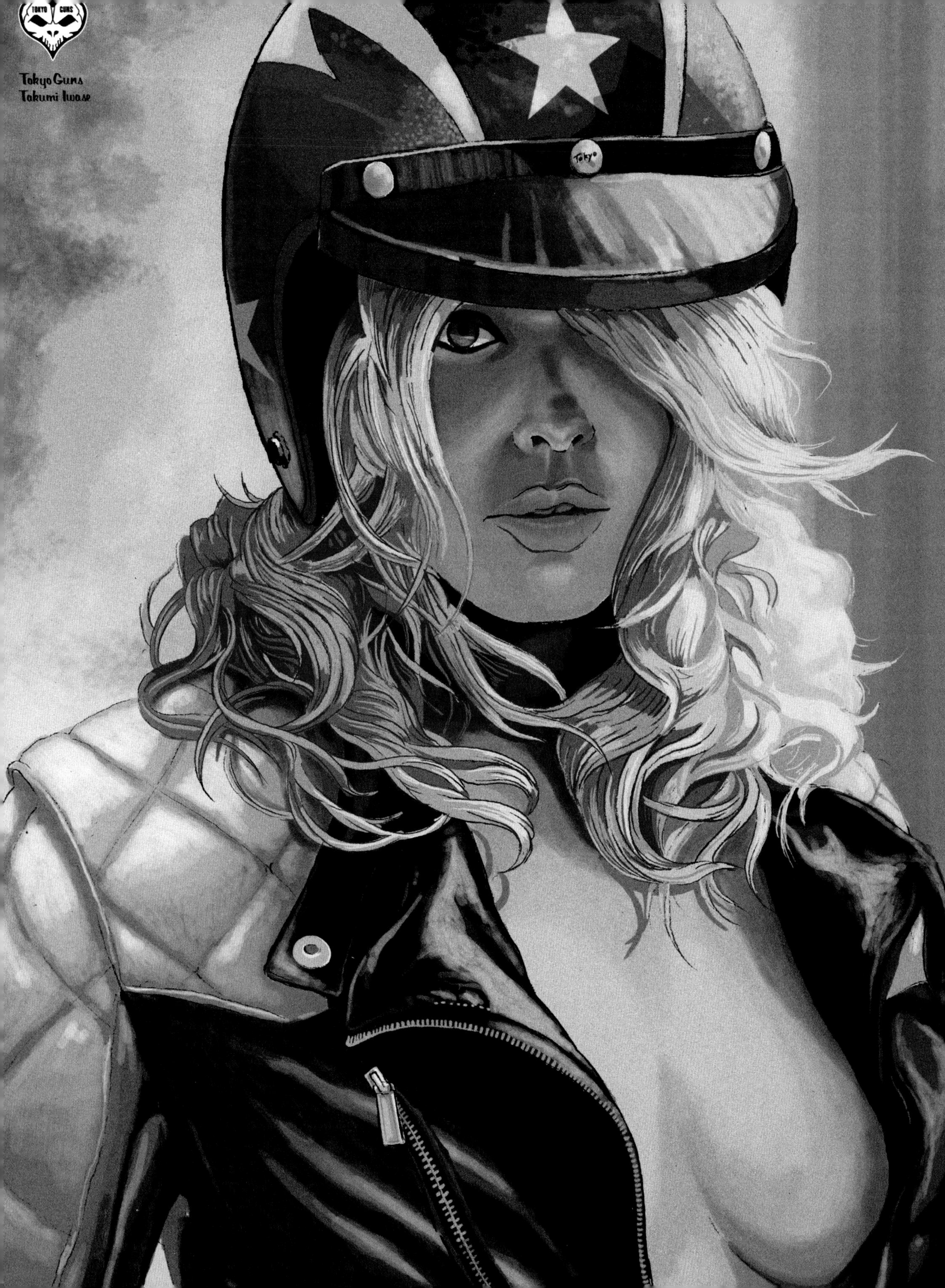
TOKYO GUNS
Tokyo Guns
Takumi Iwase
Tokyo

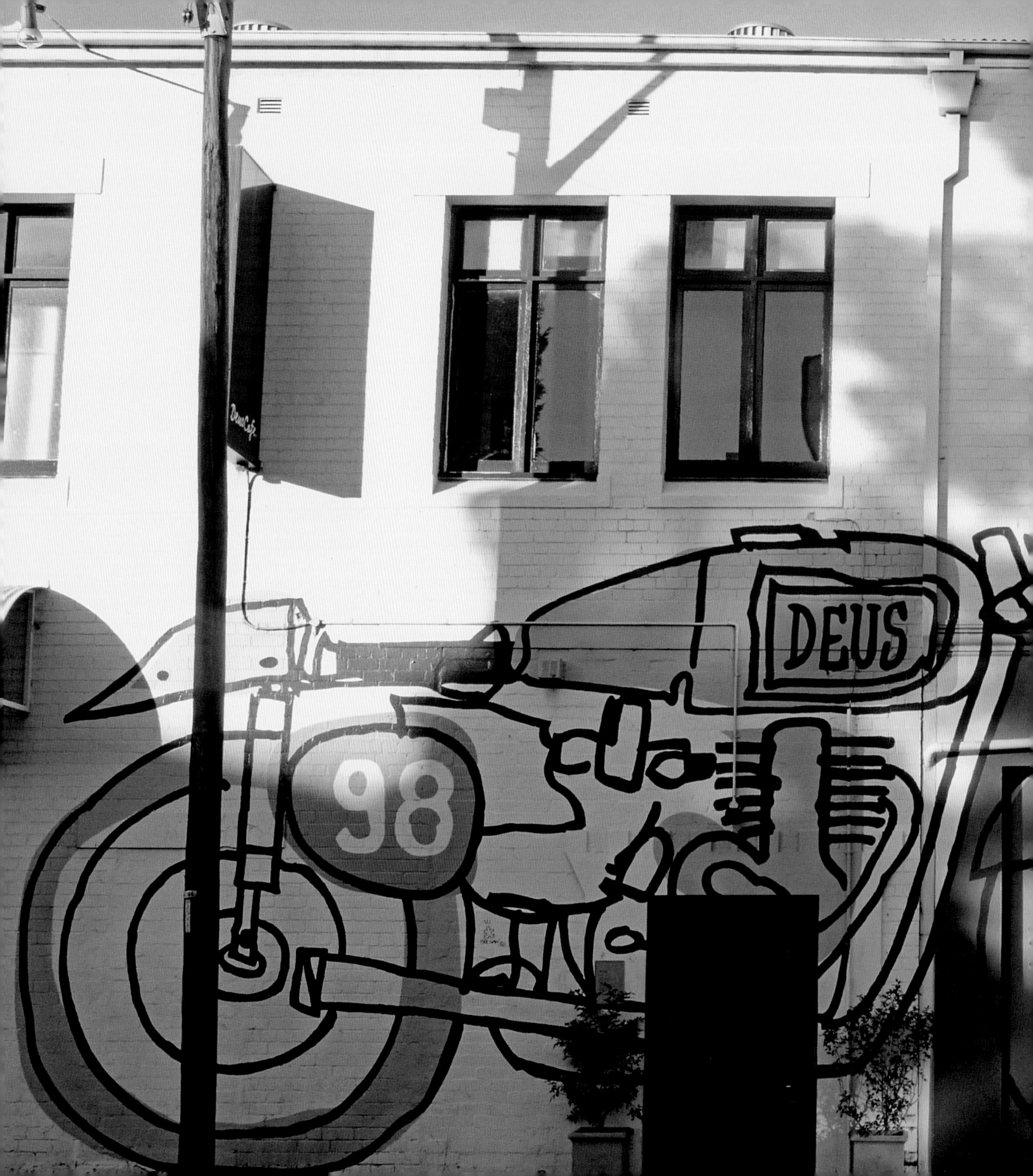
DEUS
98

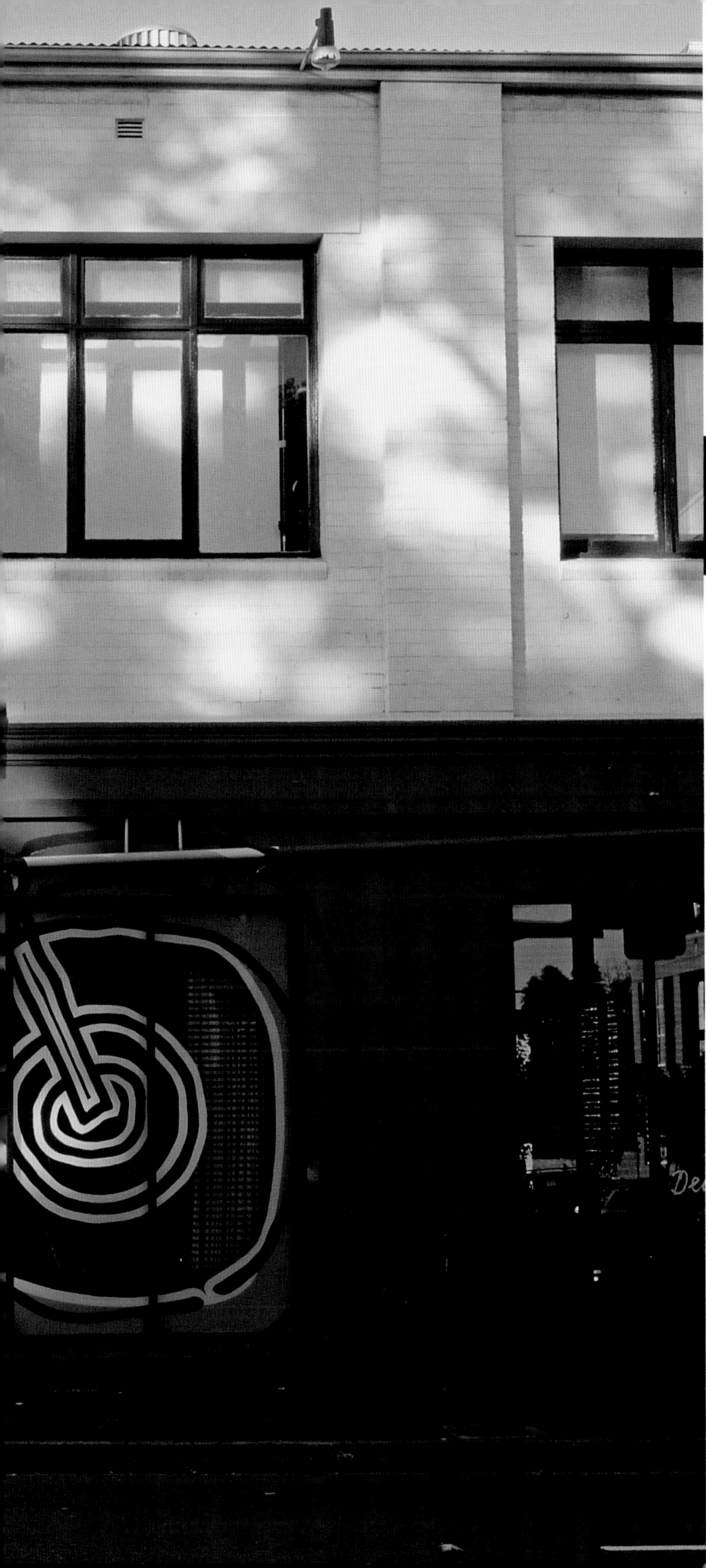

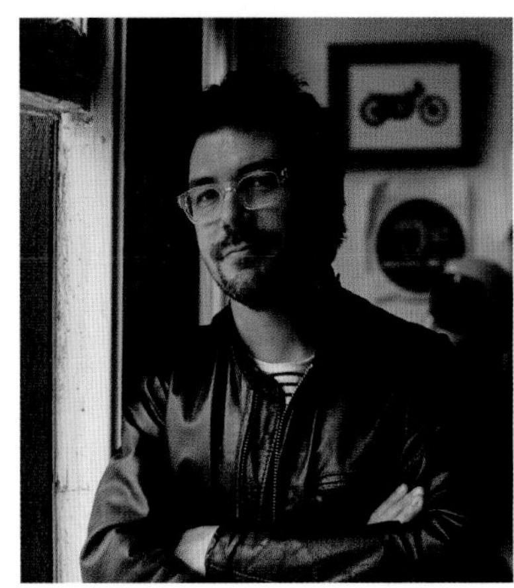

CARBY TUCKWELL

Hailing from Sydney, Australia, Carby Tuckwell is the man behind the look and feel of the Deus Ex Machina cross-cultural empire. Deus has helped introduce motorcycling to the world's urban creatives, who would otherwise be nipple-deep researching the latest moustache wax and fixed gear bicycles. That Deus also build fixies and sell facial hair pomade is neither here nor there.

Carby studied typography in Switzerland after falling for a local girl, then became the director/ partner of a major creative agency in Australia, before leaving to launch Deus Ex Machina. There he still designs t-shirts, posters, motorcycles, logos (as Carby puts it: "at 1000lph: that's logos per hour") and anything else the burgeoning brand requires."I don't think about what would make a good t-shirt design or anything else design, I just draw something and work out what it could look good for later – a logo on a gas tank, a t-shirt or maybe just a design burnt into a block of wood."

LEFT: *Deus Cafe Wall Camperdown G50.*
Oil paint on wall.

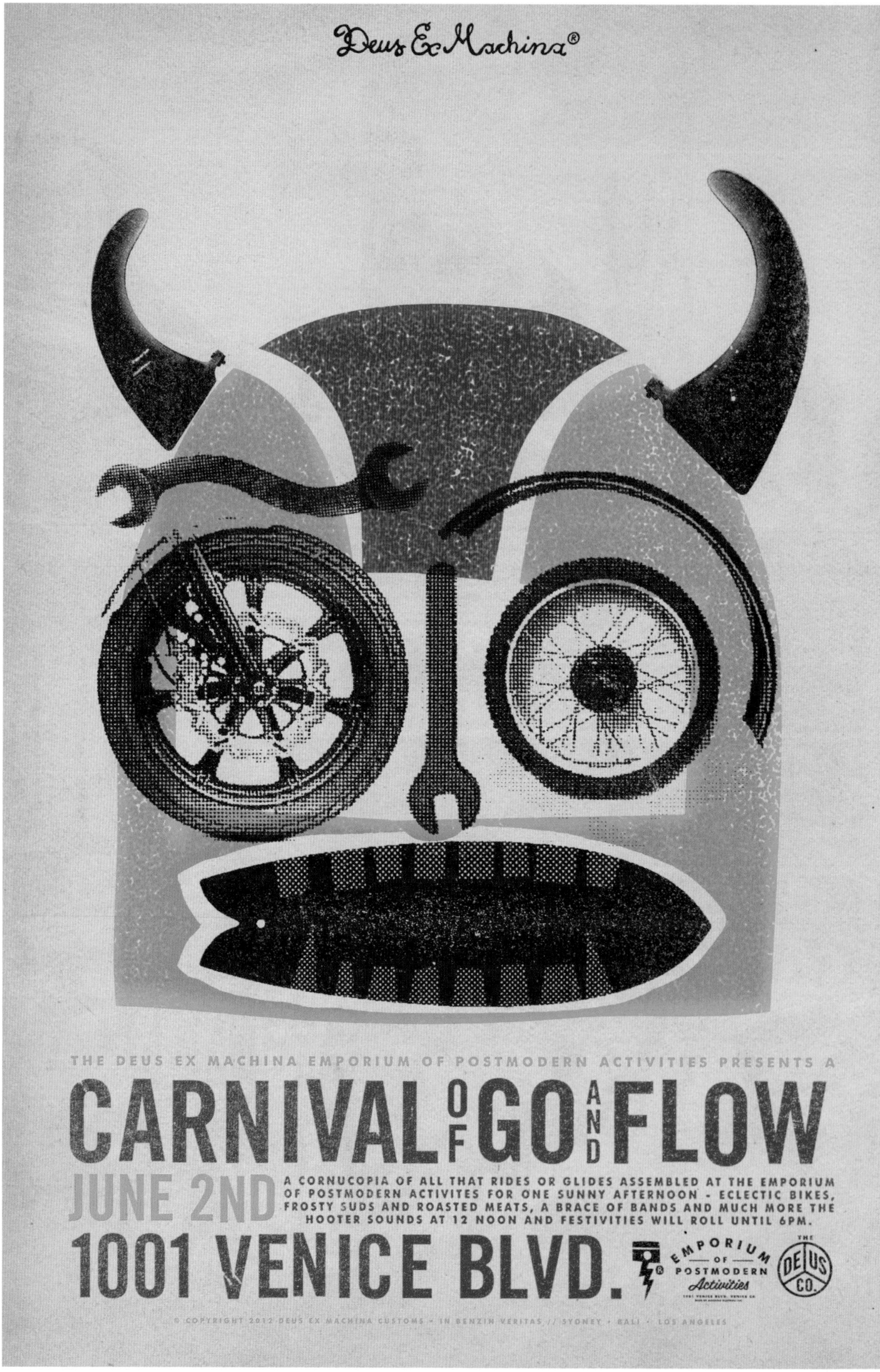

Deus Ex Machina®

THE DEUS EX MACHINA EMPORIUM OF POSTMODERN ACTIVITIES PRESENTS A

CARNIVAL OF GO AND FLOW

JUNE 2ND

A CORNUCOPIA OF ALL THAT RIDES OR GLIDES ASSEMBLED AT THE EMPORIUM OF POSTMODERN ACTIVITES FOR ONE SUNNY AFTERNOON - ECLECTIC BIKES, FROSTY SUDS AND ROASTED MEATS, A BRACE OF BANDS AND MUCH MORE THE HOOTER SOUNDS AT 12 NOON AND FESTIVITIES WILL ROLL UNTIL 6PM.

1001 VENICE BLVD.

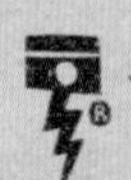

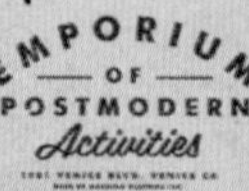

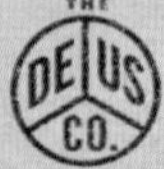

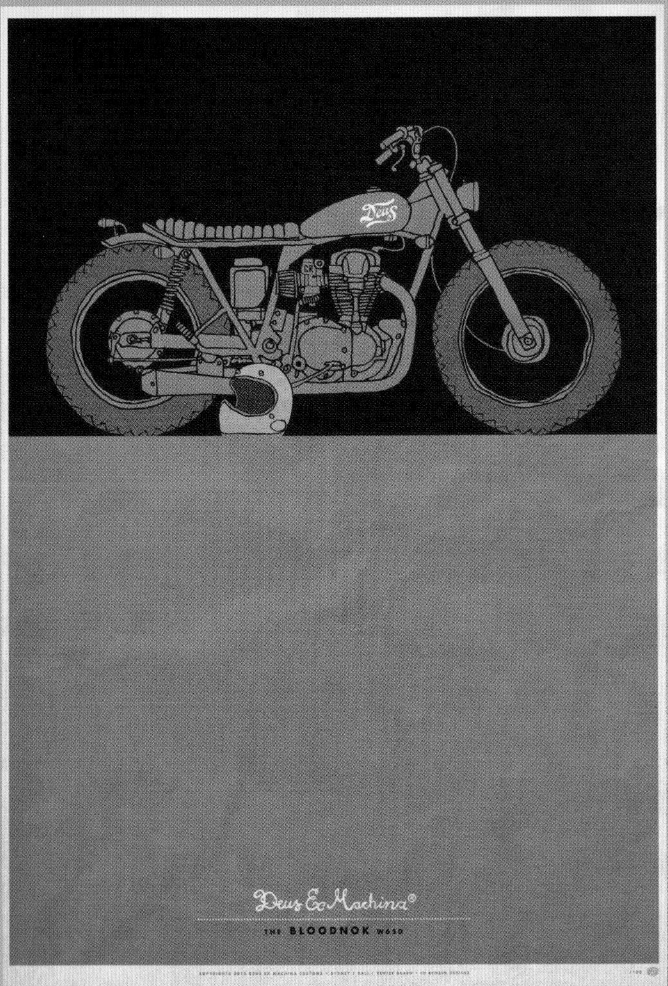

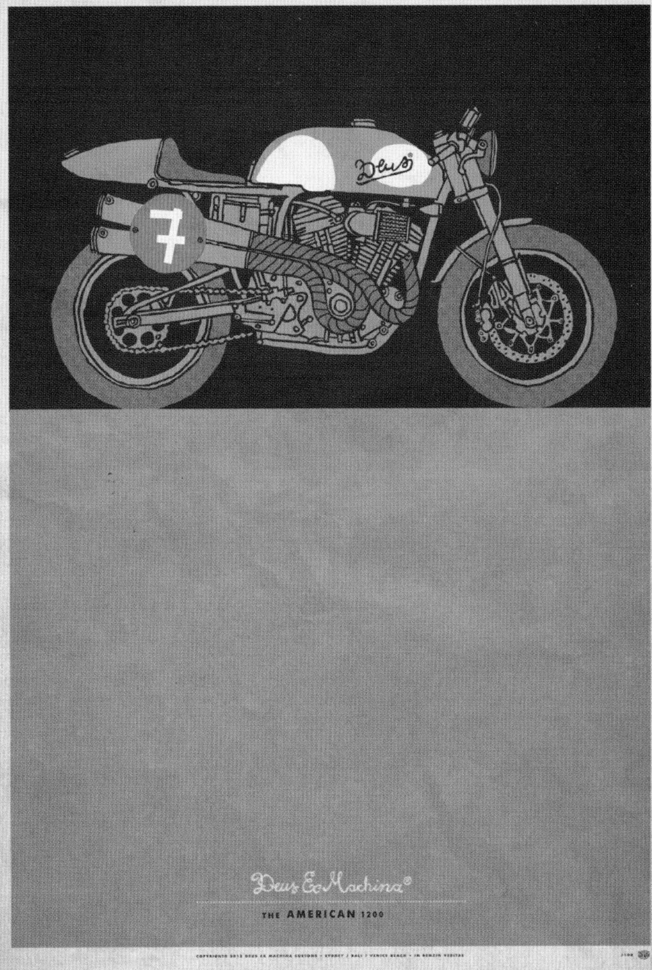

ABOVE: ***Bloodnok Poster.***
Pen and ink on paper, digital colours.

ABOVE RIGHT: ***The American Poster.***
Pen and ink on paper, digital colours.

LEFT: ***Go and Flow Poster.***
Digital artwork.

RIGHT: ***The G50.***
Marker pen on paper, digital colours.

BELOW: ***Mike's Bike.***
Paper collage, digital colours.

FAR RIGHT: ***Frontal Matchless.***
Marker pen on paper, digital colours.

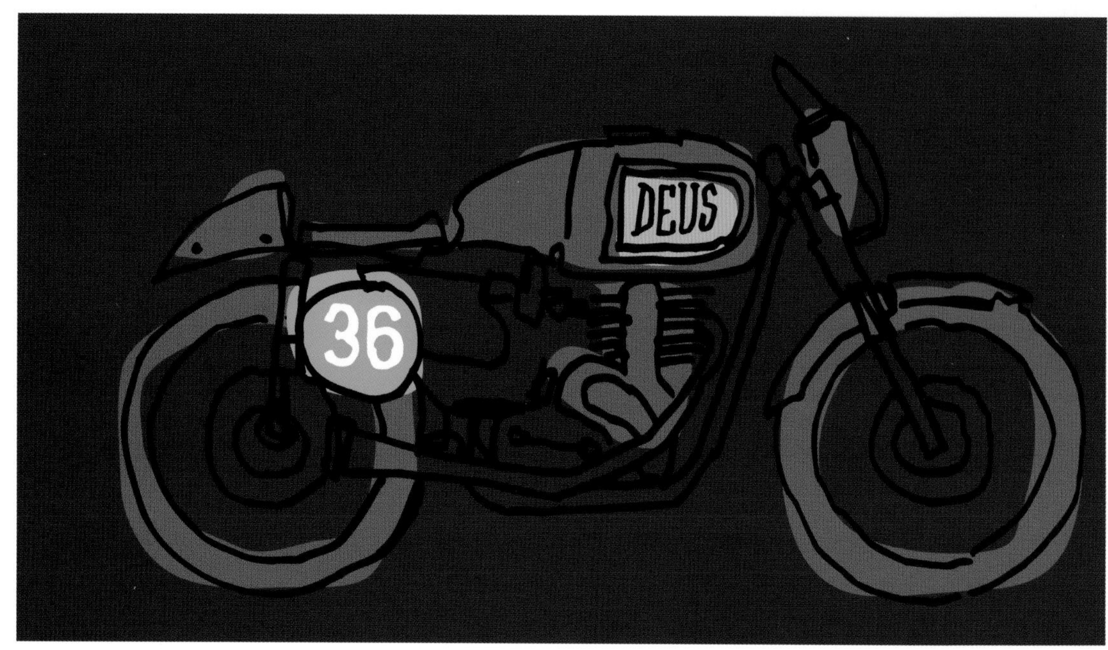

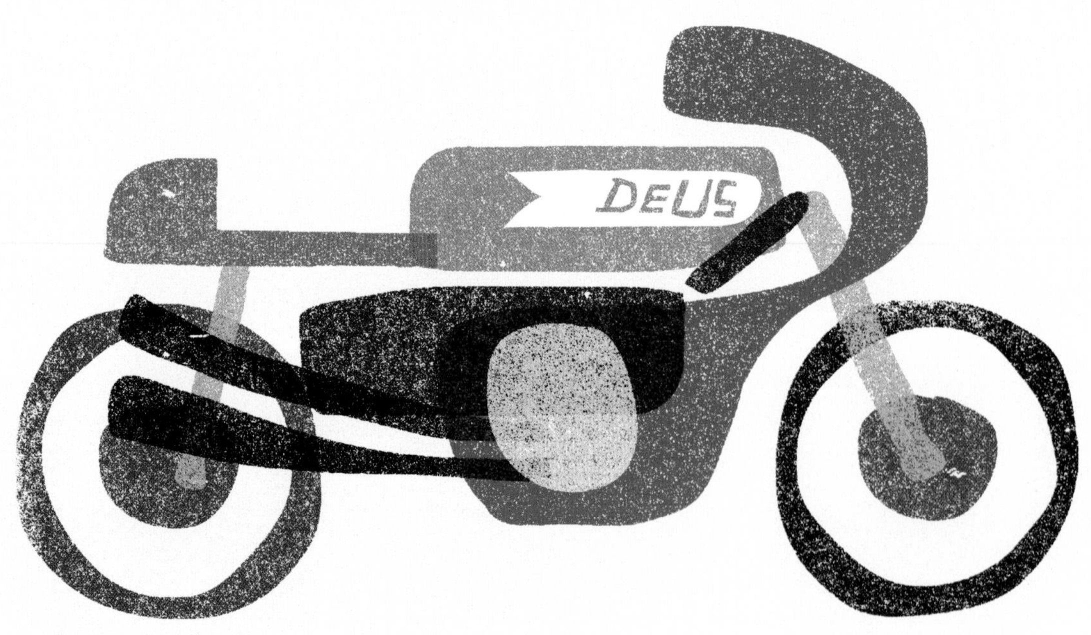

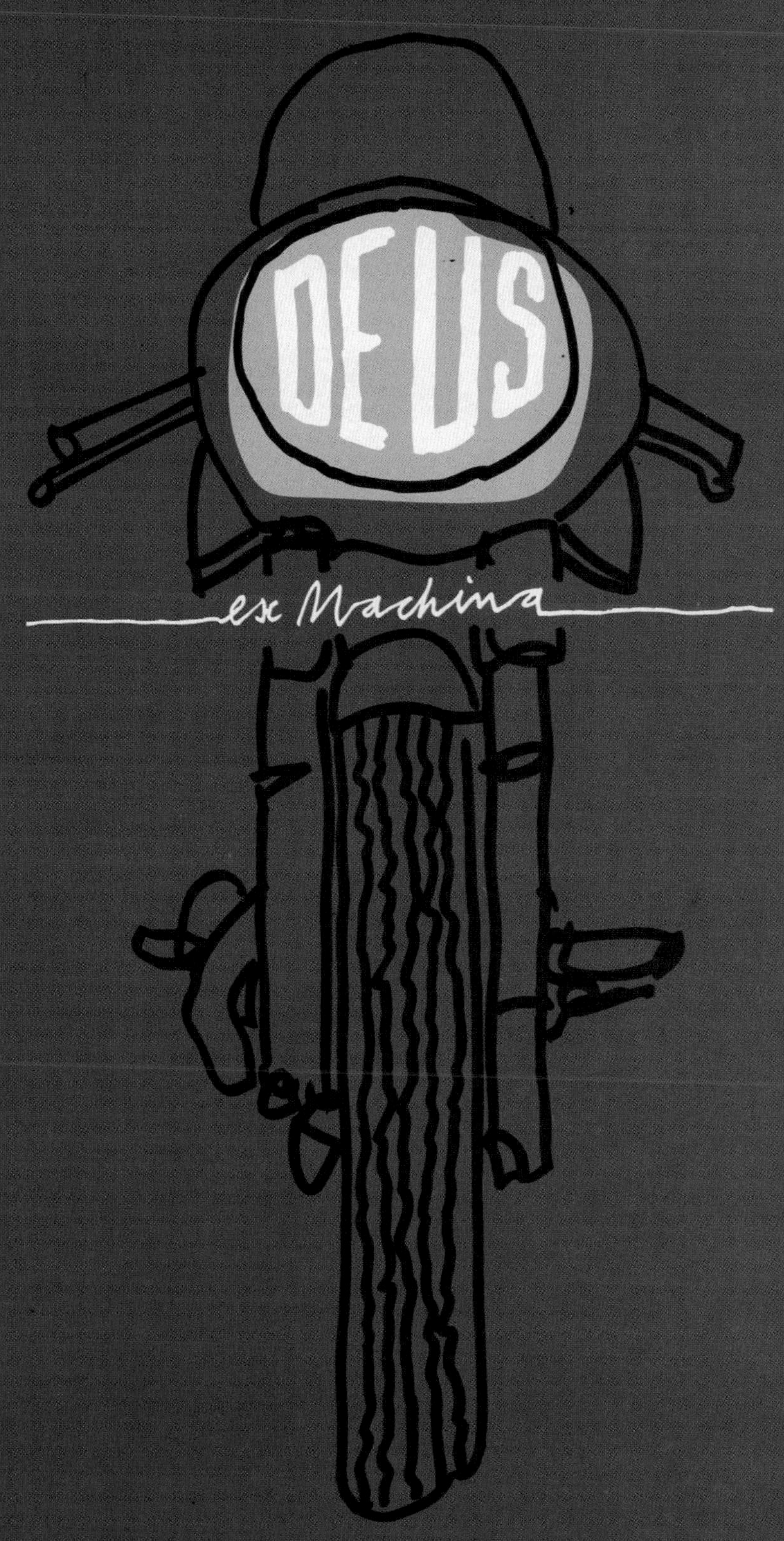
DEUS
ex Machina

BELOW: ***Cartoon Physics Poster.***
Digital artwork.

RIGHT: ***The Parallel Universe Poster.***
Digital artwork.

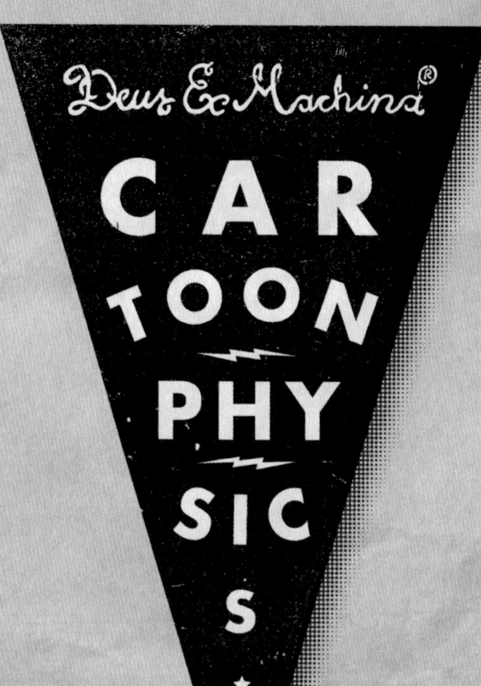

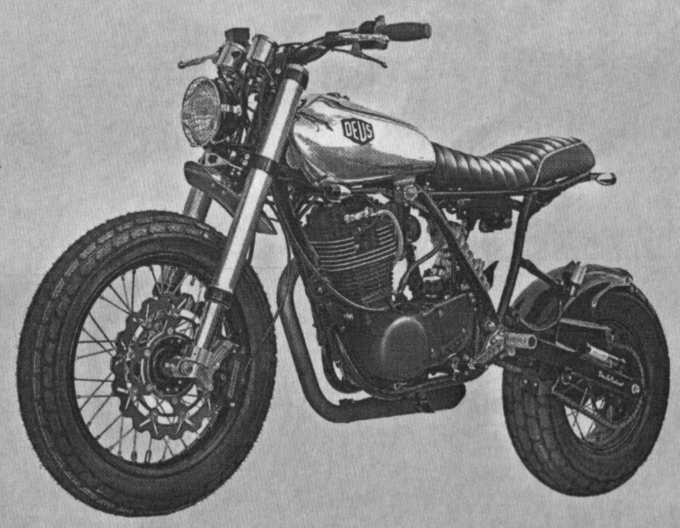

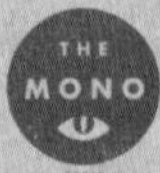

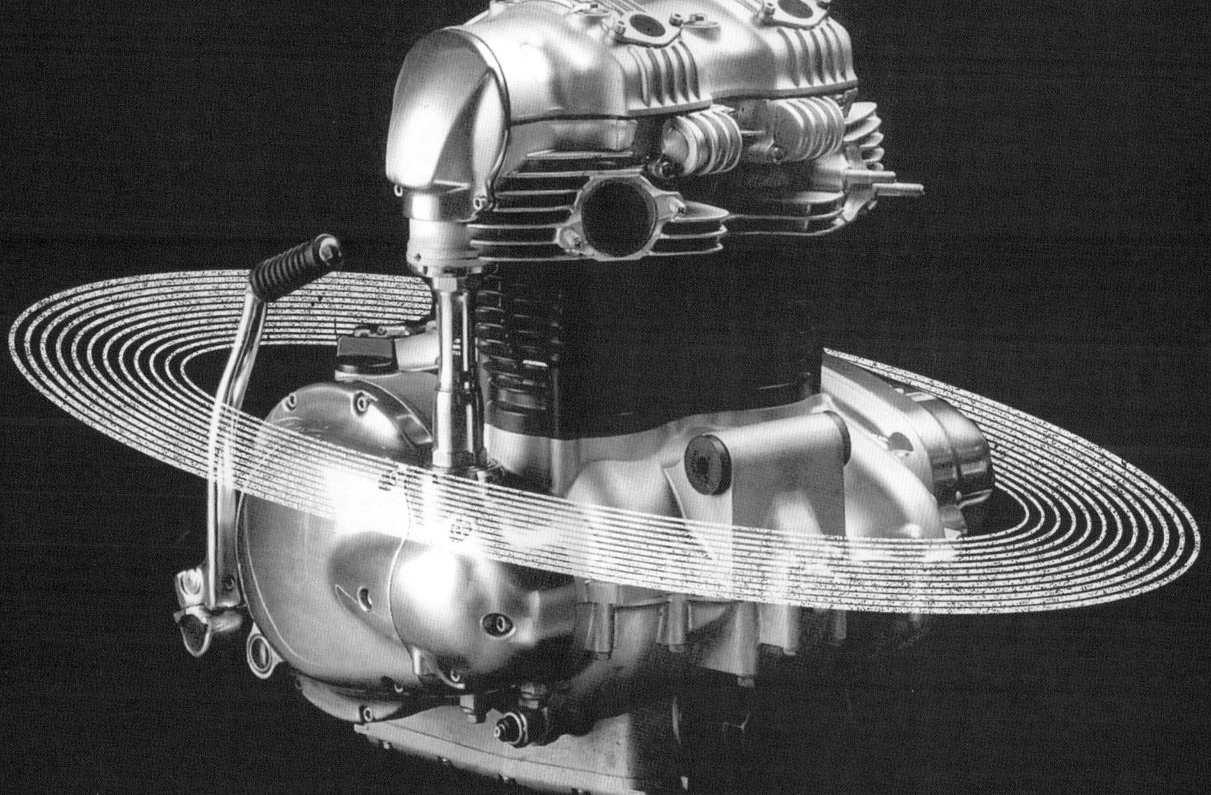

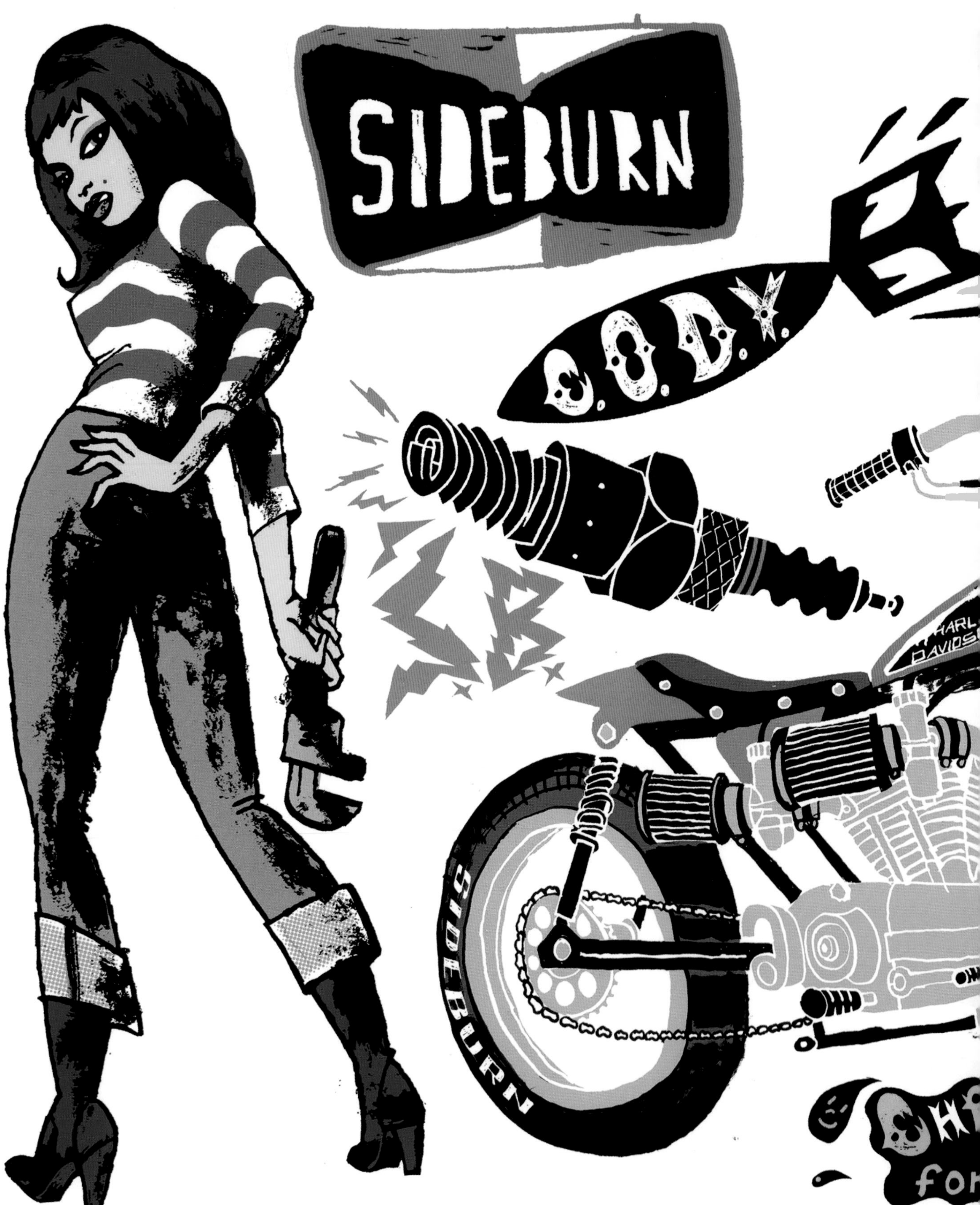
SIDEBURN
D.O.D.Y.
S.B.
HARL
DAVIDS
SIDEBURN

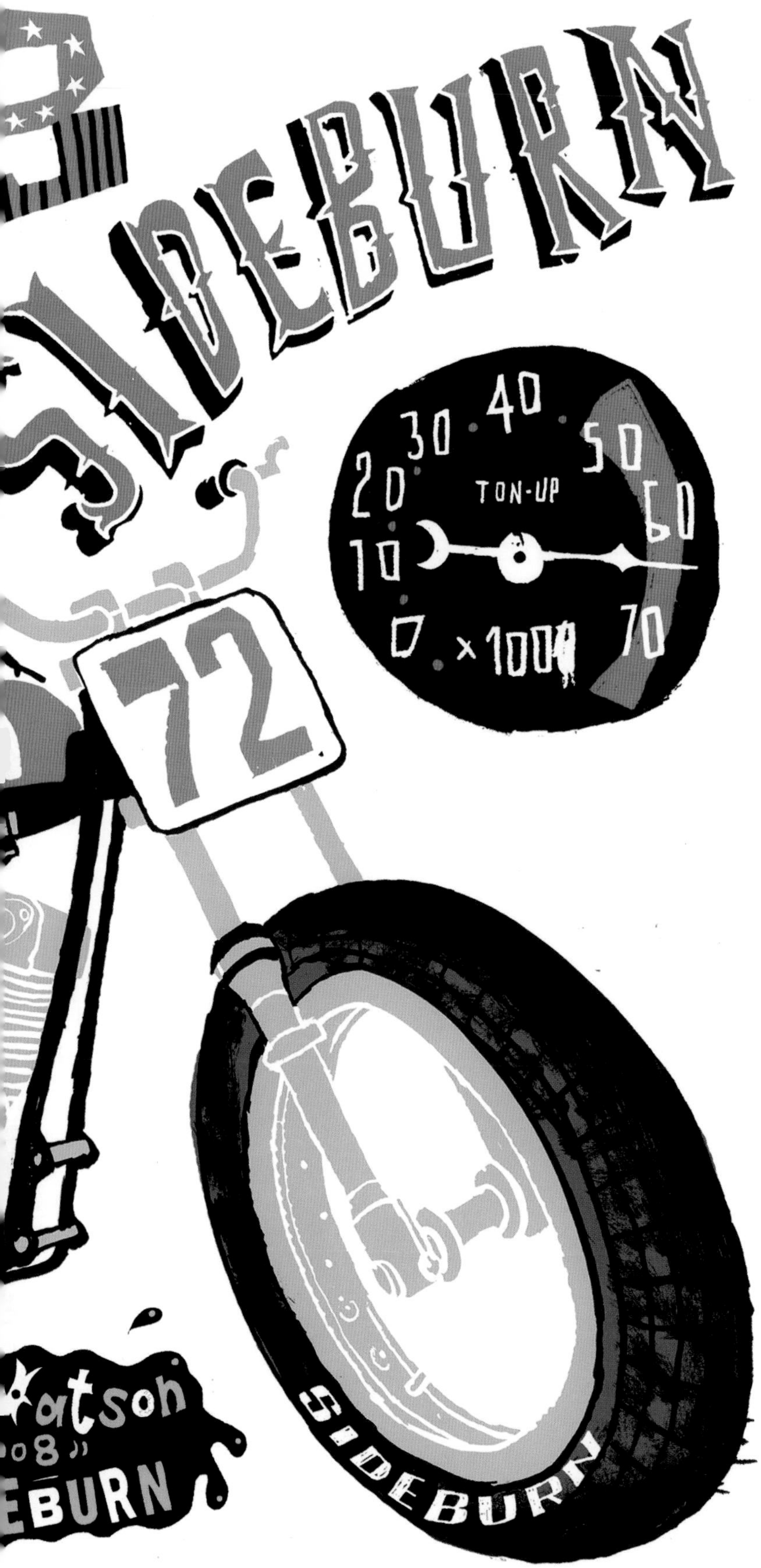

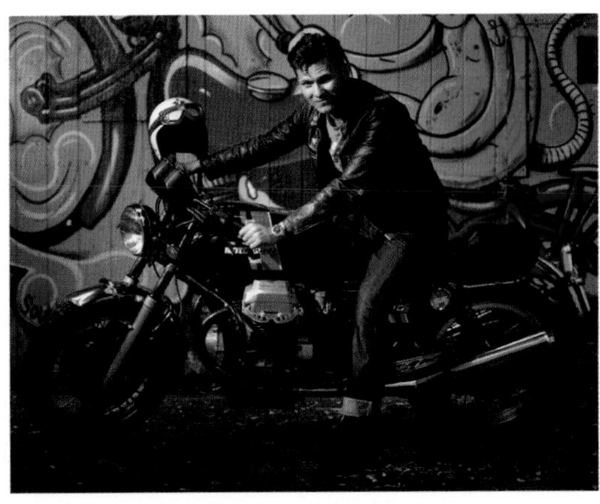

CHRIS WATSON

Growing up in Stirling, Scotland, Chris Watson was infected and fuel-injected, from an early age. "My dad gave me a pile of magazines full of choppers and there was a copy of *Hell's Angels* by Hunter S Thompson on the bookshelf outside my room. My mum caught me reading it and confiscated it. It's not normal reading material for a seven-year-old. Motorbikes were in the same boyhood area as dragons, spaceships and giant robots. In my bedroom I had posters of Barry Sheene and Judge Dredd and chopper wallpaper."

When he was old enough Chris bought a Honda 125, sewed chicken bones to his leather jacket and got through his early-20s by the skin of his teeth. Now he's a full-time illustrator working for clients like *The Guardian*, *Time Out*, Penguin books, *Cycling* and a dozen other magazines and record companies. He is also writing and illustrating his own children's books – "they're not your normal books for children" – that he's hoping to get published some day.

LEFT: *Sideburn* stickers.
Pen, ink and digital.

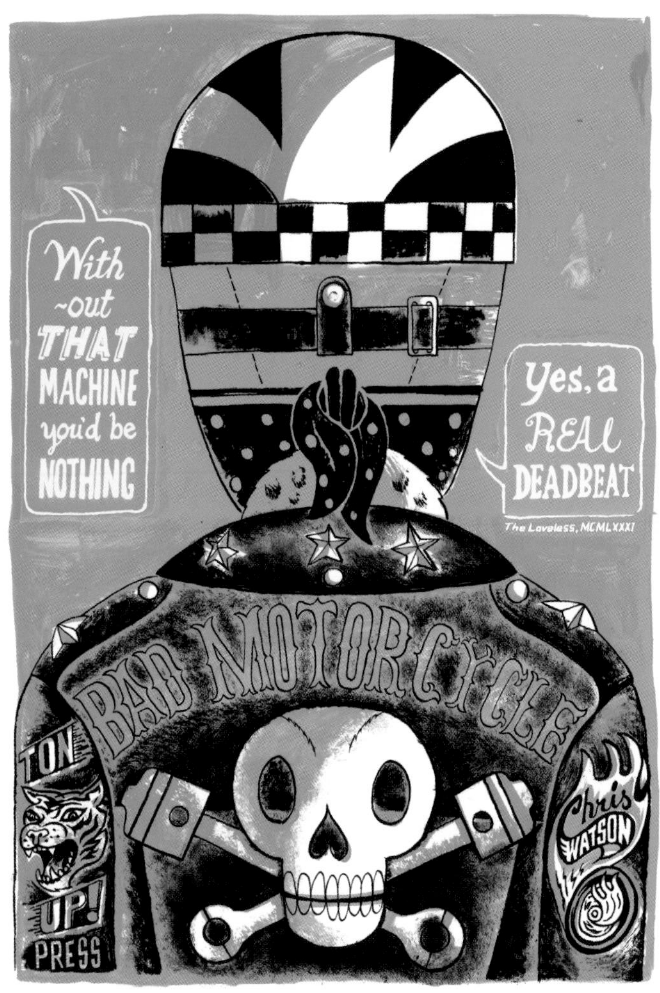

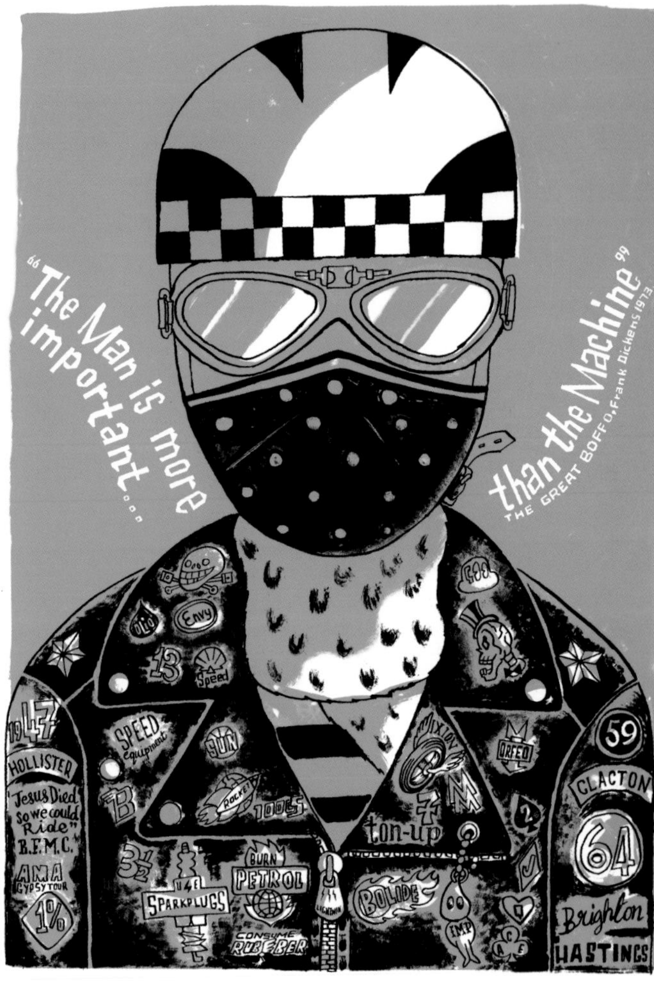

ABOVE: ***A Real Deadbeat.***
Pen, ink, opaque gouache, brush and digital.

ABOVE RIGHT: ***The Man is More Important Than the Machine.***
Pen, ink, opaque gouache, brush and digital.

RIGHT: ***Traction Control Killed the Tyre Smoker.***
Pen, brush, ink and digital.

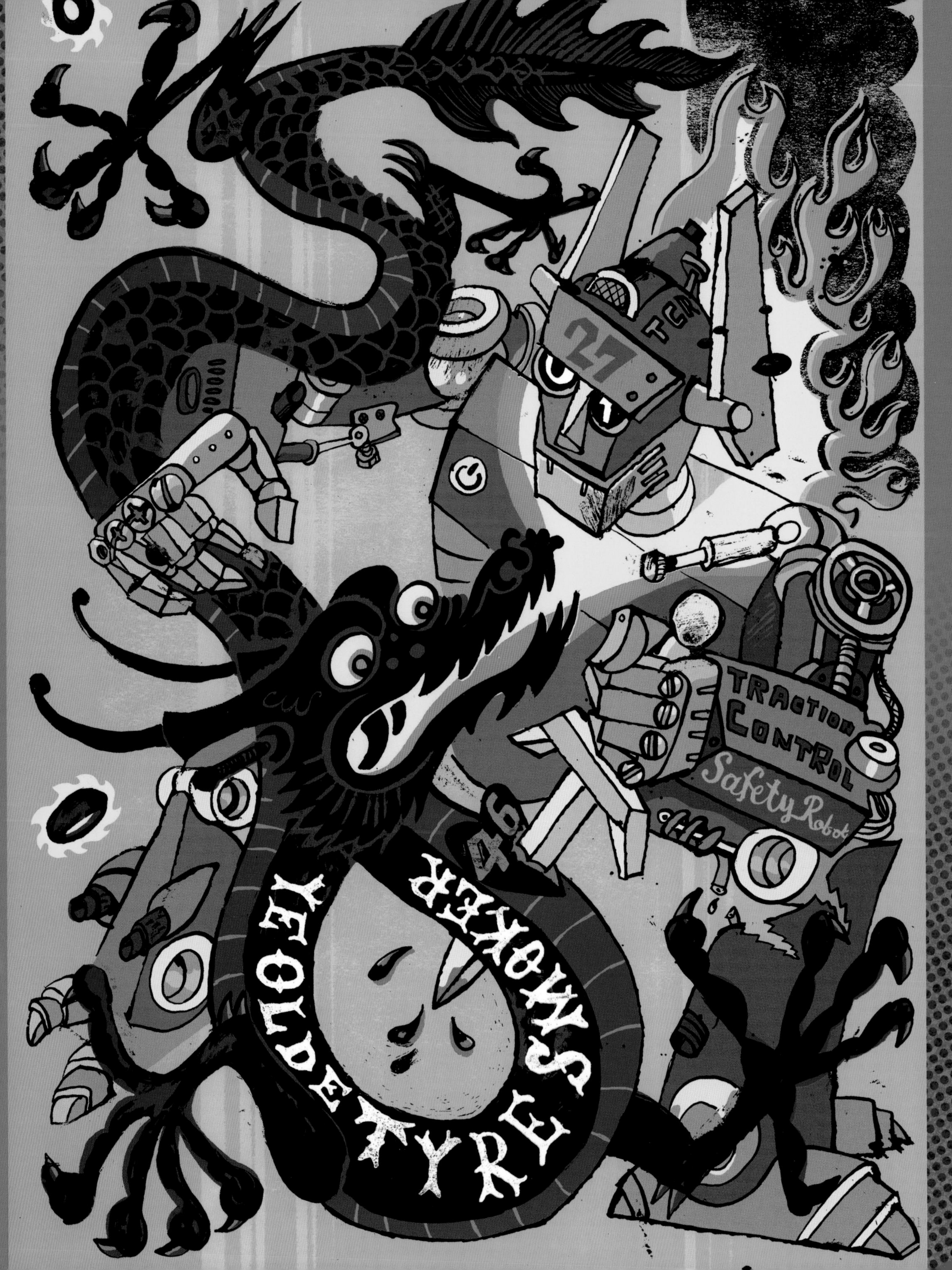
27
TCR
TRACTION CONTROL
Safety Robot
YE OLDE TYRE SMOKER

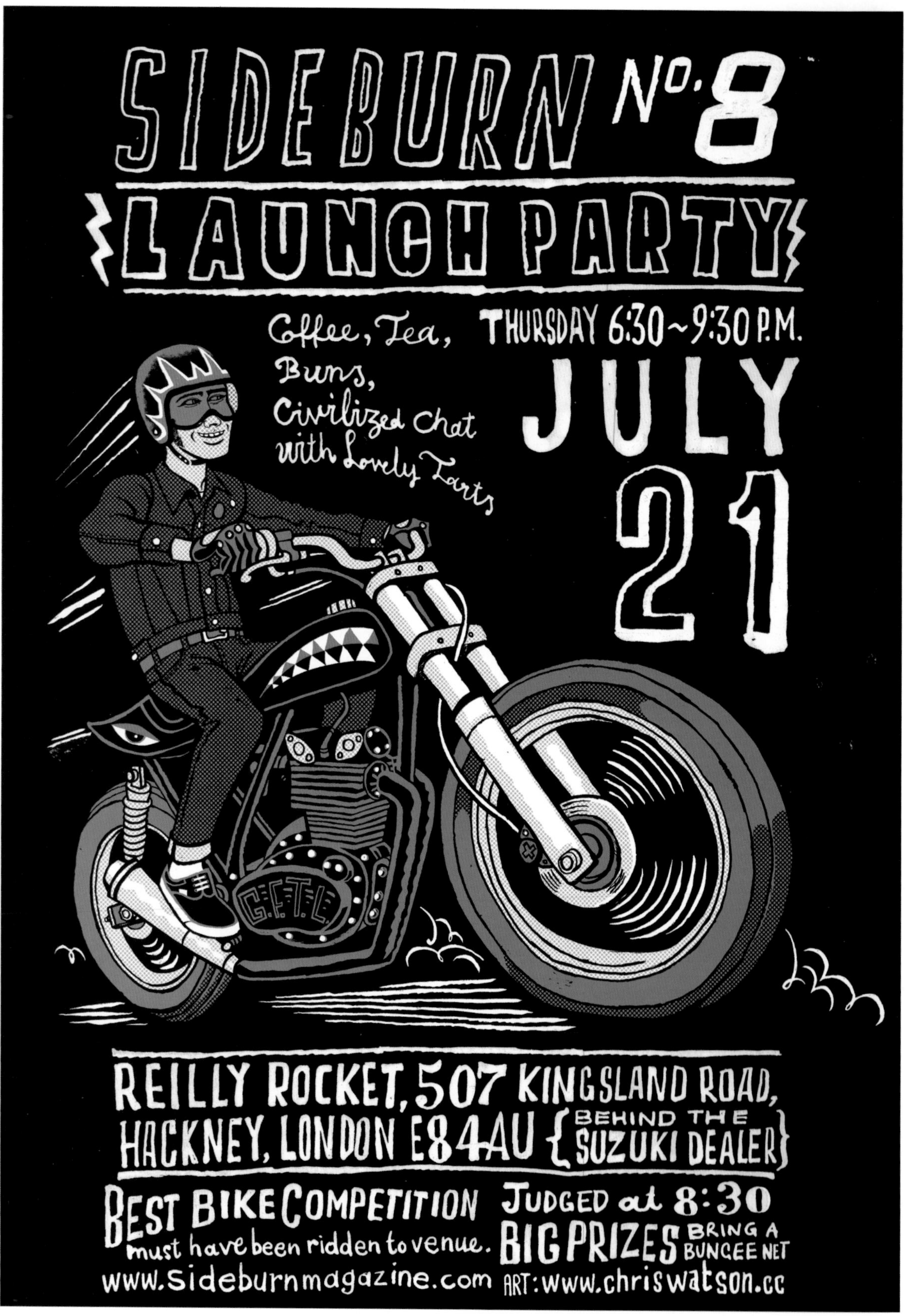
SIDEBURN No. 8
LAUNCH PARTY
Coffee, Tea, Buns, Civilized Chat with Lovely Tarts
THURSDAY 6:30~9:30 P.M.
JULY 21
G.F.T.L.
REILLY ROCKET, 507 KINGSLAND ROAD,
HACKNEY, LONDON E8 4AU {BEHIND THE SUZUKI DEALER}
BEST BIKE COMPETITION must have been ridden to venue.
JUDGED at 8:30
BIG PRIZES BRING A BUNGEE NET
www.sideburnmagazine.com
ART: www.chriswatson.cc

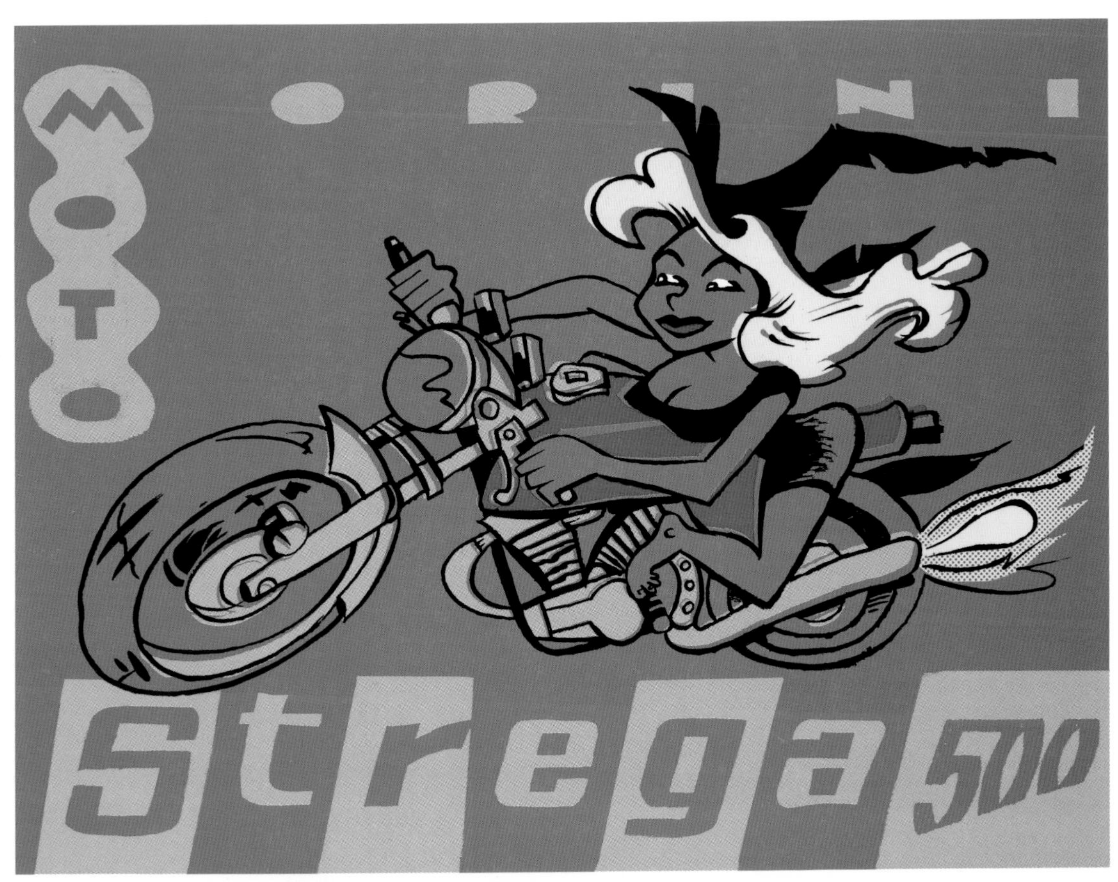

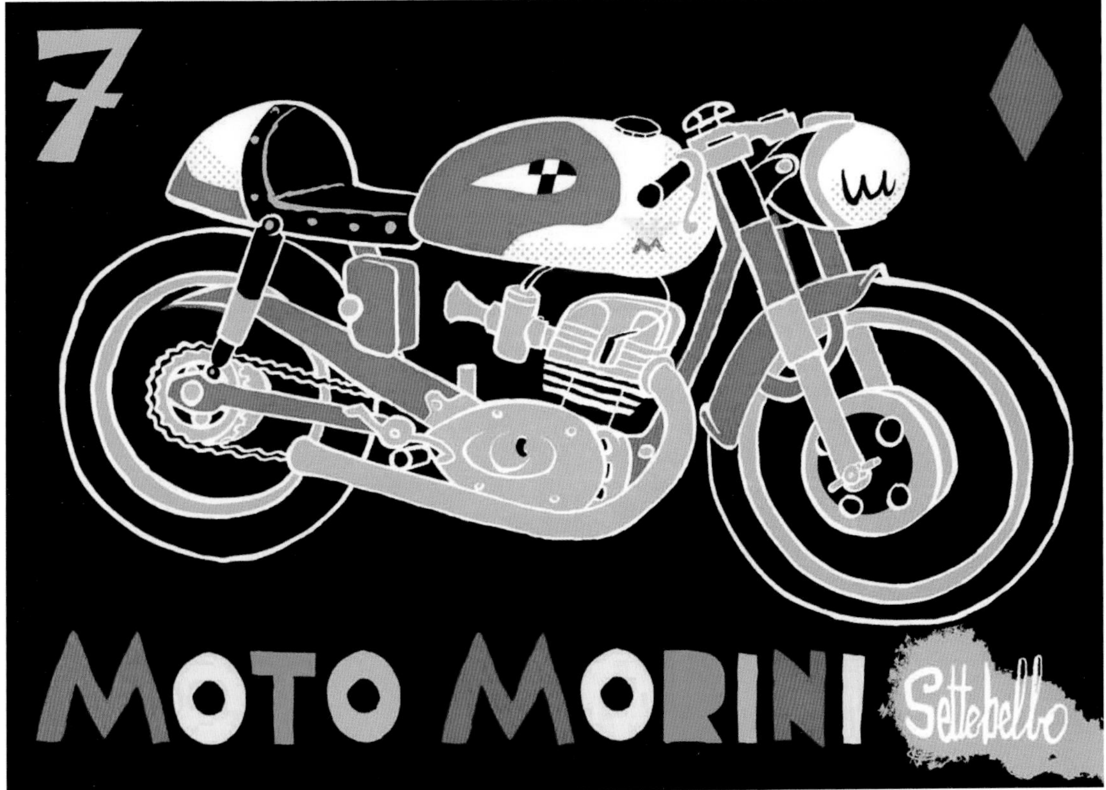

ABOVE: ***Strega 500.***
Pen, brush, ink and digital.

LEFT: ***Settebello.***
Pen, brush, ink and digital.

FAR LEFT: ***Reilly Rocket Poster.***
Pen, brush, ink and digital.

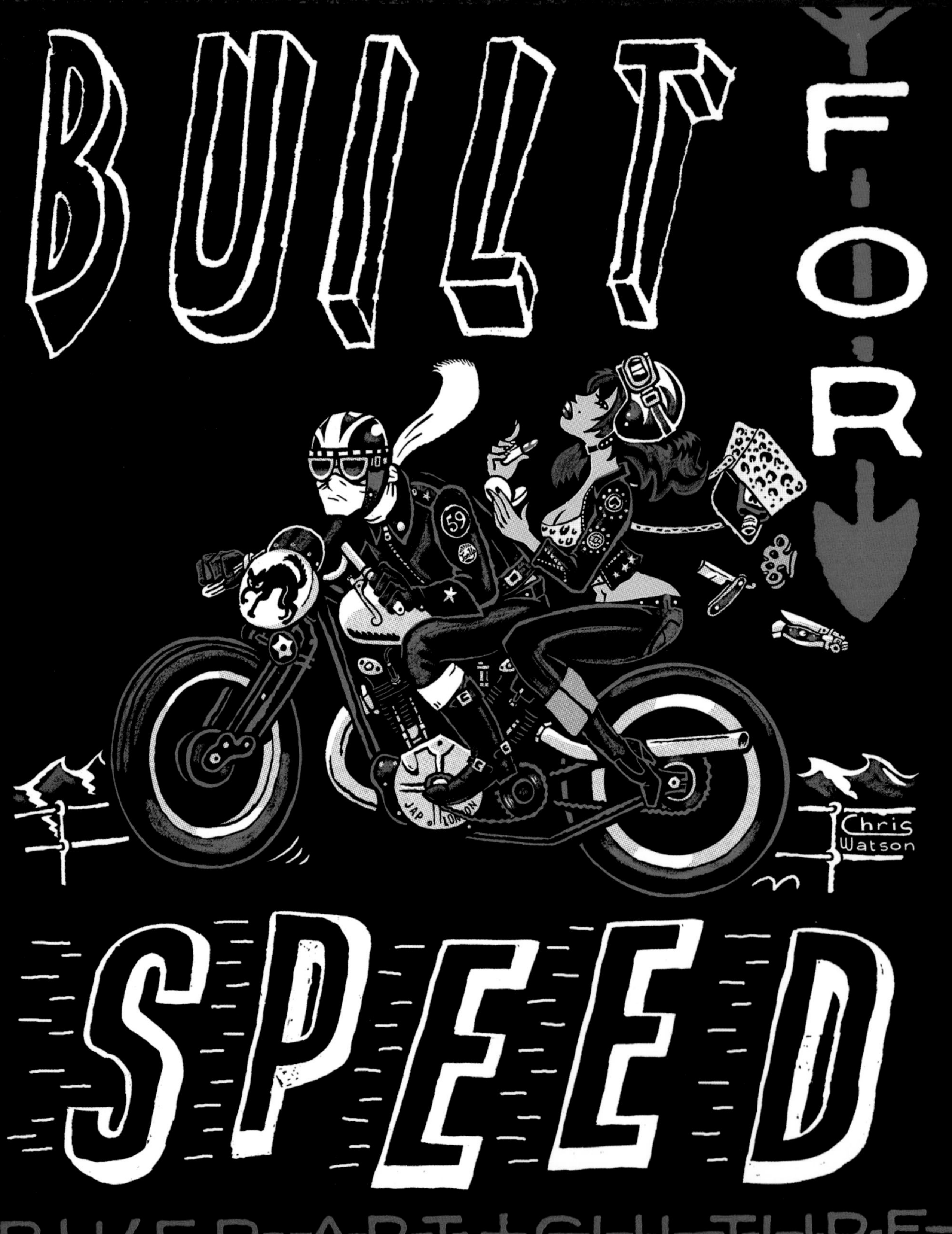
BUILT FOR
SPEED
-B-I-K-E-R- -A-R-T- + -C-U-L-T-U-R-E-
Chris Watson
59
JAP LONDON

LEFT: ***Built For Speed.***
Pen, ink, opaque gouache, brush and digital.

BELOW: ***Banda Bonnisti.***
Pen, ink and digital.

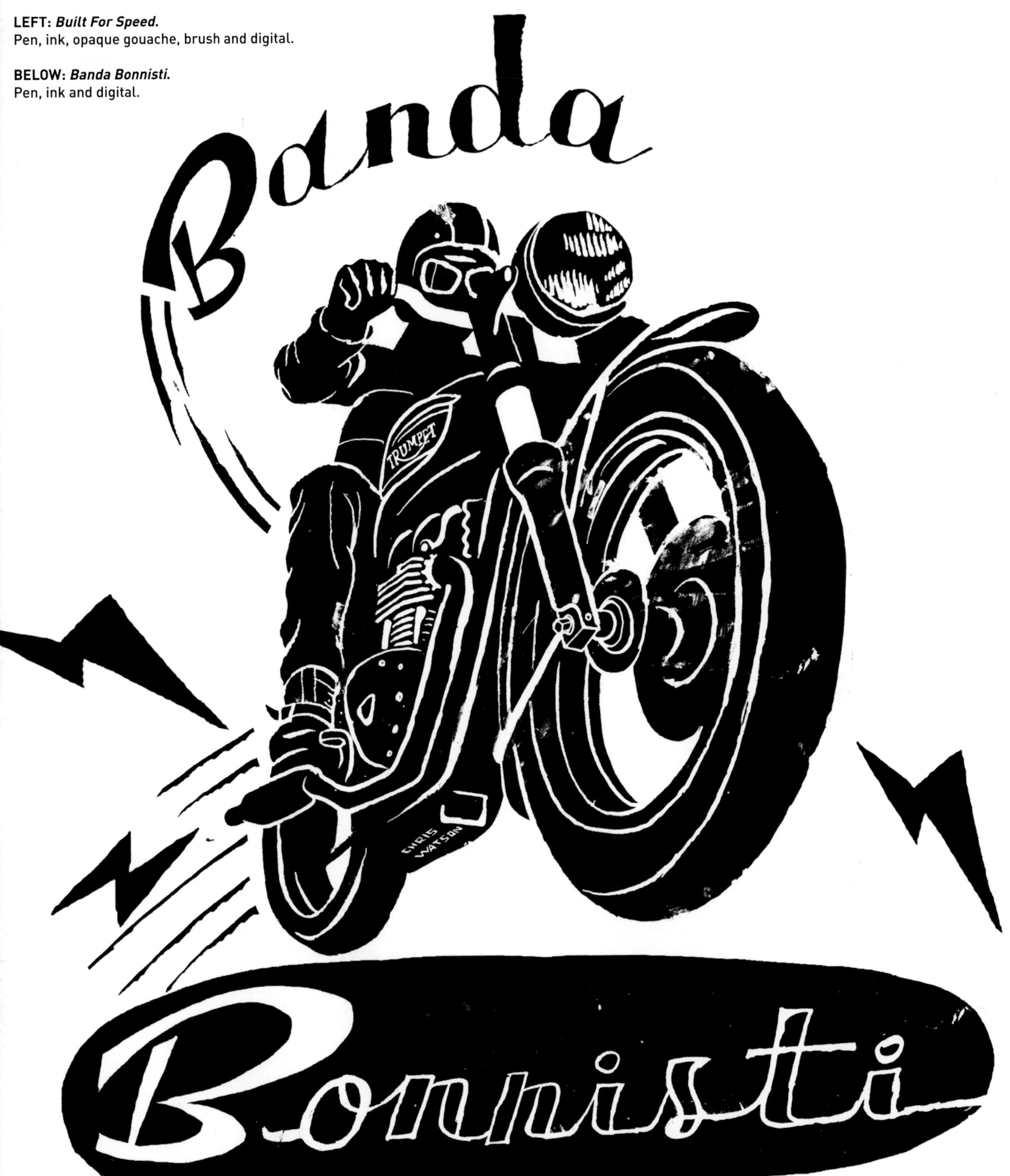

BELOW: ***Indian Girl.***
Pen, brush, ink and digital.

FAR RIGHT: ***Jesus Died So We Could Ride.***
Pen, brush, ink and digital.

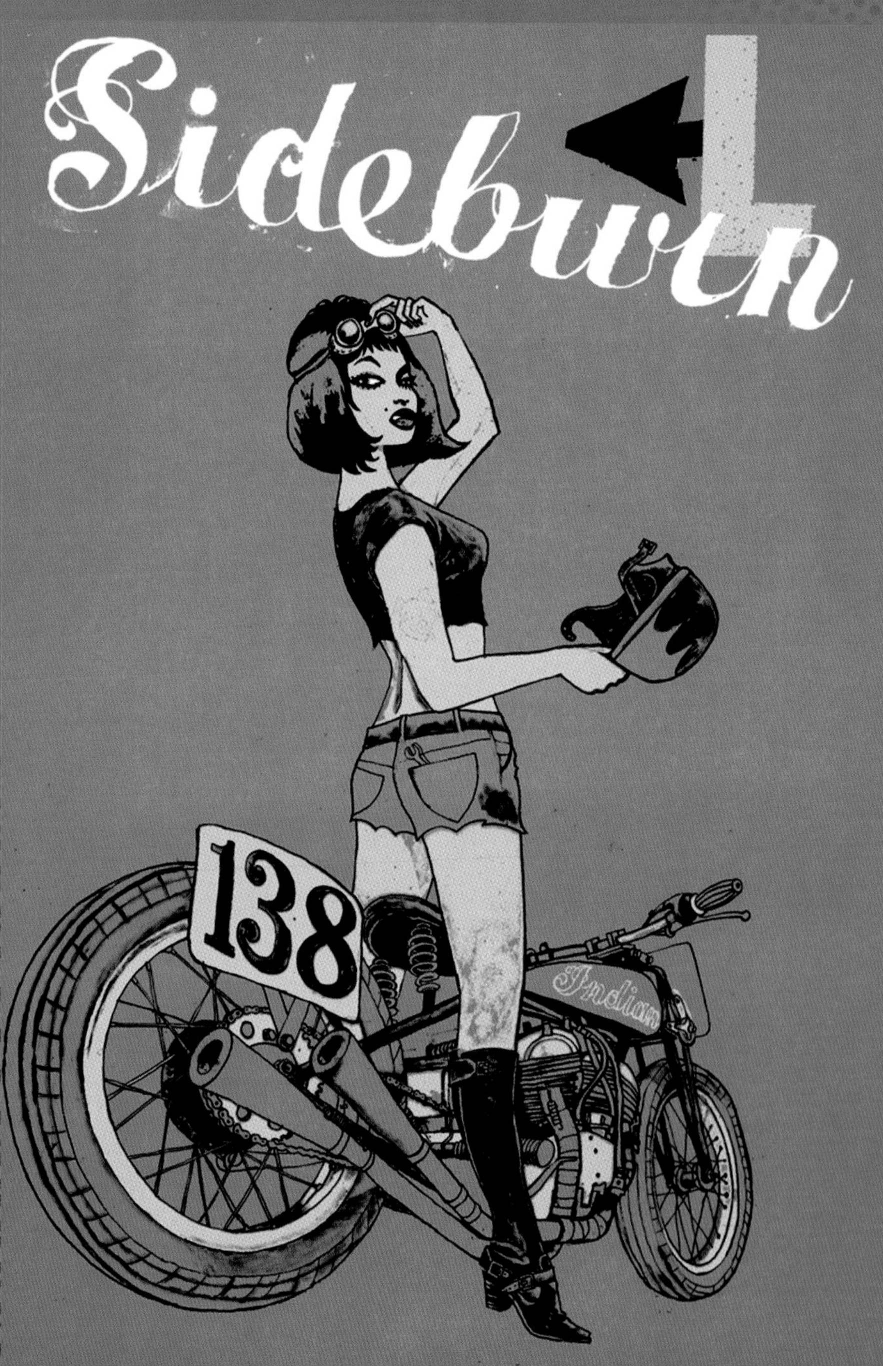

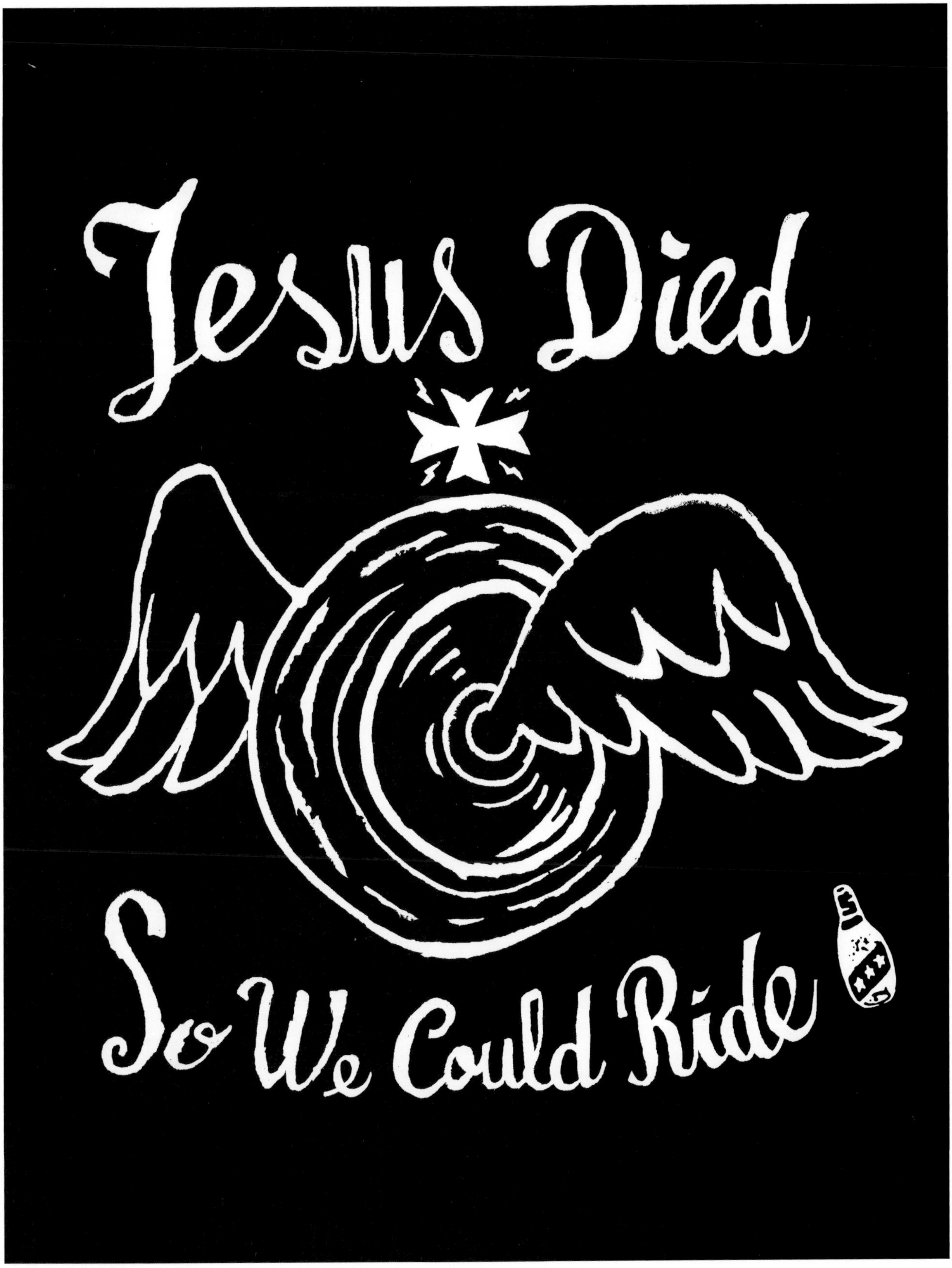

Jesus Died

So We Could Ride

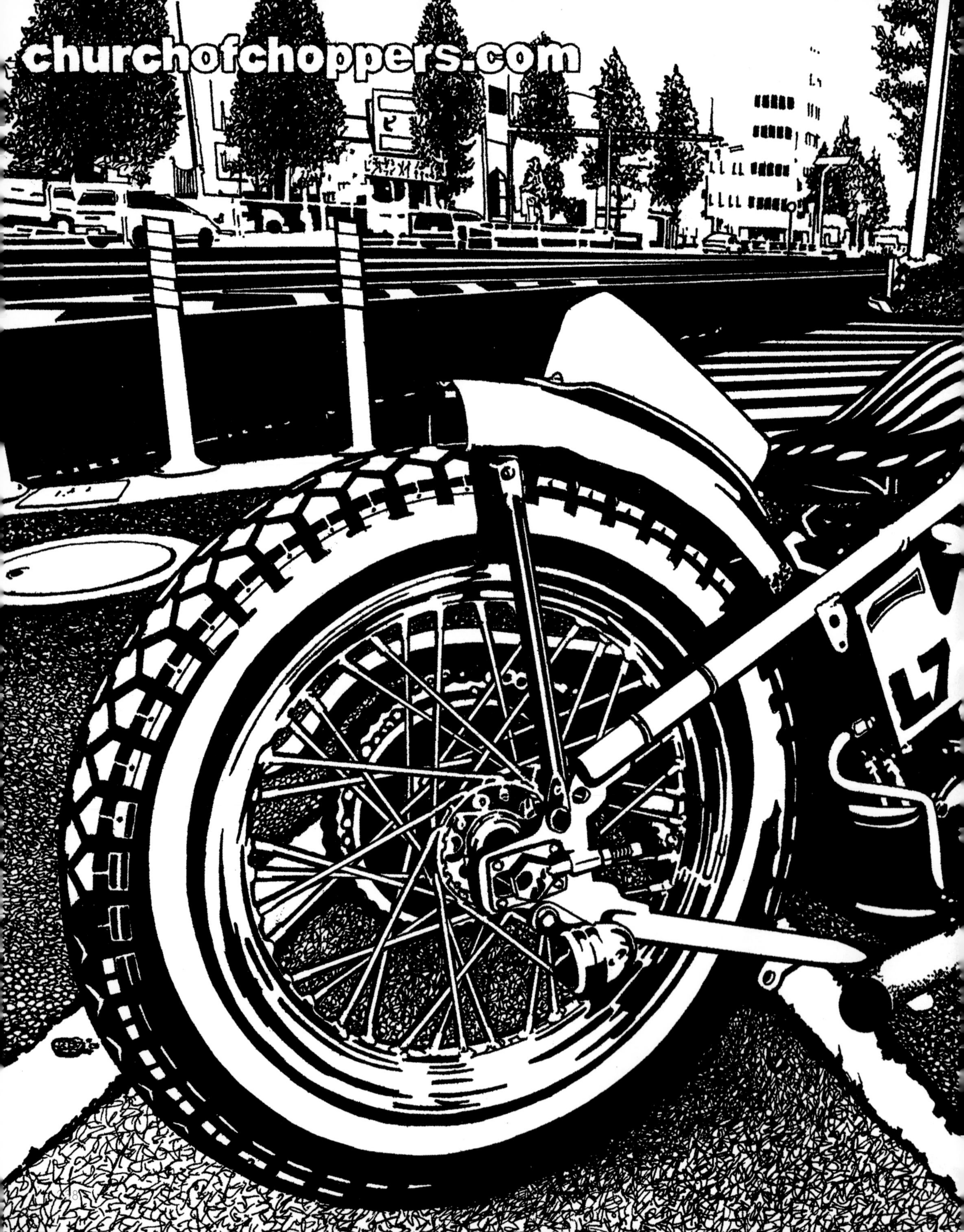
churchofchoppers.com

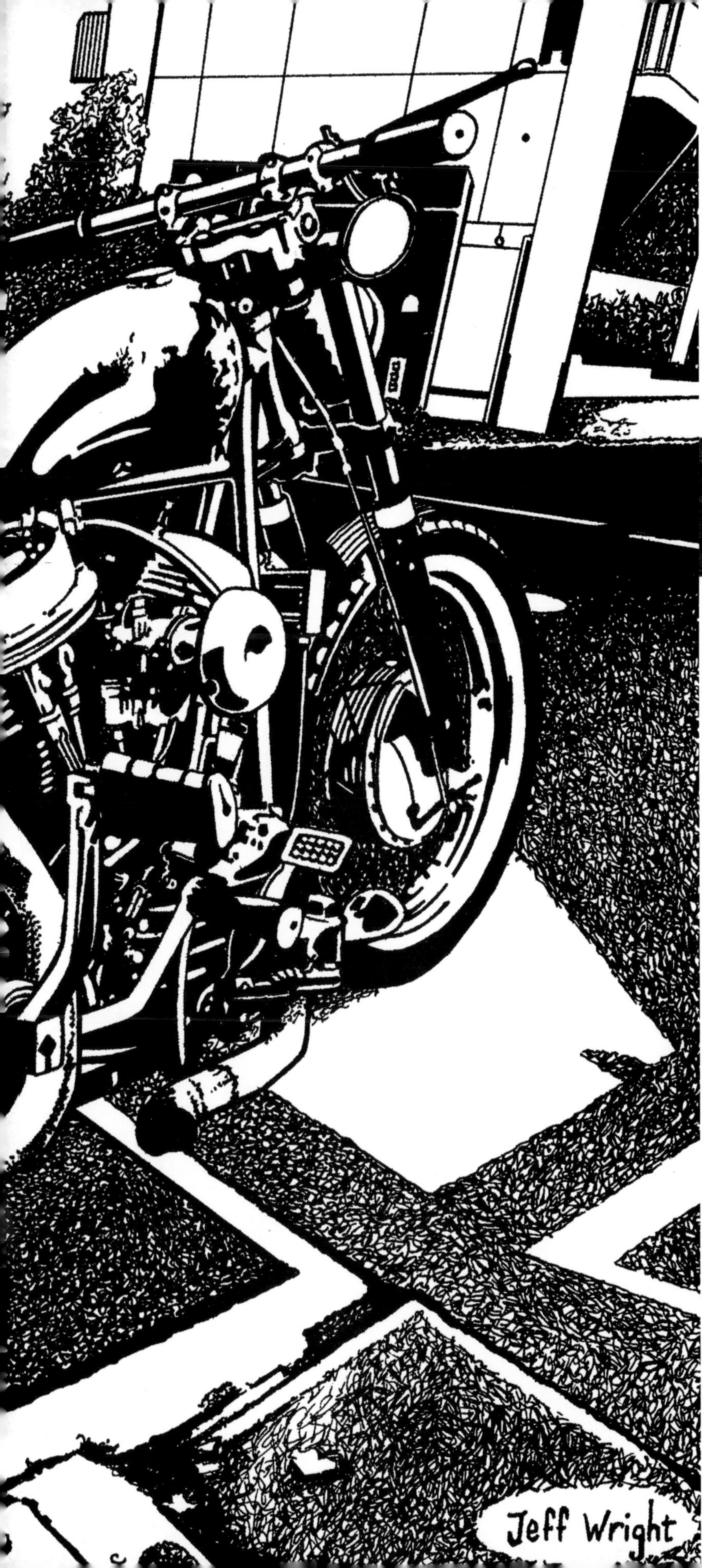

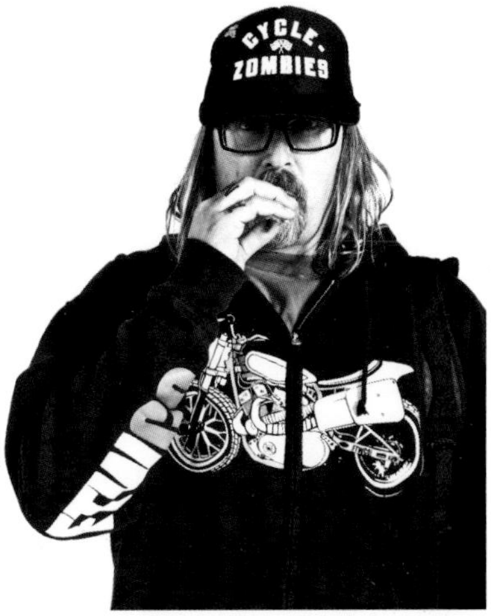

JEFF WRIGHT

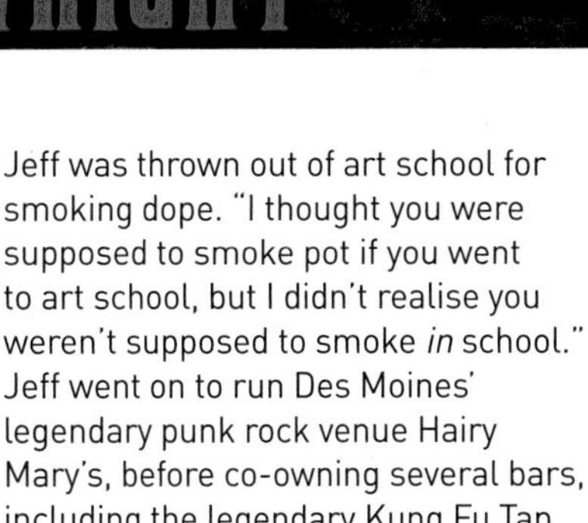

Jeff was thrown out of art school for smoking dope. "I thought you were supposed to smoke pot if you went to art school, but I didn't realise you weren't supposed to smoke *in* school." Jeff went on to run Des Moines' legendary punk rock venue Hairy Mary's, before co-owning several bars, including the legendary Kung Fu Tap and Taco, also in Iowa.

But Jeff's real interest has always been two wheels. "When I was ten I won $50 in an art competition. I stole another $50 from my step-dad and bought a Honda XR75. I got busted by the cops and they took it off me. My parents never even knew I had it. Then I bought a Yamaha RD400 that didn't work. Me and my friends used to just push it around the streets, trying to kickstart it all night, pull at some wires...We did that every night for about four weeks." Today he rides a 185mph Kawasaki ZX-10R and builds hardcore, high performance choppers. When he's not riding, he's designing for FTWCo, the t-shirt business he runs with a partner. "I hold t-shirt art at a high level. If I was a painter, all I need to find is one person who likes it enough to hang it on their wall but if I only sell one t-shirt I'm out of business."

LEFT: ***Mochi's Pan.***
Pen and ink on paper.

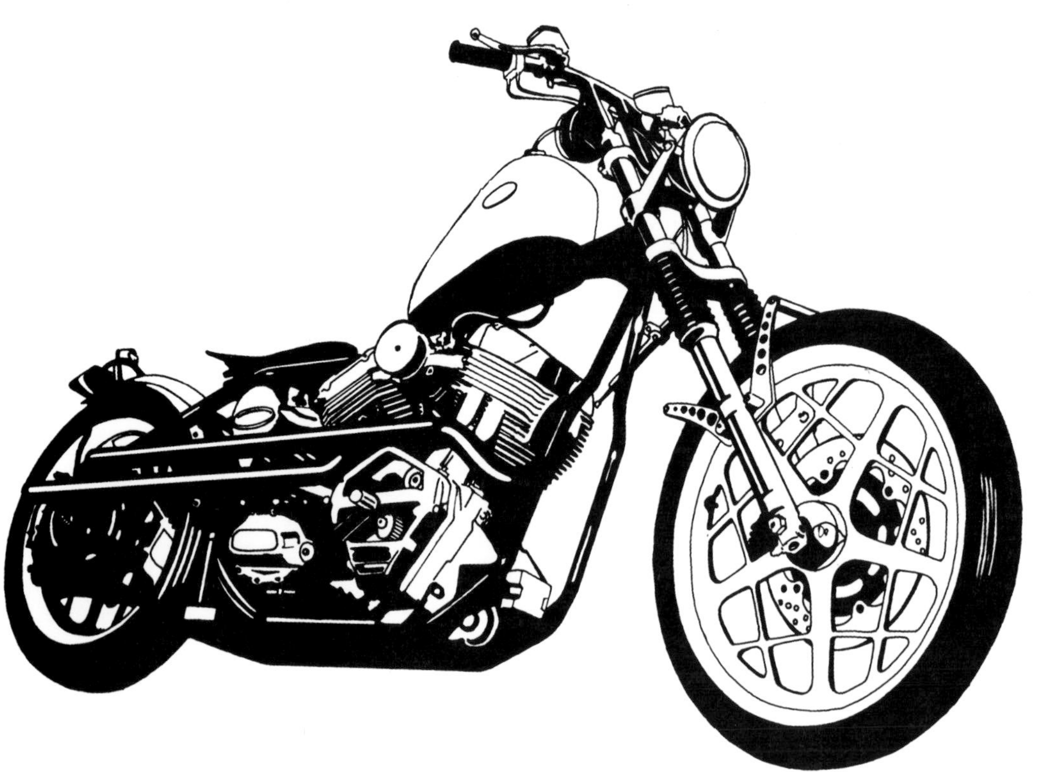

ABOVE: ***Chopper Dave's Pan.***
Pen and ink on paper.

BELOW: ***Triumphant.***
Pen and ink on paper.

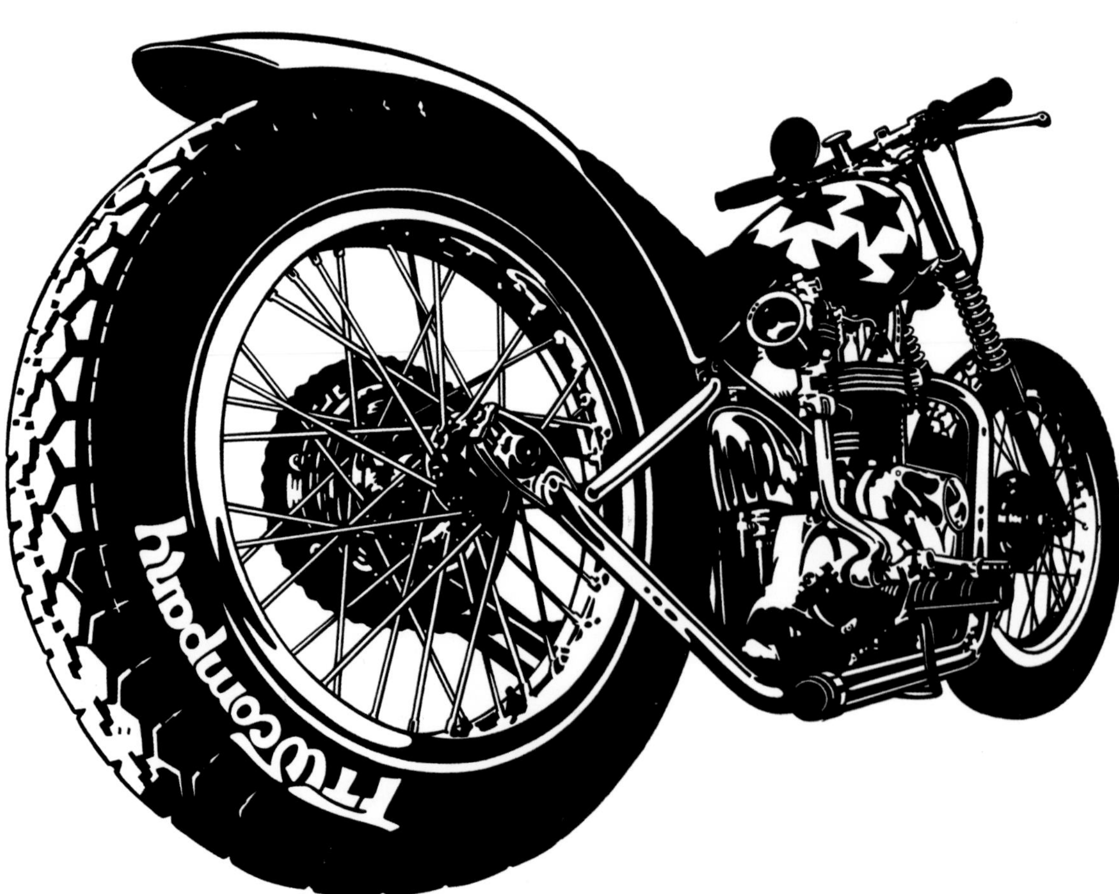

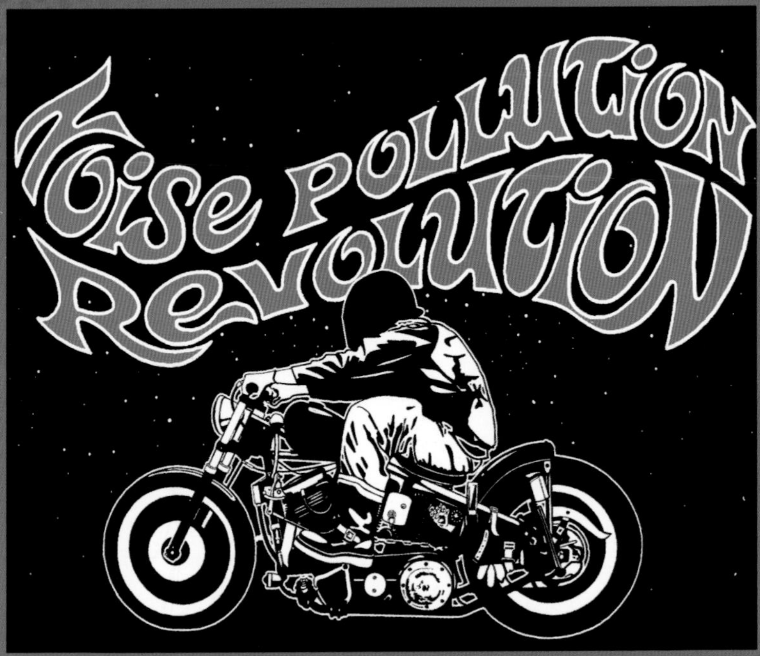

LEFT: ***Noise.***
Pen and ink on paper.

BELOW: ***Clockwork.***
Pen and ink on paper.

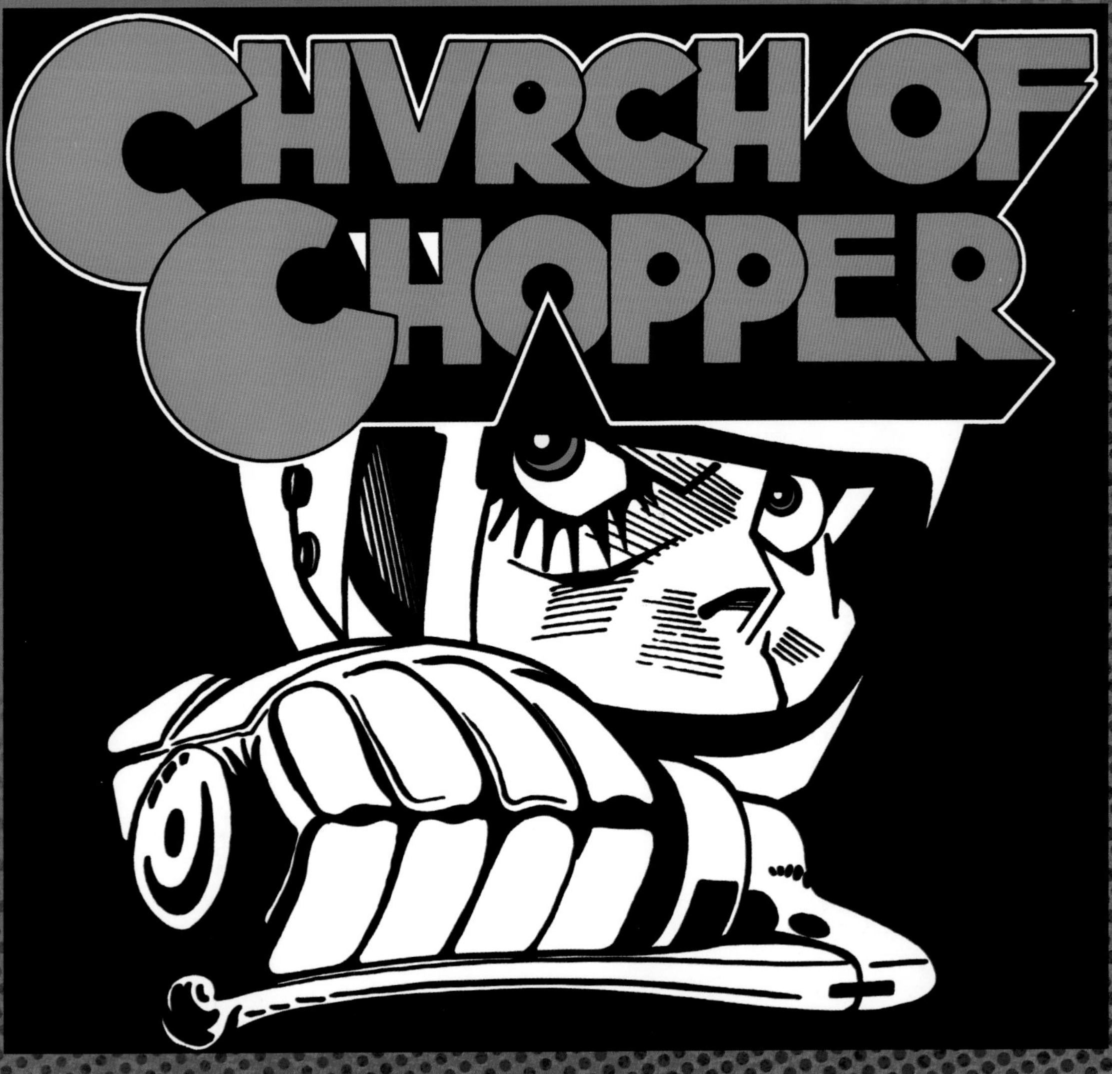

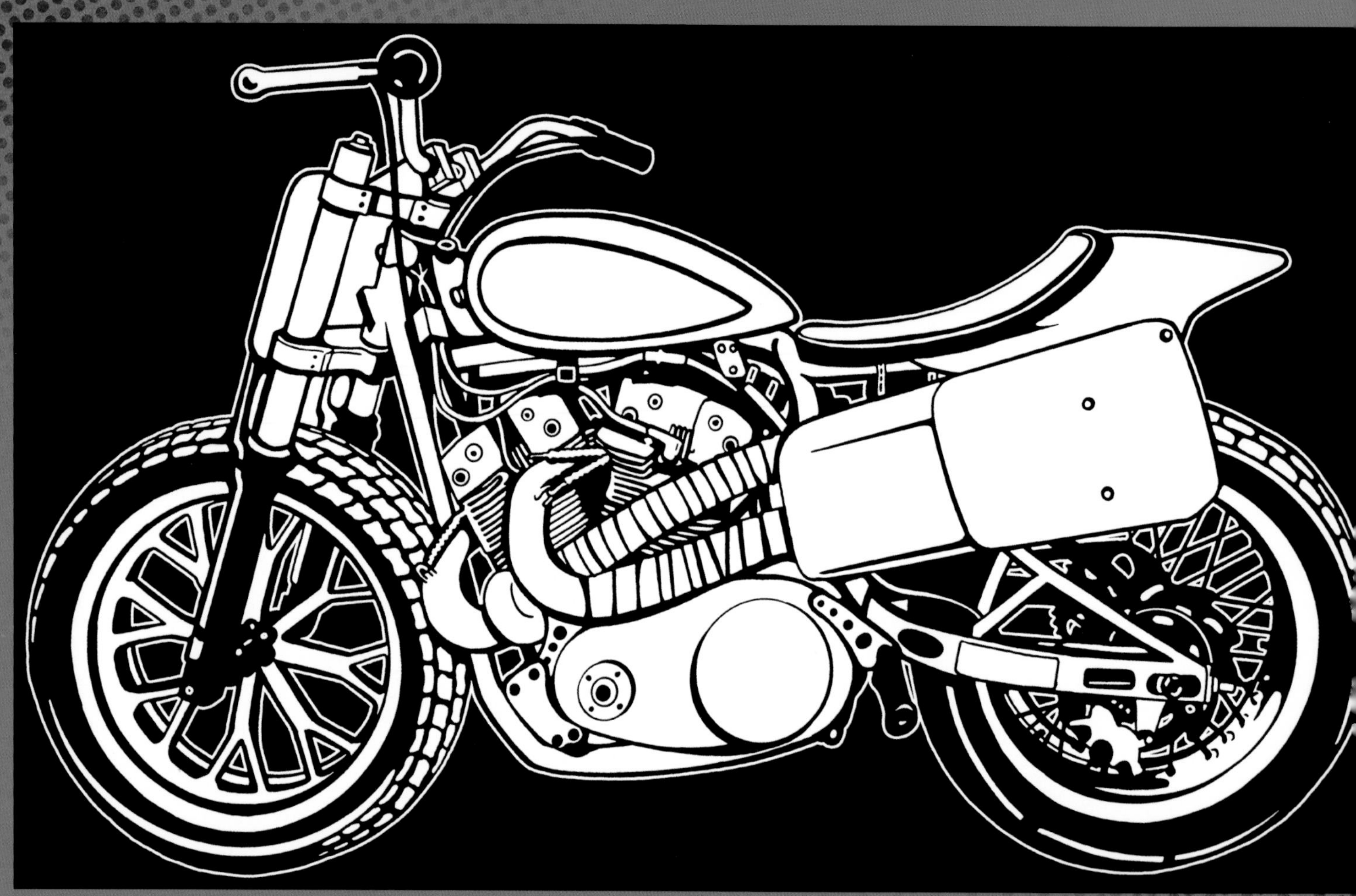

ABOVE: ***Flattracker.***
Pen and ink on paper.

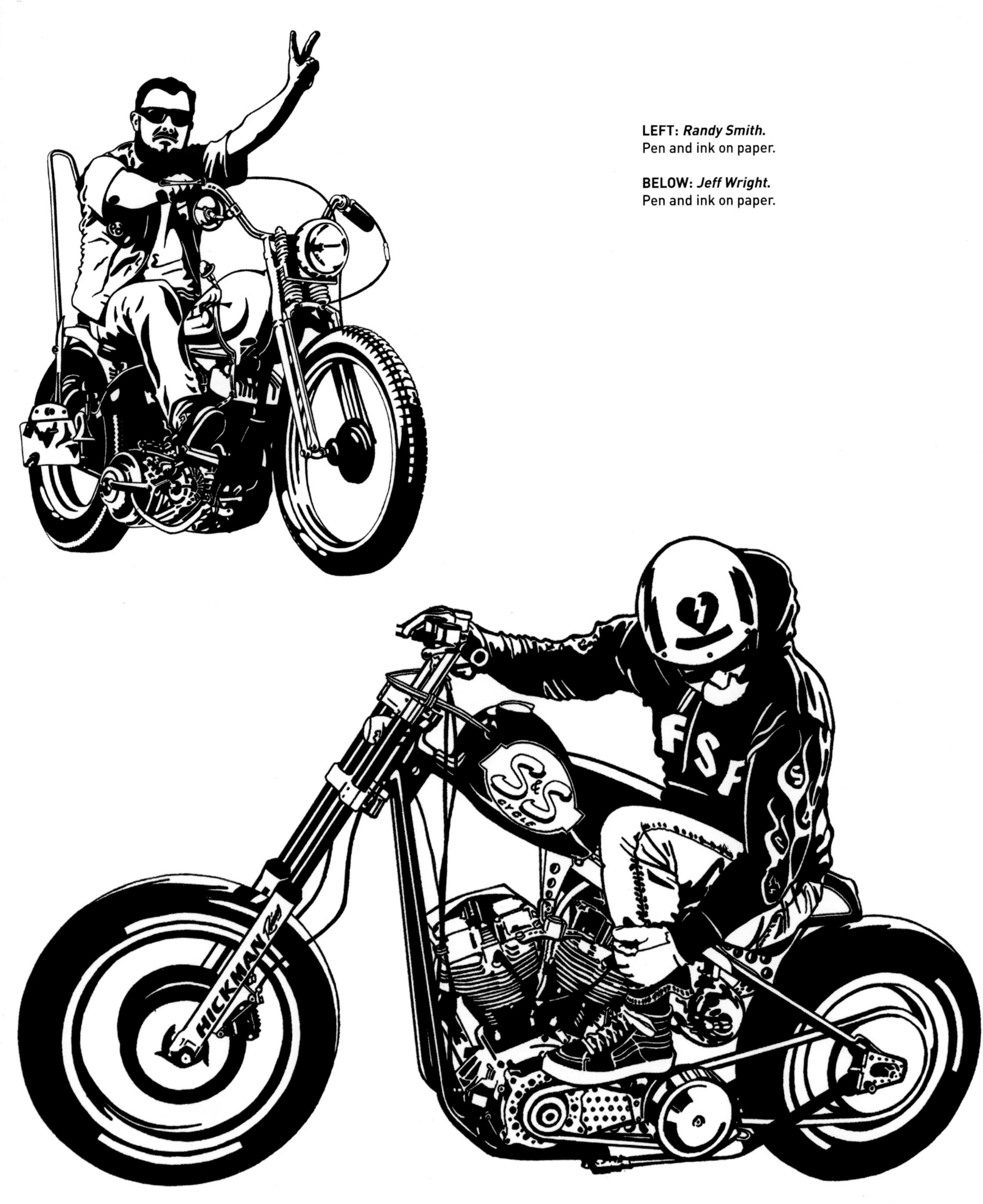

LEFT: ***Randy Smith.***
Pen and ink on paper.

BELOW: ***Jeff Wright.***
Pen and ink on paper.

RIGHT: ***Say Something.*** Digital art and serigraph on paper.

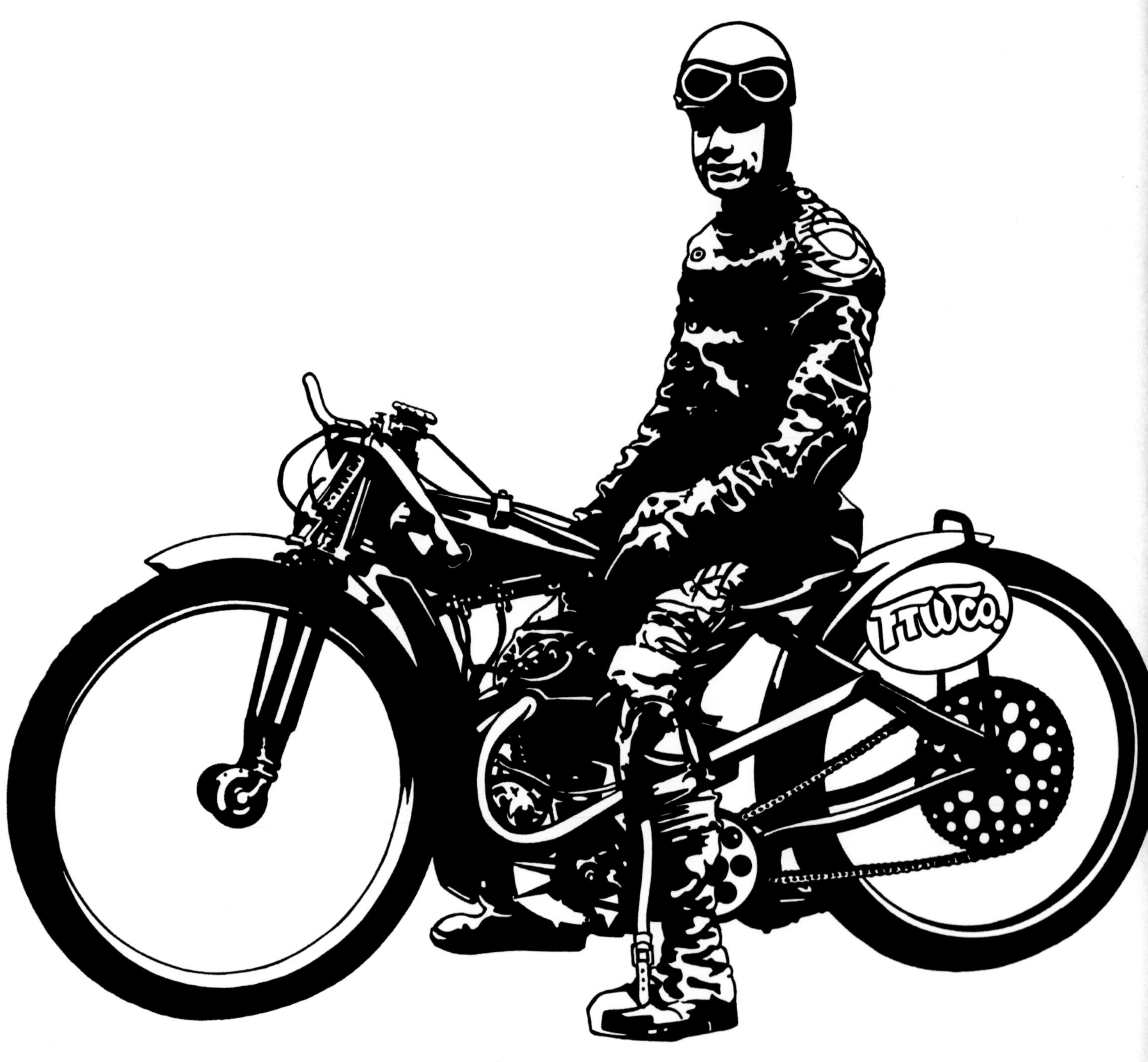

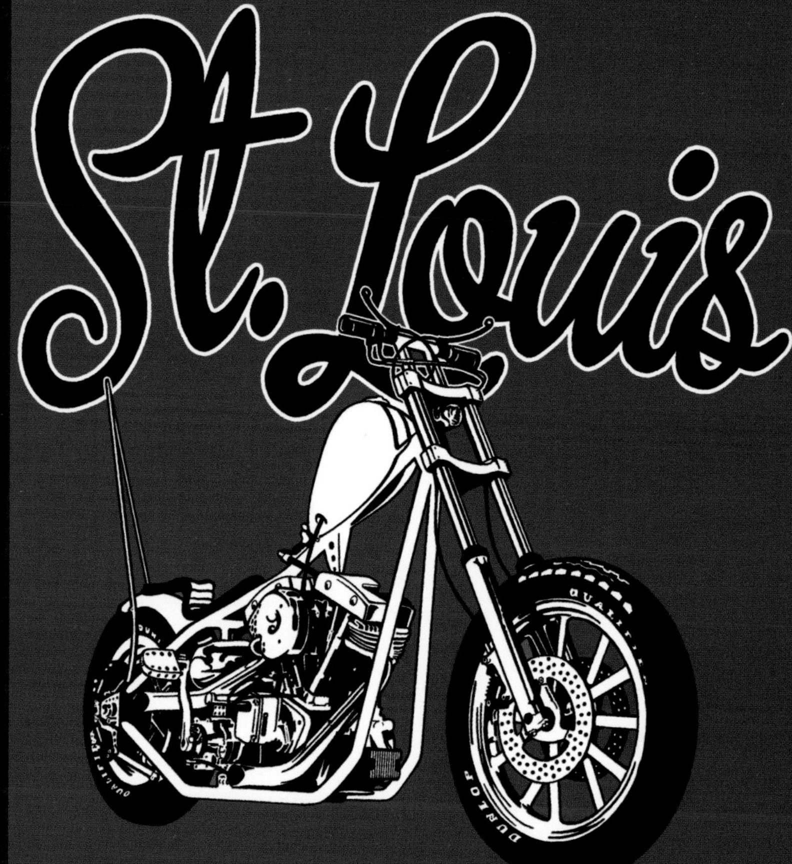

RIGHT: ***St. Louis.***
Pen and ink on paper.

BELOW: ***Wheel.***
Pen and ink on paper.

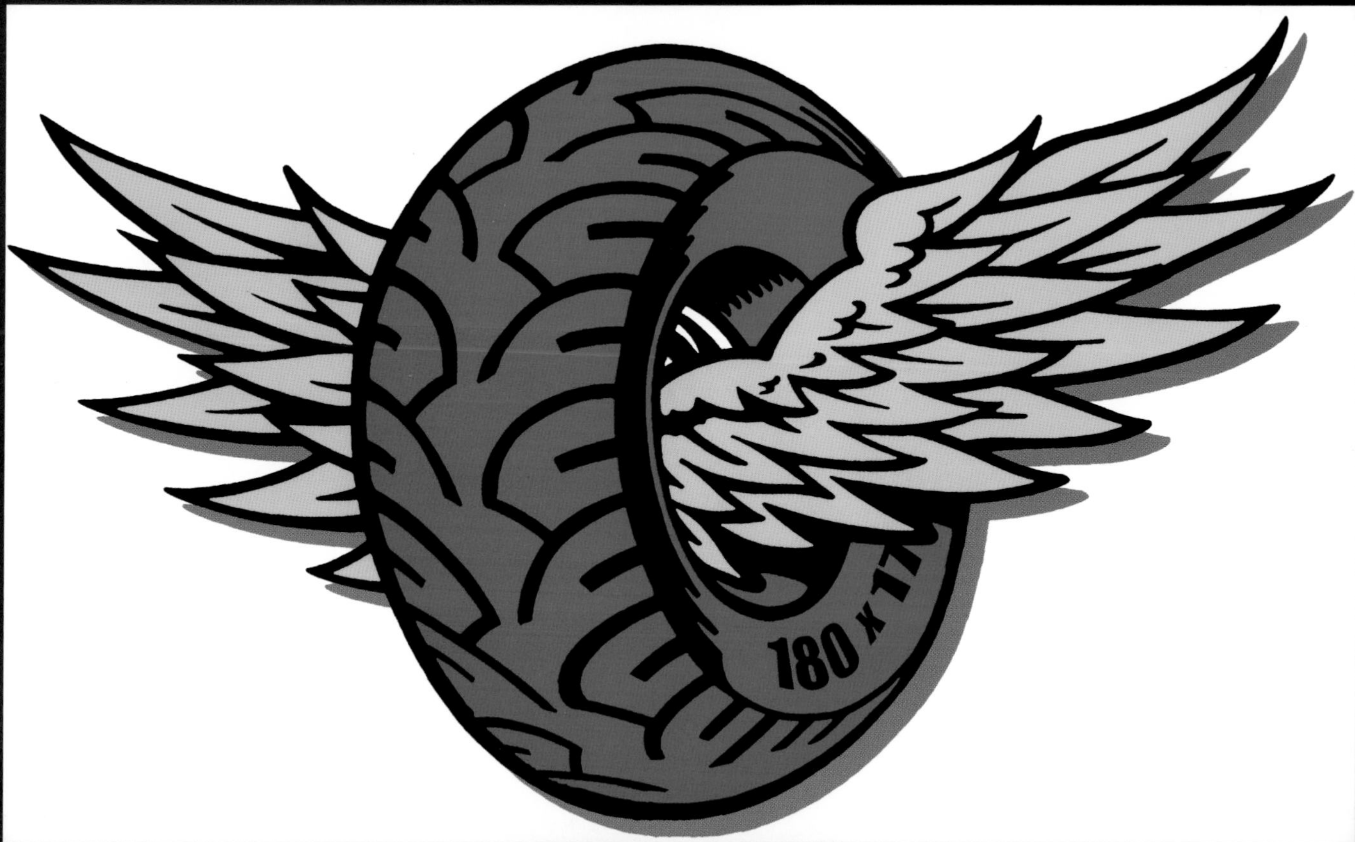

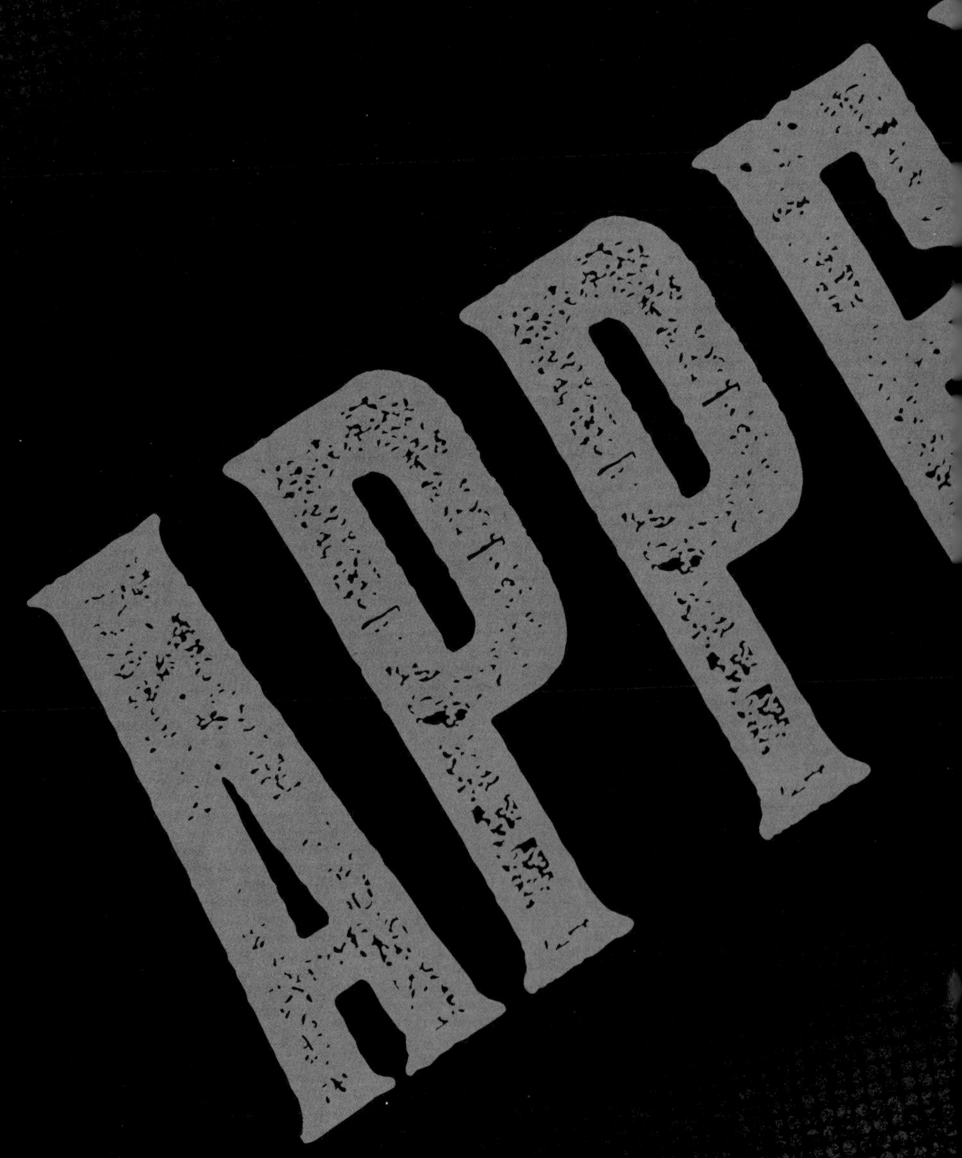
APPE

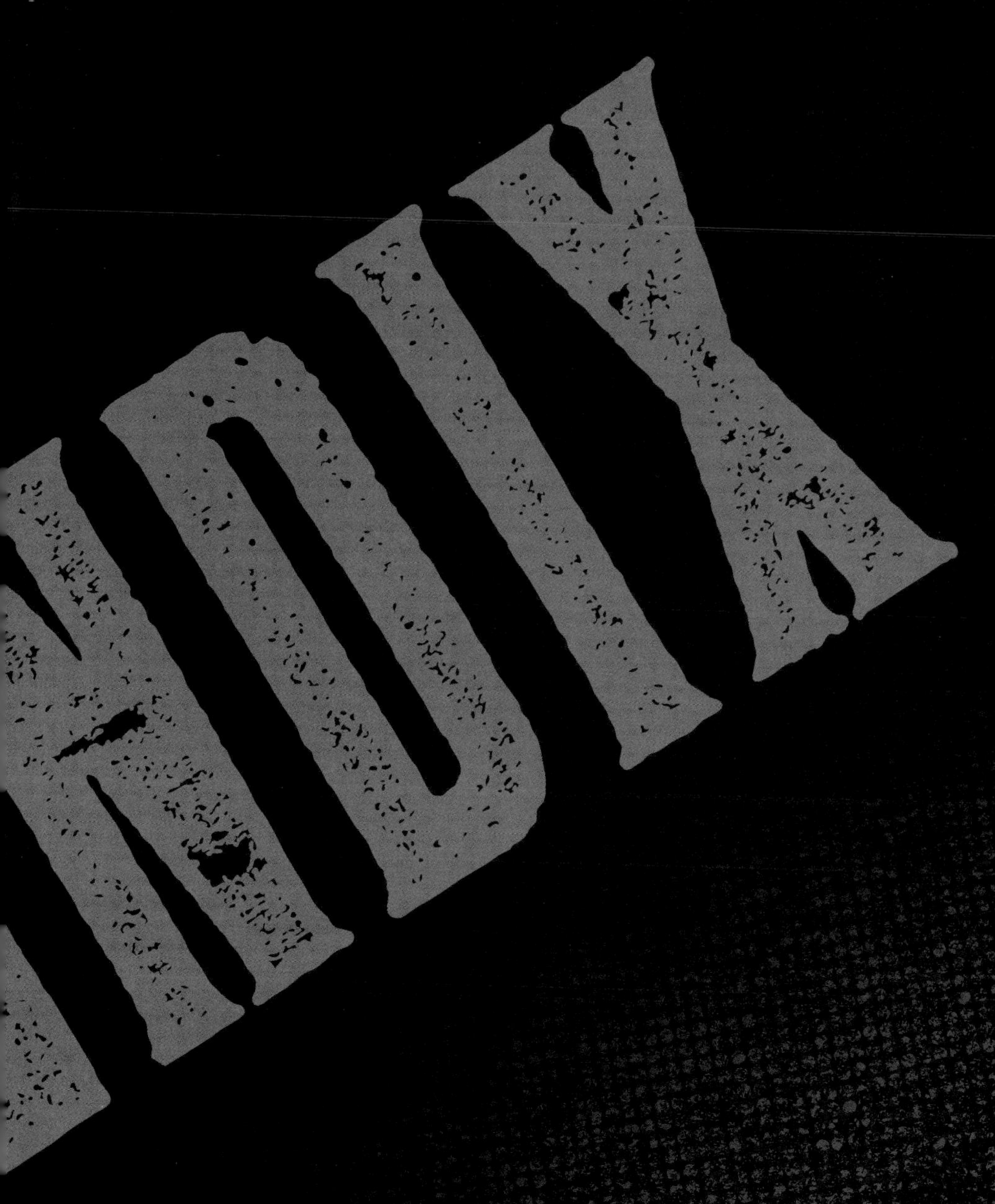

ARTIST CONTACT DETAILS
PHOTO CREDITS
ACKNOWLEDGEMENTS

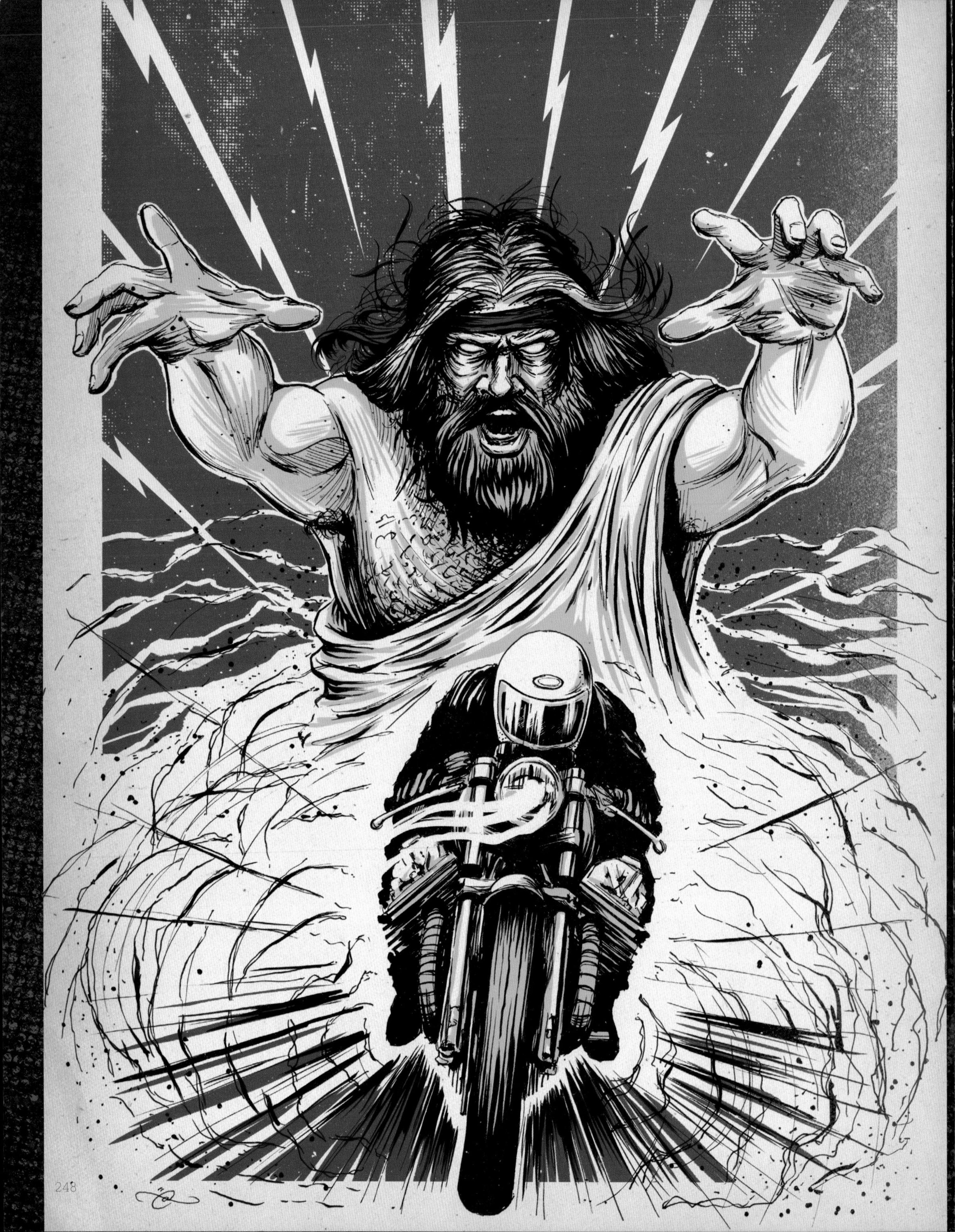

ARTIST CONTACT DETAILS

WILL BARRAS
London | UK | www.willbarras.com

CAY BRØNDUM
Copenhagen | Denmark | www.caybroendum.com

JAMES CHAPPELL
London | UK | www.jameschappell.co.uk

DIRTY DONNY
San Francisco | USA | www.dirtydonny.com

STEVIE GEE
London | UK | steviegee.tumblr.com

ADI GILBERT
Bristol | UK | 99seconds.com

STEFAN GLERUM
Amsterdam | Netherlands | www.stefanglerum.com

PHILIPPE GÜREL
Troyes | France | turboflat.blogspot.com

LAPIN
Barcelona | Spain | www.lesillustrationsdelapin.com

CONRAD LEACH
London | UK | www.conradleach.com

LEFT: ***Ton Up*** **by Adi Gilbert.** Indian ink on paper, digital art, textures.

LEVIATHAN
Valencia | Spain | www.leviathan.es

LORENZO EROTICOLOR
Paris | France | www.lorenzo-eroticolor.com

BRANDON McLEAN
Orlando | USA | www.brandontmclean.com

SHAWN McKINNEY
Los Angeles | USA | www.shawn-mckinney.com

ANTONIO MERINERO
Madrid | Spain | www.antoniomerinero.com

ADAM NICKEL
brisbane | Australia | www.adamnickel.com

NICOLAS PETIT
Mondidier | France | petit-motorcycle-creation.over-blog.com

MAXWELL PATERNOSTER
London | UK | www.maxwellp.co.uk

ALEX PATROCINIO
Barcelona | Spain | www.burnclan.com

WILL PIERCE
Houston | USA | about.me/willpierce

RYAN QUICKFALL
Gateshead | UK | www.ryanquickfall.com

RAID71
Darwen | UK | www.raid71.com

GIANNIS RAGGIAS
Athens | Greece | www.speedjunkies.gr

SCARLETT RICKARD
Folkestone | UK | www.scarlettrickard.co.uk

RAULOWSKY
Badajoz | Spain | Raulowsky.blogspot.com

LENNARD SCHUURMANS
Amsterdam | Netherlands | lennardschuurmans.com

TOKYO GUNS
Tokyo | Japan | www.tokyoguns.com

CARBY TUCKWELL
Sydney | Australia | deuscustoms.com

CHRIS WATSON
Hastings | UK | www.chriswatson.cc

JEFF WRIGHT
Des Moines| USA | www.ftwcompany.blogspot.com

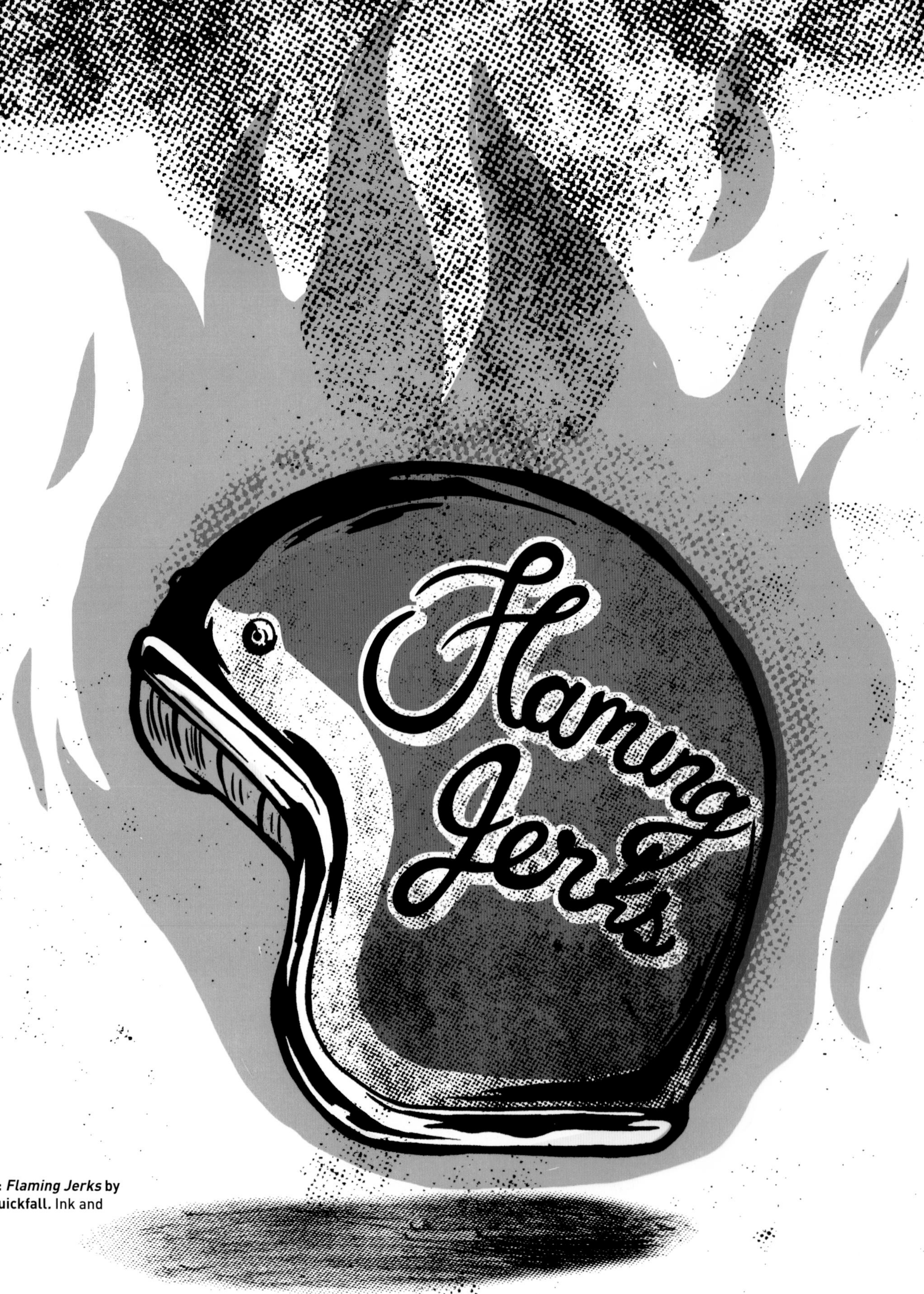

ABOVE: ***Flaming Jerks*** **by Ryan Quickfall.** Ink and Digital.

PHOTO CREDITS

P. 57 ADI GILBERT BY DIMITRI COSTE

P. 63 STEFAN GLERUM BY HARRY BRIEFFIES

P. 77 LAPIN BY MISS ALESSIA

P. 85 CONRAD LEACH BY SAM CHRISTMAS

P. 101 LORENZO BY THIBAULT STIPAL

P. 141 MAXWELL PATERNOSTER BY SAM CHRISTMAS

P. 199 SCARLETT RICKARD BY TIM RAY ROGERS

P. 229 CHRIS WATSON BY JOHN REYNOLDS

P. 239 JEFF WRIGHT BY JAMES STONE

Graffito Books Ltd also wishes to thank Pirelli for their kind permission to use the Stefan Glerum images on pages 64, 65, 66, 68, 69.

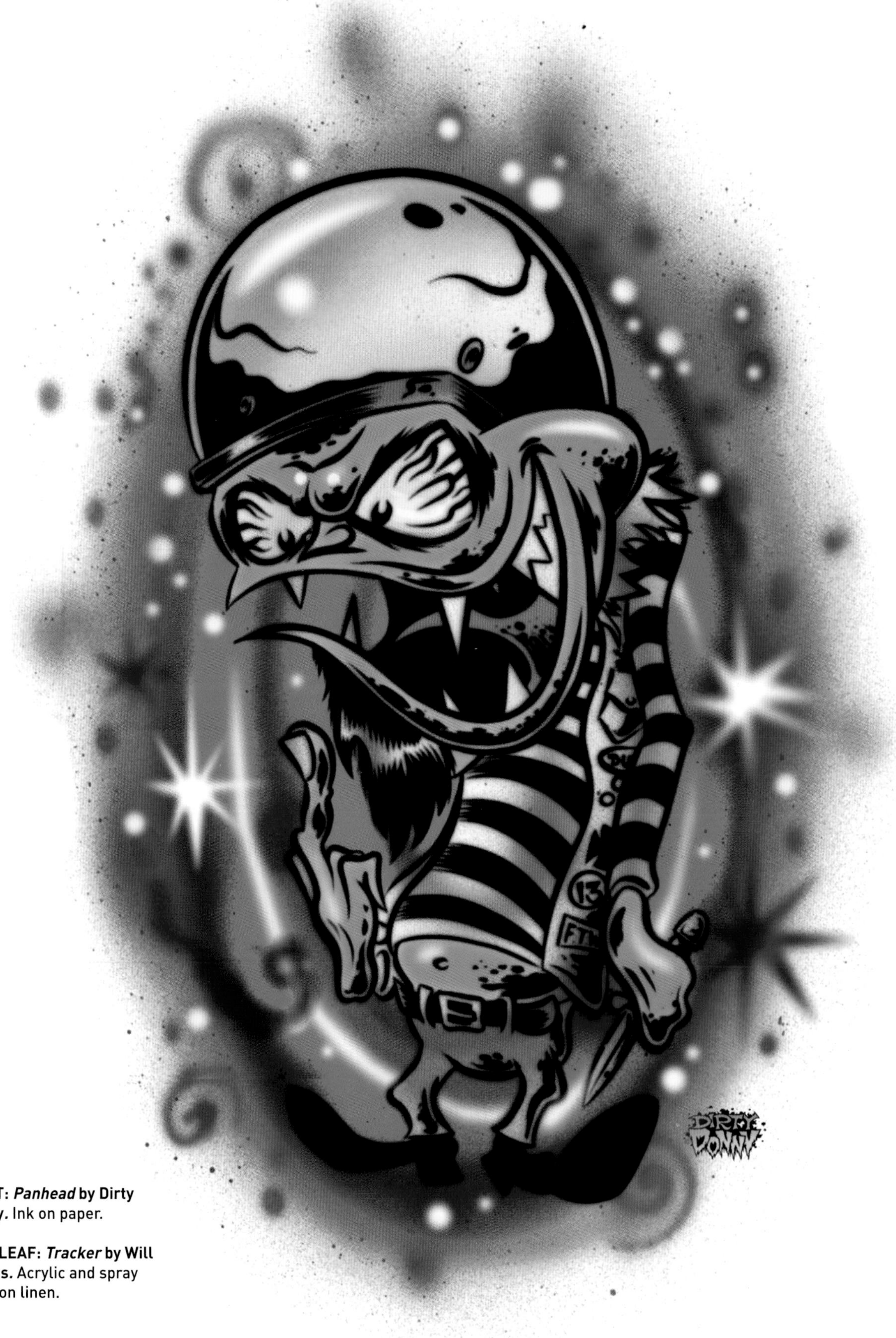

RIGHT: ***Panhead*** **by Dirty Donny.** Ink on paper.

OVERLEAF: ***Tracker*** **by Will Barras.** Acrylic and spray paint on linen.

ACKNOWLEDGEMENTS

GARY INMAN WOULD LIKE TO THANK:

BEN PART AND LENNARD SCHUURMANS FOR THEIR HELP, ADVICE AND CONTACTS; *SIDEBURN* MAGAZINE; SAM CHRISTMAS AND DIMITRI COSTE FOR SUPPLYING SOME OF THE ARTIST PORTRAITS; DEBBIE, MAX AND EVE; ALL THE ARTISTS FOR COOPERATION; GOTTLIEB DAIMLER, ARTHUR DAVIDSON, WILLIAM S HARLEY AND SOICHIRO HONDA. WITHOUT THEM...

THE PUBLISHER WOULD LIKE TO THANK:

ALL THE ARTISTS FOR THEIR STUNNING WORKS; BIARRITZ FOR PROVIDING THE BACKDROP TO SOME GREAT DISCUSSIONS ABOUT THE BOOK; SAM RATCLIFFE FOR HIS, AS EVER, TERRIFIC ART-DIRECTION; TRISTAN BALIUAG FOR HIS DESIGN INPUT; THOSE BRILLIANT, CURATED, UNIQUE OULETS, BOOKSHOPS AND DISTRIBUTORS WHO PROVIDE THE CONDITIONS THAT ALLOW SMALL PUBLISHERS LIKE GRAFFITO TO CREATE THEIR SPECIALIST BOOKS (AND WHO ALSO KEEP SHEET-FED PRINTING PRESSES ALIVE); LAST, AND MOST, EVERY ARTIST, READER AND ENTHUSIAST WHO WILL IN FUTURE BUY THIS BOOK AND PORE OVER THE ART AND DESIGNS WITHIN, LOOKING FOR IDEAS AND INSPIRATION. THAT LAST ONE IS WHAT MAKES THIS BUSINESS REWARDING.

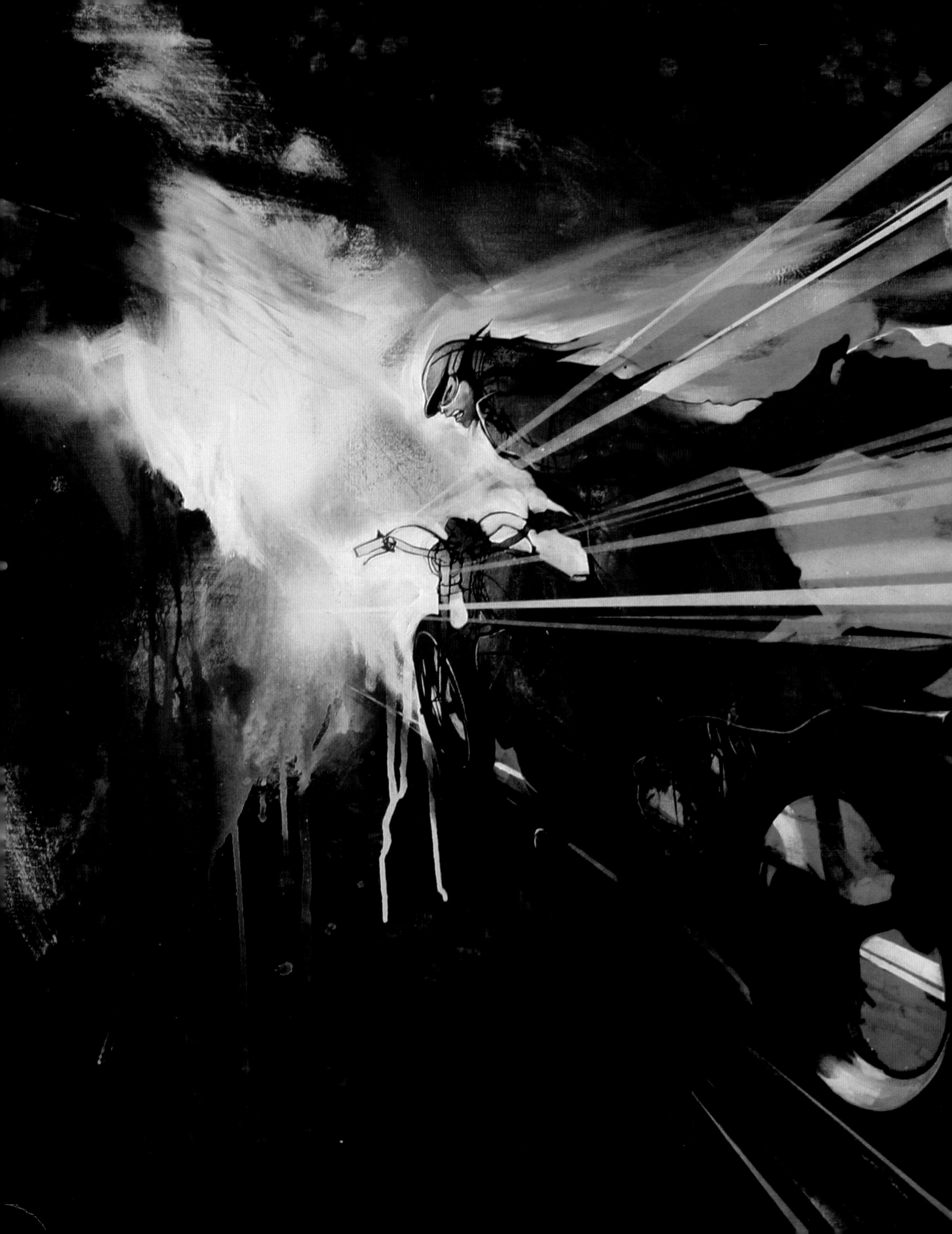

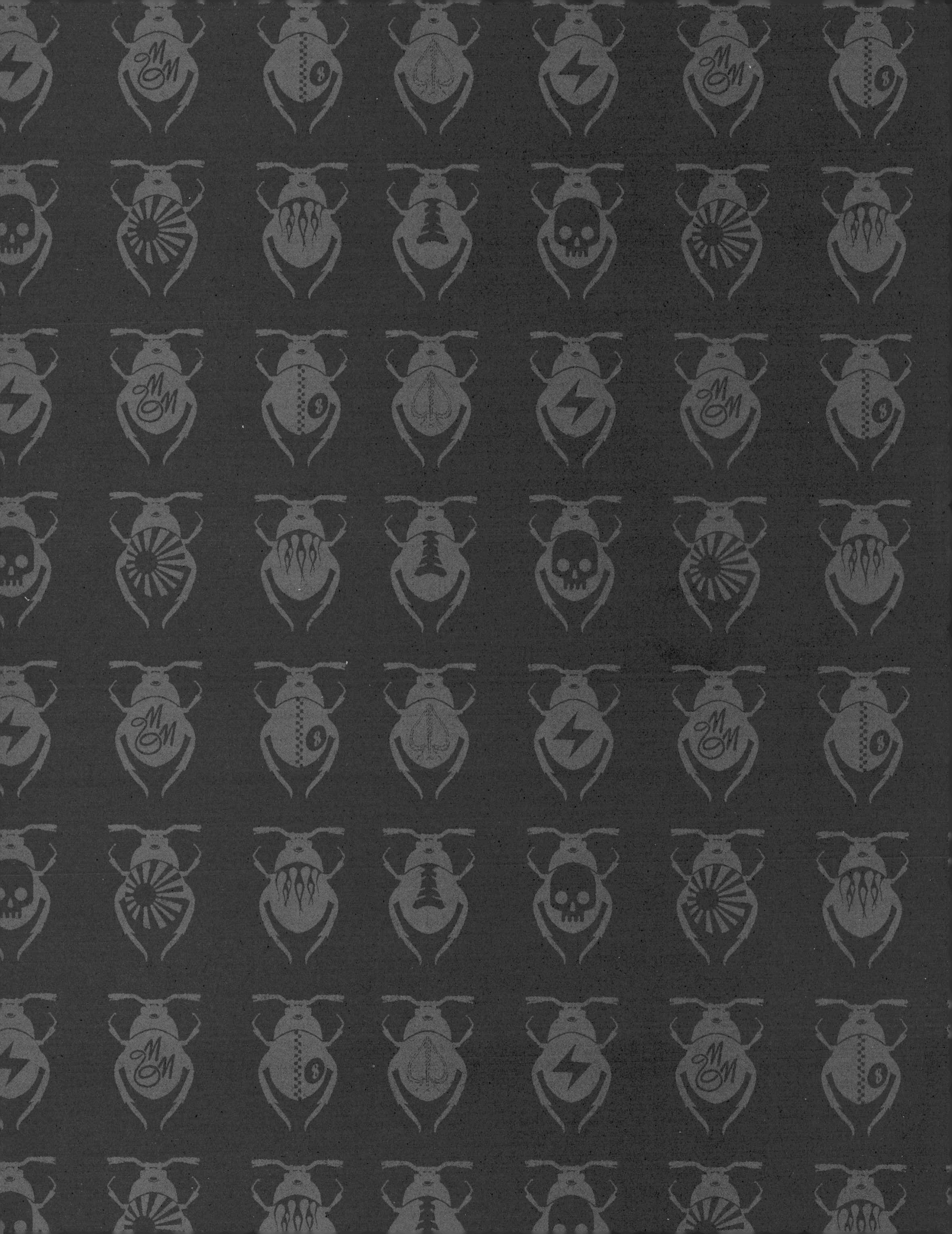